Human Development

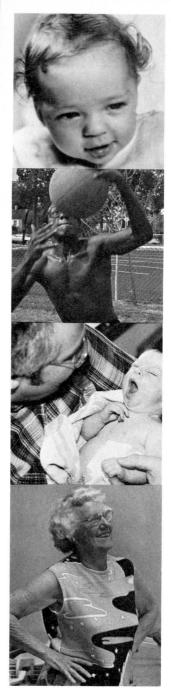

Human Development

SECOND EDITION

Lawrence B. Schiamberg
MICHIGAN STATE UNIVERSITY

with contributions by Gale Spirtas Schiamberg

Macmillan Publishing Company
NEW YORK

Collier Macmillan Publishers
LONDON

Macmillan Publishing Company
866 Third Avenue, New York, New York 10022

Collier Macmillan Canada, Inc.

Library of Congress Cataloging in Publication Data

Schiamberg, Lawrence B.
  Human development.

  Includes bibliographies and index.
  1. Developmental psychology. I. Title.
[DNLM: 1. Human Development. BF 713 S329h]
BF713.S33 1985   155   84-16996
ISBN 0-02-406870-5

Printing: 1 2 3 4 5 6 7 8   Year: 5 6 7 8 9 0 1 2

ISBN 0-02-406870-5

Dedication

For a book that deals, in part, with the vital contributions of the family to human development, it is fitting that this book be dedicated to my family—Gale, Scott, Bruce, and Elizabeth Schiamberg, Mr. and Mrs. Louis Schiamberg, and to the memory of Mr. and Mrs. Abraham Spirtas.

Preface

This book is primarily intended for introductory courses in life-span human development offered in departments of child/human development and family studies. It is appropriate for similar courses in such fields as psychology, social work, medicine, nursing, and education. The basic approach of the book is to treat human development as a process that involves the *mutual, reciprocal,* and *dynamic interaction* of the human being with the significant *contexts* of life (e.g., family, work, community, neighborhood, and culture) including the "significant others" of the life experience (e.g., parents, siblings, peers, neighbors, friends, and teachers). I shall refer to this approach as the *systems* or *ecological* perspective to human development. My intent is to organize and present to the beginning student vital and up-to-date theory and research in human development in such a *systems* or *ecological* framework. I believe that such a perspective provides the beginning student with a useful technique for approaching the significant issues and problems of human development. The systems perspective in its simplest form is a way of understanding and approaching the holistic and interactive dimensions of human development. Such an approach enables one to understand the complex nature of human development, human behavior, and related social problems. By calling attention to the mutual adaptation between the developing person and the significant contexts of life, the systems perspective helps the student to ask the right "questions" about human development rather than relying on simplistic, overly general, or convenient "solutions." Ackoff (1974) summarizes this position as follows:

*We fail more often because we solve the wrong problem than because we get the wrong solution to the right problem.**

  *R. L. Ackoff, *Redesigning the Future: A Systems Approach to Societal Problems* (New York: Wiley, 1974), p. 8.

VII

The author believes that a systems perspective provides the student with an important analytical tool as well as a beginning preparation for many significant careers and professional roles involving (but not limited to) housing and environmental design, nutrition, medicine and health sciences, nursing, child development, teaching, adolescent and youth services, gerontology, extension work, social work and social welfare, family economics, psychology, and business.

A major feature of this book is the emphasis on the vital role of contexts of development such as work, family, and neighborhood in human development. This is a unique and much needed perspective since the study of human development is much more than simply describing changes in the individual over time. Rather, the meaningful and practical application of human development concepts requires attention to the *progressive interaction* and *mutual adaptation* of human beings and the significant environments or contexts of life throughout the life span. In the same manner that biologists and zoologists have undertaken to describe plant and animal life by examining the *ecology* or mutual relationships between organisms and their environments, the study of human development becomes richer and more complete by focusing on the ecological or systems perspective. In contrast to the ecology of plant and animal development, the ecological or systems view of human development includes a major focus on the man-made and culturally evolved environments (e.g., schools, computers, television, and work arrangements) which dramatically influence human adaptation and development.

A significant aspect of this book is the complete and comprehensive consideration of the role of the family throughout the life span. Material on the family is presented in such a way that it clearly and specifically relates to the development of the individual human being at each stage of the life cycle. Furthermore, the book gives credence to the still relatively new concept of the family as a *system*. This family-systems approach is consistent with the overall approach of the book as well as providing a critical set of ideas for examining and analyzing the contributions of the family to human growth and development. Attention is given to alternative family forms including the single-parent family as well as to the impact of working mothers.

The balance of coverage of material in this book is appropriate for an introductory course. Each chapter or stage of development is thoroughly covered. The presentation of research is complete, practical, accurate, and up-to-date. A concerted effort has been made to balance necessary depth with a breadth of subjects that introduces the student to important and unique perspectives in a human development textbook (e.g., the issues of teenage pregnancy, home birth, home care for the aged, and the responsibility of middle aged adults for their aging parents).

The text is written in clear, simple, and upbeat prose. The writing style should be particularly appealing to college freshmen and sophomores. The language is straightforward. Students will find the writing style to be refreshingly direct as the more theoretical or research-oriented examples have been intentionally brought "down-to-earth" by specific examples, practical applications, and discussion questions. This has been accomplished without "watering down" the concepts or by "talking down" to the reader. Furthermore, the writing is uncluttered by jargon, flows well and, in so doing, motivates students to read on without getting them bogged down in theory or research.

Given the target audience of this book (the college freshman or sophomore), the book incorporates many useful pedagogical devices including application boxes, scenarios, discussion questions (at the end of each chapter and throughout the book), and extra ''human'' examples—all designed to elaborate on significant theoretical, practical, or research issues, such as day care or emotional stress and physical growth. They encourage students to reflect on their thoughts and opinions and to generate group discussion.

The use of pedagogical devices is designed to personally involve the student through specific questions—''your opinion''—as well as through application boxes and scenarios. In addition, the general variation of topics and the ''change of pace'' throughout the book makes it enjoyable to read. Another technique to encourage student involvement is the clarification of the ''direction'' of chapters through outlines at the beginning of each chapter and summaries at the end of each chapter. Furthermore, the text material is intentionally written in a manner that makes ideas ''flow'' in a natural order. Central ideas are clearly presented followed by clarifying examples and, in many instances, application boxes or scenarios which make the reader ''want to'' think and talk about the ideas.

The text is accompanied by an instructor's manual and a student guide. The instructor's manual contains student examination questions (including multiple choice questions, true-false questions, short-answer questions, and essay questions), lists of appropriate films, slides, television tapes, numerous student activities, and further information on the systems perspective to human development. The student guide contains chapter outlines, behavioral objectives for each chapter, student review questions, and suggested activities. Overhead projections of selected text material are available from the publisher.

There have been many individuals—family members, professional colleagues, reviewers, friends, photographers, students, typists and staff of Macmillan Publishing Co. Inc.—who have provided important assistance in the rather large and significant task of writing about human development. In particular, I would like to thank my family (Gale, Scott, Bruce, and Elizabeth) for their faithful cooperation and patience in an effort which took many years to complete.

My wife, Gale, deserves particular recognition for her numerous contributions to this book. She was responsible for arranging the vast majority of excellent photographs in the book, updating vital census information, doing thorough research on the many dimensions of human development, and carefully reading the manuscript, galley pages, and page proofs. Her insistence on accuracy, detail, and clear writing will surely be appreciated by students of human development. Were it not for these invaluable contributions, this book would not be a reality.

A special note of appreciation to parents—Mr. and Mrs. Louis Schiamberg—and sisters, brothers, and their families for their longstanding concern and interest. In addition, appreciation is extended to colleagues in the College of Human Ecology at Michigan State University for creating an atmosphere in which such a book can be written: Dean Lois Lund, Dr. Robert Giffore, Dr. Eileen Earhart, the late Dr. Beatrice Paolucci, Dr. Robert Boger, Dr. Jane Oyer, Dr. Donald Melcer, and Dr. Verna Hildebrand. The many excellent photographs in this book are largely the professional work of Darryl Jacobson, David Kostelnik, Wayne Mason, Sylvia Byers, Shan Rucinski, and Hope and Jeffrey Morris. Many students and colleagues in the College of Human

Ecology, Michigan State University provided invaluable contributions to the formulation of ideas that are central to this book.

The contribution of the reviewers was instrumental in the development of this book. Their knowledge of both the field of human development and its students was invaluable. For the first edition, I wish to thank Professors Trevor R. McKee, Joan N. McNeil, Gail F. Melson, Mary Jane S. Van Meter, and Sally Van Zandt, for the second edition, I wish to thank Professors Karen Peterson, Jean E. Poppei, and Bruce Roscoe. I also wish to thank Dr. Dorothy McMeekin of the Department of Natural Science at Michigan State University for her helpful review, suggestions, and critique of genetic factors in Chapter Four. Recognition of appreciation is also extended to the staff of the Lansing Public Library, especially Mr. Joseph Brooks, to the staff of the East Lansing Public Library, especially Sylvia Maribate and John Gleason, and to the staff of the M.S.U. and Library of Michigan Documents Division for their able assistance. Invaluable help arranging infant photographs was provided by the following Lansing, Michigan hospitals: Lansing General, St. Lawrence, and Sparrow.

The editorial and production staff of the college division of Macmillan Publishing Company provided invaluable assistance, guidance, and advice. In particular the senior editor, Mr. Peter Gordon, and the production editor, Eileen Schlesinger, were ever ready with professional advice and personal support. The manuscript was typed most ably by Martha West with contributions by Michele Meyrowitz.

Lawrence B. Schiamberg
East Lansing, Michigan

Contents

XI

9 *Adolescence*

1

Basic Concepts and General Principles of Human Development

Purposes of This Book

This book is written with essentially two purposes in mind.

1. The *first purpose* is to introduce the beginning student of human development to the excitement and challenges of studying the human being through the life span (birth to death).
2. The *second purpose* of this book is to present a framework for thinking about the developing human being in relationship to the significant environments of his or her life. For example, such environments include the family, the school, the peer group, the world of work, the neighborhood, the media, and the community. We will call this holistic approach the *systems perspective*.

Why Examine Human Development from a Life-Span Perspective?

By looking at the development of the person from birth to death, we can begin to understand how each period of development has its own challenges and frustrations and how it relates to other periods of development. The infant and the toddler learn how to control their behavior and fashion a sense of self in relation to the world of the family and of play. The school-aged child adjusts to a new environment (the school) and to a new adult (the teacher) while learning to read, write, and socialize with peers. The adolescent comes to grips with the self in terms of the world of work, career, and social development. The young adult further clarifies vocational direction and lifestyle and may begin intimate social or family relationships. The middle-aged adult consolidates self-development by generating activities that support and strengthen career and social/family associations. And finally, the aging adult

The course of human development is influenced by many people and experiences.

Photograph by Dr. Donald Melcer

2

The infant and the toddler learn to organize their behavior in relation to the world of family and play.

Right photograph by David Kostelnik

faces the prospect that life will be over—that death is inevitable. The elderly person may ask such questions as:

"Was it all worth it?"
"Have I lived a full and satisfying life?"
"Can I accept life as a process with a beginning and an end?"

Although most developmental research has traditionally focused on the periods of childhood and adolescence, there is increasing awareness that the period of adulthood contains less-explored, yet equally significant dimensions, such as vocational and career development, the crystalization of the self in social relationships, and the emerging acceptance of aging and death as realities of life.

The adolescent has many important choices.

Photograph by Darryl Jacobson

What are the reasons for the traditional emphasis on childhood and adolescence? One practical reason might be the ready availability of children and adolescents in child-care centers and schools and the relative ease of conducting experiments with such organized groups. Now suppose we want to look at the development of adults. What central location or organization provides easy access to the broad range of adults? The diversification of adult vocations and activities makes studies of adult development somewhat more difficult.

Another reason for the traditional emphasis on childhood and adolescence may well have had to do with the population distribution in the United States. Because of the high birthrate from the early 1940s through the late 1950s, the United States had a large increase in the number of births relative to previous periods as well as to later periods. This population "bulge" put pressure on educational resources and social institutions, which had to deal with these large numbers of children. These pressures served to reinforce and support an already emergent interest in research on children and adolescents. It has been projected now that we are in the middle 1980s, the last of the population bulge has moved through the educational system and has entered early adulthood. One can certainly speculate that this relative increase in the number of adults, as well as the declining birthrates after 1960, will further increase the concern of those who study human development with the period of adulthood.

Why Examine Human Development from an Interactional or "Systems" Perspective?

Although the life-span perspective helps to ensure that the milestones of human life will be covered, an interactional or systems viewpoint provides a way of understanding the relationship between the human being and the significant "contexts" or environments of life. Many of the important events throughout the life span are the result of the mutual interaction between the person and the contexts of development.

Some examples are the following:

The development of the unborn child can be viewed as a *mutual* exchange between the pregnant mother and the child (the details of this exchange process will be discussed in Chapter Four).

The growth and development of the infant and the toddler can be viewed as a *mutual* relationship between the child and the family (see Chapters Five and Seven).

The child's success in the school can be viewed as an interaction between the characteristics of the child and the characteristics of the teacher and the school. For example, some children seem to do rather well in conventional, structured classrooms, whereas others adapt better to a less-structured or "open" arrangement (Gump, 1974; Weiss, 1973).

The adaptation of the adult to the world of work is the result of many factors, including the skills and personality of the worker and the characteristics of the job and the co-workers.

The success of intimate social relationships such as friendships, parent—child interactions and marriage involves a *mutual* exchange between people and the social context in which the relationship occurs.

Was it all worth it? Do I accept what has happened and what is to come?

Photograph by Darryl Jacobson

The preceding list of human activities could be extended to include many more life-span events. Throughout the book, we will illustrate the interactional or systems features of the significant aspects of human development.

The Nature of Human Development

The study of human development emphasizes two types of change in human beings over time: *quantitative* change and *qualitative* change.

1. *Quantitative change* refers to the easily measurable and sometimes obvious features of human development, including physical growth (change in height and weight), number of years of education, and size of family.
2. *Qualitative change* refers to the alterations in human functioning through the life span (e.g., the changes in thought processes from the object-oriented thinking of childhood to the more abstract thinking of the adolescent and the adult).

Early adulthood may include marriage and childcare.

Photograph by Darryl Jacobson

PERIODS OF HUMAN DEVELOPMENT

The aim of the study of human development is to examine the qualitative and quantitative changes throughout the life span. In this book, we will look at these changes in each of the periods of the life span (see Table 1.1).

TABLE 1.1 **The Periods of Human Development**

Life Stage	Approximate Ages
Prenatal period	Conception to birth.
Infancy (includes toddler period from 2–3 years)	0–3 years.
Preschool years	3–5 years of age.
Middle childhood	5–12 or 13 years of age (the onset of puberty).
Early adolescence	Approximately 12 or 13 (the onset of puberty) until 17 or 18 years of age (the high school years).
Later adolescence	Approximately 17–18 years of age (the completion of high school) until the person attains a sense of social status or social identity in the early 20s.
Early adulthood	Early 20s to middle 30s—includes marriage, beginning of child caring, and high point of one's vocational career.
Middle adulthood	Middle 30s to middle 60s ends with completion of child caring and parenting roles.
Later adulthood	Middle 60s until death—includes grandparenting years and retirement.

PRINCIPLES OF HUMAN DEVELOPMENT

There are several general patterns or principles of growth that hold true in describing the way human beings develop. The processes of human growth and development relate to changes in the psychological, social, emotional, physical, mental (intellectual), and moral domains throughout life. The terms *growth* and *development* are used to describe this overall process.

DEFINITIONS

Growth. In this book, the term *growth* refers to the physical and physiological changes that occur in human beings. Ordinarily, these changes are quantitative and occur during the early phases of life up to and including the adolescent years. The term *growth* has traditionally had this positive emphasis. It is to be distinguished from changes in the later years of life which may include a gradual deterioration of the body organs, tissues, and senses (e.g., vision, hearing, and smell).

Development. The term *development* refers to changes in function. Such changes are nonorganic and are usually qualitative (e.g., language usage, reading skills, and relating to peers).

Growth and development, as defined above, operate in accordance with several principles:

Growth Gradients. Growth gradients or axes of growth are the *directions* of the physical and physiological changes in the human body. There are three directions of such growth:

Cephalocaudal. Physical growth occurs from the top (head) of the body downward. This is the cephalocaudal direction of growth. This principle of growth can be illustrated in many ways. For example, during prenatal development (from conception to birth), the brain and the central nervous system develop first, followed by developmental changes in the lower body (see Figure 1.1). From an evolutionary perspective, it is likely that the development of the head and the central nervous system occurs first because of their importance to the regulation of all behavior (see Figure 1.2).

After birth (the postnatal years), infants first gain control over total head movement as well as movements of the eyes and the mouth. Then they gain

FIGURE 1.1 Diagram of *axes* of human growth.

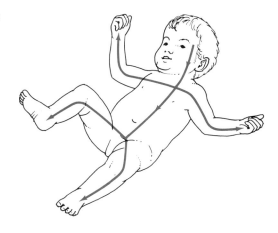

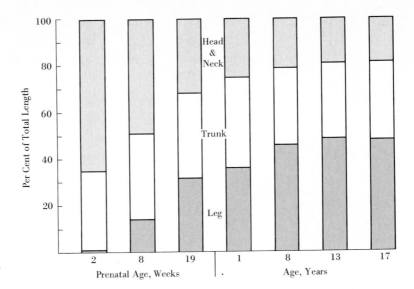

FIGURE 1.2 Percentage of total body length—head-and-neck, trunk, and legs—in boys at various stages of prenatal and postnatal growth.

From H. V. Meredith, Length of head and neck, trunk and lower extremities on Iowa City children aged 7–17 years, *Child Development,* 1939, *10,* 141.

control over trunk movements and, finally, leg movements. Babies can move their heads in several directions before they can sit up; they can sit up before they can stand; and, of course, they can stand before they can walk.

Proximodistal. Proximodistal growth means that the control of movements proceeds or matures from the central (proximal) areas of the body to the outer or peripheral (distal) areas (see Figure 1.1). For example, the infant gains control of its body, then its arm movements, then its hand movements, and finally its finger movements. Likewise, infants gain control of leg movements, then foot movements, and finally toe movements.

Differentiation. This principle suggests that a direction of growth is from "mass" or "gross" to "specific" processes or activities. Put another way, growth and development proceed from the simple to the complex. The principle of differentiation applies to growth *and* development. In the physical domain, babies learn to move their arms ("gross" movement) prior to being able to oppose their thumb and index finger while grasping a rattle ("specific" movement). Young children learn to walk before they can skip or hop.

Orderly and Sequential Development. Human growth and development are orderly processes. They are not simply random. Throughout this book, we will be examining what is currently known about the orderly and predictable pattern of development from the time of conception until death. There are, to be sure, some aspects of growth on which there is general agreement. On the other hand (as might be expected in the somewhat new and lively "science" of human development), some interpretations of the "progression" of human development have been more controversial. For example, how does one describe the course of aging in later adulthood, after retirement? At least three interpretations of this progression have been suggested.

Activity Theory. Activity theory suggests that positive adaptation in later adulthood requires the individual to maintain his or her preretirement level of involvement by either continuing the same level of involvement or by finding substitute activities (e.g., hobbies, volunteer work, or part-time work) (Mad-

The continuity theory of aging suggests that aging is the continuation of lifelong patterns of behavior and personality.

Photograph by Darryl Jacobson

dox, 1970). In other words, the individual should remain as active as possible after retirement.

Disengagement Theory. According to disengagement theory, normal aging involves two parts (Cumming and Henry, 1961):

1. The elimination or withdrawal of roles by society (e.g., through mandatory retirement from work or the death of a spouse).
2. The voluntary withdrawal from roles by the aging individual, who reduces activities and social commitments.

Continuity Theory. Continuity theory suggests that an individual's patterns of behavior are the result of a lifetime of experiences. Aging is the continuation of these lifelong adjustments or personality patterns. Therefore, positive adaptation in later adulthood means doing what is appropriate for oneself. To age successfully, an individual could disengage or become active, or combine both (Neugarten, Havighurst, and Tobin, 1968; Atchley, 1972).

Individual Variation. While individuals follow certain patterns of development in an orderly sequence, there is a considerable amount of variation among individuals. For example, young children show variation in their physical growth. Some children are shorter than others at certain ages and appear to "catch up" several years later. There are many reasons for such variations in height, including genetic endowment (genetic factors control the tempo or rate of growth), nutrition, illnesses, lack of exercise, and, in some instances, psychological disturbances.

Furthermore, the rate of growth is usually not consistent in each individual. For example, the adolescent growth "spurt" is a commonly acknowledged phenomenon (see Figure 1.3).

FIGURE 1.3   The adolescent growth spurt.

From J. M. Tanner, *Growth at Adolescence*. Oxford: Blackwell, 1962.

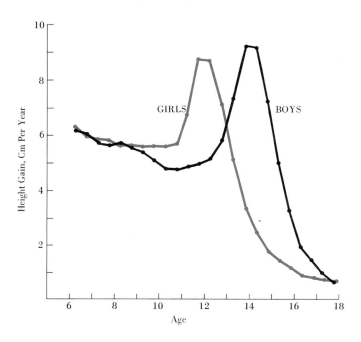

What Does It Mean to Be "Normal?"

Since one definition of "normal" is to be at the "norm," or "average," and since in statistics the "average" is a mathematical number or point, it is obvious that few, if any, [children or] adolescents can be really normal, according to this definition. Half will be above average, and the other half will be below assuming a normal distribution. This will apply to any trait that might be mentioned. Weights of adolescents will be too high or too low; breasts will be too large or too small; noses will be too long or too short; feet will be too big or too little; IQs will be too high or too low, and so on.

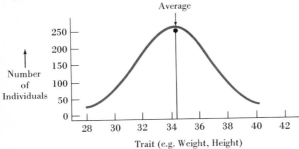

Trait (e.g. Weight, Height)

In dealing with [people], it is most important that a different concept of normality from the one defined above be used. No [person] wants to be thought of as being abnormal. Teachers, counselors, and others who work with children and young people, or other people for that matter, might well take the position that "anyone who falls under the normal curve is normal." [This definition would obviously not apply to diseases or some severe physical defects.] This, of course, includes everyone, for 100 percent of a distribution will be found under the bell-shaped normal curve [see diagram]. To be different, then, is to be normal. It takes all kinds of people to satisfy this criterion of normality. It is perfectly normal for a high school senior boy to be four feet, eight inches tall, although he is obviously short. It is likewise normal for a girl to be six feet tall. . . . [This is an] interpretation of what normality means, which at the same time takes away the stigma of being "abnormal" when one is really only different.

(G. M. Blair, R. S. Jones, and R. H. Simpson, *Educational Psychology*. New York: Macmillan, 1968, pp. 93–94.)

Sensitive or "Critical" Periods. This principle suggests that there are specific periods of time in the development of human beings when potential for growth (as well as harm from the environment) is maximal.

An example of a sensitive period for disease (environmental stress) is between the first and twelfth weeks of pregnancy. Should the mother acquire rubella (German measles) during this time, the consequences for the unborn child are far worse than if the mother has the disease at a later time during pregnancy.

Summary

1. The purposes of this book are twofold: (1) to introduce the beginning student of human development to the excitement, challenge, and importance of a life-span perspective to human development; (2) to introduce the beginning student to a holistic perspective of viewing development in terms of the interaction of contexts (e.g., family, work, and community) and the individual. We shall call this approach a "systems" perspective to human development.

Basic Concepts and General Principles of Human Development

2. By examining human development from a life-span perspective, we can begin to understand the unique features of each period of development as well as how each period relates to the entire life process.

3. An interactional or "systems" perspective to human development helps us to understand that human beings do not develop in a vacuum. Specifically, the important process and events of the life span are the result of the mutual interaction and contributions of persons and context or environment.

4. The study of human development involves two types of changes in human beings over time: (1) quantitative change and (2) qualitative change. The aim of the study of human development is to examine these qualitative and quantitative changes throughout the life span.

5. There are several general patterns or principles of growth and development. The principle of *growth gradients* or directions of growth involves the following features: the *cephalocaudal* direction and the *proximodistal* direction or differentiation. Development is *orderly* and *sequential*. Development involves *individual variation*. Development involves sensitive or "critical" periods.

Questions

1. Give a definition of the *life-span perspective*. Think of the individuals you know who are at various stages of the life span (e.g., infancy, adolescence, middle adulthood). Briefly, how would you describe their primary needs, concerns, and activities?
2. Give a definition of the *systems perspective* to human development. What do we mean when we say this approach is holistic?
3. At this point in your life, would you say that one or more of the periods or stages of life seems more important than the others? Why? Why not? Do you think your view has changed or will change? Why? Why not?
4. Do you agree with the suggested definition of "normal" presented in the application box? Can you recall situations where such a definition has been effectively used?

Bibliography

ATCHLEY, R. C. *The Social Forces in Later Life: An Introduction to Social Gerontology.* Belmont, California: Wadsworth, 1972.

BLAIR, G. M., JONES, R. S., and SIMPSON, R. H. *Educational Psychology.* New York: Macmillan, 1968.

CUMMING, E. and HENRY, W. E. *Growing Old: The Process of Disengagement.* New York: Basic Books, 1961.

GUMP, P. Operating environments in open and traditional schools, *School Review.* 1974, *84*, 575–593.

MADDOX, G. L. Themes and issues in sociological theories of human aging, *Human Development.* 1970, *13*, 17–27.

MEREDITH, H. V. Length of head and neck, trunk and lower extremities on Iowa City children aged 7–17 years, *Child Development.* 1939, *10*, 141.

NEUGARTEN, B., HAVIGHURST, R. and TOBIN, S. Personality and patterns of aging. In B. Neugarten (Ed.) *Middle Age and Aging.* Chicago: University of Chicago Press, 1968.

TANNER, J. M. *Growth at Adolescence.* Oxford: Blackwell, 1962.

WEISS, J. Openness and student outcomes: Some results (A part of the symposium with D. Musella, Closure on openness in education) Symposium presented at the meeting of the American Educational Research Association, New Orleans, 1973.

Suggested Readings

ARIÈS, P. *Centuries of Childhood*. New York: Vintage, 1962. This book presents a readable discussion of the evolution of childhood from earlier historical times up to the modern era.

LASCH, C. *Haven in a Heartless World*. New York: Basic Books, 1977. This book offers an interesting description of how the roles of the family have changed over time. Lasch suggests that the traditional functions of the family have gradually been taken over by other institutions, such as schools and health organizations. Lasch argues that the survival of the family may be threatened.

NEUGARTEN, B. L. (Ed.). *Middle Age and Aging*. Chicago: U. of Chicago; 1968. This book is an excellent collection of readings on development in adulthood and the older years. Neugarten also discusses family relationships in the aging process as well as social-psychological theories of the adult/aging personality.

TANNER, J. M. *Education and Physical Growth*. New York: International Universities Press, 1978. This book is an excellent discussion of the growth process from birth through adolescence. This is a revised edition of the popular 1961 book.

2
Theories of Human Development

Reasons for Examining Theories of Human Development

The major purpose of reviewing theories of human development is to demonstrate how such theories are used to formulate answers to basic questions of human development. Such questions may include the following: What is the basic nature of human beings? Is the human being primarily a rational creature or a creature driven by passions? Is human behavior self-regulated from within or largely determined by external factors? An important purpose of studying human development is to come to grips with these—and other—questions.

Theories of human development are ways of organizing the ''facts'' of human behavior into formulations or assumptions about the development of behavior. These formulations or assumptions can then be used to generate testable hypotheses about human development.

For example, E. H. Erikson's theory of human development predicts that a major challenge in young adulthood is developing intimate relationships with significant others. The validity of a theory of development resides, of course, in whether or not its hypotheses are accurate. Do they explain the realities of human behavior? In summary, theories of development are important because they help to organize a vast array of human behavior.

As we examine theories of development, you might ask yourself what your ''theory'' of development is. This process may help you to assess your assumptions about human development. For example, do you believe that the development of children is influenced primarily by learning or by maturation? In addition to helping in the evaluation of one's own theories or intuitions about development, a knowledge of major theories also helps one to look at behavior and development from many different perspectives. This overview can lead to an appreciation of both the strengths and the weaknesses of different perspectives.

Maturation Theories

During the early years of the twentieth century, considerable interest was generated in the United States in describing how individual patterns of growth and development differ with age. These theories of maturation were based on the idea that human development is the result of the unfolding of the human being's genetic inheritance. Therefore, behavior becomes more complex as the individual matures, both physically and mentally. Perhaps the major influence on the development of maturation theories was Charles Darwin's *On the Origin of Species,* originally published in 1859. Darwin was interested in demonstrating the general evolution of human beings from animals by identifying the ''signs'' of human behavior in animal life. In Darwin's scheme of things, infants were considered as evolutionary links between animal life and mature human beings. Animal behavior was considered to be primarily instinctual and inflexible. On the other hand, Darwin viewed human behavior as largely trainable and learned from adults. Darwin emphasized the evolutionary significance of the lengthy period of helplessness in human infancy (compared to the shorter time for animal infants). During this period, parents and adults ensured the physical survival of infants by teaching them appropriate information and skills. It followed from Darwin's notion of the evolution of species that human behavior could also be understood by studying its origins in the infant and child.

One of the leaders of this movement in the United States was G. Stanley Hall. Hall is often cited as the founder of the field of child and adolescent development. Hall believed that development through adolescence was primarily the result of biological and genetic factors. Having been heavily influenced by the work of Charles Darwin, Hall also speculated that the development of the individual human being reflected or recapitulated the evolution of the human species. For example, the infant and toddler's developing skill in using tools "recapitulated" the tool-using discoveries of the cave dwellers. According to Gallatin (1975), Hall believed that

Rather than reflecting the entire sweep of evolution, childhood was supposed to proceed in stages, each of which mirrored a primitive stage of the human species. Very early childhood might correspond, Hall speculated, to a monkey-like ancestor of the human race that had reached sexual maturity around the age of six. The years between eight and twelve allegedly represented a reenactment of a more advanced, but still prehistoric form of mankind, possibly a species that had managed to survive by hunting and fishing. (pp. 26–27)

Hall's theory of recapitulation came under criticism for several reasons, including the observation that by two or three years of age a human child has gone well beyond the abilities of monkeys, apes, and prehistoric humanlike creatures such as Neanderthal Man. That is, the verbal, social and movement skills of human three-year-olds are typically far more advanced than the adults among these other species (Gallatin, 1975).

Although Hall's recapitulation theory was never accepted as a *specific* approach to human development, his *general* emphasis on a *genetic basis* for the unfolding of development had a marked influence on the study of child development. Because of his influential position as a major figure in the establishment of human development as a scientific study, Hall exerted considerable influence on his students to adopt a "nature" or genetic perspective to human development. Two of his students turned out to be among the most prominent developmentalists of the early twentieth century—Arnold Gesell and Lewis Terman.

Arnold Gesell. Gesell founded the Clinic of Child Development at Yale University in 1911. Hall was fascinated with the stages of development that children demonstrated as they matured, and as his student, Gesell emphasized that growth and development were determined primarily by a fixed timetable of maturation. Gesell was a strong believer in the notion that innate, built-in, or genetic tendencies toward optimal development control the rate of child growth and learning in each individual. Environmental factors had a minimal impact.

Acceleration of development . . . is typically an inherent biological characteristic of the individual, most probably hereditary in nature. There is no convincing evidence that fundamental acceleration of development can be readily induced by either pernicious or enlightened methods of stimulation. (Gesell, 1928, pp. 363–64)

Gesell believed that this innate or programmed process of development could be documented through detailed observations and photographs of the

G. *Stanley Hall* (1844–1924)

G. Stanley Hall was an articulate leader who founded the field of child study in the United States at the turn of the century. In 1889, Hall went from being a professor of psychology at Johns Hopkins University to the presidency of Clark University. Like most of his contemporaries, Hall knew rather little about children's development, their behavior, their interests, and their abilities. Hall's interests were largely educational. He wanted to incorporate the study of child development into educational training. He began by developing summer workshops for schoolteachers and school administrators.

Hall's method of investigating child behavior was a questionnaire. He and his students developed questions on a wide range of child behaviors (e.g., children's play, fear, anger, dreams, and reading habits). The questionnaires were given to teachers, who, in turn, gave them to thousands of children. The results were sent to Hall for his analysis. Hall published many of the findings in a journal that he founded: *Pedagogical Seminary* (later to become the *Journal of Genetic Psychology*). Although many of Hall's results were interesting, his questionnaire method gradually fell into disfavor as a reliable technique for collecting unbiased information about children. The results of Hall's research may have been questionable, but his idea of studying the normal development of children profoundly influenced educators and psychologists.

Hall's influence was not confined to childhood. In 1904, he wrote *Adolescence*, which initiated the modern study of adolescence in the United States. *Senescence: The Last Half of Life* (1922) expanded Hall's influence to adulthood and aging. Hall was also a key figure in introducing Sigmund Freud to American psychologists (Freud's theories of personality development had a significant influence on American psychologists). In 1909, Hall celebrated the twentieth anniversary of Clark University by inviting Freud to deliver a series of lectures, which were to become both influential and controversial. G. Stanley Hall was truly a monumental figure in the study of human development.

behavior of infants and children at varying ages. This documentation would not only show the course of physical and mental development but would also provide, for Gesell, a basis for the construction of diagnostic measurements or tests.

As a result of these detailed observations, Gesell developed schedules or standards for motor, visual-adaptive, personal-social, and language behavior. These standards described the sequences of development throughout childhood (see Table 2.1).

On the basis of these observations of the sequences of behavior during development (e.g., the unvarying and predictable appearance of creeping and crawling prior to standing and walking), two logical principles of Gesell's

15 months—1. Uses massive, total-response gestures.
              2. Indicates refusal by bodily protest.
              3. Responds to a few key and catch words.
18 months—1. Communicates both by gestures and words but words are beginning to replace gestures.
              2. Responds to simple commands.
              3. Verbalizes ends of actions such as "bye-bye," "thank you," "all gone."
              4. Refusals may be expressed by "no" but more usually by bodily response.
21 months—1. Asks for food, toilet, drink.
              2. Repeats single words said to him, or last word or two of a phrase.
24 months—1. Speech accompaniment of activity.
              2. Asks questions such as "What's that?"
              3. Verbalizes immediate experiences.
              4. Much vocalization in a group, but little conversation.
              5. Refers to himself by his name.
              6. Refusals expressed by "no."

Adaptation of the table on "Communications" (p. 249) in *The First Five Years of Life* by Arnold Gesell, M.D. Copyright 1940 by Arnold Gesell. Reprinted by permission of Harper & Row, Publishers, Inc.

theory became popular during the 1930s and 1940s. These were *maturational readiness* and *behavioral stages* (e.g., the "terrible twos").

Maturational readiness meant that a given child had matured to an appropriate point where he or she could benefit from a specific type of training. In other words, the child who was ready could attain competence at a given activity. The immature child would need to spend more time and effort on that same activity and still might not perform at a comparable level. Gesell demonstrated the principle of readiness in a series of classic experiments involving identical twins. For example, one twin of a pair was given practice in stair climbing well before stair-climbing skill would be expected to occur in infants. The other twin was given no specific training in stair climbing. Gesell and his colleagues found that the twin who had received no training in stair climbing later attained stair-climbing skill at only a slightly lower pace than the trained twin. Furthermore, there was no ultimate difference between the twins in stair-climbing ability. These types of experimental results were taken as evidence that the critical determinant of development was the notion of maturational readiness. Experience and training made no difference unless the child was at the appropriate maturational level. This idea of maturational readiness was adapted to school learning by educators. The notion was that there were optimal times in the development of children when they were *ready* to learn such skills as reading or writing.

The concept of *behavioral stages* emerged from Gesell's notion that maturation, in fact, represented the unfolding of interweaving growth forces. Gesell referred to this as the principle of *reciprocal interweaving:*

Development in the human infant is orderly; it is, however, not necessarily so orderly that he achieves one function in its perfection and then develops another which he appends to the first. Two functions which are to be integrated tend to develop almost simultaneously, at first apparently unrelated to each other, first one then the other taking lead and precedence. They seem to weave in and about each other as they develop, until they finally merge, synergize, coordinate. It is a reciprocal kind of inter-weaving. So it is with the development of upright posture and locomotion. (Gesell and Amatruda, 1947, p. 192.)

Gesell applied this notion of reciprocal interweaving to personality development by suggesting that the "terrible twos" (a stage where the infant demonstrates improving locomotion and grasping combined with a seeming indifference to the verbal requests of parents or caretakers) is inevitably followed by the "conforming threes" and the "inquisitive fours." These stages of child personality were popular with many parents in the 1940s and 1950s, who were looking for some explanation of children's seemingly negative behavior. The notion of stages of personality based on maturity was, of course, a comforting idea to nervous parents.

Lewis Terman. Terman was a professor at Stanford University whose primary interest was mental measurement. Terman was one of the first to translate into English the first intelligence test developed by Alfred Binet in Paris (Binet and Simon, 1905a, 1905b). He published the test in 1916 as the Stanfod-Binet Intelligence Test.

Terman believed that intelligence was primarily a genetic or hereditary characteristic. Terman's work on mental measurement was based on two assumptions about intelligence: older children (because they are more mature) should perform better on tests of intelligence than younger children, and smarter children should do better than average children. In keeping with the influence of his mentor, G. Stanley Hall, Terman assumed that intelligence gradually unfolded with maturation, like other forms of growth and development. Although intelligence was expected to increase with age, differences between children were presumed to remain stable over time. Individual differences among people of similar age or between groups of people from varied social or family background were presumed to reflect genetic or hereditary differences in intelligence. We will examine this highly controversial notion of intelligence as well as some of the issues in the measurement of intelligence later in this book.

In addition to developing an instrument for measuring intelligence, Terman was very much interested in doing research to determine the genetic component of intelligence. His monumental project, *Genetic Studies of Genius*, begun in 1921, was a study of the development of gifted children over time (Terman, 1925; Terman and Oden, 1959). Although his research did not establish that intelligence was genetically determined, it was important for several reasons. It was one of the first major longitudinal studies (the same persons are repeatedly measured over time) conducted in the United States (Sears, 1975). (We will discuss research methods in human development, including longitudinal research, in Chapter Three.) As such, Terman's study of the intellectually gifted, which spanned almost 50 years, encouraged the development of other longitudinal studies. It provided useful information on a wide variety of developmental dimensions. Terman's work also did much to dispel stereotypes and myths about the intellectually gifted. For example, Terman's data showed that, as a group, intellectually-gifted individuals were *not* physically weak, socially maladjusted, or sickly. Rather, they tended to be just as healthy, phys-

The "terrible two's."

Photograph by Sylvia Byers

ically fit, and socially adept as nongifted individuals. In addition, Terman's research contributed to the emergence of human development as a *normative science*. (A *norm* is a statement of typical characteristics or behaviors for a specific group.) His research on gifted individuals, as well as his work with I.Q. tests, involved the development of normative descriptions about individuals. As we shall see throughout this book, much of the research, theory, and application in human development involves, in part, the careful development, evaluation, and application of normative statements about children, adolescents, and adults.

EVALUATION OF MATURATION THEORIES

The work of Gesell and Terman reached a peak of popularity during the late 1940s. The major problem with such an exclusively maturational perspective was that it ignored the significant role of the environment in development. In essence, both Terman and Gesell were suggesting that since human development was nature-based (rather than nurture-based), a full understanding of the individual required only that typical or normative changes in development be described. In the case of Terman, these norms of development could be determined through the use of intelligence tests. Both the use of psychological tests to measure intelligence and the notion that intelligence is primarily an innate or nature-based phenomenon have come under serious criticism. For Gesell, growth norms were determined through systematic and careful observation, and cataloging of child behavior. Today the extreme maturational theory that Gesell advocated has been almost totally rejected. By the mid-1960s, research was beginning to accumulate that demonstrated the importance of environmental experience and human maturation in human development (Hunt, 1961; Bloom, 1964). It became clear that both maturation and experience interact to influence the development of the individual. Many programs such as Project Head Start were launched on the assumption that experience—particularly early experience—can make a substantial difference in developmental outcomes.

Behavior and Learning Theories

In contrast to maturational theories, behavior and learning theories portray human behavior as primarily the result of environmental stimulation. Much of what an individual becomes is the result of what he or she has experienced or *learned*. This emphasis on the role of experience in human development is not new (philosophers such as Aristotle and John Locke had long ago developed notions of the importance of experience). However, it was not until the early part of the twentieth century that formal theories of learning were developed in psychology. Until that time, the prevailing emphasis in psychology was on the study of the mind through introspection or self-analysis.

THE BEGINNINGS OF BEHAVIORISM AND LEARNING THEORIES

In the 1920s, John B. Watson challenged this subjective view with an approach that he called ''behaviorism.'' Watson focused on ''stimuli'' in the environment and "responses" or behaviors of people or organisms. He was not concerned with subjective events in the mind. His major idea was that the complex behaviors of adults were built on the elementary foundation of the simple inborn reflexes of infants continually refined through life experiences. He described this complex sequential behavior as being composed of chains of S–R (stimulus–response) units that become associated through learning.

Watson's position in learning and development was strongly supported by the research of the Russian psychologist Ivan Pavlov. Pavlov's discovery of "conditioned responses" appeared to demonstrate that complex human responses are built up or derived from simple responses. A conditioned response is a behavior that is elicited by a stimulus that did not previously elicit that response. For example, Pavlov demonstrated that a dog could learn to salivate at the sound of a bell. Obviously dogs do not ordinarily salivate at the sound of a bell, but they do salivate if hungry and presented with food. Pavlov, however, arranged the situation so that the ringing of a bell always preceded the presentation of food. Eventually, the dogs learned to salivate not only when food was presented but when the bell was rung. Pavlov's discovery bolstered the idea of *associationism* (learning that occurs through the connection of two events that appear together in time).

Conditioning theory was of enormous significance to psychologists like Watson who were trying to transform the psychology of learning and human development into an objective science. Watson (1924) thought that he now had what amounted to the central features of a theory of learning and human development:

1. The S–R (stimulus–response) association, which he felt was the basic unit of behavior.
2. *Conditioning*, or the fundamental process through which learning occurred.

Watson was extraordinarily enthusiastic about his behavioristic "synthesis," as evidenced by the following statement: "The behaviorist asks for nothing to start with in building a human being but the squirmings everyone can see in the new-born infant" (Watson, 1924). His general idea was that these "squirmings" or infant reflex units could be linked in almost random sequences through conditioning. A contemporary of Watson, E. L. Thorndike (1913–1914), suggested much the same thing when he said that it is possible to "get any response of which a learner is capable associated with any situation to which he is sensitive."

Watson's general notion of human development has been challenged by recent research on infant development (we will discuss this research in Chapter Six). The following ideas of Watson have been discredited: (1) that inborn responses or reflexes are simple and initially disorganized; and (2) that learning through conditioning occurs largely by chance. For example, rather than having simple and unorganized responses, it has been shown that the infant has the visual ability, at birth, to follow a moving light with its eyes. In addition, it turns its mouth in the direction of a nipple when touched on the cheek. Contrary to the notion of the chance learning of responses, the general pattern of behavior is both defined and limited in people and in animals. For example, the ability to use the hands and fingers for operating precision tools or playing musical instruments is a characteristic of only some animal species (including humans). A bull moose cannot play the bassoon.

TYPES OF CONDITIONING

Learning theorists have generally agreed on two processes or types of conditioning that are important to human learning and development. The first process is called *classical conditioning,* the type of learning that Watson and Pavlov stressed. The second process—*operant conditioning*—was pioneered by Edward Thorndike (1911) and B. F. Skinner (1938).

Classical Conditioning. Pavlov's experiment is an excellent example of classical conditioning. In that experiment, the sight or smell of food produced salivating behavior, an unconditioned *reflex,* in the dog. *Unconditioned reflexes* are responses that—prior to any learning—are naturally combined with specific unconditioned stimuli. For example, a dog salivates when it sees or smells food, and an infant is startled at the sound of a loud noise.

In Pavlov's experiment, because the sound of a bell (originally a neutral stimulus) was repeatedly heard just before food was presented, the dog associated the bell ringing with food and began to salivate when it heard the bell. The dog now salivated at the sound of the bell whether food was presented with the bell ringing or not. Thus a *conditioned reflex* was established. *Conditioned reflexes* are formed when one associates a previously neutral stimulus (e.g., the sound of a bell) with an unconditioned stimulus (e.g., food). Because the conditioned stimulus (the sound of the bell) was repeatedly presented just before the unconditioned stimulus (food), the dog began to respond to the conditioned stimulus just as it had originally responded to the unconditioned stimulus.

Operant Conditioning. Operant conditioning is a learning process that depends on rewards and punishments. The major difference between classical conditioning and operant conditioning is that behavior in the latter cannot be automatically or naturally produced. This means that the behavior must first occur before any learning can take place. In other words, the behavior to be conditioned must first occur so that it can be strengthened or reinforced. For example, a child goes to the bathroom by himself, and this behavior is then reinforced with candy. Another example would be when a child hits a baseball, and this accomplishment is reinforced by a big smile and words of approval from mom and dad. *Reinforcement,* or the perceived consequences of behavior, influences the frequency with which that behavior occurs. For example, if a child is positively rewarded for mowing the lawn, then he/she will want to do it again in the future. On the other hand, if a child is punished or gets no reward for a behavior he/she will do it less frequently or not at all (the behavior is then said to be *extinguished*). One of the primary proponents of operant conditioning has been the psychologist B. F. Skinner.

THE LEARNING THEORY POINT OF VIEW—A SUMMARY

Sheldon White (1970), one of the leading authorities on the learning theory approach to child development, has indicated the following as the primary assumptions of such a viewpoint:

What is often called the "learning theory point of view" would seem to amount to these assumptions:

1. The environment may be unambiguously characterized in terms of *stimuli.*

2. Behavior may be unambiguously characterized in terms of *responses*.
3. A class of stimuli exist which, applied contingently and immediately following a response, increase it or decrease it in some measurable fashion. These stimuli may be treated as *reinforcers*.
4. *Learning* may be completely characterized in terms of various possible couplings among stimuli, responses, and reinforcers.
5. Unless there is definite evidence to the contrary, classes of behavior may be assumed to be learned, manipulable by the environment, extinguishable, and trainable. (pp. 665–66)

AN EVALUATION OF TRADITIONAL BEHAVIORISM AND LEARNING THEORY

After our brief review of behaviorism and learning theory in human development, several general evaluative remarks are in order:

1. *Behaviorism and learning theory tend to portray humans as reactive organisms.* People are shaped or molded by the nature of the associations in their environment and the rewards, punishments, and reinforcements to which they are subjected. This approach tends to emphasize a *mechanistic* interpretation of human life. People are set in motion by stimuli that result in behavior or responses. Little need is seen for analyzing the structure of the human "machine" (i.e., the nature of the human body, the interaction of physiology and behavior, or the nature of the self and the mind) in relation to human behavior.
2. *Behaviorism and learning theory tend to be reductionistic.* The general thrust of learning theory is that complex behavior can be derived from simple stimuli and responses or S–R units. The result of this reductionistic emphasis is the general failure of learning theory to address the broad—and more important—questions of how the human being organizes, controls, and regulates behavior.

John Dewey (1859–1952).

Drawn by Dana Wu. Copyright © 1985 by Lawrence B. Schiamberg.

JOHN DEWEY: AN EARLY CRITIC OF BEHAVIORISM

John Dewey (1896) criticized what he considered the unrealistic and overly simplistic views of behaviorism. Dewey's criticism was the forerunner of what today might be called a systems perspective to learning and development. Dewey argued that the parts of the S–R model (stimulus, brain activity or neural connections, and response) are *not* separate units. Rather, they exist only as functioning units in the *unified* activities of behavior. Dewey regarded the reflex as an artificial concept because the reflex never exists alone. Rather, he suggested that the nature of a stimulus is determined by the makeup of the organism and the activities going on inside it. In addition, he pointed out that every response produces additional stimulating properties, which themselves produce behavior. Dewey suggested that the entire process was a *dynamic* and *continuous* one that could not be realistically reduced to S–R units. For example, walking or speaking involves a continuous pattern of behavior that can be broken up into S–R units only at the risk of gross oversimplification.

3. *Behaviorism and learning theory tend to be deterministic. Determinism* means that everything about the individual and his or her behavior is the result of his or her past or present experiences. Philosophers have long debated whether human beings are free to control their behavior or whether they are the product of their environment. This long-standing debate (free will versus determinism) is resolved very neatly by learning theorists. They simply state there is no such thing as free will. All human behavior, including values, attitudes, emotional responses, and moral precepts, are determined by the external environment (past or present). B. F. Skinner, in *Beyond Freedom and Dignity* (1971), suggested that concepts such as respect, dignity, and freedom are irrelevant because an individual is simply the product of his or her previous learning history.

SOCIAL LEARNING THEORY

One of the major elaborations of learning theory was social learning theory, which examines the broad range of learning that is accomplished by means of *observation* and *imitation*. Social learning theorists have maintained that we learn much of what we learn through watching others rather than through the direct shaping or "conditioning" of responses (Bandura, 1973, 1977; Bandura and Walters, 1963). Social learning theory examines the ways people learn aggression, affiliation, generosity, and so on, through the modeling of these behaviors by significant others (e.g., parents, peers, spouses, and friends).

Some of the most recent developments in social learning theory have been made by Albert Bandura and his colleagues, (Bandura, 1977). According to

Social learning theory suggests that human beings can learn a broad range of skills by observing and following the behavior of significant others.

Photographs by David Kostelnik

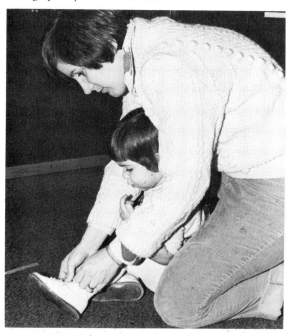
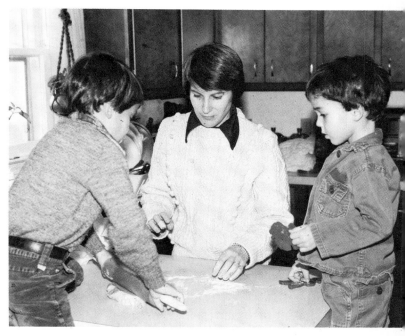

Bandura, the individual's *cognitive* (mental) processes perform a central function in behavior. For example, the child's experiences are remembered and then used by the child to form ideas about possible behavior that will guide future action. The child who observes two friends fighting with one another develops a "concept" of fighting that depends, in part, on the consequences of the fighting behavior for the friends. Did they appear to have fun without seriously injuring one another? Did one or both participants suffer cuts or bruises and begin crying? Did significant adults view the fighting with disapproval? Or did adults look on with seeming approval at displays of aggression or self-defense? Such consequences contribute to the development of a "concept" of fighting that will guide the child's future behavior.

APPLICATION BOX

Albert Bandura and Social Learning Theory

Bandura comments on the major features of social learning theory as follows:

> The capacity to learn by observation enables people to acquire large, integrated patterns of behavior without having to form them gradually by tedious trial and error.
>
> The abbreviation of the acquisition process through observational learning is vital for both development and survival. Because mistakes can produce costly or even fatal consequences, the prospects of survival would be slim indeed if one could learn only by suffering the consequences of trial and error. For this reason, one does not teach children to swim, adolescents to drive automobiles, and novice medical students to perform surgery by having them discover the appropriate behavior through the consequences of their successes and failures . . . It is difficult to imagine a social transmission process in which language, lifestyles, and institutional practices of a culture are taught to each new member by selective reinforcement of fortuitous behaviors, without the benefit of models who exemplify the cultural patterns . . .
>
> The capacity to use symbols provides humans with a powerful means of dealing with their environment. Through verbal and imagined symbols people process and preserve experiences in representational forms that serve as guides for future behavior. The capability for intentional action is rooted in symbolic activity. Images of desirable futures foster courses of action designed to lead toward more distant goals. Through the medium of symbols people can solve problems without having to enact all the various alternative solutions; and they can foresee the probable consequences of different actions and alter their behavior accordingly.

> . . . Another distinguishing feature of social learning theory is the prominent role it assigns to self-regulatory capacities. By arranging environmental inducements, generating cognitive supports, and producing consequences for their own actions, people are able to exercise some measure of control over their own behavior. (Bandura, 1977, pp. 12–13)

Photograph courtesy of Albert Bandura

Theories of Human Development

A prominent example of observational learning is the impact of television on children's behavior. To what extent is children's behavior affected by the portrayal of violence? Some research has demonstrated that the viewing of aggressive or violent behavior by children can have a dramatic effect on their subsequent demonstration of such violent or aggressive behavior (Bandura, 1973, 1977). According to social learning theory, the possibility of increased aggression as a result of the modeling of such behavior would depend on many factors. These include the consequences to the model, the child's age (e.g., is he old enough to distinguish fantasy and reality?), and the interpretation of the model's behavior by such significant others as parents, siblings, or caretakers. For example, when the Superman of television throws two crooks through a window, parents may respond in several ways (assuming that they are watching the program with their child). The parents may say that Superman is not a real person, that the two crooks are just actors, and that the window is made of special glass.

In summary, social learning theorists have made several contributions to the overall relationship of learning theory and human development:

1. The idea of "stimuli" as external events that control human behavior has been modified. Stimuli can be signals (cognitive processes) that are internalized and that serve to help human beings make decisions and control their lives.
2. The idea has been presented that other people are significant in human learning and development. The fact that human beings can learn from one another is an important theme of human development that permeates all levels of development from infancy through old age.

Cognitive Theory: Piaget

Although its roots in the traditions of European thinking are very old, cognitive theory has appeared relatively recently on the American scene. A *cognitive* approach to learning and human development emphasizes mental or internal factors as contrasted with the environmental or external factors of the traditional behaviorists. (Many social learning theorists, such as Bandura, have incorporated cognitive processes into their theories.) Perhaps the major breakthrough for cognitive psychology occurred with the gradual recognition of the work of the Swiss biologist and philosopher Jean Piaget. Although a good deal of Piaget's work was done prior to 1950, it was not until the early 1950s that his work was seriously considered by American developmentalists. In contrast to the behaviorists and traditional learning theorists, Piaget viewed the mind as central to the understanding of how human beings develop. According to Piaget, the mind is not simply a passive receiver of information but an active processor of experience. The mind is like other living and growing structures because it does not simply respond or react to experience but actively changes and adapts to the world.

INTELLECTUAL ORGANIZATION AND ADAPTATION

As a result of his early work in biology (see the biographical sketch of Piaget), Piaget came to believe that biological activities (including animal and plant behaviors) were the result of *adaptation* to the physical environment.

Jean Piaget (1896–1980)

Photograph courtesy of the
Jean Piaget Society

Piaget was born in 1896 in Neuchâtel, Switzerland. As a child, he was intellectually precocious, having published his first article at ten years of age—a description of an albino sparrow. This early interest in biology was to be reflected in all of his later work. In 1915, at the age of eighteen, Piaget received his baccalaureate degree from the University of Neuchâtel. In 1918, he received his doctoral degree in the natural sciences from the same institution. By this time, he had published twenty-one papers, mostly on mollusks, and was considered an expert in this area of biology.

After completion of his doctorate, Piaget's primary interest turned to psychology. His work in biology had led him to the conclusion that biological development was the result not only of maturation (and heredity) but also of features of the environment. Piaget's observations of structural changes in successive generations of mollusks led him to the notion that biological development was a process of *adaptation* to the environment. These concepts of biological adaptation led to Piaget's later view of human mental development as a process of adaptation to the environment. He viewed mental development as an extension of biological development. Beginning in 1921, Piaget launched a career of research that focused on the mental development of children. Piaget's first books in psychology were *The Language and Thought of the Child* (1924) and *Judgment and Reasoning of the Child* (1924).

According to Piaget, the action-oriented behavior of young children is the beginning of cognitive development.

Photograph by Gale Schiamberg

This idea led him to think of human cognitive development in the same way. In other words, thinking involves adaptation to an environment and results in the *organization* of the mind. The organized patterns of behavior and perception are called *schemata* (*schemata*, plural; *schema*, singular). Infant schemata are usually action-oriented (e.g., sucking, grasping, and looking), whereas adult schemata are abstractions (e.g., concepts of justice and the concept of the conservation of matter). The cognitive schemata of the adult are derived from the motor schemata of the child.

ASSIMILATION AND ACCOMMODATION

The processes that are responsible for this adaptation of schemata are called *assimilation* and *accommodation*. Assimilation and accommodation are complementary processes. As long as a person learns (which happens from birth to death), these processes remain important.

SOME DEFINITIONS

Assimilation. The process of using the same structure in more than one way. It is the process of applying existing habits and existing ideas to new objects. An infant sucks on a nipple, its thumb, its hand, and even its blanket.

Accommodation. The process of changing one's actions to fit a new situation. It is the process of modifying an action to fit a new object. An infant sucks on a nipple but has to adjust its sucking action in order to drink from a cup.

In assimilation, the person imposes his/her existing schemata or structures on present experiences. For example, a child who has learned what a fly is may include a butterfly in the category "fly." Assimilation is a *quantitative* change in existing schemata that are applied to many new stimuli. In accommodation, however, the development of schemata is *qualitative* because the schemata are changed to fit the new stimuli or experiences.

The processes of assimilation and accommodation work together and are necessary for cognitive growth. Of equal importance are the comparative amounts of assimilation or accommodation that occur. A balance between assimilation and accommodation is important and is referred to by Piaget as *equilibrium*. The absence of equilibrium provides the motivation for seeking a new state of balance or equilibrium. The interaction of assimilation and accommodation in the process of attaining equilibrium accounts for cognitive development from birth to death.

STAGES OF COGNITIVE DEVELOPMENT

According to Piaget, cognitive development proceeds through a series of stages, each of which is qualitatively different from the prior stage. Cognitive development can be divided into four broad periods (Piaget, 1963):

1. *Sensori-motor intelligence* (0–2 years). During this period behavior is primarily motor. Infant schemata involve action, movement, and perceptual activity (e.g., looking, hearing, and touching).

2. *Preoperational thought* (2–7 years). This period is characterized by the development of language. During this stage the child evolves from an organism that functions primarily in a sensori-motor mode to one that functions primarily in a conceptual or symbolic mode. The child is increasingly able to internally represent events (to "think") while becoming less dependent on motor activities for the direction of behavior.
3. *Concrete operations* (7–11 years). In this period, the child's reasoning processes become logical. This means that the child develops logical and rational thought processes which can be applied to concrete (actual or real) objects or experiences. The concrete operational child cannot yet apply his logic to problems that are abstract or hypothetical.
4. *Formal operations* (11–15 years). In this stage, the child's thinking reaches its greatest level of development. The child is able to apply logic to all types of problems including the abstract and the hypothetical. The child is no longer dependent on the concrete or the real.

EVALUATION

In summary, cognitive theorists such as Piaget have generally rejected the mechanistic theories of development and learning that reduce development to S–R associations and reinforcements. R. W. White (1959) has suggested that S–R theory does not explain the commonly observed phenomenon of individuals (including animals) who work or engage in any activity without any apparent reward. White seems to be saying that when people engage in some activities such as play they may well be motivated by their own basic "competence" rather than by a mere reinforcement.

Cognitive theories (in particular, Piaget's ideas) have been widely applied to educational design. Curriculum can be planned to fit the needs of children. It is possible to determine the stage of thinking that a child is at and to design educational experiences in accordance with that stage. For example, in learning mathematics, the concrete-operational child would benefit more from the use of actual objects (e.g., blocks and marbles) than from a presentation using only symbols and abstractions. There has been some criticism of the application of Piagetian theory to education. In particular, some researchers have suggested that Piaget's stages of development are unrealistically distinct, leading some educators to be much too inflexible in their expectations of child learning (Donaldson, 1979). Other criticism has focused on Piaget's theory and methods as evidenced by the following:

Although Piaget's popularity has increased dramatically in recent years, there is a great deal of concern . . . that the terms and concepts invoked by his theory more closely reflect Piaget's own cognitive structures and unique methodological approach than they do the real world of mental and behavioral phenomena. Many . . . believe that his constructs have not yet been sufficiently validated by the results of empirical investigation, and they fear that the nature of the system is such that its components may not even be subject to such validation. (Diamond, 1982, p. 21)

Another problem with cognitive theories, in general, is that they have emphasized intellectual or mental constructs as the primary organizing features of human development. While traditional behaviorists have made it a point to ignore cognitive characteristics of the organism or person in explaining development, it might be argued that some cognitive theorists have overemphasized the role of mental constructs in governing all of human behavior. While cognitive factors surely have an important role in human development, they need to be integrated with our understanding of biological, motor, emotional, and personality factors if a comprehensive appreciation of development is to occur.

The Psychoanalytic Tradition

The theories of Sigmund Freud, the neo-Freudians (Rank, Jung, Adler, Horney, and Erikson) and the so-called ego psychologists constitute the *psychoanalytic tradition.* The focus of these theories is on aspects of human development which are not addressed in any detail in the maturational, behaviorist/learning, and cognitive theories discussed so far. Specifically, the psychoanalytic tradition focuses on emotional factors and personality development.

FREUD

Like that of the learning theorists, Freud's notion of humans was essentially a deterministic one. Unlike the learning theorists, he believed that the source of determinism was not the environment but the powerful forces within the person. Psychoanalytic theory pictures humans as creatures driven by inner forces that often remain at the level of the unconscious. Human development represents the effort of the individual to channel or redirect these potentially self-destructive forces of sex and aggression in socially constructive directions. Much of Freud's theory points to the development of personality in childhood as the critical clue to understanding adult personality.

In contrast to Piaget, Freud formulated a stage theory of development relating to the development of emotions and personality. The central concept in Freud's theory is his concept of *libido.* Libido—mental or psychic energy—presumably occurs in a fixed amount at birth in each individual. The libido is centered in certain areas of the body at certain periods in life. At each location site of the libido, the individual could be gratified with the release of tensions (associated with the accumulation of libido at a specific site) or be frustrated if the appropriate stimulation did not occur. Frustration or the absence of gratification, was associated with the development of emotional or psychological problems later in life.

The movement of libido to different parts of the body determined not only the method of gratification or frustration but also the progression from one developmental stage to the next one. Freud believed that the location of the libido followed a sequence of unvarying or universal stages. He postulated that personality develops in a relatively predictable pattern of *psychosexual stages* (see Table 2.2)

1. *The oral stage.* The first location of libido is centered in the mouth region. This is for approximately the first 18 months of the child's life. Accordingly, the infant is either stimulated (gratified) or frustrated by being able—or unable—to suck on things (e.g., mother's nipple, bottle nipple, or thumb) or, when teeth erupt, to bite on things.

TABLE 2.2
Freud's Stages
of Development

Stage	Approximate Age	Characteristics
Oral	0–18 months	The sources of pleasure include sucking, biting, and swallowing. Preoccupation with immediate gratification of impulses.
Anal	18 months–3 years	The sources of gratification include urination and the expulsion or retention of feces.
Phallic	3–6 years	The child becomes concerned with the genitals. Source of sexual pleasure involves manipulating genitals. Period of Oedipus or Electra complex.
Latency	6 years–onset of puberty (approximately 12 years)	Loss of interest in sexual gratification. Identification with like-sexed parent.
Genital	puberty–the adolescent years	Concern with adult modes of sexual pleasure, barring fixations or regressions (movement to an earlier pattern of behavior).

When the infant's oral needs are blocked or frustrated, problems in the infant's development may occur. If frustration is severe enough, *fixation* may occur. That is, some of the infant's libido will remain (presumably for the rest of one's life) at the oral zone. When such an oral fixation occurs, the individual will attempt to gain the gratification which was missed earlier in life. Thus, the emotional or psychological problems that a person has as an adult may be based on fixations at early ages (Erikson, 1963). For example, an oral fixation could result in an adult who is always acquiring things (e.g., wealth and power) or taking things into the mouth (e.g., excessive eating, or smoking).

2. *The anal stage.* This stage extends from approximately 18 months to three years. According to Freud, the libido is located in the anal region of the body. The primary gratification in this stage occurs with the use of the anal muscles which control the opening or closing of the anal sphincters. The child is stimulated either by the expulsion or retention of feces.

Anal fixations result from frustrations during this period. Since the anal stage coincides in our culture with the period of toilet training, some children may have *anal expulsive* fixations (the result of overly severe toilet training). This may result in adults who are messy, wasteful or disorderly (Hall, 1954). On the other hand an *anal retentive* fixation may result in an adult who is excessively neat, orderly or "uptight" about revealing his or her emotions (Erikson, 1963).

3. *The phallic stage.* This stage involves the movement of the libido to the genital areas. The phallic stage extends from ages three to six. Because of the structural differences in male and female genitalia, it is appropriate to discuss both a male and female phallic stage (Erikson, 1963).

The male phallic stage. For the male, gratification is obtained by the stimulation of the genitals during routine care. Freud believed that it was the boy's mother who provided some of this stimulation and that, therefore, the boy would sexually *desire* his mother. However, since the father stands in the way of attaining his goal, the boy develops negative feelings toward the father. Freud labeled this entire complex of feelings the *Oedipus Complex.*

As the boy comes to recognize his father as a rival for his mother's love, he gradually comes to fear the potential retaliation of the father. Thus, as a result of the Oedipal Complex, the boy experiences *castration anxiety.* Because of the strength of this anxiety, the boy ultimately gives up his desire for his mother. He replaces it with an *identification* with his father. The identification with the father is an important development because the boy models himself after the father. In so doing, he internalizes characteristics which are required for becoming an adult male in society (Erickson, 1963).

Problems may arise in the phallic stage if, for example, the boy does not resolve his Oedipus Complex. As an adult he may identify more with his mother than with his father, and therefore adopt feminine behavior.

The female phallic stage. As with the male phallic stage, the libido moves to the genital zone. However, in this case, the girl desires to sexually possess her father. Since the mother stands in the way of the girl's goal, the girl, at first, has negative feelings toward the mother and fears punishment from her. Gradually, however, the girl transforms her dislike of the mother into a positive identification and adopts the characteristics of the mother. Freud identified this entire complex of feelings in the female as the female Oedipal Complex (sometimes called the Electra Complex)(Erikson, 1963).

As in the case of males, problems may arise if the phallic stage is not negotiated successfully. For example, the girl who does not appropriately identify with her mother may have difficulties relating to males.

4. *The latency stage.* During this stage which extends from six years of age until the onset of puberty (the biological changes associated with adolescence), the libido submerges and is not localized in a specific body zone. Freud uses the term *latency* to describe this absence or inactivity of libido.

5. *The genital stage.* With the onset of puberty, the libido emerges once again. If the individual has been largely gratified—rather than frustrated from birth until age six—he or she is now prepared for full adult sexuality. This means that the individual's sexuality can now be directed to reproductive functions (Erikson, 1963).

This summary of Freud's theory has been brief. There are additional concepts and principles which Freud discussed in his voluminous writing. The intent here has been to provide the core concepts of his developmental theory, which have served as the historical basis for considerable research and theory in human development.

ERIKSON

Erikson's theory of development has much in common with Freud's theory. In fact, he referred to Freud's work as the "rock" on which all significant improvements in personality theory would be based (Erikson, 1958). However, Erikson's theory differs from Freud's approach in three major ways (Maier, 1969):

1. Erikson emphasized the concept of the *ego* or the self whereas Freud emphasized the importance of feelings. That is, while Freud was primarily concerned with the biologically-based libido and the emerging feelings of gratification or frustration, Erikson emphasized development of the self or ego in relation to the social environment. For this reason, it has been suggested that Freud's theory is *psychosexual,* whereas Erikson's theory is *psychosocial.*

2. Erikson introduced a *social complex* or *framework* to replace the classical Freudian notion of individual dynamics in the context of the child-mother-father triangle. The Eriksonian social context in which the ego or self operates is quite broad and includes the following elements:

   • The individual and his or her parents within the context of the family.
   • The family setting in relation to the wider social–cultural setting (including the historical–cultural heritage of the family).

3. While Freud was primarily concerned with *pathological development*, Erikson focused on the *successful* or *positive solution* of developmental crises. Freud had concentrated on proving the existence and functioning of the unconscious in controlling one's fate. Erikson was trying to show that there were *developmental opportunities* which allowed one the chance to triumph over the hazards of living.

According to Erikson, the ego or the self develops as new demands are continually being placed on it by the social environment. Each new social demand produces an emotional crisis which, in turn, carries with it the opportunity for

---

THUMBNAIL SKETCH

Erik Erikson (*b.* 1902)

Erik Erikson was born in Germany. As a young adult, he met Freud, in Vienna, Austria, and became interested in the psychoanalytical approach to the study of personality development. The psychoanalytical approach was to have a pronounced influence on the direction of his career and his voluminous writings.

Erikson came to the United States when Hitler ascended to power in Germany. He assumed several positions at major universities and child guidance centers. He was on the senior staff of the Austen Riggs Center, and he participated in research on the Sioux Indians while at the Harvard Psychological Clinic. He also worked and did research at the Yale Institute of Human Relations, the Institute of Child Welfare at the University of California, and the Western Psychiatric Institute in Pittsburgh. He is now a professor of human development and a lecturer on psychiatry at Harvard University.

Erikson's books include *Young Man Luther* (1958); *Insight and Responsibility* (1964); *Identity: Youth and Crisis* (1968); *Gandhi's Truth* (1969); and *Toys and Reasons* (1976). Erikson has been a winner of both the Pulitzer Prize and the National Book Award.

Theories of Human Development

a positive resolution and healthy development. Erikson proposed a stage theory of psychosocial development which is based on a principle that is maturational—the *epigenetic principle*.

The epigenetic principle: . . . This principle states that anything that grows has a *ground plan,* and that out of this ground plan the parts arise, each having its *time* of special ascendancy, until all parts have arisen to form a *functioning whole.* (Erikson, 1959, p. 52)

According to this principle, various capabilities compose the fully-developed ego. These capabilities are not fully developed early in life. Rather, each part of the ego has a specific stage in the life cycle when it is the focus or center of development. Because the entire process is based on a maturational timetable, a person must successfully negotiate each stage at its appointed time. Development will move on to the next stage whether or not the necessary capability has been established. For this reason, Erikson views each stage of development as a critical period (Lerner, 1976).

Erikson's major idea is that the stages of development require the individual to *adapt* to the *social environment* in terms of changes in the *ego* or *self*. Erikson first discussed his model of development—the eight stages of development—in his book *Childhood and Society*. In that book, he suggested that every human being experiences eight stages or crises during the course of the lifespan. Erikson identified the following stages of development—each of which may be described as a point where individual adaptation may lean in one of two directions (see Tables 2.3 and 2.4):

1. *Stage 1: Trust versus mistrust.* This stage corresponds to Freud's oral stage and occurs from birth to approximately 18 months. If the infant develops a feeling or general expectancy of physical comfort rather than of fear or uncertainty, then he/she will develop a sense of *trust.* If the infant comes to expect that its needs will be met with some regularity (i.e., that the world is a somewhat predictable and friendly place: food is available when one is hungry, attention is available when one is distressed, and so on), then a basic foundation of trust will be established. This trust can then be extended to new experiences. If, on the other hand, a sense of fear or uncertainty is created in the infant, then adaptation will lean in the direction of *distrust.*

    Although feeding or oral interaction is surely important, it is only one mode of sensory interaction which can reassure the infant. Thus, the parent or caretaker can also develop trust through various other methods, including touching, holding, or looking at the infant.

2. *Stage 2: Autonomy versus shame and doubt.* This stage corresponds to Freud's anal stage and extends from approximately 18 months to three years of age. While Freud limited his concern in the anal stage to gratification or frustration through control of the anal musculature, Erikson expanded his approach to include the other muscles of the body. Just as the infant and toddler learns to control his anal muscles, likewise he/she learns when to "hold on" or "let go" with reference to all the body muscles.

    If the infant or toddler feels in control of its own body, then a sense of autonomy will develop. On the other hand, if the infant is incapable of controlling his/her own body movements in relation to the environment, then he/she will develop a sense of shame or doubt.

According to Erikson, infant reliance on a caregiver leads to the development of trust.

Photograph by Darryl Jacobson

TABLE 2.3 Erikson's Stages of Development: Positive and Negative Resolutions

Central Life Crisis	Positive Resolution	Negative Resolution
Trust versus mistrust (0–18 mos)	Reliance on caregiver leads to development of trust in the environment.	Fear, anxiety, and suspicion. Lack of care, both physical and psychological, by caregiver leads to mistrust of environment (e.g., fear, anxiety, or suspicion).
Autonomy versus shame and doubt (18 mos–3 years)	Sense of self as worthy. Assertion of choice and will. Environment encourages independence, leading to sense of pride.	Loss of self-esteem. Sense of external control may produce self-doubt and doubt in others.
Initiative versus guilt (3–6 years)	The ability to learn, to initiate activities, to enjoy achievement and competence.	The inability to control newly developed power. Realization of potential failure leads to fear of punishment and guilt.
Industry versus inferiority (6 years–puberty)	Learning the value of work; acquiring skills and tools of technology. Competence helps to order life and to make things work.	Repeated frustration and failure lead to feelings of inadequacy and inferiority that may affect view of life.
Identity versus role confusion (adolescence)	Experiments with various roles in developing mature individuality.	Pressures and demands may lead to confusion about self.
Intimacy versus isolation (young adulthood)	A commitment to others. Close heterosexual relationship and procreation.	Withdrawal from such intimacy: isolation, self-absorption, and alienation from others.
Generativity versus stagnation (middle age)	The care and concern for the next generation. Widening interest in work and ideas.	Self-indulgence and resulting psychological impoverishment.
Ego integrity versus despair (old age)	Acceptance of one's life. Realization of the inevitability of death. Feeling of dignity and meaning in one's existence.	Disappointment with one's life and desperate fear of death.

Reprinted and adapted from *Childhood and Society,* by Erik H. Erikson, with permission of W. W. Norton & Company, Inc. Copright 1950, © 1963 by W. W. Norton & Company, Inc.

3. *Stage 3: Initiative versus guilt.* According to Erikson, the three-to-six-year-old child is faced with the developmental dilemma of initiative versus guilt. This period corresponds to Freud's phallic stage in which exploration and manipulation of the genitals becomes a source of pleasure for the young child. Although Erikson does not ignore Freud's notion of the Oedipal Complex, his conceptualization of the conflict has broader psychosocial application than Freud's approach. That is, if the child is to resolve the Oedipal Complex, he/she must be independent of parental figures. Erikson suggested that the child must now employ the previously developed skills of autonomy and motor control by moving out into the world, thereby breaking the Oedipal "apron strings."

If the child is able to step out into this new world of experience without the prodding of the parent, then a sense of *initiative* will develop. On the

Although feeding or oral interaction is surely important, it is
only one mode of sensory interaction which can reassure the
young child.

Photograph by Darryl Jacobson

Exploring and searching the
environment are a part of the
"Initiative versus Guilt" stage of
development.

Photograph by David Kostelnik

other hand, if the child is overly dependent on the parent for permission to move out into the world, then he/she will experience a sense of *guilt.* According to Erikson, guilt will arise when the relatively immature Oedipal attachments prevent the child from doing what society now expects him/her to be able to do—independently experience the world.

4. *Stage 4: Industry versus inferiority.* This stage occurs from six years to the onset of puberty and corresponds to Freud's latency stage. Since Freud believed that the libido was submerged during this stage, he did not think that any significant *psychosexual* development was occurring in the latency phase. On the other hand, Erikson believed that this period was filled with *psychosocial* developments that were of considerable importance.

TABLE 2.4 Erikson's Eight Stages of Development

Erikson's Stages of Development

Stage	1	2	3	4	5	6	7	8
Maturity								Ego Integrity vs. despair
Adulthood							Generativity vs. stagnation	
Young adulthood						Intimacy vs. isolation		
Puberty and adolescence					Identity vs. diffusion			
Latency				Industry vs. inferiority				
Locomotor Genital			Initiative vs. guilt					
Muscular Anal		Autonomy vs. shame						
Oral Sensory	Trust vs. mistrust							

Erikson's first four stages are similar to Freud's stages, the anal, oral, phallic, and latency stages, respectively. The remaining four represent Erikson's application of interpersonal and social factors to adolescent and adult development.

Reprinted and adapted from *Childhood and Society,* by Erik H. Erikson, with permission of W. W. Norton & Company, Inc. Copyright 1950, © 1963 by W. W. Norton & Company, Inc.

Theories of Human Development

The development of a sense of industry means that children apply their skills to make things happen.

Photograph by Darryl Jacobson

According to Erikson, children begin to learn the basic skills necessary for independent functioning in adult society during this phase of life. This learning ordinarily occurs, in part, in the setting of the formal school and includes such skills as reading, writing, and reasoning. *Industry* refers to the sense of accomplishment that the child gets from applying these skills to life situations, tasks, or problems. *Inferiority* refers to the sense of *helplessness* or lack of control that occurs when children feel that their existing skill level is no match for the tasks at hand. The role of the parent or caretaker and the teacher is of prime importance during this stage, because the child who develops academic and social skills will likely emerge from this period with a sense of competence and productivity.

5. *Stage 5: Identity versus identity diffusion or role confusion.* This phase corresponds to the genital stage of Freud's psychosexual stages of development. The crisis of identity versus diffusion occurs during adolescence—the period which extends from the onset of puberty until the development of a tentative "stance toward the world" (i.e., an identity). During this phase, the adolescent begins to ask crucial psychosocial questions such as:

- Who am I in relation to society?
- What vocation or career do I wish to pursue?
- What set of values or beliefs will guide my life?
- What type of a general lifestyle do I prefer?
- Over what elements in my life can I now exercise some choice?

Two significant changes occur during this period which influence the adolescent's resolution of identity questions.

a. The first change is *physical.* The onset of puberty results in bodily changes that may encourage adolescents to view themselves, at least physically, as adults.

Role experimentation may be involved in the development of a sense of identity in adolescence.

Photograph by Darryl Jacobson

b. The second change is the development of abstract reasoning (Piaget's final stage of cognitive functioning) that enables the adolescent to deal with the concepts or ingredients of identity: values, views of self, and views of society (e.g., notions of justice, truth, and equality).

Thus, Erikson views this period of the life cycle as involving much more than the psychosexual development in Freud's genital phase. For example, adolescent maturity may make possible a new way of understanding the complexities of reality through the use of abstractions. The adolescent can now think about the vast array of possible life roles (e.g., student, mother, father, brother, teacher, lawyer, mechanic, or pharmacist) in a logical, abstract fashion such that he/she can now begin to fashion (from this vast array of possible roles) a reasonably organized description of the self or an identity. Thinking about such roles is usually accompanied by some role experimentation on the part of the adolescent. If this normal process of testing and trying out roles results in a tentative commitment to a role and accompanying set of values, then the adolescent has successfully completed this stage. On the other hand, if the adolescents cannot find a role that suits them, they may remain in a state of continual experimentation, moving from one role to another without making a permanent commitment to any role. According to Erikson, such an individual who is not able to successfully resolve the identity crisis may have a sense of *role confusion* or identity *diffusion.*

6. *Stage 6: Intimacy versus isolation.* At this point Erikson departs from Freud's psychosexual model by discussing the psychosocial implications beyond adolescence. In the stage of *intimacy versus isolation,* Erikson indicates that the social enviornment (job, education, community) helps individuals organize their identity. In this stage of young adulthood the person is beginning to find his or her place in society. The tentative identity that was fashioned in the prior stage is now being refined or corrected, as appropriate. Erikson pointed out that the *true test* of this identity is the ability to share it openly with another person or persons in an intimate relationship. A common, although certainly not the only mode of intimate relationship, is marriage. To the extent that an individual is able to attain such a relationship, he or she will have a sense of *intimacy.* On the other hand, if one has not attained a sense of identity in the previous stage and cannot intimately share the self with another, a sense of *isolation* may result.

7. *Stage 7: Generativity versus stagnation.* The developmental crisis of middle age has to do with the dimensions of "generativity versus stagnation" or "self-absorption." Although the major emphasis of development through the periods, of puberty and adolescence—and to some extent, young adulthood—has been on the development and refinement of the self, the period of middle adulthood offers the opportunity to extend the sharing tendencies of young adulthood to a broader concern for others. In this stage, the adult has the choice of becoming involved or *self-absorbed* in his or her own needs, comforts, and health or of actively initiating or *generating* concern and constructive action for the welfare of others. A common mode of generativity (although not the only one) is parental interest in the welfare of offspring. Other examples of generativity include the teacher who is concerned with the success of his or her students or the scout leader who organizes programs for children. If the adult feels that he or she is a productive and contributing member of society, then he or she will have a

sense of *generativity*. On the other hand, if the individual feels that he or she is not fulfilling the expectations of his/her role and is being unproductive, he or she will feel a sense of stagnation.

8. *Stage 8: Ego integrity versus despair.* The eighth and final stage of development occurs in old age, when the individual looks back on his or her life. If the person is satisfied that, on the whole, life has been worthwhile and meaningful, then he or she will have a sense of *ego integrity.* On the other hand, if the individual sees his life as largely disorganized, without any discernable pattern—a meaningless array of events—then a sense of *despair* may follow.

EVALUATION OF THE PSYCHOANALYTIC APPROACH

The strengths of the psychoanalytic perspective are at least twofold:

1. It takes a holistic view of human development. Unlike other cognitive theories or behaviorism, which focuses on specific dimensions of human functioning such as thinking or overt behavior, the psychoanalytic tradition treats the broad range of development, including topics such as emotions, motivation, and the broad sweep of human behavior.
2. It attempts to understand problems of human behavior in developmental terms.

A major and serious weakness of psychoanalytic theory is its inadequate attention to proving or demonstrating principles of development in a scientifically valid manner. (Scientific validity refers to the clear statement of objective procedures, methods of measurement, and findings such that other scientists can independently replicate these procedures, methods, and findings.) How, for example, did Freud prove the existence or validity of the concept of psychic energy or *libido*? Much of the so-called evidence for pychoanalytic theory comes from case studies of adults. These case studies might well be considered scientifically invalid, since the childhood experiences of adult clients or patients are reconstructed through subjective recall, which is subject to errors of memory.

Ecological or Systems Theories

Systems theories emphasize the necessary interaction between the developing person and the environment. According to this perspective, human development is the result of three major factors:

1. The *person* and what he/she brings to a particular situation or stage of development. This includes the results of experience as well as of motivation.
2. The *environment,* or what is available to the individual in a particular situation or stage of life. This includes the significant *contexts* of life such as family, school, and neighborhood/community.
3. The *interaction* between the person and the environment.

PERSON ⇆ ENVIRONMENT

EUROPEAN ORIGINS

The ecological or systems perspective has its origins in the work of the European *gestalt* psychologists. (*Gestalt* is a German word that means "pattern.") The gestalt perspective emphasizes the unity and the integration of the whole person. Whereas behaviorists are concerned with the "parts" of human behavior (e.g., stimuli and responses), the gestaltists view human behavior as a patterned or unified whole (a *gestalt*), which has to be studied as such. For gestalt theorists, the human being cannot simply be reduced to the sum of its parts (as the behaviorists imply). This tradition of looking at the whole person adapting to the environment was carried to the United States by the German psychologist Kurt Lewin. Lewin extended the gestalt approach by developing a closely related view known as *field theory*.

THE KANSAS TRADITION

In the late 1940s at the University of Kansas, Roger Barker and Herbert Wright began investigations of child life in a small midwestern town (Barker and Wright, 1955). Their research was influenced by the work of Kurt Lewin because it emphasized the adaptation of children in specific environments. Furthermore, their research was "naturalistic" because it occurred in real-life settings rather than in the laboratory. In their early research (Barker and Wright, 1955), they described a small midwestern town of 700 people (120 of the total number were children) as it functioned over a year. Later research (Barker and Schoggen, 1973) measured the environments of two towns in different countries: Midwest, Kansas, and Yoredale, England (real cities with fictitious names). What made Barker and Schoggen's research unique was that they did not simply examine beliefs expressed by children or adults, or specific actions by caretakers or children; rather, they looked at how *total environments* influenced children and how children participated in these environments. Barker and Schoggen found many interesting differences between the cities. American children (Midwest, Kansas) were presented with more situations where they were free to come and go than English (Yoredale) children. When these researchers looked at adolescents, they found that the English Yoredale system tended to delay significant participation in community life until adulthood. On the other hand, the American, Midwest system involved children in community activities earlier.

Although we have looked at only one study of person—environment interaction, it should be noted that considerable research has been done in the area, including the following:

1. *Children and housing.* (Housing provides the immediate environment of the child's early years. As the child becomes more mobile, he or she first enters the environment fairly close to the house.) Opportunities for children's activities are determined, to some extent, by how much space is available both inside and outside the home, as well as by how this space is structured (Altman, Nelson and Lett, 1972; Pollowy, 1973).
2. *Environments for preschoolers.* Research has been done in *day-care* settings, including the conditions and future needs in this area (Grotberg, 1971; Chapman and Lazar, 1971).

3. *Public school environments.* Considerable research has been directed at the examination of school environments, including the degree of involvement of pupils in school activities (Gump, 1969; Kounin, 1970); the physical structure of schools (Brunetti, 1971, 1972; Traub, Weiss, Fisher, and Musella, 1972; Gump, 1974; Fisher, 1974); and high school environments (Barker, 1968; Baird, 1969; Wicker, 1968).

THE ETHOLOGISTS

In addition to the work of the Kansas group, a relatively small group of naturalists (called *ethologists*) have attempted to describe development in real-life or natural settings. Although ethologists have been primarily concerned with the study of animal behavior, their research has been applied to human development. They view development as a process of adaptation to the environment in which the survival of a species depends on successful organism-environment interaction (Immelmann, 1980).

BRONFENBRENNER AND THE "ECOLOGY" OF HUMAN DEVELOPMENT

A relatively recent statement of an adaptation or systems theory is the work of the developmental psychologist Urie Bronfenbrenner (1979). Bronfenbrenner uses the word *ecology* to refer to the interaction of the person and his or her social and physical setting (environment).

Bronfenbrenner (1979) defined the ecology of human development as follows:

THUMBNAIL SKETCH

Urie Bronfenbrenner (b. 1917)

Urie Bronfenbrenner is currently a professor in the Department of Human Development and Family Studies, College of Human Ecology, Cornell University. Bronfenbrenner received his Ph.D. degree in psychology from the University of Michigan in 1942. He is recognized as one of the world's foremost developmental psychologists.

Bronfenbrenner has maintained that laboratory studies of child behavior (laboratory studies are the most common mode of developmental research; the subject under investigation is usually removed from a real-life setting and placed in a psychological testing room or laboratory) sacrifice too much in order to gain experimental data. He has argued that laboratory studies have led to "the science of the strange behavior of children in strange situations with strange adults for the briefest possible periods of time." If we are to understand the way human beings develop, Bronfenbrenner feels that behavior and development should be observed in natural settings. Such natural settings involve interactions with familiar people over long periods of time.

The ecology of human development involves the scientific study of the progressive, mutual accommodation between an active growing human being and . . . the settings in which the developing person lives. . . . [Development is also influenced] by the relations between these settings and by the larger contexts in which the settings are embedded. (p. 21)

According to Bronfenbrenner, these are the three significant features of the above definition:

1. The *developing person* is viewed as a growing, active individual.
2. The *interaction* between the developing person and the environment is viewed as a two-directional or *reciprocal* relationship. In other words, there is a process of mutual accommodation to which both person *and* environment make contributions.
3. The *environment* that is relevant to human development is not limited to a single, immediate setting (e.g., the home, school, or work). Rather, the *ecological environment* is much broader and includes immediate settings, interaction between immediate settings (e.g., the relationship between home and schools or home and workplace) and larger settings, including the culture (which influences specific settings).

    The *ecological environment* is composed of four structural levels:

    a. *The microsystem.* This system involves the interaction between the developing person in an *immediate* setting or context. For example, the relationship between a child and teachers or peers in the *schools* and the relationship between an adolescent and his employer in a *work* setting are topics of microsystem analysis.
    b. *The mesosystem.* This system involves the relationships among the various settings or contexts in which the developing person finds himself or

The ecology of human development is the study of the mutual interaction between the developing person and the settings or contexts of development.

Photograph by Darryl Jacobson

herself. For example, for a nine-year-old child, the mesosystem would involve the relationship between the school and the family or the relationship between the family and the peer group.

c. *The exosystem.* This system includes the primary social structures that influence the developing person. The exosystem would be the formal and informal institutions such as political/governmental structures, neighborhood and community organizations, transportation networks, and the informal communication networks within neighborhoods, communities, and workplaces.

d. *The macrosystem.* According to Bronfenbrenner, this system is the *overarching institutional patterns of a culture* (e.g., the economic, educational, legal, social, and political systems of which the micro-, meso-, and exosystems are specific and *concrete manifestations* (Bronfenbrenner, 1979, pp. 6–8, 258–291). The macrosystem consists of the most general values, beliefs, or ideologies that influence the ways in which special institutions are organized and, therefore, the way in which human development occurs. For example, the value that a particular culture or society places on the child or the family will influence how individual children and families are treated in specific situations.

SOME EXAMPLES OF "ECOLOGICAL" INTERACTIONS

1. *Interactions between the individual and an immediate environment.* When the child enters the formal school for the first time, there is an interaction between the child and the environments of the school. In states with compulsory kindergartens, children usually go to school only a half day during their first year because it is recognized that the child may still require some resting or napping and may need a gradual daily separation from mother and home.

2. *Interactions between immediate environments.* In the example cited above, the success of the child's adaptation to school is dependent not simply on the child's immediate relationship to the school. It is also a function of the interaction of at least two immediate environments—the school and the family—that influence the child's relationship to the school. For example, a child's initial performance and adjustment to the formal school is largely the result of the preparation of the child in the family context (Schaefer, 1972).

3. *Interactions between immediate environments and larger social contexts* (in which the immediate environments are embedded). Immediate environments such as school and family are embedded in larger or cultural contexts, such as economic, social, or political systems. For example, the immediate environment of the school is contained in—or exists in the context of—an economic system. The economic system determines, among other things, the method of school financing—the property tax. The property tax provides funds for schools based on the value of the property in a given neighborhood. The value of the property is, in turn, directly related to the income levels of the neighborhood residents. Under this system, lower-income neighborhoods generate fewer funds for schools through the property tax than more affluent communities. This is an example of how the economic system—an overarching cultural pattern—influences the quality of educational experiences for each child.

More on an Ecological–Systems Perspective to Human Development

Ecology, as defined by ecologists is the scientific study of the relationships of living organisms with each other and with their environments (Ambrose, 1977). In biology, ecological studies of the relationship between living communities and their nonliving environments are known as the science of *ecosystems*. These interactions are studied at a biological level with special interest in the exchange of materials between the living and nonliving parts of the total ecosystem. The ecological study of various biological species requires the description of species habitat, way of life, population characteristics, social organization, and relationship with other species.

The application of an ecosystems perspective to human development poses several initial problems (McGurk, 1977):

1. On the one hand human beings have a large diversity of habitats, styles of life, population, characteristics, and forms of social organization.
2. Unlike other animal species whose capacities for adaptation are determined primarily by biological evolution, human adaptive skills are broadly extended by cultural evolution.
3. Human beings have significant power to alter their environment both by intentional control as well as through the unplanned effects of intervention. Some have suggested that man is an "intervening animal."

Before discussing the principles of the systems approach to human development, it is necessary to define a system. A *system* is an organized sustained pattern of interaction between two or more units or components and their attributes or characteristics resulting in an integrated, self-governed adaptation of these units or components (Ambrose, 1977).

In order to reduce the generality of this definition, we will discuss its significant terms.

1. *Components*. These are the parts of the total system. Components are almost unlimited in their variety. In the physical world these parts might be genes, neurons, bones, and so on. Abstractions such as rules, laws, morality, and justice can also be components. Components in human development systems might include a whole range of both physical and social entities (e.g., family, child, neighborhood, community, language, gene, and body build) as well as derived abstractions (e.g., self—concept, morality, and cognitive processes).

2. *Attributes* or *Human Factors*. These are the properties of the components. For example, the components listed below have the following attributes:

   Family—number of total members, emotional and physical state of the members, number of children (if any), "rules" of behavior, level of activity, and so on.

   Adult—family of origin, age, occupation, emotional/psychological state, physical attributes, friendship groups, self-concept, and so on.

   Child—age, physical/body structure (e.g., hair color, height, or weight), self-concept, neighborhood and community of residence, race, and so on.

   School—location and physical setting, number of students, number of teachers.

3. *Interactions*. These are the relationships that "tie the system together." The relationships to be considered in any given situation depend on the problem or pertinent issue under consideration. The following example illustrates the concept of relationships:

   Sample Issue "Why do some children from some ethnic or minority families (e.g., Black, Spanish-American) have difficulty succeeding in school?

   Applying the tools of systems theory to this problem, we first begin by identifying the "components" of the system and their significant "attributes." In the above example, relevant components might include at least the following: Middle-class school, Black or Spanish-American child, Black or Spanish-American family, and the community support system. Relevant "attributes" might include the economic status and values of the family; the interests, skills, attitudes, and abilities of the child; the programmatic emphasis of the school (e.g., college preparation, vocational training, etc.); and the attitudes of teachers and administrators toward children and their families.

One should note that the process of accurate determination of components and their attributes is the *beginning* of the systems analysis of any significant problem or issue in human development. The next step, the specification of the *relationships* between components is also vital. It is at the level of relationships that the complexity of many human development issues becomes apparent. In the above example, the systems nature of the problem becomes clear when one examines the interaction between components. Specifically, one can raise the following *relationship* questions: What is the relationship between the school and the family? Is the relationship characterized by mutual support? Are there open and meaningful channels of communication between home and school? What is the nature of the relationship between the child and his family vis-à-vis the school? Assuming that the school and the family are at least cordial, what are the features of parent-child interaction that promote or hinder successful school experiences? What is the relationship between the child and the school? What is the nature of teacher attitudes toward the child? Are textbooks and school materials designed to maximize success in school?

These relationship questions are simply examples of the large variety of questions that could be asked. The significant contribution of the systems perspective is that it provides a framework for critically examining and raising such important questions. The assumption is that at least half the battle in dealing with issues and problems of human development is asking the "right" questions!

4. *Environment.* As Ambrose (1977, p. 5) suggests:

The most significant parts of the environment with which man interacts are his social environment and those aspects of his physical environment that have been brought about or changed by his technologies. Because the human way of life is now based upon individual participation in a multiplicity of groups, its ecological analysis is concerned not just with the biotic community and its physical environment, but, to a large extent, with the community in the sociological sense and its cultural environment. Thus, in the ecological study of the dynamic interactions of human beings within a given ecosystem, the man-made environment figures very large. This includes not only the buildings and equipment required for reproduction, child rearing, education, production, transport and communication, and servicing of all kinds, but also the many kinds of social groups which directly or indirectly affect the individual in his daily life, with their group aims and norms, social procedures and institutions.

5. *Feedback.* Feedback is the reciprocal or mutual interaction among the components of the system. Feedback allows the system, as a whole, to self-regulate itself. Some examples of feedback will help to clarify the concept:

a. *Household Thermostat.* The common thermostat used to monitor the heating and/or cooling of a home is a good example of a system which uses feedback to self-regulate its activity. If the occupant wishes to increase the heat on a cold winter day, he or she will set the thermostat at the desired temperature. The thermostat will then send a signal to the heater which will then generate enough heat to attain the desired goal or temperature. Throughout this process, information or feedback indicating the present temperature in the house is continuously monitored by the thermostat. This temperature is compared with the goal of the system or the temperature desired by a resident. If the desired temperature has been attained (i.e., a perfect match between the desired goal or thermostat setting and the actual temperature of the house), the system shuts itself off. If the desired temperature has not been reached, signals will continue to be sent to the heater until sufficient heat is generated to attain the desired room temperature.

The student should note that the critical feature of this system is that it is *feedback regulated*. This means that the total heating system is regulated by the continual exchange of information among the components of the system. This exchange process is a circular one in which the components of the system both send and receive information.

b. *Human Motor Skills*. A child (or even a professional baseball player) catching a baseball illustrates how human motor-performance can be viewed as a feedback regulated system. When the ball is tossed to the child by his parent, the child's goal is to catch it. The child receives feedback from his/her eyes as the ball approaches. How large is the ball? How fast is it coming? This feedback information goes to the brain which sends signals to the muscles of the body particularly in the arms. These signals result in specific body movements designed to catch the oncoming baseball. The child's eyes continue to monitor the oncoming baseball in relation to motor movements such as extended arms and bending knees. Visual observation of his/her own movements and the approaching ball will result in continual feedback signals to the brain which will, in turn, result in continual adjustments in limb position and body posture. This process of observation and body movement and vice versa is both continuous and circular in much the same way as the previous example of the household thermostat. The system is *feedback regulated* because it depends on the continuous exchange of information necessary to catch the baseball.

EVALUATION OF THE ECOLOGICAL/SYSTEMS PERSPECTIVE

A major contribution of the ecological or systems perspective to human development is that it focuses attention on defining issues and formulating questions relating to *social policy* matters. For example, the research of James Garbarino (1976) on child abuse and maltreatment emphasizes the necessity of moving beyond a simple ''cause–effect'' relationship for explaining child abuse (e.g., parents with particular characteristics are *the cause* of child abuse). Rather, Garbarino and his associates (Garbarino and Sherman, 1980) have done *sociological* research on the neighborhood-community characteristics as a context for child abuse.

The researchers found that *neighborhoods* could be assessed as *high* or *low risks* for child maltreatment (see Application Box: An Ecological Analysis of Child Maltreatment). Thus, the environment and its support systems can be a contributing influence on child maltreatment.

APPLICATION BOX

An Ecological Analysis of Child Maltreatment

Garbarino and his colleagues undertook research designed to illustrate the use of child maltreatment report data as a social indicator of the quality of life for families. This research addressed the feed-back function of family support systems, and linked maltreatment to the overall balance of stresses and supports in the *neighborhood context* of families. . . .

Theories of Human Development

TABLE 2.5 Illustrative Data Comparing Families in Two Neighborhoods (after Garbarino and Sherman, 1980)

	Low-Risk Neighborhood (21 families)	High-Risk Neighborhood (20 families)
1. Percent of school-aged children cared for by parents in after-school hours.	86%	25%
2. Percent of those interviewed who never engage in neighborhood exchanges.	8%	32%
3. Percent of children for whom neighborhood children regularly serve as playmates.	86%	40%
4. Average number of people mothers name as taking an interest in their child's welfare.	5.3	4.1
5. Mean score on Holmes-Rahe Social Readjustment Scale (200+ indicates moderate or major crisis).	166	258
6. Average rating by mothers of neighborhood as a place to raise children (−4 to +4).	1.66	.09

Note: All differences are significant at p less than .05

Reprinted by permission from James Garbarino, *Children & Families in the Social Environment* (Hawthorne, NY: Aldine Publishing Company) Copyright © 1982 by James Garbarino.

The. . . analyses (Garbarino and Sherman, 1980) identified two low-income neighborhoods that, although matched in socioeconomic level and demographic character differed significantly in the rates of child maltreatment. One neighborhood with a child maltreatment rate greatly exceeding what was predicted by its socioeconomic and demographic profile was termed *high risk,* while another neighborhood in which the actual rate was much less than the predicted rate was termed *low risk.* Both neighborhoods had 78 percent of their families in the low-income category, but the first had a rate of child maltreatment eight times that of the second: 130 per 1,000 versus 16 per 1,000 families (Garbarino and Sherman, 1980). Interviews with expert informants, ranging from elementary school principals to mail carriers, were used to develop profiles of the two neighborhoods. Samples of families were drawn from each neighborhood and interviews were conducted to identify stresses and supports, with special emphasis on sources of help, social networks, evaluation of the neighborhood, and use of formal family support systems. Table 2.5 presents some of the results.

As shown in the table, families in the high-risk neighborhood, though socioeconomically similar to families in the low-risk neighborhood, reported less positive evaluations of the neighborhood as a context for child and family development. Furthermore, they revealed a general pattern of "social impoverishment" in comparison with families in the low-risk neighborhood. These findings lend support to the assertion that there are neighborhood effects related to child maltreatment.

The approach used in these neighborhood studies represents a method of analyzing community effects on families and children. These and other ecologically-oriented research techniques will enable us to document in greater detail the relationships between various community characteristics and the well-being of residents. With enhanced understanding of these connections, we can identify community attributes that are most closely related to the quality of life for families and spot areas that may be high-risk places for children. This will enable us to act more effectively in minimizing the risks and maximizing the opportunities presented to the developing child.

Summary

1. The primary reason for examining theories of human development is to demonstrate the resulting variation in posing and answering important questions relating to human development (e.g., What is the basic nature of man?). In addition, theories of human development are ways of organizing the "facts" (or presumed facts) of human behavior into formulations or assumptions which can then be tested.

2. *Maturation* theory is based on the idea or assumption that human development is the result of the timed unfolding of a human being's genetic inheritance. Major contributors to this approach included G. Stanley Hall, Arnold Gesell, and Lewis Terman. Extensive research in human growth and development now supports the idea that *both* maturation and experience (or the environment) interact to influence the course of the human life span.

3. *Behavior* and *learning* theories contrast with maturation theory by portraying human behavior as primarily the result of environmental stimulation. Important contributors to this approach included J.B. Watson, Ivan Pavlov, and B.F. Skinner. This "traditional" behavior and learning theory had several problems. Human beings were frequently portrayed as primarily *reactive organisms*. These theories tended to be *reductionistic* (complex processes of human interaction and behavior were frequently and erroneously "broken down" or reduced to simplistic stimulus-response-reinforcement units). Traditional behavior and learning theory promoted an unwarranted *deterministic* view of human development. *Social learning theory* as developed by Albert Bandura represented a significant modification of traditional learning theory.

4. A *cognitive* approach to human development emphasizes mental or internal factors as contrasted with the environmental or external emphasis of the traditional behaviorists. One of the foremost cognitive theorists was Jean Piaget (1896–1980). Piaget emphasized that the human mind was similar to other living and growing structures because it actively changed and adapted to the world rather than simply responding or reacting to experience. According to Piaget, cognitive development proceeds through a series of stages, each of which is qualitatively different from, yet dependent on, the prior stage. Cognitive theorists such as Piaget have rejected mechanistic approaches which reduce human development and learning to simple associations and reinforcements. Cognitive theories (in particular Piaget's ideas) have been widely applied to educational design. A problem with cognitive theory is that it tends to overemphasize the mentalistic or thinking components of human functioning.

5. The *psychoanalytic* approach to development has focused largely on those dimensions of human functioning omitted by cognitive theorists—the emotional, personal, or "irrational" forces of behavior. Psychoanalytic theories include those of Freud and his followers Rank, Jung, Adler, and Erikson. Freud's view of human behavior was, like the behaviorists, a deterministic one. Unlike the behaviorists, however, the source of determinism was not the environment but the powerful forces within the person. Human development was the effort of the individual to channel or redirect these potentially self-destructve forces of sex and aggression in socially and personally constructive directions.

Erik Erikson's theory of human development has much in common with Freud's theory although there are some major differences. Erikson's model of development is *psychosocial* whereas Freud's model is *psychosexual*. Erikson's theory goes beyond Freud's stages by including adulthood and aging. A strength of psychoanalytic theory is that it does attempt—albeit with limited scientific evidence—to deal with such important aspects of human development as emotion, feelings, and motivation. A major weakness of psychoanalytic theory is its insufficient attention to the scientific testing of principles of development.

6. *Systems* theories of human development emphasize the necessary and mutual interaction between the developing person and the environment or contexts of life. In this perspective, three major factors are involved: the person, the environment, and the interaction between both person and environment. A relatively recent and important statement of an adaptation or systems theory is contained in the work of the developmental psychologist Urie Bronfenbrenner who has identified the ''ecology of human development.''

Questions

1. How would you describe your current view or ''theory'' of human development? Is it similar to one or more of the theories discussed in this chapter? If so identify the similarities.
2. Is your approach, view, or theory of human development similar to that of your parents, friends, or instructors?
3. Make a chart of the theories discussed in this chapter. Include the following in your chart: the name of the theory, central ideas, several proponents of the theory, and your evaluation of each theory.
4. Indicate several examples of the practical relationships between several of the theories of human development and applications in the family, community, world of work, or in public policy. In terms of your planned or current line of work or activity, cite several examples of the relationship of a theory of human development to a practical issue.

Bibliography

ALTMAN, I., NELSON, P. A., and LETT, F. E. *The ecology of home environments, final report,* Project No. 0–0502. U.S. Department of Health, Education, and Welfare, Office of Education, Bureau of Research, Jan. 1972.

AMBROSE, A. Ecology and human development. In McGurk, H. (Ed.) *An Ecological Approach to Human Development.* Amsterdam: North Holland, 1977, pp. 3–10.

BAIRD, L. L. Big school, small school: A critical examination of the hypothesis. *Journal of Educational Psychology,* 1969, *60,* 253–260.

BANDURA, A. *Aggression: A Social Learning Analysis.* Englewood Cliffs, N.J.: Prentice-Hall, 1973.

BANDURA, A. *Social Learning Theory.* Englewood Cliffs, N.J.: Prentice-Hall, 1977.

BANDURA, A., and WALTERS, R. H. *Social Learning and Personality Development.* New York: Holt, 1963.

BARKER, R. G. *Ecological Psychology: Concepts and Methods for Studying the Environment of Human Behavior.* Stanford, Calif.: Stanford U.P., 1968.

BARKER, R. G., and SCHOGGEN, P. *Qualities of Community Life: Methods of Measuring Environment and Behavior Applied to an American and an English Town.* San Francisco: Jossey-Bass, 1973.

BARKER, R. G., and WRIGHT, H. F. *Midwest and Its Children.* New York: Harper & Row, 1955.

BINET, A. and SIMON, T. Sur la necessite d'etablir un diagnostic scientific des etats inferieurs de l'intelligence. *L'Annee Psychologique,* 1905a, *11,* 162–190.

BINET, A. and SIMON, T. Methodes nouvelles pour la diagnostic du niveau intellectual des anormaus. *L'Annee Psychologique,* 1905b, *11,* 191–244.

BLOOM, B. *Stability and Change in Human Characteristics.* New York: Wiley, 1964.

BRONFENBRENNER, U. *The ecology of Human Development*. Cambridge, Mass.: Harvard U.P., 1979.

BRUNETTI, F. A. *Open space: A status report*. Mimeographed. School Environment Study, School Planning Laboratory School of Education, Stanford University, Stanford, California, 1971.

BRUNETTI, F. A. Noise, distraction and privacy in conventional and open school environments. In W. Mitchell (Ed.), *Environmental Design: Research and Practice, Proceedings of ERDA Conference*. Washington, D.C.: American Institute of Architects, 1972.

CHAPMAN, J., and LAZAR, J. *A review of the present status and future needs in day care research: A working paper*. Prepared for the Interagency Panel on Early Childhood Research and Development, Washington, D.C., 1971.

DARWIN, C. *On the Origin of Species*. London: J. Murray, 1859.

DEWEY, J. The reflex arc concept in psychology, *Psychological Review*, 1896, *3*, 357–370.

DIAMOND, N. Cognitive theory. In B. Wolman (Ed.) *Handbook of Developmental Psychology*. Englewood Cliffs, New Jersey: Prentice Hall, 1982, pp. 3–22.

DONALDSON, M. The mismatch between school and children's minds. *Human Nature*, 1979, *2*, 158–162.

ERIKSON, E. H. *Young Man Luther: A Study in Psychoanalysis and History*. New York: Norton, 1958.

ERIKSON, E. H. Identity and the life cycle. *Psychological Issues, 1*, 1959, 18–164.

ERIKSON, E. H. *Childhood and Society*. New York: Norton, 1963.

FISHER, C. W. Educational environments in elementary schools differing in architecture and program openness. Annual Conference of the American Educational Research Association, April, 1974. (Available from author: Far West Laboratory, 1855 Folsom Street, San Francisco, Calif. 94103).

GALLATIN, J. E. *Adolescence and Individuality*. New York: Harper & Row, 1975.

GARBARINO, J. A preliminary study of some ecological correlates of child abuse: the impact of socioeconomic stress on mothers. *Child Development, 47*, 1976, 178–185.

GARBARINO, J. *Children and Families in the Social Environment*. New York: Aldine Publishing Company, 1982.

GARBARINO, J., and SHERMAN, D. High-risk neighbors and high-risk families: the human ecology of child maltreatment. *Child Development, 51*, 1980, 188–198.

GESELL, A. *The First Five Years of Life: The Preschool Years*. New York Harper & Row, 1940.

GESELL, A., and AMATRUDA, C. *Developmental Diagnosis* (Second Edition). New York: Harper & Row, 1947.

GROTBERG, E. H. (Ed.). *Day care: Resources for decisions*. Washington, D.C.: Office of Economic Opportunity, 1971.

GUMP, P. Intra-setting analysis: The third grade classroom as a special but instructive case. In E. Willems and H. Rausch (Eds.), *Naturalistic Viewpoints in Psychological Research*. New York: Holt, 1969.

GUMP, P. Operating environments in open and traditional schools. *School Review*, 1974, *84*, 575–593.

HUNT, J. McV. *Intelligence and Experience*. New York: Ronald Press, 1961.

IMMELMANN, K. *Introduction to Ethology*. New York: Plenum Press, 1980.

KOUNIN, J. S. *Discipline and Group Management in the Classroom*. New York: Holt, 1970.

LERNER, R. M. *Concepts and Theories of Human Development*. Reading, Massachusetts: Addison-Wesley, 1976.

MAIER, H. W. *Three Theories of Child Development*. New York: Harper and Row, 1969.

McGURK, H. (Ed.). *An Ecological Approach to Human Development*. Amsterdam: North Holland, 1977.

PIAGET, J. *The Origins of Intelligence in Children*. New York: International Universities Press, 1963.

POLLOWY, A. M. *Children in the residential setting: A discussion paper toward design guidelines*. University of Montreal, Center of Research and Urban Innovation, 1973.

SCHAEFER, E. Report on the interagency panel on child development. Washington, D.C.: HEW, 1972.

SEARS, R. R. Your ancients revisited. In E. M. Hetherington, J. W. Hagen, R. Kron and A. H. Stein (Eds.) *Review of Child Development Research*, (Vol. 5). Chicago: University of Chicago Press, 1975, 1–73.

SKINNER, B. F. *The Behavior of Organisms: An Experimental Analysis.* New York: Appleton, 1938.

SKINNER, B. F. *Beyond Freedom and Dignity.* New York: Knopf, 1971.

TERMAN, L. M. (Ed.). *Genetic Studies of Genius I: Mental and Physical Traits of a Thousand Gifted Children.* Stanford, California: Stanford University Press, 1925.

TERMAN, L. M. and ODEN, M. H. *Genetic Studies of Genius, V: The Gifted Group at Mid-Life.* Palo Alto, California: Stanford University Press, 1959.

THORNDIKE, E. L. *Animal Intelligence.* New York: Macmillan, 1911.

THORNDIKE, E. L. Educational psychology, 3 vols. New York: Teachers College Columbia U., 1913–14.

TRAUB, R. E., WEISS, J., FISHER, C. W., and MUSELLA, D. Closure on openness: Describing and quantifying open education. *Interchange,* 1972, *3,* 69–84.

WATSON, J. B. *Behaviorism.* New York: Norton, 1924.

WHITE, R. W. Motivation reconsidered: The concept of competence, *Psychological Review,* 1959, *66,* 297–333.

WICKER, A. W. Undermanning, performances, and student's subjective experiences in behavior settings of large and small high schools. *Journal of Personality and Social Psychology,* 1968, *10,* 255–261.

WHITE, S. The learning theory approach. In P. H. Mussen (Ed.), *Charmichael's Manual of Child Psychology,* Vol. 1, New York: Wiley, 1970.

Suggested Readings

BRONFENBRENNER, U. *The Ecology of Human Development.* Cambridge, Mass.: Harvard U.P., 1979. This book is a challenge to the traditional way in which psychologists have studied human development—through ''laboratory'' studies. Bronfenbrenner argues that such studies lead to ''the science of the strange behavior of children in strange situations with strange adults.'' Brofenbrenner suggests that to really understand human behavior, it is necessary to observe human behavior in natural settings with familiar people over prolonged periods of time.

ERIKSON, E. H. *Childhood and Society.* New York: Norton, 1963. This book presents a readable introduction to Erikson's theory, including the eight stages of human development.

GESELL, A. *The First Five Years of Life.* New York: Harper & Row, 1940. Gesell and his colleagues wrote several books, including this one, that represent a maturational view of human development. The book contains much interesting, highly readable, and accurate information on the development of infants, toddlers, and preschoolers. Gesell's charts and sequential lists of age-related behaviors make interesting reading.

HUNT, J. McV. *Intelligence and Experience.* New York: Ronald, 1961. This is one of the seminal books that reoriented American views of human development away from a maturational perspective and toward an experiential view. Hunt was one of the first American psychologists to formally introduce the work of Piaget. This book provided the ideological basis for programs such as Project Head Start.

MCGURK, H. (Ed.). *Ecological Factors in Human Development.* Amsterdam: North-Holland Publishing, 1977. This volume contains the papers of the Third Biennial Conference of the International Society for the Study of Behavioral Development, held in England in 1975. The aim of the papers was to examine the contribution that an ecological perspective can make to the understanding of human development.

SKINNER, B. F. *Beyond Freedom and Dignity*. New York: Knopf, 1971. In this book, Skinner applies his learning theories to such considerations as the meaning of freedom, the origin of values, and the design of culture.

SKINNER, B. F. *Reflections on Behaviorism and Society*. Englewood Cliffs, N.J.: Prentice-Hall, 1978. Skinner is a pioneer in the development of operant conditioning. The book explores applications of his theories to social organization, the science of behavior, and education. The book is a collection of occasional papers.

WADSWORTH, B. J. *Piaget's Theory of Cognitive and Affective Development*. (3rd ed.), New York: McKay, 1984. This is an introductory overview of Piaget's theory of cognitive development for students of psychology and education. Piaget's central and major concepts are presented in a simple and readable fashion.

WATSON, J. B. *Behaviorism*. New York: Norton, 1924. This book will provide interesting reading for those who wish to explore the history of behaviorism, as written by one of its founding fathers. The book covers such topics as definitions of behaviorism and methods for studying the behavior and the emotional development of human beings.

3

The Determinants of Human Development

Three Brief Biographies

SAMUEL S.

Samuel S. was born in Russia in 1885. When he was a child, his family suffered the hardships of poverty. In his late teens, Samuel was drafted and served in the war between Russia and Japan (1905). While on duty, he contracted tuberculosis, which required hospitalization and a medical procedure for collapsing one of his lungs. In 1910, he left Russia in order to avoid the increasing dangers of religious persecution. He brought his wife and children to the United States, where they settled in Highland Falls, New York, adjacent to the United States Military Academy (West Point). At West Point, he was a tailor and made uniforms for the West Point cadets. Here he met several soon-to-be-famous people, including Dwight David Eisenhower and George S. Patton.

In the 1920s, Samuel S. and his family suffered two major setbacks. One was a family tragedy in which one of their four sons received an injury that resulted in brain damage and he had to be institutionalized. The other setback involved unemployment and family hardship due to the Great Depression of the 1930s. Despite these difficulties, Samuel S. and his family persevered. Throughout the remainder of his life, Samuel S. maintained a positive attitude toward life. He died in 1959.

VIRGINIA P.

Virginia P. was born into a well-to-do family in Boston, Massachusetts, in 1955. She did well in elementary and high school and was considered by her peers a popular girl. In 1972, she entered Wellesley College, where she majored in history and took a minor in drama. By the time she was a junior, she had become involved with a group of students who experimented with potentially dangerous and addictive drugs. Soon afterward, her grades declined, as did her participation in campus social activities. Toward the end of her junior year, she wrote a brief letter to her parents indicating that she was leaving the university to experience "the real meaning of life." Virginia's parents and friends have not heard from her in over three years.

BILL M.

Bill M. was born in San Francisco, California, in 1942. As a week-old infant, he was abandoned in a bus terminal and found by a policeman. He was placed in an orphanage, where he remained until he was adopted at the age of three. Bill's adoptive family was reasonably supportive of him, although it was clear that the "natural" children in the family were favored over Bill. Today, Bill is a highly successful factory foreman who is happily married and has two of his own children and one foster child.

In this chapter, we are going to examine the factors that influence the development of the human being. We will look at biological (genetic or inherited) determinants of development, the environments or "contexts" of development, and the interaction of the two. The biographies presented above raise several questions about the influence of these factors on human development. For example, what was the impact of the Russo-Japanese War on Samuel S.? Was it a harsh experience that made him more aware of survival and security? Why did Samuel S. leave Russia for the United States when many of his peers faced with similar dangers remained behind? What factors enabled Samuel S. and his family to work through the personal tragedy of their son and the Depression? (What personal characteristics and social supports enable people to cope with difficult life situations?) When his life was nearing an end, what enabled Samuel S. to demonstrate a positive attitude toward life? Why did Virginia P. turn to drugs and leave her family and friends despite an apparently supportive environment? How was Bill M. able to overcome a relatively adverse childhood environment to become a successful worker and family member? Is Bill M.'s behavior more likely the result of the genetic endowment he received from his natural (rather than his adoptive) parents or the result of his early environment (orphanage and adoptive family experience)? What is the relationship between early life experiences and adult development? The study of human development is about these and many related questions. In this chapter, we will introduce you to the factors of human development that will help in answering such questions.

Types of Determinants of Development

Human development and human behavior are rarely, if ever, the result of a single cause. Rather, numerous causes are involved. A convenient way of thinking about the determinants of development is to divide them into two groups: biological or genetic factors and environmental or contextual factors. The convenience of thinking about determinants of behavior in these two broad categories should not obscure the fact that both work together in the development of the human being. In fact, the biological determinants of development, the social contexts of development, and the interaction between the two represent the essential aspects of an *ecological* or *systems* perspective to human development. The basic principle of this systems view is the following:

The interactive relationship between heredity and environment is a *reciprocal or bidirectional one*. This means that the environment or contexts

of life act on the individual's characteristics (e.g., child temperament or disposition, child maturational processes) and the individual acts on his/her environment (e.g., parents, siblings, peers, or teachers). Thus, the individual plays an *active role* in contributing to his or her development (Bell, 1968; Lerner and Spanier, 1978).

A model of the determinants of life-span development was described by Dr. Robert A. Aldrich of the University of Colorado (see application box). Aldrich's "watermelon theory" of human development divides determinants into two categories that are similar to the genetic and environmental factors: biological aspects (the top half of the watermelon) and psychosocial aspects (the bottom half of the watermelon).

BIOLOGICAL FACTORS

These are the genetic or inherited aspects of development, including physical features and physiological organs:

- *Cardiovascular system* (lungs and heart).
- *Central nervous system* (brain and spinal cord).
- *Musculoskeletal system* (bones and attached muscles).
- *Endocrine system* (ductless glands such as the pituitary, the thyroid, and the adrenals, which secrete hormones directly into the blood or lymph system).
- *Skin*.

PSYCHOSOCIAL FACTORS

These factors are the *physical environment* (e.g., home, school, and neighborhood) and the *social environment* (e.g., parents, teachers, peers, and co-workers), as well as the individual's personal or psychological "interpretations" of these environments, including:

- *Cognitive development* (the development of thinking and language).
- *Personality development* (the development of the self-concept, including behavior patterns and values).
- *Social development* (the lifelong process by which individuals develop attitudes, beliefs, knowledge, the awareness of expectations, and appropriate role behaviors).

BIOLOGICAL DETERMINANTS

Each and every human being has inherited a general biological code from his or her parents. The biochemical agents which carry this code are *genes* and *chromosomes*. In the next chapter, we will discuss the operation of genes, chromosomes, and the specific mechanisms of heredity in more detail. Our focus in this section is on the general process of heredity. There are two primary types of inheritance:

1. *General inheritance*, or those attributes that make any species, including the human species, like other members of the same species. For example, all

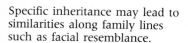

Specific inheritance may lead to similarities along family lines such as facial resemblance.

Photograph by David Kostelnik

normal human beings have a brain, two lungs, and two hands, which have four fingers and one thumb.

2. *Specific inheritance,* or those attributes that are transmitted from our family ancestors and that distinguish us from other people. This type of inheritance may lead to similarities along family lines such as facial resemblance.

Hereditary factors operate from the moment of conception in determining some features of human growth and development. For example, heredity determines eye color, hair color and texture, and susceptibility to some diseases (e.g., diabetes and some types of cancer).

In discussing the interaction of heredity and environment, it is much easier to examine genetic effects in some plants or lower animals than in human beings. The reason is that it is possible to create, in some cases, through plant or animal breeding, ''pure strains'' (or genotypes) for a specific trait. As a result of this control of genetic factors, many experiments have demonstrated the important role of heredity in animals (McClearn, 1970). Such precise control of genetic factors is much less common in studies of human beings except in the relatively few instances where specific genes have been shown to be directly related to abnormal physical traits or diseases. For example, Huntington's chorea, a degenerative disease of the nervous system, is the direct result of a single gene. In a similar vein, recent research has found that certain genes—*oncogenes*—may be directly associated with specific types of human cancer (Blair, Cooper, Oskarsson, Eater, and VandeWorde, 1982; Marx, 1982).

Given this basic limitation in the study of human genetics (serious *ethical* problems would probably arise if there were to be genetic manipulation of human breeding), we still can say some things about human heredity. Our current understanding of human genetics makes it fairly clear that many human physical traits are inherited. The physical resemblance of members of the same family provides some support for this view. We know that genetic factors are involved in the development of the human body from the time of conception. However, we do not yet fully understand the scientific mechanisms of the interaction of genetic and environmental factors in controlling human growth and development. The relationship of this nature—nurture interaction to *human behavior* is even less clear. This is particularly true for our understanding of human *intelligence* and human *personality*.

DEFINITION

Correlation coefficient. A number that indicates how similar two sets of measurements are to each other. In research in human development, correlation coefficients range from -1.00 to $+1.00$, with most scores falling in the middle range.

-1.00	0.00	$+1.00$

$+1.00$ shows a perfectly similar relationship between pairs of measurements (i.e., both measurements are in the same direction); 0.00 shows no relationship between measurements; -1.00 shows a perfectly opposite relationship between measurements (i.e., when one measurement is very high, the other is very low).

Watermelons and Human Development

Dr. Robert A. Aldrich, of the University of Colorado Medical Center, has made up a diagram that expresses the nature of the life-span continuum. Because of the diagram's shape, Buckminister Fuller promptly named it the "watermelon model" when it was first presented, and so it has been known ever since. It looks like this:

The top half of the watermelon acknowledges the biological aspects of life; the bottom half, the [social]. The model is meant to suggest visually that if you wanted to know anything about a given person at a given location on the watermelon, that point representing "now" in his life span, you must slice through the entire watermelon to be aware of the multiplicity of factors you will need to consider. The model also reminds us that from any given "now" we can learn a great deal about an individual's past history and vice versa.

From Albert Rosenfeld, "The New LSD: Life-span Development," *Saturday Review*, October 1, 1977. Copyright, 1977.

In Dr. Aldrich's "watermelon model," the C at left means conception, the D at right is for death, with question marks as to what lies beyond. The top half of the watermelon represents biological factors and the lower half represents psychological factors in the individual's life. (The word ekistic—coined by the late Constantine Doxiadis—refers to the study of human settlements, here symbolizing the environmental context.) Milestones along the way (bottom) indicate possible critical points in the life span ("Empty Nest," for example, refers to that time of life when the children grow up and leave home.)

Major Transitions in the Human Life Cycle, by Howard Spierer. New York: The Academy for Educational Development, 1977, p. 27. Copyright © Academy for Educational Development Inc.

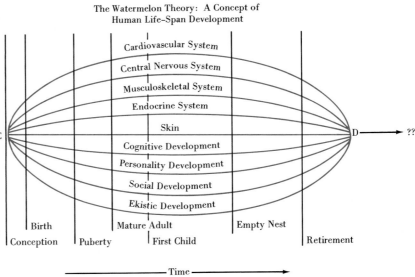

The Watermelon Theory: A Concept of
Human Life–Span Development

Cardiovascular System
Central Nervous System
Musculoskeletal System
Endocrine System
Skin
Cognitive Development
Personality Development
Social Development
Ekistic Development

C — D → ??

Birth — Mature Adult — Empty Nest
Conception — Puberty — First Child — Retirement

Time →

Intelligence. The study and measurement of intelligence in children is subject to considerable controversy and debate. Not only is there disagreement about the nature and degree of the contributions of heredity and environment but there is also some debate about the meaning and measurement of intelligence. Exactly what is intelligence? What does it mean to behave in an intelligent fashion? Do so-called intelligence tests, as used in school and vocational settings, actually measure intelligence? At this point, we will simply acknowledge these important controversies and return to a more detailed discussion of them when we discuss intelligence in later chapters. For purposes of our discussion here, we will *assume* that the abilities that constitute

The Determinants of Human Development

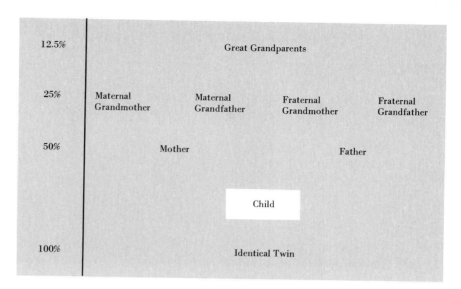

12.5%	Great Grandparents			
25%	Maternal Grandmother	Maternal Grandfather	Fraternal Grandmother	Fraternal Grandfather
50%	Mother		Father	
	Child			
100%	Identical Twin			

FIGURE 3.1 Shared heredity among family members. The percentages in the left hand column indicate the amount of heredity shared between the child and the individual(s) on the right.

intelligence reflect such traditional characteristics as verbal fluency, comprehension, reasoning, memory, spatial perception, and numerical skills. It is a fairly common observation that the more closely related people are, the more they resemble one another in physical traits such as height and facial features (see Figure 3.1 and Table 3.1). There is evidence that as relatedness between

TABLE 3.1.
Relationship Between Intelligence and "Relatedness"

Correlations Between	Degree of Relationship (Correlation Coefficient)
Unrelated persons	
Children reared apart	−.01
Foster parent and child	+.20
Children reared together	+.24
Collaterals*	
Second cousins	+.16
First cousins	+.26
Uncle (or aunt) and nephew (or niece)	+.34
Siblings, reared apart	+.47
Siblings, reared together	+.55
Fraternal twins, different sex	+.49
Fraternal twins, same sex	+.56
Identical twins, reared apart	+.75
Identical twins, reared together	+.87
Direct line	
Grandparent and grandchild	+.27
Parent (as adult) and child	+.50
Parent (as child) and child	+.56

*Descended from the same stock, but different lines. Based on A.R. Jensen, "How Much Can We Boost IQ and Scholastic Achievement?" *Harvard Educational Review*, Winter 1969, 39, 49. Copyright © 1969 by President and Fellows of Harvard College.

One way of studying the inter-action of heredity and environ-ment is with identical twins.

Left photograph by Dr. Ronald Gol-bus; right photograph by Gale Schiamberg

two people increases, the similarity of their intelligence (in this case, IQ scores) increases (Loehlin, Lindzey, and Spuhler, 1975). If we look at Table 3.1, we can see that correlation coefficients for intelligence scores between individuals who are more closely related are larger than for those who are less closely related. For example, the correlation of intelligence scores for identical twins, reared together (+.87), is much higher than for unrelated individuals reared apart (−.01). Such evidence shows that there is a relationship between intelligence and genetic factors.

Does this mean that genetic contributions are the most important factor in a person's intelligence? Not necessarily! The data in Table 3.1 can also be inter-preted in another way. For example, as "relatedness" between individuals increases, environmental similarities also increase. Thus identical twins, reared together, have more similar environments and shared experiences than two unrelated individuals reared apart. Therefore it could be argued that Table 3.1, in fact, shows that intelligence scores of more related people are similar because their environments are more similar!

The debate over heredity and environment continues to the present day. There are several ways of studying the question:

Research on Twins. Studies of the intelligence of twins usually involve comparisons of *identical twins* (identical genetic endowment) and *fraternal twins* (different genetic endowment). Identical twins are called *monozygotic* twins (a single sperm fertilizes a single ovum (egg) and early in its embryonic development an extra split occurs). Fraternal twins are called *dizygotic twins* (two separate sperm fertilize two separate ova (eggs). (Twins are either identi-cal or fraternal only because of these developmental processes—no matter how much alike or unalike they may appear later in life.) Although both monozygotic and dizygotic twins are *assumed* to share similar childhood expe-riences and therefore, to share similar environments, dizygotic twins do not have similar genetic makeup. Furthermore, dizygotic twins do not have to be the same sex nor need they physically resemble one another. In fact, they are no more genetically alike than ordinary siblings. (They are siblings with the same birth dates.)

The Determinants of Human Development

Separated at birth and reared apart, these identical twins are about to meet accidentally.

Drawn by Scott Schiamberg. Copyright © 1984 by Scott Schiamberg.

Given this natural laboratory of twins for studying the interaction of heredity and environment, we might derive the following hypotheses:

a. If *genetic factors* play a more significant role in the determination of intelligence than environment, we would expect the IQ scores of monozygotic twins (reared together) to be more similar (or more highly correlated) than the IQ scores of either dizygotic twins (reared together) or nontwin siblings (reared in the same home).

b. On the other hand, if *environment* plays a more significant role in the determination of intelligence than heredity, we might expect that the IQ scores of identical twins reared together (same genes and similar environment) would be more similar (more highly correlated) than those of identical twins reared apart (some genes and different environments).

Both of the above hypotheses have, in fact, been confirmed in research. In a review of fifty studies extending over a period of approximately fifty years, Erlenmeyer-Kimling and Jarvik (1963) found that individuals who were more genetically related were also more similar in intelligence to one another (see Figure 3.2). In fact, the similarity in intelligence increased in direct proportion to the degree of relatedness. Furthermore, the genetic contribution to intelligence is demonstrated by the fact that the degree of similarity or correlation between IQ scores increases (for individuals reared together) as one goes from unrelated individuals to siblings, to dizygotic twins, to monozygotic twins (see Figure 3.2).

Additional evidence for the important role of heredity suggests that even *variations over time* in IQ may have a genetic component (Wilson, 1972, 1974, 1975; Wilson and Harpring, 1972). Repeated measurements of intelligence for 261 identical and fraternal twins indicated a similar developmental profile (e.g., spurts and lags in measured intelligence over time) (see Figure 3.3). This

FIGURE 3.2 The contributions of heredity and environment to intelligence. Shown are the mean values for the correlation of IQ scores for monozygotic (identical) twins, dizygotic (fraternal) twins, ordinary siblings, and unrelated individuals reared apart or reared together.

Based on L. Erlenmeyer-Kimling and L. F. Jarvik, "Genetics and Intelligence: A Research Review," *Science*, December 13, 1963, Vol. 142, Fig. 1, pp. 1477–1479. Copyright © 1963 by the American Association for the Advancement of Science. Reprinted by permission.

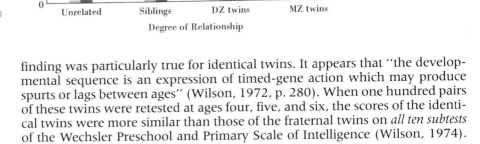

finding was particularly true for identical twins. It appears that "the developmental sequence is an expression of timed-gene action which may produce spurts or lags between ages" (Wilson, 1972, p. 280). When one hundred pairs of these twins were retested at ages four, five, and six, the scores of the identical twins were more similar than those of the fraternal twins on *all ten subtests* of the Wechsler Preschool and Primary Scale of Intelligence (Wilson, 1974).

FIGURE 3.3 Intelligence score profiles indicating the similarity in developmental status of four pairs of twins during the first twenty-four months.

From R. S. Wilson and E. B. Harpring, "Mental and Motor Development in Infant Twins," *Developmental Psychology*, 1972, 7, pp. 277–287. Copyright © 1972 by the American Psychological Association. Reprinted by permission of the author.

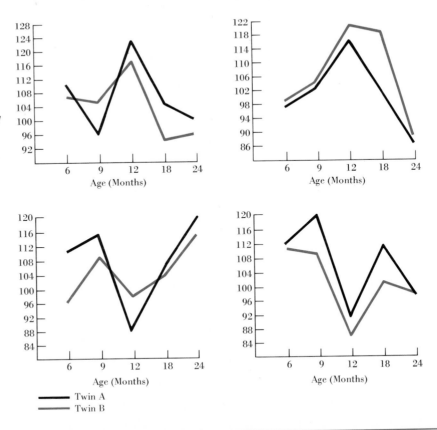

An additional follow-up study of the same twins during the preschool years found a comparable pattern of similar scores for the twins reared apart (Wilson, 1975, 1983).

Likewise, support for the strength of environmental contributions to intelligence can also be seen in Figure 3.2. That is, IQ scores of identical twins reared together (same genes and similar environment) are more highly correlated than IQ scores for identical twins reared apart (same genes and different environments).

Additional reason for an environmental perspective comes from the studies that have compared IQ scores of identical twins reared together with IQ scores of fraternal twins reared together. These studies consistently report a higher IQ correlation for identical twins than for fraternal twins (Bouchard and McGue, 1981). This result has typically been taken as supporting a hereditary perspective because it has been *assumed* that both identical twins reared together and fraternal twins reared together have *similar* environments. (Therefore, any differences may be attributed to hereditary factors). This hereditary viewpoint is misleading in light of the large body of evidence that identical twins reared together, in fact, have much more similar environments than fraternal twins reared together (Loehlin and Nichols, 1976). This situation is likely the result of the marked physical similarity of identical twins which may cause parents, teachers, and peers to treat them more similarly than fraternal twins. Furthermore, identical twins spend more time together and are more likely to sleep in the same room and dress alike than fraternal twins. Therefore, the higher IQ correlations for identical twins reared together must be attributed, at least in part, to greater similarity of environment. Currently, there is no way of knowing the exact contribution of environment or heredity to this difference between identical and fraternal twins.

Studies of Adopted Children. Another source of evidence comes from studies of adopted children (Burks, 1928; Skodak and Skeels, 1949; Honzik, 1957). These studies have compared the IQ scores of adopted children with the IQ scores of their adoptive parents and the scores of their biological parents. The findings of these studies indicate a higher correlation between adopted children and their natural parents' intellectual level than between

Fraternal twins are no more genetically alike than ordinary siblings.

Photographs by Gale Schiamberg

adopted children and their adoptive parents' intellectual level. Although these results would *appear* to support a genetic interpretation of intelligence, such a perspective would be misleading for one primary reason. Since it is usually the case that adoptive parents have been rigorously screened by adoptive agencies, one would expect them to be very special and intelligent people who would almost uniformly provide an excellent environment for the adopted child. Therefore, it is not surprising to find higher correlations or similarities between adopted children and their biological parents than between adopted children and their adoptive parents. That is, one would surely expect to find a greater similarity between the IQs of a randomly selected group of adopted children (who would represent a range of IQs) and their biological parents (who would also represent a range of IQs) than between those same adopted children and a uniformly special (and probably highly intelligent) group of adoptive parents.

Obviously many adoptive families contain not only an *adopted* child but a *biological* child of the same parents. Such families would appear to be useful for examining the relationship between heredity and environment. That is, in each of these families the biological child has received *both* genes and environment from the parents whereas the adopted child received *only* the environment from these same parents. To the extent that IQ is a primary result of heredity, then one would expect the similarity or correlation between parent IQ and biological child IQ to be greater than that between these same parents and the adopted child. Two adoption studies failed to show any significant differences between the IQ of the mother and the IQ of the biological child compared to the IQ of the same mother and the IQ of the adopted child (Scarr and Weinberg, 1977; Horn, Loehlin, and Willerman, 1979). Perhaps the best summary of the relationship of adoption studies to the question of heredity and environment is that they do *not* support the notion of a strong hereditary contribution to intelligence.

Intervention Studies. Although the purpose of intervention studies has been to improve the lives of human beings, they have shed some light on the question of heredity and environment. As might be expected in such helping programs, intervention research studies usually support an environmental position (Scarr and Weinberg, 1976; Scarr-Salapatek, 1975). Many of these studies suggest that IQ scores can be dramatically increased when young children are placed in enriched environments. Skeels' (1966) study of children raised in an orphanage and then moved to a home for retarded girls demonstrated the role of an enriched environment in substantially raising IQ scores. In a thorough review of environmental intervention research, Horowitz and Paden (1973) concluded that successful intervention programs frequently involved home visits with young children and their mothers. That is, where the value of the family as a support system was recognized, significant improvements and long-term effects were more likely (Bronfenbrenner, 1979; Garbarino, 1982).

Personality. Personality refers to the relatively consistent and unique characteristics of behavior of a person (e.g., aggressive, quiet, boisterous, shy, outgoing, and so on). Unlike some physical traits in which characteristics are specific and easily identified, personality characteristics are more general and more difficult to measure. For example, hair color, eye color, or other physical characteristics are readily apparent to an observer. On the other hand, friendliness, aggressiveness, shyness, or other personality characteristics may appear in individuals in varying degrees and in varying situations. In this section, we will review several studies which have examined the relationship of hereditary and environmental factors in the development of personality.

The New York Longitudinal Study is one of the most extensive examinations of the development of temperament from infancy through early childhood (Thomas, Chess, Birch, Hertzig, and Korn, 1963; Thomas and Chess, 1977). *Temperament* may be defined as the natural disposition of an infant which is presumably the basis of childhood and adult personality. These dispositions include characteristics as irritability or calmness, and activity or passiveness. This research has, to date, led to several major findings about the development of personality:

1. Extremely early in life children appear to possess characteristic patterns of temperament that are maintained throughout the childhood years.
2. The source of *individuality* of childhood personality has its origins in the *interaction* of both hereditary and environmental factors. Because infants and children show individually unique temperaments and reaction styles, it follows that children may react differently to what are objectively the same environmental circumstances. That is the same environmental factors—whether intentionally designed or not—will not have the same impact on different children. The child's personality is the result of this complex interaction of heredity and environment.
3. The child should be viewed as playing an *active* and *participatory* role in his or her development. The results of the New York Longitudinal Study support this conclusion. That is, the characteristics of individuality (which develop from the individually unique interaction of heredity and environment) result in a differential selection of environmental settings by the individual and differential responses to the individual by significant others (e.g., parents, teachers, friends, and so on) in that environment (Schneirla, 1957; Scarr and McCartney, 1983). These differential selections of environments and differential responses to the individual provide an arena for the *direct participation* of the individual in the self-organization of personality development.

Other dimensions of personality that are influenced by the complex interaction of heredity and environment include *activity level* and *sociability*. *Activity level* refers to the level of movement or motor behavior in young children. For example, does the child move around quite a bit or rather little? Is this activity level maintained over time and in a variety of situations such as eating, sleeping, or playing? Or is activity level inconsistent over time and more directly related to the type of activity? Some babies prior to birth are rather active in the uterus. Other babies remain rather quiet and still. Later behaviors which are related to such activity levels (including speed of reactions, anxiety or impatience in doing activities, and the number of activities engaged in) have been shown to be more closely associated for identical twins than for fraternal twins (Scarr, 1966). This research further illustrates the complexity of the relationship of heredity and environment to activity level.

Sociability refers to the general personality dimension related to how an individual approaches his or her environment. Social *introverts* tend to be more timid, shy, withdrawn, or inhibited than social *extroverts* who are more

Both hereditary and environmental contributions are intimately involved in the development of human beings. These *identical quadruplets* (possibly the only living set of identical quadruplets in the world) are part of an ongoing study at the National Institutes of Health.

Photograph by Darryl Jacobson. Copyright © 1985 by Lawrence B. Schiamberg and Darryl Jacobson.

outgoing, friendly, engaging, or active. Studies have shown that the degree of social introversion or extroversion is more similar for identical than for fraternal twins (Scarr, 1969; Gottesman, 1965; Vandenberg, 1968). Scarr (1969) in her study of the sociability of identical and fraternal twins has emphasized that the interaction of heredity and environment includes the apparent inheritance of a general disposition for "engaging" the environment. Furthermore, these dispositions can be modified and changed by environmental influence. For example, a moderately extroverted infant whose parents encourage quiet or easygoing behavior will likely be different from another infant with similar disposition whose parents encourage outgoing, uninhibited behavior.

The Interaction of Heredity and Environment. Our review of selected research on hereditary and environmental contributions to intelligence suggests that *both* factors are intimately involved in the development of human beings. If that is the case, then how to heredity and environment *interact* in the process of development? The concepts of *canalization, gene expression*, and *norm of reaction* are important to an understanding of this process of interaction and *mutual regulation* of development.

Canalization. Waddington (1957) proposed that individual development could be explained by the concept of *canalization*. Waddington suggested that the development of genetic traits could be thought of as a ball rolling down a canal (see Figure 3.4). Where the "canals" are fairly deep, it is difficult for the "environment" to change the direction of the ball. At other times (called *sensitive periods*), the moving ball may arrive at a point where several shallow canals meet. During these sensitive periods, the environment may influence the course of the ball (or of the genetic trait) (Fishbein, 1976). In research on kittens, it has been demonstrated that if they are deprived of light until three months after birth, they are never capable of seeing again (Hubel and Wiesel,

The Determinants of Human Development

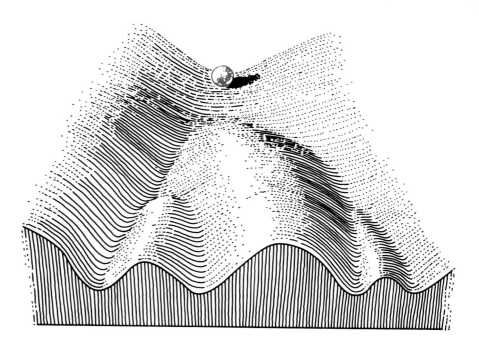

FIGURE 3.4 Waddington's model of genetic canalization.

Adapted from Waddington, C. H., *The Strategy of Genes*. London: Allen and Unwin, 1957

1963). However, deprivation of light after this sensitive period has no impact on their vision.

A remarkable feature of human development is the tendency of human beings apparently to "catch up" or recover from environmental stress to fulfill their genetic program. For example, if a five-year-old child has had his growth slowed for a year (perhaps because of malnutrition), the child will "catch up" during the next year or so, provided that the environment is supportive (in this case, if the child receives adequate nutrition). Thus, some undesirable effects of the environment that occur during canalization can be reversed.

The Concept of Gene Expression. Simply because an individual possesses a genetic endowment (*genotype*) for a particular trait does not mean that the trait will automatically be translated into a physical characteristic (*phenotype*). In other words, whether or not genetic factors are "expressed" depends, in part, on the modifying effects of the environment. For example, the genetic endowment that results in clinical diabetes for some people is not even expressed in other people (probably because of environmental factors). Another example is the expression of height in human beings, which, of course, has a genetic basis. However, the expression of height also depends on a variety of growth hormones and on nutrition, as well as on a healthy childhood.

Norm of Reaction. As we have seen we cannot simply determine the characteristics or traits of an individual (phenotype) by knowledge of the individual's genetic endowment (genotype). Rather, the phenotype represents the product or result of the complex interaction of the environment and one's genetic endowment. Therefore, our genetic inheritance is really a *range of potential outcomes* rather than a blueprint for what will occur (see Figure 3.5).

FIGURE 3.5 Several genotypes for adolescent height—*A, B, C,* and *D*—can vary in expression in relation to the environment. For example, a person with genotype *D* would have a wider range or norm of reaction for the expression of height than a person with genotype *A.*

From I. I. Gottesman, "Developmental Genetics and Ontogenetic Psychology: Overdue Détente and Propositions from a Matchmaker." In Ann Pick (Ed.), *Minnesota Symposia on Child Psychology,* Vol. 8. Minneapolis, Minnesota: The University of Minnesota Press, 1974, p. 60.

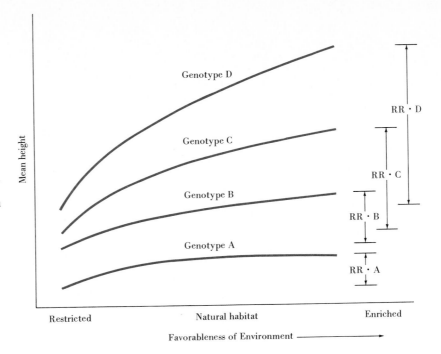

This leads us to a definition of the concept of *norm of reaction:*

The same genotype can give rise to a wide array of phenotypes depending upon the environment in which it develops. (Hirsch, 1970, p. 73)

In addition, Hirsch (1970) pointed out that the norm of reaction is almost completely unknown. The reason for this is that in order to be able to specify or predict the norm of reaction for any given genotype, one would have to be able to reproduce that genotype exactly (many times) and then expose those identical genotypes to a diverse array of environments. (The phenotypes that develop from such interactions would then provide an estimate of the norm of reaction for a given genotype.) In reality, both the development of numerous identical genotypes as well as the exposure of those genotypes to a totally inclusive set of all possible environments would be impossible. As Hirsch (1970, pp. 69–70) indicated:

Even in the most favorable materials only an approximate estimate can be obtained for the norm of reaction, when, as in plants and some animals, an individual genotype can be replicated many times and its development studied over a range of environmental conditions. The more varied the conditions, the more diverse might be the phenotypes developed from any one genotype.

Thus, it is important to note that the limits or boundaries that are set for our genetic endowment can never be accurately specified or predicted in advance. Therefore, we cannot know any individual's range of genetic potential.

The Determinants of Human Development

Heredity and Environment—An Interaction System

The organization of development is such that the processes of . . . growth are self-stabilizing or, to take another analogy, "target seeking." The passage of a child along his growth curve can be thought of as analogous to the passage of a missile directed at a distant target. The target is determined by the genetic structure; and just as two missiles may follow slightly different paths but both end by hitting the target, so two children may have slightly different courses of growth but end up with practically the same physique. This self correcting and goal seeking capacity was once thought to be a very special property of living things but now we understand more about the dynamics of complex systems . . . we realize that it is not after all, such an exceptional situation.

From J.M. Tanner, *Education and Physical Growth* (2nd ed.). New York: International Universities Press, 1978, pp. 50–51.

To further complicate the situation, Hirsch (1970) points out that even if we could know that several individuals have the same genotype, the norm of reaction would be expected to be *unique for each individual*. This means that the range of phenotypes that would develop from a given genotype in varying environments would be different for each individual. Such individual phenotypic uniqueness would make it even more difficult to predict, in advance, the likely outcome of any genetic potential.

In conclusion, the concept of the norm of reaction emphasizes the importance of viewing the development of human behavior as an *interaction* of hereditary and environmental factors. As Hirsch (1970, p. 70) has suggested,

extreme environmentalists were wrong to hope that one law or set of laws described universal features of modifiability. Extreme hereditarians were wrong to ignore the norm of reaction.

ENVIRONMENTS OR "CONTEXTS" OF DEVELOPMENT

Photograph by Darryl Jacobson

The environments or "contexts" of life play a large role in the development of human beings throughout the life span. It is acknowledged, even by the most ardent genetically oriented theorists, that the environment contributes to human development. However, it is not enough simply to state that environment is important. Rather, it is necessary to be more specific about what is meant by *environment* (how is it defined) and how it interacts with and influences human beings. In this section, we will define some of the environments that are important to human development. In order to facilitate our discussion, we will divide environments into two broad categories. "Immediate" environments are those that the human being interacts with *directly* (e.g., the infant interacts with the family, and the adult interacts with the work setting) and "larger" environments are those that the human being interacts with *indirectly*, usually through the medium of an immediate environment. For example, the child may interact with the values of his or her culture through

TABLE 3.2
Stages of the Family Life Cycle

Stage	Description of the Family
I.	Beginning families (couples without children).
II.	Childbearing families (oldest child from birth to about 2½ years).
III.	Families with preschool children (oldest child from 2½ to 6 years).
IV.	Families with school-aged children (oldest child from 6 to 13 years).
V.	Families with teenagers (oldest child from 13 to 20 years).
VI.	Families as launching centers (first child gone to last child leaving).
VII.	Middle-aged parents (empty nest to retirement).
VIII.	Aging family members (retirement to death of both spouses).

Adapted from E. M. Duvall, *Marriage and Family Development* (5th ed.). Philadelphia: J. B. Lippincott, 1977. Figure 19–3, p. 474. Reprinted by permission.

the medium of the family or the school, or the adult may interact with cultural expectations of job performance in the work setting. In other words, the *culture* of a society is a significant context that the individual experiences indirectly through the medium of other direct contexts (Bronfenbrenner, 1979).

Immediate Contexts. *The Family.* The vast majority of children grow up in a family context. This context usually includes a father and/or a mother and, in many instances, brothers and sisters. The family has been shown to have an impact on important processes, including the development of self-concept, sex roles, language, intellectual abilities, and interpersonal skills.

The developmental stages of family life. While developmental theories have emerged to describe the growth and maturation of the individual, a parallel trend has been to describe the changing pattern of the family life cycle (Duvall, 1971) as a series of developmental stages (see Table 3.2). Family developmentalists such as Duvall view the family, like the individual, as having certain primary functions at certain points in the life cycle (see the discussion of Erik Erikson in Chapter Two). Duvall believes that families, like individuals, have developmental tasks or stages. She defines a family developmental task as follows:

FIGURE 3.6 Marital-parental satisfaction over the family developmental cycle.

Adapted from B. C. Rollins and H. Feldman, "Marital Satisfaction Over the Family Life Cycle," *Journal of Marriage and the Family,* February 1970, pp. 20–28. Copyright © 1970 by the National Council on Family Relations, 1219 University Avenue Southeast, Minneapolis, Minnesota 55414. Reprinted by permission.

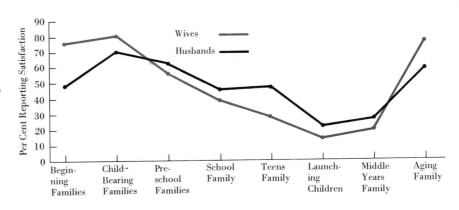

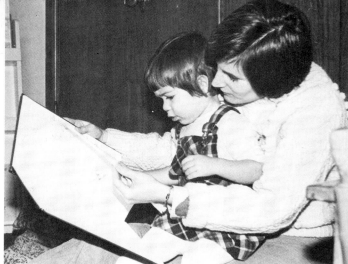

The family context creates an atmosphere of trust and security.

Group photograph by Gale Schiamberg; top right photograph by David Kostelnik; bottom left photograph by Darryl Jacobson

a growth responsibility that arises at a certain stage in the life of a family, successful achievement of which leads to satisfaction and success with later tasks, while failure leads to unhappiness in the family, disapproval by society, and difficulty with later developmental tasks (pp. 149–150).

Duvall's use of family developmental stages has resulted in considerable research on the family and its role in human development. For example, Rollins and Feldman (1970) examined the pattern of marital—parental satisfaction over the family life cycle and its implications for child development (see Figure 3.6). They found that marital—parental satisfaction begins to decline when children first arrive in the family ("childbearing families") and continues to decline until it reaches a low point when the children are adolescents (the "launching-children" phase). After the launching phase, marital satisfaction begins a climb back up and rapidly increases after the "middle-years family" phase.

Given that families are an important environment for growth and development, what are the implications of Rollins and Feldman's research? Would such results help to account for another dramatic development in American family life, that is, the substantial increase in divorce? Urie Bronfenbrenner (1979) has indicated that many of the problems that are facing both families and children come from the circumstances in which the family finds itself (and the way of life resulting from the circumstances).

When these circumstances and the way of life they generate undermine relationships of trust and emotional security between family members, when they make it difficult for parents to care for, educate and enjoy their children, when there is no support or recognition from the outside world for one's role as a parent and when time spent with one's family means frustration of career, personal fulfillment and peace of mind, then the development of the child is adversely affected.

From Urie Bronfenbrenner, "The Origins of Alienation," *Scientific American,* August 1974, 231 (2), 53–61.

Photograph by David Kostelnik

The Neighborhood—Community. Every child and adult lives in some type of neighborhood or community. Children grow up and develop surrounded by various arrangements of buildings, people, open space, and streets or roads. This neighborhood—community provides both a setting for human growth and development and a potential resource and support system for developing human beings. From the preschool years on through adulthood, the human being uses the neighborhood and community setting as a primary arena for the use of unstructured time. The neighborhood provides the settings for the child's development of competence in naturally occurring social and physical experiences. Can fences be climbed? Are the kids in the next block going to fight if someone enters their territory? Can we get the wood necessary for our treehouse? Is there a community center or some place where community people of all ages can meet to share ideas and skills? These concerns and comparable challenges are the kind of experiences that happen in neighborhoods and communities. Through exploration of the neighborhood, children gain an understanding of the social and physical characteristics of the community as well as its characteristics as a setting for play. When individuals reach adult status, they are, to some degree, in a position to reorganize or further develop the community as a setting for both child and adult.

The neighborhood has a more sophisticated psychological "meaning" as one proceeds through the life span. As the child grows and becomes increasingly mobile, as he or she has increasing experiences with the physical and social features of the neighborhood, and as the cognitive skills for representing or thinking about the community increase throughout adulthood, the child's and the adult's appreciation of the community will also increase and change.

The School. As the child moves from the preschool period to the sixth year, the formal school emerges as a major institution in the transfer of cultural

The Determinants of Human Development

The world of work.

Top photograph by Darryl Jacobson; center and bottom photographs by Gale Schiamberg

traditions and skills from society to the developing child and young person. (This cultural transfer also occurs for adults in formal adult education programs.) As cultures become more complex and more technological, they produce a more sophisticated, elaborate, and abundant collection of skills, knowledge, and information. These must be transmitted to the developing individual (as well as to adults in adult education programs) as necessary prerequisites for effective participation in the culture. Historically the role of the school in the industrialized and technological societies has been to serve this function of cultural transfer and transmission.

In serving this function, the formal school provides an environment for the growing child. This environment is made up of four major features: (1) the *curriculum*, or what is taught; (2) the *physical setting*, or the design of space (e.g., the arrangement of classrooms, hallways, and play areas); (3) the *methods of instruction*; and (4) the *characteristics of the classroom group* (e.g., the size of the group, the patterns of interactions, and the teacher's style of leadership).

The relationship of the school and the family. Both the school and the family are systems in their own right that interact in the process of educating the child and the adolescent. The school and the family are interdependent. Schools depend on parents to support the school, its activities, and its programs and to encourage the child to participate. Families depend on the school to teach their children not only how to read, write, and work with numbers but how to develop their physical skills, their communication skills, their social skills, and so on. The ability of the child to take full advantage of the school program is, in part, a function of family encouragement and support of the child and the school.

The relationship of the school and the world of work. One of the problems that adolescents in our society face is the need to make some commitment to a vocation or a career in the face of little or no direct experience in the world of work or knowledge about occupations. It has been suggested that the young are systematically excluded from the working world of adults as a function of the inherent age segregation in American society and of the American school in particular. Systematic attempts have been made to overcome this problem by reorganizing and rethinking the relationship between the school and the world of work. Such efforts include programs designed to inform high-school and grade-school students about occupations and types of jobs.

The World of Work. One of the first things that people want to know on first meeting an individual is the nature of his or her occupation. This is understandable because an individual's occupation generally defines his or her lifestyle, interpersonal relationships, and, to some extent, future potential for development. The world of work may become the central life focus for many people because it represents the primary basis for scheduling human activities on a daily, weekly, or yearly basis over the life span. Because of its economic and social significance, the world of work defines the material resources for behavior, for family life, and for development itself.

Work and the family system. If the opportunity to work is absent, or if the nature of the work is not sufficiently rewarding, severe repercussions are likely to be experienced by the individual worker and his or her family. The evidence is overwhelming that unemployment and underemployment among breadwinners is the primary factor leading to continued marital instability among the poor. The absence of work or having work that fails to fulfill the

73

Work and Families

I come at the issue of families from a roundabout direction; the factory, the office, the boardroom, the hospital, the shop. It is in these work settings that, to a large, virtually unexamined and often unacknowledged extent, the quality of American family life is decided. If this assertion was true for the past, for the somewhat mythical pairing of breadwinner—husbands and secondary-worker—wives, it will be even more apropos in the future, as ever larger numbers of young women enter the labor force with the expectation of successfully combining marriage and a career. Thus, an understanding of work settings and occupations, or organizations and public policies, may offer as much insight into the stresses, strains and challenges that families of the future will face as all the private decisions made by individuals about their relationships and households.

This is a particularly appropriate time to be looking at the dynamic intersections of work and family life, for many converging trends call attention to the nature of work, and work organizations as determinants of the quality of life for individuals and families.

Furthermore, a growing interest in adult development, in the stages of adult as well as childhood growth, naturally leads to questions about the ways in which people are shaped by and manage their multiple involvements in their private and organizational lives. The timing of events in both the work and family worlds has also begun to receive attention in this developmental perspective. (It has also been argued that historical studies of family structure also need to add this developmental focus on the family as "process," unfolding and changing during the life cycle.)

Developments in certain applied fields also pave the way for the examination of work—family linkages. In both organizational and social psychology (applied behavioral science and industrial psychology) and the growing field of family therapy, "open systems theory" has provided a useful perspective. Organization development has concerned itself with integrating social and technical aspects of work, and family therapy has taken as its central premise the notion that the problems of an individual must be seen and treated in the context of the total family system. The "open systems" perspective makes it possible to consider the inputs into each system from others in its environment.

From R. M. Kanter, "Job and families: impact of working roles on family life." Washington, D.C.: *Children Today*, March–April 1978, 7, No. 1, pp. 11–15, 45.

function of economic security, self-esteem, identity, and a sense of mastery over the chaos of one's environment prevents one from finding the stable basis required to build a lasting familial relationship.

PSYCHOLOGICAL PURPOSES OR FUNCTIONS OF WORK

1. Work contributes to self-esteem.
2. Work is the most significant source of personal identity.
3. Work is a primary way for individuals to impose order, control, or structure on their world.

Are parents who are raising children performing "work"? It may sound overly simple to ask what we mean by *work.* However, this is not a trivial question. O'Toole (1973) described the crux of the problem as follows:

It is an inconsistency to say that a woman who cares for her own children is not working, but if she takes a job looking after the children of another woman, she

The Determinants of Human Development

Peer group relationships provide valuable feedback to the developing individual.

Left photograph by Sylvia Byers; right photograph by Darryl Jacobson

is working . . . Work that is not paid is not considered to be as valuable as paid work. As a society we may have dangerously downgraded the most important work a human can perform—that is raising his children. . . . for official purposes work should be considered as any activity that produces something of value for other people.

What do you think?

Peer Group and Friends. Peer-group and friendship relationships influence development throughout the life span. From the preschool years through the years of adulthood, peer groups serve as a source of information for the individual about social expectations and behavioral roles as well as a source of mutual support.

During the preschool and early school years, the peer group offers an environment that helps the child to move out of the family. The peer group has its own values and expectations of behavior. Peer relations during these early years are marked by informality and the absence of roles in group membership. Participation in preschool peer groups is largely the result of the physical closeness of the other children. In other words, children play together because they happen to live near one another or to be in the same class (preschool class, swim class, and so on).

Peer relations during middle childhood are characterized by same-sex groups. Children learn such things as appropriate behaviors and the roles they may be expected to play in later life—what is expected of males and females in society. Peer groups also provide the opportunity for the child to learn about competition and cooperation.

Peer relations during adolescence provide several critical experiences:

- The individual develops a greater sensitivity to the needs of the "best friend." These early intimate relationships provide a valuable training ground for later interpersonal relationships.

- The peer group further develops and supports appropriate sex-role behaviors and expectations.
- Interpersonal relationships with the opposite sex often occur through support of the peer group.
- The peer group helps the adolescent to break away from the home.
- The peer group helps the adolescent to develop an identity by providing an arena for testing ideas and behaviors.

During the adult years, peers and friends provide a dynamic source of information for social behavior in work, school, or community settings. Many adults who retire from jobs report missing the supportive influence of coworkers more than they miss the work itself. In later adulthood, peers and friends are a potential resource and support network for negotiating the experiences of aging.

A Larger Context: Culture. The "immediate" environments that we have just described do not exist in a vacuum. Rather, they occur in a larger context: the culture (see Figure 3.7). The *culture* of a society is the collection of principles, beliefs, norms, rules, and expected behaviors that govern the organization of that society. Culture shapes our behavior, how we dress, what we eat, how we solve problems, what we value as important, and how our institutions (government, work and business, schools, and families) are organized. Our cultural patterns for organizing social institutions such as work and family exert a considerable influence on the conditions of human development.

FIGURE 3.7   Culture: The larger context.

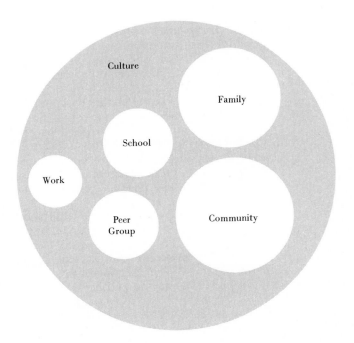

The Determinants of Human Development

For example, the family in America (and in most industrialized societies) is organized in a *nuclear* form (a nuclear family consists of a husband, a wife, and their children, if any). This form of family organization is different from family organization in other cultures (a common family form in other cultures is the *extended* family, which includes the immediate family plus other relatives). The implications of family form for human development are significant. For example, the nuclear family form provides considerable independence for the family unit (i.e., the family unit is relatively free of the influence of other relatives). On the other hand, this freedom is not without its price, as young children and their parents (in an increasingly mobile society where families may move frequently) may not benefit from the advice and support of grandparents and other relatives.

The Contexts of Life and the Stages of Human Development

The contexts of life that we have just described interact with the developing human being in a somewhat predictable pattern. That is, some contexts, such as family and school, are more prominent during the early phases of the life span, whereas other contexts, such as work, perform a primary role in adulthood. In this book, we will be looking at the total human being at different periods of the life span, and we will see how he or she interacts with the significant people of his or her life (e.g., parents, siblings, teachers, coaches, peers, co-workers, husbands, wives, bosses, religious leaders, heroes) and the significant social institutions of the social system (e.g., family, neighborhood and community, world of work, the school). This approach is both developmental and interactional, and it constitutes what we mean by a *systems perspective* for the following reasons (Table 3.3 summarizes the periods of development and the primary contexts):

1. It involves the *mutual interaction* of the developing person or self with the significant contexts of development.
2. It involves the *changing and evolving nature of the significant contexts of development* in the various periods of life. For example, the family is the central context of development during infancy; the school emerges as a significant context during middle childhood and adolescence; and the world of work is a primary context during adulthood.
3. It involves the *cumulative impact of each context of development* as the individual proceeds through the life span. This means that although a given context such as the family may have a more central or primary influence during certain stages of life, its influence does not disappear in later phases of life. For example, the family has a primary influence on development throughout the early years of life. That "primary" influence is shared with the social and the peer group as the individual proceeds through childhood and adolescence. However, when the individual is ready to leave the home and establish an independent existence, the impact of the family is still present. In fact, the influence of the family of origin continues to have an impact on many features of the adult's life (including how the adult raises his or her children).

TABLE 3.3   Human Development as an Ecosystem

Period of Development (The Individual)	←——— Mutual Accommodation ———→	Primary Contexts of Human Development
The fetus and neonate: This period begins with conception and ends shortly after birth, extending to about the first few days of life.		The *intrauterine environment* before birth. The *extrauterine environment* during the first few days after birth.
The infant: This period extends from birth to about 3 years of age (this includes the toddler period from approximately 2 to 3 years of age).		The *family* and the emerging relationship (attachment) between infant, parent(s), and other family members. The world of the "household" is a significant learning laboratory.
The preschooler: This period extends from about 3 years of age until entrance into formal school at 5 or 6 years of age.		The *family*. The *neighborhood*, particularly in the immediate vicinity of child's residence, and peer friendships within this limited range.
Middle childhood: This period begins with entrance into the formal school and continues to the beginning of adolescence with the onset of puberty (from about 5 or 6 years of age to approximately the age of 12 or 13).		The impact of the *family* is important particularly as it now contributes to the self-definition of the child in relation to the school. The *school* assumes a primary role during middle childhood as the major source of transmission of the culture (e.g., reading and writing). The *neighborhood and local community* includes the immediate vicinity as well as the larger community. The child becomes familiar with major community resources, such as the school, the library, the supermarket, and the post office. The *peer group*. Peer interactions and friendships become more formalized as organized clubs and grade-level friendships emerge. Peer relations also serve as a valuable "bridge" to negotiating newly discovered community resources.
Early adolescence: This period begins with the onset of puberty and extends through the high-school years to about 17 or 18 years of age. The organizing feature of this stage is the development of a sense of "group" identity relative to the world of high-school peer organization. Thus the central task is to come to grips with the pressure to join groups.		The *family* serves as a base from which the adolescent begins to establish his/her identity in relation to the high school and peers. In addition, the self-development skills that the adolescent has learned up to this point (reading, writing, thinking, etc.) serve as the basis for the emerging "adult-to-adult" relationship (replacing the "parent–child" relationship). From a social perspective, *the high school* and its staff tend to support the peer emphasis and orientation of early adolescence. The types of groupings that are formed in the high school (e.g., student council, service groups, athletic boosters) reinforce the peer groupings of early adolescence. The high-school student expands his/her understanding of resources in *the community* to include local, state, and national institutions.

Period of Development (The Individual)	←——————→ Mutual Accommodation	Primary Contexts of Human Development

Later adolescence and youth: This period of development begins with completion of high school (17–18 years of age) and extends until the person attains a sense of social status or social identity and a control of resources in the adult community (early 20s). In summary, this period deals with the post-high-school years and the development of the skills that the individual now uses to develop a "stance toward the world" (Erikson, 1974).

The family. A common feature of later adolescence is independent living coupled with the crystallization of autonomy from parents. Although the independence from the parents has been forming prior to this period (i.e., the skills of independent living, including reading, writing, thinking, and social cooperation, have been developing throughout childhood and early adolescence), the crystallization of these activities during later adolescence creates a situation of potential parent–adolescent conflict. The adolescent learns to resolve prior patterns of childhood dependence with the emerging needs for autonomy. The result is the development of an adult–adult relationship, which replaces the parent–adolescent relationship.

The world of work and/or postsecondary education. The end of the high school years may lead the adolescent in one of at least three directions: full-time work, additional education (college, university, or community college), which may lead to full-time employment at a later date; or a combination of both work and education. The development of an identity or stance toward the world necessitates a beginning choice of occupation during this period.

Peers. During later adolescence, peer relationships are integrated with work and/or postsecondary education, as well as with residential patterns. Peer relationships may continue to serve as a buffer between the adolescent and his/her family in the process of identity formation. Later adolescent living arrangements, school experience, and work settings represent social selection processes in the determination of associates or peers. When these selection processes become too rigid, members of ethnic, economic, and racial minorities may be excluded from advanced developmental experiences.

The community. In contrast to the early adolescent, who may have an "understanding" of the community and its resources, the later adolescent probably has some actual experience with significant community institutions and resources.

Early adulthood: During this period (from the early 20s to the middle 30s), the individual consolidates, expands, and tests his/her identity through the development of intimate and mature social relationships. This period marks the emergence of a lifestyle that will serve as a framework for the organization of experience during the rest of adulthood. Lifestyle includes the tempo of activity and the distribution of work and leisure. Three control features that constitute the lifestyle are marriage, child rearing, and work experiences.

The family. Until the period of early adulthood, the focus has been on the family of origin or the family in which the child and adolescent have grown and developed. During early adulthood, a common experience is the establishment of a "new" family through marriage and childbearing.

Work. The period of early adulthood is an experimental or preparatory phase of work and career development. The adult often tries various jobs until one is found that is compatible with their personality, likes, and values.

TABLE 3.3   Human Development as an Ecosystem (cont.)

Period of Development (The Individual)	←——————→ Mutual Accommodation	Primary Contexts of Human Development

Early adulthood (cont.):

Peer relationships. During early adulthood, peers usually fall into one of two categories: (1) other young families; (2) fellow workers.

The community. Early adulthood marks the beginning of the individual in the community as a full-fledged adult with appropriate economic, social, and personality development. The emphasis begins to shift away from getting to know and appreciate the community to the creation and support of the community for the sustenance of the individual and the family.

Middle adulthood: This period extends from about the middle 30s to the middle 60s. It represents the crystallization and maintenance of the skills acquired during early adulthood. The individual has now reached the time of life when self-development and self-regulatory skills have reached their high point. This period has the potential for creative decisions relating to family life, the world of work, and community life. The potential for influencing the lives of others (in the community, in the family, and at work) is enormous. Hence Erikson describes the developmental opportunity or crisis of this period as "generativity versus stagnation."

The family. The individual in middle adulthood has the potential for organizing a home–family environment that facilitates growth and development. The creation of such a family environment is far from the mundane activity often presented in stereotyped descriptions of parents or parenting. Positive family development requires many skills, including the ability to assess people's needs, the ability to make decisions, the ability to plan for the future, and the ability to make connections with social structures outside the family (e.g., educational institutions, other families, community groups, other individuals, relatives, and members of the extended family).

In addition to the creating of a family–home environment, the individual in middle adulthood may learn *how to raise children.* The activity of child rearing is a developmental task that stretches over a long period of time. Each stage of family development (see discussion in this chapter) and related changes in the ages of children require the adult to adopt, test, and formulate a comprehensive child-rearing strategy.

Peer relationships. During middle adulthood, peer relationships involve social interactions with other families or with fellow workers or participants in social–community activities.

The world of work. By middle adulthood the individual has completed his/her experimentation with various work settings and has now either settled into an appropriate occupation or has become so alienated from the working world that finding a satisfactory vocation may no longer be a possibility. The management of career development is an important facet of life. It influences and determines other aspects of development, including social life and self-fulfillment.

The community. Middle-adult family development includes the building of "bridges" or relationships between the family and other social structures. This requires both a knowledge of the community and its resources and the

80

Period of Development (The Individual)	←——→ Mutual Accommodation	Primary Contexts of Human Development

Middle adulthood: (cont.)

appropriate social and interpersonal skills for initiating and maintaining these relationships. The creative resources of middle adulthood allow the possibility of making a vital contribution to others (both in and outside the family) by initiating community activities.

Later adulthood: This period of development includes the time from about the middle 60s until death. The period begins with the completion of the child-rearing and parenting roles of middle adulthood and the recognition that the years of formal employment are nearing a conclusion. As life draws to an end, the individual expands the creativity and competence acquired in middle adulthood to new roles in leisure time and "grandparenting." From the perspective of experience and age, the individual renews the quest for the meaning and an understanding of life. Erikson (see discussion in Chapter Two) sees the major challenge of this period as "integrity versus despair."

The family. As children leave the nest, a new period of family development occurs that is reminiscent of the first year of marriage without children. As children emerge from the home to start their own families, the parents once again may indulge in activities as a couple or with other couples. Parenting skills may be dusted off as grandchildren arrive.

The world of work. As the years of formal employment draw to an end, the older adult may be viewed in one of two ways by his/her employer: (1) as a valuable source of experience and expertise and as a resource for younger workers; or (2) as someone who can no longer "do the job" and who therefore must be retired. Depending on the type of work, the individual's skills, the attitudes of management, and the attitudes of the person, the end of formal work can be viewed as a natural beginning for the application of competencies and creativity in a nonformal leisure setting or as the end to "meaningful work."

Peer relationships. Peer relationships are always diverse during adulthood. However, as the individual in later adulthood approaches the conclusion of parenthood and formal work, he/she will very likely find mutual interest and consolation with other individuals/couples who are experiencing the same changes.

The community. The combined expertise, competency, and creativity of the older adult represents a largely untapped community resource.

Methods for Studying Human Development

Now that we have discussed the primary determinants of human development, we will look briefly at how the determinants are studied. What research methods are used, for example, to determine what human beings are like at various stages of development?

NATURALISTIC STUDIES

Naturalistic studies are based on the observation of people in their real-life settings. No attempt is made to alter or change what people do in these settings. Naturalistic studies result in *normative* (typical) information about people and their settings. For example, we could use naturalistic studies to examine the motor development of a child or of children.

Baby Biographies. One form of naturalistic study is the baby biography. Baby biographies can provide us with useful and detailed information about a particular child. This information can help us understand the normative development of other children.

The baby biography did not gain respect until 1877, when Charles Darwin published a journal of his son's early development. In that journal, Darwin combined his emerging interest in evolution with child development. He suggested that we could best understand individual development by looking at the evolution of the species. Jean Piaget (1952) used a form of baby biography by describing the development of his three children. He used this method to illustrate his theories of children's thinking processes.

There are some problems with baby biographies that limit their usefulness in the scientific study of human development:

- Often, they simply record behavior without explaining its importance or significance.
- Often, when such biographies are written by parents, they reveal a biased perspective—somehow the positive aspects of the child's behavior are emphasized and the negative features are hardly noticed.
- Because baby biographies provide us with a great deal of specific information about a particular child, we may not be able to apply all the information to children in general.

Naturalistic Observations. Naturalistic observations are recordings of the behaviors of relatively large numbers of people. The purposes of naturalistic observations include the following:

- To record information about development at various ages.
- To suggest average ages for the appearance of skills, behaviors, and growth measurements.

Examples of this method are the work of Arnold Gesell on the maturation of the child and adolescent development and the research of M. M. Shirley (1933) on motor development.

Time Sampling. By using time sampling, researchers examine and record the number of particular behaviors (e.g., cooperation, competition, aggression, smiling) that occur during a specific period of time.

CLINICAL STUDIES

There are two types of clinical studies: the *clinical method* and the *interview method.*

The Clinical Method. The clinical method of studying human development usually involves a researcher and one individual or subject at a time,

APPLICATION BOX

The Baby Biography and Charles Darwin

Charles Darwin (1809–1882) is best known for his theories of evolution (e.g., *The Origin of Species*, 1859). These theories made a considerable impact on the study of human development. If species develop or "evolve," then societies and, indeed, human beings develop. Darwin was one of the first scientists to call attention to this development through the careful observation of infants. In the following selection, Darwin discusses anger in infants. By modern standards, he had some curiously humorous ideas about sex differences in the expression of anger.

It was difficult to decide at how early an age anger was felt; on his eighth day he frowned and wrinkled the skin around his eyes before a crying fit, but this may have been due to pain or distress, and not to anger. . . . When eleven months old, if a wrong plaything was given him, he would push it away and beat it; I presume that the beating was an instinctive sign of anger, like the snapping of the jaws by a young crocodile just out of the egg. . . . When two years old and three months old, he became adept at throwing books or sticks . . . at anyone who offended him; and so it was with some of my other sons. On the other hand, I could never see a trace of such aptitude in my infant daughters; and this makes me think that a tendency to throw objects is inherited in boys.

From Charles Darwin, "A Biographical Sketch of an Infant," *Mind, II,* 1877, 286–294.

and it combines observation with careful questioning. The clinical method has the advantage of being flexible. Tasks or questioning can be individualized for each person.

A modern-day example of the use of the clinical method occurs in the research of Piaget. In studying the development of thinking in children, Piaget was very interested in the reasons that some children were able to accomplish certain tasks and other children were not. In order to understand this, he used a combination of tests, or tasks, and individualized questions.

While the clinical method has the advantage of flexibility (allowing Piaget, for example, to probe the thought processes of young children), it has the disadvantage of producing conclusions that are highly dependent on an interviewer's ability to ask the right questions. Results that are produced in this fashion may need to be confirmed by others using the same or different methods before any faith can be placed in them. In the case of Piaget's work, many of his findings about children's thinking processes have, in fact, been supported by other investigators using other methods.

The Interview. The interview method has been used to investigate many issues of importance to human development. These include occupational satisfaction and aspirations, human sexual behavior, parent–child interaction, and attitudes toward aging, to name a few. The interviews are usually conducted with large numbers of people, so that the researcher obtains a broad picture of what these people do or think. A disadvantage of interviews is that they may depend on a subject's ability to remember correctly events or experiences from the past. Distortion can occur because of the time lag. Many early studies of parent–child interaction (e.g., Sears, Maccoby, and Levin, 1957) used interview techniques for determining the child-rearing practices of parents.

EXPERIMENTAL RESEARCH

In recent years, there has been a renewed emphasis on research in natural settings (Bronfenbrenner, 1979). Many investigators now use films and elaborate videotaping equipment to study behavior and development as it occurs in real life. Although naturalistic studies have the advantage of describing behavior that can be "generalized" to people in "natural" settings, they permit the experimenter little control over the experimental conditions (e.g., control of specific individuals in the study or of other events going on at the time of the experiment) (see Figure 3.8).

The *experimental* method is designed to provide an investigator with control over the subjects and the conditions in a study. The advantage of an experimental study is that this control allows the researcher to be more certain of the experimental results. In other words, the findings reflect what the experimenter says they reflect rather than some "uncontrolled" event. If, for example, an experiment is done for the purpose of demonstrating the relationship between parental attitudes and motor-skill development, then the findings of the experiment should demonstrate that relationship only. If they are to do that, it is necessary for the experimenter to "control" such factors as the age of the child (e.g., older children may be better at motor skills and also more responsive to parental attitudes than younger children). If the age of the children in the experiment is not controlled in some way (such as by having all of the children at the same age), then an experimental finding could be demonstrating a relationship between age and motor skills rather than parental attitude and motor skills.

ELEMENTS OF AN EXPERIMENT
Independent variables. The independent variables are the factors in an experiment that the researcher can systematically control or change. In the example of the experiment on parental attitude and motor skills, the independent variable is parental attitude. An experimenter might wish to group parents into three categories:

1. Parents who have a positive attitude toward motor skills.
2. Parents who have a negative attitude toward motor skills.
3. Parents who are neutral or indifferent toward motor skills.

Dependent variable(s). The dependent variable is the resulting behavior that is of interest to the researcher. In the experimental example, the dependent variable is the child's motor skills (e.g., running and throwing).

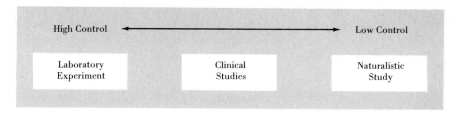

The primary advantage of experimental research compared to naturalistic studies is that the standardized procedures of experiments ensure that the study can be repeated or *replicated* by other investigators. Replication provides a test for the reliability of the experimental findings. If others get similar results using the same procedures with different subjects, then the findings have greater strength and status. A major disadvantage of the experimental method is that the precise control of experimental conditions results in findings that have limited application (except to other children in laboratory settings). Some developmentalists have argued, therefore, that the results of many laboratory studies provide unreal pictures of human development (Bronfenbrenner, 1979).

Cross-Sectional and Longitudinal Designs

Studies that deal with human development are usually concerned with one major aim: the description of how human beings change over time. There are two primary methods of data collection that serve this goal: *longitudinal* research and *cross-sectional* designs.

1. *Longitudinal designs.* The experimenter identifies a group of people and then measures them on some variable(s) of interest (e.g., behavior, attitudes, or feelings) at two or more moments in time. By examining the same people, the researcher can see the changes that occur as a result of development over a time period.

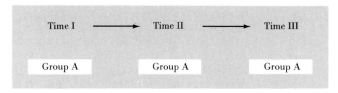

2. *Cross-sectional designs.* The experimenter compares groups of different individuals of different ages at one time.

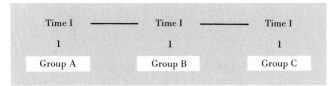

Longitudinal designs measure the changes that occur in single individuals over a period of time. Cross-sectional designs measure differences at one time among various individuals. Each approach has its strengths and weaknesses.

LONGITUDINAL RESEARCH

Advantage
- Longitudinal research is more sensitive to changes in individual behavior than cross-sectional research.

Disadvantages
- Requires several years (sometimes several decades) to collect data.
- Is usually expensive.
- Subjects may drop out of the study because of death, illness, moving, and so on.

CROSS-SECTIONAL RESEARCH

Advantage
- A sizable amount of information can be gathered in a relatively short time.

Disadvantages
- Generational or cohort effects may be present (these are effects that are the result of factors associated with being born at different times).
- Does not reflect individual changes over time.

3. *Combinations of longitudinal and cross-sectional designs.* In order to overcome some of the limitations of both the longitudinal and cross-sectional designs, the *cross-sequential* design was developed (Schaie, 1965). This design combines both the longitudinal and cross-sectional approaches by initially doing a cross-sectional sample of subjects and then following these same subjects longitudinally over time. The cross-sequential approach avoids the drawbacks and biases of both traditional designs. Research utilizing cross-sequential designs in the study of cognitive functioning in adulthood illustrates the value of this design in providing a more accurate and careful description of adult intelligence than either the longitudinal or cross-sectional designs (Baltes and Schaie, 1976). This is because cross-sectional designs typically give an *overestimate* in the drop in intellectual performance because of generational or cohort effects. For example, if we compared 20-, 40-, and 60-year-olds on a test of intellectual functioning, we would likely find a drop in performance with age. This drop would probably be due more to generational or cohort effects (e.g., given that educational experiences would have improved for the 20-year-olds compared to that of the two older groups, we might expect to find a drop in intellectual functioning as a result of such a cohort effect), than to age, per se. On the other hand, the longitudinal design tends to *underestimate* any drop in intellectual functioning with age primarily because *dropouts* from the original sample of 20-year-olds might make the sample at age 60 a much more able group of individuals than the original group. *Dropouts* from longitudinal research studies are rarely random in their characteristics. That is, those with poor health, lower occupational status, lower economic status, or, in this case, lower intelligence are far more likely to drop out of such a study). The cross-sequential design will presumably provide a more realis-

The Determinants of Human Development

Are Laboratory Experiments for "Real?"

In questions of public policy, the focus is on the enduring (and thereby familiar) social contexts in which the child lives, or might live, and in which the participants occupy enduring (and thereby familiar) roles and engage in activities that have social meaning in that setting. Such an orientation stands in contrast to many, but I hasten to add not all, laboratory situations in which the situation is of short duration and unfamiliar, the task is not only unfamiliar but artificial (in the sense that its social significance is at best unclear), and the other participants are strangers. In fact, usually there is only one other participant—a graduate student, whose prior relationship with the child is nonexistent, or, if existent, trivial in character. Indeed, it can be said that "much of American developmental psychology is the science of the behavior of children in strange situations with strange adults."

. . . More correctly, we should say the behavior of a child with "one" strange adult.

. . . These features so common in our research are hardly characteristic of the situations in which children actually live and develop. Thus, in the family, the day-care center, preschool, play group, school classroom or neighborhood, (a) there are usually more than two people; (b) the child invariably influences those who influence him; (c) the other participants are not strangers but persons who have enduring roles and relationships vis-à-vis the child; (d) finally, the behavior of all these persons is profoundly affected by other social systems [e.g., work, school] in which these same persons participate in significant roles and relationships, both toward the child and each other . . . .

By removing the child from the environment in which he ordinarily finds himself and placing him in another setting [laboratory] which is typically unfamiliar, short-lived, and devoid of the persons, objects and experiences that have been central in his life, we are getting only a partial picture both of the child and his environment.

From Urie Bronfenbrenner, "Developmental Research, Public Policy, and the Ecology of Childhood," *Child Development,* March 1974, 45(1) pp. 1–5.

tic picture of the variation of intellectual functioning by avoiding either an underestimation or an overestimation.

The cross-sequential design is not without its disadvantages. As is the case with longitudinal designs, additional time and expense are required for cross-sequential designs compared to cross-sectional research.

ETHICAL CONSIDERATIONS IN RESEARCH

In recent years increased attention has been paid to the impact of research on human beings. While it is not a common occurence for participation in research to result in abusive practices, it is nonetheless a distinct possibility. For example, ethically questionable practices could include the involvement of people in research without their knowledge or consent, coercing or forcing individuals to participate in research, invading a subject's privacy, exposing people to potential physical or psychological harm, failing to maintain the confidentiality of subject performance, and so on. As a result, the Federal government and various scientific and professional organizations have formulated ethical guidelines for the conduct of research. In addition, most institutions that engage in or sponsor research have research ethics advisory committees which evaluate proposed research and monitor ongoing projects to ensure conformity to ethical guidelines by avoiding the abuses discussed above, as well as other potentially unethical behavior.

Summary

1. This chapter has examined the factors which influence the development of the human being throughout the life span: the biological (genetic or inherited) determinants of development; the environments or "contexts" of development; and the interaction of the two. Human development and human behavior are rarely the result of a single cause. Rather numerous "causes" are involved.

2. Human heredity is of two sorts: *general* inheritance and *specific* inheritance. Heredity operates from the moment of conception—and throughout the life span—in determining various aspects of human growth and development. Although we know that genetic factors are involved in the development of the human body from the time of conception, we do *not* fully understand the scientific process in which genetic factors exercise control over growth and development. The relationship of genetic factors and human behavior is even less clear.

3. Our review of selected research on hereditary and environmental contributions to intelligence suggests that *both* factors are intimately involved in the development of human beings. The concepts of *canalization, gene expression,* and *range of reaction* are important for an understanding of this process of mutual interaction and mutual regulation of development involving both heredity and environment.

4. The environments or "contexts" of the life process play a large role in the development of human beings throughout the life span. It is not enough to simply state that heredity and environment interact. It is necessary to be more specific about what we mean by "environment." For our purposes, there are two broad categories of environments: *immediate* and *larger* environments.

5. The *family* is a significant immediate context throughout the life span. The influence of the family in childhood is critical in the development of self-concept, sex roles, language, intellectual abilities, and interpersonal skills. Duvall (1971) has described the changing pattern of the family life cycle as a series of developmental stages with primary functions at each point in the life cycle.

6. The *neighborhood-community* is another significant context for human beings throughout the life span. This context provides both a setting for human growth and development and a potential resource and support system for human beings.

7. The *school* as a context of development emerges as a major institution for the formal transfer of cultural traditions and skills from society to the developing child and young person. (This function of cultural transfer also occurs for adults in formal adult education programs).

8. *Work* as a context of development generally defines a person's intellectual level, patterns of motivation, lifestyle, and, to some degree, future potentials for development. Because of its economic and social significance, the job defines the material resources for behavior, family life, and for development itself.

9. *Peers* and *friends* are a vital source of feedback and support at all stages of human development.

10. The *culture* serves as a "larger" more indirect context of development. The immediate environments of family, school, neighborhood-community and peers do not exist in a vacuum. Rather, they occur in the context of the culture. The *culture* of a society is the collection of principles, beliefs, norms, rules, and range of behaviors that govern the organization of society. For example, our broad culture provides the framework for the organization of family, work, neighborhood-community, and peer contexts.

11. The "contexts" or environments just described interact with the developing human being in a somewhat predictable pattern. That is, some contexts such as family and school are usually more prominent during the early phases of the life span whereas others such as work perform a major role in adulthood. In this book, we will focus on this changing interactional or "systems" pattern between person and contexts throughout the life span. This developmental-interactional pattern is what we mean by a "systems" approach and has the following major characteristics: (a) It involves the *mutual interaction* of the developing person or self with the significant contexts of development. (b) It involves the *changing* or *evolving nature of these contexts* of development in each stage of development. (c) It involves the *cumulative impact of each context of development* as the individual moves through the life span.

12. Methods of studying human development include *naturalistic studies, clinical studies,* and *experimental research. Cross-sectional* and *longitudinal* designs are two primary methods of research and data collection for studying human development. The *cross-sequential* design combines both the cross-sectional and longitudinal approaches.

Questions

1. Briefly describe the "watermelon theory" of human development. How does the model integrate both genetic and environmental factors?
2. Based on your own experiences, can you cite significant physical similarities between parents and children or grandparents and grandchildren?
3. Indicate the reasons why the relationship between intelligence and heredity is unclear. If you heard someone say that a given group of people tend to do poorly in school because they are "genetically inferior," how would you counter the argument?
4. Briefly describe some of the significant "contexts" of, or settings for, human development. Do some contexts or settings play a greater or lesser role during various stages of life? Give several examples.
5. Define the following terms: naturalistic study, independent variable, dependent variable, cross-sectional study, and longitudinal study.

Bibliography

BALTES, P. B., and SCHAIE, K. W. On the plasticity of intelligence in adulthood and old age. *American Psychologist, 1976, 31,* 720–725.

BELL, R. Q. A reinterpretation of the direction of effects in studies of socialization, *Psychological Review, 75,* 1968.

BLAIR, D. G., COOPER, C. S., OSKARSSON, M. K. EATER, L. A. and VANDEWOUDE, G. F. New methods for detecting cellular transforming genes, *Science, 218,* 1122–1125, December 10, 1982.

BOUCHARD, T. J. and McGUE, M. Familial studies of intelligence: a review. *Science, 1981, 212,* 1055–1059.

BRONFENBRENNER, U. Developmental research, public policy, and the ecology of childhood. *Child Development,* March 1974, 45(1), 1–5.

BRONFENBRENNER, U. The origins of alienation. *Scientific American,* August 1974, 231 (2), 53–61.

BRONFENBRENNER, U. *The Ecology of Human Development.* Cambridge, Mass.: Harvard U.P., 1979.

BURKS, B. S. The relative influence of nature and nurture upon mental development: A comparative study of foster parent—foster child and true parent—true child resemblance. *Twenty-Seventh Yearbook of the National Society for the Study of Education,* 1928, 219–316.

DARWIN, C. A biographical sketch of an infant. *Mind, II,* 1877, 286–294.

DUVALL,, E. M. *Marriage and Family Development* (5th ed.). Philadelphia: Lippincott, 1977.

ERIKSON, E. H. *Dimensions of a New Identity.* New York: Norton, 1974.

ERLENMEYER-KIMLING, L. and JARVIK, L. F. Genetics and intelligence: a research review. *Science, 142,* 1963, 1477–1479.

FISHBEIN, H. D. *Evolution, Development, and Children's Learning.* Pacific Palisades, Calif.: Goodyear, 1976.

GAGE, N. L. Paradigms for research on teaching. In N. L. Gage (Ed.), *Handbook of Research on Teaching.* Chicago: Rand McNally, 1963.

GARBARINO, J. *Children and Families in the Social Environment.* New York: Aldine, 1982.

GOTTESMAN, I. I. Developmental genetics and ontogenetic psychology: overdue détente and propositions from a matchmaker. In Ann Pick (Ed.), *Minnesota Symposia on Child Psychology,* Volume 8. Minneapolis, Minnesota: The University of Minnesota Press, 1974, 60.

GOTTESMAN, I. I. Personality and natural selection. In S. G. Vandenberg (Ed.), *Methods and Goals in Behavior Genetics.* New York: Academic Press, 1965, 63–74.

HIRSCH, J. Behavior-genetic analysis and its biosocial consequences. *Seminars in Psychiatry 2,* 1970, 89–105.

HONZIK, M. P. Developmental studies of parent—child resemblance in intelligence. *Child Development,* 1957, *28,* 215–228.

HORN, J. M., LOEHLIN, J. C., and WILLERMAN, L. Intellectual resemblance among adoptive and biological relatives: the Texas adoption project. *Behavior Genetics,* 1979, *9,* 177–208.

HOROWITZ, F. D., and PADEN, L. Y. The effectiveness of environmental intervention programs. In B. Caldwell and H. Ricciuti (Eds.), *Review of Child Development Research,* Vol. 3. Chicago: U. of Chicago, 1973, 331–402.

HUBEL, D. H., and WIESEL, T. N. Receptive fields of cells in striate, cortex of very young, visually inexperienced kittens. *Journal of Neurophysiology,* 1963, *26,* 996–1002.

JENSEN, A. R. How much can we boost IQ and scholastic achievement? *Harvard Educational Review,* Winter 1969, *39,* 1–124.

KANTER, R. M. Job and families: Impact of working roles on family life. Washington, D.C.: *Children Today,* March–April 1978, 7, No.1, 11–15, 45.

LERNER, R. M. and BUSCH-ROSSNAGEL, N. A. (Eds.), *Individuals as Producers of Their Development.* New York: Academic, 1981.

LERNER, R. M. and SPANIER, G. B. *Child Influences on Marital and Family Interaction: A Life-span Perspective.* New York: Academic, 1978.

LOEHLIN, J. C., LINDZEY, G., and SPUHLER, J. N. *Race Differences in Intelligence.* San Francisco: Freeman, 1975.

LOEHLIN, J. C. and NICHOLS, R. C. *Heredity, Environment and Personality.* Austin, Texas: University of Texas Press, 1976.

MARX, J. L. The case of the misplaced gene (translocations of viral oncogenic genes), *Science, 218,* 983–85, December 3, 1982.

McCLEARN, E. G. Genetic influences on behavior and development. In P. H. Mussen (Ed.), *Carmichael's Manual of Child Psychology,* Vol. 1 (3rd ed.). New York: Wiley, 1970, 39–76.

O'TOOLE, J. *Senate subcommittee on children and youth, American families: trends and pressures.* Washington, D.C.: U.S. Government Printing Office, 1973, 98–109.

PIAGET, J. *The Origins of Intelligence in Children.* New York: International Universities Press, 1952.

ROLLINS, B., and FELDMAN, H. Marital satisfaction over the family life cycle. *Journal of Marriage and the Family,* 1970, 20–28.

ROSENFELD, A. The new LSD: Life-span development. *Saturday Review,* October 1, 1977.

SCARR, S. Genetic factors in activity motivation. *Child Development, 37,* 1966, 663–673.

SCARR, S. Social introversion as a heritable response. *Child Development, 40,* 1969, 823–832.

SCARR, S. and McCARTNEY, K. How people make their own environments; a theory of genotype environment effects. *Child Development, 54,* 1983, 424–435.

SCARR, S., and WEINBERG, R. A. IQ-test performance of black children adopted by white families. *American Psychologist,* October 1976, *31,* 726–739.

SCARR, S. and WEINBERG, R. A. Intellectual similarities within families of both adopted and biological children. *Intelligence, 1977, 1,* 170–191.

SCARR-SALAPATEK, S. Genetics and the development of intelligence. In F. D. Horowitz (Ed.), *Review of Child Development Research,* Vol. 4. Chicago: U. of Chicago, 1975.

SCHAIE, K. W. A general model for the study of developmental problems. *Psychological Bulletin,* 1965, 64, 92–107.

SCHNEIRLA, T. C. The concept of development in comparative psychology. In D. B. Harris (Ed.) *The Concept of Development.* Minneapolis, Minnesota: University of Minnesota Press, 1957.

SEARS, R. S., MACCOBY, E. E., and LEVIN, H. *Patterns of Child Rearing.* Evanston, Ill.: Row, Peterson, 1957.

SHIRLEY, M. M. *The First Two Years: A Study of Twenty-Five Babies, Vol. II: Intellectual Development.* Minneapolis: University of Minnesota, 1933.

SKEELS, H. M. Adult status of children with contrasting early life experience. *Monographs of the Society for Research in Child Development, 31* (Whole No. 105), 1966.

SKODAK, M., and SKEELS, H. M. A final follow-up on one hundred adopted children. *Journal of Genetic Psychology,* 1949, 75, 85–125.

SPIERER, H. *Major Transitions in the Human Life Cycle.* New York: The Academy for Educational Development, 1977.

TANNER, J. M. *Education and Physical Growth* (2nd ed.). New York: International Universities Press, 1978, 50–51.

THOMAS, A. and CHESS, S. Temperament and development. New York: Brunner Mazel Publishers, 1977.

THOMAS, A., CHESS, S., and BIRCH, H. The origins of personality. *Scientific American, 223,* 1970, 102–109.

THOMAS, A., CHESS, S., BIRCH, H. G., HERTZIG, M. E., and KORN, S. *Behavioral Individuality in Early Childhood.* New York: New York University Press, 1963.

VANDENBERG, S. G. (Ed.). *Progress in Human Behavior Genetics.* Baltimore: John Hopkins University Press, 1968.

WADDINGTON, C. H. *The Strategy of the Genes.* London: Allen & Unwin, 1957.

WILSON, R. S. Twins: early mental development. *Science, 175,* 1972, 914–917.

WILSON, R. S. Twins: mental development in the preschool years. *Developmental Psychology, 10,* 1974, 580–588.

WILSON, R. S. Twins: patterns of cognitive development as measured on the Wechsler Preschool and Primary Scale of Intelligence. *Developmental Psychology, 11,* 1975, 126–134.

WILSON, R. S. The Louisville twin study: developmental synchronies in behavior. *Child Development,* 1983, *54,* 298–316.

WILSON, R. S. and HARPRING, E. B. Mental and motor development in infant twins. *Developmental Psychology, 7,* 1972, 277–287.

Suggested Readings

DOBZHANSKY, T. *Mankind Evolving.* New Haven, Connecticut: Yale University Press, 1962. A discussion of the human condition from the point of view of a geneticist.

LERNER, R. *Concepts and Theories of Human Development.* Reading, Massachusetts: Addison-Wesley, 1976. An excellent discussion of the technical issues in research and theory building.

McKUSICK, V. A. and CHASE, G. A. Human genetics in *Annual Review of Genetics.* 1974, 7, 435–473. A well written although somewhat technical discussion of genetics.

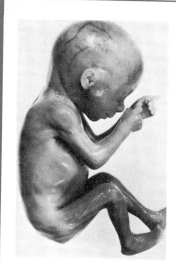

4

The Beginning of Life: Genetic Factors and Prenatal Development

The science of genetics has made extraordinary gains in the last two decades. As a result, we are beginning to accumulate a great deal of information about the mechanisms of heredity. In addition, genetic research has introduced such innovations as genetic screening and *amniocentesis* (the withdrawal of the amniotic fluid surrounding the unborn child in order to examine skin cells and other substances in the fluid for abnormality; see Application Box, "Prenatal Diagnosis of Genetic Defects"), which have led to the possibility of treating some problems before or immediately after birth and the possibility of terminating the life of the fetus early in pregnancy. Genetic advances that have made possible the treatment of some problems before or immediately after birth have received wide acceptance and support. On the other hand, the termination of pregnancy through abortion has created much debate and discussion. As is often the case with scientific and technological advances, the implications for human values and human decision-making became apparent only after the innovations were discovered.

This chapter deals with our current knowledge about genetic factors in development and about the prenatal development of the unborn child.

Life Begins

CONCEPTION

The process of conception occurs when fertilization takes place. *Fertilization* occurs when a *sperm* cell from a male unites with an *egg* from a female and forms a single cell. This single cell is called a *zygote* (see Figures 4.1–4.3).

FIGURE 4.1   Human sperm.

From *Biology,* 2nd ed., by Joan E. Rahn, courtesy of R. Uanagimachi. Copyright © 1980 by Joan E. Rahn. Reprinted by permission of Macmillan Publishing Co., Inc.

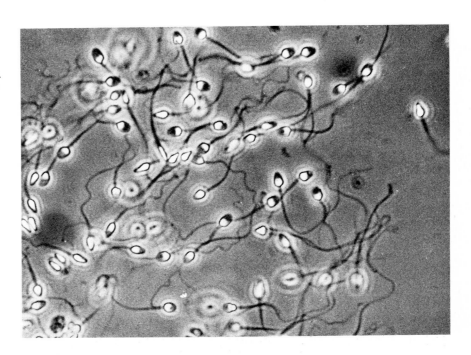

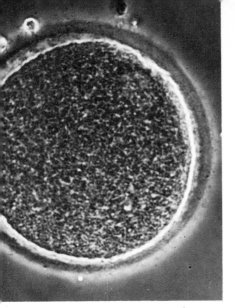

FIGURE 4.2   Human egg. A highly magnified human egg or ovum. The nucleus of the egg carries the mother's chromosomes.

Neg. no. 2A6258 Egg, Human. Courtesy of the Library Services Department, American Museum of Natural History.

(Both egg and sperm are called *gametes*.) Although we may casually state that life begins with the process of fertilization, this biological fact does not fully answer the question of when life begins.

DEFINITIONS

Zygote. The fertilized ovum formed by the union of the male sperm and the female ovum.

Embryo. The name given to the developing child during the six-week period from about the end of the second week after conception (when the egg becomes well implanted in the uterine wall) until the developing child takes on a human appearance as the result of cell differentiation (about the end of the second month after conception).

Fetus. The term used to describe the developing human organism from the end of the second month after conception (end of the embryonic period) until birth.

Indeed, the question of an abortion of an *embryo* or a *fetus* hinges, in part, on a definition of the beginning of life. Does life begin with conception? Or does life begin sometime later in pregnancy when the full assortment of human systems becomes differentiated? The notion of when life begins remains controversial among both scientists and the lay public.

FIGURE 4.3   Fertilization. Conception or fertilization occurs when the sperm cell from the father unites with the egg cell (ovum) from the mother. Fertilization marks the beginning of pregnancy. The diagram at the top right shows the union of egg and sperm. The diagram at the left center shows the location of fertilization in the female reproductive system.

Adopted from a drawing in H. Tuchmann-Duplessis, G. David, and P. Haegel, *Illustrated Human Embryology, Vol. I. Embryogenesis.* New York: Springer-Verlag, 1972, Masson, S. A., Paris, 1975.

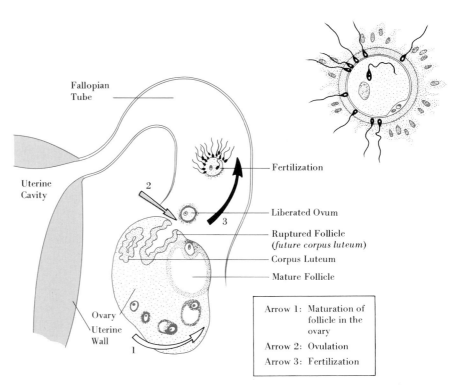

CHROMOSOMES AND GENES

Returning to biological facts, at the moment of conception there is a union of twenty-three small particles called *chromosomes* from the sperm with twenty-three chromosomes from the ovum (see Figures 4.4 and 4.5). This process of combining chromosomes from father and mother is of particular interest because these chromosomes carry *genes*.

DEFINITIONS

Chromosomes. These rod-shaped structures (see Figure 4.4) containing the genes are present in every cell. Genes contain the mechanisms for directing the activity of every cell. All normal human cells have forty-six chromosomes, or twenty-three chromosome pairs, except the germ cells (sperm and ovum), which each have twenty-three chromosomes (see Figures 4.4 and 4.5).

Genes. The basic units of heredity that are carried on the chromosomes.

It has been estimated that there are as many as 1 million genes in a human cell, or about twenty thousand genes per chromosome (Winchester, 1971). When the fertilized ovum divides, each new cell contains the same number of chromosomes and genes. Genes are composed of DNA (deoxyribonucleic acid) (see Figure 4.6.)

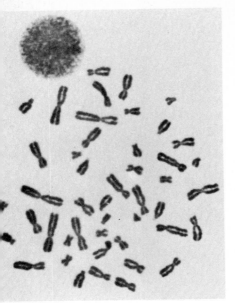

FIGURE 4.4   Human chromosomes. The photograph is of a magnified cell nucleus (top) and forty-six chromosomes of a normal human male. The chromosomes shown here are from a cell that is in the middle of cell division.

Photograph courtesy of March of Dimes Birth Defects Foundation, "Birth Defects: Tragedy and the Hope," 1977.

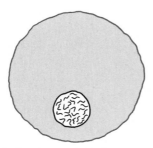

1. Female egg with 23 chromosomes.

2. Male sperm with 23 chromosomes.

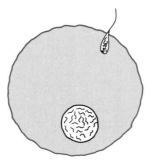

3. Sperm fertilizing the egg.

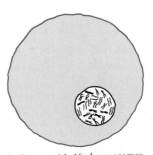

4. Zygote with 46 chromosomes.

FIGURE 4.5   The pattern of chromosomes before and after fertilization.

The Beginning of Life: Genetic Factors and Prenatal Development

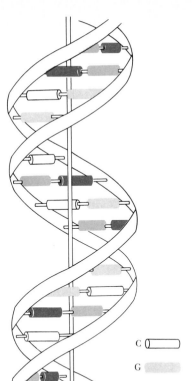

C ▭

G ▭

A ▭

T ▭

FIGURE 4.6 Model of a DNA molecule. The drawing is a theoretical representation, as DNA has never been observed. Each level of the spiral is composed of chemicals (see definition of DNA). The arrangement of these chemicals in the nucleus of each cell constitutes the genetic blueprint for the synthesis of proteins outside the nucleus of each cell.

From Lucille F. Whaley, *Understanding Inherited Disorders*. St. Louis: The C. V. Mosby Company, 1974, p. 16.

DEFINITIONS

Protein. A molecule containing amino acids (the basic building blocks of protein).

Enzyme. A protein that promotes reactions in a living system.

DNA (deoxyribonucleic acid). The chemical substance (composed of sugar, phosphate, and four bases—adenine, guanine, cytosine, and thymine) that makes up genes. The structure of DNA looks like a spiral ladder. The DNA molecule consists of two chains, which are coiled around each other in the form of a double helix (see Figure 4.6). DNA contains the genetic blueprint (genetic code) for the regulation and development of the human organism.

RNA (ribonucleic acid). RNA can be either messenger (mRNA) or transfer (+RNA). Both are structurally similar to DNA.

1. **mRNA** is formed on the DNA and carries the instructions for protein synthesis from the nucleus of the cell to the ribosome in the cytoplasm.

2. **+RNA** is also formed on the DNA. +RNA is coded to pick up one of the twenty naturally occurring amino acids, which it takes to the ribosome and places in the proper sequence to form a specific protein. Enzymes are one type of protein, as are portions of cell membranes, chromosomes, and other important cell structures.

Cytoplasm. Every thing within the cell with the exception of the nucleus.

Ribosome. Small spherical bodies in the cytoplasm; the cite of protein synthesis; composed of protein and RNA.

The elements of human heredity involve complex processes. Some of the characteristics which involve hereditary processes include physical traits (e.g., height, hair color, eye color), the timing of the onset of puberty, and susceptibility to diseases such as diabetes or heart disease. These inherited characteristics are subject to the influence of genes and their complex constituents including DNA and RNA (see definitions). DNA is the "genetic code" or "genetic blueprint" for the transmission of inherited human characteristics. DNA indicates which human traits will be transmitted and expressed in the offspring. In addition, DNA guides growth and development through the life span (e.g., rate of growth in childhood, the onset of puberty in adolescence, the onset and duration of the female menopause in adulthood, and the loss in hair in males in adulthood). DNA is composed of molecules of sugar, phosphate, and four bases (cytosine, adenine, guanine, and thymine) which combine in varying patterns with genes. The DNA molecule is in the shape of a double helix resembling a twisted ladder (see Figure 4.6). The strands of the DNA molecule which make up the "sides" of the "ladder" are composed of alternating sugar and phosphate molecules. The "rungs" of the ladder are made up of combinations of adenine and thymine or cytosine and guanine. The *order* of the chemical combinations of these bases on the rungs of the ladder determine the genetic code for a given characteristic to be inherited. Specifically, this order determines the types of proteins which will be synthesized in each human cell. Different patterns of DNA are different genes which, in turn, direct the production of different enzymes. The activity of different genes in different cells directs some cells to become bones, others to become body organs, and so on.

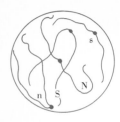
Interphase (I)

Prophase (P)

Metaphase (M)

Anaphase (A)

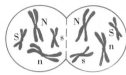
Telophase (T)

MITOSIS

FIGURE 4.7 Cell division or mitosis. The diagram shows only two pairs of chromosomes per cell instead of the twenty-three pairs usually present in humans.

Diagram drawn by Dr. Dorothy McMeekin, Michigan State University.

Because the reproductive cells formed during meiosis have only a random half of the genetic materials of the parent cell, the chance of any two siblings receiving the same random assortment of chromosomes is virtually nonexistent (except for identical twins, identical triplets, and so on). In this picture only two of the triplets are identical.

Photo by Darryl Jacobson

Since DNA is found within the nucleus of a given cell, it is necessary for the "message" of DNA to be transmitted outside the nucleus to the site of cell growth (cytoplasm). This DNA information is carried by RNA (ribonucleic acid). There are two types of RNA molecules which accomplish this transfer function (messenger RNA and transfer RNA, see definitions on page 97).

THE PRODUCTION OF BODY CELLS AND SEX (GERM) CELLS

After conception, the growth and development of the human being proceeds as a result of cell division. It is important to note that there are two different types of cells in the human body: *body* (somatic) cells and *sex* (germ) cells, from which sperm and ova develop. Body cells are reproduced through the process of cell division called *mitosis* (see Figure 4.7). Through mitosis, cells divide and make exact copies of themselves. The "directions" for the development of these new cells come from the DNA molecule in the genes.

DEFINITIONS

Mitosis. The process in which a single body cell divides into two exactly equal parts. Each of the duplicate parts has exactly the same twenty-three pairs of chromosomes as in the original cell.

Meiosis. A type of cell division that occurs only during the production of sex or germ cells (ova and sperm). During this process, each chromosome pair splits and separates so that the resulting ovum or sperm contains only twenty-three single chromosomes.

In contrast, sex or germ cells are produced by a process called *meiosis*. At the time of the final cell division during meiosis, the germ cells split, but the chromosomes do not (see Figure 4.8). Chromosome pairs separate during the formation of male and female sex cells so that each egg or sperm cell carries *half* of the total number of chromosomes. When fertilization occurs, twenty-three chromosomes from the sperm and twenty-three from the ovum unite to define the genetic potential of a new human being (see Figure 4.8).

Because the reproductive cells formed during meiosis have only a random half of the genetic materials of the parent cell, the chance of any two siblings receiving the same random assortment of chromosomes is virtually nonexistent (except for identical twins, identical triplets, and so on). Or, put another way, the chances of two peoples having identical chromosomal arrangements are about 1 in 64 trillion! In addition, the process called *crossing over* further

The Beginning of Life: Genetic Factors and Prenatal Development

FIGURE 4.8 Meiosis. During both mitosis and meiosis the chromosome containing DNA duplicates. The two processes differ: (1) After mitosis the chromosome number is the same as in the original cell; after meiosis the chromosome number is half the original number. (2) In mitosis genes/chromosomes duplicate with each of the two new cells receiving identical genotypes —NnSs. In meiosis genes/chromosomes assort or segregate independently at metaphase 1, leading to only 2 possible gamete (sperm or egg) genotypes in Telophase II. —Ns and nS *or* NS and ns represent the genes for two characteristics. With 23 chromosomes, each carrying a different expression of the gene (N/n, S/s or Brown/blue eyes, Normal/affected), the number of gamete types will be 2^{23} or $2 \times 2 \times 2 \ldots 23$ times or 8,388,608. When a sperm fertilizes an egg the chances of 2 identical independently fertilized eggs ever occuring is $8,388,698^2$ or 64 trillion to one.

In the female only one of the four cells produced by meiosis matures into an egg. In the male, all four cells mature.

Interphase in both mitosis and meiosis is not a resting cell. The very elongated chromosome material with great surface area, contains the DNA code controlling the RNA which in turn directs enzyme synthesis and all cellular reactions.

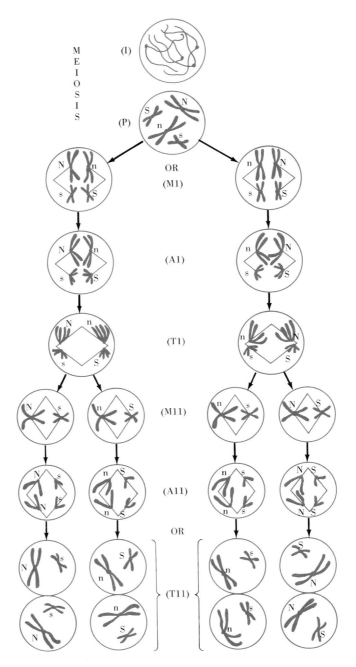

increases the likelihood that each sperm and ovum will be unique (and therefore than each child will be unique). The process of crossing over is the exchange of DNA material between chromosomes in a pair during Metaphase I of meiosis (see Figure 4.9).

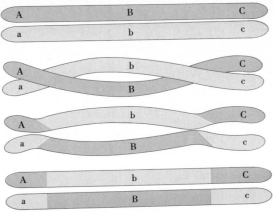

FIGURE 4.9 Crossing over. The diagram shows how the process of crossing over can result in a new organization or grouping of genes on chromosomes. Crossing over sometimes occurs during meiosis.

Adapted from J. Otto, and A. Towle, *Modern Biology*, p. 628. Copyright © 1977 Holt, Rinehart and Winston, Publishers.

SIMPLE GENETIC TRANSMISSION

A common observation is that children may or may not resemble their parents. For example, both parents may have brown eyes, and one of their children may have blue eyes. How are characteristics passed on—or not passed on—from parent to offspring?

Dominant and Recessive Genes (PKU: An Example). The genetic transmission of most traits (including eye color) is dependent not on a single gene but on several genes. In order to illustrate genetic transmission more easily, we will discuss a trait or characteristic that is, in fact, dependent on a single pair of genes: phenylketonuria (PKU). PKU is an inherited disease that results in the inability to metabolize phenylalanine, which is a component of many foods. If not treated, PKU can result in moderate to severe retardation, as well as other physical problems. (Most states require the testing of newborn children for PKU.) In order to explain the transmission of PKU, we will use *N* to symbolize the gene for normal metabolic activity and *n* to represent the gene for PKU. Related genes, such as *N* and *n*, are called *alleles*. In this case, *N* is the *dominant* gene and *n* is the *recessive* gene. Individuals can have *three* possible genetic expressions (genotypes) with reference to PKU: *NN, Nn,* or *nn*.

DEFINITIONS

Dominant gene. A gene that always expresses its hereditary characteristic. When paired with a different or subordinate gene for a given trait, the "dominant" gene will prevail in manifesting its hereditary characteristic.

Recessive gene. A gene that expresses its hereditary characteristic *only* when paired with a similar (recessive) gene. When paired with a dominant gene for a given trait, the expression of the hereditary characteristic of the recessive gene is masked. For example, blue-eyed genes are recessive to brown-eyed genes (dominant) and and expressed only when pure or exclusively blue-eyed genes are present.

     The Beginning of Life: Genetic Factors and Prenatal Development

Allele. Any of several alternative or possible genes for a given trait that might be found at the appropriate location on a chromosome.

Genotype. The fundamental hereditary constitution (assortment of genes) or an individual contained in the cells of the human body.

Phenotype. The expressed or observable characteristics of human beings that result from both a particular genotype and a particular environment.

If a mother is *Nn* and a father is *Nn* (see Figure 4.10), one of three possible *genotypes* can occur at conception: *NN, Nn,* or *nn*. At conception, *each child* of these parents has a 50 percent chance of being an *Nn* genotype, a 25 percent chance of being an *NN* genotype, and a 25 percent chance of being an *nn* genotype.

Which genotype would have normal metabolism, and which would have inherited PKU? An *NN* baby would be normal, as it has two normal genes. The *nn* baby would inherit PKU. The *Nn* babies would also be normal because the *N* gene is *dominant* over the *n* gene, which is *recessive*. It should be noted that the *Nn* offspring are considered *carriers* of the PKU trait (*n*). In other words, they have the trait in their genotypes (genetic formulas) but not in their phenotypes (actual physical characteristics).

FIGURE 4.10 The genetic transmission of P.K.U. In the diagram, both parents are carriers of P.K.U. (*Nn* genotype). Offspring may have the following genotypes: *NN, Nn* or *nn*. Only *nn* offspring will have P.K.U.

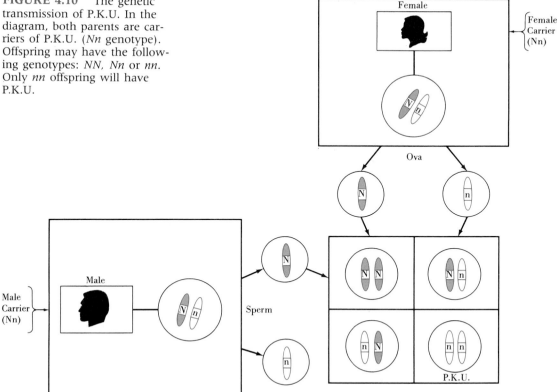

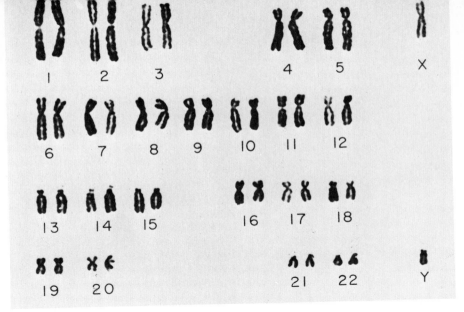

FIGURE 4.11   Male sex chromosomes. The picture shows a karyotype or arrangement of normal male chromosomes. The twenty-two paired chromosomes (the autosomes) are arranged in descending order according to size and shape. The X and Y chromosomes, which determine the sex of the individual, are easily recognized as different from the autosomes.

Courtesy of March of Dimes Birth Defects Foundation, "Birth Defects Original Article Series," Vol. IV, No. 4, Sept. 1968.

Transmission of Sex Type. One of the significant human traits that is passed on from the adult is the sex of the offspring. As we indicated earlier, each human cell contains twenty-three pairs of chromosomes (with the exception of sex cells, which contain twenty-three single chromosomes). Of the twenty-three pairs of chromosomes, twenty-two pairs are called *autosomes*, and the twenty-third pair are the *sex chromosomes* (see Figure 4.11 and 4.12).

DEFINITIONS
Autosomes. The first twenty-two pairs of chromosomes of the total twenty-three pairs of chromosomes. Autosomes are responsible for determining the physical characteristics of the child other than the sex.

Sex chromosome. The twenty-third pair of chromosomes which is responsible for determining the sex of the child.

FIGURE 4.12   Female sex chromosomes. The diagram shows a karyotype of the chromosomes of a normal female lined up in descending order by size. You may note that the paired autosomes (1–22) are not recognizably different from those of the male (Figure 4.11). There is, however, no Y chromosome (lower right corner). Instead there are two XX chromosomes (in the upper right corner).

Courtesy of March of Dimes Birth Defects Foundation, "Birth Defects Original Article Series," Vol. IV, No. 4, Sept. 1968.

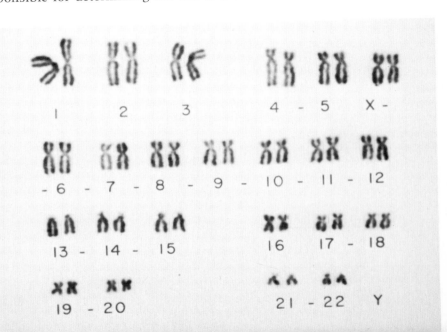

Sex determination of offspring. On the basis of chance alone, the odds are 50–50 that either a boy (XY) or a girl (XX) will be conceived.

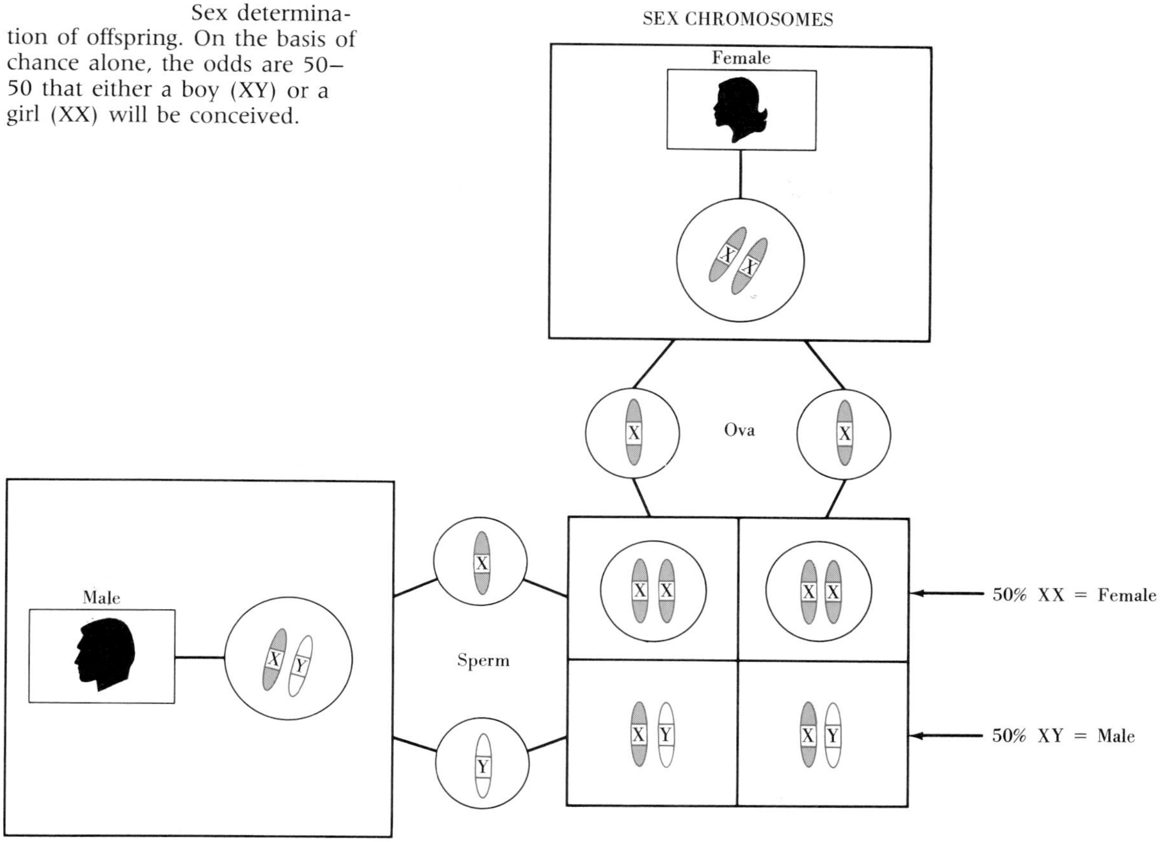

SEX CHROMOSOMES

Female

Ova

Male

Sperm

50% XX = Female

50% XY = Male

In the female, both members of the sex chromosome pair are X chromosomes (XX). In the male, one chromosome of the pair is an X chromosome and the other, much smaller chromosome is a Y chromosome (XY). Each male sperm cell, therefore, contains either an X or a Y chromosome. Because both female sex-cell chromosomes are X chromosomes, each ovum always has an X chromosome (see Figure 4.13). On the basis of chance alone, the odds are 50–50 that a boy or a girl will be conceived. However, it has been estimated that approximately 130 to 150 males are conceived for every 100 females (Beatty and Glucksohn-Waelsch, 1972). Only about 106 males are born for every 100 females (Stern, 1960; Beatty and Glucksohn-Waelsch, 1972). This birth rate difference is evidence that more male fetuses than female fetuses are lost prenatally through spontaneous abortions. This higher prenatal fatality rate for males is consistent with postnatal survival statistics. For example, males have a higher death rate during infancy than females, are less able to resist infections than females, and have a shorter life expectancy than females (Fryer and Ashford, 1972).

Transmission of Birth Defects. Included, unfortunately, in the vast array of traits that some offspring may have are birth defects.

TABLE 4.1 Selected Birth Defects, USA

Birth Defect	Type	Annual Incidence*	Prevalence**	Cause	Detection***	Treatment***	Prevention***
Down's syndrome	functional/structural: retardation often associated with physical defects	5,100	44,000	chromosomal abnormality	amniocentesis, chromosome analysis	corrective surgery, special physical training and schooling	genetic services
Markedly low birthweight† prematurity	structural/functional: organs often immature	50,000	NA	hereditary and/or environmental: maternal disorder or malnutrition	prenatal monitoring visual inspection at birth	intensive care of newborn, high-nutrient diet	proper prenatal care, genetic services, maternal nutrition
Muscular dystrophy	functional: impaired voluntary muscular function	unknown (late-appearing)	200,000	hereditary: often recessive inheritance	apparent at onset	physical therapy	genetic services
Congenital heart malformations	structural	24,800	248,000	hereditary and/or environmental	examination at birth and later	corrective surgery, medication	genetic services
Clubfoot	structural: misshapen foot	9,300	149,000	hereditary and/or environmental	examination at birth	corrective surgery, corrective splints, physical training	genetic services
Polydactyly	structural: multiple fingers or toes	9,300	184,000	hereditary: dominant inheritance	visual inspection at birth	corrective surgery, physical training	genetic services
Spina bifida and/or hydrocephalus	structural/functional: incompletely formed spinal canal: "water on the brain"	6,200	53,000	hereditary and environmental	amniocentesis, prenatal X-ray, ultrasound, maternal blood test, examination at birth	corrective surgery, prostheses, physical training, special schooling for any mental impairment	genetic services
Cleft lip and/or cleft palate	structural	4,300	71,000	hereditary and/or environmental	visual inspection at birth	corrective surgery	genetic services
Diabetes mellitus	metabolic: inability to metabolize carbohydrates	unknown (late-appearing)	90,000	hereditary and/or environmental	appears in childhood or later; blood and urine tests	oral medication, special diet, insulin injections	genetic services
Cystic fibrosis	functional: respiratory and digestive system malfunction	2,000	10,000	hereditary: recessive inheritance	sweat and blood tests	treat respiratory and digestive complications	genetic services
Sickle cell anemia	blood disease: malformed red blood cells	1,200	16,000	hereditary: incomplete recessive—most frequent among blacks	blood test	transfusions	genetic services

Disease	Description			Cause/Inheritance	Detection	Treatment	Prevention
Hemophilia (classic)	blood disease: poor clotting ability	1,200	12,400	hereditary: sex-linked recessive inheritance	blood test	clotting factor	genetic services
Congenital syphilis	structural: multiple abnormalities	(newborn only) 180	NA	environmental: acquired from infected mother	blood test, examination at birth	medication	proper prenatal care
Phenylketonuria (PKU)	metabolic: inability to metabolize a specific amino acid	310	3,100	hereditary: recessive inheritance	blood test at birth	special diet	carrier identification, genetic services
Tay–Sachs disease	metabolic: inability to metabolize fats in nervous system	30	100	hereditary: recessive inheritance—most frequent among Ashkenazi Jews	blood and tear tests, amniocentesis	none	carrier identification, genetic services
Thalassemia	blood disease: anemia	70	1,000	hereditary: incomplete recessive inheritance	blood test	transfusions	carrier identification, genetic services
Galactosemia	metabolic: inability to metabolize milk sugar galactose	70	500	hereditary: recessive inheritance	blood and urine tests, amniocentesis	special diet	carrier identification, genetic services
Erythroblastosis (Rh disease)	blood disease: destruction of red blood cells	7,000	NA	hereditary and environmental: Rh– mother has Rh+ child	blood tests	transfusion: intrauterine or postnatal	Rh vaccine, blood tests to identify women at risk, genetic services
Turner syndrome	structural/functional	575	3,100	chromosomal abnormality	amniocentesis, chromosome analysis	corrective surgery, medication	genetic services
Congenital rubella syndrome	structural/functional: multiple defects	varies with occurrence of disease; less than 50	NA	environmental: maternal infection	antibody tests and viral culture	corrective surgery, prostheses, physical therapy and training	rubella vaccine

*Incidence: the number of new cases diagnosed within a specific time period.

**Prevalence: total number living who have been diagnosed as having defect. Above statistics based on number less than 20 years of age.

***Last three columns list possible means now known for detection, treatment, and prevention. The techniques may not necessarily be applicable or successful in every case.

†Weighing 4 lbs. 6 oz. or less.

Since birth defects are not reportable conditions except when fatal, we can only estimate their incidence and prevalence. Based upon available data, the Foundation estimates that among Americans of all ages, birth defects afflict: □ 4 million with diabetes □ 580,000 born completely or partially blind □300,000 with congenital hearing impairment □ 350,000 with heart or circulatory defects □ 170,000 with severe speech problems □ millions of others with defects of the nervous, digestive, endocrine, urinary, and other body systems.

Reproduced by permission of March of Dimes Birth Defects Foundation, "Birth Defects: Tragedy and the Hope," 1977.

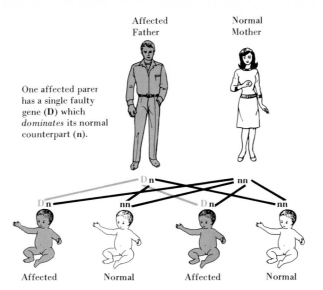

Affected
Father

Normal
Mother

One affected parer
has a single faulty
gene (**D**) which
dominates its normal
counterpart (**n**).

Each child's chances of inheriting either the **D** or the **n**
from the affected parent are 50%.

Currently, some 1,218 dominantly inherited disorders have
been catalogued. Examples include:

- achondroplasia—*a form of dwarfism*
- chronic simple glaucoma (some forms)—
  a major cause of blindness if untreated
- Huntington's disease—
  progressive nervous system degeneration
- hypercholesterolemia—
  high blood cholesterol levels, propensity to heart disease
- polydactyly—*extra fingers or toes*

FIGURE 4.14 Dominant inheritance of genetic defects. An affected child must have one parent with the same disorder. In such a family, there is approximately a 50% risk that each child will have the disorder, even though it may not be apparent at birth. There is an equal likelihood that a child will not receive the defect. Therefore both this child and his or her own children will be free of the disorder and will not carry any gene for the disorder.

Reprinted from March of Dimes Birth Defects Foundation, "Genetic Counseling," 1978.

Of all the many hundreds of potentially serious birth defects, only about 25 percent have been clearly identified as genetic "errors." Most of the remaining 75 percent are usually attributed either to *congenital* defects (caused by something going wrong in the womb or in the birth process) or to some "complex" or unknown causes. It is highly probable that a good number of the currently identified unknown causes may yet turn out to be of genetic origin.

Where there is some genetic basis for a birth defect, it usually involves one of the following methods of transmission (see Table 4.1, pp. 104–105):

1. Dominant inheritance of genetic defects (see Figure 4.14).
2. Recessive inheritance of genetic defects (see Figure 4.15).
3. Sex-linked inheritance of genetic defects (see Figure 4.16).
4. Chromosomal abnormalities (see Figure 4.17).

Congenital defects. These are abnormalities that are present at birth. They may be influenced by genetic factors or they may be due to the effect of environmental factors on the unborn child.

Figure 4.14, 4.15, and 4.16 show the first three methods of transmitting birth defects. We will now turn to chromosome abnormalities. These abnormalities are not specifically genetic in origin; they result from accidents that occur to a sperm or an egg cell, producing an abnormal assortment of chromosomes. The phenomenon of physical abnormalities and mental retardation called *Down's syndrome* is an example. This abnormality occurs in one of every

FIGURE 4.15 Recessive inheritance of genetic defects. Both parents of an affected child appear normal. However, both carry the harmful gene although neither may be aware of it. Unfortunately, recessive abnormalities tend to be more severe than dominant ones.

Reprinted from March of Dimes Birth Defects Foundation, "Genetic Counseling," 1978.

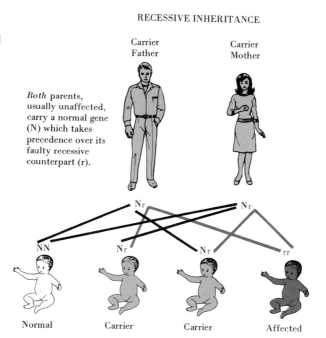

RECESSIVE INHERITANCE

Carrier Father   Carrier Mother

Both parents, usually unaffected, carry a normal gene (N) which takes precedence over its faulty recessive counterpart (r).

Nr   Nr

NN   Nr   Nr   rr

Normal   Carrier   Carrier   Affected

The odds for each child are:
1. A 25% risk of inheriting a "double dose" of r genes which may cause a serious birth defect.
2. A 25% chance of inheriting two Ns, thus being unaffected.
3. A 50% chance of being a carrier as both parents are.

Among 947 recessively inherited disorders catalogued are:

- cystic fibrosis—*disorder affecting function of mucus and sweat glands*
- galactosemia—*inability to metabolize milk sugar*
- phenylketonuria—*essential liver enzyme deficiency*
- sickle cell disease—*blood disorder primarily affecting blacks*
- thalassemia—*blood disorder primarily affecting persons of Mediterranean ancestry*
- Tay–Sachs disease—*fatal brain damage primarily affecting infants of East European Jewish ancestry*

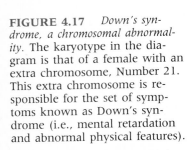

SEX-LINKED INHERITANCE

Carrier Mother   Normal Father

In the most common form, the female sex chromosome of an unaffected mother carries one faulty gene (X) and one normal one (x). The father has normal male x and y chromosome complement.

Xx   xy

xy   xx   Xy   Xx

Normal   Normal   Affected   Carrier

FIGURE 4.16 Sex-linked inheritance of genetic defects.

Reprinted from March of Dimes Birth Defects Foundation, "Genetic Counseling," 1978.

The odds for each *male* child are 50/50:
1. 50% risk of inheriting the faulty X and the disorder.
2. 50% chance of inheriting normal x and y chromosomes.
For each *female* child, the odds are:
1. 50% risk of inheriting one faulty X, to be a carrier like mother.
2. 50% chance of inheriting no faulty gene.

Among 171 catalogued disorders transmitted by a gene or genes on the X chromosome are:

- agammaglobulinemia—*lack of immunity to infections*
- color blindness—*inability to distinguish certain colors*
- hemophilia—*defect in blood-clotting mechanisms*
- muscular dystrophy (some forms)—*progressive wasting of muscles*
- spinal ataxia (some forms)—*spinal cord degeneration*

two thousand newborns. In Down's syndrome, the child is born with *three* rather than *two* of the chromosomes numbered 21 (see Figure 4.17). The mother and the father of such a child are normal; the copying or replication error occurs either in the germ cell or in the initial cell division of the embryo.

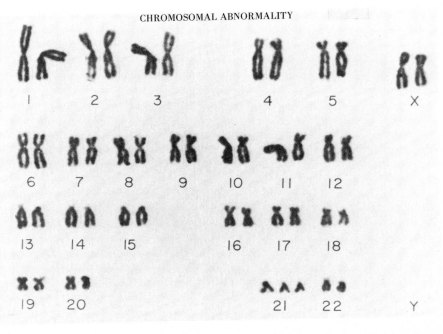

CHROMOSOMAL ABNORMALITY

FIGURE 4.17 *Down's syndrome, a chromosomal abnormality.* The karyotype in the diagram is that of a female with an extra chromosome, Number 21. This extra chromosome is responsible for the set of symptoms known as Down's syndrome (i.e., mental retardation and abnormal physical features).

Courtesy of March of Dimes Birth Defects Foundation, "Birth Defects Original Article Series," Vol IV, No. 4, Sept. 1968.

The Beginning of Life: Genetic Factors and Prenatal Development

Genetic Counseling

Genetic counseling provides and interprets medical information based on expanding knowledge of human genetics, the branch of science concerned with heredity. Its major goal is to convey understanding of birth defects to affected families, and enable prospective parents to make informed decisions about childbearing.

Birth defects may be inherited or may result from environmental factors—unfavorable "living conditions" for the fetus—during prenatal development. Often they reflect a combination of the effects of heredity and environment.

Although specific birth defects may seem relatively uncommon, together they occur in about seven percent of all births and the total number of affected families is well in the millions. Each year, about 220,000 American babies are born with physical or mental defects of varying severity. Some of these defects, though present at birth, do not become apparent until months or years later.

Using as tools the basic laws governing heredity, plus knowledge of the frequency of specific birth defects in the population, the genetic counselor can often predict the probability of recurrence of a given abnormality in the same family. Sophisticated new techniques are being rapidly developed and refined to translate statistical estimates into accurate forecasts, using tests before pregnancy and before birth to determine the chance of bearing a child with a defect, and presence or absence of a growing list of inherited defects.

Genetic counseling is concerned with all factors causing birth defects. A counselor must first determine whether the defect in question is transmitted by the genes passed from parents to children or due to infection or other influence during life in the womb. Appropriate information can enable families and physicians to prevent defects or, in some cases, to reverse or at least reduce their damaging effects.

Taken from March of Dimes Birth Defects Foundation, "Genetic Counseling," White Plains, N.Y., 1978, p. 5.

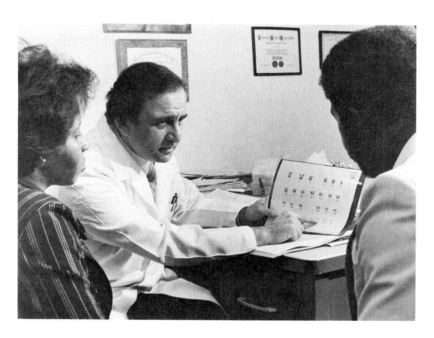

Prenatal Diagnosis of Genetic Defects

Relatively simple tests have made it possible to make a firm prediction about certain defects well before birth. One such procedure, called *amniocentesis,* is usually performed after the 14th week of pregnancy. [See diagram.] It entails withdrawing a small amount of the amniotic fluid which surrounds the developing fetus in the uterus. Since the fluid contains fetal cells, it can yield invaluable information for genetic analysis. Amniocentesis is recommended only if a woman is at increased risk for the specific defects that can be diagnosed by this means. Indications are: advanced maternal age; previous child with a metabolic defect; the finding that both parents are carriers; and certain structural defects such as open spine.

Amniotic fluid must be obtained by needle through the mother's abdominal wall, into the cavity of the uterus or womb.

The usual procedure is to locate the placenta and position of the fetus with ultrasound equipment. This prevents injury to either when the needle is inserted into the amniotic sac. The use of sound waves (ultrasonography) to show specific physical outlines avoids the harmful aspects of X-ray. In experienced hands, the entire procedure carries very low risk for mother and fetus, and the discomfort is minimal. These are small problems in view of the peace of mind gained if prenatal diagnosis reassures parents that their unborn baby does not have the defect being tested for. Indeed, 97 percent of the high risk women using amniocentesis find that their fetus is free of the suspected defect.

If a defect should be identified, the physician knowing about it early in pregnancy is able, in some instances, to minimize damage through prompt action at or soon after birth. In any event, parents are aided by firm information rather than statistical odds in deciding how to meet the problem. For some, it provides the opportunity for trying for a healthy infant without the risk of having an affected child.

Taken from March of Dimes Birth Defects Foundation, ''Genetic Counseling,'' White Plains, N.Y., 1978.

From Theodore Friedman, ''Prenatal Diagnosis of Genetic Disease,'' *Scientific American,* Nov. 1971, *225*(5), 34–42. Copyright © 1971 by Scientific American, Inc. All rights reserved.

The Amniocentesis Procedure, Step by Step

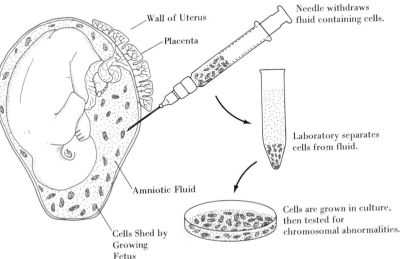

Wall of Uterus

Placenta

Needle withdraws fluid containing cells.

Laboratory separates cells from fluid.

Amniotic Fluid

Cells Shed by Growing Fetus

Cells are grown in culture, then tested for chromosomal abnormalities.

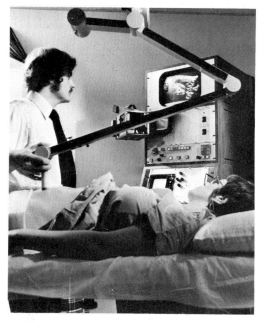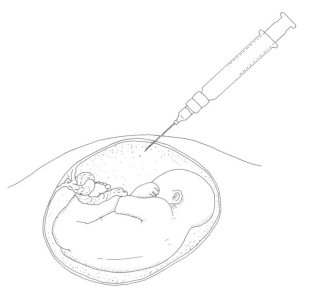

Ultrasound picture (left) shows location of fetus and placenta to help guide safe entry of the needle used in amniocentesis as shown in diagram (right).

From March of Dimes Birth Defects Foundation, "Genetic Counseling," 1978.

COMPLEX GENETIC TRANSMISSION

If all traits followed the pattern of inheritance described for PKU (controlled by one gene pair), there would be a limited number of categories of height, or pigmentation, or intelligence in humans. The fact that there is great variation in these traits means that more gene pairs are involved (polygenic)—the more diversity, the more genes.

Two blue-eyed people can produce a child with brown eyes; a modifying gene has suppressed the gene for brown in one parent. It is very rare, but a child can have two genes for PKU and be normal. For some unknown reason the PKU gene is not expressed completely.

There are several kinds of epilepsy. The type induced by physical injury is not inherited. Another form of epilepsy is inherited and is expressed. (It is a genetic-dominant trait.) Another inherited type is expressed—only if one has a predisposition—when the person is subjected to stress, high temperature, hypoglycemia (low blood sugar), or photic stimulation (e.g., flashing lights).

A Paradox. Persons with one gene for sickle cell anemia or thallisemia do not have these diseases, but they do have the trait. These people are resistant to malaria. On the other hand, people with two of these genes are debilitated by the respective diseases. There is a high frequency of sickle cell anemia only in those parts of Africa and the Mediterranean where the incidence of malaria is high. Likewise, there is a high frequency of thallisemia only in those parts of the Middle East, southern Asia, and Africa where the incidence of malaria is high. This leads to the *question* of whether those *populations* that have a high frequency of PKU, cystic fibrosis, or Tay–Sachs disease may also be more vigorous (have more surviving offspring) in a particular environment if they have the *trait* (one recessive gene for the disease and one normal gene) rather than the disease itself (two recessive genes). This, of course, is only speculation based on the *assumption* that the relatively high frequency of the disease and the trait in their populations might serve a positive evolutionary or adaptive function.

What Is Normalcy? Most of the examples given in the preceding sections deal with what have been called genetic "defects." Actually there is evidence from detailed studies of the amino acids in protein molecules (i.e., hemoglobin, which is the iron-containing protein compound in blood) that most genes, and even the changes in them (mutations), are neutral. They do not reduce or enhance one's chances for survival under present conditions. These genes have not received much attention because they are not harmful. They are not very conspicuous (Volpe, 1981, p. 50).

An example of such a neutral gene is the one for the enzyme lactase that digests lactose, a sugar in milk. Most infants produce lactase. However, only in those populations that descend from ancient dairy herders does the production of this enzyme persist into adulthood. It has been estimated that most of the world's adult population who are not of northern European descent are unable to tolerate milk to some degree (i.e., suffer from bloating, cramps, or diarrhea) because their bodies have stopped producing lactase (Kolars, Levitt, Aouji, and Savaiano, 1984). For example, descendants of some West African and Mediterranean people may stop producing this enzyme when they are adults and cannot, therefore, digest milk. Many of these people circumvent the problem by eating cheeses which have very little lactose due to the processes used in converting milk to cheese (Durham 1981). Furthermore, the inability of most adults to produce lactase may account, in part, for the longstanding popularity (in the Middle East and throughout the world) of yogurt—a dairy product that is very low in lactose (Kolars, et al., 1984). These people, which includes many of us, are all considered to be *normal.*

Prenatal Development: Three Stages

The months from conception to the birth of the child are marked by significant developments that have a profound impact on the rest of the individual's life. The poet Coleridge captured the essence of this viewpoint when he wrote, "Yes—the history of a man for the nine months preceding his birth would probably be far more interesting and contain events of greater moment than all the three score years that follow it" (from Coleridge, 1885).

THREE STAGES OF PRENATAL GROWTH

1. *Germinal stage.* This is the period of development from fertilization until approximately the end of the second week after conception. This period ends when the fertilized egg (ovum), or *blastocyst,* is implanted in the wall of the uterus.
2. *The embryonic stage.* This stage covers the six-week period from about the end of the second week until about the conclusion of the second month after conception. At the end of this period, the first bone cell is developed and the embryo appears to be a miniature human being. In other words, the embryo has all of its essential parts.
3. *The fetal stage.* This period lasts from about the end of the second month until birth.

DEFINITION: THE TRIMESTERS OF PREGNANCY

First trimester—from conception until the end of the third month of pregnancy.

Second trimester—the fourth, fifth, and sixth months of pregnancy.

Third trimester—the seventh, eighth, and ninth months of pregnancy.

FIGURE 4.18 The blastocyst. As the fertilized egg travels down the Fallopian tube, it divides. After about one week, a hollow cluster (blastocyst) of over one thousand cells is formed.

From J. Otto, and A. Towle, *Modern Biology,* p. 627. Copyright © 1977 Holt, Rinehart and Winston, Publishers.

Fertilized Egg

a

Two Cells

b

Four Cells

c

Eight Cells

d

Many Cells

e

Blastocyst

Inner Cell Mass
f

GERMINAL STAGE

When fertilization occurs, the sets of twenty-three chromosomes contributed by the reproductive cell of each parent line up to form twenty-three pairs of chromosomes. This paired arrangement will be repeated in each new cell that is developed from this first cell, or fertilized egg. Although the chromosomes and the genes on the chromosomes contain the individual's genetic potential, they are not the only determinant of development. From the very beginning—indeed, from the moment of conception—the development of the individual is a product of *both* heredity and environment.

DEFINITION

Blastocyst (blastula). A hollow ball of cells that have developed from the fertilized egg. This stage of development lasts for about a week after conception, until the sphere is implanted in the uterine wall. During the blastocyst period, cells begin to differentiate.

As the fertilized zygote or egg travels down the Fallopian tube, it continues to divide. First it divides into two cells; then the two cells divide into four in a geometric progression (2, 4, 8, 16, 32 . . .). This process of division continues as the zygote floats in the uterus and becomes embedded in the uterine wall. About five days after conception, a hollow cluster of cells has been formed. This cluster is called a *blastocyst* (see definition box and Figures 4.18 and 4.19). The cells of the blastocyst have begun to differentiate according to future functions. Two layers of cells are forming: (1) an outer layer that serves nourishing and protective functions and will become the placenta (the organ through which the baby is attached to the mother), the umbilical cord (which attaches the baby to the *placenta*), and the amniotic sac (the membrane filled with amniotic fluid that completely surrounds the embryo by the eighth week after conception); (2) an inner cell cluster that becomes the embryo. At the

FIGURE 4.19 From ovulation to implantation. (A) The ovary releases one egg (more eggs could result in multiple births); (B) the egg is fertilized; (C) the fertilized egg or zygote divides into two cells or *blastomeres* as it travels down the fallopian tube; (D) 4 blastomeres at 40–50 hours; (E) 8 blastomeres at 60 hours; (F) 12–16 blastomeres at 4 days (called *morula*); (G) by the fifth day the fertilized egg forms a central cavity and is called a *blastocyst*; (H) the blastocyst implants itself on the uterine lining or *mucosa* on the sixth day.

Based on information and drawings in H. Tuchmann-Duplessis, G. David, and P. Haegel, *Illustrated Human Embryology*, Vol. I, *Embryogenesis*. New York: Springer-Verlag, 1972. Paris: Masson, 1975.

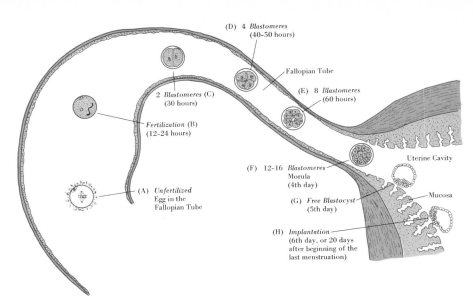

end of the germinal period, the unborn child is about the *size of the period* at the end of this sentence. The first prenatal stage, or the germinal stage, ends when the blastocyst is embedded in the uterine wall.

EMBRYONIC STAGE

After implantation in the uterine wall, the second stage, or embryonic stage, begins. The embryo now receives nourishment from the mother by means of the umbilical cord, which is attached to the placenta. The embryo (and later, the fetus) receives oxygen, water, immunities to some disease (e.g., measles, polio, and hepatitis), and nutrients (e.g., sugars, fats, and proteins) from the mother across membranes in the placenta. The mother's and child's bloodstreams are not directly connected. Waste products from the embryo also pass through these membranes to the mother. Unfortunately, some diseases and drugs from the mother (e.g., rubella, mumps, thalidomide, and heroin) also pass through these membranes.

During this period, the embryo is growing rapidly. At the end of the first month, three differentiated cell layers have developed in the embryo (see Figure 4.20):

FIGURE 4.20 The differentiation of the embryo. After implantation in the uterine wall, the embryo grows rapidly. By the end of the first month, three cell layers have been differentiated. These cell layers, in turn, give rise to the tissues and organs of the human body.

Adapted from T. J. Moon, J. Otto, and A. Towle, *Modern Biology*, p. 616. Copyright © 1963 Holt, Rinehart and Winston, Publishers. Used with permission.

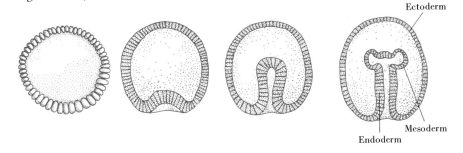

The Beginning of Life: Genetic Factors and Prenatal Development

TABLE 4.2   Structures Formed from Specific Primitive Germ Layers

Ectoderm	*Mesoderm*	*Endoderm*
Skin and skin glands	Connective tissue	Lining of alimentary canal from pharynx
Hair	Bone	to rectum
Most cartilage	Most muscles	Thyroid and parathyroids
Nervous system	Kidneys and ducts	Trachea and lungs
Pituitary gland	Gonads and ducts	Bladder
Lining of mouth to the pharynx	Blood, blood vessels, heart,	
Part of the lining of rectum	and lymphatics	
Adrenal medulla		

From J. Otto, and A. Towle, *Modern Biology,* p. 627. Copyright © 1977 by Holt, Rinehart and Winston, Publishers.

1. The *ectoderm* (outer layer) produces the skin, the sense organs, and the nervous system.
2. The *mesoderm* (middle layer) produces the muscles, the circulatory system, and the excretory system.
3. The *endoderm* (inner layer) produces the gland systems and lungs (see Table 4.2).

At this point, the embryo is ten thousand times larger than the original zygote. The embryo is crescent-shaped and about three sixteenths of an inch long. By this time, a beating heart has appeared in the embryo. Blood is flowing through very tiny veins and arteries. In addition to a heart, the embryo also has a very tiny brain, kidney, liver, and digestive tract (see Figures 4.21 and 4.22). At the end of the second month, the embryo is about one and one-eighth inches long. Virtually all of the body systems that will be found in

FIGURE 4.21   The embryo at four weeks.

Illustrations from *"Pregnancy in Anatomical Illustrations,"* appear courtesy of the copyright owner © Carnation Company, Los Angeles, Ca., 1962.

Actual Size: ¼ inch

At End of Four Weeks

Heart pulsating and pumping blood.

Backbone and spinal canal forming.

No eyes, nose or external ears visible.

Digestive system beginning to form.

Small buds which will eventually become arms and legs are present.

FIGURE 4.22   (Left) Side view of a 28-day-old human embryo. (Right) Photograph of the same embryo taken at a different angle, showing the size of the yolk sac.

From Streeter. Courtesy Carnegie Institution of Washington.

FIGURE 4.23 Human fetus at eight weeks.

Illustrations from ''Pregnancy in Anatomical Illustrations'' appear courtesy of the copyright owner © Carnation Company, Los Angeles, Ca., 1962.

At End of Eight Weeks

About 1 1/8 inches long.

Weighs about 1/30 ounce.

Face and features forming: eyelids fused.

Limbs beginning to show distinct divisions into arms, elbows, forearm and hand, thigh, knee, lower leg and foot.

Distinct umbilical cord formed.

Long bones and internal organs developing.

Tail-like process disappears.

the newborn have developed, at least to a somewhat primitive level. The head of the embryo is virtually one half of the total body length. The forehead is conspicuous because of the early development of the brain. Facial features, including eyes, ears, nose, lips, and tongue, are present (see Figure 4.23).

Thus, the first two months of embryo development are particularly crucial. By the end of the embryonic period, at around eight weeks, about 95 percent of all body parts have been developed (see Table 4.3), and the fetus has increased in size by 2 million percent. Much growth and development remain; however, they will be an extension of what already exists. Because foundational development is so rapid and critical during this period, the unborn child is extremely vulnerable to disruptions of normal growth, including influences from the environment. We discuss some of these influences later in this chapter.

TABLE 4.3 Approximate Periods of Critical Differentiation for Some Organs

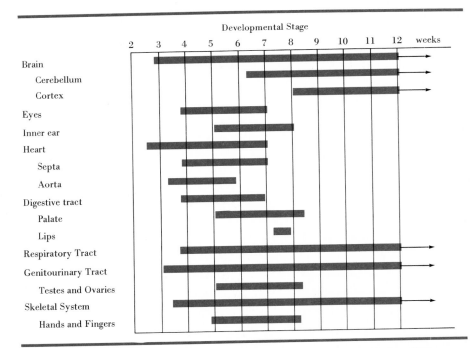

From Lucille F. Whaley, *Understanding Inherited Disorders*, St. Louis: C. V. Mosby, 1974.

The Beginning of Life: Genetic Factors and Prenatal Development

FETAL STAGE

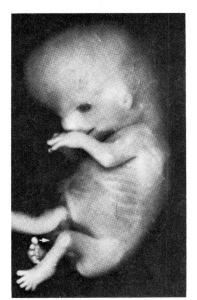

FIGURE 4.24 Photograph of a 29-mm (crown-rump length) embryo at 56 days. The intestine is still in the umbilical cord (arrow). The digits are clearly defined. The regions of the limbs are apparent, and the tail has disappeared.

Photographed by Professor Jean Hay, Department of Anatomy, University of Manitoba, Winnipeg, Canada. From K. L. Moore, *The Developing Human: Clinically Oriented Embryology,* 3rd edition, 1982. Courtesy W. B. Saunders Company.

Around the end of the second month after conception, the term *fetus* is applied to the unborn child. Technically, an embryo is called a fetus when the first bone cell appears. The fetal period lasts about seven months. It is the longest of the prenatal periods. At the end of the third month, the fetus is about three inches long and weighs about one ounce. During this stage, the fetus is capable of breathing movements, sucking movements when the mouth area is stimulated, kicking movements, and head turning. Because the fetus is so small, fetal kicking and head turning are not felt by the mother. During this stage, fingers and toes are formed, and fingernails are in the process of forming (see Figures 4.24, 4.25, 4.26, and 4.27).

One of the most interesting events that occurs during the second and early part of the third months is sex differentiation. During this period, the external genitals develop. Up to about five weeks, the fetus has undifferentiated sex gonads (the female ovaries or the male testes; germ-cell-producing organs). In the case of the male, genetic action on the Y male sex chromosome causes the fetal gonads to produce the male sex hormone androgen. As a result the previously undifferentiated sex gonads become male testes. In the case of the female, as there is no Y chromosome (females are XX), there is no production of androgen by the undifferentiated sex gonads. At about the tenth week, the gonads become ovaries.

During the fourth month, the fetus makes considerable gains in growth. The fetus is now more than six inches in length. At this time, we find the continued development of movements, including sucking, head turning, and a variety of limb, foot, and hand movements. It is during the fourth month that the mother begins actually to feel fetal movement. Usually this is a significant milestone for the father as well as for the mother (see Figures 4.28 and 4.29).

The fifth month is the midpoint of the pregnancy. The baby has grown considerably, weighs from one-half to one pound, and is about one foot in length. Evidence suggests that the fetus develops differentiated rhythms of sleeping and waking during the fifth month (see Figure 4.30).

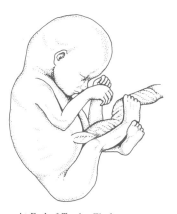

FIGURE 4.25 The fetus at twelve weeks. Illustrations from "Pregnancy in Anatomical Illustrations," appear courtesy of the copyright owner © Carnation Company, Los Angeles, Ca., 1962.

At End of Twelve Weeks

About 3 inches long.

Weighs about 1 ounce.

Arms, hands, fingers and legs, feet, toes fully formed.

Nails on digits beginning to develop.

External ears are present.

Tooth sockets and buds forming in the jawbones.

Eyes almost fully developed, but lids still fused.

Heartbeat can be detected with special instruments.

Prenatal Development: Three Stages

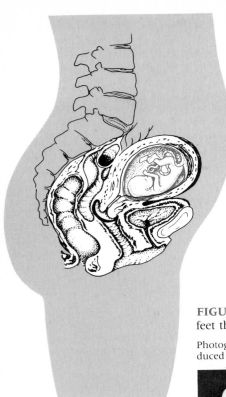

Your baby is now about 3 inches long and weighs about 1 ounce. It may continue to develop in the position shown or may turn or rotate frequently. The uterus begins to enlarge with the growing fetus and can now be felt extending about half-way up to the umbilicus.

Baby's hands are fully formed even at 12 weeks with fingers and nails all distinctly present.

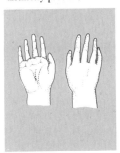

FIGURE 4.26 The fetus at three months. Illustrations from "Pregnancy in Anatomical Illustrations," appear courtesy of the copyright owner © Carnation Company, Los Angeles, Ca., 1962.

FIGURE 4.27 The development of embryonic and fetal hands and feet through twelve weeks.

Photographs from the Carnegie Institution of Washington, Davis Division. Reproduced by permission.

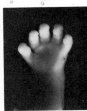

| Hand Plate 7 Weeks | Finger Ridges 7 Weeks | Definite Thumb and Fingers with Pads 8 Weeks | Regression of Finger Pads 12 Weeks |

Development of Human Hands

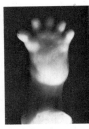
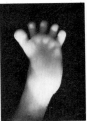
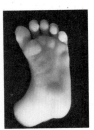

| Toe Ridges 7 Weeks | Heel Development 7 Weeks | Note Walking Pads 8 Weeks | Regression of Toe Pads 10 Weeks |

Development of Human Feet

The Beginning of Life: Genetic Factors and Prenatal Development

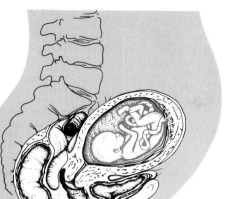

FIGURE 4.28   The fetus at four months.

Illustrations from "Pregnancy in Anatomical Illustrations" appear courtesy of the copyright owner © Carnation Company, Los Angeles, Ca., 1962.

FIGURE 4.29   Photograph of a 17-week old fetus. *Slightly larger than actual size.* Note that the ears stand out from the head and that no hair is visible. Because there is no subcutaneous fat and the skin is thin, the blood vessels of the scalp are visible. Fetuses at this age are unable to survive if born prematurely, mainly because their respiratory system is immature. The alveolar surface area is insufficient, and the vascularity of the lungs is underdeveloped.

From K. L. Moore, *The Developing Human: Clinically Oriented Embryology.* 3rd edition, 1982. Courtesy W. B. Saunders Company.

Your baby is now about 6½–7 inches long and weighs about 4 ounces. It has a strong heartbeat, fair digestion and active muscles. Its skin is bright pink and transparent and is covered with a fine down–like hair. Most bones are distinctly indicated throughout the body.

Head is disproportionately large at this stage. Eyes, ears, nose and mouth approach typical appearance. Eyebrows appear.

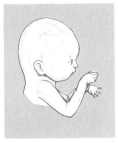

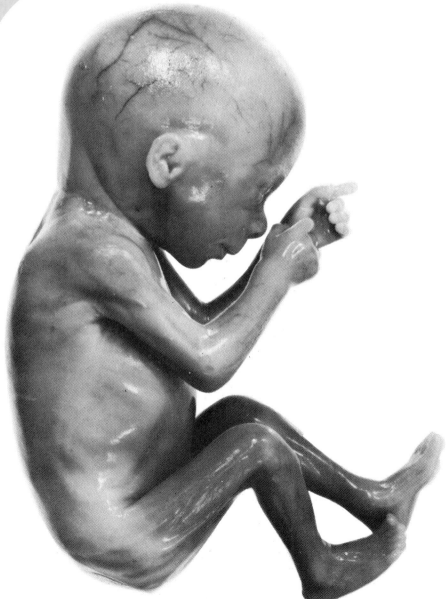

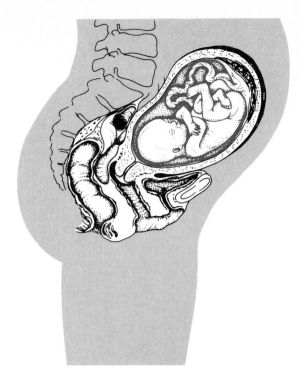

Your baby measures about 10-12 inches long and weighs from ½ to 1 pound. It is still bright red. Its increased size now brings the dome of the uterus to the level of the umbilicus. The internal organs are maturing at astonishing speed but the lungs are insufficiently developed to cope with conditions outside of the uterus.

The eyelids are still completely fused at the end of five months. Some hair may be present on the head.

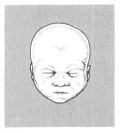

FIGURE 4.30   The five-month fetus.

FIGURE 4.31   The fetus at six months.

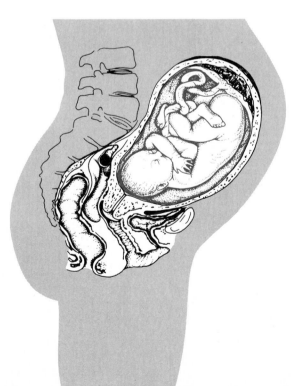

At the end of the 6th month your baby measures 11-14 inches and may weigh from 1¼-1½ pounds. The skin is quite wrinkled and still somewhat red and is covered with a heavy protective creamy coating. The eyelids are finally separated and eyelashes are formed.

Fingernails now extend to the end of the fingers.

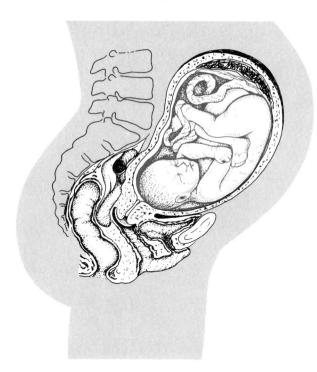

The baby's weight has about doubled since last month and it is about 3 inches longer. However, it still looks quite red, is covered with wrinkles which will eventually be erased by fat. At seven months the premature baby at this stage has a fair chance for survival in nurseries cared for by skilled physicians and nurses.

The seven month baby is wrinkled and red.

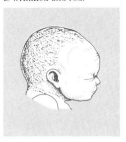

FIGURE 4.32 The fetus at seven months.

Illustrations from "Pregnancy in Anatomical Illustrations" appear courtesy of the copyright owner © Carnation Company, Los Angeles, Ca., 1962.

During the sixth month, the fetus ordinarily grows another inch or two and gains another one-half to one pound in weight. Several interesting changes occur during this month: fetal eyes open for the first time (previously the eyelids had been fused shut); the fetus can make irregular breathing movements; and it has a fairly well developed grasping reflex. Relating to the breathing movement, mothers often report feeling fetal hiccups (see Figure 4.31).

The seventh month begins the third trimester of pregnancy (see Figure 4.32). Growth begins to slow down during this period. "At seven months or twenty-eight weeks the *age of viability* is reached . . . the baby is capable of independent life and is likely to survive if born then." (Annis, 1978, p. 41).

FIGURE 4.33 Infants born prematurely usually require special care.

Photograph by Wayne Mason

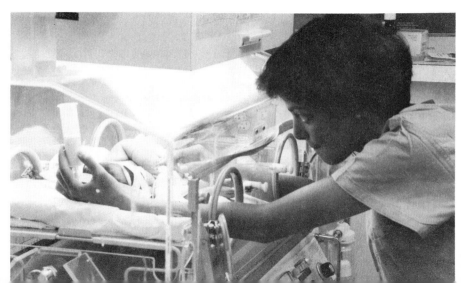

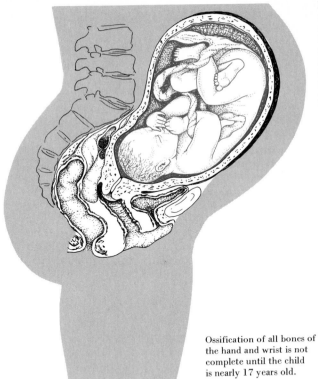

In the absence of premature labor the growth and maturation of the baby in the last two months are extremely valuable. From 2½ to 3 pounds at the beginning of the month, it will add 2–2½ more pounds and will lengthen to 16½–18 inches by the end of the eighth month. The bones of the head are soft and flexible. If born now, its chances for survival are much greater than those of a seven month fetus, although there is a popular fallacy to the contrary.

Ossification of all bones of the hand and wrist is not complete until the child is nearly 17 years old.

FIGURE 4.34 The human fetus at eight months.

Illustrations from ''Pregnancy in Anatomical Illustrations'' appear courtesy of the copyright owner © Carnation Company, Los Angeles, Ca., 1962.

Although a baby can survive if born during the seventh month, it is vulnerable to infection and needs a sheltered environment, such as an incubator (see Figure 4.33). Babies born during the sixth month may also survive, although high amounts of oxygen may be required to keep them alive. The survival of infants born during the fifth month, or earlier, is unlikely because they are unable to sustain the necessary breathing movements.

During the eighth and ninth months of pregnancy, ''the finishing touches'' are added to the unborn child (see Figures 4.34 and 4.35). The wrinkled skin of the fetus—which makes it look like an elderly person—begins to fill out with fat. The baby gains about one-half pound per week from this time until birth. Annis (1978) described some of the major features of development during this period:

the baby responds to light and sound, lifts its head, and appears to be pleased when caressed. The effects of cephalocaudal development direction (the sequence of growth from the head downward) are seen again in that at birth the fetal head is 60% of its adult size. The brain of a full-term infant is one-fourth of the adult human brain, which still makes it relatively large for the size of the infant when compared to the infant's other organs that are about ⅟₂₀ of the size and weight of adult organs (Robinson and Tizard, 1966). By the end of the ninth month all intrauterine development has been completed. The baby is now ready to enter the world. (pp. 41–42)

The Beginning of Life: Genetic Factors and Prenatal Development

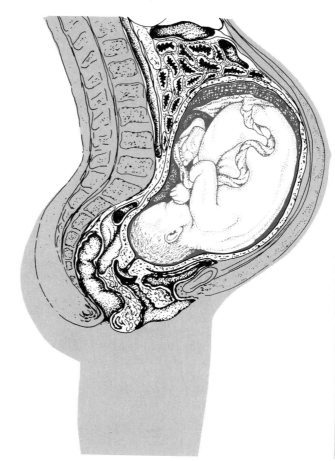

At birth or full term the baby weighs on an average about seven and a quarter pounds if a girl and seven and a half if a boy. Its length is about 20 inches. Its skin is coated with a creamy coating. The fine downy hair has largely disappeared. Fingernails may protrude beyond the ends of the fingers.

The size of the soft spot between the bones of the skull varies considerably from one child to another, but generally will close within 12 to 18 months.

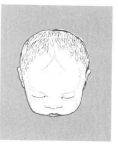

FIGURE 4.35   The human fetus at nine months.

Illustrations from "Pregnancy in Anatomical Illustrations" appear courtesy of the copyright owner © Carnation Company, Los Angeles, Ca., 1962.

Prenatal Environmental Influences

Ordinarily we think of the prenatal environment as fairly constant and rather simple compared with the more complex environments of childhood and beyond. The fact is that there are many variations in the prenatal environment, both throughout one pregnancy and from one pregnancy to another. Research on prenatal development indicates that both the mother's physical status and her emotional status may have an impact on the development of the fetus, as well as being an important influence on the future general health and adjustment of the child. The following sections describe some of the more important prenatal environmental factors that have been investigated to date.

MATERNAL NUTRITION

Because food supply for the developing fetus comes from the mother's bloodstream by way of the placenta, there is good reason to be concerned about the expectant mother's diet. Poor or inadequate nutrition is probably the greatest potential threat to the normal development of the unborn child. Malnutrition during pregnancy has been associated with stillbirth, prematurity (including low-birth-weight babies of less than five and a half pounds), and neonatal deaths.

DEFINITIONS

Premature infant. A baby having a short *gestation period* (born early, less than thirty-seven weeks after conception) or a baby born small (weighing less than twenty-five hundred grams, or under five and a half pounds). Prematurity can cause cognitive (intellectual), physical, and psychological problems (see Chapter Five).

Neonate. The newborn infant during the first month after birth.

In addition, improper maternal nutrition is also associated with a variety of problems after birth, including rickets, epilepsy, mental deficiency, general weakness, and susceptibility to disease (Tompkins, 1948; Annis, 1978). Because of the importance of nutrition, it is desirable for the woman to begin pregnancy with a history of good eating habits and in a healthy, well-nourished state. Even though expectant mothers ordinarily plan their diets carefully during pregnancy, it is difficult to reverse the effects of a past improper diet because increased nutritional demands are made on the expectant mother.

Several studies have indicated the consequences of malnutrition during pregnancy (Cravioto, deLicardie, and Birch, 1966; Vore, 1973; Drillen and Ellis, 1964). Cravioto, et al. (1966) found that children experiencing malnutrition (before and after birth) are likely to be shorter in height, lower in weight, and lagging in developmental and cognitive skills as measured by psychological tests. This study was done in Mexico, beginning in 1958, with a sample of parents and children from very similar social and economic backgrounds. Results from the study indicated that deficits in child height, weight, and developmental—cognitive skills were related to both the dietary history of the child and the child's previous experiences with diseases. These deficits were not related to differences in such factors as personal hygiene, housing, indicators of socioeconomic status, or proportion of income spent on food.

RH-FACTOR INCOMPATIBILITY

The Rh factor is a genetically determined feature of the blood. About 85 percent of Caucasians are Rh positive (compared with 93 percent of blacks). The Rh factor can become a problem in the marriage of an Rh-negative woman and an Rh-positive man. This combination occurs in only 12 percent of American marriages (Annis, 1978). About 10 percent of the children born in these marriages have some form of Rh disease (twenty-six thousand children per year). It is possible to determine whether a person is Rh positive or Rh negative by means of a specially developed serum that causes Rh-positive blood to agglutinate or clump and does not cause Rh-negative blood to clump (McCurdy, 1950).

DEFINITIONS

Anemia. A shortage of iron in the blood and a reduction in red blood cells.

The Beginning of Life: Genetic Factors and Prenatal Development

Toxemia. During pregnancy, a condition in which the woman's blood pressure increases, she retains salt and water, she develops swelling (edema), and she has albumin (a protein) in her urine.

Rh disease manifests itself in a predictable manner (see Figure 4.36). The Rh-positive fetus produces substances, called *antigens,* that pass through the semipermeable membrane of the placenta and enter the Rh-negative mother's bloodstream. The mother's bloodstream, in turn, produces Rh antibodies in response to the Rh-positive antigens of the fetus. These antibodies pass through the placenta from the mother to the unborn child and attack and destroy fetal red blood cells. The resulting disease, called *erythroblastosis fetalis,* produces severe fetal anemia. Anemia results because the level of red blood cells is reduced. The toxic substances produced by the destroyed red blood cells give the skin a yellowish color.

FIGURE 4.36 Rh disease, its cause and prevention.

Reprinted by permission of Ortho Diagnostic Systems, Inc., Raritan, N.J.

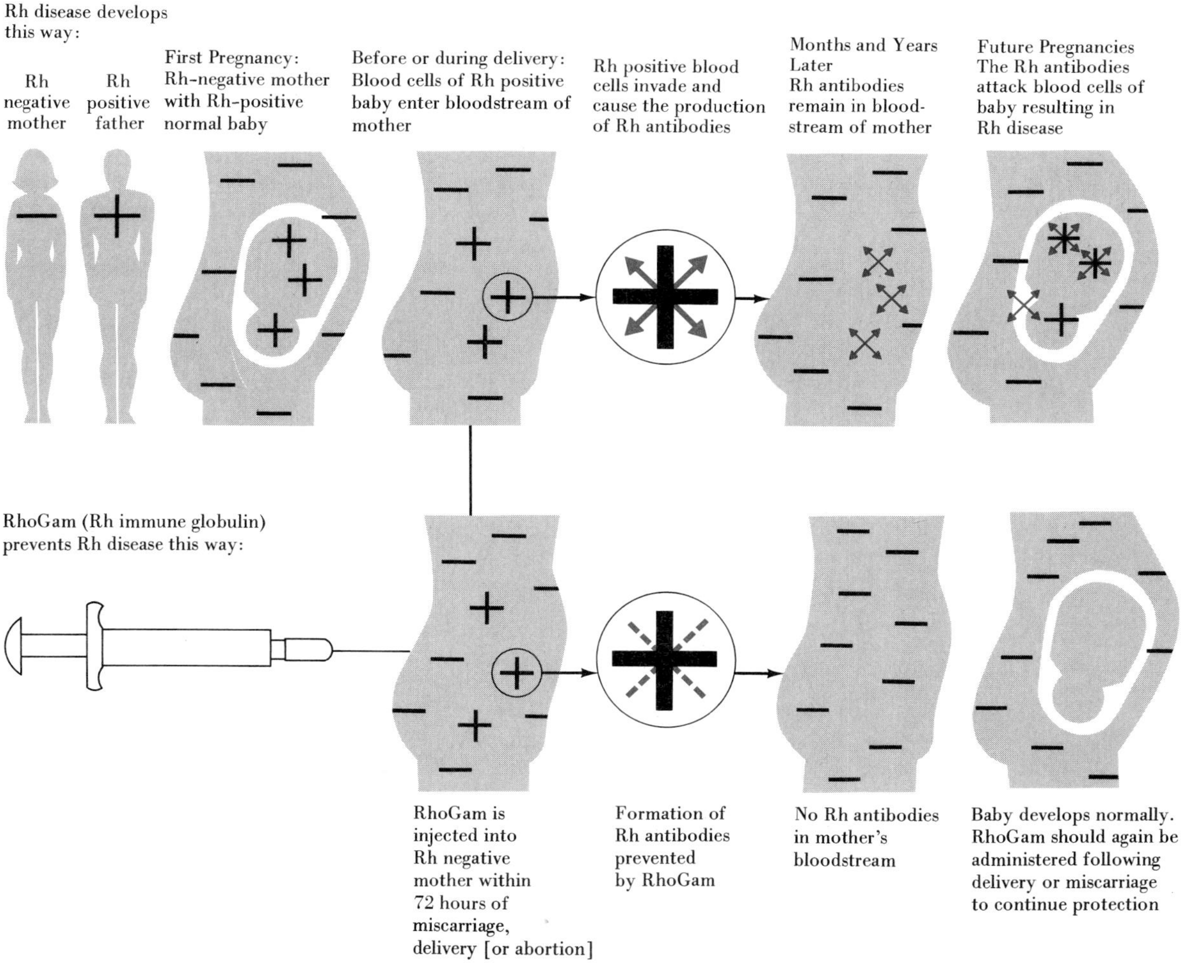

Rh disease develops this way:

Rh negative mother | Rh positive father | First Pregnancy: Rh-negative mother with Rh-positive normal baby | Before or during delivery: Blood cells of Rh positive baby enter bloodstream of mother | Rh positive blood cells invade and cause the production of Rh antibodies | Months and Years Later Rh antibodies remain in bloodstream of mother | Future Pregnancies The Rh antibodies attack blood cells of baby resulting in Rh disease

RhoGam (Rh immune globulin) prevents Rh disease this way:

RhoGam is injected into Rh negative mother within 72 hours of miscarriage, delivery [or abortion] | Formation of Rh antibodies prevented by RhoGam | No Rh antibodies in mother's bloodstream | Baby develops normally. RhoGam should again be administered following delivery or miscarriage to continue protection

Firstborn children are usually not affected by erythroblastosis because it takes the mother some time to develop the appropriate level of antibodies. Subsequent children are therefore more likely to suffer the problems of Rh incompatability. Fortunately, there are medical techniques for treating the problem when it occurs (Liley, 1963; Clarke, 1968). (See Figure 4.36.)

MATERNAL PHYSICAL CHARACTERISTICS: AGE AND SIZE

Although the average female reproductive life span extends from about age twelve through forty-five or fifty years of age, the recommended period for childbearing is between the ages of twenty and thirty-five (Rugh and Shettles, 1971). It is during this period that the highest proportion of healthy children are born. Between twenty and thirty-five years of age, there are also fewer pregnancy complications, including spontaneous abortions, stillbirths, maternal deaths, and prematurity.

More children with developmental problems tend to be born to mothers who are under twenty years of age or over thirty-five. Presumably the reason is that mothers under twenty may have inadequately developed reproductive systems, and women over thirty-five may have aging and declining reproductive systems (Pasamanick and Lilienfeld, 1955). The occurrence of such problems as miscarriages, hydrocephalus (water on the brain), and Down's syndrome are associated with the advancing age of the mother (see Table 4.4).

The frequency of Down's syndrome is usually linked to maternal age (see Table 4.4). However, recent staining techniques that permit the identification of the source of the extra 21st chromosome in the child indicate that in 20 to 25 percent of the cases it is coming from the father (Bennett and Abroms, 1979).

About two percent of Down's syndrome is inherited. In these families the parent has the 21st chromosome attached to another chromosome so that it is carried into the wrong cell. A chromosome study of the parent will determine if this is the case (deGrouchy and Turleau, 1977).

Two factors relative to maternal size may cause pregnancy difficulties for the mother. These are shortness (less than five feet in height) and obesity.

TABLE 4.4
Risk of Down's Syndrome and Maternal Age

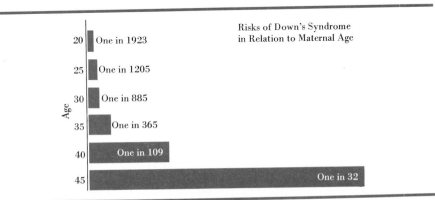

Risks of Down's Syndrome in Relation to Maternal Age

Age	Risk
20	One in 1923
25	One in 1205
30	One in 885
35	One in 365
40	One in 109
45	One in 32

The Beginning of Life: Genetic Factors and Prenatal Development

Women under five feet tall are more likely to have difficult pregnancies, more difficult labors, and somewhat higher fetal mortality (death) rates. Obesity may result in more difficult labor, higher fetal mortality rates, and a higher incidence of toxemia.

MATERNAL EMOTIONAL STATE

Although the blood systems of the mother and the unborn child are separate, it is possible for the nervous system of the mother to affect the nervous system of the fetus (Montagu, 1962). When the mother experiences such emotions as rage, anger, and anxiety, her autonomic nervous system sends chemicals into the bloodstream. In addition to these chemicals (acetylcholine and epinephrine), the mother's endocrine glands secrete hormones that combine to modify cell metabolism. As a result, the composition of the mother's blood changes, and the change agents are passed through the placenta, in turn, producing changes in the fetal blood system and in fetal activity level (Squier and Dunbar, 1946). Furthermore, the production of epinephrine in the mother as a function of stress may cause the blood flow in her body to be diverted from the uterus to other organs in her body. Such a drop in blood to the uterus and placenta may result in a deficient supply of oxygen for the fetus (Stechler and Halton, 1982).

Changes in the fetal blood system can be irritating to the fetus. The functioning of fetal-bodily systems has been known to fluctuate when mothers were under considerable stress (Sontag, 1941, 1944, 1966). Although it is quite likely that the expectant mother will experience some stress during the course of the pregnancy, it is usually when stressful and emotional situations are prolonged that enduring consequences for the child may result (Sontag, 1944). Some factors that may contribute to prolonged emotional stress are the mother's attitude toward her pregnancy and her attitude toward her marriage. The woman who does not want her child, who is unhappy about being pregnant, or who is unhappily married may be emotionally distressed for extensive periods of time.

Generally speaking, the impact of emotional stress on the unborn child probably depends on the stage of pregnancy. Severe and prolonged emotional stress early in pregnancy may result in physical abnormalities, whereas such stress later in pregnancy is more likely to result in fetal behavioral changes (rather than physical deformities). One study (Strean and Peer, 1956) of a large number of babies born with cleft palates and harelips suggested that excessive maternal stress during the seventh to the tenth weeks of pregnancy resulted in disruption of the normal process of upper jawbone development and fetal palate formation. The Strean and Peer study does not clearly implicate emotional stress as the only possible cause of abnormal upper-jaw—palate development. Some 25 percent of the mothers in the study reported past incidences of harelip and cleft palates in their family backgrounds.

Stress during the latter periods of pregnancy is more likely to result in changes in the behavioral characteristics of the fetus or the infant rather than physical difficulties. For example, increasing levels of general movement or hiccuping have been reported by mothers who had been undergoing periods of stress (Sontag, 1941, 1966; Montagu, 1964). Prenatal activity may also result in lower-birth-weight infants simply because the mother's food consumption may not have kept pace with fetal movement and energy expenditure.

Does maternal stress during pregnancy result in cranky, colicky, or hyperactive infants? Because stressful situations may not simply end with the birth of the child (that is, the stress may continue after birth), it is difficult to distinguish between prenatal and postnatal causes of infant irritability.

DRUGS

Both scientists and lay people have become increasingly aware of the impact of chemicals (in our food and in our environment) on general health. There has been an accompanying awareness of the impact of drugs on the developing fetus (see Figure 4.37 and Figure 4.38). The idea that the fetus is completely insulated from the effects of the outside environment is no longer accepted. It is now recognized that although the placenta does prevent the

FIGURE 4.37 "No-No" list of drugs for pregnant women.

From March of Dimes Birth Defects Foundation.

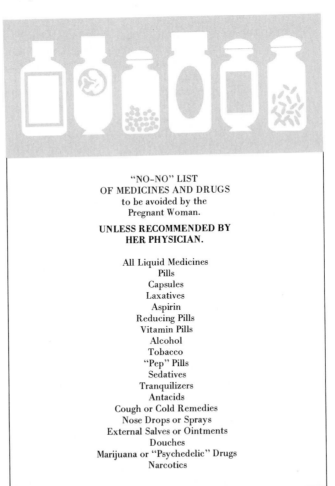

"NO-NO" LIST
OF MEDICINES AND DRUGS
to be avoided by the
Pregnant Woman.

**UNLESS RECOMMENDED BY
HER PHYSICIAN.**

All Liquid Medicines
Pills
Capsules
Laxatives
Aspirin
Reducing Pills
Vitamin Pills
Alcohol
Tobacco
"Pep" Pills
Sedatives
Tranquilizers
Antacids
Cough or Cold Remedies
Nose Drops or Sprays
External Salves or Ointments
Douches
Marijuana or "Psychedelic" Drugs
Narcotics

The Beginning of Life: Genetic Factors and Prenatal Development

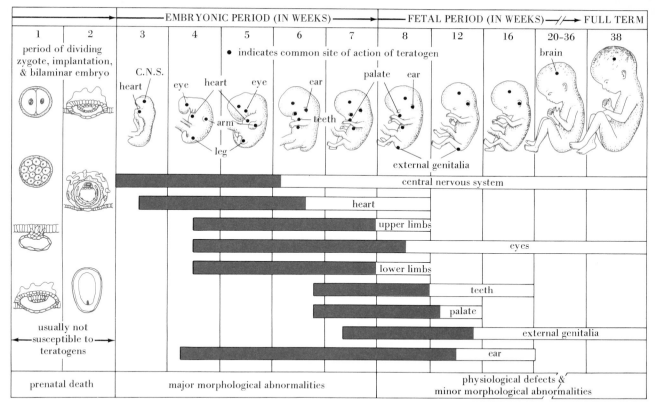

EMBRYONIC PERIOD (IN WEEKS)							FETAL PERIOD (IN WEEKS) —//→ FULL TERM				
1	2	3	4	5	6	7	8	12	16	20-36	38

period of dividing zygote, implantation, & bilaminar embryo

• indicates common site of action of teratogen

C.N.S. heart | eye heart eye | arm | ear teeth | palate ear | | | brain | | external genitalia | leg

usually not ←susceptible to→ teratogens

central nervous system

heart

upper limbs

eyes

lower limbs

teeth

palate

external genitalia

ear

| prenatal death | major morphological abnormalities | physiological defects & minor morphological abnormalities |

FIGURE 4.38 Teratogens* and critical periods in development. The diagram shows the sensitive periods of development. Colored bars indicate highly sensitive periods; uncolored bars indicate less sensitive periods. Each organ or structure has a critical period during which its development may be deranged, and physiological defects, functional disturbances, and minor morphological changes may result from disturbances during the fetal period. Severe mental retardation may result from exposure of the fetus to high levels of radiation during the 8- to 16-week period.

*Teratogen: Any agent that causes malformation. Agents that produce malformations can be direct (thalidomide), or indirect (a mother's thyroid deficiency). From K. L. Moore, *Before We Are Born,* (2nd ed.) Philadelphia: W. B. Saunders, 1983, p. 111.

passage of some harmful large-molecule substances, it does act as a passageway for small-molecule substances, which may be either necessary for life (e.g., oxygen and antibodies) or harmful (e.g., thalidomide). In the case of drugs, the stage of development is probably more important than the strength of the drug in determining the extent or the type of damage that will occur (Annis, 1978). Much of the damage from drugs occurs during the first trimester (the first three months) of pregnancy. Sometimes damage even occurs before the doctor and the woman are certain about pregnancy.

The thalidomide tragedy provides an unfortunate example of the effect of drugs on unborn children. The drug was never used in the United States but was widely available in Scandinavia, West Germany, and England in the early 1960s as a tranquilizer and sedative for "morning sickness." Unfortunately, morning sickness occurs during the critical first trimester of pregnancy. Some ten thousand children were affected by thalidomide. When thalidomide was taken from twenty-seven to forty days after conception (that is, during the critical period), it interfered with the formation of arms and legs (Taussig, 1962). When the drug was taken after this critical period, the arms and legs were already formed and there was no interference.

There is also evidence about drugs taken prior to or during delivery: analgesics (sedatives) and anesthetics (pain killers). Although these drugs affect the newborn, it is not certain what the long-term effects might be. These drugs

Drinking During Pregnancy and the Fetal Alcohol Syndrome

IF YOU DRINK,
YOUR UNBORN BABY DOES, TOO

When you're pregnant your unborn baby receives nourishment from you. What you eat, he eats. What you drink, he drinks.

So if you have a drink—beer, wine, or hard liquor—your unborn baby has a drink, too. Because he is so small, he is affected twice as fast.

That's immediate. But alcohol can also have long-lasting effects on an unborn baby.

HOW ALCOHOL DAMAGES UNBORN BABIES

Scientists have found that many children born to women who drink excessively while pregnant have a pattern of physical and mental defects. They call this "fetal alcohol syndrome" (FAS).

Growth deficiency is the most prominent symptom. Affected babies are abnormally small at birth, especially in head size. These youngsters never catch up to normal growth.

Most affected youngsters have small brains, show degrees of mental deficiency, are jittery and poorly coordinated, and have short attention spans and behavioral problems. Their IQs do not improve with age.

FAS babies usually have narrow eyes and low nasal bridges with upturned noses. These features make them look more like one another than like their parents or siblings. Almost half have heart defects, which in some cases require heart surgery.

Not every FAS baby has all defects but there *is* a relationship between the severity of physical characteristics and degree of mental impairment.

The more severely retarded are those with the most noticeable physical defects.

MANY BABIES ARE AT RISK

Fetal alcohol syndrome is a real problem in the United States today. It is estimated that there are more than one million alcoholic women of childbearing age. And the number is growing—particularly among adolescents.

Babies of teen-agers who drink heavily are in double jeopardy. They may be born too small or too soon because their mothers' bodies cannot meet the demands of pregnancy. If they also are subjected to excessive alcohol, they may suffer some symptoms of fetal alcohol syndrome.

WE NEED TO KNOW MORE . . .

No one knows how much alcohol is too much. That is one of many questions surrounding FAS—questions which researchers throughout the country are investigating. . . .

Scientists know that, as with other things pregnant women eat and drink, alcohol passes through the placenta, the organ which nourishes the unborn baby. The drink the baby gets is as strong as the one the mother takes.

It is believed that the alcohol adversely affects the baby's fast-growing tissues, either killing cells or slowing their growth. Because the brain develops throughout pregnancy, it stands to reason that it is the organ most affected. . . .

From March of Dimes Birth Defects Foundation, "If You Drink, Your Unborn Baby Does, Too," White Plains, N.Y., 1979.

appear to slow the onset of newborn respiration (Eastman, 1959; Becker and Donnell, 1952) and to affect newborn attentiveness by shortening the attention span (Stechler, 1964). However, these effects seem to be gone by the end of the first week of life. On the other hand, Brackbill (1977) found that obstetrical medication may have more lasting effects on the newborn if administered in moderate to heavy dosage levels. She reported that in a group of apparently highly healthy infants and mothers that the infants of the more heavily medicated mothers showed developmental lags in sitting, standing, and moving about when tested at four, eight, and twelve months (in comparison to the less-medicated mothers). Further research is necessary to clarify the long-term consequences of obstetrical medication.

The increase in the incidence of heroin addiction in the general population has resulted in an increasing number of infants who are born with addiction to this drug. The general conclusion of the research on this topic is that some babies born to addicted mothers are in fairly good health (Blinick, Wallach, and Jerez, 1969). Other babies, however, suffer some handicaps, such as withdrawal symptoms (Schulman, 1969). During withdrawal, infants may show fever, breathing difficulties, convulsions, excessive crying, and vomiting. However, questions remain about the direct relationship between maternal heroin addiction and infant withdrawal symptoms and pregnancy complications (Blinick et al., 1969). It has not yet been determined whether the problems of infants born to drug addicts are due to heroin or to other factors associated with maternal heroin addiction, including malnutrition and infections. Regardless of the ultimate source or sources of infant problems, pregnant women who are taking drugs are placing an added burden on their unborn children.

SMOKING AND ALCOHOLIC BEVERAGES

Cigarette smoking by pregnant women has been found to be related to some serious consequences for the fetus and the newborn infant. Some of these consequences are increased rates for lower-than-average birth weight (Evans, Newcombe, and Campbell, 1979), for premature births, for spontaneous abortions (Himmelberger, Brown, and Cohen, 1978), and for neonatal deaths (Butler, Goldstein, and Ross, 1972; Naeye, 1978). Investigators have concluded that the chances for these unfortunate consequences are increased because maternal cigarette-smoking may deprive the fetus of oxygen (Quigley, Sheehan, Wilkes, and Yen, 1979). This reduction in fetal oxygen may occur in two ways:

1. Cigarette smoking increases the levels of epinephrine and norepinephrine in the blood which constrict blood vessels reducing the blood supply (and, therefore, the oxygen level) to the placenta.
2. Cigarette smoking results in a significant increase in the amount of carbon monoxide inhaled. This, in turn, reduces the oxygenation of the blood (or the amount of oxygen in the blood) and, therefore, the amount of oxygen going to the placenta (Quigley et al., 1979).

There is some evidence that the effects of smoking are related to the degree of smoking (i.e., they are dose-related). That is, infants of heavy smokers (two or more packs a day) and of mothers who smoked continuously throughout pregnancy weighed less than the infants of light smokers or of mothers who smoked only during the first part of pregnancy (Butler et al., 1972). As a result of these disturbing findings, an increasing number of obstetricians suggest that pregnant women stop smoking.

The impact of maternal alcohol consumption seems to be rather substantial—particularly on the babies of chronic alcoholic mothers. One study demonstrated a "fetal alcohol syndrome" among children born to chronic alcoholic women that resulted in such defects as prenatal and postnatal growth deficiencies, abnormal development of the heart, defects of the joints, micrencephaly (a condition characterized by unnatural smallness of the head and severe mental retardation), and facial abnormalities (Jones and Smith, 1973). At present, it is not clear whether the cause of the fetal alcohol syndrome is the chronic alcoholism of the mother or the possible malnutrition of the mother (chronic alcoholism reduces the desire to eat or drink other foods) or both (Hanson, Jones, and Smith, 1976).

MATERNAL DISEASES AND DISORDERS DURING PREGNANCY

As is the case with drugs, the time of the onset of the disease is more important than the degree to which the mother has the disease. For example, a mild case of German measles (rubella) may be far more harmful to the unborn child during the first months of pregnancy than a more pronounced case during the end of pregnancy. Furthermore there is some evidence that the pregnant woman may have a reduced immunity to diseases and infections during pregnancy (Thong, Steele, Vincent, Hensen, and Bellanti, 1973).

The threat of rubella to the unborn child is the strongest during the first three months of pregnancy. The results of rubella may include congenital cataracts, deafness, heart disease, microcephaly, stunted growth, mental retardation, or even death. During a rubella epidemic in the United States (1964–1965), about fifty thousand children were affected because their mothers contracted three-day (an innocent-sounding name) or German measles. These children either died before birth or were born with birth defects (Rugh and Shettles, 1971).

Other diseases that may have a disastrous effect on the newborn are maternal syphilis and gonorrhea. If the mother has syphilis, the chances of a spontaneous abortion or stillbirth are drastically increased. In addition, the newborn may be deaf, blind, deformed, or mentally retarded. Fetuses under eighteen weeks of age are not susceptible to the disease. The disease can be cured by penicillin, and if it is given before the fetus is eighteen weeks old, the baby is unlikely to be affected (Thompson and Grusec, 1970).

Diabetic mothers (diabetes is a deficiency in the supply of insulin secreted by the pancreas, so that there is a high level of sugar in both blood and urine) have an increased risk of toxemia (Corner, 1961). In addition, they are more likely to have abnormally large babies (weighing more than nine pounds), with resulting delivery complications and a higher-than-average infant mortality rate. Diabetic women are more likely than normal women to have spontaneous abortions and children with malformations.

Summary

1. The science of genetics has made extraordinary gains in the last two decades. As a result, we are beginning to accumulate a great deal of information about the mechanisms of heredity.

2. The process of *conception* occurs when *fertilization* takes place. The question of an abortion of an embryo or fetus hinges, in part, on a definition of

The Beginning of Life: Genetic Factors and Prenatal Development

whether life begins at conception or sometime later in pregnancy when the full assortment of human systems becomes differentiated. The notion of when life begins remains controversial among both scientists and the lay public.

3. The elements of human heredity involve complex processes. Some of the characteristics which involve hereditary processes include physical traits (e.g., height, eye color), the timing of the onset of puberty and susceptibility to diseases such as diabetes or heart disease. These inherited characteristics are subject to the influence of *genes* and their constituents including *DNA* and *RNA*. DNA is the "genetic code" or "genetic blueprint" for the transmission of inherited human characteristics. Since DNA is found within the nucleus of a given cell, it is necessary for the "message" of DNA to be transmitted outside the nucleus to the site of cell growth. This DNA information is carried by RNA.

4. After conception, the growth and development of the human being proceeds as a result of cell division (*mitosis*). There are two different types of cells in the human body—*body* cells and *sex* (germ) cells from which sperm and ova develop. Body cells are reproduced through the process of cell division called *mitosis*. Through mitosis cells divide and make exact copies of themselves. The "directions" for the development of these new cells come from the DNA molecule in the genes. In contrast, sex or germ cells are produced by a process called *meiosis*.

5. The genetic transmission of most traits is dependent not on a single gene but on several genes. Important concepts for understanding genetic transmission are *dominant genes* and *recessive genes*. Where there is some genetic basis for a birth defect, it usually involves one of the following methods of transmission: dominant inheritance, recessive inheritance, sex-linked inheritance, or chromosomal abnormalities.

6. The months from conception to the birth of the child are marked by significant developments that have a profound effect on an individual's development. There are three stages of prenatal growth: the *germinal stage*, the *embryonic stage* and the *fetal stage*.

7. There are many possible variations in the prenatal environment. Some of the more important prenatal environmental factors that have been investigated to date include the following: maternal nutrition, Rh-factor incompatibility, maternal age and size, maternal emotional state, drugs, smoking and alcoholic beverages, and maternal diseases and disorders during pregnancy.

Questions

1. Define the following terms: amniocentesis, gene, DNA, chromosome. Why is each important to prenatal development?
2. Where there is some genetic basis for birth defects, one of four methods of transmission is usually involved. Name and briefly describe all four.
3. What is the difference between a *genetic* defect and a *congenital* defect?
4. What are the three stages of prenatal growth? What are the four major developments in each stage?
5. What is the Fetal Alcohol Syndrome (FAS)?
6. There are many important and controversial ethical questions relating to prenatal development. One of the most prominent and widely discussed issues is abortion. Carefully examine and summarize the arguments of two opposing groups on this issue.

Bibliography

ANNIS, L. *The Child Before Birth*. Ithaca, N.Y.: Cornell U.P., 1978.

BEATTY, R. A., and GLUECKSOHN-WAELSCH, S. Edinburgh Symposium on the Genetics of the Spermatozoan. Edinburgh, Scotland: University of Edinburgh, 1972.

BECKER, R. F., and DONNELL, W. Learning behavior in guinea pigs subjected to asphyxia at birth. *Journal of Comparative and Physiological Psycology*, 1952, *45*, 153—162.

BENNETT, J. W. and ABROMS, K. I. Changing perspectives on Down's Syndrome, *The Journal of the Louisiana State Medical Society*, 1979, *131*, 305—307.

BLINICK, G., WALLACH, R. C., and JEREZ, E. Pregnancy in narcotics addicts treated by medical withdrawal: The methadone detoxification program. *American Journal of Obstetrics and Gynecology*, 1969, *105*, 997—1003.

BRACKBILL, Y. Long-term effects of obstetrical anesthesia on infant autonomic function. *Developmental Psychology*, 1977, *10*, 529—536.

BUTLER, N. R., GOLDSTEIN, H., and ROSS, E. M. Cigarette smoking in pregnancy: Its influence on birth weight and prenatal normality. *British Medical Journal*, 1972, *2*, 127—130.

CARNATION COMPANY. Pregnancy in anatomical illustrations. Los Angeles, 1962.

CARNEGIE INSTITUTION OF WASHINGTON, Davis Division.

CLARKE, C. A. The prevention of "rhesus" babies. *Scientific American*, November 1968, *219* (5), 46—52.

COLERIDGE, S. T. In Thomas Ashe (ed.). *Miscellanies, Aesthetic and Literary*. London: Bell, 1885.

CONSUMERS UNION OF UNITED STATES, INC., Mount Vernon, N.Y. 10550.

CORNER, G. W. Congenital malformations: The problem and the task. In *Congenital malformations: Papers and discussions presented at the First International Conference on Congenital Malformations*. Philadelphia: Lippincott, 1961.

CRAVIOTO, J., DELICARDIE, E. R., and BIRCH, H. G. Nutrition, growth and neurointegrative development: An experimental and ecologic study. *Pediatrics*, 1966, *38* (1, Pt.2, supplement), 319—372.

DEGROUCHY, G. and TURLEAU, C. *Clinical Atlas of Human Chromosomes* New York: John Wiley and Sons, 1977, p. 192.

DRILLEN, C. M., and ELLIS, R. W. B. *The Growth and Development of the Prematurely Born Infant*. Baltimore: Williams & Wilkins, 1964.

DURHAM, W. Biology and culture meet in milk, *Science*, 1981, *211*, 40.

EASTMAN, N. J. Editorial comment. *Obstetrical and Gynecological Survey*, 1959, *14*, 34—36.

EVANS, D. R., NEWCOMBE, R. G., and CAMPBELL, H. Maternal smoking habits and congenital malformations: A population study. *British Medical Journal*, 1979, *2*, 171—173.

FRIEDMAN, T. Prenatal diagnosis of genetic disease. *Scientific American*, Nov. 1971, 225(5), 34—42.

FRYER, J. G., and ASHFORD, J. R. Trends in perinatal and neonatal mortality in England and Wales, 1960—69. *British Journal of Preventive and Social Medicine*, 1972, *26*, 1—9.

HANSON, J. W., JONES, K. L. and SMITH, D. W. Fetal alcohol syndrome: Experience with 41 patients. *Journal of the American Medical Association*, 1976, *235*, 1458—1460.

HIMMELBERGER, D. V., BROWN, B. W. JR., and COHEN, E. N. Cigarette smoking during pregnancy and the occurence of spontaneous abortion and congenital abnormality, *American Journal of Epidemiology*, 1978, *108*, 470—479.

JONES, K. L., and SMITH, D. W. Recognitions of the fetal alcohol syndrome in early infancy, *The Lancet*, 1973, *2*, 999—1001.

KOLARS, J. C., LEVITT, M. D., AOUJI, M., and SAVAIANO, D. A. Yogurt: an auto-digesting source of lactose. *New England Journal of Medicine*, Jan. 5, 1984, *310*, p. 1.

LILEY, A. W. Intrauterine transfusion of halmolytic diseases. *British Medical Journal*, 1963, *2*, 1106—1110.

MARCH OF DIMES BIRTH DEFECTS FOUNDATION. Birth defects original article series. Vol. IV, No. 4, Sept. White Plains, N.Y., 1968.

MARCH OF DIMES BIRTH DEFECTS FOUNDATION. Birth defects: Tragedy and the hope. White Plains, N.Y., 1977.

MARCH OF DIMES BIRTH DEFECTS FOUNDATION. Genetic counseling. White Plains, N.Y., 1978.

MARCH OF DIMES BIRTH DEFECTS FOUNDATION. If you drink, your unborn baby does, too! White Plains, N.Y., 1979.

MCCURDY, R. N. C. *The Rhesus Danger: Its Medical, Moral and Legal Aspects.* London: Heinemann Medical Books, 1950.

MONTAGU, M. F. A. *Prenatal Influences.* Springfield, Ill.: Thomas, 1962.

MONTAGU, M. F. A. *Life Before Birth.* New York: New American Library, 1964.

MOON, T. J., OTTO, J. and TOWLE, A. *Modern Biology.* New York: Holt, Rinehart and Winston, 1963, *616.*

MOORE, K. L. *Before We Are Born* (2nd edition). Philadelphia: W. B. Saunders, 1983, *111.*

MOORE, K. L. *The Developing Human: Clinically Oriented Embryology* (3rd edition). Philadelphia: W. B. Saunders, 1983.

NAEYE, R. L. Relationship of cigarette smoking to congenital anomalies and perinatal death. *American Journal of Pathology,* 1978, *90,* 289–294.

ORTHO DIAGNOSTICS SYSTEMS INC., Raritan, N.J.

OTTO, J. and TOWLE, A. *Modern Biology.* New York: Holt, Rinehart and Winston, 1977, 627–628.

PASAMANICK, B., and LILIENFELD, A. M. Association of maternal and fetal factors with the development of mental deficiency. 1. Abnormalities in the prenatal and paranatal periods. *Journal of the American Medical Association,* 1955, *159,* 155–160.

QUIGLEY, M. E., SHEEHAN, K. L., WILKES, M. M. and YEN, S. S. C. Effects of maternal smoking on circulating catechalamine levels and fetal heart rates. *American Journal of Obstetrics and Gynecology,* 1979, *133,* 685–690.

RAHN, J. E. *Biology.* New York: Macmillan, 1980.

ROBINSON, R. J., and TIZARD, J. P. M. The central nervous system in the newborn. *British Medical Journal,* 1966, *22,* 49–55.

RUGH, R., and SHETTLES, L. B. *From Conception to Birth: The Drama of Life's Beginnings.* New York: Harper & Row, 1971.

SCHULMAN, C. A. Sleep patterns in newborn infants as a function of suspected neurological impairment of maternal heroin addiction. Paper presented at the meeting of the Society for Research on Child Development, 1969.

SONTAG, L. W. The significance of fetal environmental differences. *American Journal of Obstetrics and Gynecology,* 1941, *42,* 996–1003.

SONTAG, L. W. War and the fetal-maternal relationship. *Marriage and Family Living,* 1944, *6,* 3–14, 16.

SONTAG, L. W. Implications of fetal behavior and environment for adult personalities. *Annals of the New York Academy of Sciences,* 1966, *134,* 782–786.

SQUIER, R., and DUNBAR, F. Emotional factors in the course of pregnancy. *Psychosomatic Medicine,* 1946, *8,* 161–175.

STECHLER, G. Newborn attention as affected by medication during labor. *Science,* 1964, *144,* 315–317.

STECHLER, G., and HALTON, A. Prenatal influences on human development. In B. Wolman (Ed.), *Handbook of Developmental Psychology.* Englewood Cliffs, New Jersey: Prentice-Hall, 1982, pp. 175–189.

STERN, C. *Principles of Human Genetics* (2nd ed.). San Francisco: Freeman, 1960.

STREAN, L. P., and PEER, A. Stress as an etiologic factor in the development of cleft palate. *Plastic and Reconstructive Surgery,* 1956, *18,* 1–8.

TAUSSIG, H. B. The thalidomide syndrome. *Scientific American,* 1962, *107,* 29–35.

THOMPSON, W. R., and GRUSEC, J. E. Studies of early experiences. In P. H. Mussen (Ed.), *Carmichael's Manual of Child Psychology,* Vol. 1. New York: Wiley, 1970.

THONG, Y. H., STEELE, R. W., VINCENT, M. M., HENSEN, S. A., and BELLANTI, J. A. Impaired in vitro cell-mediated immunity of rubella virus during pregnancy. *New England Journal of Medicine,* 1973, *289,* 604–606.

TOMPKINS, W. T. The clinical significance of nutritional deficiencies of pregnancy. *Bulletin of the New York Academy of Sciences,* 1948, *24,* 376–388.

TUCHMANN-DUPLESSIS, H., DAVID, G., and HAEGEL, P. *Illustrated Human Embryology,* Vol. I, *Embryogenesis,* Masson S. A., Paris, 1975. Springer-Verlag, New York, 1972.

VOLPE, E. P. *Understanding Evolution* (4th edition). Dubuque, Iowa: W. C. Brown Company Publishers, 1981.

VORE, D. A. Prenatal nutrition and postnatal intellectual development. *Merrill-Palmer Quarterly,* 1973, *19,* 253–260.

WHALEY, LUCILLE F. *Understanding Inherited Disorders.* St. Louis: The C. V. Mosby Company, 1974, p. 16.

WINCHESTER, A. M. *Human Genetics.* Columbus, Ohio; Merrill, 1971.

Suggested Readings

GOROWITZ, S., JAMETON, A. L., MACKLIN, R., O'CONNOR, J. M., PERRIN, E. V., ST. CLAIR, B. P. and SHERWIN, S. (Eds.). *Moral Problems in Medicine.* Englewood Cliffs, New Jersey: Prentice-Hall, 1976. An excellent discussion of the nature of ethical and moral issues confronting modern medicine including such topics as birth defects, abortion, and the difficulty of distinguishing between "killing" and "letting die."

HAMILTON, M. P. (Ed.). *The New Genetics and The Future of Man.* Grand Rapids, Michigan: Eerdmans, 1972. An excellent analysis of the impact of genetic advances with comments by biological scientists, theologians, and philosophers.

NYHAN, W. *The Heredity Factor,* New York: Grosset and Dunlap, 1976. A readable and enlightening discussion of basic factors involved in genetics, genetic counseling, and the prenatal environment.

RUGH, R. and SHETTLES, L. B. *From Conception to Birth.* New York: Harper and Row, 1971. A well written introduction to genetic mechanisms and prenatal development with excellent color photographs.

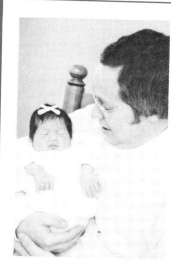

5

The Birth of the Baby: An Emerging Family Relationship

THOUGHTS ON CHILDBIRTH

Parenthood is one of the great events of a lifetime, both physically and emotionally. It is a deep human experience. Whether it is an essentially good experience or a bad one depends not only on the physical course of reproduction but also on the social and emotional impact of childbearing.

From The Boston Children's Medical Center, *Pregnancy, Birth and the Newborn Baby.* New York: Delacorte Press, 1972, pp. 3, 40–41.

Pregnancy and the birth process are neither static nor brief experiences; rather, they are periods of human development filled with growth, change, and exciting enrichment. The birth process is both rewarding and challenging because, at the end, there is literally a new life for both the parents and for the child. Only recently has the period immediately before birth, during birth, and immediately after birth been studied by behavioral scientists with the same intensity and depth as other stages in the human life cycle. All too often, pregnancy and the birth process has been viewed as rather routine although a somewhat unusual phenomena. Medical scientists, and particularly obstetrician-gynecologists, had been apt to describe most pregnancies and births as "routine" or "uncomplicated." Somehow this generalized evaluation had tended to conceal the anxieties, joys, frustrations, stresses, altered family relationships, and newly emerging relationships that many families experience during the course of a "routine" pregnancy.

The Birth Process in Context

The purpose of this chapter is to examine the birth process from a *systems* or an interactional perspective. As we indicated in Chapters 1 and 2, such a perspective emphasizes the *interaction* between the developing person and the contexts of development, which include the family, the neighborhood, the

FIGURE 5.1 An ecosystems perspective of the birth process.

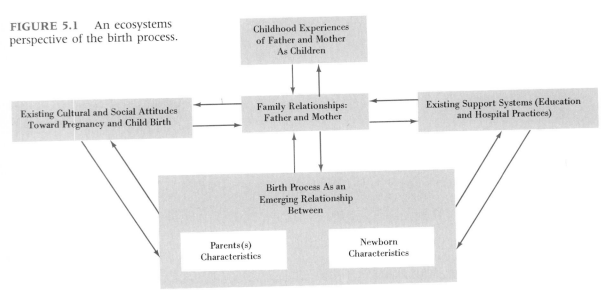

The Birth of the Baby: An Emerging Family Relationship

peer group, the schools, the world at work, and so on. The focus of this chapter is on the birth process as an emerging relationship between the newborn and his or her parent(s).

Before we discuss the birth process, however, it is important to place this process in context. Figure 5.1 illustrates some of the important factors in this context. These factors include the following:

- The childhood experiences of the father and the mother.
- The relationship of the mother and the father.
- Existing cultural and social attitudes toward pregnancy and childbirth (e.g., is childbirth an experience for the family or only for the mother, the newborn, and the physician?).
- Existing support systems (including hospital practices and available educational programs).

The Development of a Parent–Newborn Relationship

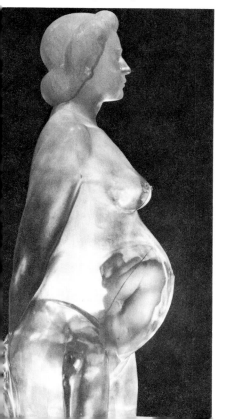

Photo courtesy Museum of Science and Industry, Chicago, Illinois

In the next chapter, we will explore in greater detail the development of maternal–infant bonding. However, in this chapter, we will sketch some of the factors that contribute to such bonding both prior to birth and immediately after birth. In discussing this most important issue, we find it important to note again that the crucial life events that surround the development of attachment (and, likewise, detachment) have been, over the past sixty years, removed from the home and transferred to the hospital. Therefore, the birth experience has been divorced and removed from long-established traditions and support systems (e.g., the immediate family members, grandparents, and friends). In the past, these support systems helped families manage and adjust to childbirth at home.

FACTORS IN THE RELATIONSHIP

The ability of both mother and father to develop a successful relationship with the newborn depends on a number of factors. These factors include the parents' own personalities and temperaments, the response of the newborn infant to the parents, the history of interpersonal relationships of the mother and the father with their own families of origin (e.g., the way husband and wife were raised by their parents) and with each other, past experiences with pregnancy, and the assimilation of cultural values and practices by the parents (Klaus and Kennell, 1982).

Figure 5.2 is a diagram of some of the primary factors and potential disturbances that may affect initial parental behavior. At the time of birth, some of these factors are unchangeable, including the mother's care by her own mother and her experiences with previous pregnancies. Other factors can change, for example, the behavior of attending physicians and the practices that result in newborn–parent separation. The figure also illustrates some potential disorders, such as disturbed mother–infant relations and the battered-child syndrome.

Klaus and Kennell (1982) identified the following events as being important to the formation of a mother's emerging relationship or attachment to her newborn:

139

Prior to pregnancy
　Planning the pregnancy
During pregnancy
　Confirming the pregnancy
　Accepting the pregnancy
　Fetal movement
　Accepting the fetus as
　　an individual

After birth
Birth
Seeing the baby
Touching the baby
Giving care to the baby

PRIOR TO PREGNANCY

　Considerable research suggests that previous experiences of the parents (in particular, their experiences as children in the family of origin) are major determinants in developing parenting styles and care-giving roles (Helfer and Kempe, 1968; Frommer and O'Shea, 1973). By observing their own parents, children learn and practice a repertoire of parenting behaviors. Parents may

FIGURE 5.2 Major influences on parenting behavior and the newborn and resulting disturbances. Solid lines represent unchangeable detriments; dotted lines represent alterable determinants.

Slightly modified from Marshall H. Klaus and John H. Kennell, *Parent-Infant Bonding,* 2nd ed., St. Louis: The C. V. Mosby Co. 1982.

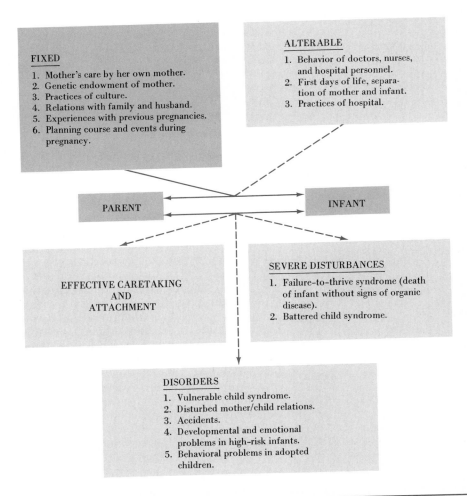

FIXED
1. Mother's care by her own mother.
2. Genetic endowment of mother.
3. Practices of culture.
4. Relations with family and husband.
5. Experiences with previous pregnancies.
6. Planning course and events during pregnancy.

ALTERABLE
1. Behavior of doctors, nurses, and hospital personnel.
2. First days of life, separation of mother and infant.
3. Practices of hospital.

PARENT

INFANT

EFFECTIVE CARETAKING
AND
ATTACHMENT

SEVERE DISTURBANCES
1. Failure-to-thrive syndrome (death of infant without signs of organic disease).
2. Battered child syndrome.

DISORDERS
1. Vulnerable child syndrome.
2. Disturbed mother/child relations.
3. Accidents.
4. Developmental and emotional problems in high-risk infants.
5. Behavioral problems in adopted children.

The Birth of the Baby: An Emerging Family Relationship

Birth–in the Hospital or at Home? What Is Your Opinion?

From a warm and comforting atmosphere surrounded by family and friends, the mother-to-be was suddenly transferred into a barren hospital ward with only a nurse and her aide running back and forth to attend to thirty-two patients with rules barring the father from the labor and delivery rooms, and more rules separating the new mother from her infant. Suddenly the mother and child were isolated. (McCleary, 1974)

An important and much debated question in modern obstetric care is whether a hospital is the best place for a baby to be born or whether some deliveries can occur at home. The fact that such a question can now be raised is not so much a criticism of modern medicine as it is a tribute to the historical development of excellent physical care for both mother and child. Only the current state of medicine has allowed the quality of childbirth from a psychological, emotional, and family perspective to become an issue.

The issue is not a simple one. For example, are parents willing to take certain risks of physical damage to child and mother in exchange for a better emotional or psychological experience of childbirth? What if complications occur during the birth process?

Dramatic improvements in health care for pregnant women during the first half of the twentieth century made the hospital the most common place for birth. Birth in the home—once the most common practice—became a rarity.

In both the United States and Great Britain an approach to childbirth developed that accompanied these medical advances in obstetric care (MacFarlane, 1977). This approach assumed that as it was not always possible to determine in advance which women or newborns were "at risk" for birth complications, all pregnant women must be treated as potentially at risk. Therefore the place for birth must be the hospital, which is uniquely equipped to deal with such situations.

While the pattern of historical development moved toward hospital delivery in the United States and Great Britain, home birth was developed to a safe and successful level in other countries. For example, the Netherlands has a lower infant mortality rate than either Great Britain or the United States, even though a very large number of deliveries take place at home. According to G. J. Kloostermann, Professor of Obstetrics at the University of Amsterdam, childbirth can be safe in the home: "childbirth in itself is a natural phenomenon and in the large majority of cases needs no interference whatsoever—only close observation, moral support and protection against human meddling" (Kloostermann, 1975). The Netherlands' approach is based on the assumption that thorough prenatal care will result in two groups of expectant mothers: (1) a low-risk group (the vast majority of pregnant women) who have no symptoms of any pathology and (2) a high-risk group (a much smaller group), in which there is at least a slight concern about some difficulty. During 1973, some 196,974 babies were born in Holland, of which 99,000 were born at home (MacFarlane, 1977).

The success of home delivery in the Netherlands depends considerably on an organized program called Maternity Home Help, which provides assistance during the delivery (the organization also provides home care for about eight to ten days after birth). In 1973, 83,088 of the 99,000 home deliveries were attended by a home helper, midwife, or doctor (MacFarlane, 1977). The infant mortality rate for the home births in this program was considerably less than the rate for the Netherlands as a whole (4.5 per 1,000 home births as compared with 16.3 per 1,000 hospital births).

Based on A. MacFarlane, *The Psychology of Childbirth,* Cambridge, Mass.: Harvard University Press, 1977.

YOUR OPINION?
- Should more infants be born at home?
- Why?
- Why not?
- If you are in favor of more home births, then what type of home support services would be necessary?

be given a vivid example of this type of imitation when their young child "plays house" and acts out the parental roles. An interesting—and alarming—feature of the American nuclear family is that most young people are rarely exposed to any formal parenting training or education before they have their own children.

DURING PREGNANCY

The Mother. During pregnancy, a woman experiences two kinds of changes within herself: (1) physical and emotional changes and (2) the growth of the fetus (Klaus and Kennell, 1982). A number of factors may contribute to how she feels about these changes, including whether there are other children, what the ages of the other children are, whether she is living with the father, and whether the pregnancy was planned (Boston Women's Health Book Collective, 1971).

Pregnancy has been defined as involving two major tasks (Caplan, 1960) (see Figure 5.3):

Acceptance of Pregnancy. During this first stage of pregnancy the mother comes to grips with the fact that she will soon be the mother of a child. Gradually, as the mother comes to realize that the growing fetus is a part of her, a number of considerations emerge. These include such things as changing interpersonal relationships with the father (Benedek, 1952) since she will now have to divide her attention between two people.

FIGURE 5.3   The fetus may develop within the uterus head down as shown or head up, and it may rotate completely before birth. It lives throughout its uterine life within the "bag of waters." The fluid filling this sac serves many purposes. It prevents the walls of the uterus from cramping the fetus and acts as an excellent shock-absorber. At term, there is usually about a quart of amniotic fluid. This fluid is not stagnant. It is completely replaced about eight times daily.

Illustrations from "Pregnancy in Anatomical Illustrations," appear courtesy of the copyright owner © Carnation Company, Los Angeles, Ca., 1962.

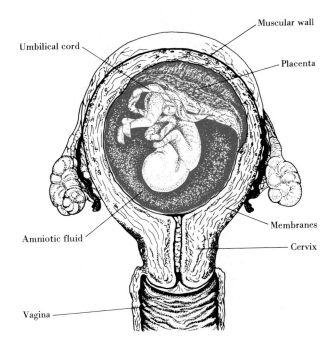

Muscular wall

Umbilical cord

Placenta

Amniotic fluid

Membranes

Cervix

Vagina

The Birth of the Baby: An Emerging Family Relationship

Differentiation. The second stage of pregnancy involves the maternal perception of the fetus as a separate individual. The significant event of this period is called "quickening" or the sensation of fetal movement. According to Bibring, Dwyer, Huntington, and Valenstein (1961), the experience of quickening lays the foundation for the relationship with a newborn who will be physically separated from the mother. . . . [The mother] . . . may demonstrate further evidence of differentiation including fantasies about what the child will be like as well as outward behavioral manifestations including purchasing a crib and selecting names.

The Expectant Father. Despite the comical stereotypes in our society of a father-to-be pacing the floor of a hospital, the father-to-be usually undergoes some changes that influence his personal image and may affect his new role as a father. Society tends to disregard the importance of the father-to-be's experience. Brazelton (1961) described this process as follows:

Each young man was forced to reevaluate his role as a provider for the family, as a model for the new child's learning about masculinity, and as a major support for his wife as she adjusted to her role as a mother. In the process, he was forced back on self-examination and his experience with being fathered. . . . In our lonely nuclear family structure in the U.S.A., the young father was often the only available support for his wife. They had moved away from their families both in physical distance and in psychological expectations, and were unwilling to fall back on them for moral or physical support. There were rarely other supportive figures nearby—such as family physicians, ministers, close friends, or neighbors who could help. The father was expected to assume the major supportive role. (pp. 259–273)

Thus it can be seen that, while the mother is undergoing physical changes, both the mother and the father undergo emotional adjustment during pregnancy.

Birth: Labor and Delivery

DEFINITIONS

Labor. The process by which the baby and placenta are expelled through the birth canal. Labor involves the muscular contraction of the uterus to aid the infant in moving through the birth canal. The primary purpose of labor is to permit the contractions of the uterus to open the cervix (the lower part of the uterus) wide enough (approximately four inches) to allow the widest part of the infant—the head—to pass. The baby then passes through the cervix and into the birth canal (the vagina).

Contractions. Contractions are the means through which labor and delivery occur. They are the movements of the uterus by means of which the cervix is opened and the baby is expelled or delivered.

There are several factors that characterize "real" labor (as distinguished from "false" labor):

• Real labor is characterized by the onset of contractions, which have a definite rhythm. For example, contractions may be fifteen or twenty minutes apart during the early phases of labor and may last about forty-five seconds. Over the next few hours, the contractions occur closer together, last longer, and become more intense. The muscles of the abdomen also harden because of the contractions.

The Role of Fathers Before and After Delivery

Does the presence of the father enhance mother–infant or father–infant bonding? Contrary to some popular biases, it is apparent that fathers are

Photograph by Shan Rucinski

capable of sensitive interaction with their infants from birth on (Lamb, 1976; Lamb and Stephenson, 1978). Parke (1974) observed parents in three different situations: (1) the mother alone with the infant (two to four days of age); (2) the father alone with the infant; (3) the father, mother, and infant (triadic interaction) together in the mother's hospital room. Most of the fathers in Parke's study had been present during labor and delivery. The results of the study indicated that in the triadic situation, the fathers tended to hold the infant almost twice as frequently as the mother and touched the infant more than the mother. In the triadic condition, the father clearly played a far more significant role than the cultural stereotype of the father would suggest.

Additional research by Parke (1974) on fathers who did not participate in the labor and the delivery demonstrated that fathers still played a more dominant and active role in holding, vocalizing to, and touching the infant immediately after birth than cultural stereotypes would lead one to believe. The implications of Parke's research are that although presence of the father during actual delivery may not be necessary to ensure appropriate interaction and bonding, early exposure of the father to the infant may be important in the formation of a positive attachment between them:

There is a lot of learning that goes on between the mother and infant in the hospital—from which the father is excluded and in which he must be included so he'll not only have the interest and a feeling of owning the baby, but also the kinds of skills that the mother develops. (Parke, 1974).

- The beginning of real labor is characterized by the appearance of a discharge ("show"). This discharge is composed of a blood-tinged mucus that serves to seal the uterus during pregnancy; when labor begins, this plug is discharged.
- In most deliveries, real labor is characterized by the bursting of the "water bag" during the last hours of labor. The result is a discharge of clear amniotic fluid. In a small percentage of pregnancies, the membranes rupture before labor has begun. In some deliveries, the doctor ruptures the membranes. There is no pain involved in this procedure.

There are three stages of labor in the birth process:

THE STAGES OF LABOR

The Stage of Dilation. The first stage involves the thinning and widening of the cervix. The cervix is the opening of the uterus at the end of the vaginal canal and is composed of muscle and fibrous tissue. Before the onset of labor, the cervix is thick and narrow, measuring less than two centimeters (four-fifths of an inch) in diameter. With the onset of contractions, the cervix thins and widens to ten centimeters (about four inches), allowing the baby to pass through. Contractions come closer together as the cervix dilates (opens).

The Stage of Expulsion. The second stage of labor begins when the cervix is completely dilated at ten centimeters and ends when the child is born. At this time contractions are usually sixty to seventy seconds in duration and about two to three minutes apart. With each contraction, the baby moves further down the birth canal (see Figure 5.4). Just prior to the delivery, the woman may be given an anesthetic (unless she is participating in a "natural" childbirth program) to ease her pain. Another common procedure at this time is an *episiotomy* or an incision to enlarge the vagina (this is done to prevent the tearing of vaginal tissue during delivery).

FIGURE 5.4 Labor and delivery. (Stages of labor, bag of waters, birth, placenta). Labor is the process by which the fetus passes from its intra-uterine environment to the outside world. Birth is the actual expulsion of the infant down the vaginal canal and through the vaginal opening.

Illustrations from "Pregnancy in Anatomical Illustrations," appear courtesy of the copyright owner © Carnation Company, Los Angeles, Ca., 1962.

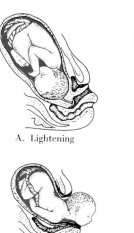
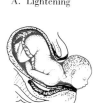

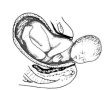
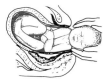
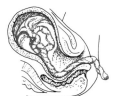

A. Lightening

B. Contractions and breaking of the bag of waters

C. Dilation of the cervix

D. Visible head. Beginning of birth.

E. Delivering the head

F. Delivering the shoulders

G. The afterbirth (placenta)

H. Expelling afterbirth

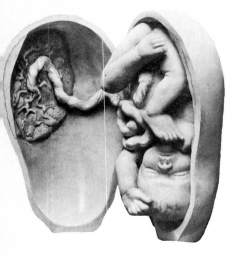

FIGURE 5.5 Labor and delivery.

Reproduced with permission from the *Birth Atlas*, published by Maternity Center Association, New York.

The actual birth of the baby occurs rather quickly after the widest part of the infant's head becomes visible ("crowning"). Once the baby's head is delivered, even before the infant is born, the physician begins the suction of mucus from the infant's mouth and nose. Sometimes the physician taps or rubs the soles of the infant's feet or its buttocks in order to get the infant to take oxygen in. As the baby exhales, it cries. (Crying forces the infant's breath through its lungs faster.)

Once the baby is free of the birth canal, the cord is allowed to stop pulsating before it is clamped and cut so that the baby receives the remaining support in the cord. The vernix, a cheesy film covering the infant's skin, may be wiped

The Birth of the Baby: An Emerging Family Relationship

off. Silver nitrate drops are administered to each eye to prevent infection and possible blindness. The baby is then usually maintained in a slightly head-down position. This position aids in mucus drainage and respiration (see Figures 5.3, 5.4, and 5.5).

The Delivery of the Placenta. The third stage of labor is the delivery of the placenta. There is seldom any pain associated with the expulsion of the afterbirth. The episiotomy is repaired at this time. The new mother is allowed to see and hold her baby. She may even be able to nurse the child before leaving the delivery room. The new mother may experience mixed emotions. Even though she has carried and known this infant for nine months, the child may seem like a stranger to her. The development of mother–child and father–child bonds is now necessary to promote family roles.

CAESAREAN BIRTH

In a Caesarean birth, the physician makes an incision through the abdominal wall and the uterus. The infant is removed, and then the incision is carefully sewn up. There are several reasons for this procedure: a fetus may be too large to emerge through the mother's pelvis; the mother might be experiencing toxemia or a hemorrhage; or the mother may have a disease, such as diabetes, that would put undue and dangerous stress on the fetus.

APPLICATION BOX

A Hospital Birth

6:00 A.M.   Six hours after the beginning of labor, Karen is admitted to the hospital. The doctor checks the baby's heartbeat. An examination indicates that Karen's cervix is dilated to 1½ centimeters. She has been experiencing regular contractions.

8:00   By the time Karen's cervix has dilated to 4½ centimeters, her membranes have ruptured. Her contractions are now closer together in time and stronger.

9:30   The doctor examines Karen. Her cervix is completely dilated. Karen is now ready to go to the delivery room.

9:40   Once in the delivery room, Karen is helped onto the delivery table. The doctor asks Karen to "push." The baby's head is visible in the vaginal canal.

9:45   Karen continues to push with each contraction. The baby's head is now outside the vaginal opening. The doctor tells Karen that she can momentarily stop pushing.

9:46   The doctor uses a suction device to remove mucus from the baby's mouth and nose. This will facilitate infant breathing. Karen pushes with the next contraction.

9:47   The rest of the baby's body glides easily through the vaginal canal. The doctor holds the baby so that Karen can see it. He says: "Looks like a bouncing baby girl!" Karen excitedly watches her new baby.

10:15   In the recovery room, Karen and her husband, Jerry, admire their daughter.

Although at one time, Caesarean births were somewhat hazardous, now they are only slightly riskier than normal births. The majority of Caesarean births are arranged well in advance by the physician and the mother. Because delivery is scheduled for when the physician feels that the baby will be ready, there is some risk of infant prematurity (Babson and Benson, 1966). New techniques have increased the accuracy of such predictions, such as the use of ultrasound. This procedure is used to "see" or measure the approximate size of the fetus and thus to estimate its age, maturity, and readiness for birth. It used to be thought that once a woman has a Caesarean delivery, the uterus and the abdominal walls were weakened. For this reason, it was believed that another pregnancy should be avoided. Today, however, a woman may have four or more Caesarean deliveries satisfactorily. In eight or nine out of ten cases of Caesarean delivery, subsequent deliveries will also be by Caesarean section (Guttmacher, 1973).

SPECIAL TECHNIQUES

In this section, we discuss two unique approaches to childbirth: the Lamaze method and the Leboyer method. Each of these methods demonstrates that philosophies and techniques of childbirth are far from static and unchangeable.

The Lamaze Method. The Lamaze, or prepared-childbirth, technique involves the father-to-be as well as the mother-to-be. A woman and her husband are taught the Lamaze method with other couples in weekly sessions during the last months of pregnancy. By teaching what is involved in labor and delivery, the Lamaze method reduces the fear and tension associated with ignorance of these processes. Also taught are exercises and breathing techniques to be used throughout labor and delivery. The husband becomes his wife's coach and helps her to learn and practice these procedures. During the birth process the husband is able to offer moral and physical support to his wife.

The basic principles of the Lamaze method are the following:

First, a thorough *understanding of the processes of labor and childbirth* alleviates unnecessary tension and apprehension, the pain multipliers; second, *muscular relaxation* helps the body's efficiency and increases comfort during labor and delivery; third, there is undeniable *pain* and discomfort during childbirth *which by a conditioning process can be displaced from a central to a peripheral location in one's consciousness through the substitution of another center of concentration*. The new center of concentration is the special body function, *breathing*. Active, difficult, and varying techniques at breathing are taught in [Lamaze]. . . . To employ them properly requires strong central concentration. (Guttmacher, 1973, p. 213)

The Leboyer Method: Birth Without Violence. There is some concern that the current medical practices of delivering babies may create unnecessary discomfort or trauma for the infant. Leboyer (1975) proposed a new approach to reduce the pain and fear experienced by the newborn. Leboyer supports

The Birth of the Baby: An Emerging Family Relationship

The Lamaze Technique

A MOTHER'S COMMENTS

In training, a woman not only learns what is going to happen to her during labor and delivery, but also acquires techniques that will help her control her body. Instead of tensing against the contractions of childbirth, she is prepared to consciously relax her body. She also learns to respond to each contraction with a specific type of breathing that helps her keep a normal amount of oxygen in her system and . . . gives her a correct response to concentrate on during each contraction. She is able to . . . take advantage of the time between contractions to replenish her reserves of energy. Her husband has been instructed how to be of utmost help at this time. To a prepared woman, a contraction is a signal to begin her work. (Ewy and Ewy, 1970, p. 30)

From Donna and Roger Ewy, *A Lamaze Guide: Preparation for Childbirth.* Boulder, Colorado: Pruett, 1970, p. 30.

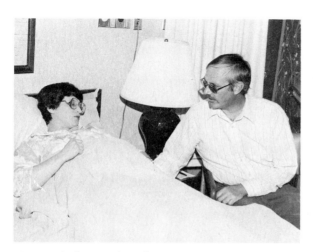

Photographs by Darryl Jacobson

the view that birth is a sensory experience. Although the infant does not organize or integrate sensations, it does perceive its surroundings through sight, hearing, and touch. For example, the blinding lamps and floodlights used in the delivery room are thought to be unnecessary and may only burn the infant's eyes. Instead, Leboyer proposed utilizing minimal light in the delivery room. In addition, the newborn's ears are sensitive to the noises and voices during delivery. Lowered voices not only relax the mother but also protect the child's vulnerable ears.

The Leboyer method encourages patience during the delivery process allowing the child to emerge from the birth canal slowly. So as to aid the baby in establishing respiration, this method also stresses refraining from cutting the umbilical cord immediately. The child's sensitivity to touch is also consid-

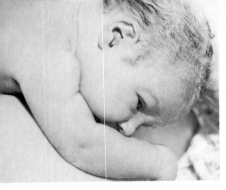

FIGURE 5.6 Leboyer method: infant is placed on the mother's abdomen.

Photograph by Darryl Jacobson

ered. The infant is placed on the mother's abdomen with its arms and legs folded under its stomach, a position that enables the child to straighten its posture at its own pace (see Figure 5.6). The child is caressed by the hands of the physician or the mother; touching is the primary language by which the obstetrician and the mother communicate with the newborn. After the cord is cut, the child is submerged in warm water much like the fetal amniotic fluid (see Figure 5.7). This procedure relaxes the infant, decreases fear, and allows the baby to explore its new environment. The similarity of the warm water to amniotic fluid minimizes the differences between the fetal environment and the new world.

Leboyer stresses that birth need not be frightening to either mother or newborn and that birth without violence creates children who are healthy, free, and without conflict. Furthermore, he maintains that impatience, nervousness, and anger may all be sensed by the infant. Those participating in the delivery need to be aware of the emotions they may be relaying to the newborn.

After the Birth

After the birth of the infant, there are many significant and exciting developments. In this section, we discuss some of these events as they pertain to the mother, the father, the baby, and the relationship between parents and newborn.

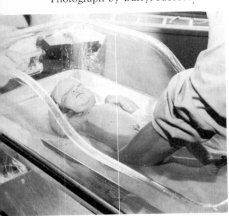

FIGURE 5.7 Leboyer method: child submerged in warm water similar to amniotic fluid.

Photograph by Darryl Jacobson

THE PARENTS

Following the birth, a mother's initial needs may include seeing, touching, and possibly holding and feeding the infant. She may wish to talk with her husband and relate her experience and feelings. She may request something to eat or may want to rest. The parent–newborn relationship begins immediately after delivery. Family-centered maternity care allows both parents to participate in the infant's care.

After the expectant parents' long months of watching the mother-to-be's abdomen gradually enlarge, their feeling the movements of the fetus, and their experiencing labor and delivery, what happens when the parents and the baby meet one another eye to eye? What are the feelings of the mother and the father when they see the child?

How do mothers respond to their infants? Observations indicate that there is an orderly and somewhat predictable pattern of behavior when the mother first examines her newborn infant (Klaus and Kennell, 1970). Klaus and Kennell were able to determine this pattern by filming twelve mothers with their full-term infants between thirty minutes and thirteen hours after birth. The films lasted about ten minutes for each mother–infant pair and covered the first contact (except for the mother's brief look at the newborn during delivery). The films indicated the following pattern: (1) with her fingertips, the mother hesitatingly touched the newborn's hands and feet; (2) within four or five minutes, she caressed the newborn's body with the palms of her hands (as she caressed the newborn, the mother became increasingly excited); (3) there was a marked increase in the total time during which the mother positioned herself and her newborn so that they could look into one

150

The Birth of the Baby: An Emerging Family Relationship

Dr. Leboyer and Gentle Birth

Dr. Frederick Leboyer was born in 1918. He graduated from the University of Paris, School of Medicine and became its clinical chief in 1954. Since that time he has devoted most of his time to his clinical practice. Since 1953 he has delivered more than ten thousand babies. In 1975, his book *Birth Without Violence* described techniques of childbirth that lessen the pain, fear, and confusion of the newborn. In the passages below, Dr. Leboyer describes some of the features of his approach to birth. He argues against cutting the umbilical cord immediately after birth.

CUTTING THE UMBILICAL CORD

To sever the umbilicus when the child has scarcely left the mother's womb is an act of cruelty. . . . To conserve it intact while it still pulses is to transform the act of birth.

First, this forces the physician to be patient; it is an invitation to both doctor and the mother to respect the baby's own life-rhythm. And it does more. When air rushes into the baby it feels like burning fire.

Before he was born, the infant made no distinction between the world and himself, since "outside" and "inside" were all one. He knew nothing of the tension of opposites—nothing was cold, since cold can only be known by contrast with what is warm. An infant's body temperature and its mother's are always identical; how could there be any separation between them? . . .

And how does the infant enter this kingdom of opposites? Through breathing. In taking its first breath, it crosses a threshold. And it is here. . . .

How do these things take place within the unborn fetus, whose lungs do not yet function? . . .

It depends on the placenta to do this—the placenta functions as its lungs. . . . The blood regenerates itself in the placenta not by contact with outside air but by contact with the mother's blood, which is restored in her lungs . . . in short: the mother breathes for her baby. . . .

[Nature] has arranged it so that during the dangerous passage of birth, the child is receiving oxygen from two sources rather than one: from the lungs and from the umbilicus.

Two systems [are] functioning simultaneously, one relieving the other: the old one, the umbilicus, continues to supply oxygen to the baby until the new one, the lungs, has fully taken its place. . . .

During this time, in parallel fashion, an orifice closes in the heart, which seals the old route forever.

In short, for an average of four or five minutes, the newborn straddles two worlds. Drawing oxygen from two sources, it switches gradually from one to the other, without a brutal transition. One scarcely hears a cry. What is required for this miracle to take place? Only a little patience. Only a refusal to rush things. Only knowing enough to wait, giving the child time to adjust.

From F. Leboyer, *Birth Without Violence.* New York: Alfred A. Knopf, 1975, pp. 44–50.

another's eyes. Klaus and Kennell indicated that the mothers showed great interest in waking their infants in order to get them to open their eyes. Nearly three-fourths of the mothers said something like "Open your eyes, oh come on now, open your eyes" or "If you open your eyes, I'll know you're alive."

Many mothers indicated that they felt much "closer" to the infant once it looked at them.

The new mother may have feelings of depression during the early days or weeks following delivery. There are emotional as well as physical adjustments to be made. The woman realizes that she must fulfill the roles of both wife and mother. She may feel dependent and require more affection and appreciation from her spouse. In attempting to establish a satisfying relationship with her baby, the mother may need temporary help from someone when she returns home. The additional help is to enable the parents to be with the baby and to decrease the mother's feelings of inadequacy in not being able to cope with the household chores as well as mothering the infant.

THE BABY

Now let us discuss the baby during the first few hours after birth (see Figure 5.8). The newborn's features and body are quite different from what they will be later on. The head is somewhat swollen and elongated from pushing against the cervix and from the passage through the bony pelvis and the birth canal. The infant's color is a bluish-purple, which gradually turns to pink. The nose is flattened and the chin recedes. There may be observable swelling of the sex organs because of maternal hormones.

Furthermore the child may have forcep marks over the cheeks, white spots on the skin due to occluded sweat glands, or visible capillaries because of the thinness of the skin. The silver nitrate used to prevent blindness that might be caused by bacteria present in the birth canal may cause temporary redness and puffiness of the eyes.

The baby's appearance may be surprising to a couple who have not seen a newborn before. Reassurance is frequently necessary to allay anxieties and to assure the parents that these seemingly strange newborn characteristics are normal and are not permanent.

APPLICATION BOX

The Psychological Impact of New Parenthood

The birth of a first baby begins an experience that is new to the parents both as individuals and as a marital pair. . . . To adjust to this new reality the parent must refocus his or her view of both the external world and also of the inner, psychic world. . . . A marital relationship undergoes irreversible change with the arrival of a first baby. Sometimes both parents, busy with the new activities generated by the needs of the newborn, remain unaware of the profound changes occurring in their own marital relationship. . . . No longer is there the exclusively one-to-one relationship between husband and wife, with all the possibilities of unlimited energy for intimacy, companionship and shared activities. . . . The directions of these fundamental changes are not always immediately apparent, and parents must search out for themselves the appropriate clues within their own lives.

From Shirley Erlich, "The Psychological Impact of New Parenthood," in The Boston Children's Medical Center, *Pregnancy, Birth and The Newborn Baby.* New York: Delacorte Press, 1972, pp. 223–229.

The Birth of the Baby: An Emerging Family Relationship

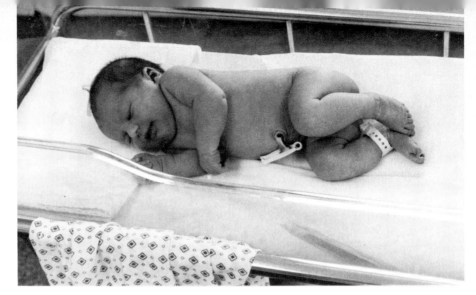

FIGURE 5.8 What a healthy week-old baby looks like.

Photograph by Darryl Jacobson

The feet look more complete than they are. X ray would show only one real bone of the heel. Other bones are now cartilage. Skin often loose and wrinkly. *The legs* are most often seen drawn up against the abdomen in prebirth position. Extended legs measure shorter than you'd expect compared to the arms. The knees stay slightly bent and legs are more or less bowed. *Genitals* of both sexes will seem large (especially scrotum) in comparison with the scale of, for example, the hands to adult size. *Weight,* unless well above the average of 6 or 7 pounds will not prepare you for how really tiny newborn is. Top to toe measure: anywhere between 18 to 21 inches. *The trunk* may startle you in some normal detail: short neck, small sloping shoulders, swollen breasts, large rounded abdomen, umbilical stump (future navel), slender narrow pelvis and hips. *A deep flush* spreads over the entire body if baby cries hard. Veins on head swell and throb. You will notice no tears as tear ducts do not function as yet. *The skin* is thin and dry. You may see veins through it. Fair skin may be rosy-red temporarily. Downy hair is not unusual. *The hands,* if you open them out flat from their characteristic fist position, have: finely lined palms, tissue-paper thin nails, dry, loose fitting skin and deep bracelet creases at wrist. *The eyes* appear dark blue, have a blank stary gaze. You may catch one or both turning or turned to crossed or wall-eyed position. *The face* will disappoint you unless you expect to see: pudgy cheeks, a broad, flat nose with mere hint of a bridge, receding chin, undersized lower jaw. *The head* usually strikes you as being too big for the body. (Immediately after birth it may be temporarily out of shape—topsided or elongated—due to pressure before or during birth.) *On the skull* you will see or feel the two most obvious soft spots or *fontanels.* One is above the brow, the other close to crown of head in back.

From W. G. Birch, M.D., *A Doctor Discusses Pregnancy.* Copyright 1980, Budlong Press, Chicago 60625.

The newborn's heart beat is rapid and may be 170 beats per minute while the infant is crying or as slow as 80–90 during rest. The average heart rate is considered 120–149 beats per minute.

Physiological jaundice (icterus neonatorum) may develop in 55 to 70 percent of all newborns. The condition is attributed to an immature hepatic (liver) system. This type of jaundice usually disappears within fourteen days after onset. Icterus neonatorum is significant in that it typifies the physiological immaturity of the newborn.

The Apgar Test—An Evaluation of Newborn Life Processes

The Apgar test was developed by Dr. Virginia Apgar, an internationally recognized specialist in the study of neonates. The test is designed to assess the basic life processes of the infant. It is usually administered to the infant approximately one minute after birth and again five minutes later. The test is both quick and safe.

The tested infant receives a score that is based on five life signs (see Apgar chart). These five signs, listed in order of importance, are

1. *Pulse or heart rate.* The infant's heart rate usually varies between 150 and 180 beats per minute during the first few moments of life and usually drops to about 135 beats per minute within an hour after birth. A heart rate less than 100 may indicate a difficulty.
2. *Respiration.* Regularity of respiration usually accompanies a healthy cry or follows shortly thereafter.
3. *Activity or muscle tone.* The newborn usually keeps its arms and legs in a fetal position. Muscle tone is evaluated by the degree of the infant's resistance when the examiner attempts to extend its limbs.
4. *Grimace or reflex irritability.* The newborn should respond vigorously to any test of reflex capability. *Grimace or irritability* is an indication of the general maturity of the nervous system. Little response could indicate impairment of the central nervous system.
5. *Appearance or color.* At first cyanosis, or blue coloring, is present in all newborns. After a few minutes, the operation of the heart and the lungs produces a rapid change to a pink coloration. The absence of the normally pink color may indicate respiratory or heart problems.

One easy way to remember these five signs is to use Dr. Apgar's name as an acronym: Appearance or coloring, Pulse or heart rate, Grimace or reflex irritability, Activity or muscle tone, and Respiration.

Apgar Scoring Chart for Evaluating Status of Newborn

Sign	0 Points	1 Point	2 Points
Pulse or heart rate	Absent	Slow (less than 100)	Greater than 100
Respiratory effort	Absent	Slow, irregular	Good strong cry
Activity or muscle tone	Limp	Some flexion of extremities	Extremities well flexed, active motion
Grimace or reflex irritability (response to catheter in nostril)	No response	Grimace	Cough, sneeze or cry
Appearance or color	Blue, pale	Body pink, extremities blue	Completely pink

(*From* Apgar, 1958, p. 1988).

The examiner takes all of the above vital signs into consideration when assigning the newborn an Apgar score. A total score of 7 to 10 points indicates that the newborn is in good condition. A score of 4 to 6 points indicates that the infant is in fair condition. In this case, the infant's air passages are further cleared and oxygen may be given. A score of 0 to 3 indicates either a stillbirth or a newborn in very poor condition requiring emergency procedures. It is important to note that an infant's Apgar may be affected by the drugs that the mother is given during birth (Apgar, 1958; Apgar and James, 1962).

The Nervous System. At birth, the infant's nervous system is relatively immature. Most of the bodily functions and responses are carried out by reflex action. The behavior of the newborn is controlled largely by processes

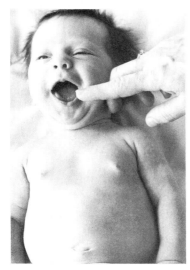
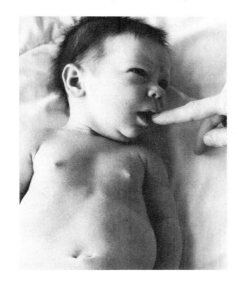
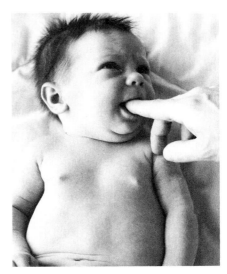

FIGURE 5.9 The rooting responses. Stimulation: the adult touches the side of the infant's mouth with a finger. Head turning: the infant turns its head in the direction of the finger. Grasping with the mouth: the infant tries to suck the finger.

Photographs by David Kostelnik

FIGURE 5.10 The sucking reflex. The infant sucks the finger placed in its mouth.

Photograph by Darryl Jacobson

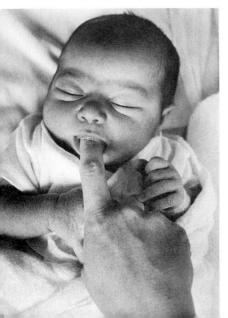

in the human brain stem rather than by processes in the cerebral cortex. The *brain stem* is located below the cortex and is responsible for such basic biological processes as breathing and circulation in addition to basic reflexes. The *cerebral cortex* is primarily responsible for memory, thought, and perception. The cerebral cortex is not fully functional in the newborn and gradually begins to exercise control over infant behavior during the first few weeks of life. As the cerebral cortex gains control, it can influence or inhibit the brain stem activities responsible for reflexes. In addition to the impact of cortical control, more complex and purposeful behavior is also made possible by the gradual and continuing process of myelinization which insulates nerve fibers. (Myelinization improves the efficiency, accuracy, and general effectiveness of nerve signals which initiate behavioral responses.)

A newborn possesses certain reflexes that are essential. These include the blinking, yawn, coughing, gagging, and sneezing reflexes. In addition, the so-called *rooting reflexes* are stimulated when one brushes the infant's cheek (see Figure 5.9), and the infant turns its head in the direction of the stimulation as if to reach for food (Prechtl and Bientema, 1964). The *sucking reflex* occurs when anything touches the infant's lips (see Figure 5.10). The *withdrawal reflex* occurs when the infant cries and recoils from a pain-inducing stimulation (e.g., being accidentally stuck with a diaper pin) (see Figure 5.11).

The *grasp (palmar) reflex* (Figure 5.12) enables the infant to hold onto an object briefly and then release its grip. This reflex diminishes with maturity. If one holds the infant upright with its feet touching a solid surface, the legs will move as if in an attempt to walk or dance. This is the *walking reflex*. The *startle (Moro) reflex* is also present at birth (see Figure 5.13). This reaction is stimulated by a sudden loud noise or loss of support; generalized, nonpurposeful muscular activity results. Another reflex which is present at birth and disappears by the sixth month is the *Babinski reflex* (Figure 5.14). This reflex can be elicited by firmly pressing the sole of the infant's foot which causes the toes to fan out and the foot to twist inward.

155

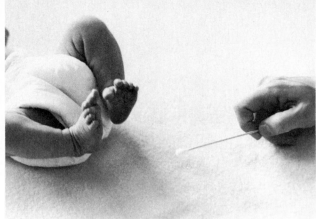

FIGURE 5.11 The withdrawal reflex. Stimulation: the examiner pricks the infant's sole with a *Q-tip* or pin. Response: the infant withdraws its foot.

Photographs by David Kostelnik

The infant's sense of equilibrium may be observed when, for example, a jarring of the infant causes it to draw up its legs and turn the soles of its feet inward. A postural reflex, the *tonic-neck reflex,* may be seen when the infant is laid on its back with its head turned to one side and its corresponding arm and leg extended at right angles to the body. The infant responds by flexing the other arm and leg and making fists with both hands.

FIGURE 5.12 The Palmar or grasping reflex. The adult presses a finger into the infant's palms, and infant's fingers flex around the examiner's finger.

Photograph by David Kostelnik

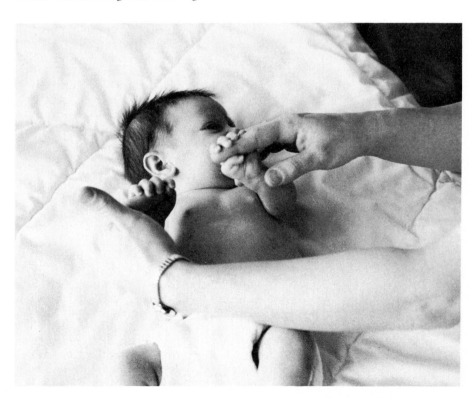

The Birth of the Baby: An Emerging Family Relationship

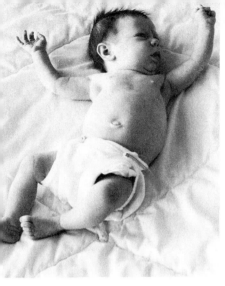

FIGURE 5.13 The Moro or startle reflex.

Photograph by David Kostelnik

FIGURE 5.14 The Babinski reflex.

Photograph by David Kostelnik

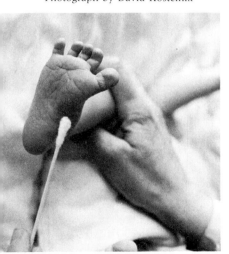

These reflex mechanisms are important because they signify normal functioning of the nervous system (see Table 5.1). The relatively brief appearance of some reflexes (e.g., the startle reflex and the Babinski reflex) may reflect the emerging control of behavior by the cerebral cortex and, therefore, the maturation of the nervous system. Those reflexes that appear early in life and then cease to exist are sometimes referred to as the *primitive reflexes* because they are shared with lower animals. For example, both the Moro and the grasping reflexes may well be evolutionary carry-overs from primates that hang onto their mothers for survival and feeding.

Sensory Capacities *Vision.* The object that a baby sees most often after birth is the face of its mother. How long does it take for the baby to distinguish its mother's face from a stranger's face? Carpenter (1974) found that such a discrimination may occur as early as two weeks after birth. Carpenter (1974) presented two-week-old babies with either their mother's face or a stranger's face in an opening in a frame in front of them. Babies spent longer looking at their mother's face than at the stranger's face. In addition, they showed an apparent aversion to the stranger's face by immediately looking away when the stranger's face was presented. Such a withdrawal may suggest that the babies found the stranger's face too novel in relation to the mother's face. Other experiments demonstrate a preference for real faces as opposed to oval-shaped constructs with scrambled arrangements of facial characteristics or oval-shaped constructs of solid color (Fantz, 1961).

Most of the studies on infant vision have dealt with this question of visual preference. An application of this approach (Fantz, Fagan, and Miranda, 1975) was used to determine visual acuity. Because newborns prefer looking at contours or contrasts rather than looking at a solid-colored field, Fantz et al., presented infants with gray cards showing black and white lines of equal width. All infants were 10 inches from the cards. The infant was then shown successive cards in which the black and white lines became progressively narrower. The assumption was that at one point (which would indicate the limit of the infant's vision), the card would appear to the baby to be an all-gray blur, which would no longer interest the infant (infant visual acuity was measured by observing the corneal reflections of objects in the infant's eyes. When an infant was looking directly at an object and, therefore, could clearly see it, the object was mirrored in the center of the eye.) On the average, this point was reached when the cards had lines one eighth of an inch wide. This finding on infant *visual acuity* as well as other research (Mauer and Lewis, 1979; Cohen, DeLoache, and Strauss, 1979) suggest that while infant vision is not nearly as fine-grained as it is in adulthood, it is better than previously thought.

Hearing. As we discussed in the previous chapter, it is apparent that hearing is present during prenatal development. As any parent will testify, a sudden loud noise such as a slamming door usually startles a newborn. During the first few days of life, however, the middle part of the ear behind the eardrum is still filled with amniotic fluid. Until this fluid gradually evaporates or is absorbed, the sounds reaching the baby's ears are dulled. At four days of age or younger, a baby can be taught to turn its eyes and head in the direction of a sound (Wertheimer, 1961).

There has been considerable research on the infant's response to sound inside the uterus early in labor (Hutt, Hutt, Lenard, Bernuth, and

TABLE 5.1   Some Newborn Reflexes

Reflex	Stimulus	Description	Significance
Rooting (see Figure 5.9)	An object touching the infant's cheek.	The head turns toward the source of stimulation, the mouth opens, and sucking actions begin. This reflex may appear within an hour after birth.	This reflex has survival value because it enables the infant to locate food.
Sucking (see Figure 5.10)	An object touching the lips.	The infant makes sucking movements. This response becomes more efficient with time.	If absent, immaturity or possible brain damage may be indicated.
Withdrawal (see Figure 5.11)	Heat (from a feeding bottle) or pinprick.	Crying and recoiling from pain.	Absence may indicate immaturity or damage to the nervous system.
Grasp or *palmar* (see Figure 5.12)	An object placed on the palms.	The infant closes its hand around the object with a firm grip. The grasp may be secure enough to raise the infant to a standing position. This reflex disappears by about the first birthday.	Absence may indicate a nervous-system problem.
Moro or startle (see Figure 5.13)	Loud noise or a sudden change in body position.	The infant throws its arms and fingers out in full extension and arches its back and extends the legs. The hands are then returned to the midline of the body. The reflex disappears between the third and fifth months.	If this reflex is weak or absent, the central nervous system may be disturbed. If present, the newborn has an awareness of equilibrium.
Babinski (see Figure 5.14)	Stimulation of the sole of the foot.	The toes fan out and the foot twists inward. After six months of age, this reflex disappears and the infant's toes curl inward when touched.	Absence may indicate immaturity of the central nervous system, defects of the spinal cord, or a lesion in the motor area of the brain.

Muntjewerff, 1973). In these unique investigations, a very tiny microphone is put on the end of a catheter, and the catheter is placed inside the uterus after the membranes have been broken (during early labor). The microphone is placed close to the baby's ear so that it can record the sounds that actually reach the baby. Because the microphone also records the baby's heart rate, it is possible to reproduce uterine noise outside the mother and to determine its impact on the infant's heart rate. From this type of research, as well as from studies done on newborns, it seems that "patterned" sounds result in more

The Birth of the Baby: An Emerging Family Relationship

infant responding than "pure" tones. Furthermore the sounds that were the most effective in eliciting infant responding were those that included the fundamental frequencies found in the human voice. Of these fundamental frequencies of sound, infants seemed to respond better to the higher frequencies than to the lower frequencies. Incidentally, it is a common observation that both parents "talk" to their babies in high-pitched voices and return to normal pitch when talking to one another or to other adults.

Research indicates that newborns can tell which side a sound is coming from by head and eye movements (MacFarlane, 1977; Muir and Field, 1979). It has been suggested that the reason is that sounds coming from one side reach one ear before they reach the other. The ability to turn toward the sound depends on these very small differences in timing and loudness as the sound strikes the two ears.

At birth to 1 month of age, infants can turn their heads to locate a sound that is directly to one side (Field, Muir, Pilon, Sinclair, and Dodwell, 1980). By at least 16 weeks of age the infant seems to be able to make more precise determinations of sounds that are only slightly to one side. This is done by differentiating the timing and loudness cues that go to both ears (Bundy, 1980).

An example of these infant sound-localization skills can be seen in everyday parent/caretaker–infant interactions. When the adult is out of the direct line of sight of the infant and begins to talk, infant head movements begin almost immediately and simultaneously with eye movements. The infant is using such head and eye movements to locate the sound of the human voice (MacFarlane, 1977).

Additional studies have demonstrated a precise interaction between newborn and adult during adult speech (Condon, 1974; Condon and Sander, 1974a, 1974b). Condon and Sander videotaped a series of infants aged twelve hours to two days old. They demonstrated that even at this very early age, the newborn babies were able to move in rather precise time to human speech. The authors stated, "The present study reveals a complex interactional 'system' in which the organization of the neonate's motor behavior is seen to be entrained by and synchronized with the organized speech behavior of adults in his environment" (Condon and Sander, 1974b, p. 461).

Olfaction: The Sense of Smell. Newborn babies can discriminate various smells (Lipsitt, Engen, and Kaye, 1963). Lipsitt and his associates observed the activity, heart rate, and breathing patterns of twenty babies who were two days old. In the experiment, each baby was presented with two aromas chosen from the following: anise oil, asafetida, acetic acid, and phenyl alcohol. When one of these aromas was initially presented to the newborn, the newborn changed its activity, heart rate, and breathing pattern. If the smell continued, the baby became habituated to it or learned to take no notice. However, when a new smell was introduced, up went the heart rate, activity level, and breathing pattern.

Other studies have demonstrated the sensitivity of the newborn's sense of smell (MacFarlane, 1975). MacFarlane took a breast pad (a piece of gauze about four inches square) that had been inside the mother's bra between breast feedings (and had therefore absorbed some breast milk) and put it next to the baby's cheek. A clean (unused) breast pad was placed next to the other cheek. MacFarlane then filmed the baby's activities for one minute and reversed the pads and filmed for another minute. Although the babies tended to turn or look more to their right (mainly because their mothers were apt to place their babies on the left when feeding), analysis of the films indicated that at five days of age, the babies spent more time with their heads turned toward the mother's used pad than toward the unused pad.

Gustation: The Sense of Taste. There is some evidence that even the fetus is sensitive to taste.

the baby surrounded by fluid swallows it continually and then pees it out again, and there is evidence that the baby may actually control the amount of fluid around him. In certain pregnancies too much fluid sometimes accumulates too fast, and forty years ago a doctor developed a novel way of treating this. He injected saccharine into the amniotic fluid in order to sweeten it, and he found that he could thereby reduce the amount of fluid, possibly by having encouraged the baby to swallow more. . . . This suggests that a fetus can taste.

MacFarlane, 1977, p. 84.

Changes in the sweetness of an infant's food have been shown to affect the baby's sucking patterns and heart rate (Crook and Lipsitt, 1976). Much earlier research (Pratt, Nelson, and Sun, 1930) demonstrated differential reactions to the tasting of various solutions. Pratt and his associates gave twenty-eight newborns (ranging in age from one to fifteen days) sweet, salt, sour, and bitter solutions. Generally, the reactions of the infants varied according to the strength of the solutions. When the solutions were fairly strong, the infants responded to the sugar solution by sucking and to the quinine (bitter) solution by grimacing. When the solutions were not very strong, the infants demonstrated rather few specific responses. This finding may indicate that a sensitivity to taste is certainly present in the newborn but not nearly as precise as in the adult.

Feeling Pain. Generally speaking, we accept the idea that newborns are not as sensitive to pain as they will be later in life (Lipsitt and Levy, 1959). For example, the circumcision of a newborn male child is done without anesthetic. Although there may be some practical reasons for researching the development of pain sensitivity in the newborn (such as setting the date of circumcision), ethical issues put stringent limits on such research. Because the infliction of pain on a newborn could well influence future emotional development, few experimenters are willing (or allowed) to take such a risk. Therefore there has been little systematic investigation of the baby's sensitivity to pain. It is interesting to note that some researchers suggest that some behavior differences between male and female babies may be due to circumcision (and the related pain) rather than to any innate differences (Richards, Bernal, and Brackbill, 1976).

Sensitivity to Touch. Touch is the most highly developed sense in the newborn, particularly on the forehead, lips, tongue, and ears. At birth, the baby shows a number of reflex actions in response to touch. Most of these reflexes are present in the uterus and disappear sometime after birth. These include the rooting reflex, the grasping reflex, and the Babinski reflex. In addition, if the back of the infant's foot is touched firmly (e.g., if the feet are drawn against the edge of a flat surface), the infant makes placing movements similar to those of a kitten (the placing reflex). At present, there is no explanation for many of these touch reflexes.

Rhythms. A recording of a heart beating at sixty to eighty beats a minute appears to have a quieting effect on a baby. In addition, a light flashing at the same rhythm has a comparable soothing effect (Salk, 1973). Other evidence also suggests infant appreciation of rhythms in rocking (Ambrose and Levine, 1970). Ambrose and Levine, who developed a crib that could be automatically rocked at varying speeds, found that the optimal rhythm was sixty rocks a minute. It has been pointed out that this rhythm of sixty to eighty beats is comparable to the mother's heartbeat, which the fetus has lived with in the uterus (Salk, 1973).

Ambrose and Levine also demonstrated that a baby appears to anticipate a future rhythmic experience from a previous one. When they gave the babies rocking for ten seconds followed by rest (no rocking) sessions for twenty seconds, then each time rocking began there were changes in baby's heart rate and breathing. Even when the rocking periods were discontinued (i.e., the rocking did not begin on schedule), the newborn's heart rate and breathing still showed changes. The experimenters suggested that these changes occurred because the baby anticipated future rocking.

Imitation. The sophisticated two-way relationship between the newborn baby and its caregiver is illustrated in research on imitation (Meltzov, 1977). Meltzov demonstrated, by careful analysis of videotape and film, that newborns of two weeks of age could stick out their tongues or clench and unclench their hands when they watched someone else making these gestures. This sort of imitation requires the newborn to do several rather complex things. First, it has to perceive another person making the gesture. Then, it has to realize that its own tongue or hand is equivalent to that of the model. Finally, without necessarily being able to observe its own behavior, the newborn must match its movements with those of the model.

Individual Differences and Newborn States. Infants behave differently from the moment of birth (Korner, 1969). Parents and caretakers attest to the differences between individual babies. For example, some newborns seem to startle rather frequently during regular sleep, whereas others startle infrequently. Some newborns seem more irritable than others. Differences of this sort are important because they may affect the newborn's interactions with its parents. Parents react differently to a baby who seems rather quiet than to one who is excitable and irritable. In addition, the parent's sense of being able to do something to calm an infant may contribute to a more positive attitude toward the infant.

In addition to the variations in infants' temperaments, there are also important variations within the daily behavior of each newborn infant. These variations—cycles of wakefulness, sleepiness, and activity—are called *states*. A baby's reaction to its environment usually depends on its state.

DEFINITION

State. A "behavioral condition that (1) is stable over a period of time, (2) occurs repeatedly in an individual infant and (3) is encountered in very similar forms in other individuals" (Hutt, Lenard, and Prechtl, 1969).

When observing babies, researchers now commonly categorize the baby's behavior by the following states (Prechtl and Beintema, 1964; Wolff, 1966; Hutt, Lenard, and Prechtl, 1973):

Regular Sleep. The newborn's regular sleep is deep, and the breathing is regular. The infant makes no movements except for an occasional and generalized startle response. On an arousal continuum, this state is the low point.

Irregular Sleep. Irregular sleep is light, breathing is irregular, and the baby shows occasional restlessness. The muscles may twitch but ordinarily no major movements are made. The sounds and noises that the infant may have been oblivious to during regular sleep now bring such responses as a smile or a startle.

Drowsiness. The infant's state, both prior to and following sleep, is drowsiness. The eyes may be open, breathing is irregular, and the body is more active than during irregular sleep. The infant is sensitive to such stimuli as the sound of a television or the sight of its mother or father.

Alert Inactivity. The state of alert inactivity occurs after the baby has been fed and diapered or has just gotten up and remains awake with eyes open for a short period of time. The infant may move its head, trunk, or limbs while looking at something in the environment such as a swinging mobile.

Waking Activity and Crying. Waking and crying can begin with either intense internal stimulation (such as hunger or pain) or external stimulation (such as restraint of the newborn or removing its pacifier). This state may begin with rather quiet movements and turn into sustained thrashing and crying. The newborn seems to be "too busy" to respond to many things that would draw its attention in the states of drowsiness or alert activity.

The Operation of States. How do states operate? What factors determine when newborn states occur? Newborn states are influenced by both internal timing mechanisms and external stimulation.

Sometimes the internal mechanisms are referred to metaphorically as *biological clocks.* These biological clocks appear to regulate human cycles of eating, sleeping, and elimination. These timing mechanisms also appear to regulate the pattern of movement from one state to another in the newborn.

Rhythms associated with the day–night cycle are called *circadian* (derived from the Latin words *circa,* which means "approximate," and *dies,* which means "day"). The most apparent human circadian rhythm is the sleep–wakefulness or activity cycle. Careful records kept of the temperature, the heart rate, and the sleeping habits of hundreds of infants showed that circadian rhythms are only slightly apparent at birth. Gradually, however, they develop during the first year of life (Hellbrugge, 1960). Figure 5.15 illustrates the development of circadian periodism in heart rate. Infants who are one week old show only a slight fluctuation above and below the norm of 100 heartbeats per minute. However, a day–night rhythm becomes apparent at about six months. The cycle is very clear for the year-old child.

How are the states of the newborn distributed over a typical day? The newborn sleeps seventeen to twenty hours during a typical twenty-four-hour cycle. Of that sleeping time, approximately 75 percent is spent in irregular sleep. The newborn spends a total time of two to three hours in a state of alert inactivity and one to four hours in the state of waking activity and crying or fussing (Hutt, Lenard, and Prechtl, 1969).

From the perspective of the infant and parent or caretaker as an interacting system, newborn states both affect parental behavior and are, in turn, affected by parental activity (see Figure 5.16). Of course, parents are interested in

The Birth of the Baby: An Emerging Family Relationship

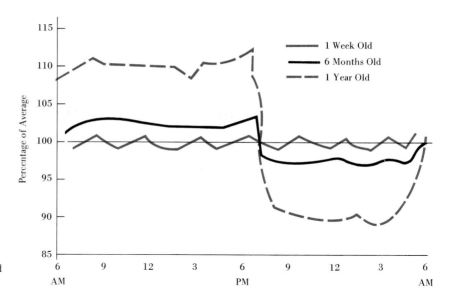

FIGURE 5.15 Development of circadian periodism in the heart rate of infants.

From S. D. Beck, *Animal Photoperiodism.* New York: Holt, Rinehart and Winston, Inc. Copyright, 1963.

FIGURE 5.16 Parent-infant interaction. The figure at the top illustrates a relationship between mother and baby in which there is limited synchrony (at beginning and end) as the mother looks intently at the infant while the infant is looking away. The figure at the bottom shows a relationship that is in synchrony as both mother and baby spend most of the time in mutually supportive and similar behaviors.

Adapted from T. B. Brazelton, B. Koslowski and M. Main, "The Origins of Reciprocity," in Lewis and Rosenblum, *The Effect of the Infant on Its Caregiver.* New York: John Wiley and Sons, 1974, p. 62.

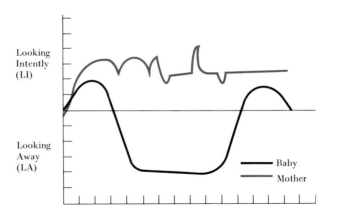

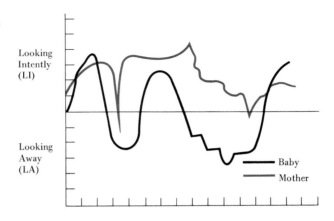

Some Famous 'Preemies'

A baby is premature if it weighs 2.5 kg. (5.5 lbs.) or less, and is born more than three weeks early. The lower the birth weight, the greater the incidence of later health problems, such as cerebral palsy and mental retardation.

Prematurity can be caused by a weak cervix, a placenta which breaks away from the uterus or is too small, an abnormal fetus, more than one fetus, or poor health of the mother.

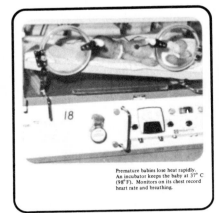

Premature babies lose heat rapidly. An incubator keeps the baby at 37° C (98° F). Monitors on its chest record heart rate and breathing.

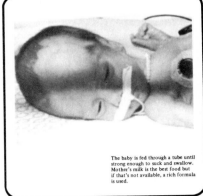

The baby is fed through a tube until strong enough to suck and swallow. Mother's milk is the best food but if that's not available, a rich formula is used.

Famous 'Preemies'

Julius Caesar
100 BC - 44 BC

A famous Roman emperor and great military leader

Sir Isaac Newton
1643 - 1727

Formulated the three fundamental laws of mechanics and invented calculus

Victor Hugo
1802 - 1885

An important French romantic writer famous for The Hunchback of Notre Dame

Charles Darwin
1809 - 1882

Expounded the theory of evolution

Sir Winston Churchill
1874 - 1965

Prime minister of Britain during World War II

Reproduced by permission of the Ontario Science Centre, Toronto, Canada

maintaining an infant state that is pleasing and satisfying to them. Not unexpectedly, this normal desire results in a number of parental activities that both soothe the baby and preserve the "sanity" of the parents. Two of the more frequent methods used by parents to influence newborn states are feeding and rocking (Wolff, 1966; Van den Daele, 1970). Research also indicates that swaddling (snugly wrapping) a newborn baby in a blanket is soothing to the infant (Lipton, Stenschneider, and Richmond, 1965).

The state of the infant determines how it responds to its world—including its parents. A drowsy or sleeping infant responds very differently than an infant that is awake and alert.

Special Issue: The Premature Infant. Prematurity can result in some problems for the newborn infant. There are two indicators of prematurity: (1) gestation time (time since fertilization) and (2) low birth weight. The infant born after a gestation period of less than thirty-seven weeks is considered premature, and an infant with a birth weight under five and one-half pounds is regarded as premature. Approximately 7.6 percent of hospital births are classified as premature.

After birth, the premature infant has greater difficulty adjusting to its environment than a full-term baby. Respiration and circulation are much more complicated and difficult for the premature infant, and because the premature infant has relatively few fat cells, it also has more limited control of body temperature. For these reasons, premature infants are often put in incubators.

What are the effects of prematurity on the long-term development of the infant? There is some indication that premature infants have more illnesses during the first three years of life, have lower IQ scores, and are more likely to have behavioral problems than full-term babies (Harper, Fischer, and Rider, 1959; Knobloch, Pasamanick, Harper, and Rider, 1959; Braine, Heimer, Wortis, and

FIGURE 5.17 Differences in mental and motor development for three groups of varying prematurity.

From M. D. S. Braine, C. B. Heimer, H. Wortis, and A. M. Freedman, "Factors Associated with Impairment of the Early Development of Prematures," *Monographs of the Society for Research in Child Development,* 1966, *31,* 139. Copyright, 1966. The Society for Research in Child Development, Inc. By permission.

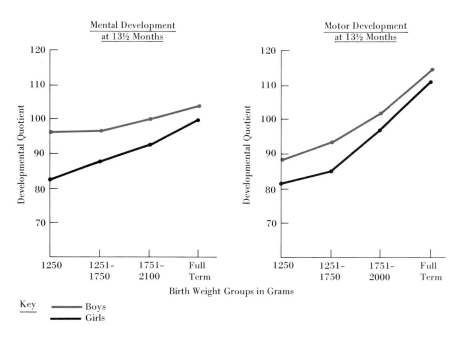

Freedman, 1966). Although prematurity may be associated with such later difficulties as learning disabilities, reading problems, and hyperactivity, prematurity does not necessarily cause these problems. Prematurity itself may be a symptom of disadvantageous maternal factors, such as malnutrition or faulty placental functioning. Therefore we cannot say that later developmental problems are caused simply by prematurity (see Figure 5.17).

In addition, it may be that some problems of the premature child may arise from parent–child interaction during infancy and early development. There is some evidence that the premature infant may not develop as well because of overprotection and/or isolation by parents or by hospital practices. Because parents or hospital personnel may be afraid of injuring the premature infant, they may fail to interact or play with the infant. Sometimes the premature newborn is in an incubator for an extended period of time, and the life-supporting mechanisms may not permit picking up, holding, and rocking the infant. The result may well be premature infants that gain less weight and are generally less healthy than full-term infants (Solkoff, Yaffe, Weintraub, and Blase, 1969).

APPLICATION BOX

Low-Birth-Weight Infants

Five and a half pounds is generally considered the dividing line between normal and low birth weight.

[Some 6.8 percent (246,000 annually) of American newborns weigh 5½ lb. (2500 gm.) or less (U.S. Department of Health and Human Services, 1982).] Babies weighing 4 lb. 6 oz. (2000 gm.) or less are particularly susceptible to critical illness.

These dangerously small infants often have severe problems with breathing, heart action, and control of temperature and blood sugar. Unless these difficulties are controlled, they may cause brain damage or death.

Learning disabilities, accompanied by emotional and behavioral problems, are often a lifetime burden for the baby born too soon or too small.

Percent of low-birth-weight infants (less than 5 lbs. 8 oz. and less than 4 lbs. 6 oz.) by age of mother.

Source: U.S. Department of Health and Human Services. Public Health Service. National Center for Health Statistics. Advance Report on Final Natality Statistics, 1980, Vol. 31, No. 8, supplement, Nov. 30, 1982. Compiled by Gale Schiamberg.

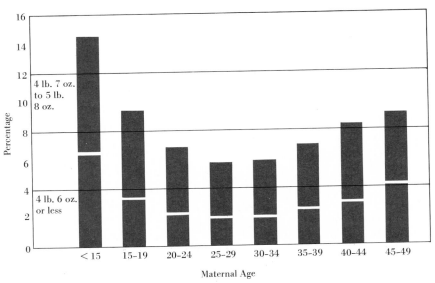

The Birth of the Baby: An Emerging Family Relationship

Structural defects occur in about 6 percent of babies weighing more than 5½ lb.; in 9 percent of those between 4 lb. 7 oz. and 5 lb. 8 oz.; and in more than 30 percent of those weighing 4 lb. 6 oz. or less.

Estimated Number of Liveborn Infants With and Without Birth Defects, by Birthweight, 1981

Condition of Newborn	More than 5 lbs. 8 oz.	4 lbs. 7 oz. to 5 lbs. 8 oz.	Less than 4 lbs. 7 oz.	Total, all birth weights
With structural or metabolic defects	188,900	13,700	30,400	233,000
Without structural or metabolic defects	2,908,100	138,500	53,700	3,100,300
Total	3,097,000	152,200	84,100	3,333,300

More than one quarter-million infants are born with structural or metabolic defects or markedly low birthweight in the United States each year.

Charts and information, courtesy of March of Dimes Birth Defects Foundation, Facts/1982.

A nurse provides medical treatment to an ill newborn.

Photograph by Wayne Mason.

Newborn intensive care.

Photograph by Wayne Mason.

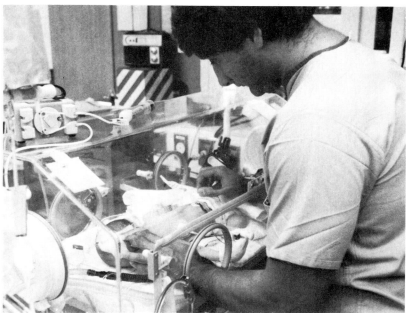

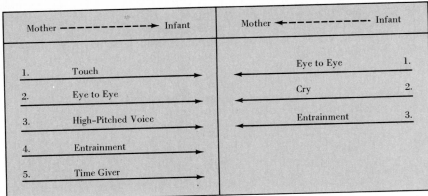

Mother - - - - - - - - → Infant		Mother ← - - - - - - - - Infant	
1.	Touch →	Eye to Eye ←	1.
2.	Eye to Eye →	Cry ←	2.
3.	High–Pitched Voice →	Entrainment ←	3.
4.	Entrainment →		
5.	Time Giver →		

FIGURE 5.18   The reciprocal interaction of mother and infant in the attachment process.

Modified from Marshall H. Klaus and John H. Kennell, *Parent-Infant Bonding,* 2nd ed., St. Louis: The C. V. Mosby Co., 1982. Photograph by Wayne Mason

THE RELATIONSHIP BETWEEN PARENT AND NEWBORN

It is quite apparent to those who have observed the interaction of parent and newborn that an attachment relationship is developing. Why does this relationship seem to progress so rapidly? What are the features of the emerging relationship that bring parent and child together? Figure 5.18 indicates some of the maternal and child factors that contribute to this relationship. We will first describe the interactions initiated by the mother and then discuss the interactions originating with the infant.

Interactions Originating with the Parent.   *Touch.* Although it is not perfectly clear which infant characteristics lead to touch by the mother, there is some agreement on the characteristic touch patterns that mothers use when making their first contact with the newborn (Rubin, 1963; Klaus, Jerauld, Kreger, McAlpine, Steffa, and Kennell, 1972). Mothers appear to follow an orderly sequence of behavior after birth while they become acquainted with newborns. Klaus et al., observed that when nude infants were placed next to their mothers either a few minutes or a few hours after birth, the mothers touched them according to the following pattern: 1. *fingertip contact* with the newborn's extremities; and 2. *palm contact,* or massaging and stroking of the trunk. During the first three minutes of the observation period, fingertip contact occurred first and 52 percent of the time. Palm contact occurred only 28 percent of the time during the first three minutes. In the second three-minute period, the mothers used palm contact and stroking for 62 percent of the total time as compared with 38 percent for fingertip contact. These results suggest that there is a sequence of tactile familiarity that mothers naturally follow. It is interesting to note that this sequence is modified and slowed down by such conditions as infant prematurity (Rubin, 1963).

TABLE 5.2 Percentage of Total Observation Time in Face-to-Face Position

Initial Contact (Minutes)	Face to Face (Percentage)
0–3	10
3–6	17
6–9	23

Based on statistics from Marshall H. Klaus and John H. Kennell, *Parent–Infant Bonding,* (2nd ed.) St. Louis: The C. V. Mosby Co., 1982.

Eye-to-Eye Contact.

Open your eyes. Oh, come on, open your eyes. If you open your eyes I'll know you're alive. (mother's comment reported in Klaus and Kennell, 1982, p. 74.)

Eye-to-eye contact seems to serve the purposes of allowing the mother to give the newborn an identity and of providing exciting feedback to the mother. When mothers are given the opportunity of holding their newborns immediately after birth, there is a dramatic increase in the time spent in the face-to-face position during the first few minutes after birth (Klaus et al., 1972; Lang, 1972; see Table 5.2).

While eye-to-eye contact may be a rewarding experience for mothers and fathers, the human eye and face also have visual characteristics that increase their "stimulus value" for the infant. Data on newborn vision suggest that infants prefer stimuli that are moving, moderately complex and ovoid like the human face (Stechler and Lantz, 1966; Haith, Kessen, and Collins, 1969). The eyes have extra stimulus features, such as shininess and black (pupil) and white (iris) contrast, that attract infant attention (Fantz, 1965).

High-Pitched Voice.
Mothers and fathers tend to speak to their newborns in a high-pitched voice (Lang, 1972). Observations indicate that parents use a high-pitched voice for their infants and then switch to normal pitch for everyday conversation with adults. The parental use of a high-pitched voice fits with the newborn's sensitivity and attraction to high-frequency sounds.

Entrainment.
When two people talk to one another, their communication is not simply verbal; it also involves movement. The analysis of sound films of human communication shows that both speaker and listener make body movements (sometimes imperceptible) "in time" to the words of the speaker (Condon and Sander, 1974a).

Condon and Sander (1974a) have also demonstrated that there is a complex interaction between newborn motor behavior and the organized speech patterns of adults. Specifically, the newborn's motor behavior is entrained by and synchronized with the speech of adults. An analysis of films of adults

A mother and a newborn in face-to-face position.

Photograph by Darryl Jacobson

talking to newborns indicated that when the infant was already moving, changes in the organization of these movements were coordinated with changes in the sound patterns of adult speech. For example, as the adult paused for a breath or accented a syllable, the infant made body movements such as raising or lowering its arms and/or legs or raising its eyebrows. Thus not only do the newborn and the parent or caretaker contribute to a shared relationship, but the shared rhythms of the relationship allow the infant to be introduced to many repetitions of linguistic forms long before it is capable of formal speech and communication.

Time Giver. The synchrony (mutual adaptation) of movement during speech is one part of a much larger picture of reciprocal interaction between parent and newborn. There seems to be a general synchrony of rhythms between the newborn and its mother that has its beginnings in the prenatal period (Klaus and Kennell, 1976; Sander, Stechler, Burns, and Julia, 1970). This synchrony of biological rhythms or biorhythmicity is thrown into a state of disequilibrium at birth. Prior to birth, the fetus is probably attuned to such intrauterine rhythms as the mother's sleep−wake cycle, the general pattern of the mother's day, the beat of the mother's heart, and the rhythmic contractions of the mother's uterus preceding birth (Klaus and Kennell, 1976). By following a routine after birth, the parent helps the newborn to reestablish biorhythmicity. This process is evident in the progressive increase of the co-occurrence of the mother's holding the newborn and the newborn's being in an alert state (Cassel and Sander, 1975). In addition, Cassel and Sander (1975) pointed out that mother−infant interaction allows the newborn to regulate its circadian rhythms. The newborn's apparent perception of this interaction was demonstrated by having a mother wear a mask and remain silent during one feeding when her newborn was seven days old. During the masked feeding, the infant took far less milk, and its sleep patterns were significantly disrupted (following the masked feeding) as compared with normal feedings. Thus, the mother serves as a time organizer or "time giver" for the reorganization of neonatal functions.

Interactions Originating with the Newborn. *Eye-to-Eye Contact.* Mutual gazing is an important affirmation of an emerging relationship for both parent and newborn. It is interesting to note that the ordinary distance between the mother or the father and the newborn during feeding is about twelve inches. Because the infant's visual system does not focus the eyes effectively beyond this distance, the feeding distance of twelve inches provides the ideal opportunity for mutual gazing. The significance of mutual gazing is reaffirmed in research with blind infants, whose mothers reported have difficulty "feeling close" to their newborns (Fraiberg, 1974). Infant-originated eye-to-eye contact may serve an important function as a releaser of caretaking responses (Robson, 1967). The emotional meaning of mutual gazing may result in such responses as an increasing desire to hold the newborn and an increasing enthusiasm about "our baby."

Cry. The sound of an infant crying can affect parents in a number of ways. As any parent who has heard this sound during the middle of the night can testify, it is difficult to ignore. The cry of the newborn is, like mutual gazing, a way of influencing the interaction between parent and infant. Specifically, it reduces the distance between them, so that the infant's needs can be identified and satisfied (Bowlby, 1969).

In the case of mothers who breast-feed, there is some evidence that the newborn's cry may cause a physiological change that increases the likelihood of nursing (Lind, Vuorenkoski, and Wasz-Hackert, 1973). For example, some women who breast-feed their infants report feeling their milk "come in" (the "let-down" reflex) when they hear their hungry babies crying. Using thermal (heat-sensitive) photography, Lind et al., demonstrated that fifty-four (of sixty-three) mothers showed a substantial increase in the blood flow to their breasts after they heard their babies cry.

Entrainment.

You cannot fall in love with a dishrag. (mother's comment reported in Klaus and Kennell, 1982, p. 82)

Another basic feature of the emerging attachment relationship between the parent and the newborn is the necessity for mutual perception of responses or signals such as eye movement, body movement, and speech sounds. This process of mutual following or mutual entrainment is supported by both members in the relationship.

Summary: Interactions of Parents and Newborns. We have sketched some of the separate components of the interactional system between parent and newborn. This description has been useful in demonstrating that *both* parent and infant may originate an interaction. In addition, such a perspective may help us to appreciate the important contribution of the newborn as an active rather than a passive organism.

Parent and newborn behaviors complement each other in various sensory systems. For example, infant crying helps to initiate the let-down reflex in nursing mothers. Parental use of a high-pitched voice complements the newborn's attraction to high-frequency sounds. Parental interest in the newborn's eyes fits the infant's interest in the parent's eyes and face:

Nature appears to have preferentially developed . . . the visual pathways so that these sensory and motor functions are ready for the newborn infant to receive stimulation from his mother and to interact with her. (Klaus and Kennell, 1982, p. 82)

PROGRAMS FOR FAMILIES

There is increasing evidence of a need to transfer the protection, warmth, and security of family support into the hospital setting, so that from the beginning, the emerging relationships between the family and their newborn are further enhanced and developed. If extended visiting of all immediate family members and "rooming-in" are encouraged, the family members can better learn to care for the baby. Confidence gained in the hospital during this postdelivery period provides a better base for child rearing.

Trends in Infant Care. Trends in infant care have gone through complete changes over the past fifty years. At the beginning of this century, babies were born in the home. Naturally the mother and the baby roomed together and the mother cared for the baby. The baby was breast-fed and allowed to eat when it wished to, and it was held and rocked when it appeared that it

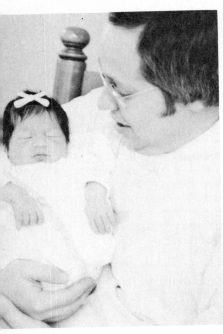

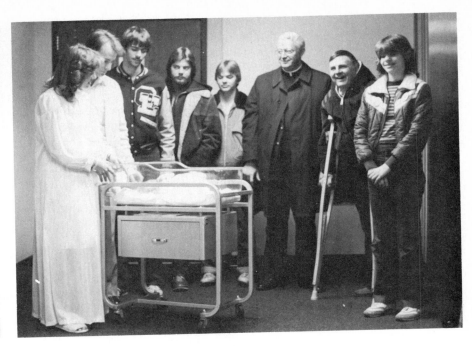

Hospital program for families.

Left photograph by Gale Schiamberg; right photograph by Darryl Jacobson

needed such attention. The father had an important part in the care of the mother and the baby.

Early in the twentieth century, infant care became increasingly strict, especially in the "scientific" 1920s, when everything was done according to schedule. Babies were fed on an inflexible schedule, were given artificial feedings according to the latest nutritional knowledge, and were allowed to cry for long periods of time, because picking them up would supposedly "spoil" them. All earlier methods of infant care were considered old-fashioned, and mothers were anxious to follow the latest scientific teachings. More and more babies were being born in hospitals, and the busy hospital staff made schedules seem even more important. There was little time to teach the mother about the care of her baby. She went home inexperienced but with a set of rules to follow. The father was considered relatively unimportant, especially during the hospitalization of the mother.

Then in the late 1930s, a change came about, with a return to many of the earlier practices. Schedules and routines became less important. The first organized effort to change infant care again began in 1942, when the Cornelian Corner was organized in Detroit, Michigan. This group was composed of a psychiatrist, a pediatrician, an obstetrician, a nurse, and workers in allied fields who planned to do research and education in child development and family life. They emphasized the importance of allowing each baby to follow its own individual schedule because it was often difficult for the baby to fit into a prearranged one. They stressed the value of such permissiveness in the development of a wholesome personality. Rooming-in, breast-feeding, and self-demand feeding schedules were given special emphasis by the Cornelians. They believed that the first step in the future development of a well-balanced, healthy adult was indulgent care for the baby.

The Birth of the Baby: An Emerging Family Relationship

Hospital Programs and Families

More and more hospitals are altering their services to give parents more information and a bigger role in decision making and to provide more homelike settings. As one hospital administrator put it, "We are treating birth as a normal process rather than a disease."

Hospitals are offering a variety of approaches to keep the mother and child together, and to bring the father and the rest of the family into the nursery. . . .

In San Francisco, the Kaiser–Permanente Medical Center offers a Family Centered Perinatal Care Program that begins with prenatal courses for both parents. A team of obstetricians, pediatricians and nurse practitioners work with the family throughout the birth period. The father attends the delivery and stays with the mother directly afterward. The mother and child are examined 12 hours after birth and are permitted to return home if all is well; in some cases, they remain for 24 hours, then are released. The nurse practitioner who was originally assigned to the mother makes daily home visits for four days afterwards

and is available for two weeks to assist the family in caring for the infant. Besides being economical and safe, the program provides concentrated and personalized care. But most important, it expedites parent–child attachment. . . .

The Booth Maternity Center in Philadelphia offers prenatal training and delivery services during labor by nurse–midwives. The physician is present only at the end of labor for infant delivery in about half the births. Full support and instruction for infant care and breast feeding are provided. Mothers are encouraged to establish physical contact with the infant as soon as possible and to nurse him or her within the first hour. An interview–questionnaire administered to new mothers indicates that the program is a success. As one mother put it, "Booth has the most natural and pleasant approach to childbirth that I have heard of in these . . . clinical times."

Reprinted by permission from S. P. Hersh and K. Levin, "How Love Begins Between Parent and Child," *Children Today*, Washington, D.C.: March–April 1978, *47*, pp. 2–6.

Rooming-in usually involves having the baby in the mother's room during a part of each day and in a central nursery for the remainder of the time.

Photographs by Darryl Jacobson

Rooming-In. Rooming-in is a hospital arrangement by which the mother and the baby are cared for in the same unit, and the father has the opportunity to care for the baby as much as he wishes, thus becoming closely acquainted with the infant. Rooming-in provides the mother with the advantages of hospital delivery and hospital care in as homelike an atmosphere as it

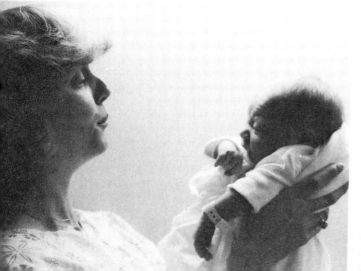

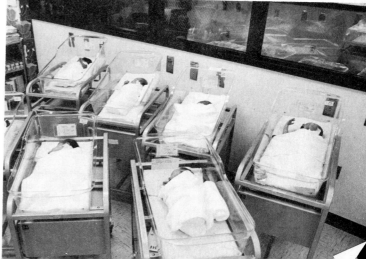

is possible to provide. This program focuses on the family, providing for the interrelationship that comes from a close association of mother, father, family, and baby. Rooming-in usually involves having the baby in the mother's room a part of each day and in a central nursery the remainder of the time. For rooming-in to be successful, the interest and cooperation of the parents and of the hospital personnel are essential, and an adequate staff for nursing care is necessary. While all mothers do not wish to have this arrangement, it is possible to provide rooming-in when requested in most hospitals.

Summary

1. *Pregnancy* and the *birth process* are neither static nor brief experiences; rather they are periods of human development filled with growth, change, and exciting enrichment. The purpose of this chapter was to examine the birth process from an interactional or systems perspective. The focus was on birth as an emerging relationship between the newborn and his or her parents.

2. The ability of parents to develop a successful relationship with the newborn depends on a number of factors. These factors include the parents' own personalities and temperaments, the response of the newborn infant to the parents, the history of interpersonal relationships of the parents with their own families of origin and with each other, past experiences with pregnancy, and the assimilation of cultural values and practices by the parents (Klaus and Kennell, 1982).

3. During pregnancy, a woman experiences two kinds of changes within herself: (1) physical and emotional changes and (2) the growth of the fetus. A number of factors may contribute to how she feels about these changes including whether there are other children in the family, the ages of the other children, whether she is living with the father, and whether the pregnancy was planned.

4. *Labor* is the process by which the baby and placenta are expelled through the birth canal. Labor involves the muscular contraction of the uterus to aid the infant in moving through the birth canal. There are three stages of labor: dilation, expulsion, and the delivery of the placenta. Two unique approaches to childbirth are the Lamaze method and the Leboyer method.

5. After the birth of the infant, many significant events happen to the mother, the father, the baby, and the relationship between parents and newborn. For parents, the birth of a first baby initiates an experience that is new to both husband and wife as individuals and as a marital pair. The newborn's features and body are quite different from what they will be later on. The baby's appearance may be surprising to a couple who have not seen a newborn before. At birth, the infant's nervous system is relatively immature. Most of the newborn's bodily functions and responses are carried out by reflex action. Newborn sensory capacities include vision, hearing, smell, taste, feeling pain, sensitivity to touch, sensitivity to rhythms, and imitative skills.

In addition to the variations in infants temperaments, there are also important variations within the daily behavior of each newborn infant. These variations in cycles of wakefulness, sleepiness, and activity are called *states*. A baby's reaction to its environment usually depends on its state. Newborn states are influenced by both internal timing mechanisms and external stimulation. The infant and parent/caretaker are an interacting system. Therefore,

The Birth of the Baby: An Emerging Family Relationship

newborn states affect parental behavior and are, in turn, affected by parental activity.

The reciprocal interaction between parent and infant in the *attachment* process is based on interactions which originate with both parent and infant. Some of the components of this *system* include touch, eye-to-eye contact, infant crying, and parental voice pitch. The contribution of the newborn to the attachment system is as an active rather than a passive organism. Parent and newborn behaviors complement each other in various sensory systems. For example, the common practice of parents using high pitched voice tones when talking to newborns and infants complements the infants attraction to high frequency sounds.

There is increasing evidence of a need to transfer the protection, warmth, and security of family support into the hospital setting. *Rooming-in* is a hospital arrangement by which the mother and the baby are cared for in the same unit and the father has the opportunity to care for the baby as much as he desires. The program focuses on the family as well as providing a home-like atmosphere in the hospital.

Questions

1. Briefly discuss both sides of the controversy of home births versus hospital births.
2. What are the factors which distinguish "real" labor from "false" labor?
3. Briefly summarize the three stages of labor.
4. What are the advantages of "prepared childbirth?"
5. Identify and briefly describe two newborn reflexes that illustrate the immaturity of the newborn's nervous system.
6. Briefly identify and describe three infant states. What is a "biological clock?"
7. Why is eye-to-eye contact important for the developing infant-caregiver relationship?

Bibliography

AMBROSE, J. A., and LEVINE, S. Discussion contribution in J. A. Ambrose (Ed.), *Stimulation in Early Infancy.* New York and London: Academic Press, 1970.

APGAR, V. Evaluation of newborn infant. *Journal of the American Medical Association,* 1958, 1988, 168.

APGAR, V., and JAMES, L. S. Further observations on the newborn scoring system. *American Journal of Diseases of Children,* 1962, 104, 419–428.

BABSON, S. G., and BENSON, R. C. *Primer on Prematurity and High Risk Pregnancy.* St. Louis: Mosby, 1966.

BECK, S. D. *Animal Photoperiodism.* New York: Holt, Rinehart and Winston, 1963.

BENEDEK, T. *Studies in Psychosomatic Medicine: The Psycho-Sexual Function in Women.* New York: Ronald Press, 1952.

BIBRING, G. L., DWYER, T. F., HUNTINGTON, T. S., and VALENSTEIN, A. F. A study of the psychological processes in pregnancy and of the earliest mother–child relationship: I. Some propositions and comments. *Psychoanalytic Study of the Child,* 1961, 16, 9–27.

BIRCH, W. G. *A Doctor Discusses Pregnancy.* Chicago: Budlong Press, 1980.

BOSTON CHILDREN'S MEDICAL CENTER. *Pregnancy, Birth, and the Newborn Baby.* New York: Delacorte, 1972.

BOSTON WOMEN'S HEALTH BOOK COLLECTIVE. *Our Bodies, Ourselves.* New York: Simon & Schuster, 1971.

BOWLBY, J. *Attachment and Loss,* Vol. 1. New York: Basic Books, 1969.

BRAINE, M. D. S., HEIMER, C. B., WORTIS, H., and FREEDMAN, A. M. Factors associated with impairment of the early development of premature. *Monographs of the Society for the Research in Child Development,* 1966, *31,* 139.

BRAZELTON, T. B. Psychophysiologic reaction in the neonate. II: Effects of maternal medication on the neonate and his behavior. *Journal of Pediatrics,* 1961, *53,* 513–518.

BRAZELTON, T. B., KOSLOWSKI, B., and MAIN, M. The origins of reciprocity. In M. Lewis and L. A. Rosenblum (Eds.), *The Effect of the Infant on Its Caregiver.* New York: Wiley, 1974.

BUNDY, R. S. Discrimination of sound localization cues in young infants, *Child Development,* 1980, *51,* 292–294.

CAPLAN, G. Patterns of parental response to the crisis of premature birth. *Psychiatry,* 1960, *23,* 365–374.

CARPENTER, G. Mother's face and the newborn. *New Scientist,* March 1974, *21,* 742–744.

CASSEL, Z. K., and SANDER, L. W. Neonatal recognition processes and attachment: The masking experiment. Presented at the Society for Research in Child Development, Denver, 1975.

COHEN, L. B., DELOACHE, J. S., and STRAUSS, M. Infant visual perception. In J. Osofsky (Ed.), *Handbook of Infant Development.* New York: Wiley, 1979.

CONDON, W. Speech makes babies move. *New Scientist,* June 1974, *6,* 624–627.

CONDON, W. S., and SANDER, L. W. Neonate movement is synchronized with adult speech: interactional participation and language acquisition. *Science,* 183, 99–101, 1974(a).

CONDON, W. S., and SANDER, L. W. Synchrony demonstrated between movements of the neonate and adult speech, *Child Development,* 45, 456–462, 1974(b).

CROOK, K., and LIPSITT, L. P. Neonatal nutritive sucking: Effects of taste stimulation upon sucking rhythm and heart rate. *Child Development,* 1976, *47,* 518–522.

ERLICH, S. The psychological impact of new parenthood. In The Boston Children's Medical Center, *Pregnancy, Birth and the Newborn Baby.* New York: Delacorte Press, 1972, 223–229.

EWY, D., and EWY, R. *Preparation for Childbirth.* New York: New American Library, 1970.

FANTZ, R. L. The origins of form perceptions. *Scientific American,* 1961, *204,* 66–72.

FANTZ, R. L. Visual perceptions from birth as shown by patterned selectivity. *Annals of the New York Academy of Sciences,* 1965, *118,* 793–814.

FANTZ, R. L., FAGAN, J. F., and MIRANDA, S. B. Early visual selectivity. In L. B. Cohen and P. Salapatek (Eds.), *Infant Perception: From Sensation to Cognition,* Vol. 1. New York and London: Academic Press, 1975.

FIELD, J., MUIR, D., PILON, R., SINCLAIR, M., and DODWELL, P. Infants' orientation to lateral sounds from birth to three months. *Child Development,* 1980, *51,* 295–298.

FRAIBERG, S. Blind infants and their mothers: An examination of the sign system. In M. Lewis and L. A. Rosenblum (Eds.), *The Effect of the Infant on Its Caregiver.* New York: Wiley, 1974.

FROMMER, E. A., and O'SHEA, G. Prenatal identification of women liable to have problems in managing their infants. *British Journal of Psychiatry,* 1973, *123,* 149–156.

GUTTMACHER, A. F. *Pregnancy, Birth and Family Planning.* New York: New American Library, 1973.

HAITH, M. M., KESSEN, W., and COLLINS, D. Response of the human infant to level of complexity of intermittent visual movement. *Journal of Experimental Child Psychology,* 1969, *7,* 52.

HARPER, P. A., FISCHER, L. K., and RIDER, R. V. Neurological and intellectual status of prematures at three to five years of age. *Journal of Pediatrics,* 1959, *55,* 679–690.

HELFER, R., and KEMPE, C. (Eds.). *The Battered Child.* Chicago: U. of Chicago, 1968.

HELLBRUGGE, T. The development of circadian rhythms in infants. *Cold Spring Harbor Symposium on Quantitative Biology,* 1960, *25,* 311–323.

The Birth of the Baby: An Emerging Family Relationship

HERSH, S. P., and LEVIN, K. How love begins between parent and child. *Children Today*, Washington, D.C.: March–April 1978, *47*, 2–6.

HUTT, S. J., HUTT, C., LENARD, H. G., BERNUTH, H. V., and MUNTJEWERFF, W. J. Auditory discrimination at birth. In S. J. Hutt and C. Hutt (Eds.), *Early Human Development*. Oxford: Oxford U.P., 1973.

HUTT, S. J., LENARD, H. G., and PRECHTL, H. F. R. Influence of "state" upon responsivity to stimulation. In S. J. Hutt and C. Hutt (Eds.), *Early Human Development*. Oxford: Oxford U. P., 1973.

HUTT, S. J., LENARD, H. G., and PRECHTL, H. F. R. Psychophysiology of the newborn. In L. P. Lipsitt and H. W. Reese (Eds.), *Advances in Child Development and Behavior*. New York: Academic Press, 1969.

KLAUS, M., JERAULD, R., KREGER, N., McALPINE, W., STEFFA, M., and KENNELL, J. Maternal attachment: Importance of the first post-partum days. *New England Journal of Medicine*, 1972, *286*, 460.

KLAUS, M., and KENNELL, J. H. Human maternal behavior at first contact with her young. *Pediatrics*, 1970, *46*(2), 187–192.

KLAUS, M. H., and KENNELL, J. H. *Parent–Infant Bonding* (2nd ed.). St. Louis: Mosby, 1982.

KLOOSTERMAN, G. J. Obstetrics in the Netherlands: A survival or a challenge? Paper presented at the Tunbridge Wells Meeting on Problems in Obstetrics, organized by the Medical Information Unit of the Spastics Society, 1975.

KNOBLOCH, H., PASAMANICK, B., HARPER, P. A., and RIDER, R. V. The effect of prematurity on health and growth. *American Journal of Public Health*, 1959, *49*, 1164–1173.

KORNER, A. Neonatal startles, smiles, erections, and reflexes as related to state, sex and individuality. *Child Development*, 1969, *40*, 1039–1053.

LAMB, M. *The Role of the Father in Child Development*. New York: Wiley, 1976.

LAMB, M., and STEPHENSON, M. Father–infant relationships. *Youth and Society*, March 1978, 277–298.

LANG, R. *Birth book*. Ben Lomond, Calif.: Genesis Press, 1972.

LEBOYER, F. *Birth Without Violence*. New York: Knopf, 1975.

LIND, J., VUORENKOSKI, V., and WASZ-HÖCKERT, O., The Effect of Cry Stimulus on the Temperature of the Lactating Breast Primipara. A Thermographic Study. In N. Morris (Ed.), *Psychosomatic Medicine in Obstetrics and Gynecology*. Basel: S. Karger, 1972.

LIPSITT, L. P., ENGEN, T., and KAYE, H. Olfactory responses and adaptation in the human neonate. *Journal of Comparative Physiology and Psychology*, 1963, *56*, 3–5.

LIPSITT, L. P., and LEVY, N. Electrocaudal threshhold in the neonate. *Child Development*, 1959, *30*, 547–554.

LIPTON, E. L., STENSCHNEIDER, A., and RICHMOND, J. B. The autonomic nervous system in early life. *New England Journal of Medicine*, 1965, *273*, 201–208.

MACFARLANE, A. *The Psychology of Childbirth*. Cambridge, Mass.: Harvard U. P., 1977.

MACFARLANE, J. A. Olfaction in the development of social preferences in the human neonate. In *Parent–Infant Interaction*. Amsterdam: CIBA Foundation Symposium 33, New Series, ASO, 1975.

March of Dimes Birth Defects Foundation, Facts/1982, Statistical Tables and Charts, Figure 1, p. 31, 1982.

MATERNITY CENTER ASSOCIATION. *A Baby Is Born*. New York: Maternity Center Association, 1964.

MAUER, D., and LEWIS, T. Peripheral discrimination by 3-month-old infants, *Child Development*, 1979, *50*, 276–279.

MCCLEARY, E. H. *New Miracles of Childbirth*. New York: McKay, 1974.

MELTZOV, A. Imitation of facial and manual gestures by human neonates, *Science*, 1977, *198*, October 7, 1977, 75–78.

MUIR, D., and FIELD, J. Newborn infants orient to sounds, *Child Development*, 1979, *50*, 431–436.

PARKE, R. Father–infant interaction. In M. H. Klaus, T. Leger, and M. A. Trause (Eds.), *Maternal Attachment and Mothering Disorders*. Sausalito, Calif.: Johnson and Johnson, 1974.

Pratt, K. C., Nelson, A. K., and Sun, K. H. *The Behavior of the Newborn Infant.* Columbus: Ohio State University, 1930.

Prechtl, H. F. R., and Beintema, D. Neurological examination of the full-term newborn infant. *Clinics in Developmental Medicine,* No. 12. London: Spastics International Medical Publications and Heinemann, 1964.

Richards, M. P. M., Bernal, J. F., and Brackbill, Y. Early behavioral differences: Gender or circumcision. *Developmental Psychobiology,* 1976, *9,* 89–95.

Robson, K. S. The role of eye-to-eye contact in maternal–infant attachment. *Journal of Child Psychology and Psychiatry,* 1967, *8,* 13–25.

Rubin, R. Maternal touch. *Nursing Outlook,* 1963, *11,* 828–831.

Salk, L. The role of the heartbeat in the relationship between mother and infant. *Scientific American,* March 1973, 24–29.

Sander, L. W., Stechler, G., Burns, P., and Julia, J. Early mother–infant interaction and 24 hour patterns of activity and sleep. *Journal of the American Academy of Child Psychiatry,* 1970, *9,* 103–123.

Solkoff, N., Yaffe, S., Weintraub, D., and Blase, B. Effects of handling on the subsequent development of premature infants. *Developmental Psychology,* 1969, *1,* 765–768.

Stechler, G., and Lantz, E. Some observations on attention and arousal in the human infant. *Journal of the Academy of Child Psychiatry,* 1966, *5,* 517.

U.S. Department of Health and Human Services. Public Health Service. National Center for Health Statistics. Advance Report on Final Natality Statistics, 1980, Vol. 31, No. 8 Supplement, Nov. 30, 1982.

Van den Daele, L. D. Modification of infant state by treatment in a rockerbox. *Journal of Psychology,* 1970, *74,* 161–165.

Wertheimer, M. Psychomotor coordination of auditory–visual space at birth. *Science,* 1961, *134,* 1692.

Wolff, P. The causes, controls, and organizations of behavior in the newborn. *Psychological Issues,* 1966, *5*(1) (Whole No. 17), 1–105.

Suggested Readings

Broen, D. *The Birth of a First Child.* London: Tavistock Publications, 1975. A very interesting examination of the results of an in-depth psychological examination of fifty women experiencing motherhood late in life and motherhood early in life.

Kitzinger, S., and Davies, J. (Eds). *The Place of Birth.* Oxford: Oxford University Press, 1978. An interesting, scholarly book on the advantages and disadvantages of home and hospital delivery.

Klaus, M. H., and Kennell, J. H. *Parent–Infant Bonding* (Second edition) St. Louis: Mosley, 1982. A very timely book on the genesis of the earliest relationships that a baby has with its caregivers including the factors that inhibit and enhance this relationship.

Leboyer, F. *Birth Without Violence.* New York: Knopf, 1975. A discussion of a novel approach to childbirth by a French obstetrician—an interesting, well-illustrated and poetic book to read.

Lewin, R. (Ed). *Child Alive.* New York: Doubleday, 1975. A collection of very readable and interesting articles by leading child development specialists on the surprising competence of babies.

MacFarlane, A. *The Psychology of Childbirth.* Cambridge, Mass.: Harvard University Press, 1977. An excellent introduction to the birth process, techniques of delivery, newborn skills and the relationship between newborn and caregiver.

6

Infancy and Toddlerhood

There is at present no known substitute for a family environment for child rearing.

M. D. S. Ainsworth, 1973, p. 77

The Infant in the Context of the Family System

The infant in the context of the family.

Photograph by Shan Rucinski

Before beginning our discussion of the infant in the context of the family, it is important for us to understand the general picture of *infancy as a system*. Figure 6.1 indicates that the most direct and most immediate context of infancy is the family. As we shall see later in this chapter, the relationship between the infant and the family is mutual or bi-directional (as indicated by the two-way arrows in the diagram). For example, this means that the influence of the infant on the family (e.g., infant characteristics and behaviors such as crying or smiling) is just as important for infant development as the influence of the family on the infant (e.g., parent characteristics and behaviors, such as level of education or feeding practices). In fact, traditional research and theory on infancy has tended to emphasize infant development as the one-way result of parents influencing their offspring.

While the mutual relationship or dyad between the infant and his/her parent is a major focus of this chapter, the *systems approach* to infancy suggests something more. That vital something is the mutual and dynamic relationship between the family of the infant and the social system in which that family exists. This social system includes at least the following components: (1) the *neighborhood and community* in which the family lives (including friendships, support networks, and services), (2) the parental work setting (the relationship of work and family is explored in the Application Box—Work and Families in this chapter on p. 185), (3) the government structure and related social policies which affect families of infants (e.g., social policies which encourage or discourage the development of quality day care programs for infants), and (4) educational institutions and programs. As in the case of the relationship between infant and parent(s), the interaction between the social system and the family of the infant is mutual and bi-directional (see Figure 6.1).

Often a consideration of the family generates strong emotions. In the words of the poet Robert Frost, the family is "the place where, when you go there, they have to take you in" (Frost, 1939). Likewise it is the place where rejection and conflict hurt the most. Over the last twenty-five years, many profound changes have occurred in American society that have had, in turn, a significant impact on the family. Some of these changes are large increases in the number of working mothers (both full- and part-time), increasing numbers of single-parent families headed by women, and changing attitudes of women regarding their place in society. The effects of these social changes on children and families include the following (Bureau of Labor Statistics, 1983):

- In 1982, 32 million children, or 55 percent of all children under 18 years of age, had a mother in the labor force (see Figure 6.2).
- The mothers of more than 45 percent of all youngsters below age 6 and of nearly 60 percent of those 6 to 17 years were in the labor force (see Figure 6.2).
- These proportions have grown rapidly in the last decade as it has become more acceptable for mothers to work (see Figure 6.2).

180

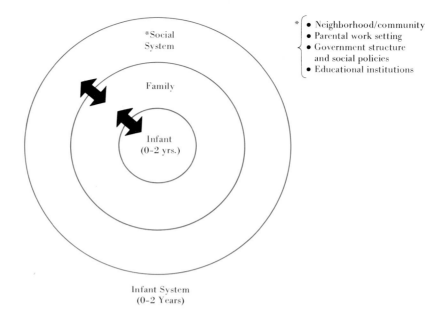

*Social
System

Family

Infant
(0-2 yrs.)

* • Neighborhood/community
  • Parental work setting
  • Government structure
    and social policies
  • Educational institutions

Infant System
(0-2 Years)

FIGURE 6.1   The system of infancy.

- In March 1982, 26 million wives, or 51 percent of all married women, were working or looking for work. Twenty years earlier, only a third were in the labor force (see Figure 6.3).
- Over half the growth in married women's labor force participation occurred during the 1970s, largely among those with school-aged children. Between 1970 and 1980, the labor force participation rate of wives whose only children were 6 to 17 years old rose from 49 percent to 62 percent. However, since 1980, most of the increase has been among those with preschool children.

FIGURE 6.2   Children with mothers in the labor force as a proportion of all children by age of children, 1972 and 1982. The proportion of children with mothers in the labor force has grown to more than half.

From Bureau of Labor Statistics, "Women at Work: A Chartbook," Washington, D.C.: U.S. Department of Labor, April 1983, Bulletin 2168, p. 21.

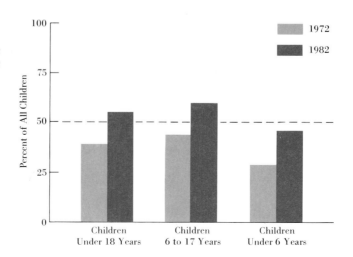

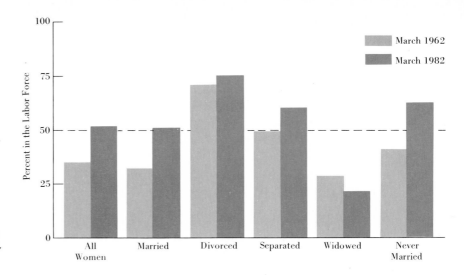

FIGURE 6.3 Labor force participation rates of women by marital status, 1962 and 1982. Half of all married women are now in the labor force.

From Bureau of Labor Statistics, "Women at Work: A Chartbook," Washington, D.C.: U.S. Department of Labor, April 1983, Bulletin 2168, p. 23.

- The proportions of divorced, separated, and never-married women in the labor force in 1982 were also greater than they had been 20 years earlier. Although the *increase* was smallest among divorced women, they remained far more likely to be in the labor force than women of any other marital status (see Figure 6.3).
- One of every six families was maintained by a woman in March 1982. During the past decade, the number of families in which no husband was present climbed steadily, reflecting the increased frequency of marital breakups and children born outside of marriage (see Figure 6.4).

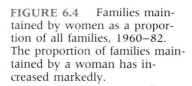

FIGURE 6.4 Families maintained by women as a proportion of all families, 1960–82. The proportion of families maintained by a woman has increased markedly.

From Bureau of Labor Statistics, "Women at Work: A Chartbook," Washington, D.C.: U.S. Department of Labor, April 1983, Bulletin 2168, p. 25.

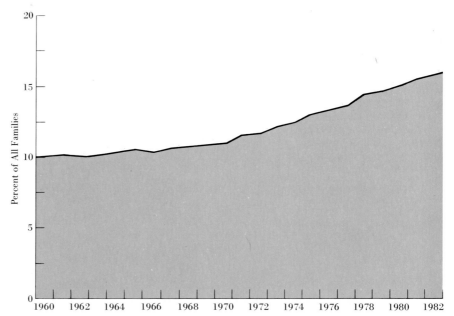

Infancy and Toddlerhood

- The growth in the number of families maintained by women far out-paced that of other families. From 1972 to 1982, their number increased by 57 percent to a total of 9.7 million, compared with a 10-percent increase for other families (see Figure 6.4).
- Three out of five women maintaining families were in the labor force in 1982. These women had, on average, completed fewer years of school than wives and were concentrated in lower skilled, lower paying jobs.

From Bureau of Labor Statistics, "Women at Work: A Chartbook" Washington, D.C.: U.S. Department of Labor, April 1983, Bulletin 2168, pp. 20–25).

WHY LOOK AT THE FAMILY?

Therefore, there are at least two major reasons for us to begin our discussion of infancy and toddlerhood with an analysis of the family.

In the first place, the family is *the* place in which early development largely occurs. Some have suggested that the social and cognitive level that the preschool child possesses on entering the formal school is largely a result of the child's experiences in the family (Schaefer, 1972). The interrelatedness of family and child is emphasized in the following statement:

A second major issue is that problems of children are inseparable from the problems of those who are primarily responsible for their care and nurture. The characteristics of each child's environment are largely determined by the environment and circumstances of one or more adults, including, but not restricted, to the child's parents. It is therefore axiomatic that one cannot attempt to help children without influencing those adults, whether intentionally or not. This is especially true in the case of very young children because of the degree of their dependence and need for close psychological attachment to a particular adult. (*Advisory Committee on Child Development*, 1976, p. 10)

In the second place, there are (as already indicated) changes occurring in families that have resulted, in part, from broader social changes. These changes have affected the ability of the family, as a unit, to cope and function. Changes in the family directly affect the children.

WHAT IS A FAMILY?

The family has been defined in many ways, and as we will see, its specific nature varies from one culture to another (Adams, 1975; Kephart, 1977; Leslie, 1973). Almost every known society has some type of family organization that is intermediate between the individual and the larger social community (Murdoch, 1949). Ordinarily, by *family* we mean a group of adults and children who live together for an extended period of time.

Most human beings belong to at least two types of family groups. The family that a child is born into is called the *family of orientation*, and the family formed by that child (usually through marriage) is called the *family of procreation* (Perry and Perry, 1977). Membership in the family of orientation is by birth, whereas membership in the family of procreation is by choice.

In addition to defining families by means of personal affiliation, one may also define families according to their structure. Some types of family structures follow.

The extended family.

Photograph by Wayne Mason

The Nuclear Family. The nuclear, or conjugal, family consists of a married couple and their children (if any). In our society, the general expectation is that the husband, the wife, and their children (if any) will live in a household or home that is separate from the family of orientation. The nuclear family is more frequently a common family structure in industrialized or technologically advanced societies. The reason for the co-occurrence is the mobility of the nuclear family. In a society—such as ours—where heads of households move about the country to different jobs (or to the same type of job in a different location), the mobility of the nuclear family is a valuable asset.

The nuclear family is not, however, without its problems—or, at least, potential problems. The strength of the nuclear family—its independence and mobility—is also a potential source of difficulty. It has been suggested that the modern nuclear family tends to be isolated from the broad network of social support inherent in the extended family. The degree or nature of such isolation is controversial.

The Extended Family. The extended family includes the nuclear family and any number of other persons, related through marriage or birth, who share a single residence or live very close by. A typical extended family might include at least three generations: grandparents; two or more of their grown children and their spouses; and the sons and daughters of these children. In such extended families, it is common for the grandmother or the grandfather to serve as the head of the entire family group.

Extended families are more commonly found in agricultural societies or preindustrial societies. Such family structures fit well with the needs of societies in which the family is the center of occupational and vocational effort. Where many hands are needed for the work of the family around the home or the farm, the extended family has been (and continues to be, in some societies and in some subcultures within our own society) an effective means of organizing the activities of family life and work. In the United States, extended families may be found, to some extent, among agricultural people as well as among the urban poor. In some farm communities and urban neighborhoods,

Work and Families

The practice of flexible working hours or *flextime* (a word coined by Willi Haller in Germany) is now in widespread operation throughout Europe and is gradually being introduced in some United States companies. Within specified limits, employees choose their own hours. There is already evidence of its positive effects. (Among other benefits, when enough organizations in a community institute flextime, it lessens traffic congestion and cuts down on commuting time.)

Close-up of a worker.

Photograph by Darryl Jacobson

In one survey of workers in a Swiss company, 35 percent (including more men than women) used the flextime hours for spending more time with their families. Married women tended to use their flextime hours to provide more time for domestic chores (in keeping with the highly traditional sex role allocation in Switzerland). Almost 95 percent of the 1,500 employees surveyed were in favor of flextime—45 percent because of the way it improved the organization of private life. Not surprisingly, married women with children were the most enthusiastic of all groups [Racki, 1975].

For working women in traditional kinds of families, single parents with sole responsibility for children, or men who expect to share family tasks, flextime seems to permit a more comfortable synchrony of work and family responsibilities. Social policy as well as scientific knowledge would benefit from further research on the use and effects of flextime. . . .

Too often in the past we have viewed families in a vacuum, as a realm unto themselves. Only now are we beginning to consider how public policy and such institutions as employing organizations may be responsible for what happens, or does not happen, in private life.

Structural rearrangements that provide people with more flexibility and options may be a first step in helping families. These would include the use of flextime; more flexible leaves and sabbaticals; greater availability of day care; income supports; explicit focus on communication about work events and work culture to workers' families; and reduction in the number of low autonomy, low opportunity jobs that create emotional tensions at home. Major changes in the world of work and the structure of work organizations may, indeed, turn out to have more profound effects on the quality of family life than all the attempts to influence individual behavior.

Reprinted from R. M. Kanter, ''Jobs and Families: Impact of Working Roles on Family Life,'' *Children Today*, Washington, D.C., March–April 1978, *45*, pp. 11–15.

families exist in the form of closely related persons staying in the same neighborhood or farm area. Such extended families carry on much of their social life together even though they do not live under the same roof. A child growing up in such a family finds it quite natural to have many aunts, uncles, and cousins living within a few blocks or a few miles. Such family structures provide the opportunity for family members to gather many opinions before making an important decision, such as marriage or a vocation.

There is a tendency to glorify the extended family as another symbol of "the good old days." Nonetheless there do appear to be positive advantages. A main advantage of the extended family, compared with the nuclear family, is that it gives family members—children and adults alike—more choices of people with whom to have close relationships.

The One-Parent Family. The one-parent family usually emerges from the breakup of a nuclear family, either through divorce or when one parent dies or leaves the family. Usually females are the heads of one-parent families. As the single-parent family is becoming more prevalent in our society, it is increasingly being treated as a normal family rather than as a damaged version of the nuclear family.

Single parenthood appears to be associated with age, sex, and income level. Figure 6.4 illustrates the dramatic increase of one-parent families maintained by women as a proportion of all families. In addition, these single-parent households with female heads comprise both a larger and an increasing proportion of families at lower income levels.

Are there more adverse characteristics associated with one-parent homes than with two-parent homes? One of the assumptions of many social scientists and lay people is that one-parent homes (sometimes called fatherless or broken homes) are more commonly associated with such problems as juvenile delinquency, low school achievement, and inadequate sex-role identification (particularly with a male model). It should be noted that the labels "fatherless" or "broken" appear to suggest a deficiency that may or may not be real. Although much of the research about the potential problems of the single-parent family is not conclusive, there does appear to be sufficient reason to reject blanket generalizations about the consequences of child development in single-parent families (Herzog and Sudia, 1973). For example, there is *not* conclusive and unequivocal evidence that for such dimensions of personality development as juvenile delinquency, school achievement, and masculine identity, the single-parent family fares any worse—or any better—than the two-parent family. The functioning of the family appears to be a more significant influence on the development of the child in the family than the simple factor of the number of parents in the home. Family functioning includes such features as the general family climate, the characteristics of individual family members (including the coping skills of the parent who is present in a single-parent family), the interactions of family members, and also the general circumstances or the environment of the family.

WHAT DO FAMILIES DO?

We have demonstrated that the family is an important institution that may take different forms. The major function is to *mediate*, or to be an intermedi-

What do families do?

Photograph by Darryl Jacobson

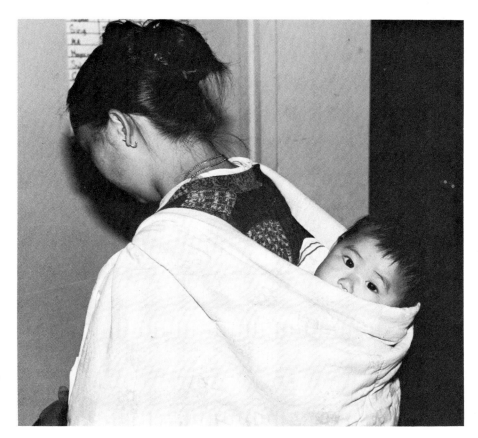

The family is an important institution that may take different forms.

Photograph by Sylvia Byers

ary, between the larger society or culture and the individual family member. Although this statement helps us to understand what families do *in general*, we can gain a better perspective of the significance of the family by examining its more *specific functions*.

FAMILY FUNCTIONS

1. *Economic cooperation and division of labor.* A basic problem that each family must deal with is the provision of food, shelter, and other amenities of life for its members. These economic responsibilities are accomplished in most societies through some sort of division of labor; that is, various family activities become the primary responsibility of certain members of the family unit. For example, a traditional division of labor in our society is that the husband is responsible for providing material goods for the family, and the woman keeps house and cares for the children. This is obviously not the *only* possible division of family labor. In fact, this "traditional" pattern is probably at the root of many of the changes—and the demands for change—that are taking place.

    Because of single-parent status or the need for a career or the need to supplement family income, women in increasing numbers have entered the work force (see Figure 6.3). In many families, the husband's

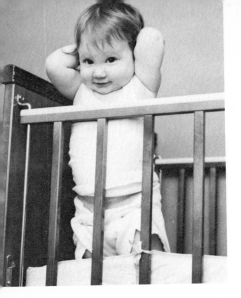

Where children are present, the family is the primary institution for their care and socialization.

Photographs by Irving Rader

income may not be sufficient, so the wife may go to work to help the family maintain the desired standard of living or to help pay for a child's college expenses.

In a society where the "traditional" pattern of family organization has come under question, more women are free to pursue their own careers if they are so inclined. Such *dual-career* households may have such patterns of organization as sharing the homemaking and child-care responsibilities (in addition to sharing the income-maintenance functions). Another reason that some women work outside the home is personal preference. They would rather work outside the home than remain at home all day.

The newer options of family organization have at least two major consequences:

- As a result of the sharing of the separated responsibilities inherent in the "traditional" division of labor, there is a shifting emphasis to shared decision-making power. When the wife works, the husband no longer has absolute (if it ever was absolute) control of finances and financial decisions.
- As a result of the increasing number of women in the work force and the larger number of choices for these women, unmarried women may perceive more options for themselves. For example, an unmarried woman who has a good job is not dependent on marriage and raising children for her identity.

2. *Care for and socialization of children.* Where children are present, the family is the primary institution for their care and socialization. Human infants and children are dependent on their parents for physical care and psychological support for a considerable period after birth. A central function of the family is the *socialization* of its children. Socialization is the process of teaching the child what he or she needs to know to be a member of society. This knowledge includes facts, skills, values, and attitudes toward society, adults, and people in general. Over the last hundred years, the socialization function has come to be shared with the school, although the primary responsibility still resides with the family.

3. *Legitimizing sexual relations.* This function is perhaps one of the most controversial. To the extent that marriage and the family make legitimate and acceptable a sexual relationship only between married partners, this function comes into collision with the sexual norms of some other segments of society. For example, some people find it appropriate to engage in sex before marriage if they are in love, have made an emotional commitment to one another, and/or have plans to get married. The advent of contraceptives such as "the pill" has made it possible to prevent unwanted births.

According to tradition, however, husband and wife are expected to have sexual relations only with each other. Tradition and law also rule out sexual relationships between persons with certain degrees of kinship. In addition, homosexual and lesbian relationships are sometimes viewed as inappropriate or even "abnormal." These views have become highly controversial.

4. *Reproduction.* Regardless of the structure that the family takes and re-

gardless of the rules that govern sexual relationships, a primary and undeniable function of the family has been reproduction. Throughout most of human history, many societies needed to produce a great number of babies. The reason, of course, was that the human life span was shorter than it now is, and infant mortality was higher. Because so many children died either in infancy or in early childhood, it made sense to have large families.

With improvements in modern medicine, better nutrition, and improved public health measures, the need for families to have many children has dramatically changed. In a world of overpopulation, families are being encouraged to have fewer children.

5. *Provision of status and role.* The family provides the child with an initial notion of who he or she is, as well as what his or her position is in the social system. What the family provides is only a beginning but, nonetheless, an important one. Social status is assigned on the basis of family attributes (e.g., where the family lives, parental income, parental occupation) over which the individual has no control. This initial status is called *ascribed status.* A child's status is based on the status of the family into which he or she is born. This notion of ascribed status is sometimes difficult to accept for people reared in a democratic society that values hard work and achievement.

There is, however, a second mode of gaining status—*achieved status.* Achieved status is accomplished through an individual's own efforts. Whereas ascribed status is largely beyond the control of the individual, achieved status is based on what the individual *does* with what he or she *can* control. Whereas ascribed status is conferred through the family, achieved status is ordinarily attained outside the family through peer, school, and work activities.

In addition to status, family membership usually provides the individual with one or more *roles*, or patterns of expected behavior. For example, there are certain kinds of behavior that are appropriate or expected (in a given family) of someone who fills the role of the father, the brother, the sister, the wife, the daughter, or the son. Most family roles are *ascribed* in the sense that family members are expected to behave in certain ways. In recent years, as we have seen, many people are moving away from "traditional" roles and are attempting to develop more flexible roles with a wider range of possible behavior. For example, fathers help with infant care and household chores, and mothers help earn a living.

6. *Emotional support and companionship.* Human beings need not only economic support—food, clothing, and shelter—but also satisfying and meaningful relationships with other human beings. They need people with whom they can share their successes, their failures, their joys, their sorrows, and all that comprises the vast array of human emotional experiences. In a society that has become increasingly task-oriented, mobile, complex, and fragmented, such *primary* relationships have become increasingly difficult to attain. Because of the apparent predominance of impersonal relationships in the world of business, school, and work, many people consider the intimacy and permanence of family relationships the most important function of the family.

Physical and Motor Development

PHYSICAL GROWTH

The physical growth of a baby is nothing short of remarkable. At birth, the average baby is about twenty inches long and weighs seven to seven and one-half pounds. During the first year of life, there is an astonishing growth spurt. Body length increases by almost a third, and weight usually *triples*. Thus at the end of the first year, the "average" baby is twenty-eight to thirty inches in length and weighs nineteen to twenty-five pounds (see Figures 6.5

FIGURE 6.5 Iowa Growth Curves for Boys. The upper curves show average weight gain in boys from birth to six years of age. The lower curves show the average increase in height for boys. These graphs can be used to assess the growth of individual children.

Copyright The University of Iowa.

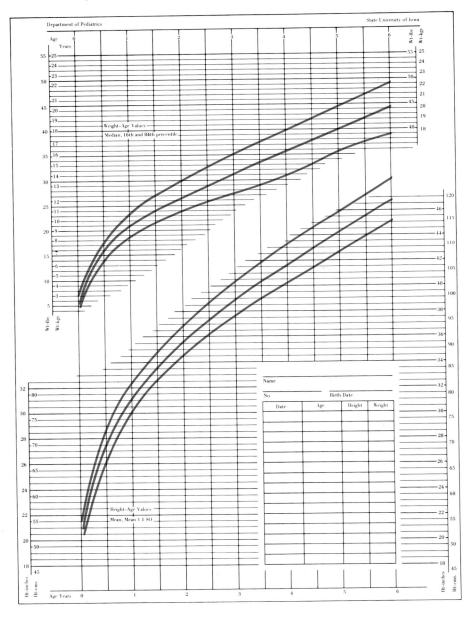

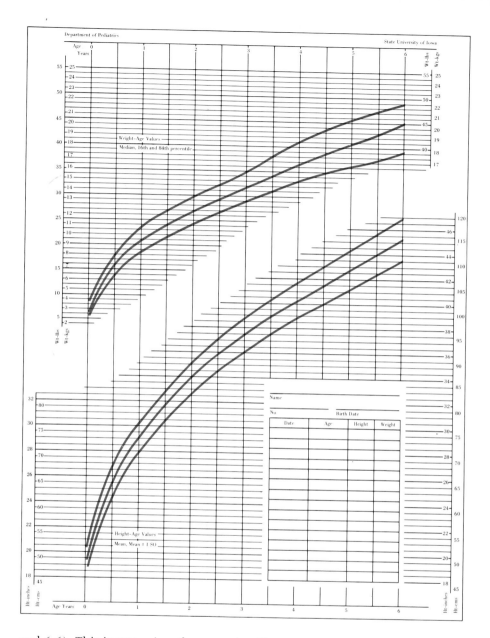

FIGURE 6.6 Iowa Growth Curves for Girls. The upper curves show average weight gain for girls from birth to six years. The lower curves show the average increase in height for girls.

Copyright The University of Iowa.

and 6.6). This increase is rather amazing if one were to imagine an adult, six feet tall and weighing 180 pounds, who increased his height by one-third and tripled his weight.

Skeletal Development. All of the bones of the body originate from soft cartilage, which, over a period of time, becomes ossified or hardened into bone by the deposit of various minerals. The process of bone ossification begins during the prenatal period and extends, for some bones, into late adolescence. Because most infant bones are not ossified, they are softer, more pliable, and more reactive to pressure and sudden movements. Parents should be careful in handling children because bones can be pulled out of their sockets or deformed.

Muscle Development. The neonate has all the muscle fibers it will ever have. These fibers are small in relation to the overall size of the infant. However, there is continuous growth in muscle length, breadth, and thickness until adulthood. At that time, the weight of the muscles is forty times what it was at birth. The striped or skeletal muscles (voluntary muscles) of the body are not completely under the infant's control during the first year of life. Therefore, the infant does not yet have efficient energy regulation and tires rapidly. As is true of the bones, different muscle groups grow at different rates. There is a general tendency for the muscles near the head and neck to develop earlier than the muscles of the torso, arms, and legs. This is an example of the *cephalocaudal principle* of development, from the head to the feet.

APPLICATION BOX

Sudden Infant Death Syndrome (SIDS) or Crib Death

The majority of infant deaths occur during the first few days of life and are typically related to maternal factors such as poor prenatal care, poor health, or malnutrition. After the first month of life, however, the majority of infant deaths are due to accidental or "unexpected" causes such as burns, suffocation, poisoning, or Sudden Infant Death Syndrome (SIDS). The most frequent cause of unexpected death in infants during the first year of life is SIDS or crib death.

CAUSES OF SIDS

There has been considerable speculation and some research on the cause(s) of SIDS. To date there are no conclusive answers and many hypotheses. Part of the problem is that the SIDS diagnosis is quite general and is applied when parents discover that their baby has died and there is no apparent or recognizable cause of death.

Since many SIDS deaths are frequently associated with mild respiratory difficulties or minor colds, some investigators have examined the relationship between respiratory/breathing processes and SIDS. It is a common observation that some infants may stop breathing for a very brief time during sleep. These pauses in breathing are called *apnea* (Baker and McGinty, 1979). In one study it was found that a high frequency of apneic episodes was associated with lower developmental test scores for sensorimotor activity at nine months (Black, Steinschneider, and Sheehe, 1979). This apparent connection between apnea and motor development has been expanded on by other investigators who have suggested that SIDS victims may suffer from a specific sensorimotor deficit which prevents their recovery from apneic pauses. That is, since almost all infants have some apneic pauses and manage to recover from them, some researchers have suggested that SIDS victims may be unable to make the appropriate motor movements and heart rate changes which would make recovery from apnea possible. (Lipsitt, 1979; Lipsitt, Sturges and Burke, 1979). There is some evidence that this motor deficit for control of breathing may be due to an inadequate perinatal (the period from one month before birth to about one month after birth) environment including a lack of oxygen or genetic factors which result in limited motor control over breathing (Naeye, 1980).

In addition to respiratory factors several other possible causes for SIDS have been suggested. Infant *botulism* or food poisoning (to which infants are very susceptible) has been known to affect the nervous system and result in paralysis of vital functions including respiration (Marx, 1978). Infant botulism is caused by a poison from a spore that may be airborne or that may be found on raw vegetables and fruits. Typically, it is not recommended that infants under twelve months of age be given these foods (Marx, 1978).

Another possible cause of SIDS is heat. Some SIDS victims have been found dressed far too warmly at the time of death (Stanton, Scott, and Downhan, 1980). It is possible that these infants had symptoms similar to heat stroke.

While genetic factors and the lack of oxygen in the perinatal period have been implicated as possible systemic (affecting the entire body) explanations for limited motor control of breathing, it is also possible that these factors are related to the inability of SIDS victims to cope with toxicity in foods or with heat. Other systemic factors have also been suggested as underlying causes for the increased susceptibility of SIDS victims to breathing problems, heat, and mild toxicity. These factors are a deficiency in a B complex vitamin called *biotin* and a hormonal imbalance (Chacon and Tildon, 1981).

PREVENTION OF SIDS

Currently, there is neither a sure method of preventing SIDS nor is there any medical treatment for the problem. However, it is possible to identify some infants who may be at risk for SIDS for the following reasons: a high rate of apneic episodes, siblings who died of SIDS, a vitamin B deficiency, an hormonal imbalance, or perinatal oxygen deprivation.

If infants can be identified as being at risk for SIDS, it may be possible to do something. One approach to preventing SIDS deaths that has been tried with some success is the home use of an electronic monitoring unit. The unit is composed of a monitor about the size of a cigar box and a soft cloth belt which is placed around the infant's chest. The belt contains sensors which measure breathing and heartbeat, relaying this information to the monitor which then detects any potentially life-threatening breathing or heartbeat episodes. The monitor emits an alarm if the infant has an irregular heart rate or stops breathing during sleep. The decision to implement such home monitoring is a complex one both for the medical staff, who carefully assess many tests to determine which infants may need such a procedure, and for the infant's family. Use of a home monitor requires training for parents in the use of the equipment, training in CPR (cardio-pulmonary resuscitation) techniques for reviving an infant, and information to help the parents understand their infant and SIDS. Research on the use of monitors in the home suggests that parents may have considerable anxiety during the first month about the use of the monitor and the resulting constriction it causes in their social life. However, once the family has adapted to the system, their recognition of its benefits far outweighed any added burdens (Cain, Kelly and Shannon, 1980).

THE IMPACT OF SIDS DEATHS ON THE FAMILY

The grieving process for the SIDS victim is similar in many ways to such patterns for other infant deaths. For example, the family of the SIDS victim may express such common reactions as disbelief, anger, shock, and guilt. However, in other ways the family of the SIDS victim requires special support and understanding from the family physician and friends because of the unique factors surrounding a SIDS death. The unexpected nature of the death as well as the general uncertainty about the causes of the SIDS may lead to extreme guilt on the part of some parents that they were somehow at fault. For this reason, an autopsy is considered an essential process for relieving extreme parental guilt (Terjesen and Wilkins, 1979). In addition, there are several major organizations whose purpose is to provide support for the families of SIDS victims:

- The National Foundation for Sudden Infant Death, Inc.
  1501 Broadway
  New York, New York 10036
- International Council for Infant Survival
  1515 Reisterstown Road
  Baltimore, Maryland 21208

FIGURE 6.7 Developmental diagram for the first year of life. The infant's figure represents a diagonal line on which is plotted the progress of behavior (right of the diagram) against chronological age. The cephalocaudal pattern of behavior is diagrammatically illustrated by position of the figure.

Reproduced by permission from G. H. Lowrey, *Growth and Development of Children* (7th ed.). Copyright © 1978 by Year Book Medical Publishers, Inc., Chicago. After C. A. Aldrich and E. S. Hewitt, "Outlines for Well Baby Clinics: Development for the First Twelve Months," *American Journal of Diseases of Children*, 1946, *71*, 131. Copyright 1946, American Medical Association.

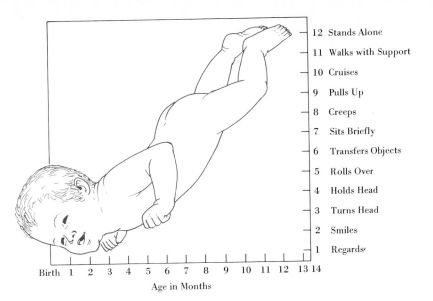

12 Stands Alone
11 Walks with Support
10 Cruises
9 Pulls Up
8 Creeps
7 Sits Briefly
6 Transfers Objects
5 Rolls Over
4 Holds Head
3 Turns Head
2 Smiles
1 Regards

Birth 1 2 3 4 5 6 7 8 9 10 11 12 13 14

Age in Months

MOTOR DEVELOPMENT

The development of movement or motor skills goes hand in hand with the development of perceptual, cognitive, and social skills. In addition to beginning language (sounds and crying), motor development is a form of communication and interaction between the infant and the significant others in his or her life. Thus motor development and movement permeate virtually all domains of infant behavior. For example, most measures of so-called infant intelligence (e.g., the Cattell Measurement of Intelligence of Infants and Young Children, 1960; the Bayley Scales, 1969; the Brazelton Neonatal Assessment Scale, 1973) are really assessments of motor performance (e.g., visual following tasks, building towers of blocks, grasping cups).

The Order of Infant Motor Development. Between birth and three years of age, infant motor development moves from very *general reflexes* to differentiated (and relatively skillful) *movements*. The so-called *gross* (large) *motor system* regulates movement of the head, body, arms, and legs. The *fine* (small) *motor system* governs the movement of hands, fingers, feet, toes, eyes, and lips. Both gross motor activity and small motor skills become more precisely regulated and controlled by the infant as it grows. Tables 6.1, 6.2 and Figure 6.7 summarize the major features of infant motor development.

All of the stages of motor development follow the principles of cephalocaudal (from head downward) and proximodistal (from the center of the body to the outer areas) development. In this section, we will give an overview of some of the milestones of motor development during the first three years.

The Four-Month-Old. By about four months of age, the average infant is usually sleeping through the night and has developed a somewhat regular

Infancy and Toddlerhood

TABLE 6.1 **Summary of the Major Stages of Infant Motor Development**

Age	Stage	Some Behavioral Activities
0–1 months	Exercise of basic reflexes	Sucking, reflex grasp
1–4 months	Perfection of visual control	Coordinates eye movement with head movements; develops differential viewpoints for moving and stationary objects; no prehensive (*Prehension* is the ability to grasp objects between the fingers and opposable thumb) contact.
4–7 months	Head and arm control	Able to raise chin and chest while flat on stomach; raises head while on stomach; rudimentary reaching movements.
7–10 months	Trunk and hand control; emerging prehension	Sits alone (5–6 months); immature grasp.
10–13 months	Control of legs, feet, fingers, thumb; refines prehension	Stands alone; mature grasp; walks alone (approximately 13 months).
13 months to 2 years	Perfection of prehension, mobility skills	Walks sideways; walks backwards; walks up and down stairs; fast walk—run; emerging fundamental motor skills (e.g., throwing, catching); uses mature grasp.

TABLE 6.2 **Development of Motor Skills**

0.2 Months—crawling movements	7.6 Months—complete thumb opposition
0.5 Months—lifts head at shoulders	8.5 Months—sits alone with good coordination
1.7 Months—arm thrusts in play	9.2 Months—prewalking progression
1.9 Months—head erect—vertical	9.3 Months—fine prehension with pellet
2.6 Months—dorsal suspension—lifts head	9.4 Months—raises self to sitting position
2.9 Months—head erect and steady	10.5 Months—pulls to standing position
3.4 Months—turns from side to back	10.6 Months—stands up
3.5 Months—sits with support	11.6 Months—walks with help
4.1 Months—beginning thumb opposition	12.5 Months—stands alone
5.0 Months—turns from back to side	13.0 Months—walks alone
5.4 Months—effort to sit	16.5 Months—walks sideways
5.7 Months—sits alone momentarily	16.9 Months—walks backward
6.2 Months—pulls to sitting position	20.3 Months—walks upstairs with help
6.2 Months—sits alone thirty seconds or more	24.3 Months—walks upstairs alone—marks time
7.0 Months—rolls from back to stomach	24.5 Months—walks downstairs alone—marks time

Abridged from Nancy Bayley, "The Development of Motor Abilities During the First Three Years," The Society for Research in Child Development, Inc., Monograph No. 1, 1935; 1–26.

schedule. The baby has organized the timing of its behavior to coincide more with family patterns of eating and sleeping. The infant can do a number of things, including being able to hold its head steady from a sitting position. This is an important behavioral attribute because it allows the infant to observe its surroundings carefully. Most four-month-olds can reach for and grasp an object (Frankenburg and Dodds, 1967). Grasping objects is an important developmental milestone because it allows the infant to experience both the sensation of touching objects and the sensation of controlling and manipulating them.

The process of self-discovery seems to be well on its way during this period. The infant may look at its hands and fingers for several minutes. This experience of discovery may also be marked by various movements such as hand clasping or hand clapping. The infant may also discover its feet and toes during this period.

By about four months, the social relationship between the parent or caretaker and the infant may include mutual "games" involving touch, sights, and sound. For example, imitative sound-play games may occur in which the parent mimics the cooing or babbling sounds of the infant. The infant, in turn, may sustain these vocalizations in a fashion that amuses the parent. Tactual interactions might include simple social games in which the parent holds the infant and gently turns so as to swing the infant. The infant, of course, tactually follows the parent by grasping and holding onto the parent. Visual following games include such activities as peek-a-boo, patty-cake, and simple movement observation by parent and infant.

The Eight-Month-Old. Almost all babies at eight months can get themselves into a sitting position, and most infants can sit without support. About half of the eight-month-olds can pull themselves to a standing position. Once the eight-month-old is in a standing position, he or she can probably move about by holding onto fixed objects such as tables, chairs, or crib sides.

Most eight-month-old babies are rather proficient crawlers and tend to rely on this mode of transportation as a major way of seeing the environment. Crawling is the primary means by which the infant gets *to* things and—sometimes to the amusement of parents—*into* things.

An eight-month-old uses his/her hands quite proficiently in grasping objects. Some are able to use the thumb and forefinger to grasp things, and almost all are able to pass objects from one hand to the other. Infants continue to enjoy playing interaction games such as peek-a-boo and patty-cake. Infants seem particularly to enjoy handing objects or toys to adults and then receiving them back. Another popular "game" seems to be for the infant to drop an object for the adult to pick up. This game may continue until one of the participants tires (usually the adult).

The Twelve-Month-Old. At twelve months of age, many babies are walking without any assistance. There is, however, a range of variability. It is usually between eleven and thirteen months that walking occurs (Frankenburg and Dodds, 1967). Walking provides increased mobility, and mobility means that the infant is actively involved in many things. At twelve months, the child can open cabinets, climb stairs, climb on furniture, pull table cloths (with or without dishes on them), bite lamp cords, feed themselves, and much more. The word *no* becomes an important part of the vocabulary for both parents and infants.

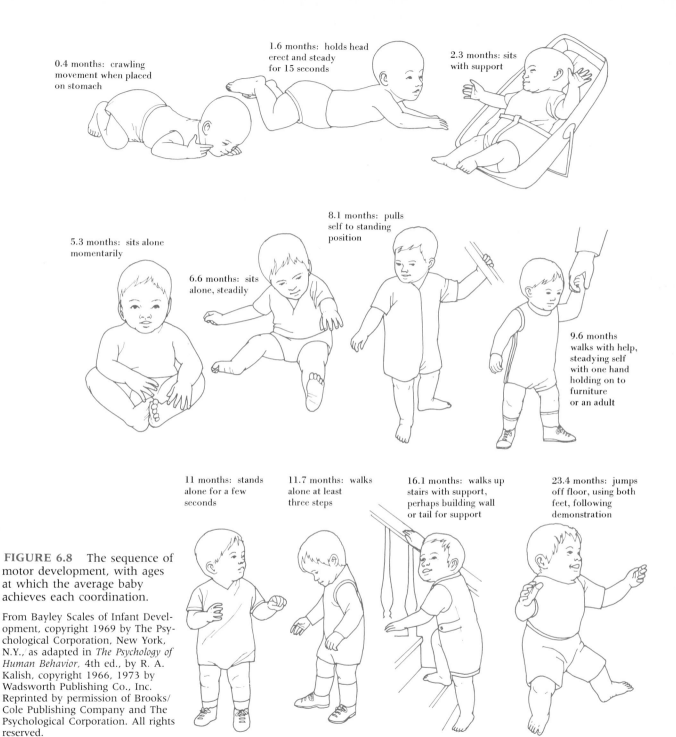

0.4 months: crawling movement when placed on stomach

1.6 months: holds head erect and steady for 15 seconds

2.3 months: sits with support

5.3 months: sits alone momentarily

6.6 months: sits alone, steadily

8.1 months: pulls self to standing position

9.6 months walks with help, steadying self with one hand holding on to furniture or an adult

11 months: stands alone for a few seconds

11.7 months: walks alone at least three steps

16.1 months: walks up stairs with support, perhaps building wall or tail for support

23.4 months: jumps off floor, using both feet, following demonstration

FIGURE 6.8 The sequence of motor development, with ages at which the average baby achieves each coordination.

From Bayley Scales of Infant Development, copyright 1969 by The Psychological Corporation, New York, N.Y., as adapted in *The Psychology of Human Behavior,* 4th ed., by R. A. Kalish, copyright 1966, 1973 by Wadsworth Publishing Co., Inc. Reprinted by permission of Brooks/ Cole Publishing Company and The Psychological Corporation. All rights reserved.

Eighteen Months and Beyond. The period that begins at about eighteen months and extends through two and one-half years is often called *toddler-hood* (see the detailed discussion of this period at the end of this chapter). Walking skills become refined, and the toddler is quite proficient at getting about. He or she may like to push or pull something while walking. By the age of two years, the child can not only walk but also run and jump. The child can also climb up steps and can probably walk down without assistance. The toddler can move things, push and pull objects, put things into containers, and stretch and bend objectives, to name only a few accomplishments.

Two Major Developments: Locomotion and Prehension. The two primary motor events of infancy are *locomotion* and *prehension* (reaching and grasping). The development of locomotion is described in Figure 6.8. Shown are several important phases in the process of learning to walk.

Walking is a monumental event for the child and the parents. The child is now capable of improved self-regulation by being able to move toward (or away from) objects and people.

Prehension constitutes one of the most important achievements in child development. Prehension is monumentally significant because it is the basis for a wide range of important infant–toddler skills. These skills include feeding oneself, block building, and scribbling with crayons. As White (1971) pointed out:

> . . . until the infant acquires the ability to use his hands to reach for and examine objects, all he can do to explore the external world is to either lie on his back and stare, or, if prone, he can with increasing skill raise his head and peer about. (p. 86)

FIGURE 6.9 Stages in the development of grasping.

From "An Experimental Study of Prehension in Infants by Means of Systematic Cinema Records," by H. M. Halverson, *Genetic Psychology Monographs*, 1931, *10*, 212–215. Reprinted by permission of The Journal Press.

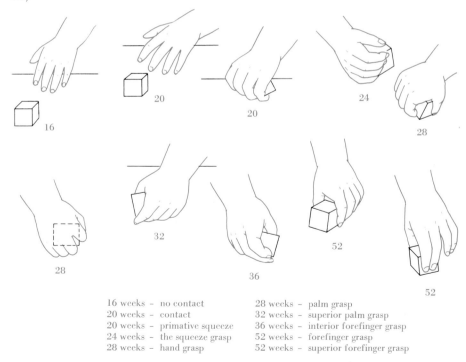

16 weeks – no contact	28 weeks – palm grasp
20 weeks – contact	32 weeks – superior palm grasp
20 weeks – primitive squeeze	36 weeks – interior forefinger grasp
24 weeks – the squeeze grasp	52 weeks – forefinger grasp
28 weeks – hand grasp	52 weeks – superior forefinger grasp

When the baby extends its arm in a reaching movement after about three and one-half months, parents or caretakers are witnessing a dramatic event.

For the first few months after the infant is born, it possesses a strong grasp, which is a reflex action. This reflex grasp disappears and is gradually replaced by grasping that is under voluntary control. Halverson (1931) identified ten stages in the development of prehension (see Figure 6.9). These stages appear in a sequence ranging from "no contact" at sixteen weeks to a mature grasp ("superior forefinger" grasp) at fifty-two weeks.

Infant Cognitive Development

Cognitive development is the development of mental processes such as thinking, understanding, and perceiving (using the senses to gather information about the world). Mental development is a process that begins at least as early as the day the infant is born and probably earlier. The motor and sensory skills (which we have already described) serve as the basis for cognitive development.

THE SENSORIMOTOR PERIOD

Jean Piaget has observed and written extensively on the development of intelligence in infancy and throughout life. His research indicates that the processes of intelligence evolve from the sensorimotor activities of infancy. As the infant procedes through the sensorimotor period, the changes in mental skills are dramatic. At birth, the infant has only a few patterns of action or reflexes including grasping, sucking, and crying. By the age of two, the child's repertoire of activities has become more sophisticated.

AN INTERLUDE: PIAGET SAYS . . .

The period that extends from birth to the acquisition of language is marked by an extraordinary development of the mind. Its importance is sometimes underestimated because it is not accompanied by words that permit a step by step pursuit of the progress of intelligence and the emotions, as is the case later on. This early mental development nonetheless determines the entire course of psychological evolution. . . . At the starting point of this development, the neonate grasps everything . . . to his own body—whereas at the termination of the period, i.e., when language and thought begin, he is . . . in a universe that he has gradually constructed himself, and which hereafter he will experience as external to himself.

From Piaget (1968), pp. 8–9.

Piaget has divided the stage of sensorimotor operations into six substages (Table 6.3 summarizes the major characteristics of development during the sensorimotor period).

Jean Piaget.

Drawn by Dana Wu; copyright © by Lawrence B. Schiamberg.

Stage 1 (Birth to One Month). Throughout most of Stage 1, the behavior of the infant is largely reflexive; that is, infants respond to the world largely in terms of the reflexes that they are born with (e.g., crying, grasping, sucking, and specific movements of head, trunk, legs, and arms). For example, whenever an object is placed in the mouth of an infant, the infant sucks

TABLE 6.3   Characteristics of Development During the Sensorimotor Period

Stage	General	Object Concept	Space	Causality
1 Reflex 0–1 mo.	Reflex activity	No differentiation of self from other objects	Egocentric	Egocentric
2 First differentiations 1–4 mos.	Hand–mouth coordination; differentiation via sucking, grasping	No special behavior re: vanished objects; no differentiation of movement of self and external objects	Changes in perspective seen as changes in objects	No differentiation of movement of self and external objects
3 Reproduction 4–8 mos.	Eye—hand coordination; reproduction of interesting events	Anticipates positions of moving objects	Space externalized; no spatial relationships of objects	Self seen as cause of all events
4 Coordination of schemata 8–12 mos.	Coordination of schemata; application of known means to new problems; anticipation	Object permanence; searches for vanished objects; reverses bottle to get nipple	Perceptual constancy of size and shape of objects	Elementary externalization of causality
5 Experimentation 12–18 mos.	Discovery of new means through experimentation	Considers sequential displacements while searching for vanished objects	Aware of relationships between objects in space, between objects and self	Self seen as object among objects and self as object of actions
6 Representation 18–24 mos.	Representation; invention of new means via internal combinations	Images of absent objects, representation of displacements	Aware of movements not perceived; representation of spatial relationships	Representative causality; causes and effects inferred

Source: From *Piaget's Theory of Cognitive Development,* Second Edition, by Barry J. Wadsworth. Copyright © 1971 and 1979 by Longman Inc. Reprinted by permission of Longman Inc., New York.

it—regardless of what it is (e.g., bottle nipple, blanket, rattle). The infant's hand also grasps whatever comes into it.

During this stage, active groping or "searching" for objects begins to replace the simple exercise of reflexes. For example, an infant may begin to search actively for a nipple to suck on when the nipple is not present. Such searching behavior was not present at birth; therefore it cannot be attributed to the simple exercise of reflexes.

By the end of this stage, the infant can distinguish between objects. When hungry, for example, the infant may actively suck a milk-producing nipple and repel other objects placed in its mouth. Such behavior was not present at birth.

As the infant proceeds through the sensorimotor period, the changes in mental skills are dramatic.

Photograph by Sylvia Byers

Stage 2 (One to Four Months). The second stage begins with the alterations in reflexive behaviors. Several new behaviors appear that represent such changes.

- *Hand—mouth coordination* develops and is reflected in repeated thumb-sucking.
- *Eye coordination* is the ability of the eyes to follow moving objects.
- *Eye—ear coordination* is reflected in the ability of the infant to move its head in the direction of sounds.

Stage 3 (Four to Eight Months). Prior to Stage 3, the infant's behavior is oriented largely toward the self. In addition, the infant cannot distinguish itself from the objects of the environment, nor can it coordinate eye—hand movements. During Stage 3, however, all these things change.

1. The infant's behaviors are increasingly directed to events or objects beyond its own body.
2. The infant recognizes the difference between the self and other objects.
3. The infant grasps or manipulates objects that it can reach. This activity reflects the coordination of the eyes and the hands.

Another important characteristic of this period is that infants seem to *repeat events* that are interesting to them. When this occurs, the beginning of *intentional* action is evident. During Stage 2, behavior was random and was not designed to attain an object or goal.

Stage 4 (Eight to Twelve Months). Prior to Stage 4, behavior has usually resulted in the *direct* action of the infant on objects. Interesting phenomena may even have been repeated. During Stage 4, *three* very interesting and related things begin to happen:

1. The infant begins using *means* to attain *ends* that may not be attainable in a direct way. The infant *intentionally* selects appropriate or available means to achieve a goal. A significant difference between the *intentionality* of Stage 3 and the *intentionality* of Stage 4 is that both end and means in Stage 4 are chosen *prior* to behavior.

Piaget described this means—end relationship in the following example:

Observation 121—At [8 months, 20 days] Jacqueline tries to grasp a cigarette case which I present to her. I then slide it between the crossed strings which attach her dolls to the hood [of her bassinet]. She tries to reach it directly. Not succeeding, she immediately looks for the strings which are not in her hands and of which she only saw the part in which the cigarette case is entangled. She looks in front of her, grasps the strings, pulls and shakes them, etc. The cigarette case then falls and she grasps it.

From Piaget (1952), p. 215.

2. The infant begins to *anticipate* events. Certain "signs" or "signals" seem to be associated with actions that follow.

Observation 132—At [8 months, 6 days], Laurent recognizes by a certain noise caused by air that he is nearing the end of his feeding and, instead of insisting on drinking to the last drop, he rejects his bottle. . . .

At [1 year, 1 month, 10 days] he has a slight scratch which is disinfected with alcohol. He cries, chiefly from fear. Subsequently, as soon as he again sees the bottle of alcohol, he recommences to cry, knowing what is in store for him. Two days later, same reaction, as soon as he sees the bottle and even before it is opened.

From Piaget (1952), pp. 248–249.

3. For the first time, the infant recognizes that objects (besides itself) can *cause* things to happen. The infant is now aware that external objects can be the cause of actions.

Piaget described this change as follows:

. . . the cause of a certain phenomenon is no longer identified by the child with the feeling he has of acting upon this phenomenon. The subject begins to discover that a spatial contact exists between cause and effect and so any object at all can be a source of activity (and not only his own body).

From Piaget (1952), p. 212.

[8 months, 7 days] . . . [Laurent] . . . A moment later I lowered my hand very slowly, starting very high up and directing it toward his feet, finally tickling him for a moment. He bursts out laughing. When I stop midway, he grasps my hand or arm and pushes it toward his feet.

From Piaget (1954), p. 261.

Stage 5 (Twelve to Eighteen Months). In Stage 4, the infant was able to coordinate familiar behavior patterns to attain goals. In Stage 5, the infant is able to develop *new* means (through experimentation) to attain goals. When the infant is presented with a new problem that cannot be solved through existing behavior patterns, the infant experiments with new means. Through trial and error, new strategies of behavior are developed. During this period, the infant appears to be interested in how objects adapt to new situations. The child playing in the bathtub may experiment by pushing objects underwater and splashing as if in a minor squall.

Observation 167—At [1 year, 3 months, 12 days], Jacqueline throws a plush dog outside the bars of her playpen and she tries to catch it. Not succeeding, she then pushes the pen itself in the right direction! By holding onto the frame with one hand while with the other, she tried to grasp the dog, she observed that the frame was mobile. She had accordingly, without wishing to do so, moved it away from the dog. She at once tried to correct this movement and thus saw the pen approach its objective. These two fortuitous discoveries then led her to utilize movements of the playpen and to push it at first experimentally, then systematically.

From Piaget (1952), p. 315.

Stage 6 (Eighteen to Twenty-four Months). Stage 6 provides evidence that the child has moved from a sensorimotor level of intelligence (as reflected in the five prior stages) to a *representational* level of thinking. By *representational* is meant the ability of the infant to symbolize objects or events mentally.

This new development allows the infant to solve problems cognitively (by means of representations or symbols).

In Stage 5, the infant arrived at new means for problem solving through active experimentation. In Stage 6, the invention of means for problem solving is suddenly apparent, suggesting to Piaget that such invention occurs through representation and mental activity.

> Observation 181—At [1 year, 6 months, 23 days] for the first time Lucienne plays with a doll carriage whose handle comes to the height of her face. She rolls it over the carpet by pushing it. When she comes against a wall, she pulls, walking backward. But as this position is not convenient for her, she pauses and without hesitation, goes to the other side to push the carriage again. She therefore found the procedure in one attempt, apparently through analogy to other situations but without training, apprenticeship or chance.
>
> *From* Piaget (1952), p. 338.

The infant's ability to represent objects and events internally also enhances its concept of *causality*. In Piaget's example, the infant was able to think of a "cause" (pushing the carriage in the opposite direction) without having to perceive or immediately experience its "effect" (freeing the carriage). Therefore true causality relationships had become understandable.

CONSTRUCTION OF THE PERMANENT OBJECT

Piaget demonstrated that during the sensorimotor period, children begin to recognize that their environment is made up of objects and that they are part of the total environment in which they participate. The infant comes to recognize many objects, such as mother, father, food, toys, feeding bottle, brother, and sister. However, the infant does not seem to understand that these objects exist when they are out of sight. A prominent milestone in cognitive development comes when the infant recognizes that objects can be permanent (i.e., that objects can exist when they are not in view; see Figure 6.10). The construction of the permanent object is significant because it signals the beginnings of the ability to "think" about what is not present or in immediate view.

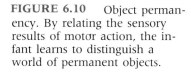

FIGURE 6.10 Object permanency. By relating the sensory results of motor action, the infant learns to distinguish a world of permanent objects.

Photograph by David Kostelnik

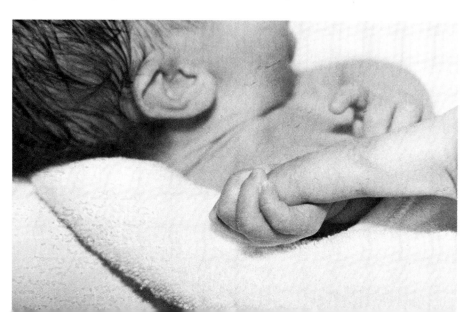

Much of cognitive functioning in later life involves the development and analysis of symbols regarding what is not immediately present or even abstracted from "real" objects.

Piaget observed and recorded the development of object permanence during the first three years of life. According to Piaget, object permanence occurs in six stages as follows.

Stages 1 and 2: "Out of sight, out of mind." The first two stages occur during the first four months of life. During these initial stages of object permanence, the infant's behavior indicates that an object that is out of sight is, in fact, out of mind or may not exist.

Stage 3 (Four to Eight Months of Age). Infants begin to indicate that they can maintain some contact with an object that is not present.

Example: Baby Elizabeth is sitting in her feeding chair. Her father places a cooked noodle before her. Baby Elizabeth grasps her noodle and is about to place it in her mouth when she accidentally drops it on the floor (to the dismay of her father). Instead of staring into space and forgetting about the noodle (as she might have done in Stages 1 and 2 when she dropped an object), Elizabeth leans over and looks down to the floor in the general area where the noodle now lies. She indicates that she can maintain some contact with an absent object.

In addition to contact-maintenance behavior, the Stage 3 infant can grasp and retrieve a partially hidden object if a large enough part remains visible.

Example: Baby Elizabeth is comfortably sitting at her feeding table. Elizabeth's father holds a toy next to one of her brother's books. When he has Elizabeth's attention, her father puts the toy behind the book so that a large part of the toy is visible to her. Elizabeth now reaches for the toy, at which point her father makes less and less of the toy visible. When the visible part becomes relatively small, Elizabeth's reaching hand seems to stop rather abruptly.

As illustrated by Elizabeth, Stage 3 infants usually make no attempt to recover objects that are barely visible or that have disappeared behind an obstruction.

Stage 4 (Eight to Twelve Months of Age). During Stage 4, the infant will search for an object, but only in the *first* place where they saw the object. For example, if a toy is continually hidden behind one object (and the child repeatedly finds it there) and then (in full view of the child) is hidden behind a different object, the infant will probably continue to look for the toy behind the *first* object. The Stage 4 infant has made conspicuous progress because it realizes that objects continue to exist. However, it continues to indicate (by virtue of its searching behavior) that objects cannot exist in multiple places.

Stage 5 (Twelve to Eighteen Months). By Stage 5, the infant has clearly developed the idea that objects can exist in multiple places. The Stage 5 infant–toddler always looks for an object in the place in which it was *last* seen. In the Stage 4 example, for instance, even if a toy is continually hidden behind one object (and found there) and then is hidden behind a second object, the Stage 5 infant will always look behind the second, or last, object to find the toy. Thus, no matter where it was previously hidden, the infant will search for the toy where it was last seen.

Although the notion of object permanence has developed considerably during this stage, it is nonetheless not perfect or complete. For example, if an object (in full view) is moved behind one object and then (covered by the adult's hand) is moved behind another object, the child will look for the object where it was *last seen*. Stage 5 infants apparently do not *reason* that the toy must have been moved to another place under the cover of the adult's hand.

Stage 6 (Beginning at Eighteen Months). The Stage 6 infant–toddler has acquired the concept of object permanence with all of its subtle manifestations. The infant has the notion that an object continues to exist when it is moved from place to place and will continue to search for an object until it is found. The infant–toddler can understand the possibility that an object can be covered or hidden in an adult's hand and still exist. For example, if a small object is hidden in an adult's hand and is then placed behind one object after another, the toddler will search each hiding place (including the adult's hand) until the object is found.

SPACE AND TIME

The construction of object permanency makes the world a more predictable and simpler place in which to live. Objects no longer have a dual existence in one space and then in another space or in one time period and then, several minutes or seconds later, in another time period. The discovery of object permanency helps the infant to separate the existence of the object from a particular or unique space and time, so that the object can exist in many different spaces and at different times. The ability of the infant to sort out the existence of an object from a particular time or place provides the foundation for the emerging concepts of space, time, and causality.

For the young child, the concept of space seems to derive primarily from the child's own movement experiences, rather than from an abstract notion of distance. For example, children under three years of age tend to think that the distance between two points (A and B) is increased when an object or obstacle (around which the child must walk) is placed between the two points. In other words, the infant–toddler's concept of distance is a *practical* one based on movement and motor experience rather than the *abstract* notion that (in plane geometry) the shortest distance between two stationary points is a straight line of constant length.

According to Piaget, the infant–toddler's concept of time is confounded with his/her notion of space. Piaget showed that young children who see a toy demonstration in which one man runs a distance of four feet in the same time that another man runs one foot usually report that the second man stopped before reaching the end. Young children report that the second man has stopped, even though they have seen both men running from beginning to end, without any evidence of stopping (Flavell, 1970). This example illus-

By recording what she has done in the past, memory helps the infant learn what to expect in the future.

Photograph by Sylvia Byers

trates how the ideas of time and space are intertwined and are not yet, for infant–toddlers, separated and distinguished.

The concept of time, although not clearly distinguished from the notion of space, is an important dimension of comprehending simple causal relationships. By the time toddlerhood arrives (at about 18 months), children have acquired simple notions of causality based on the close proximity, in *time*, of many events that occur on a daily basis in many families and households. For example, children see that a switch turns on a light, that a knob starts a television set, that pushing a doorbell produces a ringing noise, that putting a key in the car ignition starts the motor, and so on. Although there is a *physical distance* between the behavior that "causes" an activity and the activity itself (e.g., between the switch and the light), the infant–toddler appears to understand the simple, causal relationship as long as there is no extended *time* delay.

MEMORY

Many people have thought of the infant's and child's memory as a storehouse of past experiences but have failed to suggest how this storehouse is built. Memory is more than haphazard recall of past perceptions and activities. Memory is a process of *expecting* and *predicting* future events based on past events. What purpose would memory serve if it only recorded the past? By recording what he/she has done in the past, memory tells the infant what to expect in the next few minutes, in the next hour, and, perhaps, in the next day.

Piaget (1952) showed how memory develops in children below two years. The one-year-old baby who has just begun to crawl has a far more limited memory (yet memory it has) than a brother or sister of four. For example, the infant who watches its parent walk behind a screen and come out on the other side does not have the active memory to remember this sequence of behavior should the parent once again walk behind the screen. To find its mother, the baby will crawl to the side of the screen where the mother entered and disappeared. Or if a ball rolls behind a box, the baby will crawl to the side where the ball disappeared and will not go to the other side, where the ball would be expected to emerge.

Language Development

All over the world the first sentences of small children are being as painstakingly taped, transcribed and analyzed as if they were the last sayings of great sages. Which is a surprising fate for the likes of "That doggie," "No more milk," and "Hit ball." (Brown, 1973)

Language represents one of the most mysterious events of biology and culture. Many who have studied language have marveled at its vast detail and organization. Although the most complex of all psychological and cultural adaptions, language is uniform in structure throughout the endless cultures of the world. The striking characteristic of language is that infants acquire all of the main forms of speech and language before the end of the second year—the end of infancy. This fact defines the theme of this section: speech and language are developed in a parallel fashion—on a moment-to-moment basis—with general behavior and adjustment, beginning early in life and continuing thereafter throughout all stages of development. People have wondered about the nature of language for thousands of years, but there are still major differences of opinion about its nature and how to study it. Psychologists and linguists have written at great length about the functions of language.

FUNCTIONS OF LANGUAGE

Language is used diversely throughout the human life span in various forms of communication, in thinking and problem solving, and in creative activity and writing. Although language therefore has many other specific functions that depend on the nature of the activity, three major functions are fundamental to language:

PRIMARY FUNCTIONS OF HUMAN LANGUAGE

- Language is a mechanism of self-stimulation and control of individual activity.
- Language is a self-guidance mechanism for predicting and thinking about future behavior.
- Language is a mechanism that organizes social behavior and interactions of people with each other.

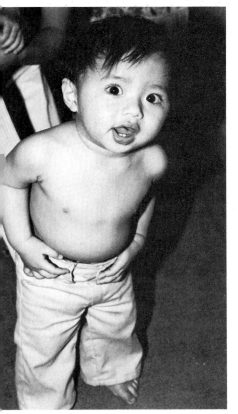

FIGURE 6.11 Language represents one of the most mysterious events of biology and culture.

Photograph by Sylvia Byers

WHAT IS LANGUAGE?

Although we customarily think of language and communication as the same thing, actually they are not. Language is only one form of communication (a verbal–symbolic form). As we have seen in our earlier discussions of the infant, there are many ways in which the infant (and people, in general) communicates its feelings, emotions, and thoughts. For example, a baby's social smile may convey to the parent general information about the infant's physical or emotional state. Such a mode of communication does not require verbal processes—speech or words—and, therefore is *nonverbal*. For our purposes, we will use the term *language* to mean the transmission and reception of ideas and feelings by means of *verbal symbols* (Critchley, 1975).

PROPERTIES OF LANGUAGE

Language has several properties that are important for us to define if we are to understand the miraculous development of language in infants and young children:

1. The *phonological* component of language represents its sound structure. Every spoken language is composed of a limited number of primary sounds, or *phonemes*, usually three or four dozen (e.g., the sounds of the letters *p, t, d,* and *o* are *phonemes*). There are between 45 and 50 phonemes represented by the 26 letters of the alphabet used in the three main dialects of English spoken in the United States (Darley and Spriestersbach, 1978).

Vowel sounds (*a, e, i, o, u*) are produced first by infants because they are easier to utter than consonant sounds, which appear later as the infant develops better thought and tongue control.

2. The *morphological* components of language are *morphemes,* or the smallest meaningful elements of a language. Morphemes may be words or parts of words (e.g., *a, no, ma, play, s, ing*).

3. The *grammar* of a language is the "rules" or principles for organizing the sounds (phonemes) of a language into meaningful units (morphemes and words). For example, there are numerous words in the English language that begin with the morpheme *be* (e.g., *be, become, because*). We might say, then, that there is a grammatical "rule" in the English language that "allows" people to make these combinations. On the other hand, there is no word in the English language that begins with *zb*. In other words, there is no grammatical "rule" that allows for that letter combination.

4. *Syntax,* or the syntactical component of language, is made up of the rules that govern the organization of meaningful units (such as words) into meaningful utterances (such as phrases, clauses, or sentences).

5. The *semantic* component of language constitutes its meaning. "The semantic system of a language is the knowledge that a speaker must have to understand sentences and relate them to his knowledge of the world. It includes both knowledge of individual lexical [vocabulary] items and knowledge of how the meaning of a sentence is determined by the meanings of individual lexical items and the structure of the sentence." (Dale, 1976, p. 166).

6. The *expressive* component of language consists of the emotion, feeling, motivation, or action that accompanies the utterance of speech. It may be defined by emphasis, rhythm, loudness, and patterning of speech. Because the expressive factors in language denote the state and feeling of the speaker, they give additional meaning to particular phrases or sentences. The expressive component of speech is closely interlocked with the gestures, facial expressions, and "body language" that accompany speech. The expressive components of vocal behavior are the first aspects of speech to develop in infancy and are seen in the varied patterns of crying, whimpering, cooing, gurgling, and babbling in the first year, before significant speech articulations emerge.

THEORIES OF LANGUAGE ACQUISITION

Although the significance of speech and language is certainly undeniable, the explanations of these processes are very controversial. Three major theories of language development are learning theory, psycholinguistic theory, and social learning theory.

Learning Theory. Learning theory explains speech and language development as the products of reinforcement of infant responses. In other words, language and speech are attained in much the same fashion as other behaviors, which are learned through the pairing of stimulus (S) and response (R) in the presence of appropriate reinforcement. According to this theory, the infant's production of sounds and words is the result of caretaker's reinforcement of these activities by increased attention to the infant or by the provision of desired objects (e.g., milk, toys, cookies).

There are at least two major difficulties with this theory. First, the individual infant cannot possibly be reinforced for every utterance it makes. How do the infant and child "learn" to make utterances that they have never heard before? Second, learning theory provides little or no insight into the development of the complex "rule" systems that govern languages. Where do these rules come from? Learning theory implies that these rules are attained through association and reinforcement. However, as we have indicated, infants generate speech and language that they have never heard before. Furthermore observation of parent–child language interaction indicates that parents pay more attention to the ungrammatical but "cute" linguistic responses of their child than to "correct" responses.

Psycholinguistic Theory. *Psycholinguistics* is the study of the development of language from the cooing and babbling of the infant to the organized words and sentences of the older child. Whereas learning theory tends to emphasize association and reinforcement as major components of language development, psycholinguistic theory emphasizes the role of "built-in" or "preprogrammed" structures as the major determinants of language development. According to Noam Chomsky (1965), the major proponent of psycholinguistic theory, the rules of language are imbedded in something called *deep structure*. Deep structure is described as if it were a built-in mechanism in the brain that generates actual speech and language.

As with learning theory, there are several difficulties with the psycholinguistic approach. First, it assumes that human beings are always capable of grammatical sentences whether or not they have anything meaningful to say. Psycholinguists tend to minimize the role of meaning in the development of language. A second difficulty is that psycholinguists attribute important functions of language generation to unverifiable structures of the mind. What exactly is "deep structure?" How do we know it exists except by *assuming* that it is the source of grammatical utterances? It is a fact that the child can generate a vast number of grammatical utterances without having heard them before. It is a matter of conjecture whether these utterances are generated by means of a "deep structure."

Social Learning Theory. Social learning theorists maintain that children learn language by listening, observing, and *imitating* models. This theory appears to explain language development as being the result of interactions between parent or caretaker and child. There is considerable evidence that mutual imitation does occur and is a factor in language learning (Dale, 1976). On the other hand, imitation does not seem to be a sufficient explanation, in itself, for language development.

Several kinds of evidence suggest that imitation in the sense of a child's attempt to reproduce the actual adult utterances he hears, does not play an important role in the acquisition of syntax. Many of the very earliest utterances of children cannot be viewed as imitations or even reduced imitations of adult speech; for example "Allgone sticky." Furthermore, even when children do imitate parental speech (which is not uncommon), they reformulate the sentences using their own grammars. Children can hardly acquire new grammatical features through imitation when it is precisely these new features that are omitted in imitations. (Dale, 1976, p. 138)

THE COURSE OF EARLY LANGUAGE DEVELOPMENT

Infants, of course, begin to make vocal sounds at birth. At first, their "language" is undifferentiated; however, they quickly develop a variety of cries. By six weeks, infants are also making a variety of cooing sounds. Two fundamental ideas underlie our notions of the child's language development (Dale, 1976):

1. The child does not simply speak a garbled form of adult language. Rather, infants and children speak a language of their own, with its own patterns and characteristics.
2. Infants and children act as their own "language specialists." That is, they are faced with an unlimited set of possible utterances from which they must somehow extract the underlying rules. The child is continually trying out hypotheses about these rules of the language. For example, if the child hears the parent make a plural noun by adding s (e.g., boys, dogs, cats), the child may extend the "rule" to *sheeps* and *peoples*.

Photograph by David Kostelnik

A SCENARIO:
THE BABY ELIZABETH AS LANGUAGE SPECIALIST

Most of the "hypotheses" of language usage that infants and young children develop are based on what they hear. Witness the following conversation between Elizabeth and her parents:

Father: (to Elizabeth's mother) By looking at the grass outside, I think it's time for me to mow the lawn.
Mother: This is a good time to do it.
Elizabeth: (repeating her mother) Daddy, *do* it.

(Sometime later in the day).

Father: (wiping his brow) Well, I mow*ed* the lawn.
Mother: You complet*ed* your work.
Elizabeth: Daddy, *doed* it.

Elizabeth, on learning the past tense of such verbs as *mow* and *complete* may have developed the following hypothesis: All past-tense forms are produced by adding *d* or *ed*. The application of this hypothesis led to her utterance—*"doed."*

BIOLOGICAL AND MATURATIONAL FACTORS

The interactional process by which the infant develops the use of speech and language in the family is based, in part, on biological and maturational features. The development of speech and language has a supporting basis, therefore, in the biological maturation of the infant. The sequence of speech development seems to be parallel to motor development (see Table 6.4). The human brain has many *association areas* that organize specific sensory functions such as touch, hearing, vision, and speech. The speech centers of the brain are generally located in the left brain hemisphere. The process by which the various brain centers mature and develop with regard to their functions is called *lateralization*. There is some evidence that where this process of lateralization of brain hemisphere functions is incomplete, interference with such activities as speech is possible (Levy, 1976). Thus biological maturation appears to be an important undergirding feature of speech and language (Dale, 1976).

Preliminaries to Language: Cooing, Babbling, and Crying. Shortly after birth the infant is capable of making gestures and sounds. Infants may spend considerable time making cooing and babbling sounds to themselves. Usually, by the end of the first year, the infant is able to use single words. How does this important event occur?

The transition from cooing and babbling to the use of words is not well understood. Screaming and crying occur during the first six months of life; however, these are not considered real language. Although infant crying may lead to an adult response—and it usually does—there is no evidence that the infant is aware of the meaning of its cries. Babbling (the playful repetition of sounds) usually occurs during the second six months of life and represents a limited form of communication (Engel, 1973). It seems to appear at a time when infants understand the meaning of a few words, and to disappear when

TABLE 6.4 The Relationship Between Speech and Motor Development

Age	Language Activity	Motor Activity
Birth	Cries.	Limited voluntary control.
12 Weeks	Infant can smile and make cooing sounds.	Infant can support its head (when in a prone position).
16 Weeks	Infant can turn head in response to human voice.	When a rattle is placed in its hands, infant can play with it.
20 Weeks	Infant can make vowel-like and consonant-like cooing sounds.	Infant sits up when propped.
6 Months	Infant cooing changes to single-syllable babbling sounds (e.g., *ma, mu, di*).	Infant can grasp or reach toward people or objects.
8 Months	Infant can repeat many single-syllable sounds (e.g., *mama, gaga*).	Infant can stand by holding on to objects (e.g., crib sides, tables).
10 Months	Infant distinguishes between adult words by responding differently to them.	Infant creeps, pulls self to a standing position, and takes steps while holding on.
12 Months	Infant can utter words such as *ma-ma* or *da-da* and seems to understand other words.	Infant can sit on floor and can walk with assistance.
18 Months	Infant has vocabulary of 3–50 words and begins to use two-word combinations.	Infant can grasp and manipulate objects; infant can walk proficiently.
24 Months	Infant's vocabulary exceeds 50 words; infant uses two-word phrases.	Infant can run and walk up and down stairs.
30 Months	Variety of infant's words increases dramatically; infant can use three- to five-word phrases.	Toddler refines walking behavior by being able to move on tiptoes and to stand on one foot alone.
3 Years	Toddler has clear pronunciation vocabulary of about 1,000 words.	Toddler can ride a tricycle.
4 Years	Language well established.	Preschooler can hop and jump over a rope.

Based on E. H. Lenneberg, *Biological Foundations of Language*, 1967, pp. 128–130. © John Wiley & Sons, Inc. Reprinted by permission.

infants become more proficient language users. Table 6.4 provides a summary of the developments.

Some research suggests that the infant may well be "preprogrammed" for language learning from as early as the first day of life. Condon and Sander (1974) demonstrated that long before the infant has any notion of the meaning of language, its physical movements are matched to or synchronized with the speech sounds of its parents. This finding suggests that parents and caretakers can provide a supportive environment for the development of formal language well in advance of its emergence.

The Child's First Words. Sometime around the first birthday, the child achieves a milestone in language: the utterance of the first word. The range from ten to thirteen months includes most recorded observations of the first word (McCarthy, 1954; Nelson, 1973). The infant's first words are distinctive in at least three ways (Dale, 1976):

212

1. *Phonetically* (their pronunciation). Typically the words consist of one or two syllables. Each syllable is ordinarily of the form "consonant–vowel."
2. *Their meanings.*
3. *The ways in which they are used.*

The Meaning of First Words. There appears to be a great deal of similarity between children in the first fifty words or so that are acquired. Nelson (1973) used the following classification system to describe the infant's first words:

CATEGORIES OF FIRST WORDS

- *General nominals* (51 percent): e.g., doggie, ball, house.
- *Specific nominals* (14 percent): e.g., daddy, mommy, pet, names.
- *Action words* (14 percent): e.g., give, bye-bye, go.
- *Modifiers* (9 percent): e.g., dirty, mine, outside, nice.
- *Personal–social words* (8 percent): e.g., no, yes, please.
- *Function words* (4 percent): e.g., what, for.

The important individuals in the infant's life are commonly found in the infant's first words. Among the more common *general nominal* words are *juice, milk, cookie, shoes, ball,* and *car* (Nelson, 1973). An important factor in whether a word will be included among the first words is whether it is something that the *child can act on* fairly easily. For example, large objects that are simply "there" (e.g., stove, table, trees) are usually not found among the child's first words, whereas words such as *key, blanket, toy,* and *brush* (objects toward which the child acts) are common (Dale, 1976).

Regardless of the type of first words used by the infant, most likely they do not *mean* the same thing to the infant that they mean to the parent.

A SCENARIO:
THE BABY ELIZABETH (AT 1 YEAR)

Our bouncing baby girl—Elizabeth—has been doing many things since we last saw her. Just the other day, she uttered what her parents thought was her first word: "Dada." Daddy, of course, was quite pleased because he assumed that he was clearly differentiated from Elizabeth's mother, her brother, and various neighbors or strangers. Daddy's relative state of euphoria lasted only until 6:00 P.M. that evening, when dinner guests arrived. At that time, Baby Elizabeth cheerfully greeted one of the male guests with a loud, booming "Dada!!"

A common phenomenon in almost every language is the child's *overextension* of the use of a word to refer to a broader category than appropriate in adult usage (Clark, 1973) (see Table 6.5). In the example, Elizabeth's word *dada* was extended to refer to adult males other than her father. Another example would be the word *ball*, which may sometimes be extended to include or "mean" other round objects, such as stones, gumballs, or radishes. Such overextensions appear to be most common during the period from thirteen to thirty months. It seems that the basis for overextensions (as well as for word meaning) is the *perceptual* attributes of objects (e.g., all round objects are "balls") or functional attributes (small round objects called *balls* are to play with) (Dale, 1976).

TABLE 6.5   Some Perceptually Based Overextensions

Source and Language	Lexical Item	First Referent	Extensions in Order of Occurrence
Shape			
Lewis (1951) English	tee (from name of cat)	cat	dogs; cows and sheep; horse
Pavlovitch (1920) French	bébé	reflection of self in mirror	photograph of self; all photographs; all pictures; all books with pictures; all books
Imedadze (1960) Russian	buti	ball	toy; radish; stone spheres at park entrance
Size			
Moore (1896) English	fly	fly	specks of dirt; dust; all small insects; his own toes; crumbs of bread; a toad
Taine (1877) French	bébé	baby	other babies; all small statues; figures in small pictures and prints
Sound			
Shvachkin (1948) Russian	dany	sound of bell	clock; telephone; doorbells
Leopold (1949) German-English	sch	noise of train	music; noise of movement; wheels; balls
Movement			
Moore (1896) English	bird	sparrows	cows and dogs; cats; any animal moving
Taste			
Leopold (1949) English	candy	candy	cherries; anything sweet
Texture			
Shvachkin (1948) Russian	kiki	cat	cotton; any soft material
Idelberger (1903) German	bow-wow	dog	toy dog; fur piece with animal head; fur piece without head

Source: Adapted from E. V. Clark, "What's in a Word? On the Child's Acquisition of Semantics in His First Language." In T. E. Moore (Ed.), *Cognitive Development and the Acquisition of Language*. New York: Academic Press, 1973, Table 6.1.

Gradually the child narrows the meanings of words that have been overextended. One of the explanations for this process of limiting word meaning is the acquisition of new words. That is, new words take over parts of the broader, overextended meanings (Clark, 1973). An example with Baby Elizabeth may help us:

The Baby Elizabeth who had been using the word *dada* rather freely for any adult male now begins to refine her meaning of the word (to the joy of her father). Let's look at the evolution of the word *dada* as she learns new words.

1. The first "meaning" apparently referred to her father, her grandfather, and other adult males.

2. When Elizabeth learns the word *papa* to refer to her grandfather, the word *dada* comes to be limited to her father and other males.
3. When Elizabeth learns the word *man* to refer to male adults other than her father and her grandfather, she limits her meaning of *dada* to her father alone.
4. Baby Elizabeth's "dada" is—to say the least—pleased.

Words That Are Sentences. The child's first words seem to be more than single words. They are used for more than description. They appear to express complex ideas (ideas that would be expressed in sentences by adults). The term *holophrase* is used to describe this use of words as sentences.

SCENARIO

Baby Elizabeth sees her father's pipe and says, "Daddy."

Baby Elizabeth is seated comfortably at her feeding table and is presented with some peas. She touches them and says, "Eat."

Baby Elizabeth is sitting on the grass and hears an airplane. She points to the airplane, follows it across the sky, and says, "Bye-bye."

In each of the examples, the infant's first words might be interpreted as comments on *experiences* or *actions* in the environment rather than simply as names for objects (Antinucci and Parisi, 1973; Ingram, 1971). First words are closely related to the child's experiences. In particular, they describe those experiences in which the child participates and over which he/she gains control (Dale, 1976).

Learning First Words: Family Contribution. Although there may be a pattern to the learning of first words, there may also be a contribution resulting from adult–child interaction. Nelson (1973) determined that the children in her experiment could be divided into two major groups: children who were talking more about *things* (referential or R group) and children who were talking more about *self and other people* (expressive or E group). She found that all of the *first-born children of parents with high educational achievement* were in the referential group (see Table 6.6). Nelson then examined the nature of adult–child interaction to see if there might be differences between R-group interactions and E-group interactions. In other words, did family behavior make a difference? The mothers of the R-group children did *not* name objects more frequently than the mothers of E-group children. Rather, R-group mothers did talk about objects more, whereas E-group mothers

TABLE 6.6
Distribution of Groups by Birth Order and Education of Parents

Birth Order	Education	Referential	Expressive
First	High	5	0
Later	High	2	2
First	Low	3	3
Later	Low	0	3

Source: K. Nelson, "Pre-syntactic Strategies for Learning to Talk." Paper delivered to the Society for Research in Child Development, Minneapolis, March, 1971.

Roger Brown on Telegraphic Speech

Roger Brown is currently Professor of Social Psychology at Harvard University. He has contributed numerous books and research articles to the study of child language development.

Brown and Bellugi described the child's use of telegraphic speech as follows:

When words cost money there is a premium on brevity or to put it otherwise, a constraint on length. The result is "telegraphic" English . . . One does not send a cable reading: "My car has broken down and I have lost my wallet; send money to me at the American Express in Paris" but rather "Car Broken down; wallet lost; send money American Express Paris." The telegram omits *my, has, and, I, have, my, to me, at, the, in*. All of these are *functors*. . . .

A telegraphic transformation of English generally communicates very well. It does so because it retains the high-information words (contentives) and drops the low-information words (functors). . . . If you say aloud sentences you will find that you place the heavier stresses . . . on contentives rather than on functors. In fact, the heavier stresses fall, for the most part, on the words the child retains (when the child repeats or tries to imitate adult utterances). We first realized that this was the case when we found that in transcribing tapes, the words of the mother that we could hear most clearly were usually the words that the child reproduced. We had trouble hearing the weakly stressed functors and, of course, the child usually failed to reproduce them. . . .

We are fairly sure that differential stress is one of the determinants of the child's telegraphic productions. For one thing stress will also account for the way in which children reproduce polysyllabic [many-syllable] words when the total is too much for them. Adam, for instance, gave us *'pression* for *expression* and Eve gave us *'raff* for *giraffe;* the more heavily stressed syllables were the ones retained.

From R. Brown and U. Bellugi, "Three Processes in the Child's Acquisition of Syntax," *Harvard Educational Preview*, Spring 1964, *34*, 138–139. Copyright 1964 by the President and Fellows of Harvard College.

talked more about their children. Although the long-term implications of these family differences were not explored, there appears to be evidence that family interactional style may be a significant feature of language development (Dale, 1976).

From One Word to Two. Sometime around eighteen or twenty months of age, children begin to make two-word combinations. These two-word combinations are significant for the following reasons (Dale, 1976):

1. Two-word phrases represent an important milestone in the expansion of language as a tool for expressing complex ideas.
2. Two-word phrases reflect the child's language-organization strategies. When the child first begins to use two-word phrases, there are no con-

Adult Sentence	Child Utterance
Daddy will be gone.	Daddy gone.
Mommy can help us.	Mommy help.
Daddy's briefcase.	Daddy case.

FIGURE 6.12 Sample telegraphic utterances.

straints on the order of the words. For example, Baby Elizabeth, on noticing an open door, is as likely to say, ''Open, door,'' as ''Door, open.'' In the two-word stage, observable patterns and emerging rules of organization become apparent.

Telegraphic Speech. One of the primary characteristics of children's speech that is noted with the onset of two-word phrases is that it is *telegraphic*. In other words, there is a pattern to the words that are included and excluded in the child's utterances, compared with the ''ideal'' adult sentence for expressing a similar idea. Children's sentences or two-word utterances tend to omit the following types of words: prepositions (e.g., *to, for, be*); auxiliary verbs (e.g., *was, has, been*); and articles (e.g., *a, the*). It is as if the child were sending a telegram to those with whom he/she is trying to communicate (see Figures 6.12 and 6.13).

The Meaning of Two-word Utterances. The decade of the 1960s was marked by a consideration of the structure of two-word phrases (Braine, 1963; Slobin, 1968; McNeill, 1970). Braine (1963) suggested that two-word phrases were composed of two classes of words: *pivot* words and *open* words.

DEFINITION OF PIVOT WORDS

The *pivot* class is small, and each word in it is used with many different words from the much larger open class. For example, a child might say *bandage on, blanket on,* [and] *fix on . . . on* is a pivot word. It is always used in the second position, and many other words can occur with it. Or a child might say *allgone shoe, allgone lettuce, allgone outside,* and others. . . . A pivot word may be the first or the second in two-word utterances, but *each pivot word has its own position.* (Dale, 1976, p. 21)

FIGURE 6.13 Children's speech is telegraphic.

Where *pivot* words come *first,* the Baby Elizabeth might say the following:

P	+	O
see		dog
see		cat
see		Bruce
see		Scott

In the above examples, *see* is the *pivot* word (P), and *dog, cat, Bruce,* and *Scott* are *open* (O) words.

Where pivot words come in second position, Elizabeth might say:

O	+	P
dog		all gone
cat		all gone
man		all gone
diaper		all gone

In the above examples, *all gone* is the *pivot* word, and *dog, cat, man,* and *diaper* are the *open* words. [Elizabeth's parents were particularly relieved to discover that, in fact, her diaper was not "all gone."]

Over the last decade, the accumulation of evidence has indicated that, as might have been expected, children's two-word phrases do not always conform to the structure described (Bowerman, 1973; Bloom, 1970a). In addition to *structural* descriptions (e.g., word classes and their combinations), children's sentences can also be described in terms of the *functions* that the words serve in the sentence (Schlesinger, 1971). In the latter case, the *context* in which the child's utterance occurs and the child's *intentions* are critical factors in the organization of two-word phrases. For example, the child's utterance "Mommy hat" could mean "Mommy, put on a hat" or "Mommy, give me a hat" (Dale, 1976).

SCENARIO

The irrepressible Baby Elizabeth is practicing her two-word phrases when she encounters an object on which she can act (an important criterion for language development): Daddy's shoe. Elizabeth promptly announces to her father (who is reading the newspaper in his easy chair), "Daddy shoe." She then hands the shoe to her father, who is only slightly startled when the shoe lands in his lap. Quickly recovering his dignity (an indispensable characteristic for the parent of a toddler), Elizabeth's father smiles at her and returns to his reading. Elizabeth again states—slightly louder this time—"Daddy shoe." At this point, Daddy concludes that if he wishes to finish the newspaper, perhaps he ought to put on his shoe. He does so. Elizabeth looks on with a rather astonished expression. She temporarily leaves the scene, circles the kitchen table, stares at her brother, and again spies her father quietly reading in his chair. She returns to her father's chair, where she indicates her presence by putting her hand against the back of the newspaper and gently shakes the paper. Her father lowers his newspaper to discover the smiling face of Elizabeth, who says, "Daddy shoe." Her father (wondering if there might not be a better time to read the newspaper) says to her, "Yes, Daddy shoe." Elizabeth seems pleased. She moves on to other adventures.

Comment. How do we explain why Elizabeth seemingly relented in her assault on her father? There are many possible answers, including the obvious fact that Elizabeth may simply have tired. Another explanation may involve the meaning or the *intent* of Elizabeth's statement: "Daddy shoe." There are at least two meanings: "Daddy's shoe" and "Daddy put on the shoe." It is quite possible that Elizabeth simply wished her father to acknowledge that the shoe belonged to him.

Some of the most common relationships that children use in their speech are presented in Table 6.7. One way of thinking about the semantic relationships expressed in Table 6.7 is as a set of statements or propositions that verbally describe the sensorimotor world of the toddler as he/she emerges from infancy. You will remember from our discussion of infant cognitive development that the major achievements of infancy include the establishment of a stable world (object permanency), the distinction of the world from the self, and the ability to organize and self-regulate behavior directed at objects. Linguistic expression (and, in particular, the relationships in Table 6.7) can be viewed as the extension of action as a mode of self-regulation to include language as a technique for both self-control and object control (Bloom, 1970b; Brown, 1973; Smith and Schiamberg, 1973).

Other Changes in Language. Out of the basic set of "rules" described in Table 6.7, the child generates three-word and four-word sentences. It is rather amazing that no new relationship rules beyond those for two-word phrases are required to generate more lengthy utterances that describe the exciting realities of toddler life (Dale, 1976).

TABLE 6.7
Semantic Relations in Two-word Sentences

Semantic Relation	Form	Example
1. Nomination	that + N[1]	That book
2. Notice	hi + N	Hi belt
3. Recurrence	more + N	
	'nother + N	More milk
4. Nonexistence	all gone + N	
	no more + N	All-gone rattle
5. Attributive	adjective + N	Big train
6. Possessive	N + N	Mommy lunch
7. Locative	N + N	Sweater chair
8. Locative	V[2] + N	Walk street
9. Agent–action	N + V	Eve read
10. Agent–object	N + N	Mommy sock
11. Action–object	V + N	Put book

[1]N = noun.
[2]V = verb.

Adapted from R. Brown, *Psycholinguistics.* New York: Free Press, 1970, p. 220. Copyright © Free Press, 1970.

The Development of Inflections. Word inflections (e.g., verb endings for the past tense), going from the present tense "I beg" to the past tense "I *begged*" by adding the inflection *ed,* are acquired in a consistent order by children.

The acquisition of inflections demonstrates one of the most interesting characteristics of language development: *overregularization.* Specifically, over-regularization happens when children who are first learning language inflect the irregular (or strong) verbs of English for the past tense in the same way that regular (or weak verbs) are inflected. For example, children produce such verbs as *comed, breaked,* and *doed* by this process of overregularization. They use the inflection *d* or *ed,* which is appropriate for regular verbs such as *walk* (*walked*) or *talk* (*talked*), and apply it to irregular verbs. Although the phenomenon of overregulation is interesting in its own right, it also demonstrates an important feature of early language development: *the child is searching for patterns of organizing words.* When a pattern is acquired, it will very likely be applied as broadly as possible (Dale, 1976).

Another interesting way in which the development of language inflections has been studied is by the use of nonsense nouns or verbs. This method ensures that the child has never heard the word before, and therefore it eliminates the possibility of rote memory. Berko (1958) has used this technique (see Figure 6.14). A typical language problem using this technique is the following: "This is a wug. Now we have another one. We have two of them. We have two _____." Results of this kind of experiment with toddlers and preschoolers indicate that children do overgeneralize by applying their known inflection patterns to all situations.

This extraordinary capacity for applying language patterns is illustrated by an interesting situation. One might expect that toddlers and young children begin their language development by using regular verb forms correctly (e.g.,

FIGURE 6.14   Berko's experimental method for examining children's use of inflections. Nonsense verbs and nouns are used so that results will indicate generalized patterns of language rather than memory of spoken words.

Adapted from U. Bellugi and R. Brown, Eds., "The Acquisition of Language," *Monographs of the Society for Research in Child Development,* 1964, *29*(1), 43–79. Reprinted by permission.

This is a wug.

Now there is another one.
There are two of them.
There are two _____ .

walked or *helped*) and then gradually extending these learned patterns to irregular verb forms (e.g., *come, do,* and *tear*), producing grammatically incorrect words such as *comed, doed,* and *teared*. This commonsense expectation, however, is not what happens. Observations indicate that toddlers at first use the correct forms of the past tense for irregular verbs *even before* they learn the correct inflections for regular verbs. Why should this be the case? It is probably not so surprising in light of two things (Dale, 1976):

1. Irregular verbs (*come, do,* and so on) express *common actions* and are therefore used more often to describe simple behaviors.
2. Irregular verb forms are four times *more common in parental speech* than regular verb forms (Slobin, 1971).

Soon, the regular-verb past-tense inflection (*d* or *ed*) appears and is extended by the toddler to both regular and irregular verbs (Ervin, 1964). The correct irregular past-tense forms that preceded may coexist with the regular and generalized pattern for a time, but they are ultimately abandoned (Cazden, 1968). Later they are discovered again or relearned as "exceptions" to the new-found inflection patterns.

Modification of Simple Sentences. After the child has mastered the basic principles of the formation of two-word phrases (or simple sentences), the next period of language development is characterized by the *modification* of these simple sentences, including such transformations as the creation of *negative* and *imperative* forms and *asking questions.*

The Development of Questions. The development of questions illustrates the general development of complex transformations of simple sentences (Bellugi, 1965; Brown, Cazden, and Bellugi, 1969; Klima and Bellugi-Klima, 1966; Ervin-Tripp, 1974). Like most other languages, the English language has two types of questions (Dale, 1976):

1. *Yes/no questions* are those that can be formed from almost any declarative sentence; they ask if the declarative statement is true or false. *Declarative statement:* "Johnny plays with his blocks." *Yes/no question:* "Does Johnny play with his blocks?"
2. *"Wh" questions* are those that ask for specific information. They are called "wh" questions because they usually begin with "wh" words, such as *which, what, why,* and *who* (see Table 6.8)

TABLE 6.8
"Why" and "Why Not"
Questions

Mother	Child
I see a seal.	Why you see seal?
You bent that game.	Why me bent that game?
I guess I'm not looking in the right place.	Why not you looking in the right place?
You can't dance	Why not me can't dance?

Source: R. Brown, C. Cazden, and U. Bellugi, "The Child's Grammar from I to III." In John P. Hill (Ed.), *Minnesota Symposium on Child Psychology*, Vol. 2. University of Minnesota Press, Minneapolis, 1969.

The general pattern of development for question asking follows the same form as language development as a whole. That is, the toddler's questions are telegraphic at first, and then over time, they approximate adult questions. Initially questions differ from their declarative equivalents only by a rising intonation (Dale, 1976):

Declarative statement: "See cat"
Question: "See cat?" In this case, a rising intonation is symbolized by a question mark.)

Complex Sentences. An important milestone in the development of language is the formation of *complex sentences*. These are formed by the joining of two simple sentences together by conjunction or by embedding. With the use of a conjunction, the two simple sentences *I can read* and *I can write* can be made into the complex sentence *I can read and write*. Using embedding, one can combine the two simple sentences *Where's a book?* and *I can read a book* into *Where's a book I can read?* Another example of two simple sentences combined by embedding would be *You can watch me* and *I can draw pictures*, formed into the simple sentence *You can watch me draw pictures*. The first complex sentences used by children are usually embedded in simple sentences (Limber, 1973).

The appearance of these apparently embedded complex sentences seems to occur between two years and three and one-fourth years. At this point, it is not clear whether the child is really creating *complex* sentences or simply juxtaposing elements in a given context (Clark, 1974; Ingram, 1975).

THE CONTEXT OF LANGUAGE DEVELOPMENT: THE ROLE OF THE FAMILY

As we will see in the next chapter, there is a distinction between learning a language and the effective *use* of language in interpersonal communication. Even though the infant and the toddler may possess *competence* in such language activities as communicating needs, emotions and various points of view, it is not until the school years that the "mutual following" skills that underlie effective adult communication begin to develop. For example, the ability to understand another person's point of view—and to design communication in line with this understanding—is not present in early language development. In fact, this mutual following skill does not ordinarily occur until the child is about ten years old. Language development occurs in a social system that involves *both* active, adult models and the creative, active child.

The Contribution of the Adult. The verbal interchange between parent and child serves an important function in the development of language. The adult speaks to the child in language forms that are simpler than ordinary adult–adult speech. However, the adult's language is more effective as a language-teaching technique if it remains just above the level of the child's own language productions. In other words, the child is more likely to learn language through mutual verbal interaction if the parent's utterances are challenging rather than overwhelmingly new or simple repetitions of what the child can already say (Dale, 1976).

The problem for the language learner is that to develop competence in language, he/she can work only with the information available: the caretaker's or parent's speech heard by the child and the responses to the child's own speech. Because most of the language the young child hears is that of the parent or caretaker, we might ask, what kind of language environment do parents or caretakers provide for their children? As we have already indicated, the speech of the parent (usually the mother) is simpler than ordinary adult conversation. Maternal utterances are shorter in length, the rate of speech is slower, and there are fewer complex sentences (Vorster, 1974). As the child acquires the patterns of language, maternal speech gradually increases in complexity (Dale, 1976).

What about the father's role in early language development? Fathers may not be ignored by their children or their spouses, but typically they have been overlooked in psychological research. There are very few studies of the role of father–child verbal interaction during early language learning. The consensus is that fathers just do not spend very much time talking to their young children (Rebelsky and Hanks, 1971). Because it is not clear whether what happens at three months will determine or predict language development at one or two years of age (or whether the *quality* or *quantity* of verbal interaction is more important), it is important not to underestimate the role of fathers. This is important to bear in mind when one looks at Rebelsky and Hanks' results. They found that, on the average, there were 2.7 verbal interactions between father and three-month-old infants during a twenty-four-hour period. These verbal interactions totaled an average of thirty-eight seconds a day!

Several interesting *types of verbal exchange* between parent and child have been observed (Brown, Cazden, and Bellugi, 1969; Brown and Hanlon, 1970). These interchanges provide important opportunities for the infant and the toddler to refine language competence. The most interesting mode of exchange between parent and child is *expansion*. Expansion involves the mutual imitation of child by parent and parent by child. There are several types of expansion that a parent can initiate (see Table 6.9).

The Role of the Child. In the social system of language development, the child is an *active*, autonomous investigator of the world. Mastering language is not a simple task. As we have indicated, the child constantly formulates hypotheses about the "rules" of language and tests these.

TABLE 6.9
Expansions of Child's Speech Produced by Mothers

Child	Mother
Baby highchair	Baby is in the highchair.
Mommy eggnog.	Mommy had her eggnog.
Eve lunch.	Eve is having lunch.
Mommy sandwich.	Mommy'll have a sandwich.
Sat wall.	He sat on the wall.
Throw daddy.	Throw it to daddy.
Pick glove	Pick the glove up.

Source: R. Brown and U. Bellugi, "Three Processes in the Child's Acquisition of Syntax," *Harvard Educational Review,* Spring 1964, pp. 34, 141. Copyright © 1964 by President and Fellows of Harvard College.

Social and Personality Development

During the first three years of life, the child makes many important advances in development: learning to walk and to grasp objects and acquiring a language. Another extraordinarily important facet of development is the *sense of self* that the baby organizes. How does this sense of self develop? What are the factors that contribute to its evolution? What are the characteristics of self that emerge in the infant and the toddler? In this section, we examine these questions.

THE ATTACHMENT RELATIONSHIP: THE CONTEXT OF SELFHOOD

How does the infant's sense of self develop? It develops in the *context* of relationships with other people, including family members, peers, and adults outside of the family (e.g., teachers and neighbors). During infancy, the sense of self emerges from the affectional relationship between parents and infants that is called *attachment*.

Ainsworth (1973) defined attachment as follows:

An attachment is an affectional tie that one person forms to another specific person, binding them together in space and enduring over time. Attachment is discriminating and specific. One may be attached to more than one person. . . . Attachment implies affect. . . . We usually think of attachment as implying affection or love.

One way to view attachment is as a set of behaviors (by *both* parent and infant) that result in a *mutual* parent–infant relationship. This attachment relationship promotes the goal of parent–infant closeness or *proximity*. Proximity between parent and newborn is very important for human beings (and for many animals). Closeness between parents and infants allows for the

FIGURE 6.15   Components of the attachment relationship.

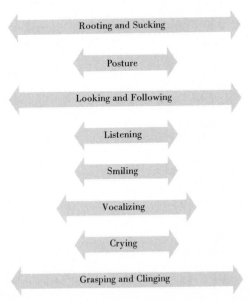

satisfaction of infant and parent needs (e.g., feeding, looking, and affection). The sense of self is forged in this relationship.

Components of the Attachment System. The attachment relationship involves interaction in a number of areas (Ainsworth, 1973) (see Figure 6.15).

Rooting and Sucking. The behavior of the infant includes many responses that both facilitate feeding and provide "signals" to the mother to help her meet the infant's needs. The *rooting reflex* (see Chapter 5) is an infant behavior that makes it likely that the infant will find the nipple of the mother (if breast-fed) or the bottle (Ainsworth, 1973). Rooting behavior is often a signal to the mother that the infant is hungry (Blauvelt and McKenna, 1961; Prechtl, 1958). If the baby is being breast-fed, it moves its head in such a way that it will be likely to find the mother's nipple. The mother, in turn, adjusts her behavior so that the baby's search is likely to be successful (e.g., in the way in which she holds the baby or in the way she positions the breast). Once the breast or bottle nipple reaches the infant's mouth, the sensation of touch

---

APPLICATION BOX

John Bowlby on Attachment as a System

Attachment develops over time. It is not something that is present at birth, although there are certain biological mechanisms that predispose such a relationship. Bowlby (1958) identified five behavioral systems that contribute to attachment. These behavioral systems emerge at different times and serve to "bind" mother to child and child to mother

Behavior System	Descriptions	Behavior System	Descriptions
Fixed-Action Behaviors Crying Smiling	These infant behaviors activate parental responses that bring the adult into close proximity with the infant. Infant crying and smiling behaviors during early infancy (usually after the first year) are called "fixed-action" systems. *Fixed-action behaviors* are those that promote proximity but that are not altered or changed by the infant in relation to adult responses. For example, crying may continue at the same level of intensity even though the adult may be about to pick up the infant.	*Goal-Corrected Behaviors* Sucking Following Clinging	Sucking, following, and clinging also generate parental responses that bring both infant and parent closer together. These three behaviors are called *goal-corrected behaviors* because the infant takes an *active* role in maintaining proximity by adjusting its responses to the parent's behavior (e.g., the infant may "cling" more tightly to the parent when the parent attempts to put the child down than simply while being held by the parent).

The Beginnings of Love Between Parent and Child

The expectant mother, no less than the father, often finds it hard to imagine how she is going to feel about the unborn infant. But once the child arrives the mother love that so strongly shapes the infant's future unfolds in a complex and wonderful pattern. This mysterious process begins before birth. As our knowledge increases, all who bother to look at the process find themselves instilled with awe and respect.

The newborn, it turns out, is not the passive creature most people have assumed him to be. Recent research shows that the newborn comes well-endowed with charm and a full potential for social graces. His eyes are bright and equipped with surprisingly good vision. Shortly after birth, he likes to watch the human face. He looks at his mother and soon recognizes and prefers her. Dr. Robert Emde, of the University of Colorado Medical School, observes, "Little in life is more dramatic than the mother's moment of discovery that the baby is beaming at her with sparkling eyes." This is the time, mothers often say, when affection begins. The infant's cry alerts her and causes a biological as well as emotional reaction. Swedish studies using thermal photography have shown that the cry increases the flow of blood to her nipples, increasing milk secretion. The newborn hears the mother's or caretaker's voice and turns his head towards that person. The infant's ability to cling and cuddle communicates a pleasurable warmth to the mother. The infant's odor, too, is pleasant and uniquely his own. Although some experts say the smile is not "real" until some weeks after birth, the newborn does smile. Dr. Burton L. White of Harvard University says, "God or somebody has built into the human infant a collection of attributes that guarantee attractiveness." . . .

To get a close look at what happens between mother and the new infant, Dr. T. Berry Brazelton of Harvard has studied video-tapes of their interactions. Frame-by-frame "micro-analysis" of the pictures shows that the baby moves in smooth, circular "ballet-like" patterns as he looks up at the mother. The baby concentrates his attention on her whole body and limbs move in rhythm;

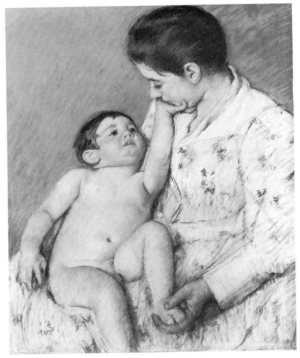

"First Caress" by the American artist Mary Cassatt. From the collection of the New Britain Museum of American Art, Harriet Russell Stanley Fund.

Photograph by E. Irving Blomstrann

the infant then withdraws briefly, but returns his attention, averaging several cycles a minute. The mother falls in step with the baby's cycles by talking and smiling, in a kind of "dance." If the mother falls out of step and disappoints the infant by presenting a still, unresponsive face when he gazes at her, the baby becomes "concerned" and keeps trying to get her attention. If he fails, the baby withdraws into a collapsed state of helplessness, face turned aside, and body curled up and motionless. If the mother becomes responsive again, the baby looks puzzled but returns to his cyclical motions. . . .

Reprinted from S. P. Hersh and K. Levin, "How Love Begins Between Parent and Child," *Children Today*, Washington, D.C., March–April 1978, pp. 2–6, 47

produces *sucking* movements. The presence of milk in the mouth, in turn, produces swallowing. This whole chain of events ensures that food will be taken in and, as an important by-product, that the infant and the parent will be brought together in an attachment relationship (Ainsworth, 1973).

Adjustment of Posture. During the feeding process, there is a mutual or reciprocal adjustment of posture between infant and parent (Blauvelt and McKenna, 1961). This mutual adjustment also occurs when the infant is being held by the parent or the caretaker for reasons other than feeding. When being held in a feeding or "cuddling" position, the infant characteristically relaxes and "molds" its body against the adult (Ainsworth and Bell, 1969; Ainsworth and Wittig, 1969; Bell and Ainsworth, 1972). There is some limited evidence of the interaction between cuddling and attachment. Infants identified as "noncuddlers" had "less intense" attachments, as well as being somewhat slower to develop an attachment relationship (Schaffer and Emerson, 1964a, 1964b; Ainsworth, Bell, and Stayton, 1971; Prechtl, 1963).

Looking and Following. The infant's looking behavior appears to be stimulated by certain properties of objects (see the discussion of vision in Chapter 5; Fantz, 1958, 1961, 1963, 1964, 1965, 1966, 1967; Fantz and Nevis, 1967). The objects that the infant encounters that are most likely to possess these properties are *human faces* (Haaf and Bell, 1967; Kagan, Lewis, Campbell, and Kalafat, 1966; Carpenter and Stechler, 1967; Robson, 1967). As the infant develops increasing control over its visual responses, it is able to establish eye-to-eye contact. The *mutual process* in which the infant looks at an adult and the adult looks at the infant serves as a *signal* for both; the parent notes the attention of the infant, and the infant notes the attention of the parent (Wolff, 1963; Robson, 1967; Stechler and Latz, 1966). In the same way, the infant's ability to look away acts as a signal. Mutual gazing has affectional or emotional aspects, particularly when mutual social smiling occurs (see the discussion of smiling later in this chapter). Looking also enables the infant to supplement other mediums of attachment (e.g., touch) by helping the infant to discriminate between people while they are various distances away. All of these factors suggest the vital role that vision plays in the development of early social behavior and attachment.

Listening. Although there has been considerably less research on infant hearing than on vision, there is reason to think that *mutual following* does occur (Bowlby, 1969; Wolff, 1966; Wertheimer, 1961). For example, an infant's interest in its parent's voice is likely to lead the parent to talk more. This, in turn, will probably cause the infant to attend more to the sounds of the parent's voice (Bowlby, 1969).

In the development of attachment, the infant seems to show a progression in listening (Wolff, 1959):

1. By the second week of life, a soft sound (rather than a loud one) and especially a human voice are quite successful in causing the baby to smile (Wolff, 1959). A high-pitched voice is most effective (see Chapter 5). Through about the fourth month of life, the *human voice alone* tends to calm the infant.
2. After the fourth month, the infant seems to want not only the sound but the sight of the parent as well.

Smiling. There is reason to think that the motor ability to smile is probably "built into" the human being from birth (Ainsworth, 1973). We will discuss

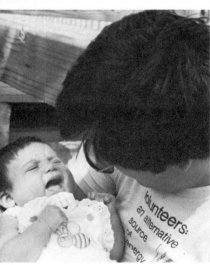

Babies, like all human beings, can be close to many different people. Fathers can "bond" with their children.

Top photograph by Shan Rucinski; bottom photograph by Sylvia Byers

the development of smiling more specifically later in this chapter, but from the beginning, some stimuli are more likely to cause a smile than others (Wolff, 1963; Freedman, 1964). These effective stimuli are more apt to come from a parent. Through learning, the *mutual interactions* that result in a sometimes irresistible infant smile come to be restricted to mutual following involving the human face and voice (Wolff, 1963; Piaget, 1952). Through further learning, smiles become more frequently elicited by one person, or a few specific persons, rather than by others. Finally, the baby's smile is itself a stimulus to reciprocal social behavior on the part of its parents and others. Therefore, the smile serves to increase the probability of interaction with, proximity to, and contact with the parents and potential attachment figures (Ainsworth, 1973).

Vocalizing. The role of an infant's babbling in the formation of attachment has a similar function to that of smiling (Ainsworth, 1973). According to Bowlby (1969, p. 11), "Both occur when a baby is awake and contented and both have as a predictable outcome that the baby's companion responds in a sociable way and engages with him in a chain of interaction." It is quite likely that an adult's vocal responses to an infant's vocalization strengthen the infant's tendency to vocalize in social transactions (Wolff, 1963, 1969; Piaget, 1952; Rheingold, Gewirtz, and Ross, 1959; Weisberg, 1963). Although language is significant throughout the life span as a mode of social communication, vocalizing is most important at the preverbal level of infancy as a source of attachment.

Crying. During the early phases of infancy, crying is usually activated by the infant. The causes of infant crying are fairly well known and include pain, hunger, and intestinal distress.

As a focus of attachment interaction, there appears to be a developmental progression for crying (Wolff, 1959):

1. *Physical–physiological activation.* This phase extends from birth through about the first month. Crying is usually caused by stomach pains, general discomfort, or hunger.
2. *Psychological activation.* This phase begins at about one month with the onset of "fake" cry (a low-pitched, nonrhythmical crying, without tears). Many parents feel that this cry usually means that the baby wants attention; often such crying stops when the baby gets attention.

   At about the sixth week, babies tended to stop crying when parent–infant eye-to-eye contact begins. By three months of age, thumb-sucking reduces crying. Of all the modes of reducing crying (including the above two), physical contact is the most effective (Bell and Ainsworth, 1972).
3. *Differential crying.* Somewhere between two months of age and twenty-two months of age, infants may protest the departure of a parent, although not the departure of other adults (Ainsworth, 1967; Wolff, 1969). Thus different persons may activate and terminate crying. This differential crying suggests that the baby is becoming attached to specific people.

Grasping and Clinging. Through its reflex responses, the human neonate grasps and clings to a figure with whom it is in close contact. Perhaps in the original environment of evolutionary adaptation, these reflexes gave way to voluntary grasping and clinging so that the infant could help to support itself while being transported. (There is no evidence that contemporary Western

TABLE 6.10 Four Stages in the Development of Attachment

Stage	Age	Characteristics
Stage 1	0–3 mos.	Infant uses sucking, rooting, grasping, smiling, gazing, cuddling, and visual tracking to maintain closeness with caregiver.
Stage 2	3–6 mos.	Infant is more responsive to familiar figures than to strangers.
Stage 3	7 mos. to 2 years	Infant begins actively to seek proximity with the object of attachment.
Stage 4	Toddlerhood and beyond	Infant uses a variety of behaviors that influence behavior of object of attachment in order to satisfy the need for closeness.

From B.Caldwell and H. Ricciuti (Eds.), Review of Child Development Research, Vol. 3, pp. 1–94, 1973. Reprinted by permission of The University of Chicago Press, Copyright © 1973. Table by M. D. S. Ainsworth.

infants can do so in any voluntary way until considerably later in the first year of life, and then perhaps only under special circumstances). Nevertheless, it seems reasonable to assume a genetic basis for clinging, and to consider clinging an attachment behavior.

The Development of Attachment in the Family: Four Phases. Attachment does not occur suddenly; rather, it is a process that takes place over many years of the child's early development. *Four major phases* have been identified in the development of attachment: a phase during which the infant's social behavior is undiscriminating; a phase of discriminating social behavior; a phase characterized by active infant initiative in seeking physical closeness and contact with the caregiver; and a final phase characterized by a finely tuned relationship guided by the mutual following skills of the parent and the child (Bowlby, 1969) (see Table 6.10).

Phase of Undiscriminating Social Responsiveness (birth to two or three months).

Two primary activities occur in the first phase:
Infants begin to examine their environment, especially people. These activities include listening, visual following, and sucking. The infant's exploration of people may be aided by crying, smiling, and vocalizing. These behaviors serve as "signals" by bringing adults closer to the infant.
Infants display their perceptual skills (e.g., vision and hearing) in distinguishing various stimuli. The infant seems to be most responsive to the sights and sounds of human adults (Ainsworth, 1973). However, in spite of these skills, the infant cannot yet distinguish between the different persons who provide these stimuli.

Phase of Discriminating Social Responsiveness (three to six months of age). The infant continues to explore the environment. However, during this phase, the infant can distinguish a few familiar figures (e.g., mother and father) from unfamiliar adults. Ainsworth (1967) pointed out that this phase is divided into two parts:

1. *Responsiveness to people close at hand.* The infant distinguishes between familiar and unfamiliar adults by demonstrating different smiling or vocalizing patterns in their presence.

2. *Responsiveness to people at a distance.* The infant demonstrates its awareness of differences between people by showing different greeting behaviors when a familiar figure and an unfamiliar figure enter a room and different crying patterns when a familiar figure and an unfamiliar figure leave a room.

Phase of Activity Initiative in Seeking Proximity and Contact (seven months to two years). During this phase, there is a marked increase in the infant's ability to initiate behaviors that are likely to result in proximity or contact. Whereas in the previous phases the infant's signals were expressive, "fixed-action" signals, the baby's actions are now more carefully adjusted to the behavior of adults in order to promote proximity or contact. By this phase, infant locomotion and voluntary hand and arm movements are prominent techniques for initiating attachment. Also, parents may begin to notice that when they come into the infant's view, they may be "greeted" in a more active and affectionate way. Following, approaching, and clinging behaviors become significant in this phase.

"Goal-corrected" sequences of behavior also emerge during this phase (Bowlby, 1969). These are behavioral interactions that are mutual and are guided by a *constant stream of feedback.* In these sequences of behavior, the infant (as well as the parent) can guide and change the behavioral direction, speed, or motive in accordance with what the other is doing. In other words, this behavior is based on *mutual following.*

In addition, the onset of this phase of attachment coincides with the fourth phase of Piaget's first stage of intelligence—the stage of *sensorimotor development* (see discussion of cognitive development). A major feature of this stage is the development of the *concept of object permanence.* In other words, the child's ability to search for a "missing" object may be a cognitive basis for attachment.

Phase of Goal-Corrected Partnership (two years and beyond). In the third phase, the infant could, to some extent, predict its mother's movements and adjust its own movements in order to maintain the desired degree of proximity. The infant could not, however, understand the factors that influenced its mother's movements and could not plan means to change her behavior. As the child begins to understand and "infer" the parent's set goals, it begins to attempt to alter them to fit better with its own needs for contact, proximity, and interaction. This relationship is characterized by Bowlby as a "partnership." In his or her early efforts to change the set goal (the degree to which the parent wants to maintain proximity) of the parent's behavior, a young child may have some difficulty because he/she cannot see things from the parent's point of view. The reciprocity of the partnership develops gradually.

SCENARIO:
THE DAY BABY ELIZABETH ANTICIPATED
HER PARENTS' EVENING OUT

Our Elizabeth is now a full-fledged toddler (two years, seven months). She has begun to anticipate separations from her parents. One evening, her parents were preparing to leave for an evening at another couple's home. Elizabeth became "suspicious" that something "unusual" was going on when her father began putting on his suit. As he was putting on his tie, Elizabeth marched into the bathroom and confronted him.

Elizabeth: Daddy, going away.
Daddy: Yes, your mother and I are going out to see Jeff, Brian, and Todd's mommy and daddy.
Elizabeth: Daddy, can stay with me and . . .

(At this moment, the bell rang. Elizabeth walked to the front door. Her mother opened the door. It was the baby-sitter, Mark. Elizabeth recognized him.)

Mark: Hi, Elizabeth.
Elizabeth: Mark . . . go home.

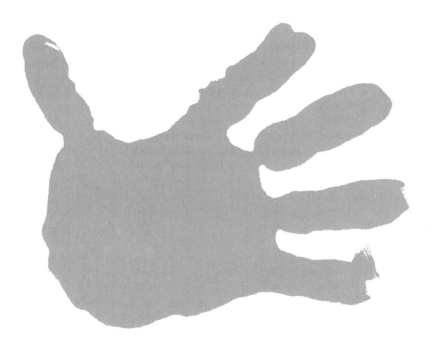

Sometimes you get discouraged
Because I am so small
And always leave my finger prints
On furniture and walls.
But every day I'm growing up
And soon I'll be so tall
That all those little hand prints
Will be hard to recall.
So here's a special hand print
Just so that you can say.
This is how my fingers looked
When I placed them here today.
                    Author Unknown
                    Artist: Elizabeth

Relationship Between Attachment and Other Infant Behaviors.

The biological and cultural functions of attachment are fulfilled when the infant and the young child remain "close enough" to the parent(s) to survive and to learn valuable social skills. Attachment is also related to other behaviors that are important in human development. In this section, we explore the relationship between attachment behavior and exploration (and, therefore, cognitive development and competence) and behavior with strangers and in strange situations. The ability of the infant and the child to learn to extend social horizons and relationships using attachment as a base is significant in later development. The attachment relationship is the basis for more complex interaction in peer groups, school groups, and play relationships.

Play, Exploration, and Attachment. When a baby achieves locomotion, it is often eager to move away from its mother to explore the world around it (Ainsworth, 1967). The parents seem to provide a secure base from which the baby can undertake explorations without anxiety. The baby keeps track of the parents' whereabouts, however, and will probably return to this base from time to time before venturing out again. The infant may explore objects and environments whose novelty might be frightening in the absence of the attachment figure. The smoothness and integration of the balance is affected by the characteristic interaction that has been built up between parent and infant. The infant's behavior in new situations can be a sign of the quality of infant–mother attachment (Ainsworth and Bell, 1969).

Fear of Strangers. Fear of strangers is the result of an infant's first attachment. When an infant becomes attached to its parents, it can be easily upset by unfamiliar adults. When in the presence of a strange adult, the infant may cry or show other signs of distress.

Stranger anxiety is primarily a reaction to discrepancies between what the infant sees and what it expects to see, not a reaction to the stranger as such. The infant has come to expect the adult person to have certain characteristics (those of the familiar caretakers).

Stranger anxiety usually appears in American children at about six months of age. It reaches a peak at about eight months and is usually gone by twelve months. Whether an infant is frightened or alarmed by a stranger depends on many factors including the following (Ainsworth, 1973):

1. The infant's developmental stage.
2. The infant's previous experience with strangers or with people generally (Schaffer, 1966).
3. The infant's temperament or predisposition to fearfulness.
4. The behavior of the stranger, including how "close" he or she is or how "strange" he or she seems.
5. Whether the parent is *present or absent* (and, if present, how close).
6. The behavior of the mother (if present), including whether she herself is alarmed or anxious or whether she encourages or rebuffs the infant's attempt to cling.
7. The *quality of the infant–mother attachment relationship*, including whether it is secure or has been disturbed in any way by special circumstances such as illness or extended separations.

Separation Anxiety. Separation anxiety usually appears in American infants sometime around eight to twelve months, and it usually disappears around twenty to twenty four months (Ainsworth, 1967, 1973). Separation anxiety is produced when a parent or caretaker physically leaves the child and is no longer in view. Adverse effects may result if a child is separated for long periods from his or her mother once he/she is old enough to be attached to her and before he/she is mature enough to withstand a period of absence (Bowlby, 1952; Ainsworth, 1962; Winnicott, 1964).

Separation anxiety involves a level of infant cognitive competence. The infant has to be able to compare being separated from the parent with being with the parent. Because this skill does not occur before about eight months, children under this age do not experience separation anxiety (Ainsworth, 1973).

The issue of separation raises two related questions:

1. What is the impact of the lack or loss of mothering on infants("maternal deprivation")? For example, do institutionalized infants suffer from the absence of a single caregiver?
2. Can multiple caregivers successfully assume a child-rearing function, not only for institutionalized infants but for other children? This is an issue because of the increasing numbers of parents whose children are in some form of day care.

Maternal Deprivation. Early studies of children reared in institutions showed that these children suffered devastating effects to their cognitive and social development (Dennis, 1960; Dennis and Sayegh, 1965). Some early interpretations of these studies attributed the disastrous results to the lack of mothering, or *maternal deprivation*. However, "maternal deprivation" is a catchall phrase that can refer to a broad range of early experiences (e.g., the lack of a single primary caregiver or the lack of stimulation for proper development) (Rutter, 1971). It is now apparent that the institutionalized infants in many of the early studies suffered from the lack of stimulating, enriching experiences in addition to the lack of a stable, concerned caregiver. When some of these infants experienced more stimulating and responsive interactions, their social and cognitive skills improved, sometimes dramatically.

Multiple Caregiving. Does the absence of a single or primary caregiver *result in* harmful effects on children? Research evidence suggests that the most important feature of caregiving is its stability and responsiveness, rather than the number of caregivers (Rutter, 1971). Rutter (1971) found that children who experience multiple caregiving demonstrate perfectly normal development.

Children raised in Israeli kibbutzim show normal development (Gewirtz, 1965; Beit-Hallahmi and Rabin, 1977). In an Israeli kibbutz, young children are raised communally by several caregivers. While the parents are working, the children are cared for in residential nurseries. The parents see their children for only a few hours a day or on weekends. The conclusions of research on kibbutz children are that parents can, in fact, be away from their children for a significant time period without any adverse effects on the children. Nonetheless, it is important that children and infants in such multiple caregiving settings be with sensitive, responsive adults.

The Role of the Father. As we have pointed out, attachment has an important role in the healthy development of human beings. Historically the

What Is the Impact on the Developing Infant When Mothers Are in the Work Force?

Put another way, one might ask, Can a child tolerate daily separations of eight to ten hours without distressing effects? As we pointed out earlier in this chapter, mothers may hold a full-time job for any number of reasons, including economic necessity or career aspirations. When it is necessary or appropriate for both parents to work, they find substitute care for the child. This care has usually taken one of two forms: (1) *family day care*, or care by (a) the father or another relative (e.g., grandparent, uncle, aunt, cousin), a neighbor, or a stranger in the *child's home* or (b) care by a relative or nonrelative in *that person's home*; (2) *institutional day care*, in which the infant is cared for by a specific organization whose purpose is day care. The vast majority of such care has been provided through family day care (see the table).

Whether separation from both parents could be harmful to the child depends on a number of factors:

1. *Characteristics of the parents.* What are the parents' attitudes toward their child? How good is their attachment relationship to their child? What is the effect of parental personality and attitudes on the child's response to separation? Is it true that good parent–child interaction in the evening and on weekends can make up for long absences during the work week? Are the parents reasonably well adjusted to their work activities?

2. *Characteristics of the child.* Is the child "anxious" in his/her attachment to the parents? If the child is already insecure in the attachment relationship, separation from the parents may be irritating and disturbing. On the other hand, if the child is neglected, day care may be more beneficial.

3. *Characteristics of the substitute care.* What is the quality of the relationship between the child and the substitute care giver? There is reason to think that the child can develop healthy multiple attachments to adults other than the parents (e.g., care givers) (Ainsworth, 1973). Is quality care available? Is substitute care provided by a caregiver who does not have to distribute his or her attention over too many children?

Percent Distribution of Principle Type of Child Care Arrangement Used by Mothers 18 to 44 Years Old for Their Youngest Child Under 5 Years, June 1982.	
Mother Employed Full-time	
Care in Child's Home	25.7%
By father	10.3
Other	15.4
Care in Another Home	43.8
Relative	19.7
Nonrelative	24.1
Group Care Center	18.8
Other Arrangements	11.7
Mother Employed Part-Time	
Care in Child's Home	39.3%
By father	20.3
Other	19.0
Care in Another Home	34.1
Relative	15.7
Nonrelative	18.4
Group Care Center	7.6
Other Arrangements	19.0

Source: Calculated from U.S. Bureau of the Census, "Child Care Arrangements of Working Mothers: June 1982," *Current Population Reports*, Series P23, No. 129, Table 2, Parts B and C, Nov. 1983.

research on attachment has focused largely on the relationship of the mother and the infant. This, of course, was no accident, as the "traditional" (sex biased) cultural expectation has assured that the place of the mother was in the home—with her children. Over the last decade, this expectation has been

Infancy and Toddlerhood

called into question. Many women seek fulfillment in careers in the world of work, in addition to (and sometimes instead of) the roles of homemaking and child rearing. These changing values have generated research on the role of fathers in child development (Lynn, 1974; Lamb, 1977). In other words, the historical or traditional expectation that the father's place will be in the world of work has also come into question.

Fathers can—and do—become as attached to infants and young children as mothers. A common observation in middle-class families is that both father and mother interact with their newborn for about the same amount of time during the first few days after birth. When given the opportunity, working-class fathers also demonstrate responsive and nurturant behavior toward newborns (Parke and Sawin, 1977). Studies of fathers' attachment to infants show that fathers look and smile at their babies, kiss their babies, and give them their bottles. These behaviors are similar to those of the mothers.

Lamb (1977) found that there may be some differences between fathers and mothers in the way that they interact with babies and children. For example, mothers are likely to be gentle in handling infants and young children, whereas fathers seem more prone to rough-and-tumble play with youngsters.

THE EMERGENCE OF THE SOCIABLE SELF

During the first two years of life, the infant "builds on" the attachment relationship. Infants expand their social horizons, refining their competence and autonomy in all relationships with people and things. They extend themselves to interact with new adults and with peers.

As we pointed out earlier, an important determinant of the infant's efforts to gain *competence* in exploring the environment and in being "sociable" with others is the quality of the infant–parent attachment. Research has demonstrated that the infant is naturally a "sociable" person from birth on (Sander, 1977; Schaffer, 1977). Detailed observations of parent–infant interactions indicate that the mother and the infant adjust mutually to each other's behavior (Stern, 1977). Through this interaction, the baby learns to control its experiences and to develop a primitive sense of "me."

Who Am I? When do infants recognize who they are? When can they distinguish between the "me" and the "not me"? Research evidence demonstrates that by twenty to twenty-four months, infants have developed a self-concept (Brooks and Lewis, 1976). They recognize themselves as distinct from others, and they recognize differences between people (including height and facial differences).

One of the ways of studying the question of self-recognition has involved infant responses to their images in mirrors and to films or videotapes of their own behavior. Papousek (1967) found that younger infants (five months old) showed more interest in films or videotapes of their behavior than in looking at themselves in a mirror. Older infants became more interested in the behavior that they created and could observe in mirrors. Papousek suggested that as infants grew older, their concept of self expands to include what they are actively *doing* (i.e., the relationship between their behavior and that of the mirror image).

Amsterdam (1972) identified the time of mature self-recognition as occur-

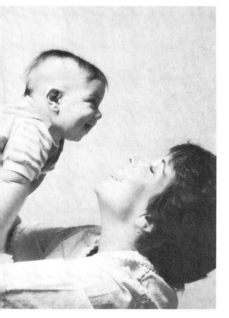

The emergence of the "sociable" self.

Photograph by Wayne Mason

The Role of the Father in Infancy

"Fathers are a biological necessity but a social accident," Margaret Mead once observed. Contemporary women might take issue with this traditional image of the father as the helpless parent with little talent for or interest in child-rearing. They are likely to argue that the father is just as capable of caring for babies as the mother, and ought to at least share the burdens.

Interestingly, research by developmental psychologists tends to support their view. Our studies of fathers confirm that they are not a social accident at all. They contribute significantly to an infant's social and intellectual growth, although in ways that are different from the mother's. The father is not just a poor substitute for the mother; he makes his own unique contribution to the care and development of infants and young children. . . .

Our . . . studies have confirmed that fathers, when given the opportunity, become actively involved with their newborns. While mothers and fathers are equally involved with their infants, they are involved in different ways right from the start. When they have the chance, fathers are

Photograph by Sylvia Marabate

more visually attentive and playful (talking to the baby, imitating the baby), but they are less active in feeding, and care-taking activities such as wiping the child's face or changing diapers.

From Parke, R. D. and Sawin, D. B., "Fathering: It's a Major Role," *Psychology Today*, November, 1977.

ring somewhere between twenty and twenty-four months. The experimenter put a rouge spot on the noses of children and watched their reaction to seeing the spot in the mirror. Amsterdam reasoned that mature self-recognition would occur when the infant used the mirror to identify and touch the rouge spot. Few babies under a year old seemed to recognize that the rouge spot and the nose belonged to them. It was not until twenty to twenty-four months that infants grabbed at the rouge spot, using the mirror as a guide.

Whom Do I Trust? The development of an attachment relationship between the infant and his or her parents provides the stable basis for all further social and personality development. As we have suggested, the attachment relationship can be viewed as a *system* in which the infant and the caregiver *interact mutually* with one another. In this context, the infant develops a sense of trust.

The beginning of social and personality development occurs with the establishment of a sense of trust (Erikson, 1950). For the infant to "trust" the environment and the people in it, he or she needs to feel that these "others" are in some sense "predictable" or "controllable." This process of learning to *predict* and *control* one's own behavior in relation to and in mutual interaction with others is what is meant by the term *self-regulation*. A sense of trust emerges from this give-and-take relationship between the infant and its caregiver. The baby comes to learn that his or her responses, in turn, generate the caregiver's responses, which, in turn, generate more infant responses. For example, in the process of feeding, the baby learns that its needs will be satisfied somewhat predictably. In turn, the caretaker also learns that the infant needs to be fed on a generally predictable schedule. Through such a process of *mutual accommodation*, a sense of trust is established.

The Infant Smile. One of the best "common sense" indicators that a healthy, trusting relationship is being established is the "dialogue" between the smiling infant and the parent. Infants smile for many reasons, including as a response to their recognition of familiar objects, as a simple response to internal physiological changes, as a response to controlling objects by making them move, or as a response to surprises such as the game of peek-a-boo (Piaget, 1952; Watson, 1970; Wolff, 1963). In addition to these reasons, the smile may develop into a social means of communication between infant and caretaker.

The infant's smile appears to go through the following phases (Bowlby, 1969; Sroufe and Waters, 1976):

1. *Spontaneous smiling.* This phase begins at birth and lasts until the age of about five weeks. These smiles seem to occur spontaneously and not as a response to any particular environmental event or stimulus. For example, the infant may smile during sleep.
2. *The transition from unselective to selective social smiling.* This phase begins at about the fifth week and extends to about the fourteenth week. The major characteristic of this phase is that at its onset, smiling can be produced by a rather broad range of moving and/or noise-making objects and by human faces, whereas at its conclusion, smiling is produced by a much narrower range of social stimuli (e.g., the stationary face).
3. *Differential social responsiveness.* This final phase, which begins at about six or seven months of age, has as its distinguishing characteristic the ability of the infant to use the social smile differently in response to different individuals. For example, the infant may smile more freely at familiar faces and may smile somewhat more cautiously at strangers.

Thus the smile is an important indicator of emerging attachment and trust. The emergence of the social smile (after the fifth week) and its refinement thereafter constitute a landmark in the development of the relationship between infant and caretaker. The change or transition from unselective smiling to social smiling is usually noted with some enthusiasm by the parent (Wolff, 1963). Such parental comments as "My baby seems more like a person" or "I'm beginning to enjoy my baby" are not uncommon responses to this change. Both the parent and the infant are beginning to gain a feeling of control in their mutual relationship.

What Can I Do? By the end of the second year, the period of social development, including autonomy, or self-direction, emerges. As the child becomes aware of his or her competence in language, object manipulation, and interpersonal relationships, he or she wants to do things for himself or herself. Although two-year-olds possess the skills and the will to move out into the world, they are obviously not yet aware of the potential consequences of their behavior. For example, the child who recognizes that a lengthy cord is attached to a lamp and that the lamp can be pulled by the cord may not yet understand that the lamp could break in transit. This venturesome attitude on the part of toddlers has led to the toddler period's being humorously called the "terrible twos."

The development of autonomy may sometimes result in a clash of wills between the parent and the toddler. The parent may be all too aware of the consequences of pulling lamp cords, yet the child may be determined to establish a sense of control over the environment. The parent may say "no" to the child, and the child may offer a hearty "no" back to the parent.

There are several areas of behavior in which autonomy is developed and tested. Two of these are peer relationships and play. Competence with other people emerges in many forms, including peer relationships, during the toddler years. For many years, peer relationships between infants and toddlers were not often examined. The thought may have been that infants were too involved in their own world to relate successfully to peers. Mounting evidence has shown that this is not the case (Rubenstein and Howes, 1976; Becker, 1977). Infants and toddlers are, in fact, sociable creatures. It appears that infants and toddlers learn to expand their social skills in the presence of peers. Becker (1977) demonstrated that nine-month-old babies could relate to one another by reaching toward each other and handing toys to one another. By the end of the first year, these infant interactions also included occasional fights and screams over disputed toys. One-year-olds appeared to imitate one another's play activities. For example, when one child started playing with blocks, others wanted to participate. One-year-olds demonstrated the emergence of mutual excitement about play activity. Peer interaction continues to develop throughout the second year as infants and toddlers learn to relate mutually to one another in play situations with greater satisfaction and delight.

Summary

1. There are at least two primary reasons for us to begin a discussion of infancy and toddlerhood with an analysis of the family. First, the family is the place in which early development largely occurs. Second, changes in the family affect the ability of the family, as a unit, to cope and function in child rearing.

2. For our purposes, we will define family as a group of adults and children who live together for an extended period of time.

3. The general function of the family is to mediate between the larger society or culture and the individual family member. More specific functions of the family include: economic, cooperation and division of labor, socialization of children, legitimization of sexual relations, reproduction of the species, provision of status and roles, and emotional support and companionship.

4. The physical growth of a baby is nothing short of remarkable. The development of movements or motor skills goes hand in hand with the development of perceptual, cognitive, and social skills. In addition to beginning language (sounds and crying) motor development is a form of communication

and interaction between the infant and the significant others in his or her life. Thus, motor development permeates virtually all domains of infant behavior. The two *primary* motor events of infancy are *locomotion* and *prehension.*

5. *Cognitive development* is the development of mental processes such as thinking, understanding, and perceiving. Piaget's research indicates that the process of intelligence evolves from the sensorimotor activities of infancy. As the infant progresses through the sensorimotor period the changes in mental skills are dramatic.

The emerging understanding of *object permanency* in the infant makes the world a more predictable and simpler place in which to live. The discovery of object permanency helps the infant to separate the existence of the object from a particular or unique space and time and, therefore, provides the foundation for the emerging concepts of space, time, and causality.

The development of *memory* in infants involves more than the simple recall of past perceptions and activities. Memory is a process of *expecting* and *predicting* future events based on past events.

6. *Language* represents one of the most mysterious events of biology and culture. The striking characteristic of language is that infants acquire all the main forms of speech and language before the end of the second year—the end of infancy. Language has many critical functions in individual self-regulation and social interaction. Language has several important properties: phonological components, morphological components, grammatical features, syntactical components, semantic features, and expressive components. Three major theories of language acquisition include learning theory, social learning theory, and psycholinguistic theory.

Two fundamental ideas underlie our notions of infant-child language development. (1) The child does not simply speak a garbled form of adult language. Rather, children speak a language of their own with unique patterns and characteristics. (2) Infants and children act as their own language specialists by continually experimenting with various utterances as a way of determining the "rules" of language.

The interactional process by which the infant develops the use of speech and language in the family is based, in part, on biological and maturational factors. Sometime around the first birthday, the infant attains a milestone of language—the utterance of the first word. One of the primary characteristics of children's speech that is noted with the onset of two-word phrases is that it is *telegraphic.*

After the child has mastered the basic principles of the formation of two-word phrases (or simple sentences), the child creates such transformations as *negative* and *imperative* statements and *questions.*

Language development occurs in a social system that involves *both* active adult models and the *creative,* active child.

7. The infant's organization of a sense of self is an extraordinary facet of social and personality development during the first three years of life. The sense of self develops in the context of relationships with other people including family members, peers, and adults outside the family. During infancy, the sense of self emerges from the affectional relationship between parents and infants that is called *attachment.* The components of the attachment relationship or system include rooting and sucking, posture, looking and following, listening, smiling, vocalizing, crying, and grasping and clinging.

The development of attachment is a process that takes place over many years. Four major phases in the development of attachment have been identified. During the first two years of life the infant "builds on" the attachment relationship. Infants expand their social horizons refining their competence and autonomy in relationships with people and things. Research evidence suggests that by 20 to 24 months infants have developed a self-concept. They recognize themselves as distinct from others, and they recognize differences between people. Social and personality development in infancy may be viewed as the emerging resolution to three questions: Who am I? Whom do I trust? What can I do?

Questions

1. Give two reasons why it is crucial to begin a description of the infant-toddler period with a discussion of the family.
2. Briefly identify and describe three family forms.
3. Two major features of motor development in infancy and toddlerhood are prehension (grasping) and locomotion. Briefly describe the developmental sequence associated with each of these motor skills.
4. Provide a detailed description of infant cognitive development in one of the six substages of Piaget's sensorimotor stage. What role do you see for parents or caregivers in that substage?
5. What is telegraphic speech and why is it important?
6. In what sense is attachment a system? Discuss one component of that system with particular reference to the mutual relationship between infant and caregiver.

Bibliography

ADAMS, B. N. *The Family: A Sociological Interpretation.* New York: Rand McNally, 1975.

ADVISORY COMMITTEE ON CHILD DEVELOPMENT. *Toward a national policy for children and families.* Washington, D.C.: National Academy of Sciences, 1976.

AINSWORTH, M. D. S. The effects of maternal deprivation: A review of findings and controversy in the context of research strategy. In *Deprivation of maternal care: A reassessment of its effects.* Public Health Papers No. 14. Geneva: World Health Organization, 1962, 97–165.

AINSWORTH, M. D. S. *Infancy in Uganda: Infant Care and Growth of Love.* Baltimore: John Hopkins U. P., 1967.

AINSWORTH, M. D. S. The development of infant–mother attachment. In B. Caldwell and H. Ricciuti (Eds.), *Review of Child Development Research,* Vol. 3. Chicago: U. of Chicago, 1973, pp. 1–94.

AINSWORTH, M. D. S., and BELL, S. M. V. Some contemporary patterns of mother–infant interaction in the feeding situation. In J. A. Ambrose (Ed.), *Stimulation in Early Infancy,* London: Academic Press, 1969, pp. 133–170.

AINSWORTH, M. D. S., BELL, S. M. V., and STAYTON, D. J. Individual differences in strange-situational behavior of one-year-olds. In H. R. Schaffer (Ed.),*The Origins of Human Social Relations.* London: Academic Press, 1971, pp. 17–52.

AINSWORTH, M. D. S., and WITTIG, B. A. Attachment and exploratory behavior of one-year-olds in a strange situation. In B. M. Foss (Ed.), *Determinants of Infant Behavior.* New York: Wiley, 1969, pp. 111–136.

AMSTERDAM, B. Mirror self-image reactions before age two. *Developmental Psychology,* 1972, *5,* 297–305.

ANTINUCCI, F., and PARISI, D. Early Language acquisition: A model and some data. In C. A. Ferguson and D. I. Slobin (Eds.), *Studies of Child Language Development.* New York: Holt, 1973, pp. 607–619.

BAKER, T. L., and McGINTY, D. J. Sleep apnea in hypoxic and normal kittens. *Developmental Psychology,* 1979, *12,* 577–594.

BAYLEY, N. *Bayley Scales of Development*, New York: The Psychological Corporation, 1969.

BAYLEY, N. The development of motor abilities during the first three years. *The Society for Research in Child Development, Inc.,* Monograph No. 1, 1935, 1–26. abridged.

BECKER, J. M. A learning analysis of the development of peer-oriented behavior in nine-month old infants. *Developmental Psychology,* 1977, *13,* 481–491.

BEIT-HALLAHMI, B., and RABIN, A. I. The kibbutz as a social experiment and child-rearing laboratory. *American Psychologist,* 1977, *32,* 532–541.

BELL, S. M., and AINSWORTH, M. D. S. Infant crying and maternal responsiveness. *Child Development,* 1972, *43,* 1171–1190.

BELLUGI, U. The development of interrogative structures in children's speech. In K. Riegel (Ed.), *The development of language functions.* University of Michigan Language Development Program, Report No. 8, 1965, pp. 103–138.

BELLUGI, U., and BROWN, R. (Eds.). The acquisition of language. *Monographs of the Society for Research in Child Development,* 1964, *29*(1), 43–79.

BERKO, J. The child's learning of English morphology. *Word,* 1958, *14,* 150–177.

BLACK, L., STEINSCHNEIDER, A., and SHEEHE, P. R. Neonatal respiratory instability and infant development. *Child Development,* 1979, *50,* 561–564.

BLAUVELT, H., and MCKENNA, J. Mother–neonate interaction: Capacity of the human newborn for orientation. In B. M. Foss (Ed.) *Determinants of Infant Behavior, Vol. 1.* New York: Wiley, 1961, pp. 3–36.

BLOOM, L. *Language development: Form and function in emerging grammars.* Cambridge, Mass.: MIT, 1970a.

BLOOM, L. *Semantic features in language acquisition.* Paper presented at the Conference on Research in the Language of the Mentally Retarded, University of Kansas, 1970b.

BOWERMAN, M. *Early Syntactic Development: A Cross-Linguistic Study with Special Reference to Finnish.* Cambridge: Cambridge U. P., 1973.

BOWLBY, J. *Maternal Care and Mental Health* (2nd ed.). Monograph Series, No. 2. Geneva: World Health Organization, 1952.

BOWLBY, J. The nature of the child's tie to his mother. *International Journal of Psychoanalysis,* 1958, *39,* 350–373.

BOWLBY, J. *Attachment and Loss, Vol. 1: Attachment.* London: Hogarth; New York: Basic Books, 1969.

BRAINE, M. D. S. The ontogeny of English phrase structure: The first phrase. *Language,* 1963, *39,* 1–13.

BRAZELTON, T. B., *Neonatal Assessment Scale.* Philadelphia, Pennsylvania: J. B. Lippincott, 1973.

BROOKS, J., and LEWIS, M. *Infant's response to strangers: midget, adult and child. Child Development,* 1976, *47,* 323–332.

BROWN, R. *Psycholinguistics.* New York: Free Press, 1970, pp. 220.

BROWN, R. *A First Language: The Early Stages.* Cambridge, Mass.: Harvard U. P., 1973.

BROWN, R., and BELLUGI, U. Three processes in the child's acquisition of syntax. *Harvard Educational Review,* Spring 1964, *34,* 138–139, 141, 224.

BROWN, R., CAZDEN, C., and BELLUGI, U. The child's grammar from I to III. In J. P. Hill (Ed.), *Minnesota Symposium on Child Psychology, Vol. 2.* Minneapolis: University of Minnesota Press, 1969, pp. 28–73.

BROWN, R., and HANLON, C. Derivational complexity and order of acquisition. In J. R. Hayes (Ed.), *Cognition and the Development of Language.* New York: Wiley, 1970, pp. 11–53.

BUREAU OF LABOR STATISTICS, Women at Work: A Chartbook, Washington, D. C.: Department of Labor, April 1983, Bulletin 2168, 20–25.

CAIN, L. P., KELLY, D. H., and SHANNON, D. C. Parent's perceptions of the psychological and social impact of home monitoring. *Pediatrics,* 1980, *66,* 37–41.

CARPENTER, G. C., and STECHLER, G. Selective attention to mother's face from week 1 through week 8. *Proceedings of the 75th Annual Convention of the American Psychological Association,* 1967, 153–154.

CATTELL, P. *The Measurement of Intelligence of Infants and Young Children.* New York: Psychological Corporation, 1960.

CAZDEN, C. The acquisition of noun and verb inflections. *Child Development,* 1968, *39,* 433–438.

CHACON, M. A., and TILDON, J. T. Elevated values of triiodothyronine in victims of sudden infant death syndrome. *Journal of Pediatrics,* 1981, *99,* 758–760.

CHOMSKY, N. *Aspects of the Theory of Syntax.* Cambridge, Mass.: MIT Press, 1965.

CLARK, E. What's in a word? On the child's acquisition of semantics in his first language. In T. E. Moore (Ed.), *Cognitive Development and the Acquisition of Language.* New York: Academic Press, 1973.

CLARK, R. Performing without competence. *Journal of Child Language,* 1974, *1,* 1–10.

CONDON, W. S., and SANDER, L. W. Synchrony demonstrated between movements of the neonate and adult speech. *Child Development,* 1974, *45,* 456–462.

CRITCHLEY, M. Language. In E. H. Lenneberg and E. Lenneberg (Eds.), *Foundations of Language Development: A Multidisciplinary Approach,* Vol. 1. New York: Academic Press, 1975.

DALE, P. *Language Development,* New York: Holt, 1976.

DARLEY, FREDERIC L, and SPRIESTERSBACH, D. C. *Diagnostic Methods in Speech Pathology.* New York: Harper and Row, 1978, 222.

DENNIS, W. Causes of retardation among institutional children: Iran. *Journal of Genetic Psychology,* 1960, *96,* 47–59.

DENNIS, W., and SAYEGH, Y. The effect of supplementary experiences upon the behavioral development of infants in institutions. *Child Development,* 1965, *36,* 81–90.

ENGEL, W. R. An example of linguistic consciousness in the child. In C. A. Ferguson and D. I. Slobin (Eds.), *Studies of Child Language Development.* New York: Holt, 1973, pp. 155–158.

ERIKSON, E. H. *Childhood and Society,* New York: Norton, 1950.

ERVIN, S. Imitation and structural change in children's language. In E. H. Lenneberg (Ed.), *New Directions in the Study of Language,* Cambridge, Mass.: MIT Press, 1964, pp. 163–189.

ERVIN-TRIPP, S. The comprehension and production of requests by children. *Papers and Reports on Child Language Development,* Committee on Linguistics, Stanford University, 1974, No. 8, 188–196.

FANTZ, R. L. Pattern vision in young infants. *Psychological Record,* 1958, *8,* 43–47.

FANTZ, R. L. The origin of form perception. *Scientific American,* 1961, *204,* 66–72.

FANTZ, R. L. Pattern vision in newborn infants. *Science,* 1963, *140,* 296–297.

FANTZ, R. L. Visual experience in infants: Decreased attention to familiar patterns relative to novel ones. *Science,* 1964, *146,* 668–670.

FANTZ, R. L. Visual perception from birth as shown by pattern selectivity. In H. E. Whipple (Ed.), *New Issues in Infant Development, Annals of the New York Academy of Sciences,* Vol. 118, 1965, 793–815.

FANTZ, R. L. Pattern discrimination and selective attention as determinants of perceptual development from birth. In A. H. Kidd and J. L. Rivoire (Eds.), *Perceptual Development in Children.* New York: International Universities Press, 1966, pp. 143–173.

FANTZ, R. L. Visual perception and experience in early infancy: A look at the hidden side of behavior development. In H. W. Stevenson, E. H. Hess, and H. L. Rheingold (Eds.), *Early Behavior; Comparative and Developmental Approaches.* New York: Wiley, 1967, pp. 181–224.

FANTZ, R. L., and NEVIS, S. Pattern preferences and perceptual–cognitive development in early infancy. *Merrill-Palmer Quarterly,* 1967, *13,* 77–108.

FLAVELL, J. H. Concept development. In P. H. Mussen (Ed.), *Carmichael's Manual of Child Psychology* (3rd ed.) Vol. 1. New York: Wiley, 1970.

FRANKENBURG, W. K., and DODDS, J. B. The Denver developmental screening test. *Journal of Pediatrics,* 1967, *71,* 181–191.

FREEDMAN, D. G. Smiling in blind infants and the issue of innate vs. acquired. *Journal of Child Psychology and Psychiatry,* 1964, *5,* 171–184.

FROST, R. *The Collected Poems of Robert Frost.* New York: Holt, 1939.

GEWIRTZ, J. L. The course of infant smiling in four child-rearing environments in Israel. In B. M. Foss (Ed.), *Determinants of Infant Behavior*, Vol. 3. London: Methuen, 1965, 205–260.

HAAF, R. A., and BELL, R. Q. A facial dimension in visual discrimination by human infants. *Child Development*, 1967, *38*, 893–899.

HALVERSON, H. M. An experimental study of prehension in infants by means of systematic cinema records. *Genetic Psychology Monographs*, 1931, *10*, 107–286.

HERSH, S. P. and LEVIN, K. How love begins between parent and child. *Children Today*, Washington, D. C.: March-April 1978, *47*, 2–6.

HERZOG, E., and SUDIA, C. E. Children in fatherless families. In B. M. Caldwell and H. N. Ricciuti (Eds.), *Review of Child Development Research*, Vol. 3. Chicago: U. of Chicago P., 1973, pp. 141–232.

IDELBERGER, H. Hauptoproblemen der kindlichen sprachentwicklung. *Zeitschrift fur Pedagogische Psychologie*, 1903, *5*, 241–297.

IMEDADZE, N. V. K. Psikhologicheskoy prirode rannego dvuyazychiya. *Voprosy Psikhologii*, 1960, *6*, 60–68.

INGRAM, D. Transivity in child language. *Language*, 1971, *47*, 888–910.

INGRAM, D. If and when transformations are acquired by children. Paper presented to the Georgetown University Round Table, Washington, D. C., March 1975.

KAGAN, J. LEWIS, M., CAMPBELL, H., and KALAFAT, J. Infant differential reactions to familiar and distorted faces. *Child Development*, 1966, *37*, 519–532.

KALISH, R. A. *The Psychology of Human Behavior* (4th ed.), Belmont, Calif: Wadsworth Publishing Co., Inc. 1966, 1973.

KANTER, R. M. Jobs and families: Impact of working roles on family life. *Children Today*. Washington, D. C., March–April 1978, *45*, 11–15.

KEPHART, W. M. *The Family, Society, and the Individual.* Boston: Houghton Mifflin, 1977.

KLIMA, E. S., and BELLUGI-KLIMA, U. Syntactic regularities in the speech of children. In J. Lyons and R. J. Wales (Eds.), *Psycholinguistic Papers*, Edinburgh: Edinburgh U. P., 1966, pp. 181–208.

LAMB, M. E. The development of mother–infant and father–infant attachments in the second year of life. *Developmental Psychology*, 1977, *13*(6), 637– 648.

LENNEBERG, E. H. *Biological Foundations of Language.* New York: Wiley, 1967.

LEOPOLD, W. F. *Speech Development of a Bilingual Child.* Evanston: Northwestern U. P., 1949.

LESLIE, G. R. *The Family in Social Context.* New York: Oxford U. P., 1973.

LEVY, J. Evolution of language lateralization and cognitive function. In S. R. Harnad, H. D. Steklis, and J. Lancaster (Eds.), *Origins and Evolution of Language and Speech.* New York Academy of Sciences, *Annals*, 1976, pp. 280, 810–820.

LEWIS, M. M. *Infant Speech.* London: Routledge and Kegan Paul, 1951.

LIMBER, J. The genesis of complex sentences. In T. E. Moore (Ed.), *Cognition and the Acquisition of Language.* New York: Academic Press, 1973, pp. 169–186.

LIPSITT, L. P. Infants at risk: Perinatal and neonatal factors. *International Journal of Behavioral Development*, 1979, *2*, 23–42.

LIPSITT, L. P., STURGES, W. Q., and BURKE, P. Perinatal indicators and subsequent crib death. *Infant Behavior and Development*, 1979, *2*, 325–328.

LOWREY, G. H. *Growth and Development of Children* (7th ed.). Copyright © 1978 by Year Book Medical Publishers, Inc., Chicago. After C. A. Aldrich and E. S. Hewitt. Outlines for well baby clinics: Development for the first twelve months. *American Journal of Diseases of Children*, 1946, *71*, 131. Copyright © 1946, American Medical Association.

LYNN, D. *The Father: His Role in Child Development.* Monterey, Calif: Brooks/Cole, 1974.

MARX, J. L. Botulism in infants: a cause of sudden death? *Science*, 1978, *201*, 799–801.

McCARTHY, D. Language development in children. In L. Carmichael (Ed.), *Manual of Child Psychology*. New York: Wiley, 1954, pp. 452–630.

McNEILL, D. *The acquisition of language: The Study of Developmental Psycholinguistics*. New York: Harper & Row, 1970.

MOORE, K. C. The mental development of a child. *Psychological Review, Monograph Supplements*, 1896, *1*(3).

MURDOCH, G. P. *Social Structure*. New York: Free Press, 1949.

NAEYE, R., Sudden infant death. *Scientific American*, 1980, *242*, 56–62.

NELSON, K. Pre-syntactic strategies for learning to talk. Paper delivered to the Society for Research in Child Development, Minneapolis, March 1971.

NELSON, K. Structure and strategy in learning to talk. *Monographs of the Society for Research in Child Development*, 1973, *38*(149), (whole issue).

PAPOUSEK, H. Experimental studies of appetitional behavior in human newborns and infants. In H. W. Stevenson, E. H. Hess, and H. L. Rheingold (Eds.), *Early Behavior: Comparative and Developmental Approaches*. New York: Wiley, 1967, Huntington, N.Y.: Krieger, 1975, pp. 249–278.

PARKE, R. D. and SAWIN, D. B. Fathering: It's a major role. *Psychology Today*, November, 1977.

PAVLOVITCH, M. *Le Language Enfantin: Acquisition du Serbe et du Francais par un enfant Serbe*. Paris: Champion, 1920.

PERRY, J., and PERRY, E. Pairing and parenthood. San Francisco: Canfield Press, 1977.

PIAGET, J. *The Origins of Intelligence in Children* (2nd ed.) New York: International Universities Press, 1952.

PIAGET, J. *The Construction of Reality in the Child*. New York: Basic Books, 1954

PIAGET, J. *Six Psychological Studies*. New York: Random House, 1968.

PRECHTL, H. F. R. The directed head turning response and allied movements of the human body. *Behavior*, 1958, *13*, 212–242.

PRECHTL, H. F. R. The mother–child interaction in babies with minimal brain damage. In B. M. Foss (Ed.), *Determinants of Infant Behavior*, Vol. 2, New York: Wiley, 1963, pp. 53–66.

RACKI, G. The effects of flexible working hours. Ph.D. dissertation, University of Lausanne, 1975.

REBELSKY, F., and HANKS, C. Father's verbal interaction with infants in the first 3 months of life. *Child Development*, 1971, *43*, 63–68.

RHEINGOLD, H. L., GEWIRTZ, J. L., and ROSS, H. W. Social conditioning of vocalizations in the infant. *Journal of Comparative and Physiological Psychology*, 1959, *52*, 68–73.

ROBSON, K. S. The role of eye-to-eye contact in maternal–infant attachment. *Journal of Child Psychology and Psychiatry*, 1967, *8*, 13–25.

RUBENSTEIN, J., and HOWES, C. The effects of peers on toddler interaction with mother and toys. *Child Development*, 1976, *47*, 597–605.

RUTTER, M. Parent–child separation: psychological effects on the children. *Journal of Child Psychology and Psychiatry and Allied Disciplines*, 1971, *12*, 233–260.

SANDER, L. W. The regulation of exchange in the infant–caretaker system and some aspects of the context–content relationship. In M. Lewis and L. Rosenblum (Eds.). *Interaction, Conversation, and the Development of Language*. New York: Wiley, 1977, pp. 133–156.

SCHAEFER, E. *Report of the interagency panel on child development*, Washington, D. C.: HEW, 1972.

SCHAFFER, H. R. Activity level as a constitutional determinant of infantile reaction. *Child Development*, 1966, *37*, 595–602.

SCHAFFER, H. R. *Mothering*. Cambridge, Mass.: Harvard U. P., 1977.

SCHAFFER, H. R., and EMERSON, P. E. The development of social attachments in infancy. *Monographs of the Society for Research in Child Development*, 1964a, Vol. 29, No. 3 (Serial No. 94) (whole issue).

SCHAFFER, H. R., and EMERSON, P. E. Patterns of response to physical contact in early human development. *Journal of Child Psychology and Psychiatry*, 1964b, *5*, 1–13.

SCHLESINGER, I. M. Production of utterances and language acquisition. In D. I. Slobin (Ed.), *The Ontogenesis of Language*, New York: Academic Press,1971, pp. 19–20.

SHVACHKIN, N. KH. Razvitye fouematichekogo vospriyatiya rechi v rannem vozraste, (Development of phonemic speech perception in early childhood). *Izv. Akad. Pedagog. Nauk RSFSR*, 1948, *13*, 101–132.

SLOBIN, D. I. Imitation and grammatical development in children. In N. S. Endler, L. R. Boulter, and H. Osser (Eds.), *Contemporary Issues in Developmental Psychology*. New York: Holt, 1968, pp. 437–443.

SLOBIN, D. I. (Ed.). The ontogenesis of grammar. New York: Academic Press, 1971.

SMITH, K. U. and SCHIAMBERG, L. The Infraschool: The Systems Approach to Parent–Child Education. Madison, Wisconsin: Behavioral Cybernetics Laboratory, University of Wisconsin, 1973.

SROUFE, L. A., and WATERS, E. The ontogenesis of smiling and laughter: A perspective on the organization of development in infancy. *Psycological Review*, 1976, *83*, 173–189.

STANTON, A. N., SCOTT, D. J. and DOWNHAN, M. A. Is overheating a factor in some unexpected infant deaths? *Lancet*, 1980, 1054–1057.

STECHLER, G., and LATZ, E. Some observations on attention and arousal in the human infant. *Journal of the American Academy of Child Psychiatry*, 1966, *5*, 517–525.

STERN, D. N. *The First Relationship: Infant and Mother*. Cambridge, Mass.: Harvard, U. P., 1977.

TAINE, H. Acquisition of language by children. *Mind*, 1877, *2*, 252–259.

TERJESEN, N. C., and WILKINS, L. P. A proposal for a model of sudden infant death syndrome act: help for the "other" victims of SIDS. *Family Law Quarterly*, 1979, *12*, 285–308.

U. S. Bureau of the Census, Child Care Arrangements of Working Mothers: June 1982, *Current Population Reports*, Series P23, No. 129, Table 2, Parts A and B, Nov., 1983.

VORSTER, J. Mother's speech to children: some methodological considerations. Instituute voor Algemene Taallwetenschap, Universiteit von Amsterdam, 1974.

WADSWORTH, B. J. *Piaget's Theory of Cognitive Development*. (2nd ed.). Copyright © 1979, New York: Longman.

WATSON, J. S. Smiling, cooing and "the game." Paper presented at the annual meeting of the American Psychological Association, Miami Beach, 1970.

WEISBERG, P. Social and nonsocial conditioning of infant vocalizations. *Child Development*, 1963, *34*, 377–388.

WERTHEIMER, M. Psychomotor coordination of auditory and visual space at birth. *Science*, 1961, *134*, 1692.

WHITE, B. L. Human infants: Experience and psychological development. Englewood Cliffs, N. J.: Prentice-Hall, 1971.

WINNICOTT, D. W. Separation from parents during early childhood. In M. L. Hoffman and L. W. Hoffman (Eds.), *Review of Child Development Research*, Vol. 1 New York: Russell Sage Foundation, 1964, pp. 89–136.

WOLFF, P. H. Observations on newborn infants. *Psychosomatic Medicine*, 1959, *21*, 110–118.

WOLFF, P. H. Observations on the early development of smiling. In B. M. Foss (Ed.), *Determinants of Infant Behavior*, Vol. 2. New York: Wiley, 1963, pp. 113–138.

WOLFF, P. H. *The Causes, Controls and Organizations of Behavior in the Neonate*. New York: International Universities Press, 1966.

WOLFF, P. H. Crying and vocalization in early infancy. In B. M. Foss (Ed.), *Determinants of Infant Behavior*, Vol. 4. London: Methuen; New York: Wiley, 1969, pp. 81–110.

Suggested Readings

BOWLBY, J. *Attachment and Loss. Vol. 1. Attachment.* New York: Basic Books, 1969. A thorough and comprehensive examination of attachment and the early infant–caregiver relationship.

BRAZELTON, T. B. *Toddlers and Parents.* New York: Delacorte, 1974. An interesting and readable collection of case-histories on toddler behavior.

FOGEL, A. *Infancy: Infant, Family, and Society.* St. Paul, Minnesota: West, 1984. An excellent overview of infant development with up-to-date coverage of theory and research.

FRAILBERG, S. *Every Child's Birthright: In Defense of Mothering.* New York: Basic Books, 1977. The author makes a strong case for the need of babies to develop loving attachment relationships to a caring person as the basis for sound growth and development.

KAYE, K. *The Mental and Social Life of Babies—How Parents Create Persons.* Chicago: The University of Chicago Press, 1982. Kaye suggests that the behavior of infants depends on the universal interaction patterns of both infants and parents.

LEWIS, M. and ROSENBLUM, L. A. *The Effect of the Infant on Its Caregiver.* New York: Wiley, 1974. A collection of articles which emphasize the theme that infant development must be understood in terms of the mutual and reciprocal relationships between caregiver and child.

SMITH, K. U. and SCHIAMBERG, L. *The Infraschool: The Systems Approach to Parent–Child Interaction.* A readable book designed to provide an examination of feedback and social tracking skills, and their application to parent–infant/child interaction. Numerous activities involving tactual, visual, and auditory tracking are discussed.

WHITE, B. L. *The First Three Years of Life.* Englewood Cliffs, New Jersey: Prentice-Hall, 1975. A well written and authoritative discussion of infant behavioral development during the first three years, accompanied by practical advice and techniques for parents.

7

The Preschool Child

CHILDREN LEARN WHAT THEY LIVE

If a child lives with criticism,
  He learns to condemn.
If a child lives with hostility,
  He learns to fight.
If a child lives with ridicule,
  He learns to be shy.
If a child lives with tolerance,
  He learns to be patient.
If a child lives with encouragement,
  He learns confidence.
If a child lives with praise,
  He learns to appreciate.
If a child lives with fairness,
  He learns justice.
If a child lives with security,
  He learns to have faith.
If a child lives with approval,
  He learns to like himself.
If a child lives with acceptance and friendship,
  He learns to find love in the world.

                                        Anonymous

The preschooler begins to move into a larger world of interpersonal relationships.

Photograph by Jeffrey Morris

248

The Preschool Child in Context

In this book, we emphasize that the human being grows, develops, and functions in a *system* or set of contexts. This system, which includes the family, progressively changes as the individual matures from infancy through adulthood (see Figure 7.1). The transition from the infant system to the preschool system is marked by a gradual movement of the child into the larger society. The social world of the infant is contained within the family. The preschooler begins to move out into a larger society, which becomes differentiated into neighborhood and peer group. As we will see, this process of differentiation of the larger society continues throughout the life span. The growing individual continually encounters "new" aspects of the social world, such as school and work, and integrates them with the family.

THE FAMILY

The family performs the primary function of socializing the child from birth through at least adolescence. This process of socialization is accomplished through mutual interactions between parent and child. These interactions include the transmission and interpretation of cultural standards of values and behavior. The family can be viewed as a dynamic system that changes over time, as do its members.

The Family as a System. The family can be viewed as a *system* in its own right.

A system is a "set of objects together with relationships between the *objects* and between their *attributes . . . objects* are the components or parts of the system, *attributes* are the properties of the objects, and *relationships* tie the system together" (Hall and Fagen, 1956).

FIGURE 7.1 The transition from infancy to the preschool world.

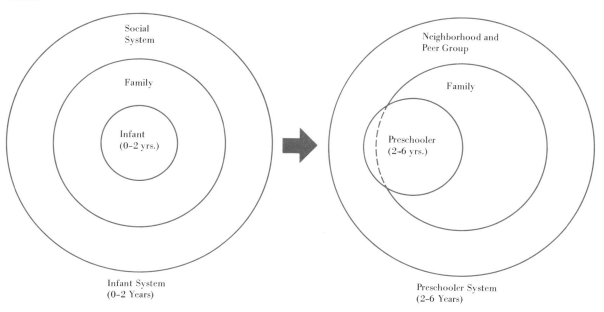

If we view the interpersonal relationships of the family as a system, then the *objects* of the system are the people (husband, wife, children, relatives). The *attributes* are the relevant characteristics of the family members, such as age, personality, and previous experiences. The *relationships* are the interactions or communications between the objects, or people.

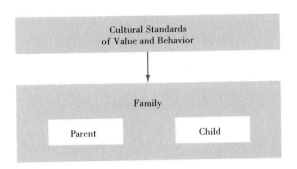

It is becoming increasingly apparent in the social sciences that any workable theory of family behavior is greatly advanced by the idea of the family as a system. The model suggested here views the activity of the family as "a complex interplay of systemic structures and forces which elaborate and change in response to both internal and external phenomena" (Kantor and Lehr, 1975).

Kantor and Lehr (1975) identified the following characteristics of the family as a system:

1. *Organizational complexity.* Families evolve networks of interdependent relationships.
   - These interactional networks involve relationships that are mutual in the sense that all parties contribute something to the relationship. That is, the components of family systems are *reciprocally influencing*.
   - These interactional networks may be either *internal* (between members of the family, for example, parent, child, sibling, and grandparent) or *external* (between the family, as a unit, and other institutions or organizations, for example, school, other families, doctors, and health specialists).
   - These interactional networks are rule-governed in the sense that either formal or informal "understandings" largely direct and influence the very nature of these relationships. For example, some family "rules" or organizational principles may result in an authoritarian, or *closed*, style of family functioning. Authoritarian parents may operate on the "rule" that the parent can simply hand down family decisions (including expectations about children's behavior) without consulting other family members. Other families may have "rules" that generate more democratic, or *open*, styles of family interaction and decision making (see Figure 7.2).

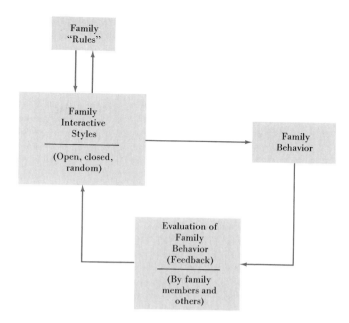

FIGURE 7.2   The family as a "rule-governed" system.

2. *Openness*. The family is influenced by external (outside-the-family) forces, and it also influences these external forces. Therefore, the family is said to be an "open" system because it depends on mutual interaction with an environment to grow and develop. In order for the family to accomplish its many functions (child rearing, economic maintenance and so on) it must interact with institutions such as the school and the world of work.

3. *Adaptiveness*. Open family systems develop and grow as a consequence of interaction with factors external to the family as well as adjustments to internal changes in the family system. Internal changes in the family or changes in one component of the family have an impact on all other parts of the family system. Such changes may promote adaptiveness. For example, when a father becomes ill or is permanently disabled, the mother and/or the older children may assume the father's role as economic provider. If a mother becomes ill or dies, then maternal responsibilities might be taken on by a grandmother, other relatives, and/or the father. In summary, the family as a system adapts in order to survive.

Parenting Styles. One of the important components of the family system is the parenting style. By *styles of parenting*, we mean simply the attitudes and behaviors of parents. At least three dimensions of parenting style are related to the social and personality development of the preschool-aged child.

Parental Modeling. Parents provide models with which the preschool child can interact and identify. Parents provide models of behavior that the child can adopt and use. If parents shout at one another, then it is possible that the child will use this behavioral technique.

Some of the most dramatic examples of the modeling of behavior by the preschooler often occur during free play time. It is during these moments that the child may imitate parental behaviors that were learned and observed at an earlier time.

SCENARIO:
THE DAY PRESCHOOLER BRUCE DISCIPLINED
"CHARLIE McCARTHY."

Our irrepressible preschooler, Bruce, has many playmates. In addition to his friends Michael, Patrick, Susie, and Dana, Bruce also enjoys the company of "Charlie McCarthy." Charlie is a toy "dummy" modeled after the one used by the famous ventriloquist Edgar Bergen.

Yesterday, when Bruce was sitting at the dinner table, he reached for his fork and unintentionally knocked over his glass of milk. The milk spilled over Bruce's dinner plate, which now contained milky chicken and even milkier potatoes, over Bruce's trousers, and, of course, on the floor. Needless to say, Bruce's mother was not pleased with this turn of events. As she began the task of wiping up the milk, cleaning the floor, and replacing Bruce's trousers, the following dialogue occurred:

Mother: Bruce, you have to be more careful.
Bruce (surprised expression): Okay, Mom.
Mother: When you reach for something at the table always look while you are reaching.
(A demonstration of reaching carefully immediately follows.)

The next day, Bruce was seen playing with Charlie McCarthy. Charlie was seated at a small table with a small cup of water before him. Somehow the cup was knocked over, and the following dialogue occurred:

Bruce: Now Charlie, you just have to be careful not to spill the water.
Charlie (voice supplied by Bruce): I'm sorry.
Bruce: See, this is how you do it.

FIGURE 7.3 Children develop work habits largely in terms of the way in which parents work with them to develop their skills and talents.

Photographs by Gale Schiamberg

Parenting behaviors are not confined to one-way modeling (i.e., the model or parent demonstrating a behavior that is then imitated by the child). A good deal of parent–child interaction involves *mutual following.* For example, parents and children engage in activities or play games in which the parents adjust their behavior to the child's movements in much the same way that the child observes the parents and organizes his or her behavior in relation to what the parents are doing (see Figure 7.3).

Parental Expectations Concerning Children's Behavior. Each family might be characterized, in part, by what they expect of their children. Often these expectations are embedded in the ''rule'' structure or organizing principles of family behavior (see Figure 7.2). For example, some families might wish their children to participate in family decision-making, whereas other families would find such involvement completely out of character with their expectations concerning child behavior (e.g., ''Children should be seen and not heard.''). Sometimes expectations about children's performance are so influential that they actively structure the way in which the parent or teacher acts toward the child, resulting in a self-fulfilling prophecy (i.e., if we believe something, then our behavior may be altered in the direction of making the belief come true) (Rosenthal and Jacobson, 1968).

Parental Disciplinary Techniques. Parents usually control the entire area of discipline. For example, parents determine not only *what* the child is disciplined for but *how* the child is disciplined; the parent may use rewards, punishments, verbal support, physical spanking, scolding, and so on.

Dimensions of Parent–Child Interaction. Parent–child relationships are *reciprocal,* or two-way. This is important to bear in mind because almost any episode of behavior between a parent and child could be interpreted as

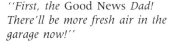

''First, the Good News Dad! There'll be more fresh air in the garage now!''

DENNIS THE MENACE ® used by permission of Hank Ketcham and © by Field Enterprises, Inc.

being one-way. For example, a sullen child could be viewed as the product of a rejecting parent. On the other hand, a rejecting parent could just as well be viewed as the product of a sullen, unresponsive child.

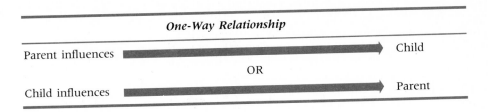

What is actually happening, however, is a *two-way* process of *mutual influence* to which both parent and child contribute. In the remainder of this section, we will examine some of these mutual relationships as well as parental disciplinary patterns.

Parental Disciplinary Patterns. Parents play an important role in their children's development—either by direct action or, in some cases, by inactive default. In the past, many parents in the United States believed that maintaining order in the family was the highest calling of the parent. This responsibility, of course, included dominating and controlling the child, a pattern of discipline that came to be called the *authoritarian* approach. Children were perceived as being prone to uncivilized behavior, and the only way to cultivate and civilize children was to subdue this urge.

Sometime after World War II, a challenge emerged to the legitimacy of unquestioned, unilateral, and unrestrained parental authority. This approach—which came to be known as the *permissive* approach to discipline—had many advocates (Farson, 1974; Holt, 1974; Neill, 1960). The major premise of this approach is that the child has a natural tendency toward self-actualization (the development and fulfillment of human potential), which—left unfettered by adult intervention—will naturally result in appropriate, socially approved behavior. The following statements by Neill (1960) summarize the permissive approach:

I believe that to impose anything by authority is wrong. The child should not do anything until he comes to the opinion—his own opinion—that it should be done. (p. 114)

Every child has the right to wear clothes of such a kind that it does not matter a brass farthing if they get messy or not. (p. 115)

Communicating with Children—Effective Ways of Confronting Children

Dr. Thomas E. Gordon, a clinical psychologist, has developed communication techniques which can be taught to parents for the purpose of improving parent–child interaction. The techniques are described in detail in Dr. Gordon's book, *Parent Effectiveness Training* (New York: Peter H. Wyden, Inc., 1975). The success of the parent training is based, in part, on Gordon's observation that once parents become aware of the destructive power of "put-down" messages, they are eager to learn effective modes of confronting children. Gordon indicates that neither he or any of his staff have ever encountered a parent who intentionally tried to damage a child's self-esteem.

"YOU-MESSAGES" AND "I-MESSAGES"

One way for parents to understand the difference between effective and ineffective communication is to learn the distinction between "You-messages" and "I-messages." When Gordon and his staff ask parents to think carefully about "put-down" messages, the parents are frequently surprised to find that such messages begin with the word "You" or include that word. Examples of "You-messages" include the following:

"*You* had better stop doing that."

"Why didn't *you* do that?"

"*You* are behaving like a big baby."

"*You* are naughty."

"Why don't *you* try something else?"

In contrast, a parent can learn to simply and honestly tell a child how some unacceptable behavior is making the parent feel by using an "I" message. Such a communication is called an "I-message" because it typically begins with the word "I."

"*I* don't feel like playing with you when I am so tired."

"*I* can't say what I wish when you interrupt me like that."

"*I* can't rest when someone is climbing on my legs."

"*I* get very upset when someone puts their dirty shoes on the couch."

"I-MESSAGES" ARE MORE EFFECTIVE THAN "YOU-MESSAGES."

According to Gordon, "I-Messages" are more effective in parent–child interaction because they promote a healthy, open relationship. In so doing, they are much more successful in influencing the child to control behavior that may be unacceptable to the parent, maladaptive for the child, or both. "I-messages" are effective because they place the responsibility for changing or modifying behavior squarely on the shoulders of the child. For example, when a parent says to a child "I dislike your shouting," not only is the parent openly communicating a feeling but is leaving the child with the responsibility for doing something about the situation.

An "I-message" tells a child that you are leaving the responsibility with him, trusting him to handle the situation constructively, trusting him to respect your needs, giving him a chance to start behaving constructively.

Because "I-messages" are honest, they tend to influence a child to send similar feelings *whenever he has a feeling.* "I-messages" from one person in a relationship promote "I-messages" from the other. (Gordon, 1975, p. 118).

Unfortunately, "You-messages" from one person in a relationship tend to promote "You-messages" from the other. Typically, in deteriorating relationships between parents and children, conflicts degenerate into mutual blaming and name-calling.

This is typical of many conversations between parents and children when the parent starts his confrontation with a "You-message." Invariably, they end up in a struggle . . . (Gordon, 1975, p. 118).

Based on T. E. Gordon, *P.E.T.—Parent Effectiveness Training.* New York: Peter H. Wyden, Inc., 1975, pp. 115–119.

A parent or educator is not necessarily limited to either the authoritarian or the permissive approach. Baumrind (1972) suggested that the *authoritative* mode may combine the best features of both. The characteristics of the authoritarian, permissive, and authoritative approaches to discipline were summarized by Baumrind (1978) as follows:

(1) The *authoritarian* parent values obedience as a virtue and favors punitive, forceful measures to curb self-will at points where the child's actions or beliefs conflict with what the parent thinks is right. . . . The authoritarian parent believes in keeping the child in a subordinate role and in restricting his autonomy, and does not encourage verbal give and take, believing that the child should accept a parent's word for what is right. Authoritarian parents may be very concerned and protective or they may be neglecting.

(2) The *permissive* prototype of adult control requires the parent to behave in an affirmative, acceptant, and benign manner towards the child's impulses and actions. The permissive parent sees him—or herself as a resource for the child to use as he wishes but not as an active agent responsible for shaping and altering the child's ongoing and future behavior. The immediate aim of the ideologically aware permissive parent is to free the child from restraint as much as is consistent with survival. Some permissive parents are very protective and loving, while others are self involved and offer freedom as a way of evading responsibility for the child's development.

(3) The *authoritative* parent . . . attempts to direct the child's activities in a rational issue oriented manner. He or she encourages verbal give and take, shares with the child the reasoning behind parental policy, and solicits the child's objections when the child refuses to conform. Both autonomous self-will and disciplined conformity are valued by the authoritative parent. Therefore, this parent exerts firm control when the young child disobeys, but does not hem the child in with restrictions. The authoritative parent enforces the adult perspective, but recognizes the child's individual interests and special ways. Such a parent affirms the child's present qualities, but also sets standards for future conduct, using reason as well as power and shaping by regimen and reinforcement to achieve parental objectives. . . .

Authoritative discipline tends to foster in children a particular kind of social competence which is associated with success in Western society. This kind of social competence is called *instrumental competence*. (pp. 224–225)

What are the results of these modes of discipline for preschool children? It appears that authoritative parents are most effective in controlling undesirable behavior such as aggression. Authoritarian parents tend to have children who are withdrawn, distrustful, less assertive, and less independent. Children of authoritative parents are more likely to be self-reliant, content, explorative, self-satisfied, and self-controlled. Children of permissive parents tended to be the least self-controlled, self-reliant, and explorative of all three groups (Baumrind, 1972, 1978).

THE NEIGHBORHOOD AND THE COMMUNITY AS CONTEXTS FOR PRESCHOOLER DEVELOPMENT

Although the family is undoubtedly a vital context for the developing child, there is another, more global context in which the family and the child are merged—the neighborhood and the community. Every child develops, matures, and grows in some type of community and lives in some type of shelter.

Photograph (right) by Bruce Hecht

Children's understanding of their communities, neighborhoods, and housing spaces comes about gradually. Pastalon (1977) described the emergence of this understanding as follows:

as a child develops physically and intellectually his home range begins to expand. For instance, the child begins to make sense out of his surroundings. . . . He begins to sort out the various arrangements of objects and spaces that he can see and relate to. As soon as the child begins to develop his ability to walk, his home range expands even further, going beyond the crib, his nursery, out into the other rooms of the house, and soon the child is exploring not only spaces within the dwelling unit but outside as well and begins to sort out and respond to his immediate areas outside the dwelling unit. Then as he increases in age and development he continues to expand his home range until he reaches maturity where he has almost an unlimited home range in the sense that there can be a large number of spaces, objects, and people with sensed relationships that he experiences.

The Community and Neighborhood: An Ecological Perspective.
People use the term "community" in many ways including the development of a "sense of community" or fellowship. Our concern in the study of human development is, however, with the idea of a territory-based place in which such relationships might occur (Anderson and Carter, 1978).

A community may be defined as follows:

Community consists of persons in social interaction within a geographic area and having one or more additional common ties. (Hillery, 1955).

A more recent characterization of community is in terms of the functions accomplished, including the following (Warren, 1973):

- Mutual support.
- The socialization of children.
- Economic production and consumption.

According to this approach, a community has both social and economic functions.

Child Development and Personal Social Networks

An important emphasis of this book is on the interaction of the developing human being with the significant contexts of life (e.g., family, community-neighborhood, work, peers, and the school). One of the most promising and potentially fruitful approaches to understanding the nature of child and community-neighborhood interaction is through the examination of *personal social networks* (Cochran and Brassard, 1979).

Families have always been embedded in networks of relatives, neighbors, and friends. Those network members have undoubtedly influenced the rearing of children, sometimes directly and often indirectly. Yet such social influences have gone virtually unrecognized by those studying child development. While the prominent role played by the parents in that development has been a subject much in vogue during the past decade, little attempt has been made to place the family in a social context. . . .

[The personal social] network is defined as those people outside the household who engage in activities and exchanges of an effective and/or material nature with the members of the immediate family. . . .

There are at least three major ways in which the parent's social network influences the performance of the parental role and, in turn, affects the child. . . .

1. ACCESS TO EMOTIONAL AND MATERIAL ASSISTANCE

A substantial body of research documents the existence of network helping patterns for parents living in many different kinds of social circumstances. Persons with both middle and low income, from a variety of ethnic and cultural groups and from both single and two-parent families share child care, personal distress, information about jobs, and housing and leisure time (. . . Furstenberg, 1976; Gottlieb, 1979 . . .). . . . The emotional and material support flowing along the network system to the parents [may affect] . . . the child. By providing a loving and relatively consistent social environment that allows the doubts and frustrations of parents, the social network may enable them to be more sensitive to the needs of their children. . . .

2. PROVISION OF CHILD-REARING CONTROLS

Members of the parents' social network may influence actual child-rearing behavior through the control they exert via direct sanctions. Friends, relatives, or neighbors of parents may encourage or discourage particular patterns of parent–child interaction. . . .

3. AVAILABILITY OF ROLE MODELS

A third process of influence is at work when parents adopt or modify some child-rearing practices as a consequence of watching the behavior of network members. . . .

From Cochran, M. and Brassard, J. A., "Child Development and Personal Social Networks," *Child Development,* 1979, *50,* pp. 601–603.

Based on these functions and characteristics, the community can exert a strong influence on the quality of life for families living in it and, therefore, on the quality of child and human development. The ecological or systems perspective used in this book allows us to understand more fully the impact of the community on the family environment at both direct and indirect levels (Garbarino, 1982) (See the discussion of systems theory in Chapter Three).

1. *Direct influence of community on the family and human development.* The community may have an effect on the *microsystem* of family dynamics and interaction. For example, a disturbance in the economic resources of a community, such as the closing of a factory, could have an impact on the rate of violence in families (Steinberg, Catalano, and Dooley, 1981; Straus, Gelles, and Steinmetz, 1980).

2. *Indirect influence of the community on the family and human development.* The ecological perspective helps us to appreciate the ways that the community indirectly influences families and development by influencing the *interaction between microsystems*. For example, the school and family as microsystems interact to influence the quality of the child's education. These relationship patterns between microsystems are called *mesosystems* (see Chapter Three). Mesosystems have an important role in influencing the daily lives of children and adults in families. That is, the quality or the richness of the mesosystems for the developing human being is indicated or measured by the *number* and *quality* of the connections or *linkages* between microsystems. If we use the example of the interaction of the home and school, then we can make some estimate about a child's likelihood of success or achievement in school based on the linkages between the school and the home. If the participation of people (e.g., parents/caretakers and teachers), other than the child, in both settings supports the similarity between the two settings, then the child's academic success is more likely.

The central principle here is that the stronger and more diverse the links between settings, the more powerful the resulting mesosystem will be as an influence on the child's development (Garbarino, 1982, p. 23).

Another way of examining the indirect impact of the community is the consideration of *exosystems* (the formal and informal institutions such as political/governmental structures, neighborhood and community organization, transportation networks, and the informal communication networks within neighborhoods, communities, and workplaces) (see Chapter Three). That is, how is the family treated by the institutions of a community? For example, are employers aware of and responsive to the needs of families and children for day-care services (Garbarino, 1980)? Is the local government sensitive to the needs of families and children through tax policies and zoning regulations (Garbarino and Plantz, 1980)?

Still another source of indirect community effects on families and developing individuals is through the *macrosystem* or the broad ideological or value patterns of a particular culture.

Macrosystems are the "blueprints" for the ecology of human development. These blueprints reflect a people's shared assumptions about "how things should be done" (Garbarino, 1982, p. 24).

The organization or institutional arrangements of a specific community can be viewed as the embodiment or the "carrying out" of the ideologies, beliefs, or values of the macrosystem. For example, communities having ethics or values that are opposed to child abuse or other forms of domestic violence are more likely to have reduced rates of such violence compared to communities that appear to allow or tolerate such violence (Garbarino, 1977).

While the term *community* refers, as indicated, to a broad range of general and very specific relationships, the term *neighborhood* is used to refer to a part of the community. The *neighborhood* is the specific setting or place where parents interact with their children, as well as with other people. Children are also participants in the neighborhood and are typically given the freedom to interact with other people in the neighborhood (particularly with other children) independently of parents or caretakers. The quality of support and feedback given to the family through neighborhood relationships also has an influence on human development in the family context (see Application Box: Child Development and Personal Social Networks).

Why Look at Communities and Neighborhoods? There are many reasons to examine the neighborhood and the community as contexts of human development:

1. The neighborhood and community provide the major setting in which the child organizes free or unstructured time. Most outdoor play occurs in the neighborhood.
2. The neighborhood and community are a setting where certain activities are more likely or less likely to occur. For example, urban children can probably play with several age-mates in the immediate vicinity of their homes. A child in a rural setting might have to be driven several miles to play with the nearest peer.
3. The neighborhood may provide a broader or a more limited set of experiences for the child's socialization and development. For example, some neighborhoods contain a diverse range of people with varying occupations, income, social class, and racial or ethnic background. Other neighborhoods provide much less variety.

The Role of the Neighborhood. In our discussion of the role of the neighborhood and the community in the development of the child, we are going to focus on the urban environment. More than 70 percent of the population of the United States lives in cities or suburbs (compared with a rather meager 6 percent in 1800). A number of features of city life affect child development.

Stress. The urban neighborhood (particularly the inner-city neighborhood) is thought to be contaminated by noise, polluted air, and various levels of congestion occasioned by many people. The density of inner-city neighborhoods has been blamed for creating special conditions that make it an unhealthy and stressful environment (Milgram, 1970; Meier, 1962).

Sociability and a Sense of Community. Although we may think of large cities as made up of large numbers of anonymous people, this stereotypical characterization is not always correct. On the contrary, sections of large cities provide inhabitants with a sense of identity based on territory or place. In fact, many of the satisfactions of living in an urban neighborhood or community have to do with the individual child's or adult's perception and use of both the social and the physical "spaces" provided in the neighborhood (Ittelson, Proshansky, Rivlin, and Winkel, 1974).

What Are the Effects of Density and Crowding? *Crowding* refers to the number of persons occupying a unit of living space (e.g., a house). *Density* usually refers to the distribution of these "units" (e.g., houses) over a particular area (e.g., a neighborhood). Simply because a neighborhood has a high density does not mean that the neighborhood is necessarily crowded (e.g., living areas in many cities have a number of tall apartment buildings, which may provide more than adequate living space). Density becomes a problem when it creates crowding. Although there are numerous studies that have purported to demonstrate the undesirable social and physical effects of crowding and high density (Schorr, 1963; Loring, 1956), a simple "one-way" cause-and-effect relationship is not a safe assumption. In other words, high density and crowding are only one dimension of the total urban system. Therefore, many other research studies have not found simple relationships between crowding and social or physical ills (Fried and Gleicher, 1961; Gans, 1962; Schmitt, 1966). These apparently contradictory findings are reconciled if one recognizes that different people—as well as different cultures—tolerate varying degrees of crowding and that these differences work to neutralize the effects of crowding. In other words, families may develop successful approaches to dealing with potentially stressful events such as crowding.

The Overloaded Environment. It has been suggested that one of the factors which may be at the root of the crowding problem is the *overloaded environment*. The large city is usually in a state of constant change. Much is happening and many people are congregating in a rather limited space. When the total amount of what is happening (including the number of people present) exceeds the individual's capacity to deal with all of it, the condition of overload exists. To conserve energy, the individual develops "priorities" that may force him/her to avoid all but superficial relationships. In other words, a "people overload" may result in a "turning off" or a withdrawal from social relationships.

The depersonalization and routinization of human relationships and activities in large cities affects the environment for families and for child rearing. This problem of depersonalization has been summarized as follows:

the concept of overload helps to explain a wide variety of contrasts between city and town behaviors: (1) The differences in "role enactment" (the urban tendency to deal with one another in highly segmented, functional terms; the constricted time and services offered customers by sales personnel); (2) The evolution of "urban norms" quite different from traditional town values (such as the acceptance of noninvolvement, impersonality and aloofness in urban life); (3) The adaptation of the urban-dweller's "cognitive processes" (his inability to identify most of the people seen daily; his screening of sensory stimuli; his development of blasé attitudes toward deviant or bizarre behavior; and his selectivity in responding to human demand); and (4) The far greater competition for scarce "facilities" in the city (the subway rush; the fight for taxis; traffic jams; standing in lines to await services). I would suggest that contrasts between city and rural behavior probably reflect the responses of similar people to very different situations, rather than intrinsic differences between rural personalities and city personalities. The city is a situation to which individuals respond adaptively (Milgram, 1970, p. 1465).

INTERLUDE: THE PRIVILEGED POOR

I was raised in a section of New York that was called a slum by sightseeing guides and a depressed area by sociologists. Both were right. Our neighborhood fulfilled all the sordid requirements with honors. We were unquestionably above average in squalid tenements, putrid poolrooms, stenchy saloons, cold flats, hot roofs, dirty streets and flying garbage. Yet, paradoxically, I never felt depressed or deprived. My environment was miserable; I was not.

I was a fortunate child. Ours was a home rich enough in family harmony and love to immunize eight kids against the potentially toxic effects of the environment beyond our door. Since the social scientists do not, as far as I know, have a clinical name for the fortunate possessors of this kind of emotional security, I might suggest they label them "the privileged poor."

From Levenson, S. *Everything But Money.* New York: Simon and Schuster, 1966, p. 12.

Housing and Child Development. Although the overall organization of neighborhoods and streets is an important aspect of the growing child's environment, the nature of the child's housing is also important in several ways. As in the case of crowding and social or physical ills, the relationship between housing and such factors as stress is again not a simple cause–effect relationship. Human beings have different levels of tolerance of stress as well as individualized strategies for handling it. Therefore, dilapidated slum dwellings are not necessarily more stressful than comfortable suburban homes. Stress in family members may result from coping with features of slum dwellings such as lack of sanitary facilities, inadequate space, lack of privacy, and the inadequacy of household design for raising children (Schorr, 1963). On the other hand, the suburban home that has a large number of appliances and rooms to clean and organize could well be as stressful as a slum dwelling (Ittelson, et al., 1974).

Again, the relationship between physical dilapidation and "social dilapidation" is not a simple one. It appears that subjective elements such as the kind of neighbors one has and the friendship relationships that have been developed are far more important than more objective measures of physical inconvenience or difficulty. People in slum areas tend to have many friends and to be involved in the social life of their neighborhoods. In an interesting study, Rossi (1955) found that of four urban areas, one area that rated very low on an objective assessment of physical quality, ranked the highest on subjective satisfaction.

The Meaning of the Neighborhood to the Child. As the preschool child ventures forth out of the house and into the immediate surroundings of the home, he or she begins to recognize the boundaries of the neighborhood in a very general sense. The preschooler comes to recognize such things as "my house," "my driveway," and "my street." Although he/she may recognize these general features, the preschooler also tends to estimate distances inaccurately. A distance of two hundred miles to a grandmother's house may seem closer than it really is. The preschooler tends to view the things in the neighborhood as larger than they really are. Streets, alleys, houses, and fences seem much larger from the viewpoint of one who must look up to most people and things.

Play and Play Settings. Play occupies a considerable amount of the preschooler's waking hours. The environments in which play occurs are of two major types: (1) planned play settings for children (e.g., playgrounds) and (2) unplanned play areas (neighborhood and household areas that promote play behavior although they were not originally designed for that purpose). Play in planned play areas usually accounts for a small part of the child's total play experience. Most play occurs during the unplanned daily agenda of the preschooler, for example, while walking in the house or running outside.

Two important criteria for evaluating play settings are availability and responsiveness. *Availability* refers to the relative ease with which the child can get to the play setting. *Responsiveness* refers to whether or not the play setting (and the objects or equipment located there) can engage or involve the child. Responsive play settings have the potential through diversity of design to meet a broad range of the needs of individual children. The opportunities available to children vary considerably in terms of geographic location (e.g.,

Urban Renewal and Child Development

During the 1950s many cities became involved in so-called urban-renewal projects. The major idea of these programs was to replace the dilapidated structures of the inner-city ghetto with modern, efficient, and clean buildings that would have low rents and be subsidized by the cities.

The failure of the Pruitt–Igoe project in St. Louis, Missouri, is often taken as an example of the problems inherent in large-scale public housing. In 1972, a significant part of the complex was ordered to be dynamited by city authorities (see the photograph). The project had become such a social disaster for the residents that St. Louis city authorities felt there was no other alternative but to destroy it. Indeed, most of the housing complex had been abandoned by its residents. There have been many reasons offered for this dramatic failure in public housing:

1. The entire population of Pruitt–Igoe was black. In effect, a modern ghetto replaced a dilapidated one.
2. The project failed to provide places where social networks could form and where people could meet. The social opportunities for support that prevailed in the dilapidated slum structures were eliminated by the institutionalized efficiency of the Pruitt–Igoe housing complex.
3. Although the original buildings (which Pruitt–Igoe replaced) may have lacked some privacy, the new complex created a vast no-man's-land of hallways and public spaces. These spaces were no one's "property" and quickly became a source of vandalism and crime.
4. The people in the Pruitt–Igoe housing complex became isolated from the surrounding neighborhood as well as from the project complex itself. The project (which contained largely vertical buildings) was so enormous that the project's residents as well as their neighbors in surrounding homes found that the project's rigid physical barriers prevented easy interaction with people.

Not all public housing projects have been failures. Many cities have tried to avoid the serious mistakes of Pruitt–Igoe. The city of Jackson, Mich. developed a low-cost housing project that emphasized the privacy of the individual families while maintaining social networks and interactional opportunities (see Figures 7.4 and 7.5).

One of the apartment complexes of the Pruitt–Igoe project in St. Louis, Missouri being dynamited.

Photograph courtesy of United Press International

urban or rural) and family socioeconomic status. The child in an inner-city slum area has available a different kind of play environment than a preschooler from a suburban middle-class neighborhood or a child from a rural

FIGURE 7.4 A Jackson, Michigan Housing Project. Low-rise town houses provide opportunity for social interaction as well as a mixture of young couples, single families, and the elderly.

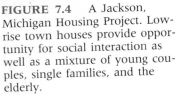

Photographs courtesy of Oxford Development Corporation, Okemos, Michigan

area. Each of these children has play settings that have limitations as well as strengths.

Although both availability and responsiveness are important characteristics for play settings, they are not always present. For example, although planned play spaces in urban areas may be more available in suburban middle-class neighborhoods, they may be somewhat less responsive than the informal

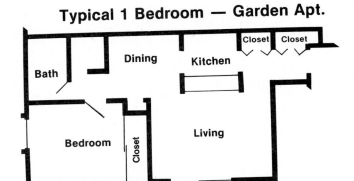

FIGURE 7.5 Plan of Woodland Hills (Jackson, Michigan) residential apartments.

Courtesy of Oxford Development Corporation, Okemos, Michigan

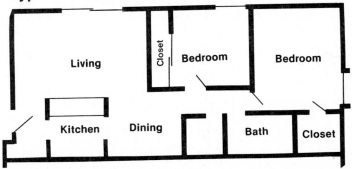

collection of varied objects and assorted "junk" that might characterize inner-city slum areas. Hart (1973) pointed out that children in suburban middle-class neighborhoods are often encouraged to stay in their nicely landscaped yards, which are usually supplied with toys and equipment. Unfortunately, much of this equipment may be unresponsive, thus discouraging exploration and creativity. On the other hand, inner-city neighborhoods may have a much larger collection of potentially "responsive" objects and materials and fewer organized and planned play areas. Unfortunately many of the responsive objects in inner-city neighborhoods may be potentially dangerous to the child (e.g., boards with exposed nails). Recognition by urban planners of the limitations of available and planned play spaces in urban areas has led to the creation of the so-called adventure or junk playground. Adventure playgrounds provide the opportunity for the child to deal with responsive play objects such as sand, scrap metal, wood, and rubber tires at the level of complexity that he/she is ready for (Nicholson, 1971). The adventure playground, in fact, simulates the elements of street play in the inner-city neighborhood and the "vacant lot" of previous generations.

How often do children really use planned playground facilities? Preschoolers appear to use planned play facilities more frequently than school-aged children. However, most planned play facilities are largely unused, particularly after the child reaches the age of six or seven (Bangs and Mahler, 1970; Dee and Liebman, 1970; Gold, 1972). By the time children reach school age, they appear to blend their play into the adult world of the neighborhood.

Hayward, Rothenberg, and Beasley (1974) examined the use of play areas as a function of the design of the play setting. Three different types of play settings were studied (see Figure 7.6):

1. *The "traditional" play setting.* This setting includes equipment such as slides, swings, see-saws, or a sandbox.
2. *The "designed" play setting.* This setting includes traditional activities such as swings and slides that are integrated into a continuous sculptured pattern with sand commonly used as a base.

FIGURE 7.6 Three types of playgrounds.

Left photograph by Darryl Jacobson; center and right photographs by David Kostelnik

3. *The "adventure" or "junk" play setting.* In this setting, children "create" their own play equipment from objects such as old tires, lumber and used packing crates, rocks, and bricks.

The general conclusion of the study is that the play environment was instrumental in determining the use of a play setting. In other words, the amount of time spent by a child in a given play area, as well as the type of activity that occurred, was a function of the *opportunities* provided in the play setting. Some play settings had more "potential" for generating creative and sustained interest than others.

THE PEER GROUP AS A PRESCHOOL CONTEXT

During the first two years of life the infant and the toddler usually play with family members. As the child matures, interaction expands to include other children in the neighborhood or, perhaps, in the setting of a preschool program. These early childhood years mark the beginnings of the first real peer group (see Figure 7.7). The first signs of a shifting dependency pattern from parents to peers emerge during these years. The preschooler may seek approval from peers as well as asking them for assistance. This trend increases until adolescence, when dependence on peers is usually greater than dependence on parents.

Research evidence suggests that peers encourage one another's behavior (Charlesworth and Hartup, 1967; Patterson, Littman, and Bricker, 1967). For example, peers may influence behavior by the use of mutual approval, praise, or affection. Modeling is also a powerful source of peer influence (Bandura, 1977; Hartup and Coats, 1967). Children can learn to do things by watching others do them. For example, aggressive behaviors are imitated by children under the appropriate circumstances. The consequences to the model (pleas-

FIGURE 7.7 A preschool-aged peer group.

Photograph by Gale Schiamberg

The Preschool Child

ant or unpleasant) and the child's judgment of the appropriateness of modeled behavior appear to influence the imitation of aggressive behavior (Hicks, 1971). In addition to aggression and disobedience, children may learn to imitate the cooperative and sharing behaviors of their peers.

THE PRESCHOOL AS A CONTEXT FOR DEVELOPMENT

DEFINITION

Preschool. "A school serving the needs of two-, three-, and four-year-old children . . . by offering them experiences adapted to what is now known about growth needs at these age levels. It shares with parents the responsibility for promoting sound growth and learning in a period when growth is rapid and significant. Respect for the individual child and his needs is the basis for a good . . . program" (Read, 1971, p. 27).

Although the preschool is not a context of development for all children, it has become an important experience for increasing numbers of young children. With the increase in the number of working mothers (see Chapter Six) and the development of early-childhood-education programs for special children (e.g., children from disadvantaged backgrounds), participation in a preschool program has become a common experience for young children. In this section, we examine some of the characteristics and types of preschool programs.

Some Characteristics of Preschool Programs. In a well designed preschool program, there are several distinguishing characteristics (Read, 1971, p. 27).

Small Groups. Preschool-aged children are usually put in small groups of two, three, or four. It is unusual for all children to be together doing the same things at the same time. On the other hand, a good amount of talking between the children is usual and acceptable. Talking among peers is one way of improving language skills.

Activity. The preschool is a place for involvement in a variety of activities and with many people. It is not unusual for an observer to enter a preschool program and find one group of children engaged in a homemaking activity (e.g., pretend cooking), another group building with blocks, another group playing a game under the guidance of the teacher, another group playing outdoors, and a single child painting a picture.

Play. Play is the primary mode of learning for the preschool child. Play might be thought of as the "work" of the child. The many activities of the preschool usually occur in a playful context. The spontaneous energy and curiosity of preschool children are channeled toward mastery of self and experiences. Such mastery occurs through playful learning involving the child's senses—seeing, touching, smelling, hearing, and tasting—and movement. Through play, the child learns to use his/her senses and his/her body.

Indirect Teaching. Much of the teaching at the preschool level involves facilitating the child's own learning. Such teaching is said to be *indirect*. The teacher sets the stage for learning by providing a variety of materials and possible experiences for the child to choose: "She makes comments or asks questions and, above all, she listens" (Read, 1971, p. 28).

Direct Teaching. Direct teaching is usually done with individual children and in small groups. Read (1971) described such teaching as follows:

It may occur through conversations about experiences the children have had. In these conversations the teacher encourages the children to express their thinking. It may occur through the use of resource materials, by drawing conclusions, and by making plans. A large part of the teacher's role is in helping the children learn how to learn. Some teaching may be done through games that encourage the use of the senses, the imagination, and problem-solving capacities. (p. 28)

Team Teaching. Preschool children in the process of discovering themselves and their world require individual attention. Therefore, more than one teacher is required for each group of children. Team teaching, which involves more than one teacher in planning and carrying out activities, is an effective way of meeting preschool children's needs.

The Structure of the Day (Session). The structure or plan for a particular day can be modified, as necessary. Such a plan depends on several factors, including the needs of the children, the interests of the teachers, and the resources of the school and the community. Often such plans are organized on a weekly basis around a given theme.

Types of Programs. There are many different types of early-childhood-education programs. These programs are designed to meet a wide range of needs among families and preschoolers. Some of these programs are as follows:

CHILD CARE CENTERS

Child-care centers provide full day care for children of working mothers. Increasingly, care is given to crib infants and toddlers. . . . Those agencies sponsoring child-care centers typically hope to provide a well-rounded educational program. [However], their first priority is to keep the child safe, nourished, and rested. It is not uncommon to find these centers understaffed and thus incapable of providing the educational programs their directors know would be desirable (Hildebrand, 1981, p. 11).

LABORATORY SCHOOLS

Laboratory schools have been established on college and university campuses since the 1920s to provide students a laboratory for observing and working with children of nursery school and kindergarten age. Research and teacher-preparation programs are usually carried out in these groups (Hildebrand, 1981, pp. 13–14).

PARENT-COOPERATIVE NURSERY SCHOOLS

Parent-cooperative nursery schools . . . are operated by parents who organize to provide schooling for their own children. They pool their time, energy and money and hire a qualified teacher. In addition, they take turns serving as the teacher's assistant. Parents meet to build equipment, paint the facility, or plan outings for the children. Tuition is lower than at . . . private schools. . . . Some parent cooperatives include well-organized classes for parent education in addition to the child's participation in the school. Since the parents . . . must participate, cooperatives are ordinarily not feasible for working mothers (Hildebrand, 1981, pp. 11–12).

Physical Characteristics and Motor Development of Preschool Children

PHYSICAL CHARACTERISTICS

The physical growth of children follows an order in which one activity comes after another. For example, the mature grasp (prehension) follows after more primitive grasping efforts. This sequential pattern of development is again apparent at the preschool or early childhood ages (two to five years). Most of the physical skills developed during these years are built on the foundation of perceptual skills (e.g., vision, hearing, and touch) and motor skills (e.g., walking and grasping) of infancy and toddlerhood.

The Pattern of Growth. There is an overall pattern for the growth and maturation of physical characteristics. As indicated in Figure 7.8, there are at least four major types of organs and tissues that grow according to a predictable pattern. These four types of organs are lymphoid (e.g, thymus and lymph nodes), brain and head (e.g., eyes and spinal cord), general (e.g, the body as a whole, muscles, and digestive organs), and reproductive (e.g., the testes and the ovaries).

General body growth increases rather rapidly during the first two years of life. During this time, dramatic growth in most bones and muscles can be observed. After the beginning of the third year, there is a slower and more gradual increase. At puberty, there is a distinct growth spurt (the adolescent growth spurt).

Brain and head growth increase rapidly during infancy and the preschool years. The brain and the head grow the fastest. The lymphoid system has the second most rapid growth rate. By age six, about 80 percent of the lymphoid growth has occurred. The lymphatic system supports the immunity of the body to illness and helps to fight infections.

FIGURE 7.8 Growth curves of different parts and tissues of the body, showing the four chief types. All the curves are of the size attained (in percentage of the total gain from birth to maturity) and plotted so that size at age twenty is 100 on the vertical scale.

From J. A. Harris, C. M. Jackson, D. G. Patterson, and R. E. Scammon, *The Measurement of Man.* University of Minnesota Press, Minneapolis. Copyright © 1930 by the University of Minnesota.

Lymphoid type: thymos, lymph nodes, intestinal lymph masses.

Brain and head type: brain and its parts, dura, spinal cord, optic apparatus, head dimensions.

General type: body as a whole, external dimensions (except head) respiratory and digestive organs, kidneys, aortic and pulmonary trunks, musculature, blood volume.

Reproductive type: testes, ovary, epididymis, prostrate, seminal vesicles, fallopian tubes.

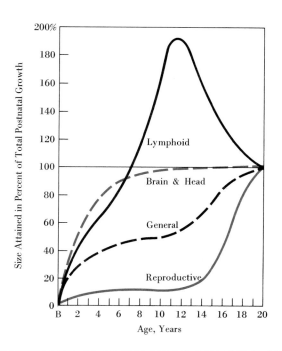

At age two, almost 60 percent of neurological development has occurred, and by age six, almost 90 percent has occurred (see Figure 7.9). Development of the reproductive system occurs at a much slower pace. It is not until the onset of puberty that the reproductive organs are functionally mature.

Brain Growth. From the early fetal period and beyond, the brain is nearer its adult size (in terms of weight) than any other organ of the body with the exception of the eyes. At two and one-half years the brain is about 75 percent of its adult weight; at five years, it is 90 percent of its adult weight, in contrast with the weight of the body as a whole, which is only about 50 percent of its adult weight at age ten (Tanner, 1978).

Prior to about age two, most of the *myelinization* of brain fibers has occurred.

DEFINITIONS

Myelin. This is a white, fatty substance that covers many neural fibers. It serves to channel brain impulses along appropriate fibers and to reduce the random spread of brain signals.

Myelinization. The process through which neural fibers acquire a myelin covering or sheath.

A number of areas in the brain have not completed myelinization until three or four years after birth. The *cerebellum* is the part of the brain concerned with the smooth and even performance of voluntary movements. In human beings, the *cerebral cortex* constitutes the major portion of the brain and occupies

FIGURE 7.9 Brain development.

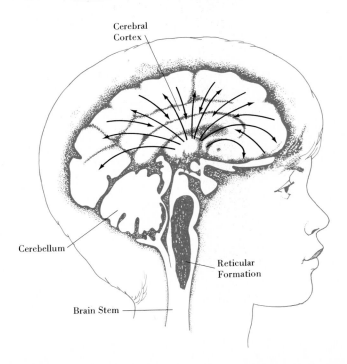

Cerebral Cortex

Cerebellum

Reticular Formation

Brain Stem

The Preschool Child

the upper part of the cranium. It contains the most highly developed functions of the nervous system, including intelligence and memory, and the centers for sight, hearing, smell, taste, and general body sensations. The neural fibers that connect the cerebellum and the cerebral cortex do not complete myelinization until about age four. These fibers are responsible for the fine control of voluntary movement. In addition, the *reticular formation* (the part of the brain concerned with the maintenance of attention and consciousness) does not complete myelinization until puberty or after (Tanner, 1978). There is some reason, therefore, to suppose that the fine motor movements characteristic of such skills as writing and the attentional skills necessary to accomplish them are, in part, the result of brain maturation.

Specific Characteristics: What Does a Preschooler Look Like? The typical two-year-old (see photographs) weighs somewhere between 25 and 28 pounds and is from 32 to 36 inches tall. By age two, the arms have lengthened 60 to 75 percent over what they were at birth. The legs are about 40 percent longer than at birth. Soon the legs will catch up and eventually become longer than the arms. At the age of three, the average child weighs over 30 pounds and is over 3 feet tall. The average four-year-old weighs about 36 pounds and is about 40 inches tall. The average five-year-old weighs about 43 pounds and has grown to about 44 inches in height (Corbin, 1980) (see Iowa Growth Charts in Chapter Six).

APPLICATION BOX

A Typical Day in a Day-Care Center

In a day-care center, the day . . . must fit the working hours of parents. The program will include more of what a home offers, meeting more of the child's needs for learning, for personal relationships, and for rest.

The morning will probably start more slowly. The children who arrive first may play quietly inside, and the teacher will help them make the transition from home to school as a place to live. She may put an arm around one, give another a pat, and listen to another talk about what happened at home. She may have a snack ready for the children to supplement their hurried breakfast. As more children arrive, they will separate and go to their different groups. . . .

The long day will include both a morning and afternoon snack as well as a main meal at noon. . . .

Planning for a full day means that the school is providing a larger share of the children's experiences. There will be excursions to the park, a farm, the city zoo, the grocery store. . . . There may be visitors to the school—a friendly policeman, or a fireman . . . or people who play different kinds of instruments. . . .

Through the days and weeks, children need new experiences to talk about, to broaden their concepts of the world, and to stimulate their thinking. The teachers will encourage conversation. Children need experience with verbal communication and the clarification of ideas which comes through expressing them. In a day-care center, especially, they must depend on finding this in their nursery school experience.

From K. Read, *The Nursery School.* Philadelphia: W. B. Saunders Company, 1971, pp. 31–32.

Clockwise from top left: three-year-old; two-year-old; two-year-old.

Photographs by Teresa Mayville, David Kostelnik, and Jeffrey Morris

There are, of course, individual variations in the growth of children. Girls tend to be slightly shorter than boys, although they both develop at about the same rate throughout the preschool years and the rest of childhood. An important difference between boys and girls is that boys tend to have more muscle tissue per body weight than girls. Girls tend to have more fatty tissue than boys (Breckenridge and Murphy, 1969).

There are other important facets of preschool growth. Body proportions change during this period. By the time children are six years old, they have the body proportions of the adult; the child's legs are about half the length of the body, which is the adult proportion. Most of the weight gained by the preschool child is the result of muscle development.

ENVIRONMENTAL FACTORS INFLUENCING GROWTH

Human growth is the result of the interaction of hereditary and environmental factors. Any gene is dependent for its expression on two types of environment: (1) an internal environment composed of all other genes and (2) an external environment (Tanner, 1978). It is difficult, if not impossible, to specify the precise relationship between heredity and environment. For example, a 10 percent increase in nutrition will not result in a similar increase in height for all individuals. Different genotypes respond differently to the same stimulus. In this section, we examine the effects of several environmental factors on growth, including nutrition, illness, exercise, and emotional stress.

The Preschool Child

de Montbeillard's Son (1759–1777)

The pattern of *general body growth* can be illustrated by the increase in height in human beings. The oldest published study of the physical growth of a child was made by Count Philibert Gueneau de Montbeillard from 1759 to 1777. Count de Montbeillard followed the growth in height of his son. The graphs provide a summary of the results of these observations. These data represent an accurate description of normal growth in height some two-hundred years after they were initially recorded and described. (Of course people are taller today than they were in eighteenth-century France. However, the pattern of growth in terms of rate is similar to modern times). The left diagram shows the pattern of increase in height. This pattern is similar to the "general" curve in Figure 7.8.

The graph on the right shows that the "velocity" or the rate of growth in height decreases from birth onward. This deceleration is interrupted briefly during the adolescent growth spurt. Count de Montbeillard's son experienced his adolescent growth spurt between thirteen and fifteen years of age. From birth through about age four or five years, the rate of growth in height declined quickly. The rate of decline is almost constant from about five or six years up to the adolescent growth spurt.

From J. M. Tanner, *Education and Physical Growth* (2nd ed.). New York: International Universities Press, 1978

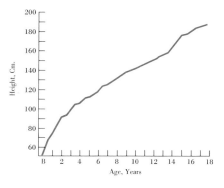

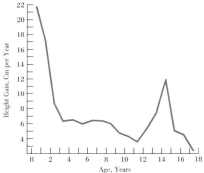

Growth in height of de Montbeillard's son from birth to eighteen years, 1759–1777.

From J. M. Tanner, *Growth at Adolescence.* Oxford, England: Blackwell Scientific Publications, Ltd., 1962.

Nutrition. Appropriate diet is necessary to the adequate growth of children. Such a diet includes the following:

Proteins provide the raw materials of growth.
Carbohydrates provide the energy necessary for activity.
Vitamins, fats, minerals, and water provide important support for growth.

What happens when children have too little to eat? In order to answer this question, we need to distinguish between two types of malnutrition: temporary and chronic. Considerable research and studies have been done on the effects of temporary malnutrition in children (Tanner, 1978; Richardson, 1975). During short periods of malnutrition, children's growth may be delayed. When better times arrive and food is available, rapid growth occurs

Photograph by Darryl Jacobson

until the child "catches up." At the end of this catch-up phase, the child's growth is almost indistinguishable from what it would have been had no malnutrition occurred at all. On the other hand, when children experience chronic undernourishment, they may become smaller adults.

What happens when children have too much to eat? Although malnutrition is certainly an important problem in some parts of the world, "overnutrition" is probably more prevalent and no less dangerous in its potential outcomes. There is some evidence that overfeeding during the first eighteen months of life may permanently contribute to adulthood obesity by increasing the number of fat cells (Dwyer and Mayer, 1969). In addition, as bottle feeding has replaced breast feeding in industrialized nations, the likelihood of excessive feeding also increases.

Illnesses. Minor or short-term illnesses (e.g., influenza and measles) have rather little impact on the growth rate of well-nourished children. Preschool children catch a large number of such communicable diseases with no apparent effect on their growth.

Major illnesses that require extended periods of hospitalization may result in a marked slowing of children's growth. A "catch-up" phenomenon ordinarily occurs after such illnesses. However, depending on the severity of the disease, chronic illness can result in a reduction in size.

Socioeconomic Status. There is evidence that children from families of differing socioeconomic level differ in average body size. This difference is apparently true for all ages of childhood, with upper socioeconomic groups being larger (Tanner, 1978). The British National Child Development Survey of 1958 showed differences between the height of children in relation to their family social status (Tanner, 1978). Children of professional- and managerial-class families were found to be approximately three centimeters taller than children of unskilled laborers at age three and four or five centimeters taller at adolescence (Tanner, 1978). This more rapid rate of growth may reflect better diet and health care (fewer illnesses). Some of this difference in height persists into adulthood.

Emotional Stress and Growth. Some investigators have found a relationship between severe psychological stress and retardation of growth. Widdowson (1951) found that children living in a German orphanage in 1948 grew more slowly under the tutelage of a punitive matron than children in another orphanage who received food with fewer calories (see the application box). Furthermore, some children under severe stress appear actually to switch off the secretion of growth hormone. This condition has been identified as *deprivation dwarfism* (Gardner, 1972). When the severe stress is removed, the secretion of growth hormone resumes and a growth "catch-up" occurs.

PERCEPTUAL DEVELOPMENT

Perceptual processes have to do with the reception or taking in of information about the environment. Various sensory systems are involved in providing this important information to the individual (touch, taste, sight, smell, and hearing). Perceptual information and the activity of the brain are important prerequisites to motor learning and development. Perceptual development has to do with age-related changes in the process of taking in information. In this section, we examine some of the major changes in perceptual skill that occur during the preschool years.

As children grow, there are at least three major changes in perceptual processes (Corbin, 1980; Nash, 1970):

1. A shift in the dominance of sensory systems.
2. An increase in communication between sensory systems.
3. An improvement in the functioning of individual sensory systems.

The earliest developmental change in perception is the *shift from primary reliance on tactual–kinesthetic* (*tactual* refers to the sense of touch; *kinesthetic* refers to the sense of one's body movement) *sensory systems to primary reliance on the visual system* for regulation of behavior. The visual system is the most advanced of all human perceptual processes in terms of the speed and the precision of information that it supplies to the individual (Corbin, 1980).

A second distinct change in perception is the improved *intersensory functioning* of the child. As children grow and mature, they are better able to interrelate information received from many sensory systems at the same time (Corbin, 1980). For example, children can ''match-up'' what they see with what they hear, what they see with what they smell, what they feel with what they see, and so on. Such multisensory functioning is important for several reasons; for example, it allows the child to make more precise judgments before action or movement is initiated. Multisensory functioning also indicates the appearance of integrative powers in the brain.

The third major change in perception is an increasing sharpness of discriminatory skill of the individual sensory systems. Preschool children begin to make finer distinctions in what they see and hear. The child preparing to catch a thrown ball, for example can now make a more precise determination of the location and speed of the ball than at an earlier age.

MOTOR DEVELOPMENT

The period of early childhood (from two to five years of age) is a significant period of motor learning and development. Most of the fundamental motor patterns develop to a relatively high level of precision during this period, although many of the underlying motor skills, such as walking, have their beginnings prior to this period. Such basic activities as walking are the basis for such fundamental motor skills as jumping, climbing, hopping, skipping, and galloping. The number of activities that can be learned by a young child is almost unlimited. That is, the child at this age can learn almost any motor skill to some level of effectiveness. Catching, throwing, swimming, and bicycle riding are examples of motor skills (or combinations of motor skills) that can be learned by age six if the opportunity is given.

General Characteristics of Motor Learning: Learning as Play and Play as Learning. For preschoolers, it is important to have a good start at what will most likely be a lifelong process of learning, a start in which they

APPLICATION BOX

Emotional Stress and Physical Growth

"Better a dinner of herbs where love is than a stalled ox and hatred therein" (quoted in Widdowson, 1951).

Quality of care proved more important than quality of food in two postwar German orphanages studied by Elsie M. Widdowson. For six months during 1948 the fifty-odd war orphans in each home received nothing but basic rations, yet the children in Orphanage A, supervised by a kindly matron, gained more weight than most of those in Orphanage B, whose matron was a stern disciplinarian. An exception was a group of favorites of the stern matron at B; they did better than their companions. After six months the matron at B was transferred to A and brought her favorites with her. Simultaneously the children at A were given extra rations, whereas the children at B remained on the same basic diet. (The transition is indicated by the vertical . . . line.) Relieved of the stern matron's discipline, the children at B began to show a sharp increase in weight; those at A showed a weight gain that averaged somewhat less than it had during the preceding six months in spite of the larger ration. Again matron's favorites were an exception; their gain was greatest of any. (Taken from L. I. Gardner, "Deprivation Dwarfism," p. 82. Copyright © July 1972 by Scientific American, Inc. All rights reserved.)

Gardner (1972) has suggested that serious deprivation of affection in the parent (caretaker)-child relationship may lead to a physical and emotional disturbance in the child called *deprivation dwarfism.* This disturbance is registered first in the *higher brain centers* where signals are sent to the *hypothalmus.* In turn, the hypothalmus regulates

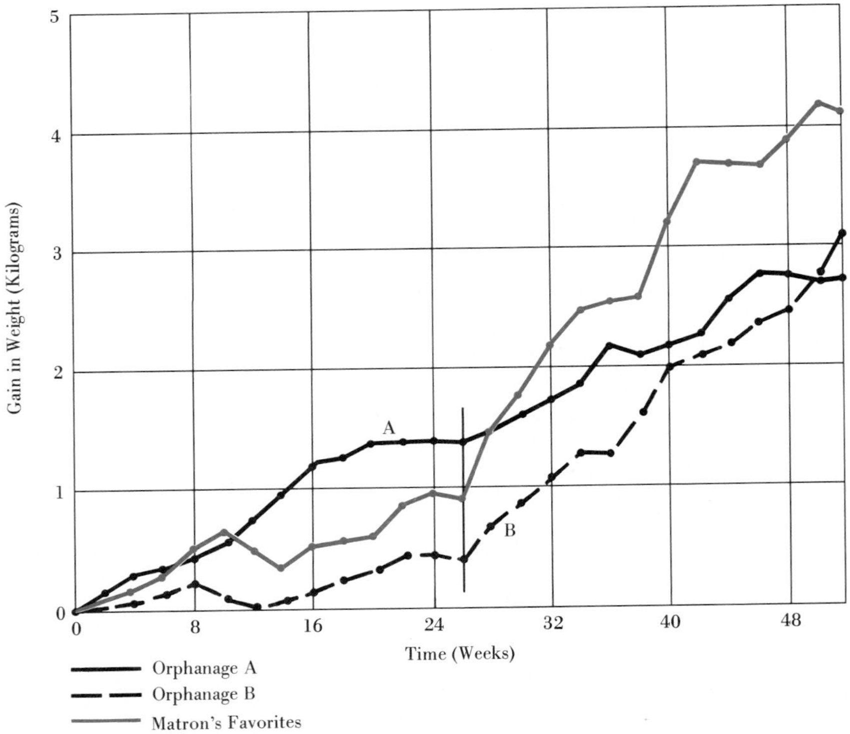

the pituitary gland (the "master gland" of the entire *endocrine system*). The pituitary gland, in turn, regulates the secretion of *somatotrophin* or *growth hormone*. Deprivation dwarfism results from reduced production of growth hormone (Gardner, 1972).

The emotional disturbance resulting from deprivation of affection, in turn, leads to disturbed sleeping modes. It is known that growth hormone is released during a mode of sleep when the higher brain centers are the least active. Deprivation dwarfism leads to irregular sleeping patterns which, in turn, result in reduced secretion of growth hormone. Normal growth is accompanied by a return to normal sleeping patterns (Gardner, 1972).

Although not as severe as deprivation dwarfism, the young child who is small and physically weak could possibly have diminished growth due to an emotionally disturbing family life. This assumes, of course, no nutritional deficiencies or diseases.

---

are free to set their own pace. Such a situation encourages competence and the desire to learn, particularly as much of preschool learning occurs in the context of "play," whereas, most learning beyond age six occurs in the context of school, or "work." Children who are two to six years old do not seem to want rules and regulations imposed on their play and motor games that are characteristic of such "play" beyond the age of six. In fact, preschoolers seem to be spontaneous in "inventing" their own play games (and the minimal rules that accompany them) using the "raw materials" of objects around the house or in the immediate neighborhood (e.g., pots, pans, tables, chairs, balls, sandboxes, ropes, wagons, puddles).

Use of toys in play is an important way in which the child learns to refine motor development and movement skills. On the whole, toys that effectively develop motor skills are sturdy, simple, and not overly realistic. In addition, objects and toys that can be moved and manipulated by the child seem to promote both motor skill and strength.

SCENARIO:
THE LOVE OF A MUD PUDDLE AND MOTOR DEVELOPMENT
Like other children of her age, Elizabeth seems to be drawn to mud puddles. She appears to derive great delight from riding her bicycle (with training wheels) through such puddles. Little boys and girls and mud puddles seem to have an affinity for one another. It is as if the mud puddle is a world all its own, over which the child exercises total control. Coupled with this control and the delight of the water splashing on both sides of the bicycle, the child is, of course, refining and practicing a basic motor skill: bicycle riding. The situation is a natural play context in which motor development as well as development of self-confidence occurs as the child learns what she or he can do.

Fundamental Motor skills. By the time children are four years old, they have mastered the underlying motor skills of infancy and toddlerhood, including locomotion, postural adjustment, and the manipulation or handling of objects. One way to look at the motor development of the preschooler is to look at those motor activities that seem to be common in the experiences of most children from two or three to six years of age. We will call these common motor activities *fundamental motor skills*. This category includes such ac-

Tricycles, bicycles, and motor development.

Left photograph by Wayne Mason, right photograph by Sylvia Byers

tivities as throwing, catching, skipping, hopping, jumping, and balancing. In this section, we focus on fundamental motor skills that develop, to some degree of competency, during the preschool years and that are a basic part of childhood games and play activities.

Such fundamental skills as running, jumping, throwing, catching, and hitting are the basis for sports, dance, and many recreational skills of middle childhood, adolescence, and adulthood. For this reason, the preschool period is a fundamentally significant period for motor development. Figure 7.10 shows the developmental pattern of motor skills ranging from the reflexes of early infancy to the advanced movement skills of older children, adolescents, and adults. It is important to note that there is a "proficiency barrier" that follows the preschool period of fundamental motor skills. This means the fundamental motor skills are the prerequisites for any advanced motor-skill performance. Table 7.1 summarizes the significant aspects of the developmental progression of these skills.

The following are some fundamental motor skills and their pattern of development:

Climbing. Climbing behavior emerges initially from infant crawling. In fact, many infants can climb steps before they can walk. Often, when infants reach the top of a staircase, they may try to descend in the same fashion in which they ascended: head first. After a few unsuccessful head-first attempts, the child discovers that it may be better to descend backwards. Studies of children's climbing ability suggest that there are several stages of climbing (Corbin, 1980).

1. *Mark-time pattern.* By the time children are about two years old, they can ascend steps using a mark-time pattern. This means they can go up one step at a time leading with the same foot each time.
2. *Alternating pattern.* By about forty-one months, children can climb stairs leading with each foot in an alternating pattern.

By age six, 92 percent of children are proficient climbers (Corbin, 1980). There are no significant differences between boys and girls in climbing skills (Corbin, 1980).

Jumping. Jumping can occur shortly after the child has learned to walk. More strength is required for jumping than for running because the body must be lifted upward in jumping (Corbin, 1980). The first attempt at jumping may appear as an emphatic step from an elevated level. At about twenty-eight months, children are able to jump with both feet simultaneously (Corbin, 1980). According to Corbin (1980), about 81 percent of children are proficient jumpers by age five.

FIGURE 7.10 The sequential progression of motor skills.

Based on V. Seefeldt and J. Haubenstricker, Pattern, phases or stages: an analytical model for the study of developmental movement. Michigan State University, Department of Health, Physical Education and Recreation, 1982.

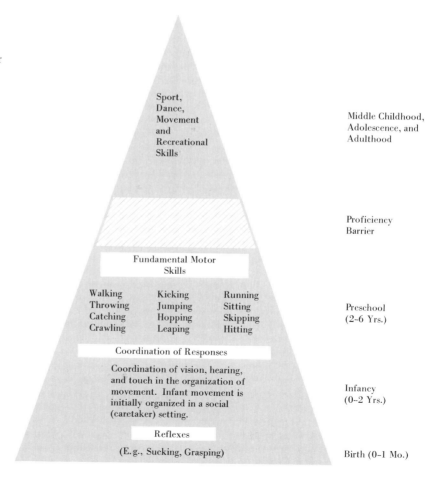

TABLE 7.1 Motor Characteristics of Perceptual–Motor Development: The Preschool Child

Motor Pattern	Skill Characteristics		
	The Three-year-old	*The Four-year-old*	*The Five-year-old*
Walking, running	Run is smoother and stride is more even than at two. Cannot turn or stop suddenly or quickly. Can take walking and running steps on the toes. Can walk a straight line. Can walk backwards long distances. Walks path (1 inch wide, 10 feet long) without stepping off. Cannot walk circular path (1 inch wide, 4 feet in circumference).	Run is improved in form and power. More effective control over stopping, starting, and turning. In general, greater mobility than at three. Coordinates body parts better in independent activities. Walks 6-cm. board partway before stepping off. Walks circle (1 inch wide, 4 feet in circumference) without stepping off.	Has effected adult manner of running. Can use this effectively in games. Runs 35-yard dash in less than 10 seconds.
Jumping	Jumps distance of 36–60 cm. 42% rated as jumping well. Clears rope less than 20 cm. high. Can jump down from an 8-inch elevation. Leaps off floor with both feet. Jumps down from heights of 8, 12, and 18 inches *alone, feet together.* (This preceded at early stages of jumping with help followed by jumping alone, one foot in front of the other.) Jumps down from a 28-inch height with help.	Jumps distance of 60–85 cm. 72% skilled in jumping. Most show difficulty in executing jump over a barrier. Jumps down from 28-inch height with feet together. Crouches for a high jump of 2 inches. Standing broad jump 8–10 inches. Running broad jump up to 23–33 inches. Jumps down from 28-inch height, alone with feet together.	80% have mastered the skill of jumping. More adept at jumping over barriers. Makes running broad jump of 28–35 inches. Makes vertical jump and reach of 2½ inches.
Hopping, galloping, skipping	Some attempt at hopping by 29 months. Hopping is largely an irregular series of jumps with some variation added.	Hops 2 meters on right foot. Only 14% skip well. 43% are learning to gallop.	22% skip well at end of fifth year. 78% gallop but are not rated as skilled. Hops distance of 16 feet easily.

Motor Pattern	Skill Characteristics		
	The Three-year-old	The Four-year-old	The Five-year-old
	Executes one to three consecutive hops with both feet: 38 months. Executes ten or more hops on both feet: 42 months (rapid skill development). Executes one to three consecutive hops 1 foot: 43 months. Performs a shuffle skip.	Hops four to six steps on one foot. Skips on one foot. Executes one to ten hops consecutively: one foot.	Ten or more consecutive hops: one foot. Alternates feet in skipping.
Climbing	50% rated as proficient in climbing on jungle gyms, packing boxes, inclined planks, etc. Ascends stairway unaided, alternating feet. Ascends short stairway unaided, alternating feet: 31 months. Ascends long stairway unaided, alternating feet: 41 months. Descends both short and long stairways, marking time; not supported. Ascends small ladder, alternating feet.	Further increase in proficiency. Descends long stairway by alternating feet, if supported. With no support; marks time. Ascending skills mastered (stairways). Descends long stairway, alternating feet if supported. Descends short stairway, alternating feet unaided. Ascends large ladder, alternating feet. Descends small ladder, alternating feet.	Still further increase in proficiency. Descends long stairway or large ladder alternating feet. Descends long stairway, alternating feet, unaided. Ascending skills mastered (ladder). Descends large ladder, alternating feet.
Throwing	Frequently engaged in ball throwing, but does not throw well. Throws without losing balance. Throws approximately 3 feet; uses two-hand throw. Anteroposterior movement dominant in throwing. Body remains fixed during throw. Arm is initiating factor.	20% are proficient throwers. Beginning to assume adult stance in throwing. Can toss ring toss successfully at peg 4 feet 10½ inches away. Distance of throw increases. Horizontal-plane movements dominate. Whole body rotates right, then left. Feet remain together in place. Arm is the initiating factor.	74% are good throwers— great variation at each age level. Assumes adult posture in throwing. Some throw distances of 17 feet; use primarily unilateral throw. Introduction of weight transfer; right-foot-step-forward throw. At 6–6½ years: mature throw: left-foot-step-forward; trunk rotation, and horizontal adduction of arm in forward swing.

TABLE 7.1 (cont.)

Motor Pattern	Skill Characteristics		
	The Three-year-old	*The Four-year-old*	*The Five-year-old*
Catching	Attempts to stop rolling ball with hands or corrals it with legs. Gradually synchronized movements with speed of rolling ball and hands reach around object. Aerial ball: first attempts—hands and arms work as a single unit in an attempt to corral the ball against the body. Catches large ball with arms extended forward stiffly. Makes little or no adjustment of arms to receive ball. Catches large and small ball; arms straight.	29% are proficient in catching. Catches large ball tossed from 5 feet away with arms flexed at elbows. Moves arms in accordance with direction; definite efforts to judge position at which ball will land. Depends more on arms than hands in receiving ball. Catches both large and small balls; elbows in front of body.	56% are skilled at catching. Catches small ball; uses hands more than arms. Judges trajectory better than at four; not always successful. Attempts one-hand catches. Catches both large and small balls; elbows at side of body.
Bouncing	Bounces small ball distance of 1–5 feet; uses one hand. Cannot perform this task with a large ball.	Bounces large ball distance of 4–5 feet; uses two hands.	Bounces large ball 6–7 feet; uses two hands. One-hand bounce; large ball attempted at 72 months.

Hopping. Hopping skill is more difficult than jumping because it requires balancing on one foot. It is not until almost thirty months that children can balance themselves by standing on one foot (Corbin, 1980). Most children can hop for short distances at around four years, but it is not until children are about six that they are proficient at hopping (Corbin, 1980).

Throwing. Throwing emerges through four stages (Milne, Seefeldt, and Reuschlein, 1975; Corbin, 1980). The last stage occurs at the end of the preschool period and into the school-aged period (roughly six and one-half to seven years of age). We will discuss all four stages in detail in Chapter Eight.

Catching. The ability to catch a moving object such as a ball requires good eye–hand coordination as well as space–time perception (Corbin, 1980). Toddlers are usually able to stop or gather in a rolling ball. First attempts at catching a ball in flight are somewhat awkward. The arms may be held out stiffly in anticipation of the ball. Eventually the preschooler learns to adjust arm movements in relation to the oncoming ball.

Thinking, Play, and Art

In Chapter Six we examined the sensorimotor intelligence of the infant. In this section, we continue our discussion of the development of thinking. According to Piaget's theory of intelligence, early-childhood cognitive development includes the period of preoperational thinking (eighteen months to seven years). The preoperational period is sometimes subdivided into two parts: the preconceptual stage (two to four years of age) and the intuitive stage (five to seven years). Although the intuitive stage includes part of the preschool years and beyond, we discuss it here briefly because many preschool children may function at that level.

THE PREOPERATIONAL PERIOD

The Preconceptual Stage (Two to Four Years). The highlights of the preconceptual stage include the emergence of language, symbols, and symbolic play. The use of both symbols and symbolic play are significant because they indicate the emerging ability of the child to think about what is *not immediately* present. For example, the child may call a teddy bear a "baby," indicating that the teddy bear represents or symbolizes the idea "baby." The teddy bear is a "symbolic" baby. In the previous period of sensorimotor intelligence, cognitive functioning was limited to what was immediately present or before the infant. Furthermore the development of language, or linguistic symbols, for action provides the opportunity to use verbal symbols as a way of extending the sensorimotor control of the environment (e.g., instead of walking toward the refrigerator and staring at it as a sensorimotor technique for getting some milk, the preschooler uses the word *milk,* or some facsimile thereof, to control the behavior of adults). The preconceptual child is able to use words to categorize objects; however, this process is limited by the *egocentrism* of the child's thinking (i.e., the inability to distinguish between one's own perceptions and the perceptions of others). Because their perception of the world is colored by their own relatively limited experiences, preschoolers cannot readily distinguish among mental, physical, and social realities. For example, if the child experiences living things as moving (e.g., dogs, cats, people, birds), then he or she may extend this meaning to include the moon and the clouds as "living" because they also move.

The Intuitive Stage (Five to Seven Years). The intuitive stage begins at approximately age five. It is closer to adult thinking because the child is now able to separate mental from physical reality. The child is somewhat less egocentric than in the previous stage and therefore is able to distinguish between his or her own perceptions of the real world and the reality of physical and social behavior. For example, this ability to distinguish aspects of reality—and to categorize these features—helps the child differentiate between living objects that move and other objects (e.g., clouds, moon, or stars) that also move but are not "alive." The child begins to grasp the force of other powers and can more readily appreciate multiple points of view. Thinking skills are improving; however, at the intuitive level, children still depend on what they actually perceive (or think they perceive) as the basis of reality (see Figure 7.11).

Symbolic Representation. The most significant cognitive difference between the infant and the preschooler (two to five years of age) is the *use of symbols* by the preschooler. The preschooler's use of symbols includes a wide range of behavior, such as the use of action images or words to represent experience. For example, on being given a toy car, the twelve-month-old

Top photograph by David Schiamberg; bottom photograph by Gale Schiamberg

FIGURE 7.11 *The intuitive stage of thinking (ages five to seven).* Because the child's thinking is more a function of *perception* (how things appear) rather than *logical* necessities, he/she solves problems in a "perceptual" manner. For example, the child is given a square piece of paper and asked to draw both the largest possible square and the smallest possible square on the paper. In order to solve this problem, the intuitive-stage child probably needs to draw many squares on the paper in order to compare them visually to see if each is larger or smaller than the previous one. This "perceptual" mode of problem solving can be contrasted with the "logical" or "abstract" mode of older children and adolescents (e.g., the largest possible square must "logically" be very near to the borders of the paper, whereas the smallest possible square must be very tiny).

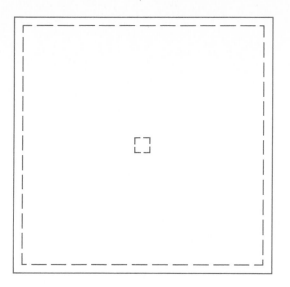

infant might do various things with it, including putting it in his or her mouth, banging it on the floor, throwing it, or simply looking at it. The two-year-old, however, on being presented with a similar car, will probably demonstrate by his or her use of the toy car that he or she knows what a car is or does. For example, the two-year-old may put the car down on the rug (as if the rug were a road) and move the car, making a sound like a running motor. In other words, the two-year-old uses movements and vocal sounds to imitate past events and roles with which he/she is familiar. Observation of the preschooler in play settings may indicate the development and acting out of extensive sequences of behavior relating to the use of the family car to go shopping or for other family activities.

When children first begin to use words, they may use them in idiosyncratic ways. As we saw in Chapter Six, Baby Elizabeth was somewhat general in her use of the word *father*. As symbol use becomes more effective and specific, more complex modes of thinking are possible. For example, the refined use of language allows children to demonstrate to themselves (and to others) both the similarities and the differences of objects by assigning them labels (Piaget, 1950, 1951). In addition, children can use words as a way of interpreting their past and predicting their future.

Limitations of Preoperational Thinking. Although the child at the preoperational level of thinking has made substantial improvements in thinking skills, preoperational thought has several *limitations*:

1. Preoperational thinking is *concrete*. That is, the child works best with the world of his or her immediate surroundings and his or her own perceptions of reality. The child is usually involved with the present and with objects or experiences that can be easily represented by images and simple words.

2. Preoperational thinking is *irreversible*. That is, the child can understand how events happen in the present but has difficulty imagining the return of

The Toddler Elizabeth and Her Brother Bruce—An Example of the Dominance of Sensory Systems

Our indefatigable toddler Elizabeth is a rather sociable creature who enjoys mingling with human beings of all ages. The emerging dominance of her visual system is apparent when one observes her efficient walking and improving running skills. In young children visual dominance increases with age. For example, Elizabeth spied Bruce (now five years old) playing baseball with his friends. Bruce swung a plastic bat at a pitched ball, hitting it a good distance. Bruce's ability to do this is based on his ability to establish his bat swinging (motor skill) in relation to perceptual information (the size and speed of the oncoming baseball) from his visual system. His visual system is *dominant* in that it organizes his swinging movements.

Not to be outdone, Elizabeth, noting Bruce's success, approaches him and requests his bat. Elizabeth swings the bat, indicating that she has the basic motor skill to manipulate the bat. However, in response to a pitched ball, she simply cannot coordinate her body movements in relation to the ball's movement. This inability suggests that Elizabeth is still largely dependent on tactual–kinesthetic information. In contrast, Bruce's ability to hit the ball suggests that there is—or, at least, there is in progress—a shift toward a visual dominance, which allows for his rapid and precise regulation of movement.

Photograph by David Kostelnik

present events to their original state. For example, if a large ball of clay is made into several smaller balls of clay in full view of the child, the child continues to think of the clay as several small balls and has difficulty thinking of the clay in its original form, as a large ball.

3. Preoperational thinking tends to be *egocentric.* The child focuses on the environment from the perspective of his or her own limited experience.

4. Preoperational thinking tends to focus on only *one aspect or dimension of a problem at a time.* For example, when looking at the height of an object, the child may be almost oblivious to its width. The child perceives one set of relationships while being unable to think of other relationships simultaneously (see Figure 7.12).

5. Preoperational thinking tends to involve "transductive reasoning" (Piaget, 1951); the preschooler reasons from one specific and immediate (here-and-now) event to another equally specific and immediate event. Reasoning from particular to particular is a matter of thinking by association. For example, if the child sees the wind blowing leaves, trees, and paper about,

the child might arrive at the conclusion that he or she, too, will be blown away, never to be seen again. Because the child reasons from particular to particular, somewhat illogical and sometimes humorous conclusions are reached. Transductive reasoning differs from two types of reasoning employed by older children and adolescents:

a. *Inductive reasoning,* or moving from specific instances to generalities (e.g., a baseball, a golf ball, and a tennis ball are all examples of the general category *ball*).

b. *Deductive reasoning,* or reasoning from generalities to specifics (e.g., foods include cheese, tomatoes, meat, and cake).

Conservation. Several of the features (as well as limitations) of children's thinking are illustrated in what Piaget and others have called *conservation problems* (see Figures 7.12 and 7.13). According to Piaget, one of the most important cognitive achievements of child development is the construction of permanent concepts ("invariances") in the face of an environment that involves continuous changes. As we have mentioned before, around two years of age the child constructs the notion of the permanence of objects. Having acquired this idea, the preschool child is ready to refine the notion of the permanence of objects to include the *invariability* or conservation of object characteristics, such as weight, volume, number, or amount.

Piaget and others have studied the development of conservation using the following experimental arrangement (see Figures 7.12 and 7.13):

1. The child is shown two amounts or quantities that are, in fact, equal. The child is then asked to affirm that the two amounts are equal. Most four-year-old children are able to recognize such equalities.

286

FIGURE 7.12 Conservation of volume. Two beakers with equal amounts of water in them are presented to the child, and the child is asked to recognize the equality (most children can do this by the time they are four years of age). While the child watches, a transformation occurs: one beaker of water is poured into a tall, cylindrical beaker and the other is poured into a flat beaker. This child is now asked whether the amounts of water in the tall and the short beakers are the same or different. The preoperational child will say that they are different. The tall, cylindrical beaker will appear to have more water in it.

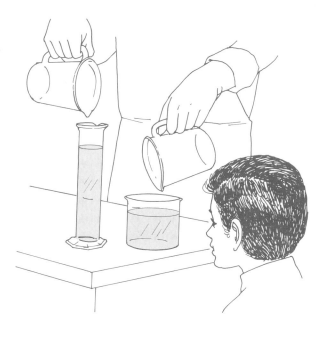

FIGURE 7.13 Conservation of number. When shown the arrangement of candy at the top, four- to five-year-old children generally respond that both lines contain the same number of candies. In the configuration at the bottom, the lower line of candy has been spread out so that it appears to be wider and longer. When asked whether the candies in the lines of the bottom configuration are the same or different, the preoperational child insists that the line that appears longer has more candy in it, even if the child has counted the candies in each line.

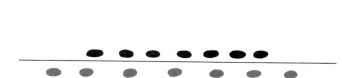

Based on J. Piaget, *The Child's Conception of Number.* London: Routledge & Kegan Paul, Ltd., 1952.

2. While the child watches, the equal objects are transformed so that they "appear" to be different.
3. The child is then asked whether the two amounts are now the same or different.

In the developmental pattern of conservation, the four- to five-year-old child can usually recognize that the quantities presented in the first step of the conservation problem are equal. For example, when children are presented (as in Figure 7.13) with equal amounts of candy, they will say that both lines of candy are the same, probably because they "look" the same. In other words, the child's conclusion is based on his or her perception that the candy in both lines covers the same total distance. This reliance on perception becomes clear when a *transformation* is made in the perceptual characteristics of the candy arrangement (see bottom of Figure 7.13), so that one line is longer than the other. When this happens, the child has difficulty understanding that there are still equal amounts of candy in both lines. The five- to six-year-old child seems to be in a transitional phase and may respond inconsistently. At one time, the child will say that the transformed arrangements contain the same amounts and, at another time, will insist that the transformed arrangements are not equal. By the time the child reaches age seven, the concept of conservation seems to have been perfected. The acquisition of conservation accompanies the change from preoperational thinking to the concrete operational thinking of the school-aged child.

Classification. The process of refining the idea of conservation during the preoperational phase of thinking is accompanied by other developments in the preschooler's thinking skills. In particular, the child's ability to organize and *classify* objects according to categories is also limited in certain ways. When asked to classify and organize objects, the preoperational child puts them in categories that reflect his or her egocentric perception of how the world is structured. In other words, the *basis* for classification arises out of the free association of objects and perceptions.

SCENARIO:
THE CLOUDS IN THE SKY, GRAMPA'S PIPE,
AND A PREOPERATIONAL GRANDSON.

Bruce's grandparents have come from Chicago to see their grandchildren. One evening, grandfather was smoking his pipe and pipe smoke began to rise over his head in a visible gray pattern. On noting this "cloud" of smoke, Bruce arose from his preoccupation with a small cardboard box and made the following observations to his grandfather:

1. "Grampa, your cloud is the same as the clouds outside in the sky."
2. "Grampa, did you make the clouds outside?"

In the scenario, Bruce organizes his world according to a classification in which the clouds from his grandfather's pipe can be easily and seriously grouped with the clouds in the sky. The preoperational child who is given a collection of objects that vary along a number of dimensions, including size, shape, color, and texture, will probably not organize or *classify* the objects in the same fashion as an older child or an adult. As we pointed out, the preoperational child can usually focus on only one dimension or attribute of an object or a collection of objects. The preoperational child may have no difficulty grouping together objects on the basis of use, for example, plates, knives, forks, and spoons. The arrangement of objects on the basis of many characteristics at the same time is much more difficult.

Space, Time, and Sequence. The understanding of time concepts develops very gradually in the child (see Table 7.2). In the first year, the child usually acts on objects only in terms of their relationships in space, rather than their relationships in time. Delayed responses to cues appear only after about one and a half years. The ability to remember time sequences and the

TABLE 7.2
**Age and Recognition
of Temporal Spans**

Age	Time Spans Recognized
4 years old	Recognize a special day of the week, such as Sunday
5	Tell whether it is morning or afternoon
	Use the words "yesterday" and "tomorrow" with their true meaning
6	Indicate the day of the week
7	Indicate the month
7–8	Indicate the season
8	Indicate the year
8–9	Indicate the day of the month
12	Estimate the duration:
	a. of a conversation
	b. "since the holidays"
	c. "until the holidays"
	Give the time to within 20 minutes

Source: Fraisse, P. *The Psychology of Time* (Translated by J. Leith). New York: Harper and Row, 1963, p. 180.

repetition of events in particular places seems to develop between ages three and four (Hunter and Bartlett, 1948). Concepts of time of day and clock time develop around age five and six (Vinacke, 1951). Children's early concepts of concrete space contribute to their first concrete concepts of clock time and calendar time. A mature understanding of time (which develops at age eleven to twelve) precedes the development of abstract concepts and the use of logical strategies in problem solving (Bruner, Oliver, and Greenfield, 1966; Piaget, 1966).

An extensive study by Michaud (1949) surveyed changes in cognitive structures between the ages of ten and fifteen years by asking hundreds of children what happens to time when we put the clock forward in the spring for daylight savings time. The respondents were classified into four categories: (1) those who regarded time as a real quantity affected by the clock; (2) those who dealt with the change as a practical problem of losing an hour that would have been useful; (3) a relatively small number who treated the clock shifting as a mathematical problem of equalizing spring and fall changes; and (4) those who recognized that clocking time is a pure convention and that changing the clock creates a discrepancy between clock time and sun time. Classifying the first two types of response as concrete and the last two as abstract, there was an increase in abstract responses from age ten to age fifteen.

PLAY: THE INTEGRATION OF DOING, THINKING, AND LANGUAGE

Both adults and young children engage in what is called *play*. For adults, play is primarily recreation; however, for children, play is recreational as well as being an important feature of development. We refer to play as an *ecosystem* of development because it represents the integration of activity, thought, and language in the natural settings of the family, the neighborhood, or preschool. In a sense, play is the "work" of the child.

What Is Play? Play is not easy to define. As a matter of fact, it is probably easier to define what play is *not* than what it is. That is, play is not routine, nor is it work. For our purposes, we will define play as nonserious activity that is engaged in for itself or simply for the satisfaction that results (Dearden, 1967). Other descriptive characteristics of play are often cited in a definition of play (Garvey, 1977):

1. Play is enjoyable and pleasurable.
2. Play has no extrinsic purpose or external goals (the motivation to play is intrinsic or internal and serves no particular end except, perhaps, enjoyment for its own sake).
3. Play is undertaken *spontaneously* and *voluntarily.*
4. Play involves active participation on the part of the child.
5. Play is *related* in a coordinated way *to other aspects of development* (e.g., creativity, problem solving, language learning, motor activity, and development of social roles).

In summary, play enlarges the child's understanding of the world in which he or she lives. Play allows the child to explore objects, social roles, language, and feelings without serious risk. In play situations, the child is free to choose an activity without regard to its consequences or to the achievement of a particular goal. Play is certainly behavior, but with two important qualifications (Garvey, 1977):

1. Play does not have any behavioral patterns that are unique to it (rather, the behaviors of play are all borrowed from other domains, e.g., movement or language).
2. Play behavior (e.g., simulated aggression in a play situation) is "buffered" from the normal consequences associated with the behavior.

Types of Play. As there are many definitions of play, there are many ways of categorizing play. One way is to categorize play in relation to cognitive ability (Piaget, 1951). Piaget divided play into three major types:

Sensorimotor play extends into the second year of life. The child acquires and exercises control over his or her movements and learns to coordinate these movements and their effects. Play during this stage often takes the form of motor behaviors that are repeated and varied. According to Piaget, the infant derives pleasure simply from the experience of seeing, hearing, touching, and holding. In addition, the infant seems to enjoy making things happen.

Symbolic or representational play extends from approximately two to six years of age. As we pointed out in our discussion of symbolic representation and cognitive development, the preschool child begins to interpret experience in terms of symbols or images. The child's improved memory facilitates the recall of images of previous experiences that serve as one basis for organizing play. The child begins to organize the play with symbols, and *pretending* becomes a common play mode (e.g., holding a stick against the back of a toy car and pretending that the car is at a gasoline station and being filled with gasoline).

Games with rules ordinarily start at the beginning of the school years. The child becomes interested in structured games that involve the social concepts of cooperation and/or competition. It is probably no accident that this interest in games with rules and structure coincides with the emergence of the ability to do conservation problems (i.e., to recognize the invariant "rules" of environmental phenomena).

Another way to view play (which is different from Piaget's perspective) is to focus on the resources or materials involved in various categories of play (Garvey, 1977). This perspective is based on the idea that as the child matures and grows, new resources and materials emerge as sources of play. Resources for play can be viewed as categories of experience.

Play as Motion and Interaction. Motion or the sensation of movement are probably the first play experiences that adults provide for infants. As the infant learns to control its own movements, the joy and pleasure of play as body movement comes under the infant's own control.

An important step in normal socialization is learning to interact—and play— with others, including adults and peers. Playing with other children is different than playing with adults and objects in two ways: (1) other children are less predictable, and (2) other children are less subject to control. As might be expected, a two-year-old child has much to learn about sustaining successful play interaction with peers. The social skills of the two-year-old are largely organized in terms of mutually *predictive relationships* with adults and/or objects (Eckerman, Whatley, and Kutz, 1975; Bronson, 1975). Infants and toddlers appear to be more interested in objects and toys than in other children. Although they may be attracted to other toddlers, they sometimes find these relationships erratic and threatening. About half of these peer encounters end in minor struggles (Garvey, 1977).

Another category of motion–interaction play is sometimes called *rough-and-tumble play,* a term that refers to a number of behavior or action patterns performed by a group at a high level of activity. For example, rough-and-tumble may include any of the following sample *cluster* behaviors: running, hopping, chasing, falling over one another, fleeing, wrestling, and laughing. These playful group interchanges are frequently observed among preschool children and, in particular, during outdoor free-play sessions in nursery schools (Blurton-Jones, 1972). In nursery-school settings, rough-and-tumble activities are usually organized according to sex. Toddlers probably spend more time watching than actually participating, a form of exploration that precedes actual involvement.

Play with Objects. Interaction with objects in the environment (e.g., toys), constitutes a large part of the play experiences of the toddler and the pre-

An important step in normal socialization is learning to interact through play.

Photograph by David Schiamberg

school child. Toys are objects designed by adults to elicit the interest of the child. As might be expected, most of the other objects in the home and the neighborhood are probably at least as interesting.

How does object play begin? The following pattern describes the progression of object play (Garvey, 1977; Lowe, 1975):

Nine months. The child grasps objects that are close to him/her and brings them to his or her mouth. After the object has been brought to the mouth, the child may wave it about and bang the object. Action patterns are rather limited.

Twelve months. The child is likely to manipulate, investigate, or examine the object *before* doing anything with it.

Fifteen months. Investigative behaviors clearly occur before the child does anything else with an object. In addition, objects begin to be treated in accordance with their typical or conventional uses (e.g., a cup may be placed in a saucer, or the child may pick up a brush and put it in his or her hair).

Twenty-one months. The child now begins to search for objects that normally go with other things. For example, the child may look for a spoon or a fork to go with a cup and saucer with which he or she is playing.

Thirty to thirty-six months. The child's play has become considerably more realistic. For example, dolls sit at tables and are made to pick up and drink from glasses; dishes may be washed after the "dinner"; and the dolls may wipe their mouths with napkins.

Throughout childhood, objects provide a basis for the initiation of play and for promoting social contacts. For example, when a young child encounters a novel object for the first time, there is a progression of activity leading from discovery and exploration to imaginative and playful use of the object. Garvey (1977) gave the following example of this progression:

A three-year-old boy saw a large wooden car in our playroom for the first time. (a) He paused, inspected it, and touched it. (b) He then tried to find out what it could do. He turned the steering wheel, felt the license plate, looked for a horn, and tried to get on the car. (c) Having figured out what the object was and what it could do, he got to work on what he could do with it. He put telephones on it, took them off, next put cups and dishes on it. These activities were a form of trying out ideas to see how they would work. Finally, the car was understood, its properties and immediate usefulness reasonably clear. (d) He then climbed on it and drove furiously back and forth with suitable horn and motor noises. (p. 47)

As the child grows and matures, his or her playful interaction with objects becomes more complex and sophisticated. As symbolic representation becomes a more refined cognitive skill, objects take on more and more meaningful associations. Later, objects become part of dramatic play and games with rules. Throughout these changes, objects are always a source of curiosity and interest.

Play with Language. Almost all aspects of children's speech are potential resources for play. For example, most levels of language organization (sound formation, word and sentence development) are sources of playful use of language. For young children, there is an infinite variety of play combinations of language forms.

Language play occurs when the child is alone as well as when he or she is with others in a social situation. There are three types of social play with language (Garvey, 1977).

1. *Spontaneous word play and rhyme making.*

Boy (5 years, 2 months)	Girl (5 years, 7 months)
(inspects stuffed animals) 1. Teddy bear's mine.	(busy with suitcase)
	2. The fishy fishy is mine.
3. No, the snakey snakey is yours.	

From C. Garvey, *Play.* Cambridge, Mass.: Harvard University Press, 1977, p. 69.

2. *Word play with nonsense and fantasy.* Nonsense words or short stories become a useful source of playful language for the preschool child.
3. *Play with conversation.* As we pointed out earlier in this chapter, the preschool child becomes increasingly acquainted with the rules and norms of language organization. Accompanying this development is the use of play conversations in which it appears to be understood that rules of accuracy and truth are in temporary or creative suspension.

Speech enters into other aspects of play as a way of organizing dramatic play and of controlling games with rules. In addition, many of the simple rituals of childhood play are organized by language.

Play with Social Materials (Dramatic or Pretend Play). The principle resources of play with social materials are social expectations and social roles. When recognizable "roles" or "characters" are involved, this type of play is referred to as *dramatic or pretend play.* This type of play is one of the most sophisticated forms of childhood play because it involves the *integration* of other play forms (motion and interaction, object play, and language games).

There are two primary modes for organizing such dramatic play (Garvey, 1977):

1. An action play or the organized arrangements of events into a coherent episode.
2. A role assumed by the play participants.

It is thought that pretend play does not appear before about age three, and it seems to disappear sometime before adolescence. There are two explanations for the demise of dramatic or pretend play:

1. Although overt make-believe play decreases, it is replaced by covert play, or fantasy (Klinger, 1967). Fantasy, daydreaming, or "thinking" about make-believe situations becomes a part of the adolescent experience (e.g., concern about popularity, appearance, and vocation).
2. The beginning of games with rules and the onset of more realistic play serve as replacements for pretend play (Piaget, 1951).

The Meaning of Dramatic Play

. . . dramatic play . . . centers around episodes and relationships that seem significant to the children. Through play they reveal themselves and their concepts of the world to us.

What meaning does such play have for children?

Dramatic play is one way to handle the problem of being "little."

We can be sure that children want to understand what it is like to be grown up and do grown-up things. In their play they are preparing themselves for these roles someday. Play is also one way to handle their own special problem of being "little" in a world of big people. In play they have a chance to be big mother or father, or the important workman. . . .

Play makes children feel less helpless.

Taking adult roles in play also gives the child the chance to feel in control of situations. He can make things come out as he would like in his dramatic play. He can be the one to put the baby to bed, to do the scolding and spanking, to make decisions. . . .

Play offers an opportunity to drain off negative feelings.

In their play children often act out aggressive, destructive feelings. These are the kinds of feelings which create anxiety and need to be drained off. It is important to accept them in play, being sure only that the children are safe and that the impulses are under control and kept on a "pretend" level. An adult may need to remain near to "steady" a group which is acting out negative feelings. . . .

From K. Read, *The Nursery School.* Philadelphia: W. B. Saunders Company, 1971, pp. 356–359.

Top photograph by Gale Schiamberg, left photograph by David Kostelnik, right photograph by Dr. June Youatt

Games, Rituals, and Competitive Play. The play of children involves rules in games with a specific (although usually not a serious) purpose once they move beyond the stage of dramatic play. Children make decisions about such things as taking turns and making guidelines about what behavior is permitted in the game. Such games as tag, Red Rover, and hide-and-seek are common in this stage of play.

CHILDREN'S DRAWING: THE INTEGRATION OF MOVEMENT, THINKING, AND SELF-PERCEPTION

As we have pointed out before, human behavior involves the *integration* of many specific components into a unified whole or *system.* This integration is well illustrated by the development of children's drawing, which involves the integration of motor skills (e.g., eye–hand coordination), cognitive development, and expression of feelings about the self and the world. In its broadest context, children's drawing is the playful, nonserious representation of symbols on paper. In a narrower context, children's drawing has been interpreted (like adult artistic works of painting, sculpture, and design) as purposive and goal-oriented (and therefore, not really play). We will not try to resolve this issue. However, it is clear that children's drawing (whether or not an "official" mode of play) is an important indicator of child development. Children's drawing often occurs in the context of the family or the preschool.

From the very moment that he or she picks up a crayon, pencil, paintbrush, or other drawing implement, the child is taking significant steps toward the organization of his or her development (see Figure 7.14). Children's drawing skills progress through four stages (Kellogg, 1970).

FIGURE 7.14 Children express their creativity in drawing.

Left photograph by David Kostelnik; right photograph by Sylvia Byers

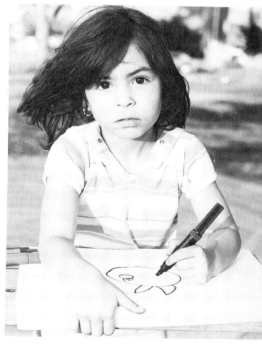

FIGURE 7.15 The placement stage of children's drawing. "The importance of the Placement Patterns lies in the developmental sequence that follows from them. The Patterns are the earliest evidence I have discerned of controlled shaping in children's work. The Basic Scribbles themselves suggest shapes, mainly circles, but also rectangles, and triangles."

Based on R. Kellogg, *Analyzing Children's Art.* Palo Alto, Calif.: Mayfield Publishing Company, 1969, 1970.

The Placement Stage. In the placement stage, the child is experimenting with various scribble marks. Much of the child's activity is exploratory as he or she tries different ways of holding the crayon as well as drawing on different places on the paper. Sometimes the child's drawing is confined to one small part of a paper, and at other times, the child's drawing is composed of broad strokes that take up the entire paper (and sometimes beyond). By the time the child is two and one-half to three years of age, he/she has probably mastered most of the basic scribble movements (see Figure 7.15).

The Shape Stage. In the shape stage, children begin to draw actual forms. They can make the outline or the approximation of such shapes as circles, squares, Xs, and so on.

The Design Stage. In the design stage, the child begins to make imaginative arrangements that combine the basic shapes and forms mastered in the previous stage.

FIGURE 7.16 A chart depicting shape, design and pictorial stages.

Source: Rhoda Kellogg, Child Art Collection, San Francisco

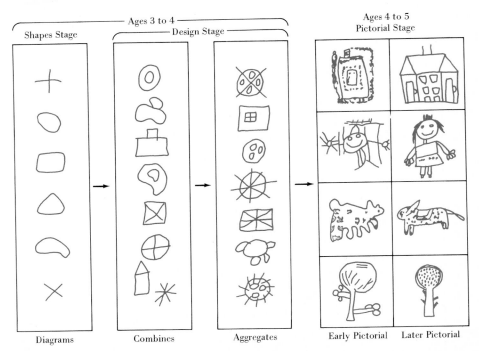

The Preschool Child

The Pictorial Stage. By the time the child is four or five years old, he/she is able to combine the basic shapes and combinations (learned in earlier stages) to depict or represent familiar objects in the family, the neighborhood, or the preschool environment. For example, the child may draw reasonable facsimiles of houses, cars, dogs, cats, faces, and other people. (see Figure 7.16).

APPLICATION BOX

Children's Art and Creativity

Art is valuable because it is a means of self-expression. It is a language to express feelings—to draw off tensions or to express well-being. The young child needs avenues of expression. His speech is limited. His feelings are strong. . . .

A child uses creative materials in different ways during the following three stages of a developmental process:

- *Exploration* (also called Manipulation or Kinesthetic). In this state a child explores the media and learns its [sic] capabilities. He scribbles, he bangs and breaks clay and he makes drips and lines with paints.
- *Intuitive Design* (Transitional). During this phase a child exploring an art medium will see a shape or form in the material that suggests something to him. A drawn curved line may suggest a face, or a thin roll of clay a snake.
- *Intended Design* (Realistic or Representational). At this point the child decides in advance what he wants to make and then draws, paints or models his subject.

A child may remain at any one stage for a certain length of time, or he or she may move back and forth among these stages.

From J. Danhoff, "Children's Art: The Creative Process," Children Today. Washington, D.C., July–August 1975, pp. 7–10.

Bruce

Scott

BY ELIZABETH

Language and the Preschool Child

Now that we have some understanding of how the preschool child thinks, we might ask how such thinking is related to the emerging skills of language. Is language essential for thinking? Or are thinking skills a prerequisite for language development?

LANGUAGE AND THINKING

There appears to be increasing evidence that the development of language is affected by the course of thinking. As you may recall from Chapter Six, this is the position that Piaget took toward the language–thought controversy. For example, children's ideas of time are a function of their cognitive level and "understanding" of the concepts of order or sequence rather than merely knowing the words (e.g., *before, after, later, now*) (Cromer, 1974).

Because the ability to *conserve* and to think about the unchanging or permanent attributes of objects in a changing world is a milestone of cognitive development, we might ask about the relationship of language to conservation skills. Specifically, can nonconserving children be taught the language expressions of conserving children and then be able to solve conservation problems? In an interesting experiment designed to test this language-training–conservation hypothesis, Sinclair-de-Zwart (1969) reached the following conclusions:

1. Children who conserved used *more "relational" words* than those children who did not conserve. For example, conserving children said things like "One has more than the other one" or "One has more and the other has less."

   Children who did not conserve did not use these relational terms. They tended to use terms that reflected absolute quantities rather than relations: "This has a lot" or "That one has a little."
2. Children who conserved used more *highly differentiated terms* than those who did not conserve. For example, conservers used specific terms for each dimension (e.g., *long, short, fat, thin*). Nonconservers used undifferentiated terms for describing two dimensions; for example, they might refer to the long, thin pencil as *big* and short, fat pencil as *small.*
3. When an attempt was made to teach nonconservers to use the words used by conservers, the results indicated that language, at best, could help the child *focus* on the significant dimensions of the problem (e.g., length, width, height). Of the children who learned to use the expressions of the conservers, very few made the transition to conservation. These results were confirmed by other unsuccessful attempts to train for conservation using language (Peisack, 1973; Holland and Palermo, 1975). These results suggest that thinking skills are probably a prerequisite for true language and development.

LANGUAGE AND COMMUNICATION

Language is learned in a social setting. That is, adults talk to children, children talk to adults, children talk to peers, peers talk to children, and children overhear both adults and peers talking. Communication, therefore,

would appear to be an important function of language. For yo[ung]
however, language is not as effective in communication as it w[ill be]
later, primarily because of the young child's egocentrism. In parti[cular, the]
child does not have the ability to adopt the perspective of another [person.]
Communication requires at least two participants who *mutually follo[w]* [one]
another's movements, gestures, and words so as to understand "where [the]
other person is coming from."

The limited skill of preschoolers in mutual following or social tracking in
communication is illustrated in an interesting experiment (Glucksberg,
Krauss, and Weisberg, 1966; Glucksberg and Krauss, 1967; Krauss and
Glucksberg, 1969). In the experiment, the two participants are seated at a
table, separated by an opaque screen. Each person has a set of six blocks on
the table before him/her. Each block has a unique design on it that is easy to
distinguish from another design, yet some sets are novel enough so as to be
difficult to name. One person (the decoder) selects one block at a time (from
the given six blocks) on the basis of a verbal message supplied by the other
person (the encoder). As might be expected, adult performance in this experiment is nearly perfect. Preschool children appear to understand what the
"game" is about and can play rather effectively if the block designs are simple
(e.g., colors, familiar objects) and can be easily described by the "encoder"
(e.g., "red," "dog," "blue"). However, if the block designs are novel, the
preschool child's success rate (choice of appropriate blocks) is almost random.
The results of the experiment showed that it was much more difficult for
preschool children than for adults to take the listener's perspective. Older
children demonstrate an improved ability to adjust their communications to
the point of view of the listener.

On these communication tasks, one striking difference between children
and adults was illustrated by their reactions to *feedback* from the decoder
about his/her understanding of the encoder's verbal directive. For example,
when decoders requested more information (e.g., "I don't know which one
you mean"), adult encoders were likely to provide elaboration on previous
messages or to provide completely new verbal messages that addressed the
perceived selection problems of the decoder. On the other hand, child encoders were more likely to repeat the very same descriptions given before or
simply to remain silent.

The experiment just described also illustrates one of the critical features of
communication between preschool children: although there may be many
verbal messages, there is relatively little communication. For example, the
youngest children (kindergartners and first-graders, in the experiment) often
communicated in particularly egocentric ways, such as by saying "this one"
or even pointing to the appropriate block—even though there was an opaque
screen separating the participants. The following interaction between decoder
and encoder is another example of the private or egocentric nature of communication:

Decoder: "Do you mean that one?"
Encoder: "Yes."

Whether or not preschoolers are actually communicating, they assume that
they are understanding the other child as well as being understood by that
child.

uld the Child Be Able to Do with
ly Age Five?

ge begins as early as birth
ut one's entire life. Lan-
es the very form of adult–child in-
on. It mediates every aspect of a human
being's experience. Dale (1976) has suggested the
following uses of language that children should
have by age five:

1. *Instrumental.* Children should understand that
language is a tool for accomplishing things.
The phrase "I want . . . " helps the child express needs.
2. *Regulatory.* Children come to understand that
language can be used to control their behavior.
In turn, they can use language to influence the
behavior of other children and adults. The regulatory function becomes elaborated into rules
stated with language.
3. *Interactional.* Language can be used to organize
and define relationships with other people, for

example, stating who can play a particular
game or defining the make-believe roles to be
assumed by playmates.
4. *Personal.* Through the use of language, children become more aware of their individuality. The ability to label facets of the personality
with words or phrases helps the child to develop a more objective sense of self in relation
to other children.
5. *Heuristic.* Children use language to discover
the dimensions of reality. Asking questions is a
common technique for accomplishing this
goal.
6. *Imaginative.* Language can be used in pretend
play and games as well as in playing with combinations of real and "made-up" words.
7. *Representational.* Children use language to represent aspects of reality. Language, then,
becomes a system of mutually understood
symbols that facilitate thinking and communication with others.

It is interesting to note that verbal exchange between preschool-aged children appears to be more effective in "natural" as opposed to "laboratory" or
artificial settings (Mueller, 1972). Mueller introduced pairs of three- to five-
year-old children and let them play together naturally. The results indicated
that the children not only played well together but also "communicated"
effectively and successfully with one another:

> Almost all the utterances provided adequate information to the listeners, and 85 per-
> cent of them received replies or at least attracted the listeners' attention. The difference
> between successful communication in this natural and unstructured setting, as as-
> sessed by the maintenance of the verbal exchange, and the failure of children of this
> age in laboratory communication tasks . . . must lie primarily in the fact that, in
> playing together, the two children in each pair shared a common context of toys and
> books and of interests. Speech was about the "here and now," which was shared by
> the listener. (Dale, 1976, pp. 257–258)

In the experiment, the responses of the children included both verbal and
nonverbal behaviors (e.g., shaking the head). Mueller demonstrated that the
best predictor of successful communication between preschoolers was the
behavior of the listener. For example, communication was more likely if the
listener was looking at the speaker when the exchange began. In other words,

Opportunities for language-learning occur in many different settings.

Photographs by David Kostelnik

where both participants were mutually following one another, communication was more likely.

Other evidence suggests that the egocentrism of the preschooler's communications may be overemphasized. For example, preschool children are often able to make adjustments to a listener in accordance with characteristics of the listener. Four-year-olds tend to generate simpler and shorter utterances when they are talking to five-year-olds than when talking to adults or older children (Shatz and Gelman, 1973). In summary, preschoolers' communication is an interactive process that is based on the ability of both participants to adjust mutually and to modify their behavior so as to "follow" the other person.

LANGUAGE LEARNING IN THE FAMILY

As we have indicated in our discussion of infant language development, parents are important to the child's overall language development. Several important dimensions of parental behavior seem to be significantly related to language development:

1. Parents appear to be influential in the *type of words* that young children use (Nelson, 1973). For example, where parent–child interactions are marked by more parental reference to *objects* than to *interpersonal relationships* or *personal* qualities, the child's language reflects this emphasis (likewise, if parents emphasize personal–interpersonal words).
2. Parents adjust their speech to their children in at least two ways: (a) the length of parental utterances and (b) the topics or content of the interactions (Moerk, 1975). The length of parental utterances to children is shorter than speech to adults but longer than utterances used by the child.

Thus, parental speech requires the child to reach toward higher skill levels.

As the child gains in language competence, the type of content in parent–child communication changes. Simple child imitation of parental action and words diminishes, and child-generated questions and descriptions increase (Moerk, 1975).
3. Parents' use of language appears to be related to the level of the child's performance, achievement, and success in accomplishing tasks (Hess and Shipman, 1965; Tulkin, 1972; Bee, 1974).

LANGUAGE AND CULTURE

Most of us are aware that cultural features of our environment can enhance and support the development of both children and adults. Culture has an impact on how children learn to speak and develop language skills. A central question that emerges—and that has resulted in a great deal of heated controversy—is whether there is a "right" way to speak and use language. For example, in the United States, there is a variety of forms of spoken English. Some forms may differ in somewhat minor ways (e.g., differences in accent in various parts of the country). Other differences may include variations of standard spoken English such as so-called black English. Other problems arise when different languages (e.g., Spanish or American Indian languages) are spoken in neighborhoods or communities more frequently than the so-called standard English, which is taught in school. As a result of these concerns, the following important questions arise:

Is "nonstandard" English necessarily "substandard" English?
Should bilingualism (the use of two languages) be encouraged for some ethnic or cultural groups? Would a policy of bilingualism be a help or a severe handicap if and when a child grows up to live and work in the majority cultural and language system?
Are cultural *differences* the same as cultural deficits?

Such issues become critical when one considers the important role of language skill as a basic tool for negotiating and controlling aspects of culture.

THE CULTURAL FUNCTIONS OF LANGUAGE

How is language related to a human being's functioning in a culture? There is considerable agreement that language plays an important role in guiding the thinking of human beings (Sapir, 1958; Bruner, 1966). Although language is undeniably an important component of the cultural environment of the growing, thinking, and developing child, there remains a controversy whether thinking is preeminent and therefore directs language or whether language conditions thinking.

Difference or Deficit? When we make comparisons between the language of middle-class children and children from economically poor situations, there are many obvious differences. When these differences are acknowledged there are at least two interpretations:

1. *The deficit hypothesis:* Although we have rather little knowledge of language development among poor and, specifically, young black children, many psychologists, educators, and public servants have proceeded to develop the deficit hypothesis. In its simplest terms, this hypothesis suggests that the well-documented failure of many black children (particularly in school) is the result of an "impoverished" language. As we shall see later in this chapter, this hypothesis rests on some shaky assumptions.
2. *The difference hypothesis.* This hypothesis asserts that English, like other languages, has a number of forms (dialects), none of which is superior. Therefore asserting that academic failure results simply from a different dialect may be a gross oversimplification of the child's total environment in contributing to "success" in school and in life.

"Black English": A Case Study. In order to put the language concepts we have been discussing in concrete terms, we have reproduced a sample of black English in the box.

AN ANNOTATED TRANSCRIPTION
OF A SAMPLE OF BLACK ENGLISH

Calvin: One day I was walking. Then I met Lennie. Lennie say,[1,2] "Calvin, what happened to your lip?" I said, "Nothing." And then Lenn came over to me and he say,[1,2] "What you mean by nothing?" Like he always say[2] because he's always interested in me and me and him is[3] good friends. So I told him what happened. "This guy named Pierre, he about fifteen . . ."
Lennie: Yeah?
Calvin: He came over to me . . .
Lennie: Uh huh.
Calvin: And he hit me in my lip because . . .
Lennie: Yeah?
Calvin: I . . .
Lennie: Done[4] what?
Calvin: Had done copied[4] off his paper in school.

Annotations

1. Some verbs, like "come" and "say," are not marked for past tense in Black English narratives, even when the context is past time.
2. Black English lacks the -*s* suffix which marks the present tense with third person singular subjects in Standard English.
3. Occasionally (and particularly with coordinate constructions), the singular conjugated forms of "be" ("is," "was") occur with the plural subject in Black English.
4. The use of "done" plus the past tense of a verb is a construction indicating completed action. Some speakers occasionally include a form of "have" as in "had done copied . . ."

Adapted from W. Wolfram and R. Fasold, "Toward Reading Materials for Speakers of Black English: Three Linguistically Appropriate Passages." In J. C. Baratz and R. W. Shuy (Eds.), *Teaching Black Children to Read.* Washington, D.C.: Center for Applied Linguistics, 1969. pp. 144–147, 152–154.

Black Children and Their Language Development. As indicated in the example, it would be wrong to infer that black English is without a meaningful structure or communication value. Although it is possible that some black children have problems learning and using standard English as taught in the public school, it is unlikely—as the deficit hypothesis suggests—that failure of black children could be attributed to language problems taken alone. Cognitive development may be slowed by poverty and other social factors. The following are some reasons to question the deficit hypothesis (Dale, 1976, p. 278):

1. In the first place, the deficit hypothesis assumes that language plays a determining role in thinking. It is, of course, possible to be a perfectly logical thinker using either Standard English or Black-English.
2. Are black children inadequate in their mastery of Standard English or in their inability to apply such a language system? The deficit hypothesis does not make this distinction.
3. The deficit hypothesis blurs the distinction between *race* and *social* class as contributing factors to language development. It is a fact of American life that blacks are overrepresented in the lower socioeconomic groups. It is certainly possible that differences between black children and white children are due more to social class factors than to some unspecified "racial" distinctions. Evidence suggests that the poor language performance of children from poverty settings appears to be limited primarily to vocabulary rather than to mastery of the total language system (Ginsburg, 1972; Stodolsky and Lesser, 1967).

Black English and Black Culture. In keeping with our emphasis in this book on the total *system* of the child and the adult as the major arena for growth and development, we would point out that the black child and the black adult live in such a total ecosystem. The overall development of the child—and in particular, the language development of the black child—can be profitably viewed from such a systems perspective.

Specifically, one of the major reasons that the language deficit hypothesis is on such shaky ground is that it tends to ignore these systems features of development. One of the questions raised by those who have investigated black English is the *methods* of investigation used to assess such language development (Labov, 1970, 1972). Simply placing a black child in a room with a white adult (otherwise known as the "experimenter") may create defensive responses on the part of the black child, including withdrawal and nonfluent speech. Even placing the child in a room with a black adult may not eliminate the artificiality of the experimental situation.

The fact that some "experimental" situations are not "real" (*real* in the sense of representing or evoking behavior that would occur in the black child's ecosystem) is effectively demonstrated when the experimental situation is changed. Labov (1970) reported the following change in the context or setting for a language development experiment for black children:

in the next interview with Leon, Clarence

1. brought along a supply of potato chips, changing the "interview" into something more in the nature of a party;
2. brought along Leon's best friend, 8-year-old Gregory;
3. reduced the height imbalance (when Clarence got down on the floor of Leon's room, he dropped from 6 ft. 2 in. to 3 ft. 6 in.);

4. introduced taboo words and taboo topics, and proved to Leon's surprise that one can say anything into our microphone without any fear of retaliation.

From Labov, W., "The Logic of Nonstandard English." In J. E. Alatis (Ed.,) *Twentieth Annual Roundtable.* Washington, D.C.: Georgetown University Press, 1970, p. 8.

This change in procedure resulted in much more active, fluent, and argumentative speech from Leon (an eight-year-old) than had occurred outside of his ecosystem.

Furthermore, the so-called deficit hypothesis seems to be contradicted even further by observations of many social scientists that in the black culture, there is indeed an emphasis and importance placed on verbal fluency. There is considerable evidence that black children have a good knowledge of standard English. Furthermore, when the speech of black children is translated from black English to standard English, there are no differences in the overall language competency of lower class black children and middle class white children (Stodolsky and Lesser, 1967; Copple and Suci, 1974; Anastasiow and Hanes, 1974; Johnson, 1974). It appears that once one understands the "rules" of black English, many instances of what seems to be illogical statements are really dialect differences. For example, in black English, the use of a double negative may be meaningful, particularly when one recognizes that other languages (e.g., Russian, Old English) may use not only two but three negatives (e.g., black English double-negative: "He don't know nothing").

One of the interesting features of black language development is the important role of peers in language formation. In some cases involving black families in which the parents speak standard English, the children's language is more similar to the black English of their peers (Stewart, 1969). These children are approximately seven to eight years old when the dialect shifts from the parental dialect to the peer-group dialect. The dialect shift seems to be a function of interaction with a peer group in which the black English dialect is seen as normal. For both white and black children in the New York City area, dialect shifts have also been observed that are an apparent result of interaction with the child's peer group. This not-uncommon phenomenon raises some interesting questions about the relative role of parents and peers in language development. Do children learn more about language from their peers or from their family members? Would an educational emphasis on the quality of language in the home be misplaced? (Dale, 1976).

Personality Development

The years from two to six have sometimes been called the magic years of childhood (Fraiberg, 1959). These years are special or "magic" primarily because so many new things happen. Children are gradually moving from exclusive relationships with parents or caretakers toward interaction with other adults and children. For the first time, children experience many new challenges as well as conflicts and anxieties. These challenges and anxieties result from the process of *socialization* (i.e., the ways in which a young child's behavior and attitudes are influenced by parents, other adults, and the institutions of society). In this section, we examine several aspects of personality that result from socialization: self-concept formation, sex-role identity, prosocial behavior, and aggressiveness.

THE SENSE OF SELF

In our discussion of infancy, we pointed out that the child has already begun the gradual process of self-definition. During infancy, cognitive developments occur that provide the basis for an emerging sense of self. In the first place, the infant learns to distinguish the self from other things in the environment. Although this distinction may appear to be rather basic, Piaget and others have shown that the very young infant does not make this distinction. The separation of "self" from "nonself" develops as early as the first six months of life when the infant recognizes that objects other than itself exist in its world (e.g., caretakers, rattles, feeding nipples). In addition to recognizing the separation of self and objects, the infant comes to recognize the permanency of objects (and, by implication, the permanence of self). By age two or three, the infant has a view of the self as stable and organized. This view is enhanced by feelings of trust and autonomy.

Early social development of preschool children may include friendships.

Photograph by Sylvia Byers

SCENARIO:
CAN GRANDPARENTS BE PARENTS?—AN ELIZABETHAN PERSPECTIVE

Elizabeth (now four years old) is sitting at the dinner table with her family. The topic of discussion is the upcoming Thanksgiving holiday.

Elizabeth's father (announcing to all): Next week gramma and grampa will be coming for Thanksgiving. (Looking at Elizabeth) Your gramma and grampa are *also* my mother and father.

Elizabeth: *No* (pause), gramma and grampa are *not* your mother and father, they're *my* gramma and grampa.

Elizabeth's father (smiling at Elizabeth): My mother and father are *also* your . . . .

Elizabeth (with a look of mild outrage, she forcefully and promptly replies): No! They're *my* gramma and grampa.

By about age four, a new extension of the self appears. Children begin to attach importance to their possessions. Commonly heard phrases include "my dolly," "my toy," "my book," or "my cereal." Objects seem to be extensions of the self and may be shared somewhat grudgingly. The possessiveness of the four-year-old may also be due to other factors. For example, it is quite likely that four-year-olds are involved in more frequent cooperative play situations in which competition over toys might occur. In addition, the four-year-old is still somewhat egocentric and, as a result, may not understand that grandparents can simultaneously be parents.

By the time children are five years old, they have been exposed to many evaluations of themselves by other people. These early evaluations influence the child's overall self-image. For example, the child may have developed a self-image that is largely positive or largely negative. The evaluations of others as well as the child's own evaluation (based on experiences of competence or inadequacy) contribute to the child's self-concept.

WHAT DO CHILDREN HEAR ABOUT THEMSELVES?

Throughout the early childhood years, young children are given many evaluations of themselves by parents. Based on your experiences with young children, you might be able to add to the list:

The Preschool Child

- "You're a good helper."
- "Why do you always spill your milk?"
- "You look handsome today."
- "Can't you ever stay out of the way when I'm doing something?"
- "You're a bad girl."
- "That's good! You can do that by yourself."

By the time children are five or six years old they begin to verbalize their self-concepts. Parents or caretakers may be pleased to hear such statements as "Let me help you—I'm a good helper." On the other hand, a negative self-concept is evident when the child says, "I can't do it—I can't do anything right." The family atmosphere and the parenting styles discussed in the beginning of this chapter contribute to the formulation of a child's self-concept.

SEX-ROLE DEVELOPMENT

An important dimension of self-concept is the development of the child's sex role. What does it mean to say, "I am a male" or "I am a female?" How do children come to think of themselves as sexual beings? How do children learn the "appropriate" behaviors for their sex? Are these "appropriate" behaviors useful guidelines for all children? Do they limit self-development for others?

Developmental Progression. Children's understanding of the sex roles appears to follow a progression. By about three years, the child is able to *label* his or her own gender *correctly*. In other words, he/she knows whether he or she is a boy or a girl. Correct labeling does not imply that the child understands the full meaning of sex-role identity. For example, a three-year-old does not yet understand that the gender of others is constant. The three-year-old typically classifies other children as "boy" or "girl" based on external characteristics such as clothes or hairstyle. Consequently classifications are not always consistent.

This concept of gender constancy is not perfectly understood until age five or six. At that time, the child is able to classify males and females correctly and consistently on the basis of a more complete understanding of sex roles. This more complete understanding of sex-role identity is based on a knowledge of the behaviors and the appearances that are "appropriate" for each sex.

Major Theories. Three major theories have been proposed to describe the acquisition of sex-role identity in young children. The major concepts of these theories have already been discussed in Chapter Two.

Psychoanalytic Theory. Freud used the concept of *identification* to describe the acquisition of sex-role identity. The process of identification is different for males and females.

For boys, identification occurs as a result of the *Oedipus complex* (the boy has fantasies of replacing his father and possessing his mother). The boy resolves the Oedipus complex by identifying with the father. According to Freud, such an identification represents an "If you can't beat 'em, join 'em" approach. As a result, the male child takes on the sex-role behaviors of the father. Freud suggested that male sex-role development is largely the result of "identification with the aggressor" or more powerful figure (the father).

In the case of the female, identification with the mother is the result of the *Electra complex* (the girl has fantasies of possessing her father, whom she envies because he has something that she lacks: a penis). The girl fears that her mother will punish her for desiring her father by not loving her. Presumably because of her need to be loved, the girl tries to be like her mother.

What is the status of the psychoanalytic interpretation of sex-role identification? It is difficult—if not impossible—to arrange an experimental study to test Freud's conception of identification. Identification is a complex process that cannot be easily broken down into measurable parts. Where this has been done, experimenters have not been able to demonstrate the Freudian theory of identification (Sears, Rau, and Alpert, 1965). That is, there is no evidence that sex typing results from identification with a same sex parent who is *thought by the child* to be a hostile rival for the opposite-sex parent's affection.

Although there is no evidence of this Freudian notion of identity, there is some evidence that child identification with the parent does influence sex typing. Unlike the Freudian explanation of identification based on "fear of an aggressor," considerable evidence suggests that the important factors in strengthening child imitation and identification with an adult are the adult's *warmth* and *perceived power* (Perry and Bussey, 1984). For example, there is considerable evidence that masculine boys have fathers who are perceived by their sons to be both affectionate and authoritative (Perry and Bussey, 1984; Drake and McDougall, 1977; Hetherington, 1967). Apparently, these affectionate fathers are more likely to spend time interacting with their sons.

It is interesting to note that despite the substantial body of evidence for a strong relationship between fathers' personality characteristics and sons' masculinity, there is less evidence of a parallel relationship between mothers and daughters. The dramatic increase in maternal employment (see Chapter Six) has, in recent years, been suggested as an important factor in girls' sex typing. The evidence appears to suggest a significant relationship between maternal employment and girls' sex typing. For example, daughters of working mothers have more flexible ideas concerning sex roles than daughters of nonworking mothers. They believe that *both* men and women can work, make important decisions, raise children, do household chores, and so on. They think of women as capable of successful competition and not, as in stereotyped depictions, easily hurt emotionally. Of particular interest is the fact that these daughters were most likely to nominate their mothers as *the person they would most want to be* if they had their choice of being anyone in the world. Thus, daughters of working mothers appear to develop egalitarian notions of sex roles and are likely to emulate their mother's sense of independence (Miller, 1975; Marantz and Mansfield, 1977).

Social Learning Theory. Social learning theorists such as Walter Mischel have assumed that sex-role development is the result of both imitation and reinforcement. In other words, children learn appropriate sex-role behaviors and imitate others when they think they will be rewarded for doing so.

In social-learning theory, sex-typed behaviors may be defined as behaviors that typically elicit different rewards for one sex than for the other. In other words, sex-typed behaviors have consequences that vary according to the sex of the performers. . . . According to social-learning theory, the acquisition and performance of sex-typed behaviors can be described by the same learning principles used to analyze any other aspect of an individual's behavior. . . . Sex-typing is the process by which the individual acquires sex-typed behavior patterns: first he learns to discriminate between sex-typed behavior patterns, then to generalize from these specific learning experiences to new situations and finally to perform sex-typed behavior.

Mischel, W., "Social Learning Theory and Sex Roles." In E. E. Maccoby, *The Development of Sex Differences.* Stanford, Calif.: Stanford University Press, 1966, pp. 56–57.

To date, research efforts have not demonstrated the validity of a social learning approach to sex typing *prior* to the start of the *elementary school years* (5 to 6 years of age). Maccoby and Jacklin (1974) concluded (after an extensive review of the research) that few differences existed in the treatment of boys and girls by parents during the *preschool years*. Although some differences were evident (e.g., boys tended to be treated more roughly than girls), there was nothing resembling a systematic difference in the treatment of boys and girls. In other words, preschool boys and girls were not systematically rewarded for behaving in accordance with stereotypes of maleness or femaleness. Of course, this is *not* to suggest that young children's observations of so-called "appropriate" sex-role behaviors are irrelevant. Rather, the evidence suggests that it is not until the elementary school years (when the concept of gender constancy has been attained) that children *actively* and *systematically* incorporate these observations into their personalities.

Cognitive Development Theory. Kohlberg (1966) described the cognitive approach to sex-role development as being directed primarily by the development of the child's thinking skills. At first, children learn to label themselves as a "he" or a "she." Labels may be used inconsistently during this early period. It is not until age five or six that children's conceptual thinking is refined to the point of consistent use of labels and concepts. As we indicated earlier, there are cognitive underpinnings for this refined usage of concepts (e.g., the development of the notion of object permanency). Both cognitive development theory and the social learning approach are similar because both suggest that once children know their gender label, they strive to incorporate "appropriate" behaviors and attributes into their personalities.

The research evidence for the cognitive development approach is strong (Kohlberg and Zigler, 1967; Kohlberg, 1969; Slaby and Frey, 1975). Kohlberg and Zigler demonstrated that a child's mental or "conceptual" age was a far more important determinant of the development of sex roles in children than was simple chronological age. A problem with cognitive developmental theory is the implication that the motivation for sex typing is entirely an *intrinsic* or *internal* process. That is, the internal striving for competence interacting with the internal process of cognitive development provides the sole basis for sex-role typing. In contrast, social learning theorists suggest that internal cognitive processes *interact* with external pressures (e.g., pressures from parents, peers, or the media) to produce sex typing. Slaby and Frey (1975) demonstrated that the degree to which children observe like-sexed models is related to the level of their gender concepts. Regardless of their chronological age, children with more sophisticated gender concepts spent more time watching same-sex models. Observation is an important prerequisite for later imitation or modeling of behaviors.

Furthermore, the *interaction* of observation and cognitive processes provides a more convincing description of individual differences in sex typing than cognitive processes alone. For example, the fact that some girls adopt androgynous sex roles (combining traditional male behaviors such as assertiveness with traditional female behaviors such as nurturance) and some girls do not is more easily explained as a combined result of cognitive processes and environmental experiences than as a result of solely cognitive processes (as cognitive development theory would suggest).

PROSOCIAL BEHAVIOR

SCENARIO

In the early 1970s a shocking event occured in New York City. A night club manager named Kitty Genovese was returning home from work when she was attacked by a man with a knife in the courtyard of her apartment building. She screamed, and thirty-eight of her neighbors came to their windows and watched her being murdered. For one-half hour they watched, and not one of them even so much as called the police.

For what reasons do people help or not help one another? Why would thirty-eight people watch Kitty Genovese being attacked and ultimately murdered without providing some help or at least calling the police? Concerns about such issues have raised questions about the situational conditions that might influence helping behavior in children and adults and the developmental origins of prosocial behavior in children.

Observations of human behavior indicate that people do try to assist and help one another even when there appears to be little apparent "payoff" to the sacrificing individual (Bryan and London, 1970; Krebs, 1970; Rosenhahn, 1970, 1972). What are the circumstances and motivation that result in child or adult helping behavior in the face of risk of injury or inconvenience or when neither material gain nor social acclaim are likely results? Two important features of development appear related to the child's acquisition of prosocial (helpful, cooperative, or altruistic) behavior: *modeling* and *cognitive development*.

Anyone for a helping hand—or how about an apple? Prosocial behavior can be seen in the early years of life.

Photograph by Irving Rader

Modeling: Observing Parents and Adults Who Help. Helpful models affect the child's learning and performance of helpful behavior. When a child observes an adult or peer giving or helping, the likelihood that the child will imitate that behavior is increased (Bryan, 1975). The effects of observation and imitation have been demonstrated with rescue acts (Staub, 1971 a, b), gift donations (Schwartz and Bryan, 1971), and other prosocial acts (Bryan and Walbek, 1970; White, 1972; Grusec and Driscoll, 1973). Furthermore, there is evidence that the effects of prosocial models may be relatively long-lasting (White, 1972).

There is evidence that what a parent or other model says is much less influential than what the model actually does (Bryan, 1975). For example, if parents or other models say things like "Giving is good" or "Helping other people will make them feel better," these statements are not motivating factors for child behavior unless they are coupled with appropriate actions. In other words, for young children the dictum "Do as I say not as I do" does not work.

Cognitive Development and Prosocial Behavior. There are important relationships between prosocial behavior in children and their cognitive development. Several cognitive factors are important, including the following (Perry and Bussey, 1984):

- The extent to which children understand and use *social norms.*
- The sophistication of children's *moral reasoning* used in justifying prosocial action (or inaction).
- The *evaluations* that children make about the situation or plight of another person (*empathy* and *role taking*).
- The degree to which prosocial behavior is important to the *self-concept* of the child.

The prevalence of prosocial behavior depends, in part, on the child's understanding and use of norms such as *social responsibility, deserving, reciprocity, equity,* and *equality.*

Norm of Social Responsibility. This is the idea that help should be given to others strictly on the basis of their need, regardless of the possibility of any reward to the giver. In the case of young children, the need of another person may not be clear enough to arouse helping behavior.

Norm of Deserving. This norm suggests that "people get what they deserve" (Long and Lerner, 1974). Belief in this norm presumably causes people to try to ensure that help and resources are fairly distributed. Research suggests that children and adults are more helpful to those who do not deserve their plight than those who appear to bring dire consequences on themselves (Miller and Smith, 1977). Likewise, there is some evidence that children who receive an unearned windfall gain (e.g., being overpaid for doing a task) often try to redistribute their gain by sharing it with other children (Miller and Smith, 1977). Also, children who think they have received less than their fair share on one occasion may react selfishly at a future time (Miller and Smith, 1977).

Norm of Reciprocity. This is the principle that individuals should help those who have helped them. This norm develops during the preschool years but is more consistently understood and followed during the school years (Berndt, 1979). Research suggests that both children and adults will return favors with some regularity (Peterson, 1980).

Because the norm of reciprocity suggests that favors should be returned, child and adult helping behaviors may be motivated by the expectation of future reciprocity (rather than by an unselfish desire to give assistance or aid). Research evidence supports this possibility (Dreman, 1976).

Norms of Distributive Justice (Equity vs. Equality). These are the norms used by individuals in order to determine rewards among members of a group in relation to their contribution to a given task. For example, how do children divide rewards on a group task when the contributions of the children are different? Do the children divide the rewards carefully in relation to the relative contribution of each child (the norm of *equity*)? Or do they simply give each child an equal amount (the norm of *equality*)? Do the norms of distributive justice used by children change with age and development?

Children under 4 or 5 years of age generally tend to operate without any norms of distributive justice. When asked to divide rewards on a group task, they simply take the largest share for themselves regardless of their actual contribution (Nelson and Dweck, 1977). By the first grade children are capable of using both equity and equality norms (Enright, Franklin, and Manheim, 1980).

In addition to the use of norms, children's prosocial behavior is determined by their *moral reasoning* (their reasons for giving or withholding help). In Chapter Eight we will explore the development of moral reasoning in children. Here we will simply indicate that children's moral reasoning becomes developmentally more sophisticated moving from largely hedonistic motives (based primarily on what satisfies the self) to motives based on self-determined standards of "right" action. Furthermore, children who use more sophisticated moral reasoning methods are more likely to exhibit prosocial behaviors. For example, preschoolers who justify their behavior based on the "needs" of another child rather than on their own hedonistic desires are more likely to engage in the prosocial behavior of spontaneous sharing (Eisenberg-Berg and Hand, 1979).

The development of *empathy* and *role-taking* are also related to prosocial behavior. Empathy involves reacting to another individual's situation with the same emotion as that other individual. For example, the child who feels sad when another child is sad, happy when another child is happy, and so on, is exhibiting empathy. However, role-taking involves the correct understanding of what another individual is thinking or feeling without having to feel the same way (see Chapter Eight for a detailed discussion of role taking).

The relationship between empathy and prosocial behavior becomes greater with age. Empathetic preschool children may or may not exhibit more prosocial behavior (Marcus, Telleen, and Roke, 1979; Eisenberg-Berg and Lennon, 1980). Older children and adults who are empathetic are more consistently prosocial in their behavior (Eisenberg-Berg and Mussen, 1978).

From a rather early age, role-taking ability relates positively to prosocial behavior (Buckley, Siegel and Ness, 1979). Furthermore, there is evidence that children who are given practice in role-taking can increase their level of prosocial behavior (Iannotti, 1978).

Although empathy and role-taking are important in the development of prosocial behavior, the child's self-concept is an equally important ingredient. For example, children who learn to value prosocial behavior, to consider such behavior essential for their own self-esteem, and to have confidence in their ability to help another person will demonstrate more prosocial behaviors (Grusec and Redler, 1980).

Prosocial Behavior: Family and Neighborhood Contexts. What types of family experiences lead to the development of prosocial behaviors? How do specific dimensions of child rearing influence prosocial behavior? How important is it for parents to encourage or prompt prosocial behavior in children?

The dimension of parental warmth–parental hostility is related to child behavior. Research indicates a positive relationship between parental warmth and prosocial behavior. Children who think of their parents as particularly loving and warm are more generous, supportive, and cooperative (Hoffman, 1975). However, parental warmth is most helpful in promoting prosocial behavior when it is given in response to the child's expressed need for attention (Bryant and Crockenberg, 1980). On the other hand, when adults offer warmth and rewards excessively and needlessly, they may foster an atmosphere of indulgence that restricts prosocial behavior (Weissbrod, 1980).

In addition, parents may play a vital role in encouraging prosocial behavior in children. It appears essential for parents to *actively* encourage the development of positive and desirable (prosocial) behaviors and *not limit* their disciplinary efforts only to the elimination of unwanted behavior. In other words nurturing prosocial behavior in children appears to require parental *strictness* in encouraging positive behavior rather than parental *permissiveness* either in the form of indifference or only focusing on the elimination of undesirable behavior. Numerous studies support the conclusion that demanding prosocial behaviors, in fact, promotes future prosocial behaviors. For example, prosocially oriented toddlers tended to have mothers who forcefully stated to their children that socially responsible behavior was expected (Zahn-Waxler, Radke-Yarrow, and King, 1979). Furthermore, parents who use discipline as a means of promoting positive and prosocial behaviors in children (*prescriptive* parents) rather than only to eliminate undesirable behaviors (*proscriptive* parents) have children who are more generous (Olejnik and McKinney, 1973).

In a similar vein, parents who try to get their children to act prosocially (e.g., to share toys) by simply issuing warnings enforcing principles of social responsibility (e.g., "You ought to help others in need") are usually not very successful. In order to be effective, such statements of social norms must include some reasonable justification for such action. The use of *victim-centered reasoning* (i.e., spelling out to the child the consequences of their behavior to other people) by parents is particularly helpful (Hoffman, 1975). For example, the parent might explain to the child how his/her behavior has emotionally or physically hurt another person and what corrective measures can be taken by the child. Research supports the conclusion that victim-centered reasoning promotes prosocial behavior for the following reasons (Perry and Bussey, 1984):

- It encourages empathy and role taking in the child.
- It helps children understand the rationale for parent discipline.
- It suggests how children can atone for their wrongdoing.

Perhaps one of the most obvious and most successful modes of encouraging prosocial behavior is through adult recognition and reinforcement. For example, if parents and other significant adults respond to child prosocial behavior with lavish praise and undivided attention, such behavior is more likely to occur again in the future (Grusec and Redler, 1980).

Other factors, in addition to the family, operate to influence children's prosocial behavior. Neighborhood, relatives, school system, and peer relationships are some of the factors that influence prosocial behavior. A particular neighborhood may foster the feeling of closeness and mutual sharing or "we-ness" (Hornstein, 1976). Other neighborhoods may breed suspiciousness, antagonism, or an atmosphere of "them-ness" (Hornstein, 1976). Within neighborhoods, there are models (e.g., neighbors, merchants, relatives) who also provide children and parents with prosocial input.

Preschool programs may also influence children's prosocial behavior. It should come as no surprise that schoolteachers are powerful modeling figures. They may emphasize and exhibit altruism in any number of ways and ultimately help shape a child's altruistic repertoire, in the same way that they influence so many other facets of a child's development.

It should be noted that all of these factors are present in varying degrees for each child. Children are influenced by their parents, their neighbors, their peers, and their schools to value—or not to value—prosocial behavior. The subtle combination and integration of all these factors result in each individual's unique prosocial attitudes and behavior.

AGGRESSION IN PRESCHOOLERS

As in the case of prosocial behavior, aggression is learned in a context that includes the family, the neighborhood, peer groups, and in some cases, television. Before we begin our discussion, it is important to keep in mind a distinction between *aggression* and *aggressive* or *assertive behavior*. *Aggression* means behavior *motivated* primarily by the desire to hurt another person. On the other hand, *aggressive behavior* means assertive responses that are not intended to hurt another person; for example, the preschooler who eagerly seeks to gain the attention of his or her parent or caretaker might be considered aggressive.

Developmental Patterns. There appears to be a developmental progression in the frequency of aggression during the preschool years. Quarrels among young children appear to reach a peak around age three (Green, 1933). Furthermore, diffused and undirected temper tantrums increase until about age three and then begin to decrease throughout the remaining preschool years. These undirected tantrums are replaced by retaliatory attacks (either verbal or physical). Sulking and resentment may follow these retaliations when children are reminded that such aggression is not appropriate. Because parental intervention usually increases as child aggression increases, preschool children may develop techniques for sustaining this attention by increasing their verbal aggression or verbal assertiveness and reducing their physical aggression (Feshbach, 1970).

Explanations for Aggression. What are the causes or origins of aggression in children (and adults)? We discuss several theories in the following paragraphs.

The Frustration–Aggression Hypothesis. The central idea of this theory is that aggression is the inevitable, or at least the most common, result of frustration (defined as the blocking of a goal) (Dollard, Doob, Miller, Mowrer, and Sears, 1939). However, a number of research studies failed to confirm the inevitability of aggression in a frustrating situation (Barker, Dembo, and Lewin, 1943; Fawl, 1963; Dollard and Miller, 1950). Fawl examined preschool children in nursery-school settings and found a wide variation of responses (including aggression) to daily events that might be described as at least potentially frustrating. It has been suggested that the occurrence of aggression, in response to a frustrating situation, depends on the "availability" or "primacy" of the aggression response in the individual's total hierarchy of behaviors (see Figure 7.17). Therefore, although frustrating situations produce emotional arousal, aggression is only one possible response.

Ethological–Biological Theories. The major idea of the ethological–biological theories is that aggression is an evolutionary product of human (and animal) survival in dangerous and threatening environments. Aggres-

FIGURE 7.17 The occurrence of aggression in a frustrating situation depends, in part, on the "primacy" of the aggression response (arrow indicates direction of increasing likelihood of response.)

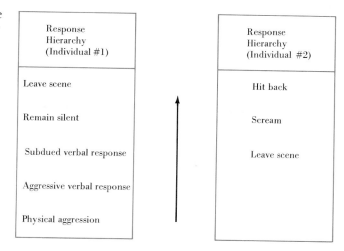

Response Hierarchy (Individual #1)

Leave scene

Remain silent

Subdued verbal response

Aggressive verbal response

Physical aggression

Response Hierarchy (Individual #2)

Hit back

Scream

Leave scene

sion is the result of our biological inheritance. Given this state of affairs, one of our major modern-day problems is that there are relatively few outlets for these tendencies toward aggression. For example, preschool children learn that they are not to strike their parents or caretakers as a way of lessening frustration. Likewise, an adult learns not to punch the boss in the nose.

The major problem with ethological–biological theories is that they may be an overgeneralization from theories of animal and plant evolution. The assumption of the biological inheritance of aggression is presumably supported by general observations of behavior of animals and human beings rather than by any direct assessment of genetic evidence.

Reinforcement Theory. Simply put, reinforcement theory suggests that aggression, like other behaviors, can be influenced by rewards or punishments. Where aggression "works" by gaining attention or desired objects for the child it is rewarded and will probably occur again in the future.

Punishment as a parental response to aggression is a little more complex. The success of punishment as a disciplinary technique is profoundly affected by the context in which it occurs. When punishment (e.g., spanking a child) is reported as an effective mode of discipline, it is usually in the context of a warm, affectionate relationship between parent and child (Sears, Maccoby, and Levin, 1957). It appears that punishment is not an effective technique for suppressing undesirable behavior if administered in a cold or harsh manner by a rejecting or hostile parent.

Caution should be exercised in the use of punishment because it can have undesirable effects. For example, in certain situations, punishment of aggression in children "generalizes" from the painful consequences of a specific behavior to the painful consequences of being in a particular context or situation. For example, punishment for taking a toy away from another child could generalize to anxiety and relative unhappiness on being in peer play contexts. In other cases, the use of physical punishment by a parent can lead to inhibition of aggression only in a specific circumstance and not in other contexts. For example, a child may learn to inhibit aggression only in the presence of an adult or a caretaker, while showing aggression toward playmates when adults are not present. Furthermore, parents who use physical punishment as a mode of curbing child aggression may, unwittingly, be "modeling" the very aggression that they are trying to reduce in their children. It should be noted, however, that many of the adverse effects of punishment can be traced to the rejecting and hostile parents who administer it (Berkowitz, 1973).

Modeling Theory. The major idea of the modeling theory of aggression (and behavior) is that behavior can be learned from observation (from watching someone else do something) as well as from being rewarded or punished. The proponents of modeling theory (Bandura and Walters, 1963) begin by criticizing reinforcement theorists for failing to make a distinction between learning and *performance*. That is, reinforcement may, in certain circumstances, influence the *performance* of an already learned response. However, reinforcement does not explain the *existence* of that learned response.

APPLICATION BOX

Aggression in the Young Child

Infants occasionally hurt others by pushing too hard or striking another with a hard toy held in wobbly and uncertain grasp. The pushing is often a form of "Hello," a way of greeting for a child short on vocabulary. The striking is seldom done with any malice but more from lack of coordination. It isn't sensible to scold infants for these transgressions. We need only to keep them apart or free from toys or other objects that might be hurtful. . . .

Toddlers, too, are still short on vocabulary and on social skills. They learn to defend their space with shrieks, which may sound like they are badly hurt when they usually aren't. The shrill shriek serves a purpose. It causes adults to come running and scold anyone in sight, assuming the "poor baby" was the victim. This technique is successfully used on older siblings. . . .

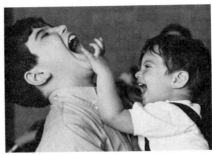

Photograph by Irving Rader

HITTING AND KICKING

Very seldom is a preschooler maliciously hitting and kicking. Rather these children strike out because of frustration or because of some interference or assumed interference from another child. . . .What can adults do about hitting or kicking? First, stop the behavior without blame or punishment—neither of these stops negative behavior except in a short-run sense. Second, make adjustments in indirect guidance, arranging the space, . . . routine, and so on in ways that more readily fit the children. Third, recognize the child for his strengths and good behavior. . . . In other words, give him attention for his "good" works, not for his "bad." Fourth, give him opportunities to talk out his feelings. Fifth, find a diversion for his energy.

From V. Hildebrand, *Guiding Young Children.* (2nd ed.). New York: Macmillan Publishing Company, 1980, pp. 311–313.

Examples of the effectiveness of observation as a source of learning are evident in the experiments of Bandura (Bandura, Ross, and Ross, 1961). One group of children viewed a model who displayed physical and verbal aggression toward a "Bobo" doll. Another group of children viewed an adult who sat quietly and virtually ignored the same doll. Later, the children were observed in free play. Children who had observed the aggression model displayed more aggression than children who did not see an aggression model.

Aggression in the Family and the Neighborhood: A Systems Perspective. Aggression may be viewed as one type of response to a particular situation. Furthermore, aggression, like attachment behavior, can be viewed as a *mutual interaction* in the context of family, neighborhood, and peers. In other words, like attachment behavior, aggression can be viewed as a characteristic of a *relationship* rather than as the characteristic of only one of the participants (e.g., parent or child).

Like prosocial behavior, the support or nonsupport of aggression is a characteristic of a complex, interacting system. The components of this system include the family, the neighborhood, and social—cultural values (as transmitted through such media as the television). Family relationships have an impact on the occurrence of aggression in children. Children's temperaments and personalities (i.e., what they bring with them to a particular family encounter or activity) *interact* with the general "rule" structure of the family (e.g., closed, open, or random) and the characteristics or demands of the particular situation to produce many types of behavior (including, in some instances, aggression).

Whereas children bring with them a history of experience and a personal style of coping, the parents likewise bring their own experiential history and coping style. In addition, parents bring with them a specific mode of responding to aggression.

Summary

1. The transition from the infant world to the preschool world is marked by a gradual movement of the child into the larger society. The social world of the infant is contained largely within the family. The preschooler begins to move out into the larger society which becomes differentiated into neighborhood-community and peer contexts.

2. The role of the family in the preschool years can best be understood by viewing the *family as a system* in its own right. The characteristics of this system include the following: organizational complexity, openness, and adaptiveness. These characteristics govern the relationship of the people in a family as well as the interaction of the family unit with the larger society. The family as a system provides the framework for understanding the development of the preschool child.

3. One of the important components of this family system is parenting style (the attitudes and behaviors of parents or caretakers in child rearing activities). There are at least three dimensions of parenting style which are related to the social and personality development of the preschool child: parent modeling, parent expectations, and parent disciplinary techniques.

4. Parent–child relationships are a *reciprocal* or two-way interaction. This is important to bear in mind because almost any episode of behavior between a parent and child could be interpreted as being one-way. For example, a sullen child could be viewed as the simple product of a rejecting parent. What is actually happening is a *two-way process of mutual influence* to which both parent and child contribute.

5. Although the family is undoubtedly a vital context for the developing child, there is another more global context in which the family and the child are embedded—the neighborhood and community. There are many reasons for examining the neighborhood/community context. The neighborhood/community provides the major setting in which the child organizes free or unstructured time. The neighborhood/community is a setting where certain experiences or activities are likely to occur.

6. As the preschool child matures, interaction expands to include other children in the neighborhood or, perhaps, in a preschool program. The first emergent signs of a beginning shift in dependency pattern from parents to peers emerges during these years.

7. Although the preschool is not a context of development for all children, it has become an important experience for many young children.

8. There is an overall pattern for the growth and maturation of physical characteristics. There are at least four major types of organs and tissues that grow according to a predictable pattern: lymphoid, brain and head, general body, and reproductive. Although human growth is the result of the interaction of hereditary and environmental factors, it is difficult, if not impossible, to specify the precise relationship between both. Several environmental factors do have an influence on growth: nutrition, illnesses, socioeconomic status, and emotional stress.

9. Perceptual processes involve the reception or taking-in of information about the environment (e.g., touch, taste, sight, smell, and hearing). As preschool children grow and develop there are at least three major changes in perceptual processes.

10. Preschooler motor development is woven into the fabric of play activities.

11. The primary task of motor development in the preschool years is the development of the *fundamental motor skills* (e.g., jumping, running, throwing, catching, and climbing). These fundamental motor skills are the basis for all advanced motor skill and sport activities throughout childhood and adulthood.

12. According to Piaget, early childhood cognitive development occurs in the period of *preoperational* thinking (eighteen months to seven years). This preoperational period is sometimes divided into two parts: the *preconceptual* stage (two to four years) and the *intuitive* stage (five to seven years). There are several important limitations of preoperational thinking. Several of the features of the preschool child's thinking (including limitations) are illustrated in what Piaget and others have called *conservation* problems. The process of refining conservation skills is accompanied by other developments in thinking including *classification* skills and better understanding of space, time, and sequence.

13. Both adults and young children engage in *play*. For adults, play is primarily recreation; however, for children play is recreational as well as

being a central feature of growth and development. Play is the "work" of the child. We will refer to play as an *ecosystem* of development because it represents the integration of activity, thought, and language in the natural setting of family, neighborhood, or preschool.

14. Children's drawing involves the integration of motor skills, cognitive development, and the expression of feelings about the self and the world.

15. Language development in the preschooler is affected by the course of the development of thinking. The language learning of the preschool child occurs in a social-interactional context. Language is not as effective in communication as it will later become because of the young child's egocentrism. Several important dimensions of parent behavior seem to be significantly related to language development. Culture has an impact on how children learn to speak and develop language skills. Black English is an example.

16. Preschooler personality and social development involve the movement from exclusive relationship with parents or caretakers and siblings to interaction with other adults and children. For the first time children experience many new social challenges as well as conflicts and anxieties. These challenges and anxieties result from the process of socialization. We examined several critical aspects of preschooler personality development and socialization: sex-role identity, self-concept formation, prosocial behavior, and aggression.

Questions

1. Briefly identify and describe three characteristics of the family as a system. Why is this approach useful in understanding the contribution of the family?
2. Briefly identify and describe several types of preschool settings.
3. Why is the process of myelinization important for brain growth?
4. What is "deprivation dwarfism?"
5. Identify one fundamental motor skill and briefly describe how it changes from age three to five.
6. Briefly describe the major differences between the preconceptual stage of thinking and the intuitive stage of thinking.
7. Define play. Why is it important for the preschooler?
8. What is prosocial behavior? How can it be developed in the preschooler?

Bibliography

ANASTASIOW, N. J. and HANES, M. L. Cognitive development and acquisition of language in three subcultural groups. *Developmental Psychology,* 1974, *10,* 703–709.

ANDERSON, R. E., and CARTER, I. *Human Behavior in the Social Environment: A Social Systems Approach* (2nd ed.). New York: Aldine, 1978.

BANDURA, A. *Social Learning Theory.* Englewood Cliffs, N.J.: Prentice-Hall, 1977.

BANDURA, A., ROSS, D., and ROSS, S. A., Transmission of aggression through imitation of aggressive models. *Journal of Abnormal and Social Psychology,* 1961, *63,* 575–582.

BANDURA, A., and WALTERS, R. H. *Social Learning and Personality Development.* New York: Holt, Rinehart and Winston, 1963.

BANGS, H. P., and MAHLER, S. Users of local parts. *Journal of the American Institute of Planners,* 1970, *36,* 330–334.

BARKER, R. G., DEMBO, T., and LEWIN, K. Frustration and regression. In R. G. Barker, J. S. Kounin, and H. F. Wright (Eds.), *Child Behavior and Development.* New York: McGraw-Hill, 1943.

BAUMRIND, D. Socialization and instrumental competence in young children. In W. Hartup (Ed.), *The Young Child: Reviews of Research*, Vol. 2. Washington, D.C.: National Association for the Education of Young Children, 1972.

BAUMRIND, D. Parental disciplinary patterns. *Youth and Society*, 1978, *9*, 223–276.

BEE, H. *Social Issues in Developmental Psychology*. New York: Harper & Row, 1974.

BERKOWITZ, L. Control of aggression. In B. M. Caldwell and H. N. Ricciuti (Eds.), *Review of Child Development Research*, Vol. 3, Chicago: U. of Chicago P., 1973.

BERNDT, T. J. Lack of acceptance of reciprocity norms in preschool children. *Developmental Psychology*, 1979, *15*, 662–663.

BLURTON-JONES, N. Categories of child–child interaction. In N. Blurton-Jones (Ed.), *Ethological Studies of Child Behavior*. Cambridge: Cambridge U. P., 1972.

BRECKENRIDGE, M. E., and MURPHY, M. N. *Growth and Development of the Young Child* (8th ed.). Philadelphia: Saunders, 1969.

BRONSON, W. Developments in behavior with agemates during the second year of life. In M. Lewis and L. Rosenblum (Eds.), *Peer Relations and Friendship*. New York: Wiley, 1975.

BRUNER, J. S. *Toward a Theory of Instruction*. Cambridge, Mass.: Belknap Press of Harvard U. P., 1966.

BRUNER, J. S., OLIVER, R. R., and GREENFIELD, P. M. *Studies in Cognitive Growth*. New York: Wiley, 1966.

BRYAN, J. H. Children's cooperation and helping behaviors. In E. M. Hetherington (Ed.), *Review of Child Development Research*, Vol. 5. Chicago: U. of Chicago P., 1975, 127–280.

BRYAN, J. H., and LONDON, P. Altruistic behavior by children. *Psychological Bulletin*, 1970, *73*, 200–211.

BRYAN, J. H., and Walbek, N. H. Preaching and practicing generosity: Children's actions and reactions. *Child Development*, 1970, *41*, 329–353.

BRYANT, B. K., and CROCKENBERG, S. B. Correlates and dimensions of prosocial behavior: A study of female siblings with their mothers. *Child Development*, 1980, *51*, 529–544.

BUCKLEY, N., SIEGEL, L. S., and NESS, S. Egocentrism, empathy, and altruistic behavior in young children. *Developmental Psychology*, 1979, *15*, 329–330.

CHARLESWORTH, R., and HARTUP, W. W. Positive social reinforcement in the nursery school peer group. *Child Development*, 1967, *38*, 993–1002.

COCHRAN, M., and BRASSARD, J. A. Child development and personal social networks. *Child Development*, 1979, *50*, 601–603.

COPPLE, C. E., and SUCI, G. J. The comparative ease of processing standard English and black nonstandard English by lower-class black children. *Child Development*, Dec. 1974, *45*, 1048–1053.

CORBIN, C. *A Textbook of Motor Development* (2nd ed.). Dubuque, Iowa: Brown, 1980.

CROMER, R. The development of language and cognition: The cognitive hypothesis. In B. Foss (Ed.), *New Perspectives in Child Development*. Hammondsworth, England: Penguin, 1974.

DALE, P. S. *Language Development* (2nd ed.). New York: Holt, Rinehart and Winston, 1976.

DANHOFF, J. Children's art: The creative process, *Children Today*. Washington, D.C.: July–August 1975, 7–10.

DEARDEN, R. F. The concept of play. In R. S. Peters (Ed.), *The Concept of Education*. London: Routledge and Kegan Paul, 1967.

DEE, N., and LIEBMAN, J. C. A statistical study of attendance at urban playgrounds. *Journal of Leisure Research*, 1970, *2*, 145–159.

DOLLARD, J., DOOB, L. W., MILLER, M. E., MOWRER, O. H., and SEARS, R. R. *Frustration and Aggression*. New Haven, Conn.: Yale U. P., 1939.

DOLLARD, J., and MILLER, M. E. *Personality and Psychotherapy: An Analysis in Terms of Learning, Thinking and Culture*. New York: McGraw-Hill, 1950.

DRAKE, C. T., and McDOUGALL, D. Effects of the absence of a father and other male models on the development of boys' sex roles. *Developmental Psychology*, 1977, 13, 537–538.

DREMAN, S. B. Sharing behavior in Israeli school-children: Cognitive and social learning factors. *Child Development*, 1976, 47, 186–194.

DWYER, J., and MAYER, J. Psychological effects of variations in physical appearance during adolescence. *Adolescence, 3*, Winter 1968–1969, 353–380.

ECKERMAN, C., WHATLEY, J., and KUTZ, S. The growth of social play with peers during the second year of life. *Developmental Psychology*, 1975, 11, 42–49.

EISENBERG-BERG, N., and HAND, M. The relationship of preschoolers' reasoning about prosocial moral conflicts to prosocial behavior. *Child Development*, 1979, 50, 356–363.

EISENBERG-BERG, N., and LENNON, R. Altruism and the assessment of empathy in the preschool years. *Child Development*, 1980, 51, 552–557.

EISENBERG-BERG, N., and MUSSEN, P. Empathy and moral development in adolescence. *Developmental Psychology*, 1978, 14, 185–186.

ENRIGHT, R. D., FRANKLIN, C. C., and MANHEIM, L. A. Children's distributive justice reasoning: A standardized and objective scale. *Developmental Psychology*, 1980, 16, 193–202.

FARSON, R. *Birthrights*. New York: Macmillan, 1974.

FAWL, C. L. Disturbances experienced by children in their natural habitats. In R. G. Barker (Ed.), *The Stream of Behavior*. New York: Appleton-Century-Crofts, 1963, pp. 99–126.

FESHBACH, L. Aggression. In P. H. Mussen (Ed.), *Carmichael's Manual of Child Psychology* (3rd ed.), Vol. 2. New York: Wiley, 1970.

FRAIBERG, S. *The Magic Years*. New York: Scribner, 1959.

FRAISSE, P. *The Psychology of Time* (translated by J. Leith). New York: Harper & Row, 1963.

FRIED, M., and GLEICHER, P. Some sources of residential satisfaction in an urban slum. *Journal of the American Institute of Planners*, 1961, 27, 305–315.

FURSTENBERG, F. *Unplanned Parenthood: the Social Consequences of Teenage Parenthood*. New York: Free Press, 1976.

GANS, H. *The Urban Villagers*. New York: Free Press, 1962.

GARBARINO, J. The human ecology of child maltreatment: A conceptual model for research. *Journal of Marriage and the Family*, 1977, 39, 721–736.

GARBARINO, J. Latchkey children: Getting the short end of the stick? *Vital Issues*, 1980, 30(3).

GARBARINO, J. *Children and Families in the Social Environment*. New York: Aldine, 1982.

GARBARINO, J., and Plantz, M. C. *Urban Environments and Urban Children*. ERIC/CUE Urban Diversity Series, #69. New York: ERIC Clearinghouse on Urban Education, 1980.

GARDNER, L. I. Deprivation dwarfism. *Scientific American*, 1972.

GARVEY, C. *Play*. Cambridge, Mass.: Harvard U. P., 1977.

GINSBURG, H. *The Myth of the Deprived Child*. Englewood Cliffs, N.J.: Prentice-Hall, 1972.

GLUCKSBERG, S., and KRAUSS, R. M. What do people say after they have learned to talk? Studies of the development of referential communication. *Merrill-Palmer Quarterly*, 1967, 13, 309–316.

GLUCKSBERG, S., KRAUSS, R. M., and WEISBERG, R. Referential communication in nursery school children: Method and some preliminary findings. *Journal of Experimental Child Psychology*, 1966, 3, 333–342.

GOLD, S. Nonuse of neighborhood parks. *Journal of the American Institute of Planners*, 1972, 38, 369–378.

GORDON, T. E. *P.E.T.—Parent Effectiveness Training*. New York: Peter H. Wyden, Inc., 1975.

GOTTLIEB, B. The primary group as a supportive milieu: applications to community psychology. *American Journal of Community Psychology,* 1979.

GREEN, E. H. Group play and quarreling among preschool children. *Child Development,* 1933, *4,* 302–307.

GRUSEC, J. E., and DRISCOLL, S. A. Saying and doing: Effects on observer performance. Unpublished manuscript, University of Toronto, 1973.

GRUSEC, J. E., and REDLER, E. Attribution, reinforcement, and altruism: A developmental analysis. *Developmental Psychology,* 1980, *16,* 525–534.

HALL, A. D., and FAGEN, R. E. Definition of systems, revised introductory chapter of *Systems Engineering.* New York: Bell Telephone Laboratories, 1956.

HARRIS, J. A., JACKSON, C. M., PATTERSON, D. G., and SCAMMON, R. E. *The Measurement of Man.* Minneapolis: U. of Minnesota Press, 1930.

HART, R. A. Personal communication, 1973. In W. H. Ittelson, H. M. Proshansky, L. G. Rivlin, and G. H. Winkel *An Introduction to Environmental Psychology.* New York: Holt, 1974.

HARTUP, W. W., and COATES, B. Imitation of a peer as a function of reinforcement from the peer group and rewardingness of the model. *Child Development,* 1967, *38,* 1003–1016.

HAYWARD, D. G., ROTHENBERG, M., and BEASLEY, R. R. Children's play in urban playground environments: A comparison of traditional, contemporary and adventure playground types. *Environment and Behavior,* 1974, *6, 2,* 131–168.

HESS, R. D., and SHIPMAN, V. Early experience and the specialization of cognitive modes in children. *Child Development,* 1965, *36,* 869–886.

HETHERINGTON, E. M. The effects of familial variables on sex typing, on parent–child similarity, and on imitation in children. In J. P. Hill (Ed.), *Minnesota symposia on child psychology* (Vol. 1). Minneapolis, Minnesota: University of Minnesota Press, 1967.

HICKS, D. J. Girls' attitudes toward modeled behaviors and the content of imitative private play. *Child Development,* 1971, *42,* 139–147.

HILDEBRAND, V. *Guiding Young Children* (2nd edition). New York: Macmillan, 1980.

HILDEBRAND, V. *Introduction to early childhood education* (3rd ed.). New York: Macmillan, 1981.

HILLERY, G. A., JR. Definitions of community: Areas of agreement. *Rural Sociology,* 1955, 20, 111–123.

HOFFMAN, M. L. Altruistic behavior and the parent–child relationship. *Journal of Personality and Social Psychology,* 1975, *31,* 937–943.

HOLLAND, V. M., and PALERMO, D. S. On learning "less": Language and cognitive development. *Child Development,* 1975, *46,* 437–443.

HOLT, J. *Escape from Childhood: The Needs and Rights of Children.* New York: Dutton, 1974.

HORNSTEIN, H. A. *Cruelty and Kindness: A New Look at Aggression and Altruism.* Englewood Cliffs, N.J.: Prentice-Hall, 1976.

HUNTER, W. S., and BARTLETT, S. C. Double alternation behavior in young children. *Journal of Experimental Psychology,* 1948, *38,* 558–567.

ITTELSON, W. H., PROSHANSKY, H. M., RIVLIN, L. G., and WINKEL, G. H. *An Introduction to Environmental Psychology.* New York: Holt, 1974.

JOHNSON, D. L. The influences of social class and race on language test performance and spontaneous speech of preschool children. *Child Development,* 1974, *45,* 517–521.

KANTOR, D., and LEHR, W. *Inside the Family.* San Francisco: Jossey–Bass, 1975.

KELLOGG, R. *Analyzing Children's Art.* Palo Alto, Calif.: Mayfield Publishing Co., 1969.

KELLOGG, R. Child Art Collection, San Francisco: 1974.

KLINGER, E. The development of imaginative behavior: Implications of play for a theory of fantasy. *Psychological Bulletin,* 1967, *72,* 277–298.

KOHLBERG, L. A cognitive-developmental analysis of children's sex-role concepts and attitudes. In E. E. Maccoby (Ed.), *The Development of Sex Differences.* Stanford, Calif.: Stanford U. P., 1966, pp. 82–83.

KOHLBERG, L. Stage and Sequence: The cognitive-developmental approach to socialization. In D. A. Goslin (Ed.), *Handbook of Socialization Theory and Research.* Chicago: Rand-McNally, 1969.

KOHLBERG, L., and ZIGLER, E. The impact of cognitive maturity on the development of sex-role attitudes in the years 4 to 8. *Genetic Psychology Monographs,* 1967, *75,* 84–165.

KRAUSS, R. M., and GLUCKSBERG, S. The development of communication: Competence as a function of age. *Child Development,* 1969, *40,* 255–266.

KREBS, D. Altruism—an examination of the concept and a review of the literature. *Psychological Bulletin,* 1970, *73,* 258–302.

LABOV, W. The logic of nonstandard English. In J. E. Alatis (Ed.), *Twentieth Annual Roundtable.* Washington, D.C.: Georgetown U. P., 1970.

LABOV, W. *Language in the Inner City: Studies in the Black English Vernacular.* Philadelphia: U. of Pennsylvania P., 1972.

LEVINSON, S. *Everything But Money.* New York: Simon and Schuster, 1966.

LONG, G. T., and LERNER, M. J. Deserving the "personal contract," and altruistic behavior by children. *Journal of Personality and Social Psychology,* 1974, *29,* 551–556.

LORING, W. C. Housing and social problems. *Social Problems,* 1956, *3,* 160–168.

LOWE, M. Trends in the development of representational play in infants from one to three years: An observational study. *Journal of Child Psychology,* 1975, *16,* 33–48.

MACCOBY, E. E., and JACKLIN, C. *The Psychology of Sex Differences.* Stanford, Calif.: Stanford U. P., 1974.

MARANTZ, S. A., and MANSFIELD, A. F. Maternal employment and the development of sex-role stereotyping in five-to–eleven-year-old girls. *Child Development,* 1977, *48,* 668–673.

MARCUS, R. F., TELLEEN, S., and ROKE, E. J. Relation between cooperation and empathy in young children. *Developmental Psychology,* 1979, *15,* 346–347.

MEIER, R. A. *A Communications Theory of Urban Growth.* Cambridge, Mass.: MIT, 1962.

MICHAUD, E. Essai sur l'organisation de la connaissance entre 10 et. 14 ans. *Etudes Psychol. Philos.,* No. 11. Paris: J. Vrin, 1949.

MILGRAM, S. The experience of living in cities. *Science,* 1970, *167,* 1461–1468.

MILLER, D. T., and SMITH, J. The effect of own deservingness and deservingness of others on children's helping behavior. *Child Development,* 1977, *48,* 617–620.

MILLER, S. M. Effects of maternal employment on sex role perception, interests, and self esteem in kindergarten girls. *Developmental Psychology,* 1975, *11,* 405–406.

MILNE, C., SEEFELDT, V., and REUSCHLEIN, P. Relationship between grade, sex, and motor performance in young children. *Research Quarterly,* 1975, *47,* 726.

MISCHEL, W. Social learning theory and sex roles. In E. E. Maccoby, *The Development of Sex Differences.* Stanford, Calif.: Stanford U. P., 1966, pp. 56–57.

MOERK, E. L. Verbal interactions between children and their mothers during the preschool years. *Developmental Psychology,* 1975, *11,* 788–794.

MUELLER, E. The maintenance of verbal exchanges between young children. *Child Development,* 1972, *43,* 930–938.

NASH, J. *Developmental Psychology: A Psychobiological Approach.* Englewood Cliffs, N.J.: Prentice-Hall, 1970.

NEILL, A. S. *Summerhill.* New York: Hart, 1960.

NELSON, K. Structure and strategy in learning to talk. *Monographs of the Society for Research in Child Development,* 1973, 38.

NELSON, S. A., and DWECK, C. S. Motivation and competence as determinants of young children's reward allocation. *Developmental Psychology,* 1977, *13,* 192–197.

NICHOLSON, S. How not to cheat children: The theory of loose parts. *Landscape Architecture,* 1971, *62,* 30–34.

OLEJNIK, A. B., and MCKINNEY, J. P. Parental value orientation and generosity in children. *Developmental Psychology,* 1973, *8,* 311.

PASTALON, L. The empathic model. *Journal of Architectural Education,* 1977, 10.

PATTERSON, G. R., LITTMAN, R. A., and BRICKER, W. Assertive behavior in children: A step toward a theory of aggression. *Monographs of the Society for Research in Child Development*, 1967, *32* (5, Serial No. 113).

PEISACK, E. Relationship between knowledge and use of dimensional language and achievement of conservation. *Developmental Psychology*, 1973, *9*, 189–199.

PERRY, D. G., and BUSSEY, K. *Social Development.* Englewood Cliffs, New Jersey: Prentice-Hall, 1984.

PETERSON, L. Developmental changes in verbal and behavioral sensitivity to cues of social norms of altruism. *Child Development*, 1980, *51*, 830–838.

PIAGET, J. *The Psychology of Intelligence.* New York: Harcourt, Brace, 1950.

PIAGET, J. *Play, Dreams and Imitation in Childhood.* New York: Norton, 1951.

PIAGET, J. *The Child's Conception of Number.* London: Routledge & Kegan Paul, Ltd., 1952.

PIAGET, J. Time perception in children (translated by B. B. Montgomery). In J. T. Fraser (Ed.), *The Voices of Time.* New York: Braziller, 1966, pp. 202–216.

READ, K. *The Nursery School.* Philadelphia: Saunders, 1971.

RICHARDSON, S. A. Physical growth of Jamaican school children who were severely malnourished before 2 years of age. *Journal of Biosocial Science*, 1975, *7*, 445–462.

ROSENHAHN, D. L. Conceptual structures for preschool behavior. Paper presented at the annual meeting of the American Psychological Association, Miami Beach, 1970.

ROSENHAHN, D. L. Learning theory and prosocial behavior. *Journal of Social Issues*, 1972, *28*, 151–163.

ROSENTHAL, R., and JACOBSON, L. *Pygmalion in the Classroom: Teacher Expectations and Pupil's Intellectual Development.* New York: Harper & Row, 1968.

ROSSI, P. H. *Why Families Move: A Study in the Social Psychology of Urban Residential Living.* New York: Free Press, 1955.

SAPIR, E. Language and environment. In D. G. Mandelbaum (Ed.), *Selected Writings of Edward Sapir in Language, Culture, and Personality.* Berkeley: U. of California P., 1958, pp. 89–103.

SCHMITT, R. C. Density, health and social organization. *Journal of the American Institute of Planners*, 1966, *32*, 38–40.

SCHORR, A. L. *Slums and social insecurity.* Washington, D.C.: U.S. Government Printing Office, 1963.

SCHWARTZ, T., and BRYAN, J. H. Imitation and judgements of children with language deficits. *Exceptional Children*, 1971, *38*, 157–158.

SEARS, R. R., MACCOBY, E. E., and LEVIN, H. *Patterns of child rearing.* Evanston, Ill.: Row, Peterson, 1957.

SEARS, R. R., RAU, L., and ALPERT, R. *Identification and child rearing.* Stanford, California: Stanford U. P., 1965.

SEEFELDT, V., and HAUBENSTRICKER, J. Pattern, phases or stages: an analytical model for the study of developmental movement. Michigan State University, Department of Health, Physical Education and Recreation, 1982.

SHATZ, M., and GELMAN, R. The development of communication skills: Modification in the speech of young children as a function of listener. *Monographs of the Society for Research in Child Development*, 1973, *38*, (No. 152).

SINCLAIR-DE-ZWART, H. Developmental psycholinguistics. In D. Elkind and J. H. Flavell (Eds.), *Studies in Cognitive Development.* New York: Oxford U. P., 1969, pp. 315–366.

SLABY, R. G., and FREY, K. S. Development of gender constancy and selective attention to same-sex models. *Child Development*, 1975, *46*, 849–856.

STAUB, E. A. A child in distress: The influence of implicit and explicit rules of conduct on children and adults. *Journal of Personality and Social Psychology*, 1971(a), *17*, 137–144.

STAUB, E. A. A child in distress: The influence of nurturance and modeling on children's attempts to help. *Developmental Psychology*, 1971(b), *5*, 124–132.

STEINBERG, L., CATALANO, R., and DOOLEY, D. Economic antecedents of child abuse and neglect. *Child Development*, 1981, *52*, 975–985.

STEWART, W. A. On the use of Negro dialect in the teaching of reading. In J. C. Baratz and R. W. Shuy (Eds.), *Teaching Black Children to Read.* Washington, D.C.: Center for Applied Linguistics, 1969, 156–219.

STODOLSKY, S., and LESSER, G. Learning patterns in the disadvantaged. *Harvard Educational Review,* 1967, *37,* 546–593.

STRAUS, M., GELLES, R., and STEINMETZ, S. *Behind Closed Doors.* New York: Doubleday, 1980.

TANNER, J. M. *Growth at Adolescence.* Oxford, England: Blackwell Scientific Publications, Ltd., 1962.

TANNER, J. M. *Education and Physical Growth* (2nd ed.). New York: International Universities Press, 1978.

TULKIN, S. R. An analysis of the concept of cultural deprivation. *Developmental Psychology,* 1972, *6,* 326–339.

VINACKE, W. E. The investigation of concept formation. *Psychological Bulletin,* 1951, *48,* 1–31.

WARREN, R. L. *The Community in America* (2nd ed.). Chicago: Rand-McNally, 1973.

WEISSBROD, C. S. The impact of warmth and instructions on donation. *Child Development,* 1980, *51,* 279–281.

WHITE, G. M. Immediate and deferred effects of model observation and guided and unguided rehearsal on donating and stealing. *Journal of Personality and Social Psychology,* 1972, *21,* 139–148.

WIDDOWSON, E. M. Mental contentment and physical growth. *Lancet, I,* 1951, 1316–18.

WOLFRAM, W., and FASOLD, R. Toward reading materials for speakers of black English: Three linguistically appropriate passages. In J. C. Baratz and R. W. Shuy (Eds.), *Teaching Black Children to Read.* Washington, D.C.: Center for Applied Linguistics, 1969, 144–147, 152–154.

ZAHN-WAXLER, C., RADKE-YARROW, M., and KING, R. A. Childrearing and children's pro-social initiations toward victims of distress. *Child Development,* 1979, *50,* 319–30.

Suggested Readings

CLARKE, A. M. and CLARKE, A. D. B. (Eds.). *Early Experience: Myth and Evidence.* New York: Free Press, 1976. An excellent discussion of the resiliency of young children in recovering from deprived early environments.

CLARKE-STEWART, A. *Child Care in the Family: A Review of Research and Some Propositions for Policy.* New York: Academic Press, 1977. A thorough analysis and review of research on the impact of various modes of child care on child development and some provocative recommendations for child-care policy.

CLARKE-STEWART, A. *Daycare.* Cambridge, Massachusetts: Harvard University Press, 1982. A comprehensive discussion of daycare including its history, ecology, and effects along with suggestions on selecting daycare programs for young children.

DE VILLIERS, PETER A. and DEVILLIERS, JILL G. *Early Language.* Cambridge, Massachusetts: Harvard University Press, 1979. A concise and well-written discussion of major advances in language development from birth to six years.

GARVEY, C. *Play.* Cambidge, Massachusetts: Harvard University Press, 1977. An excellent discussion of the evolution of children's play from simple peek-a-boo infant games to games with rules.

GINSBURG, H. and OPPER, S. *Piaget's Theory of Intellectual Development* (2nd edition). Englewood Cliffs, N.J.: Prentice-Hall, 1979. A well organized and thorough description of all the stages of Piaget's theory of cognitive development.

HILDEBRAND, V. *Introduction to Early Childhood Education* (3rd edition). New York: Macmillan, 1981. A well written introduction to professional preparation for nursery school, child care, and kindergarten teachers with an emphasis on parent involvement.

HILDEBRAND, V. *Guiding Young Children* (3rd edition). New York: Macmillan, 1983. Provides excellent discussion of interpersonal interaction of adults with infants and preschool children in addition to many excellent practical suggestions for self direction in such activities as toileting, sleeping, dramatic play, and science.

LEWIS, M. and ROSENBLUM, L. A. (Eds.). *The Child and Its Family.* New York: Plenum, 1979. Excellent collection of reviews of research on family and child development.

RUBIN, Z. *Children's Friendships.* Cambridge, Massachusetts: Harvard University Press, 1980. A well-written discussion of friendships in early childhood with descriptions of contributions of school and social setting.

8
Middle Childhood: A Cultural Beginning

A Systems Overview: The Developing Self in the Contexts of Middle Childhood

Development during the years of middle childhood is an exciting phenomenon. The period of middle childhood begins at age five or six with entrance into the formal school, and it concludes with the onset of puberty, which heralds the arrival of adolescence. Development during the years of middle childhood is filled with many exciting and sometimes dramatic changes in the child. As children enter the formal school, the stage is set for developments in the way they think, learn, interact with others, and organize their behavior.

A good way to capture the total picture of what is happening during this period is to think of development in middle childhood from a *systems perspective*. This means that we look at the child as a self who is growing and developing in the contexts of middle-childhood experience. These contexts include the family, the neighborhood and the community, the school, and the peer group. You will remember that in Chapter Seven we examined the development of the preschooler in a similar manner. The major differences between the world of preschooler and the world of school-aged child are summarized in Figure 8.1. During middle childhood, the child usually begins more extensive interactions outside of the family (e.g., in school and with peers) than in the preschool years. The relationship between child and family remains important but is now expanded to include the school, the peer group, and the neighborhood-community. In this chapter, we examine the contributions of each of these contexts to middle childhood as well as the personality development of the child.

Before doing that, however, we will present a brief overview of personality development and the contributions of each context.

THE CHILD AS A ''COMPETENT'' PERSON

During middle childhood, there is an increasing degree of ''seriousness'' about life as children begin to concentrate on what can be done and how well they can do it. This attitude contrasts with that of the preschool years, when learning to do things was more incidental to the total life activities of the child. We refer to the increasing seriousness of middle childhood as an emerging *sense of competence*. Two important elements relate to this sense of seriousness or competence: the refinement of the self-concept and skill learning.

FIGURE 8.1 The transition from the preschool system (two to six years) to the middle childhood system (six to twelve years). The mutual relationship between family and child is expanded during the middle-childhood years to include a larger society (school, neighborhood-community, and peers).

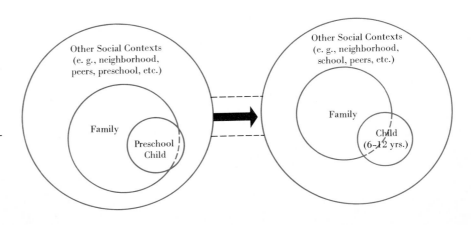

In middle childhood there is curiosity about the world—and much to learn.

Photograph by Dr. Donald Melcer

The Refinement of the Self-concept. During middle childhood, there is an emphasis on the building of child skills such as reading, writing, interpersonal relationships, and game activities. For this reason, children may become occupied with the process of *self-evaluation.* Two primary sources of feedback for such self-evaluation are adults (e.g., parents, neighbors, relatives, and teachers), and peers. As a result of children's evaluations of themselves, two things happen:

1. Children refine their self-concepts in light of firsthand experiences.
2. Children learn to approach the world with a sense of relative self-confidence or relative self-doubt.

In addition, children's sense of competence in relating to their world is based on the development of their personalities up to middle childhood. For example, Erikson (1963) maintains that a sense of industry or competence is based on the prior development of trust (rather than mistrust), autonomy (rather than shame), and initiative (rather than guilt) (see the discussion of Erikson in Chapter Two and the discussion of the preschooler's personality development in Chapter Seven).

As children develop standards for evaluating their performance, they begin to assess the extent to which they can readily learn skills (Erikson referred to this stage as "industry versus inferiority"). In so doing, they develop a basic idea of how well they enjoy being "industrious," both in learning skills and in

During middle childhood, children begin to concentrate on what can be done and how well they can do it.

Photograph by Mark Kubinec

performing them, in comparison with others. This early sense of industriousness marks the beginning of vocational–occupational development—a process that will come to a head during adolescence.

Skill Learning. Learning skills is one of the most important and impressive facets of middle childhood. During this period, children develop many significant skills in thinking, interacting with others, body movement, writing and drawing, and reading, to name a few. Reading is one of the most important skills a child will learn. It is essential to success both in the school and, afterward, in the working world. In addition, reading skills allow the child to move beyond the world of immediate concrete experience to explore the past and the future and what others are thinking or feeling.

THE SCHOOL: A CULTURAL TRANSFER MECHANISM

When children enter the formal school at five or six years of age, they become involved with a primary institution for the transfer of cultural information and skills from one generation to the next. In the school, children are formally introduced to such cultural skills as reading, writing, thinking, problem solving, and interpersonal relations.

From a historical perspective, the formal public school is a relatively recent phenomenon (educational reformers such as Horace Mann supported free public education which became a reality in the United States in the latter half of the nineteenth century). In primarily agricultural societies (e.g., the United States prior to the Industrial Revolution of the latter nineteenth century), the transfer of cultural skills and information was traditionally a role of the family because the level of cultural knowledge and skills was sufficiently simple as to be known and communicated by most adults. In modern industrialized socie-

Right photograph by David Kostelnik; left photograph by Sylvia Byers

ties, such simplicity of cultural information and skills is no longer the case. Over the last hundred years in the United States, the school has come to serve as the primary means of cultural transmission.

For the most part, the formal school has succeeded fairly well in accomplishing this transfer of information and skills. One important factor that influences the success of the school is the relationship between the family and the school. For example, where there is some measure of agreement between school and family on the value and the purposes of education, the child's adaptation to the school will very likely be enhanced (see Figure 8.2).

FIGURE 8.2   The family and the school as interacting contexts. Where the family and the school share similar values toward education, the success of the child in school will be enhanced.

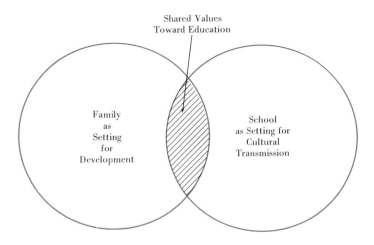

"The First Grader's Rites of Passage"

Do you remember the day you began first grade? Can you recall the anticipation, apprehension, mystery, and excitement of the first days and weeks when small events took on great importance as you searched desperately for order and meaning in the new world of "real" school? Many adults report more vivid memories of first grade than of any other school grade. They especially remember the feeling of having "arrived," of being no longer a little kid (nor yet a big one), but someone to be reckoned with.

Is there really something special about first grade, or is it simply one more new experience on the road to growing up. It *is* special in many ways because first grade represents a rite of passage—from a family world to a peer and school world—at a time when the child is beginning to think in ways adults recognize as reasonable or logical.

Reprinted from J. Costello, "The First Grader's Rites of Passage," *Parents Magazine*, November 1978, p. 104.

Photograph by Darryl Jacobson

THE FAMILY

Although the child is making a major transition to the school, the family continues to act as a vital resource for development. The socializing function of the family continues to be significant, but it is now shared with the school. Several features of family life that are of vital concern to the child's development are the support and enhancement of the child's self-concept and self-esteem, the development of relationships between family members, the general quality of family life, and the development of relationships and linkages between the family and the other contexts of middle childhood (e.g., the school, the community and the neighborhood, and the peer group).

Bigner (1979) described the importance of the parents during the school years as follows:

Parents remain a source of security and stability for the school-aged child during this relatively busy time in life. Children value their parents and other family members, although there is a gradual tendency not to admit this openly during the later years of this period.

School-aged children generally view their parents in an idealistic way. Their dad is the greatest in every matter he undertakes and their mom is the very best in the whole world! . . . Relations with parents can become strained at the end of the middle childhood period because of the harsh unacceptance of parental imperfections. . . .

From J. J. Bigner, Parent–Child Relations. New York: Macmillan, 1979, pp. 177–178.

THE COMMUNITY AND THE NEIGHBORHOOD

The community and the neighborhood provide support for the family in its child-rearing activities in several major ways, including the provision of resources such as playgrounds and community centers and the existence of informal communication and support networks between neighbors and friends.

In addition, the community-neighborhood is a place where the child learns to negotiate the challenges of the out-of-school environment. Because of the changes in children's thinking during middle childhood, they are able to "cognitively map" their neighborhoods. That is, the child's understanding of the spatial arrangement of neighborhood landmarks (e.g., home dwelling, friend's house, large tree) comes to include a more accurate and detailed representation than that of the preschooler.

Bigner (1979) discussed some of the community supports for families of school-aged children:

Children of this age respond to more structured group activities. Communities respond to this need of school-aged children by providing programs that are peer group oriented.

Larger communities and cities usually have extensive recreational programs for school-aged children. Arts and crafts programs are especially popular with children of this age as well as organized sports and game activities. . . . These programs are often held during after-school hours or on weekends.

School-aged children have a particularly strong desire to belong to groups. As they progress through the years of middle childhood, children become eligible for . . . more formal groups [such as] Cub Scouts, Brownies, Camp Fire Girls, 4-H, and so on. . . .

From J. J. Bigner, Parent–Child Relations. New York: Macmillan, 1979, pp. 186–187.

THE PEER GROUP

Children's interaction with their age-mates provides a major contribution to their development in both the school and the community. Peer interactions may occur in several settings including the school, organized group activities, or informal relationships in the neighborhood. As a result of peer relationships, children come to learn that some peers share their thoughts and feelings, although others may not. An awareness of these differences may have the positive effect of helping children to rethink their own perspectives. The peer group also provides a unique experience for sharing feelings and emotional experiences. Children come to realize that they are not the only ones in

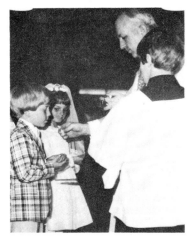

School-aged children frequently become acquainted with their religious heritage.

the world who feel a certain way. These unique emotional experiences are important because they provide an arena for handling many of the challenges and difficult feelings associated with self-evaluation and growing up. The friendship group offers a transitional allegiance between the family and the larger social system. By the time the individual reaches adolescence, the transition from reliance on family relationships to commitment to a larger culture is much more prominent.

During the middle school years, a new feature is added to the quality of children's play. They develop a sense of the group and start to channel energy into team or group goals as well as into personal goals. Three significant characteristics of the group or peer experience are relevant to the child's development: (1) the subordination of personal goals to group goals; (2) the principle of division of labor; and (3) the principles of competition and cooperation.

The Contexts of the Middle Childhood System

THE FAMILY CONTEXT AND THE EMERGING SELF

In this section, we examine in more detail the contexts of development in middle childhood, through a look at the family, the community-neighborhood, the peer group, and the school. Children learn and discover much about themselves in the family context. Childhood is a period of *self-discovery* in which children learn about themselves in the course of engaging in activities and relating to other persons. Before beginning our discussion of the role of the family in the child's emerging self-concept, we need to stress two features of the total family system as they pertain to the developing child:

1. In the first place, the relationship between children and their parents is marked by *inequality* in both power and authority. Many of the unpleasant aspects of child behavior seem to revolve around this imbalance of authority and power, which is a natural concern of children. It is not uncommon for children to act against it. The inequality of power and authority is a normal part of a healthy parent–child relationship.
2. In the second place, whereas the problem of the child may be the inequality of the parent–child relationship, the problem of the parent is how best to use this power and authority. This problem leads to one of the major concerns of modern society: Specifically, how can people be prepared for the challenging role of parenthood? Indeed, there seem to be many parents who are quite unclear about how to handle their authority as parents.

The Parent–Child Relationship and Child Self-esteem. One of the most significant tasks of the parent–child relationship is nurturance of the child's self-esteem. The primary task of the school-aged child is to develop a sense of self largely from experiences in the formal school and with peers. (We will discuss the contributions of peers to the development of the child's self-concept later in this chapter). Although there is a shift to peer interactions, the role of the parent is still vital. The school-aged child lives in two worlds: the adult or family world and the world of her or his peers. The parent not only provides support for the child as a family member but also helps the child to manage the sometimes harsh judgments of the peer world.

Coopersmith (1967) found that certain parental or family characteristics were closely related to the development of self-esteem in school-aged children:

Thus, although there is no evidence that the mothers of high self esteem subjects are more successful (and only limited differences in the social and occupation status of their husbands), our results suggest that they are stable, resilient, and self-reliant women, whose actions are likely to convey the sense they know what they are about and are doing it well. Their children are likely to perceive this posture and this conviction of confidence. (p. 117)

In addition, Coopersmith found that the parents of children with high self-esteem were characterized by higher levels of compatibility in their relationship than parents of children with lower self-esteem.

Coopersmith (1967) identified four major factors contributing to the development of child self-esteem:

1. The degree of acceptance that individuals receive from the significant others in their lives;
2. One's history of successes and the status and position one holds in the world;
3. The individual's aspirations—living up to aspirations in areas which the individual values leads to high self esteem;
4. The individual's manner of responding to criticism. The ability to defend self esteem reduces the experience of anxiety and helps to maintain personal equilibrium. (p. 37)

In addition to the general characteristics of the parents, Coopersmith (1967) found a number of specific family experiences to be associated with the development of the child's self-esteem.

The Imposition of Limits. In general, Coopersmith (1967) found that parents of children with high self-esteem were both concerned and attentive toward their children. These parents structured their children's world in ways that they believed to be both proper and appropriate and allowed their children a great deal of freedom within these limits.

The families of children with high self-esteem established a more extensive set of rules than families of children with low self-esteem. The former parents were more zealous in enforcing these rules. The pattern for the low-esteem group consisted of few and poorly defined limits and harsh control techniques. These parents either did not express their authority to their children or were so vague in their expression that it lacked clarity and force. These parents demanded absolute compliance without providing the guiding limits that would indicate what types of behavior they really valued. As a result of this lack of standards, the children in these families were uncertain whether they were behaving appropriately. Feelings of insignificance or powerlessness often accompanied such uncertainty.

Coopersmith concluded that the imposition of limits was important to children. These limits serve to define the expectations of others, and their enforcement helps children to understand that such limits are real. The existence of these limits contributes to the child's sense of reality that can be understood and successfully negotiated.

The Sign on His Bedroom Door Says "Don't Enter without My Permishum"— The Self in Middle Childhood

Baby Elizabeth, whom we have previously visited, has two older brothers, Scott and Bruce. Scott is now nine years old and in the fourth grade.

One day, Scott's father approached his son's bedroom only to find the door closed and a handwritten sign taped to it. The sign read as follows: "KEEP OUT—DON'T COME IN WITHOUT MY PERMISHUM." Well now, what is an innocent parent supposed to think about this?

This harsh notice bears happy tidings: Junior is bearing down on the "homework" of self; he is refining his separateness. . . .

The middle years of childhood are directed toward extending mastery and autonomy. . . .

. . . "Keep out" signs, secret drawers complete with lock and key and collections jealously hoarded accentuate autonomy.

What benefits come from collecting 376 rusty bottle caps, 208 green marbles, 452 unmatched playing cards and a string of 1,000 paper clips? They are "symbols"—psychological tools—that nourish self-esteem. They bring the joy of initiating, the excitement of the hunt, the comfort of status, the fascination of management, and the pride of ownership. The youngster gets experience in controlling, possessing, planning and trading. It is easier to treat junior-sized junk heaps with proper respect when you know the purpose they serve. If, in a fit of spring house cleaning, you dispose of them, you work against autonomy and control. You emphasize helplessness and nurture seething resentment.

Have you ever noticed that "big secrets" told to chums with all kinds of ceremonial flourish are later casually revealed to you? The "content" of the secret is unimportant: the process of shutting out a brother or friend (maybe even you!) is vital. Deciding whom he will let into his confidence accentuates a child's separateness. This bit of power gives control in a world where so much is still beyond his control. So, signs and secrets and locked diaries are not poor manners nor evidence of rejection. They are part of normal growth.

From D. C. Briggs, *Your Child's Self Esteem*, New York: Doubleday, 1975, pp. 139–143.

The Seven-to-Ten-Year-Old Child as Backseat Driver

"Mommy!" calls out an eight-year-old voice from the backseat, "That sign we just passed says, Speed Limit 25 Miles Per Hour, and you're still going 30. You'd better slow down!"

Or later at home: "Dad, you always tell us to turn out the lights when we're not going to stay in a room, but you don't always do it. You're wasting energy!"

These common scenes surface regularly during the years from seven to ten, and often cause parents feelings of mild guilt (because the children are usually right, at least in the technical sense), mixed with a bit of irritation, at the notion that a seven- or eight-year-old has become the self-appointed "enforcer" for the whole family.

. . . Of course, the central reason for the child's interest in our adult behavior is that he is beginning to look closely at what adults really do. These are the years when children are beginning a crucial search for adult models. They are moving out of the home and into school settings, neighborhoods, playgrounds, camps, and eventually beyond. What they are seeking is a style of behavior and a general code that will fit more than one kind of

situation. They find it best by observing us as we negotiate our daily lives.

Reprinted from F. Roberts, "The Little Backseat Driver," *Parents Magazine,* November 1978, p. 106.

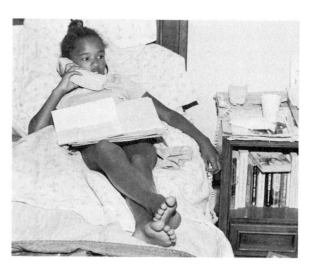

The school-aged child is becoming a social creature.

Photograph by Darryl Jacobson

Acceptance. Coopersmith found that mothers of children with high self-esteem were more loving and had closer relationships with their children than mothers of children with less self-esteem. Greater acceptance of the child was demonstrated by interest in the child, concern about the child's companions, and the availability and willingness of the parent to participate in joint activities.

Coopersmith found that in families of children with low self-esteem, the parents were more likely to withdraw from their children. This isolation produced an environment for child self-esteem that was relatively deprived of meaningful contact with adults.

Success. Favorable attitudes and treatment by persons significant to an individual, whether parents or peers, were likely to enhance self-judgments (Coopersmith, 1967). The most favorable self-judgments were not associated with uncritical, unrestricted, and totally favorable attitudes and treatment. In families of children high in self-esteem, there were greater and more defined limits to behavior, parents were more apt to lead active lives outside their families, and there was a clear expression of parental authority.

Values. Coopersmith found that although individuals are theoretically free to select their values, the childhood years spent in home, school, and peer groups

Maturing self-esteem.

Photograph by Sylvia Byers

generally lead to acceptance of group standards and values. Furthermore, parents who had definite values, who had a clear idea of what they regarded as appropriate behavior, and who were able and willing to present and enforce their beliefs were more likely to rear children who valued themselves highly.

The Influence of Siblings in the Family. Although the impact of the parents on the child is of primary importance, the child's relationship with his or her siblings, if any, exerts some influence on personality formation. The number of siblings a child has and his or her relationship to them are important components of the total system in which the child develops. For example, the social learning environment of the firstborn is different from that of younger siblings. The oldest child may have greater responsibilities placed on him or her and is the *only* child in the family to lose the "only-child" status. The impact of siblings on the development of the child is not a simple one and depends on the interaction of a number of factors, including the sex and age of the siblings, the spacing of siblings (proximity in age), the size of the family (the total number of children), and the mode of parent–child interaction.

Birth Order: Sex of Siblings and Spacing. Birth order appears to have some impact on personality development even when factors such as social class, the sex of siblings, and the size of the family are held constant. Research indicates the firstborn children are more adult-oriented, more achievement-oriented, more conscientious and prone to guilt feelings, more conforming to social pressures, and more concerned with being cooperative and responsible (Altus, 1967; Fenton, 1928; Kagan and Moss, 1962; Rosenberg, Goldman, and Sutton-Smith, 1969; Sears, 1951; Sears, Maccoby, and Levin, 1957). From an early age, it appears that the oldest child may be expected to take responsibility for younger siblings.

The effect of ordinal position is not independent of such factors as the *sex* of the siblings and the *spacing* between them (Koch, 1956a,b,c). Children with brothers had more "masculine" traits than children with sisters. For example, girls with brothers, as compared with girls with sisters, were more ambitious and aggressive (Koch, 1956a,b,c). When siblings were of the same sex and separated by less than two years, there were few differences between them; when the spacing increased to four years and the siblings were of the opposite sex, the differences between them were more apparent.

A two-year period is often seen as optimal *spacing* between siblings (Koch, 1956a,b,c). It gives the older child sufficient time as the "only child" who receives the most attention, without the child's developing a lasting perception of being in that role. When a new baby arrives after less than two years, the older child is more likely to be jealous than if the new baby comes later. Likewise, a baby who comes three or four years after the arrival of the last child may also be resented by the older child. Presumably the reason for this resentment is that the older child may have become accustomed to the comfortable and satisfying position of being an only child and the center of attention. It is assumed that the three- to four-year-old child is in a particularly vulnerable position relative to a new sibling for two reasons:

1. The three- to four-year-old child's *self-concept* is sufficiently organized and rooted in the experience of being the parents' "only child." Children younger than three to four years may not have self-concepts that are so organized and differentiated.

Middle Childhood: A Cultural Beginning

Sibling relationships.

Top left photograph by Gale Schiamberg; right photograph by David Kostelnik; bottom photograph by Irving Rader

2. The three- to four-year-old is still "in the family," both physically and socially. However, the five- to seven-year-old child has already entered school and has begun the process of self-evaluation relative to school skills and peer relationships.

Siblings' position is important because it duplicates many of the significant social interaction experiences of adolescence and adulthood (e.g., high or low power, siding with authority or rebelling against it).

The Development of Self in Single-Parent Families. What happens to children in families where the father is absent? This question has become increasingly important as the number of single-parent families has increased. (A high percentage of these families are headed by females. See the discussion of the family in Chapter Six.) Three areas have received significant attention in the research literature (Herzog and Sudia, 1973):

- Juvenile delinquency.
- School achievement.
- Masculine identity.

In the areas of juvenile delinquency and masculine identity, the evidence is neither clear enough nor strong enough to demonstrate beyond doubt that fatherless boys are negatively affected. In the case of school achievement, the evidence is clearer. The finding of "no difference" between fatherless boys and boys with fathers on school achievement seems to be solid (Herzog and Sudia, 1973).

According to Herzog and Sudia (1973), the following conclusions are warranted:

There is good reason to reject blanket statements about the consequences of father absence on boys. It appears that the impact of father absence is much less handicapping than has been assumed. For example, the contribution of father absence to juvenile delinquency is probably less than the impact of such factors as the socioeconomic level of the family or the characteristics of the community. Such findings are consistent with the idea that father absence would primarily affect the mother's ability to supervise family members and to maintain a harmonious family atmosphere.

The number of parents in the home is likely to be less crucial to the child's development than the family functioning of the present members . . . Family functioning would include the mother's role and coping ability as well as the general family climate. (Herzog and Sudia, 1973, p. 214)

THE NEIGHBORHOOD — COMMUNITY AND THE EMERGING SELF

The child's discovery of the various aspects of the self occurs in several settings, one of which is the community. On the whole, the child tends to have a rather limited perspective of the community and probably knows only the parts of the community with which he/she is familiar, such as stores, zoos, parks, police department, or fire department. Most children know little about the workings of government, nor are they familiar with public service agencies. In other words, the child's perception of the community is ordinarily fragmented. There is, of course, variation among children; for example, middle-class youngsters may be familiar with private physicians and dentists and may have little experience with social service agencies. Children whose families live in poverty may be less familiar with private doctors and more aware of public welfare or health agencies. It is not until the end of middle childhood or the beginning of adolescence that the individual can differentiate the various levels of government bodies—local, state, and national—and the related social service and administrative agencies. Most children's perceptions of the community are positive even though their knowledge is limited. Children are usually enthusiastic about visiting the firehouse, meeting police officers, and going on shopping trips with their parents. As the child moves into adolescence, some of this enthusiasm tends to disappear as the novelty of the situations wears off.

The child's changing attitude toward the community and the neighborhood is influenced by a changing conception of spatial relations. The preschooler's "cognitive map," or conception of the neighborhood, usually focuses on the largest, most noticeable elements of the neighborhood and on simple boundaries (e.g., between buildings and houses). These rather simple perceptions of preschoolers reflect their limited experience in the world. As their experiences and skills increase, so do their conceptions of their neighborhood.

Children's conception of space—including the neighborhood—is not a simple mirror image of what they see. Rather, it is a picture of the world that they develop as if they were actually acting, moving, or manipulating things in it (Ittelson, Proshansky, Rivlin, and Winkel, 1974). This skill of representing space was present in the preschool years (probably as early as age two). However, it is not until age seven or eight that children have become sufficiently "decentered" to be able to view their spatial environment in a coordinated way. *Decentering* means that children are able to explore many aspects and viewpoints in looking at objects and in thinking about them (Piaget,

Inhelder, and Szeminska, 1960). The objects of the environment for the seven- or eight-year-old begin to acquire a quality of more "total" representation than for the preschooler.

In an interesting experiment conducted by Piaget, et al. (1960), children between the ages of four and ten were asked to make a sandbox model of their school and its immediate environment. Piaget found that the children in the preoperational stage of thinking (usually preschoolers) used an "active-centered" organizational framework, in which the focus of the sand design was on the routes in and out of the school. Details of significant landmarks were added later, if at all. In contrast, the operational child tended to organize details into a whole pattern, including the routes in and out of the school.

Spatial concepts are influenced not only by cognitive development but also by experience in the environment and the "freedom" to explore. There appears to be a relationship between the distance from home that a child plays and selected spatial tasks such as block copying (Munroe and Munroe, 1971; Nerlove, Munroe, and Munroe, 1971). Both inside and outside the home, various adults (e.g., parent, teacher, playground supervisor, home owner, police officer) serve as "gatekeepers" to the environment by determining the accessibility and use of community-neighborhood spaces. This situation was well described by Madge (1950) in discussing housing developments in England:

It seems probable that the relationship between the house and neighboring houses has a lot to do with early social development. Under living conditions where a child is able to move freely into other people's houses and gardens, and where other children visit its own house and garden, the parental body will be extended by a series of analogies, to include a whole group of houses and even a neighborhood, village or town. Early restriction on this freedom of movement would tend to produce a generation that keeps itself to itself. (p. 193)

One indicator of the maturing spatial conceptualization of children are their *cognitive mapping skills*. There is considerable evidence that school-aged children are capable of rather sophisticated mapping skills. When children are asked to draw a map of their neighborhood, the results indicate a good understanding of major features of the area (Ladd, 1970). Figure 8.3 shows two cognitive maps of the same neighborhood—one by a preschooler, the other by an eight-year-old child.

Children learn about the environment in two ways (Ittelson, et al., 1974):

1. First, children learn to orient themselves in an environment by relating to certain objects or reference points. This is a basic prerequisite for all future activity in the neighborhood—the knowledge of "what is where" and the resulting boost in self-esteem.
2. In the second place, the children learn the *social* features of the environment; specifically, they learn what spaces are accessible to them, what "rules" govern the use of those spaces, and *how well* they perform activities in those spaces. Some of these self-evaluative activities will be discussed later when we examine children in the peer group and the

FIGURE 8.3 Cognitive maps of a neighborhood. (The top drawing is by a 5-year-old pre-schooler; the bottom map is by an eight-year-old child.)

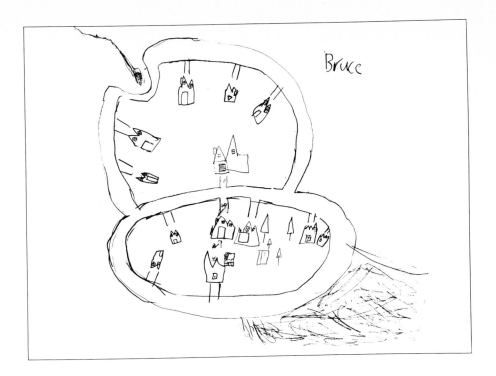

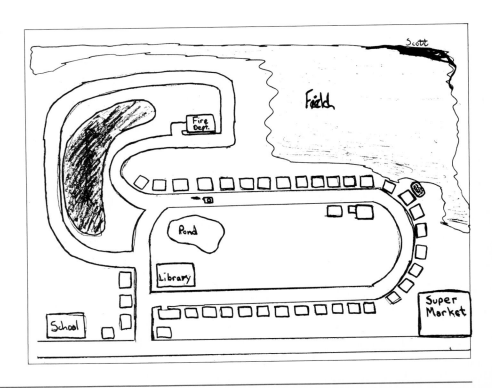

Middle Childhood: A Cultural Beginning

school. As children move gradually "out" of the home and family and "into" the community, they become aware of relevant social factors that have an impact on the self-evaluation or self-concept (e.g., the race, religion, and socioeconomic status of the family).

THE SCHOOL AS A CONTEXT FOR DEVELOPMENT

Almost all children between the ages of six and sixteen spend a considerable amount of time in a classroom. The learning of school skills, as well as the social changes in the child that the school fosters, produces changes in the child's self-concept. In this section, we focus on these changes in the child's conception of self and the characteristics of the school that support these changes.

The education of children has been a field that has spawned numerous debates on many issues, including the following:

- Is it more important for schools to train people for specific jobs or to provide them with a general or "liberal" education?
- Should all children be exposed to the same curriculum, or should there be special programs for the gifted or the disadvantaged?
- Should school programs be designed to foster learning directed by the teacher ("traditional" classroom), or should learning be organized around the children's interests ("open" classroom)?

In our examination of the school-aged child, we shall be concerned not only with some of these issues but with those that specifically address the situation of the child in the elementary school, including the following:

- What are the characteristics of teacher–child relationships?
- How do teachers help the child develop a positive self-concept?
- What impact do family and peers have on the child's performance in school?
- What challenges confront the child on entering the school?

The First Time in School: Some Adjustments. When the child enters the formal school for the first time, two major adjustments are made.

Learning to Read and to Write. Once the child has mastered the basic structures of his or her language by developing speech and oral communication skills in the preschool years, the child has now to direct his or her efforts toward understanding the relationship between *oral* communication and *written* language.

Social Adjustments. When the child first enters the school, he or she is confronted with several social changes that require some adjustment.

In the first place, the child must adjust to a change of schedule. Instead of the freedom of doing almost whatever she/he wanted to do in the home setting, the child must adjust to a planned set of activities that may or may not be to her or his liking.

Second, the child is exposed to a new adult known as the teacher. The teacher may not be like the child's parent(s), or like other adult figures whom the child may have been around.

Child Vulnerability, Learned-Helplessness, and Parents: A Systems Perspective

While it is undoubtedly important for parents to provide appropriate support and nurturance for the growing child, the contribution of the child to his or her own development is equally important. Put another way, why is it that children from apparently similar environments "turn out" so differently? How much influence do parents really have?

THE MYTH OF PARENTAL DETERMINISM

Theoretical perspectives on parenting—and child care based on these perspectives—have frequently focused on two major ideas. The first is that children are *vulnerable* and sensitive beings who are easily damaged by traumatic events or, in some cases, by too much affection. This viewpoint has emerged from Freudian theories of childhood trauma as the root cause of adult problems. (See discussion of Freudian theory in Chapter Two). Secondly, children have, with equal frequency, been viewed as completely *malleable* or capable of being shaped into any type of person by conscientious parents. This view has emerged from the traditional behaviorist perspective (see discussion of this theory in Chapter Two). This viewpoint is well exemplified by the behaviorist J. B. Watson (1928) who once said, "Give me a dozen healthy infants, well-formed, and my own specified world to bring them up in and I'll guarantee to take any one at random and train him to be any type of specialist I might—doctor, lawyer, artist, merchant, chief, and yes, even beggarman and thief." Both the notions of vulnerability and malleability emphasize the power of the parent and the relative passivity of the child. *Only* if parents do the *right* things will their children turn out alright. The corollary to this is, of course, that if something goes wrong, then it is entirely the parent's fault.

Current research provides a correction for such an overemphasis on parental power and control. It is now recognized that children are not passive receivers of information and, furthermore, that all children do not respond in the same way to what

may seem to be similar environmental situations. Rather, children's needs, as well as their developing physical and mental qualities, influence their perceptions of external events (Lerner and Spanier, 1978; Lerner and Busch-Rossnagel, 1981).

Furthermore, many studies that claim to demonstrate the impact of parents on children could just as easily be interpreted as demonstrating, instead, the impact of children on parents (Bell, 1968). For example, a study that indicates a correlation between severe parental punishment and child aggression might be interpreted as suggesting that punishment leads to aggression. However, such a study could just as well be interpreted as showing that aggressive children produce harsh disciplinary practices in their parents.

In addition, the notion of parental determinism does not take into account the fact that parent–child interactions occur in the *context* of the complex reality of daily life. In *systems* terminology, this means that the quality of parent–child relationships is influenced by the significant contexts in which the family finds itself (e.g., community, neighborhood, and parental work arrangements).

The reciprocity of parent–child interaction, as well as the fact that parent–child interaction is imbedded within other contexts, should *not* be taken to imply that parents exercise no influence over or responsibility for the outcomes of child development. Rather, the distinction should be carefully made between *influence* and *control*. Parents exercise influence over their children but so do other forces. Parents do not have complete control over their child's development, nor should they, as some would argue.

RETROSPECTIVE AND LONGITUDINAL RESEARCH ON THE CONSEQUENCES OF CHILDHOOD EXPERIENCE

The notion that childhood stress must inevitably result in an adult who is scarred for life is all too frequently accepted uncritically. Frequently, evidence for this notion is based on retrospective studies in the clinical literature that begin with adults who have problems and then trace these problems back to their childhood origins. It is, of course, true that when clinical psychologists, psychiatrists, or counselors examine the background experiences of delinquents or mental patients they may indeed find that a substantial number came from "broken" homes or homes characterized by disturbed interactions. Frequently, the conclusion is that these conditions of childhood have *caused* the delinquency or emotional disturbances of adulthood. However, the fact remains that the majority of children who are exposed to such conditions in childhood still manage to emerge later as adequate, normal adults. In addition, studies of "normal" or "superior" people (e.g., scientists, professionals, executives, or well-known artists) also find "unhealthy" childhood environments in the same or greater proportion as that of troubled adults (Goertzel and Goertzel, 1978).

Longitudinal research has, for the most part, failed to support the notion of inevitably troubled and scarred adults emerging from disturbed childhood backgrounds. MacFarlane (1964) followed approximately 200 children from infancy through early adulthood (age 30). Initial predictions were that those children from troubled backgrounds would grow up to be troubled adults and that those from good backgrounds would turn out to be well-adjusted adults. The researchers were *wrong* in approximately two-thirds of their predictions. They had overestimated the impact of *both* traumatic and seemingly positive environments on children. Surprisingly, many of the children who had come from apparently "good" childhood backgrounds turned out to be unhappy or immature adults (this pattern was particularly the case for boys who had been athletic stars and girls who were popular and attractive in high school).

Further support for the weak link between early traumatic or pathological conditions and later development comes from research on children who do well despite genetic or environmental disadvantage. Garmezy studied children who were thought to be at high risk to develop schizophrenia as adults (because of possible genetic predisposition, environmental circumstances, or both) (Garmezy, 1976; Garmezy and Rutter, 1983). He found that only 10 to 12 percent actu-

ally became schizophrenic, while the vast majority did not. The British psychiatrist Michael Rutter has also done extensive research which suggests that a surprisingly large number of children turn out to be normal and successful adults despite disadvantaged or even brutalized childhoods (Garmezy and Rutter, 1983).

A SYSTEMS PERSPECTIVE TO VULNERABILITY AND COMPETENCE IN CHILDREN

If there is no perfectly clear or precise relationship between childhood background and adult status, then why are some children *vulnerable* to stress and others not? As we might expect the answer is neither simple nor complete at this time. However, the application of the systems orientation which has been used in this book may help one to understand the issue more clearly.

In the first place, the fact that family relationships occur in the context of a neighborhood and a community suggests a possible relationship between the community and both family and child competence (i.e., a positive adaptive response to the environment). In fact, the local community may have a distinct role in modulating the impact of stressful home environments on the child (Cochran and Brassard, 1979). In a study of child rearing in six cultures, Whiting and Whiting (1975) found that parent behavior toward children was based less on the parent's principles or beliefs about child rearing than on a whole host of community or ecological factors. These factors included such things as the design of neighborhoods and housing, the social support networks within the community, work pressures, the pressures of daily household work, and the availability of alternate adults (other than parents) to help with the responsibilities of child care (see Application Box—Child Development and Personal Social Networks, p. 258).

In addition to the fact that parent–child relationships do not occur in a vacuum, the apparent vulnerability (or invulnerability) of children to stress may be related to learned aspects of children's personalities. From time to time, various terms such as *resilience, competence,* or *coping skill* have been used to describe this positive and adaptive quality of child personality. More recently, the psychologist Martin Seligman has used the term *learned-helplessness* to describe what makes a child vulnerable to stress (Seligman, 1975; Garber and Seligman, 1980). He suggests that people may "give up" in despair when faced with a potentially frustrating or traumatic situation *not* necessarily because of the actual severity of the experience but because they *feel* they have little or no *control* in changing it. According to Seligman, this sense of incompetence or helplessness is actually *learned* when people experience situations or events which they cannot control or are led to believe they cannot control.

By applying the concept of *learned-helplessness* to the findings of MacFarlane and others discussed above, we may be able to resolve some apparent contradictions. For example, why was it that children from apparently good or "ideal" homes in the MacFarlane study turn out to be somewhat discontented or poorly adapted adults? Or why was it that so many children from apparently troubled families turned out to be normal and stable adults? The theory of *learned-helplessness* suggests that a child's sense of competence or self-esteem depends not on whether positive or negative things happen but on whether the child perceives that he or she has some control over what happens. Is it possible then, that in some "ideal" homes good things happened to the children completely *independent* of any effort or control by the child? Likewise, is it possible that some children from troubled families were able to actively adapt or "make the best" of a given situation? Thus, the principle of learned-helplessness suggests that a sense of competence is more likely to emerge from a sense of "controlled stress" than from good or bad things happening without any contribution on the child's part. The late poet Dylan Thomas put it best when he said, "There's only one thing that's worse than having an unhappy childhood and that's having a too-happy childhood" (Ferris, 1977).

In summary the roots of vulnerability lie in the relationship of the child to the family and, in turn, in the relationship of the family to the community. We refer to these relationships as the *system* of childhood. Within this system parents do not exercise unrestricted and absolute control, however, they make a valuable contribution to the development of child competence by both encouraging and modeling positive self–control and adaptation.

Along with these differences of teacher personality and role, the child may, at first, feel lost in a crowd of children. Whereas the ratio of adults to children was much lower in the informal setting of the home, the child may now be one of fifteen or twenty children in a classroom with only one adult—the teacher.

The Role of Teachers. The kinds of teachers that children have greatly influence whether their school experience will foster development or will simply increase difficulties and frustrations. The teacher's general attitudes and actions may appear to the child to be similar to those of the child's parents. This is particularly true if they are from the same social class. Many young children, therefore, react to the teacher as though he/she were a substitute parent. The motives, attitudes, fears, and overt behavior that children have developed in relation to their parents are likely to be generalized to the teacher. Because most elementary-school teachers are women, children, especially boys, sometimes view school activities as more related to femininity than to masculinity (and, therefore, as more appropriate for girls than for boys) (Kagan, 1964; Kellogg, 1969). In this country, the teacher's values are usually middle-class. He or she rewards neatness, obedience, cooperation, and cleanliness; he or she punishes waste, lack of responsibility, lying, and aggression. Many teachers feel that stealing, cheating, lying, and disobedience are the most serious offenses that a young child can commit.

Teachers can have a profound influence on students.

Photograph by Gale Schiamberg

Most children respond to the beginning of school with favorable anticipation, and these feelings are usually maintained by most children, at least through the earliest school years (Stendler and Young, 1951). Young children exposed to warmer, more encouraging teachers were found to be more constructive when faced with possible failure and to be more involved in classroom activities (Pippert, 1969). Most children seem to do best under well-trained teachers who are *authoritative* but not either *authoritarian* or *permissive*. The *authoritative* teacher, unlike the *authoritarian* teacher, encourages individual initiative, self-esteem, and social responsibility. Unlike the *permissive* teacher, the *authoritative* teacher provides guidance, ultimate direction, and sets standards and goals.

Teacher Expectations and Student Behavior. Most educators are in fairly close agreement that a talented teacher is a vital force in influencing the child's performance in school. There is disagreement, however, on exactly why and how teachers influence students.

One of the most interesting ideas about the interaction of teachers and children is the so-called Pygmalion hypothesis (Rosenthal and Jacobson, 1968). The major idea is that teachers' expectations (whether high or low) may influence the level of student performance (high or low) independently of the child's actual ability (as measured by standardized tests). Rosenthal and Jacobson (1968) arbitrarily divided a group of children from low-income families into two groups, which they labeled "potential bloomers" and "nonachievers." The children in each group were matched so that both groups were comparable in measured IQ. The experimenters then informed the teachers of the "groups" to which each child belonged. At a later time, it was found that the children who were labeled "potential bloomers" had done significantly better than the "nonachievers." Rosenthal and Jacobson concluded that the teachers' expectations of the children had been influenced by the arbitrary grouping and labeling of the children.

Although there has been some support for the Pygmalion hypothesis (Pippert, 1969), there have been many criticisms. Specifically, the teacher's expectations are transmitted through the teacher's actual behavior and not in some general or unspecified manner. Furthermore, the teacher's expectations are a function of "realistic" indicators of performance, such as cumulative records and other teachers' recommendations, rather than general statements from "outside" sources, as in the Rosenthal and Jacobson research.

Given the significance of teachers' expectations in influencing children's success in the school, an important question concerns the *source* of these expectations. Where do teachers' expectations come from? Several factors appear to influence the development of teachers' expectations about children's academic and social behavior, including socioeconomic status and race, and social setting of the school.

Socioeconomic status and race. As a result of many factors, including the transmission of values and attitudes toward people through child-rearing experiences and through such media as television, people (including teachers) develop expectations about many minority, ethnic, and social-class groups. Attitudes about racial and socioeconomic group can be easily transmitted and, unless questioned or examined, can become part of one's belief system. Furthermore, the very organization of neighborhoods in some cities may make it less likely that individuals will know people from various socioeconomic, racial, or national backgrounds. Unfavorable and even untrue biases can easily be developed about those people with whom we have little direct contact. As a result of these and other influences, some teachers may come to expect middle-class students to perform better than lower-class students (Cooper, Baron, and Lowe, 1975).

The social setting of the school. The child gradually comes to develop both a cognitive map of the neighborhood of residence and an understanding of how others "evaluate" her/his neighborhood and general social background (e.g., parents' occupational and social standing). These evaluations are often transmitted to the child, for the first time, by the teacher. Such communications are usually not "direct," in the form of overt statements about the teacher's perceptions of the child's racial or socioeconomic background. Such evaluations are often communicated in an indirect form, through the teacher's perceptions and evaluations of the *social setting* of the school. It is not very surprising, therefore, to find middle-class teachers who neither empathize with nor understand children from lower socioeconomic neighborhoods or different racial groups. Howe (1972) made an interesting study of novice teachers who had been warned to use the "firm" approach in dealing with ghetto youngsters. This approach led, unfortunately, to further defiance and low academic performance in the students that it was supposed to help. In many ghetto neighborhoods, the tendency for teachers to generate expectations based on social setting is even further aggravated by the tendency of most teachers to base their expectations of children on the performance of the children's older siblings (Seaver, 1973).

How Are Teachers' Expectations Transmitted? There are several ways in which teachers actively transmit their expectations of students' academic and social performance:

1. Teachers tend to *spend more time* with students who are perceived to be high achievers (Brophy and Good, 1970).

Middle Childhood: A Cultural Beginning

Technological innovations, such as home computers, can influence children's success in school.

Photograph by Janet Merchant

2. Teachers encourage more interaction and *generate more responsiveness* from children from whom they have high expectations (Rosenthal, 1973). For example, teachers call on students more often and pose harder and more challenging questions to them when the teachers have higher expectations.
3. Teachers may differentially assign students to particular reading or study groups on the basis of expectations of student performance. In an interesting study (Tuckman and Bierman, 1971), children who were placed in classes based on an overestimation of their abilities tended to perform better on standardized tests than children who had been placed in classes based on an underestimation of their talents.

The transmission of expectations can occur in several ways. The results may be good or bad, depending on what is transmitted. At any rate, it is usually a *self-perpetuating cycle* (see Figure 8.4). Teachers develop expectations that are then transmitted to the child. The child (particularly the child in the early school grades) may internalize these expectations and thus perform in accordance with these expectations (Tuckman and Bierman, 1971). This performance, in turn, leads to confirmation of the expectations of both the student and the teacher, which, of course, leads to the same expectations, and so on. Where expectations are low, there is always the danger that children will become locked into a self-perpetuating cycle of poor performance or failure.

The Role of the Family in Educational Development. Whatever the expectations that are encountered by the child in the school, it is the family that provides the cornerstone and the foundation of self-concept, self-esteem, and formal school skills. The role of the family in the educational development of the child is critical and sometimes goes unappreciated by both the school and the family itself. Although children may start their formal schooling as early as age five, it is the family that has been a dominant feature of their lives for many years before and that remains a vital force for many years after.

Ordinarily it is not until the child is in the sixth or seventh grade that the peer influence becomes more prominent than the influence of the family.

FIGURE 8.4   The transmission of teachers' expectations: a self-perpetuating cycle in the development of the child's self-concept.

Photograph by Mark Kubinec

Therefore, the child's values and behavior are significantly influenced by the family. An increasing amount of research has supported the critical role of the family (Coleman, Campbell, Hobson, McPartland, Mood, Weinfeld, and York, 1966; Jencks, Bartlett, Corcoran, Crouse, Eaglesfield, Jackson, McClelland, Mueser, Olneck, Schwartz, Ward, and Williams, 1979). For some 600,000 students, Coleman, et al. (1966) assessed the role of many factors in the academic success of the child, including the classroom (school characteristics), classmate–peer variables, and family background. He concluded that home environment (including parents' income and educational level) was the single most important factor in predicting the child's academic success. Next in importance were school characteristics (such as curriculum, quality of teachers, diversity and organization of instructional programs). Coleman's data seem to indicate that a supportive home environment can compensate for deficient school or community resources.

Parental Behavior and the Child's School Performance. In addition to parental income and educational level, which provide an overall level of support in the home environment, there is evidence that the parents' actual behavior with the child may be an important factor in the child's academic success. Parents of high achievers tend to be more accepting of their children than parents of underachievers (Hilliard and Roth, 1969). Furthermore, it is quite likely that underachievers may sense parental rejection and may attempt to gain parental attention by creating problems in school or even failing. When failure results in attention—and academic success does not (sometimes the most direct or easiest route to parental attention is failure)—the child can incorporate incompetence as part of the self-concept.

Other evidence (Bernstein, 1965; Hess and Shipman, 1965) suggests that there is a relationship between the language that parents use in working with their children and success in academic or problem-solving tasks. Bernstein (1965) suggested that parents of different social classes use different "behavioral or language codes" in organizing their children's behavior. For example, lower-socioeconomic-group parents may rely more than other parents on gestures, facial expressions, vocal intonations, and a general collection of "unwritten rules" to communicate with their children. Middle-class parents may use much more elaborate verbal communication, complete with detailed

Two different types of classrooms: on the far right is a traditional classroom; in the middle and below are two open classrooms.

Photographs right and center by Gale Schiamberg; photograph below by Darryl Jacobson

descriptions of the features of problems and school-related tasks (Bernstein, 1965, 1966; Hess and Shipman, 1965, 1966, 1968). Research has shown that these language differences were reflected in the manner in which parents interacted with children in both informal and formal problem-solving situations in the home. For example, middle-class parents tended to use language that was specific, instructive, varied, and tailored to the child's level of competency. On the other hand, lower-class parents tended to give very general and ambiguous directions, such as "Do it right!" or "Make sure it's good!" However, as we pointed out in our discussion of black English (see Chapter Seven), it is possible that the controlled environment of laboratory experiments does not reflect the permanent environment of the lower-socioeconomic-group or minority family. Therefore, the elaborate and effective language codes of these groups may not be apparent (Labov, 1970; Fein and Clarke-Stewart, 1973).

The Role of Classroom Organization. As we indicated in our discussion of the family, the role of the school and the classroom is clearly significant to the child's academic performance. The way the school or classroom is organized may go a long way toward supporting the child in the school. Although there have been numerous curricular and educational experiments—some more successful and some less—we will examine here only one feature of classroom organization: classroom type, that is, *traditional* or *open*.

The *traditional* classroom is ordinarily characterized by a structured arrangement of lessons and discipline as the best ways to achieve student learning. In such a classroom, the teacher is the authority (in both subject areas and discipline). The desks are typically arranged in rows, each child has an assigned seat, and the activities of the day are organized by the teacher.

Although the so-called traditional classroom has worked rather well for some children, the general awareness that educational development involves self-regulated and self-determined mastery of subject areas has led to the development of the *open* classroom. Although the open-classroom movement received a large boost from the transplantation of the so-called British primary school in the United States (Featherstone, 1971) and the "rediscovery" of Piaget in the 1960s, the origins and ideas of the open classroom can be traced back to the educational philosophy of John Dewey and the progressive education movement in the United States during the 1930s and 1940s (Dewey, 1943). The philosophy of the open classroom stresses the idea of the teacher and the student as cooperating partners in the learning process. The basic assumption is that children are naturally motivated to learn socially valued skills. Therefore, the function of education should be to tap this spontaneous interest in learning by providing the child with interesting choices of classroom activities. In other words, the classroom should be arranged so that each child moves at his or her own pace by making a choice of activities during the course of a school day. The child is viewed as an active "doer" and the teacher is considered a "facilitator" of learning. The child progresses in skill development by involvement with *concrete* materials and everyday problems and issues as the primary mode of developing competency in the formal school skills of reading, writing, mathematics, social studies, geography, and so on. Socially and emotionally, the emphasis of the open classroom is on the "here and now," as well as on the expression of the child's feelings and creativity (Spodek, 1971).

Furthermore, in the open classroom, the meaning of "good behavior" is different from its counterpart in the traditional classroom. In the traditional classroom, being "good" means attending to the lessons of the day, adjusting to the established routines, and, of course, looking to the teacher for help in difficult situations. In an open classroom, good behavior consists of exploration and interaction with peers initiated by the student. Talking in the classroom—a sometimes forbidden behavior in the traditional classroom—is favorably viewed in the open classroom as a way of seeking out the help and resources of peers.

Which type of classroom is the best? Although this issue is important, we need to ask "best for whom?" Although there is a great deal of *diversity* in what are called traditional and open classrooms, there appears to be an emerging consensus that, like anything else in education, no single method is perfect for everyone. Attempts to compare the effects of the traditional and the open classroom have supported this position. For example, Minuchin, Biber, Shapiro, and Zimiles (1969) found that some bright children in the least-structured or "open" classrooms floundered unproductively. They seemed "unable or unwilling to . . . express themselves even in their own terms" (p. 406). For some children, the open classroom was a stimulating experience, whereas for others, it was a source of tension and stress (Minuchin, 1976).

In addition, Minuchin, et al. (1969) found that there was little difference between children in either type of classroom in cognitive skills, but there were differences in pupil self-perceptions. Children from the open classrooms were more varied in their perceptions of themselves and seemed to be more open to variation in sex roles. On the other hand, children in traditional classrooms seemed to be more conventional in their perceptions of development and roles and to be more impersonal. Since the investigators were unable to control for the parent's reasons for selecting the classroom types for their children, it is possible that home influences might have been as likely an explanation for pupil differences as the classroom type.

THE PEER GROUP

Definition. The peer group in middle childhood is composed of same-sex individuals who all interact with one another to some extent. Its size is limited by the qualification that its members must interact with one another. Furthermore, its members usually share many common values as well as norms that govern the behavior of each child and the interaction between children. Usually there are status divisions in the peer group, so that some individuals assume a leadership role whereas others are followers. Peer groups are stable over time. A peer group is defined by Hartup (1970) as follows:

a relatively stable aggregation of two or more children who interact together, who share norms and goals, and who have developed some division of roles and status which governs their interaction. (p. 457)

Functions. Children learn valuable things about themselves as a result of peer interaction. The peer group provides an opportunity for the following experiences.

Which Type of Classroom Is Best?

This research (Minuchin, et al., 1969) . . . concentrated on an intensive study of fourth-grade, middle-class children in a small number of modern and traditional schools. The schools, parents, and 105 children were studied over a two-year period. Each child was seen in six individual sessions involving interviews; intelligence, achievement and problem-solving tests; and a variety of projective and semistructured activities, including a play session, story telling . . . The aims were to tap the child's development in areas of intellectual mastery, interpersonal perception and self concept, and to compare children from the different school environments.

The clearest differences appeared in relation to self-perception and attitude. In these matters, a different value system was in formation and there appeared to be a different style of thought as well. Children from traditional environments had the more impersonal self images and the more conventionally structured images of social roles and possibilities. They were generally more oriented toward the future and saw their own development as a growth into organized, preordained roles. Children from modern environments, especially the girls, were more differentiated in their self-perceptions. They had more open conceptions of the boundaries and value of typical social roles, were more psychologically invested in their current lives as children, and projected more individualized images of the future.

From Minuchin, *The Middle Years of Childhood.* Monterey, Calif.: Brooks/Cole, 1977, pp. 119–120.

The Opportunity to Learn How to Interact with Age-mates. Mutual interaction skills that have been developing during the infant, toddler, and preschool years are now extended and refined in group activities. The ability to interact with parents, siblings, and a few playmates (the social skills of the preschool period) are extended to include relations between the self and numerous peer group members.

Peer relationships in middle childhood.

Photograph by Sylvia Byers

The Contexts of the Middle Childhood System

Man wishes to be confirmed in his being by man, and wishes to have a prescience in the being of the other. . . . secretly and bashfully he watches for a Yes which allows him to be and which can come to him only from one human person to another.

Martin Buber, *The Knowledge of Man.* New York: Harper & Row Publishers, 1965.

This total relationship has the characteristics of a *dynamic system* as individuals interact together in governing and organizing both individual and group behavior.

Included in the social skills that are learned are the ability to deal with hostility and dominance. How does the child learn to handle hostility in both herself or himself and other children? This skill is usually developed in the *context* of the peer group. Here the individual child learns to organize his or her responses in terms of peer-group norms that establish appropriate patterns of responding to hostility.

SCENARIO:
"BAD DAY AT SANDBOX FLATS" OR
THE RESOLUTION OF PEER CONFLICTS

Our two brothers, Scott and Bruce, have been playing in the neighborhood sandbox-playground area with several of Scott's eight-year-old age-mates. Things have been going fairly well as everyone seems involved in "developing" what appears to be an interstate highway system complete with toy automobiles, rest areas, and several campers and recreational vehicles. Unbeknownst to our industrious road workers, a danger to their work is approaching. Baby Elizabeth (now one and a half years old) and her friend Todd the Toddler (who have been playing together in another area of the playground under the supervision of Elizabeth's mother) have spied what looks like something going on at the other end of the playground—beyond the swings and the monkey bars. With the direct speed of a tornado about to happen, Elizabeth and Todd make a beeline directly to the sandbox. Our brothers, Scott and Bruce, and their friends (Jeffrey, Michael, Brian, and Johnny) have meanwhile gone to fetch some water for construction. While they are gone, the irrepressible Elizabeth and her assistant have traveled through the sandbox (after all, what is a highway system for, anyway?) when our boys return to find the remains of a once formidable development.

Hostility and conflict ensue. It turns out that during a debate prior to going for water, it was suggested by one faction that some of the group remain behind to guard the road construction. Jeffrey and Michael are upset with the others for not listening to them. "See, I told 'ya what would happen!" comes the refrain.

There are, of course, several possible resolutions to the conflict—some constructive and some not: (1) physical aggression; (2) verbal aggression; (3) leaving the scene; (4) crying; (5) pouting and tantrums; and (6) starting the project again. Although each child might prefer one or more of these solutions, it is the total group that arrives at a consensus as to what constitutes appropriate responses to the conflict. As the boys try to decide what to do, it is apparent that they are watching one another to determine mutually appropriate responses to the situation. Johnny starts to shout at Bruce and vice versa. Both boys are quickly told by the older boys that shouting isn't going to help matters. The solution that the boys finally decide on is to rebuild the road project.

Meanwhile the Baby Elizabeth and her friend Todd are looking for something to do . . .

The Opportunity to Organize and Evaluate One's Self-concept. The way in which peers react to the child and the bases on which he or she is accepted or rejected give the child a clearer and a perhaps more realistic picture of personal assets and/or liabilities.

If we watch a group of children during a free-play period such as recess or lunchtime at school, it is apparent that a process of selection is going on. One child may appear to be surrounded by numerous children. Another child may be alone in a corner of the lunchroom. Still another group of children may sit together in one area of the lunchroom almost every day, forming a tightly knit group.

One technique that psychologists and other social scientists use to study these group relationships is called the *sociogram* (Moreno, 1934). The sociogram is a relatively simple map of the relationships within a group (see Figure 8.5). Usually children are asked preference questions such as "Which three of your classmates do you like the best?" or "Which three of your classmates would you pick as your teammates for a game of tag?" The preference questions may refer to a number of tasks, for example, going on trips, working on a classroom project, or playing together on a sports team. As a result, a number of status skills can be tapped in addition to simple "popularity." Where a sociogram indicates a large number of arrows going toward a particular child, that child is sometimes called a *star*. Likewise, where a disproportionately small number of arrows are drawn toward an individual, that child may be called an *isolate*.

FIGURE 8.5 A sociogram is used to determine the network of relationships within a group. In this diagram, the members of a fifth-grade class have indicated their choice of classmates as best friends.

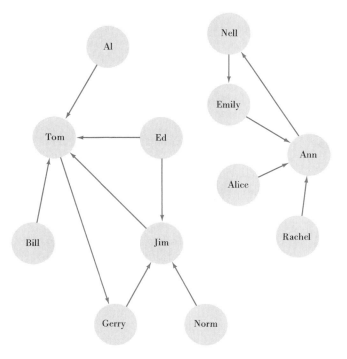

The Contributions of the Gang (Peer Group)

Gang influence . . . provides important benefits. Playmates force a child to face the realities of his world. In short order and in no uncertain terms, they teach what is acceptable and what is not.

"You brag too much," "I don't want to play with a cheater!" "You poor sport! You always pout when you lose," "Why don't you wash your hair once in a while? It stinks!" "Quit griping; he didn't mean to do it!" "Drop dead!" No, children are not noted for tact and gentleness. They are brutally frank, if not downright cruel, in their honesty with one another. They socialize with blunt, sledge-hammer comments.

As if sensing that moving from the family causes insecurity, youngsters pad their world with rigid rituals that are passed on to succeeding groups of children. . . . It may be only a game of hide-and-seek, but if Paul is "it" and doesn't say, "Here, I come, ready or not" after he's counted to ten, he has eight important people in his life screaming, "Cheater!" "Unfair!" "You didn't do it right!" Tempests in teapots. But they underscore the need for solid structure outside as the youngster edges away from the family nest.

From D. C. Briggs, *Your Child's Self-Esteem.* New York: Doubleday, 1975, pp. 141–142.

Ordinarily each peer group has members who are popular and others who are not as popular. Several factors seem to be related to this differentiation:

1. *The individual child's overall personality and adjustment.* On the whole, peer acceptance seems to be related to such personality factors as enthusiasm, sensitivity, active participation in group activities, and a cheerful, friendly disposition. This type of general adjustment (or lack of it) seems to be supported in a "circular" fashion; that is, children who are liked have their popularity supported, which probably encourages them to continue to be well adjusted, which, in turn, leads to popularity, and so on. For unpopular children, negative personality features such as dejection and dourness also tend to be circularly supported (Glidewell, Kantor, Smith, and Stringer, 1966).
2. *The intelligence of the child.* Usually children who are popular with their peers are intelligent and have reasonably high IQs (Roff and Sells, 1965). Slow learners do not usually enjoy the broad support of their peers.
3. *Athletic skills.* An important factor in contributing to popularity among boys—particularly in the early elementary-school grades—is athletic skill. One of the organizing features of the early elementary period— particularly in the school setting—is the playground and related sports areas.

Developmental Trends in the Formation of Peer Groups. As we have indicated, the role of the peer group is important throughout middle childhood. Between ages six and eleven, there is a general shift in the overall structure and meaning of the peer group to the child.

During the early years of middle childhood, peer groups are largely *informal* and usually have the following characteristics:

1. They are usually formed by the children themselves (as opposed to such organizational groupings as the Scouts or Campfire Girls, which are organized and supervised by adults).

Middle Childhood: A Cultural Beginning

2. They have few formal rules for governing their operation or the interaction of the participants.
3. There is a rapid turnover in membership. Children come and go with relatively little difficulty. Expediency and proximity appear to be the major criteria for membership.
4. Groups are organized according to sex.

When children reach the age of about ten, the peer group takes on a more intense meaning for its members. The structure of the peer organization becomes more formal and solidified. Aspects of formal organization, such as special membership requirements and rituals for initiation, become common.

APPLICATION BOX

Huckleberry Finn, Tom Sawyer, and the "Rules" of the Peer Group

One of the important functions of the peer group is to familiarize the child with the nature of group goals, expectations, and rules. In the following passage from *Huckleberry Finn*, Mark Twain describes what happens when Huck and Tom Sawyer try to help the slave Jim escape. At first, Huck wants simply to open the shack door. However, Tom reminds him that it must be a "proper escape" in accordance with the unwritten rules of the peer group.

Well, if that ain't just like you, Huck Finn. You can get up the infant-schooliest ways of going at a thing. Why, hain't you ever read any books at all?—Baron Trenck, nor Casanova, nor Benvenuto Chelleeny, nor Henri IV, nor none of them heroes? Who ever heard of getting a prisoner loose in such an old-maidy way as that? No, the way all the best authorities does is to saw the bed leg in two, and leave it just so, and swallow the sawdust, so it can't be found, and put some dirt and grease around the sawed place so the very keenest seneskal can't see no sign of its being sawed, and thinks the bed leg is perfectly sound. Then, the night you're ready, fetch the leg a kick, down she goes; slip off your chain, and there you are. Nothing to do but hitch your rope ladder to the battlements, skin down it, break your leg in the moat—because a rope ladder is nineteen foot too short you know—and there's your horses and your trusty vassles, and they scoop you up and fling you across a saddle, and away you go to your native Languadoc, or Navarre or wherever it is. It's gaudy, Huck. I wish there was a moat to this cabin. If we get time, the night of the escape, we'll dig one.

From Clemens, S., *Huckleberry Finn*, 1962.

Peer pressures become more apparent and assume a sometimes coercive influence.

Play: Games with Rules. During early childhood, play is characterized by make-believe games and the use of symbols or imagery. Such sociodramatic play reaches its peak during the period from four to six years. With the onset of middle childhood, games, often competitive or team activities, become structured by rules. These rules may specify such things as who may participate, how many participants may play, what the participants can or cannot do. From a developmental perspective, the appearance of organized play with games at age five or six occurs at a time when children are now able to do things that they were unlikely to do at an earlier age. These new skills include the following (Garvey, 1977):

1. The ability of the child to engage in sustained social interactions of a cooperative or competitive nature.
2. The ability to plan and carry out purposeful activities over a longer period of time.
3. The ability to use self-control and to submit voluntarily to the restrictions of game rules.

Games with rules appear to have a "natural history" that goes back to the infant's early social interactions with caretakers. Bruner and Sherwood (1976) observed how regularities or patterns of interaction evolve into rule-structured events in mother–infant interactions. Bruner found that most of the mother–infant pairs he studied played the game of peek-a-boo. Peek-a-boo is a game that depends on mutual interaction and the repetition of the same movements. Garvey (1977) described the rule structure of this *mutual following game* in this way:

Initiator's Turn	Recipient's Turn
Round 1:	
Move 1 Attract R's attention	Give attention to I
Move 2 Hide object, self, or R, optional vocalization	Look for
Move 3 Reveal	Appreciate
Move 4 Reestablish contact	Reestablish contact
(simultaneous)	
Round 2:	
Optional repetition of the whole game, with or without permissible variations.	

Much like these infant–caretaker interactions, games in middle childhood require cooperation and rules. The rules are, however, more explicit and can be communicated and learned by the participants. The first peer games are usually cooperative ventures such as ring-around-the-rosy (Garvey, 1977). At ages seven to nine, competitive games become popular.

Far right photograph by Wayne Mason; right photograph by Darryl Jacobson

THE IMPACT OF THE CULTURE ON THE DEVELOPING CHILD: TELEVISION — A SPECIFIC EXAMPLE

A discussion of the contexts of development in middle childhood would be incomplete without a look at the role of television. The reason is that television occupies a great deal of time in the child's life as well as providing children with many ideas and impressions about facets of life such as sex roles, violence, occupational roles, and family life. Bronfenbrenner (1970) has expressed some concern about the impact of television on families and children:

"Don't you understand? This is life, *this is what is happening. We* can't *switch to another channel."*

Drawing by Robert Day; © 1970 The New Yorker Magazine, Inc.

Why Bother with Play?

Why bother with play? The main reason is that life is generally dull. Often it is downright boring. Anything that makes life a little more interesting is an improvement; and if it makes life exciting, that is a special event. . . . Play makes us enjoy being with each other a lot more. It makes us think life is a little more worth living. As such, play is a rare and life-giving feast. That is why we should bother with it. . . . You may say that children first have to learn how to work; and furthermore, you may be too busy to show them how to play. . . .

But work is not what it used to be. For most people work is not carpet weaving or cattle herding or road shoveling any longer. Work is going in to an advertising agency, a marketing research company, or a classroom and coming up with a new idea. To be successful in the modern world, to keep up with the enormous amounts of new information, and to try to handle the new ways of life thrown at you by a changing society, you

have to be versatile. You have to be able to create, but you also must be able to adapt to other points of view. The word "versatile" means two things here: creative and flexible. If a person is creative but not flexible, he may put out the wrong product. If he is flexible but not creative, he may know what the smart thing to do is, but he may not be able to produce. A versatile person has both qualities. . . .

What do we know about versatile people? We know they are more playful. Stated in another way, playful people are more versatile.

This is a staggering discovery. For centuries we have believed that playful people were wasting their time.

From Brian and Shirley Sutton-Smith, *How to Play with Your Children (and When Not to).* Copyright © 1974 by Brian and Shirley Sutton-Smith. Reprinted by permission of the publisher, Hawthorn Books, a Division of Elsevier-Dutton Publishing Co., Inc.

Like the sorcerer of old, the television set casts its magic spell, freezing speech and action, turning the living into silent statues so long as the enchantment lasts. The primary danger of the television screen lies not so much in the behavior it produces—although, there is a danger there—as in the behavior it prevents: the talks, the games, the family festivities and arguments through which much of the child's learning takes place and through which his character is formed. Turning on the television set can turn off the process that transforms children into people. (p. 5)

Television and Violence. Because preschool children have relatively little ability to distinguish between fiction and reality, they are more likely than other age groups to be affected by television violence. On the whole, it appears that violent cartoons may instigate young children to aggressive behavior (Ellis and Sekyra, 1972; Lovaas, 1961; Mussen and Rutherford, 1961; Siegel, 1956). Repeated exposure to violent programming seems either to increase or to maintain whatever effects have been initially created by the viewing of violence (Friedrich and Stein, 1973).

Developmental changes during middle childhood tend to reduce the likelihood of children's demonstrating aggression. These developmental changes include more behavioral cognitive controls, the ability to separate fact from fiction, and more sensitivity to adult prohibitions against aggression. School-aged children are more likely than preschoolers to experience anxiety reactions to violence, which may initially reduce the expression of aggression.

However, even these anxiety reactions appear to decline with increased viewing of violence (Bandura, 1969; Goranson, 1970; Cline, Croft, and Courrier, 1973).

In summary, viewing television violence appears to increase the likelihood of aggressive behavior across all age groups, including the adolescent (Hartmann, 1969; Stein and Friedrich, 1975; Feshback and Singer, 1971, 1972; Leifer and Roberts, 1972). Children of both sexes from a wide range of social classes and of varying ages appear to respond to television violence with aggression. Children who by habit are more aggressive are more likely to respond aggressively to violent television programs. The children who are likely to have aggression anxiety are least likely to behave aggressively in response to televised violence. However, the impact of aggression anxiety appears to be lessened with repeated viewing of violent television programs. This finding has led some to suggest that repeated viewing of violence tends to "harden" children or to make them indifferent to violence happening in real-life situations (see the discussion of prosocial behavior in Chapter Seven). Also, if children are frustrated or are aroused by a competitive experience, they are more likely to behave aggressively by acting out viewed violence.

"The Farmer in the Dell"

For centuries small children of five to seven years of age have played ring games in which one person in the center got to act in a special way. The best known modern example is "The Farmer in the Dell," where the person in the center gets to choose the next person to come into the middle with him/her. So the farmer chooses a wife and the wife chooses a child, and the child chooses a dog, etc.

The choices are made as the children sing the following lyrics:

> Farmer in the dell,
> Farmer in the dell,
> Hi-ho the dairy-o,
> The farmer in the dell.
>
> The farmer takes a wife,
> The farmer takes a wife,
> Hi-ho the dairy-o,
> The farmer takes a wife.
>
> The wife takes a child . . .

It is clear that marriage and lover are imitated obliquely in these games. What is more important about them, however, is choosing and being chosen to go into the center. Here in game form is the experience of acceptance and rejection . . . as inclusion and exclusion . . .

Although today children do not express their apprehension about acceptance and rejection so often in ring games, they tend to show it more clearly in informal conversation about boy and girl friends. They also show it in informal games of chasing, in which the girls chase the boys or the boys chase the girls. . . . These games begin between five and seven years and may be played throughout childhood, getting more boisterous and rough until about twelve years. After that age children show more earnest concern for acceptance on grounds of personal appearance, adequacy and the like.

The Contexts of the Middle Childhood System

Children and Television

In order to understand the impact of television on children it isn't necessary to study all the latest reports on behavioral research. As an alternative, you can simply watch a child watching television.

What you will usually observe is an immobile, uncommunicative subject, oblivious to his surroundings, with a face devoid of expression and eyes that stare vacantly into space. . . .

It is television's subtle, "narcotic" effect on children which is concerning more and more parents and educators. . . .

Until now, we've barely scratched the surface in this area. Instead, the public pressure concerning television and children has focused on two more obvious issues: violence and advertising.

Limiting violence and advertising on programs for children, though, is only the first step toward making television a useful member of the average American family. To some extent, violence and advertising are issues that can be handled through laws and regulation. Dealing with the more subtle and complex effects of television, on the other hand, will require creative, individual responses from parents and children.

There is so much we don't know about television's long-term effects on children. But we have suspicions, and many, many questions. What role does television play in developing role models and value systems for children? Does it encourage a passive attitude toward life? Does it blunt a child's own imaginative powers, or his ability to play in a natural, creative way? Do "flashy" educational programs such as "Sesame Street" spoil children for the more regimented, difficult learning that comes in the classroom? By filling so much leisure time, does television inhibit the kind of personal, emotional discoveries that children so often make when they are truly alone with themselves?

Most important, what effect does television have on interaction within the family? . . . When the set is on, it discourages communication between brothers and sisters, children and parents. A family watching television is alone with each other. There is no need for the games, questions and even arguments that can help cement the family relationship. As one researcher recently asked after completing a 10-year study of how Americans use their leisure time: "I wonder if we aren't moving toward, or have arrived at, a society in which mass communication is more prevalent than interpersonal communication?"

In many cases, answers to these questions will be more personal than scientific.

Reprinted from E. Kittrell, "Children and Television: The Electronic Fix," *Children Today,* May–June 1978, pp. 20, 24–25, 36–37.

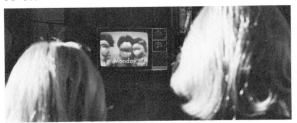

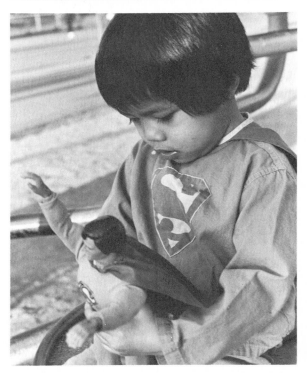

Top photograph by Janet Merchant; bottom photograph by Sylvia Byers

Watching Television and Physical Fitness— Coronary Prone Kids?

"Over the past fifteen to twenty years there has been a concerted effort by the allied medical professions to identify individuals who are susceptible to premature development of coronary heart disease (CHD)" (Gilliam, Katch, Thorland and Weltman, 1977, p. 21). Research by Gilliam and his associates has shown that young children are demonstrating increasingly high levels of conditions that are typically associated with heart disease in adults (e.g., high cholesterol levels, high blood pressure, and obesity). They found that almost 50 percent of a sample of 47 boys and girls aged 7 to 12 years showed one or more such risk factors.

In a preliminary study of the effects of exercise on the incidence of these risk factors in children, Gilliam found a reduction in risk factors due to exercise. He tested 63 third and fourth grade boys and girls, half of whom participated in a 12 week rigorous exercise program (25 minutes, four days a week) while the other half were in a typical physical education class (twice a week). Gilliam found that children in the experimental group with high blood lipids or fats (a risk factor) were able to significantly reduce these in the rigorous

12-week exercise program. Gilliam concludes that vigorous exercise programs should begin as early as the preschool years. Furthermore, these programs should be designed in such a fashion as to motivate youngsters to engage in strenuous exercise for health maintenance throughout their lives.

Adapted from Gilliam, T. B., Katch, V. L., Thorland W., and Weltman, A. "Prevalence of coronary heart disease risk factors in active children, 7 to 12 years of age," "Medicine and Science in Sports, 1977, 9, pp. 21–25.

The sedentary habits of young children may make them high-risk candidates for coronary heart disease.

Photograph by David Kostelnik

Television and Prosocial Behavior. Although the vast majority of research on children's television has focused on violence, television can—and does—teach children many forms of prosocial behavior. For example, children can learn about positive social behavior, self-regulation, and imagination. The majority of research on prosocial behavior has focused on the television program "Mr. Rogers' Neighborhood." This program appears throughout the United States on the Public Broadcasting Service (PBS) and focuses on social and emotional development. Kindergarten children who saw four episodes of "Mr. Rogers" learned about several themes, including helping a friend, trying to understand another's feelings, distinguishing between wanting something to happen and actually having it happen, and learning to value a person for inner qualities rather than for physical appearance (Friedrich and Stein, 1975; Collins, 1974). In some instances, these changes were accompanied by a reduction in aggression or a replacement of aggressive behavior by prosocial activity (Shirley, 1974; Singer and Singer, 1974). Prosocial programs for elementary-school-aged children (as opposed to preschoolers) are recent in origin. There is some evidence that such programs can be effective in conveying positive social messages. For example, the program "Fat Albert and the Cosby Kids" successfully communicated messages involving such events as the arrival of a new baby, divorce, and being proud of a father's job in spite of its social status (CBS Broadcast Group, 1974).

Social Knowledge and Cultural Stereotypes. Television is a potential influence on the quality and tenor of family life and the child's self-development through the information it provides about the world and its social structure and relationships. What social values are conveyed to child viewers about ethnic groups, sex roles, and age groups?

American television portrays white, middle-class, male adults as the most powerful figures of our society. Lower-class men, foreigners, blacks and women have been traditionally restricted to a limited—if not demeaning—set of roles (Barcus, 1971; Mendelson and Young, 1972; Ormiston and Williams, 1973). There has been an increasing attempt to portray blacks in more pres-

"AND NOW AN IMPORTANT MESSAGE FROM YOUR SPONSOR: GO OUTSIDE AND PLAY!"

DENNIS THE MENACE ® used by permission of Hank Ketcham and © by Field Enterprises, Inc.

Middle Childhood: A Cultural Beginning

tigious and powerful roles. The images and stereotypes presented on television are particularly important for activities and people with whom the child has little or no personal contact.

Although females predominate in the population, males are found far more frequently in television programming. For example, in prime-time television, 70 to 75 per cent of the leading characters are male (Tedesco, 1974; Gerbner, 1972). The differential power of men and women is often portrayed by males who have prestigious occupations and females who have no occupation aside from homemaker (Tedesco, 1974; Stein and Friedrich, 1975).

The portrayal of such stereotypes raises serious questions about the power of the television industry. Does television simply reflect the main-stream of existing biases and stereotypes? Whose ideals or values should be implemented? The implications of such questions are important to families and growing children:

One solution is for television to present a wider diversity of life as it is and as it might be. Children could then be made aware of a variety of possibilities for interpersonal relations, social roles, occupational activities and ethnic group attributes (Stein and Friedrich, 1975, p. 245).

Motor Development and Athletic Skills

By the end of early childhood, children have almost completed the development of the fundamental motor skills that will allow them to accomplish the sport and dance skills of middle childhood, adolescence, and adulthood (see Chapter Seven). The learning of these fundamental motor skills represents a proficiency barrier; that is, the development of motor skills in middle childhood is extremely difficult unless foundational early-childhood skills are de-

"There is so much we don't know about television's long term effects on children."

Drawing adapted from E. Kittrell, "Children and Television: The Electronic Fix." *Children Today*, May–June, 1978, p. 20, USDHEW.

veloped to a reasonable level. During middle childhood, fundamental motor skills are extended to simple games in play situations. For example, the child may begin to participate in such activities as street hockey or tag.

The types of activities in which children participate are very much related to the play activities common to middle childhood. Many of the games that are played involve the use of rules and the social understanding involved in coordinating one or more people in a mutual activity. For example, the game of tag requires the understanding of the rule that one child begins by trying to tag other children, who all join to try and tag the remaining children as they run within a bounded area. Such a game involves the fundamental motor skill of running coupled with more sophisticated dodging and balancing movements. As the child progresses through middle childhood, other fundamental motor skills such as catching, throwing, and hitting are coordinated in the performance of specific dance and sport skills such as baseball, football, volleyball, diving, and swimming. Relative competence in the performance of these skills is one part of the child's developing self-concept.

GENERAL CHARACTERISTICS (SIX TO TWELVE YEARS)

On the whole, the period between six and twelve years is a period of skill learning. The range and depth of the child's motor learning are determined largely by at least two factors:

1. The completion and refinement of fundamental motor skills.
2. And the child's opportunities for combining fundamental motor skills (e.g., throwing, hitting, and running) into game skills (e.g., baseball, volleyball, and Red Rover).

During this period, it is important that children engage in these motor activities, which will support their self-concepts and enhance their relationships with peers. Although much of this activity probably happens during free play, it is not always a certainty. The organization of neighborhoods and homes does not always ensure the development of motor skills.

Children who are six or seven years old are still perfecting fundamental motor skills and therefore may need more simple and less organized motor activities than older youngsters:

The younger learners like rhythmic and dramatic activities, movement exploration, simple stunts and games of low organization. They progress best with individualized instruction and individualized challenges. Beginning with the younger learners and then continuing instruction throughout the six to twelve period, youngsters should be taught how to use force and space, how to improve timing and coordination; this means that they should be helped to gain "good form" in their movements for this makes possible the greatest amount of precision, force, ease and poise. (Corbin, 1973, p. 156)

By about the age of twelve, children have developed about 90 percent of their potential mobility and speed of reaction (Corbin, 1980). Balance, speed, strength, and coordination seem to improve with time and minimal practice. All of these prerequisites for motor skill can be improved through physical activity (see Figure 8.6, p. 368).

Right photograph by Darryl Jacobson; photograph above by Wayne Mason

SPECIFIC SKILLS

Running. At the ages of four and five, there is continued improvement in the form and power used in running. This improvement results in the gradual development of the necessary control for efficient stopping, turning, and starting. By the time the child reaches five or six, the adult manner of running is fairly well established. Furthermore, running skills are now effectively integrated into most play activities. The level of achievement of skill in running (see Figure 8.7) is similar for both sexes and increases with age until adolescence, when the rate of girls' performance declines slightly and the performance of boys continues to improve (we will discuss the reasons for these apparent sex differences later).

Photograph by Darryl Jacobson

FIGURE 8.6 The aspects of physical fitness.

From Corbin, Charles B. *Becoming Physically Educated in the Elementary School*, 2nd ed., p. 54. Copyright © 1976 Lea and Febiger Publishing Company, Philadelphia. Reprinted by permission.

PHYSICAL FITNESS

Definition: Physical fitness is composed of many different aspects including health-related physical fitness aspects and motor fitness (skill-related) aspects. To function effectively in our society without undue fatigue and to have reserve energy to enjoy leisure time require adequate development of both the health-related and skill-related aspects of physical fitness. The important aspects of physical fitness are:

HEALTH-RELATED ASPECTS

Cardiovascular Fitness. The ability to persist in numerous repetitions of an activity. Specifically, this aspect involves development of the respiratory and circulatory systems of the body.

Flexibility. The ability to move joints through a full range of motion.

Strength. The ability to exert force such as lifting a weight or lifting your own body.

Muscular Endurance. The ability to persist in numerous repetitions of an activity involving strength.

COMBINED ASPECT

Explosive Power. The ability to display strength explosively or with speed.

MOTOR-FITNESS ASPECTS

Agility. The ability to change directions quickly and to control body movements (total body).

Reaction Time. The ability to perceive a stimulus, begin movement, and finally complete a response.

Balance. The ability to maintain body position and equilbrium both in movement and in stationary body positions.

Coordination. The ability to perform hand-eye and foot-eye tasks such as kicking, throwing, striking, and the like.

Speed. The ability to move from one place to another in the shortest possible time.

Jumping. Like running, jumping requires complex motor skills of form, balance, and maintenance of equilibrium. Because jumping requires the advanced skills of equilibrium and balance in negotiating an accelerated leap

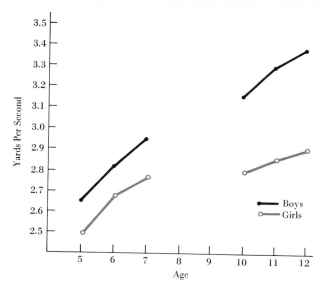

FIGURE 8.7 Endurance run performance in yards per second.

After Milne, Seefeldt, and Reuschlein [1975], Jackson and Coleman [1975], and Gutin, Fogle, and Stewart [1975]. From Corbin, Charles B., *A Textbook of Motor Development*, 2nd ed., p. 80. © 1973, 1980. Wm. C. Brown Publishers, Dubuque, Iowa. All rights reserved. Reprinted by permission.

and a decelerated stop, the child usually does not undertake jumping until some degree of proficiency has been attained in more basic locomotion skills. About 80 percent of children usually have a good mastery of jumping skills at around five years of age (Hellebrandt, Rarick, Glassow, and Carns, 1961). Like running, jumping proficiency increases in both sexes until around adolescence, when girls' performance begins to level off and boys' performance continues to increase (see Figure 8.8).

Throwing. Analysis of movies of youngsters (two to seven years old) throwing indicates that there are four types of throws (Wickstrom, 1977) (see Figure 8.9).

Anterior–Posterior Throw. The anterior–posterior throw is the least mature throw and is seen at two to three years of age. The major characteristic of this throw is that the movements of the arms and the body are confined to the anterior–posterior plane.

For the preparatory phase, the arm is drawn up either obliquely or frontally with a corresponding extension of the trunk until the object to be thrown is at a point high above the shoulder. During delivery the trunk straightens with a forward carry of the shoulder as the arm comes through in a stiff, downward motion. Both feet remain firmly in place with the body facing in the direction of the throw during both the preparatory phase and delivery of the projectile. (Eckert, 1973, p. 166)

Throwing with Horizontal Arm and Body Movement. During the period of three and one-half to five or six years of age, there is a major shift to throwing with horizontal arm and body movements. The horizontal arm movements and the body rotation provide additional momentum for the object being thrown. The feet remain together and in place during throwing (Corbin, 1980).

Weight Transfer in Throwing. At five or six years of age, a dramatic change in the throwing pattern occurs. This change is marked by the transfer of weight from one foot to the other during throwing. For example, a right-

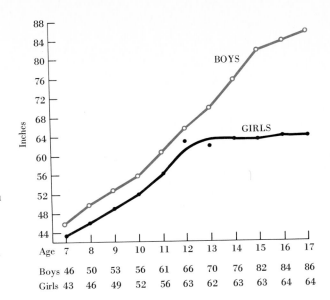

FIGURE 8.8 Standing long jump (based on data from seven studies [Keogh]).

From Corbin, Charles B. *A Textbook of Motor Development*, 2nd ed. Copyright © 1973, 1980. Wm. C. Brown Publishers, Dubuque, Iowa. All rights reserved. Reprinted by permission.

Age	7	8	9	10	11	12	13	14	15	16	17
Boys	46	50	53	56	61	66	70	76	82	84	86
Girls	43	46	49	52	56	63	62	63	63	64	64

Stage I
Anterior–Posterior
Throw

Stage II
Horizontal Arm and
Body Movement
Throwing

Stage III
Weight Transfer
in Throwing

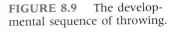

FIGURE 8.9 The developmental sequence of throwing.

From Wickstrom, R. L., *Fundamental Motor Patterns*, 2nd ed. Copyright © 1977 Lea and Febiger Publishing Company, Philadelphia. Reprinted by permission.

Stage IV
Mature
Overhead
Throw

Middle Childhood: A Cultural Beginning

handed child transfers his or her weight from the left foot to the leading right foot while throwing with the right hand. The transfer of weight coupled with the horizontal movement of arms and body produces greater power and distance in throwing than in the previous stage.

Mature Overhand Throw. The major characteristic of the mature overhand throw is a rearrangement of the foot patterning during the throw. For example, a right-handed child transfers body weight to the right rear foot during the preparatory phase of throwing and then takes a step forward onto the leading left foot as the object is thrown (Corbin, 1980).

By about the age of six, most children are proficient at the mature overhand throw. There appears to be a similar developmental pattern for throwing as for running and jumping, as the performance of boys continues to improve and girls' throwing tends to level off (Corbin, 1980) (see Figure 8.10).

SEX DIFFERENCES IN MOTOR SKILLS

The preceding discussion of running, jumping, and throwing indicates a similar pattern of slightly higher performance levels for boys than for girls until the onset of adolescence, when the differences become more marked in favor of boys. We will discuss the differences in adolescent physical growth that contribute, in part, to these sex-related performance differences in Chapter Nine. Here we will discuss several factors—both physical and social—that could contribute to the relatively slight performance differential between girls and boys six to eleven years of age.

In the first place, performance differences may be a reflection of the relationship between the greater height, weight, and limb length of boys from birth to adolescence. These factors give boys a slight mechanical and strength advantage in throwing objects. Averages in bone and muscle tissue favoring boys may also relate to the differential performance of boys and girls (Corbin,

FIGURE 8.10   Distance throw.

Figure 24.6, p. 330, in "Motor Development" by Anna Espenschade and Helen Eckert from *Science and Medicine of Exercise and Sport* (2nd ed.), edited by Warren R. Johnson and E. R. Buskirk. Copyright © 1974 by Warren R. Johnson and Elsworth R. Buskirk. Copyright © 1960 by Warren R. Johnson. Reprinted by permission of Harper & Row, Publishers, Inc.

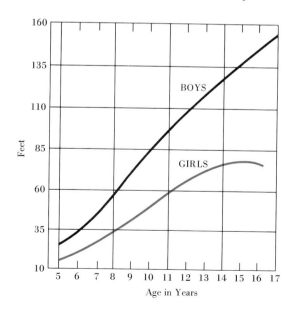

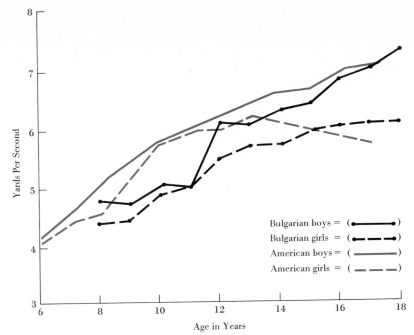

FIGURE 8.11 Curves of running performance for Bulgarian and American boys and girls.

From Espenschade, A. and Eckert, H. M., "Motor Development." In *Science and Medicine of Exercise and Sport*, 2nd ed. Edited by Warren R. Johnson and Elsworth R. Buskirk. Copyright © 1974 by Warren R. Johnson and Elsworth R. Buskirk. Copyright © 1960 by Warren R. Johnson. Reprinted by permission of Harper & Row Publishers, Inc.

1980; Espenschade and Eckert, 1980). However, it should be emphasized that although these differences in physical characteristics may account for a *slight* difference in performance between the sexes from six to eleven years, they are *not* great enough to account for the rather large sex differences at adolescence and beyond. It is possible that *social* and *cultural* factors influence the mean performance in throwing, jumping, and running so that performance differences are magnified at adolescence and beyond. In other words, it may be that the individual's efforts to consolidate and formulate an "identity" during the adolescent period may make him or her organize behavior in accordance with social–cultural sex-role expectations. Some evidence of the role of social–cultural factors in performance differences between sexes may be seen in cross-cultural comparisons. A comparison of scores of Bulgarian and American youngsters in running indicated that performance leveled off for American girls at ages thirteen to fifteen years, whereas Bulgarian girls continued to improve through age eighteen (Mangarov, 1964; Espenschade, 1960) (see Figure 8.11).

Cognitive Skills

During the years from five to seven, a number of qualitative changes occur in the child's thinking processes. These changes accompany the child's first years in the formal school. In our discussion of the preschool child's cognitive development, you will remember that Piaget characterized the four- to seven-year-old child as being in the *intuitive period*. Children in the intuitive period rely primarily on their perceptions and their direct experiences rather than on logical operations. Two major characteristics of the intuitive level of thinking (from which the school-aged child is emerging) are the following:

Middle Childhood: A Cultural Beginning

1. *Centering*. This is the ability of the child to focus on only one dimension or feature of a configuration at a time.
2. *Reversibility*. This is the ability of children to return in their thinking to the beginning of a sequence of behavior (e.g., when two equal beakers of water are poured into different-sized containers, the child can return, in his/her thinking, to the original condition of two equal amounts of water). The thinking of children in the intuitive period is *not* reversible.

As the intuitive period comes to an end, the child's thinking becomes more flexible, less dependent on perceptions, more dependent on logical operations, and more reversible.

Somewhere between five and seven years, the child begins to use what Piaget has called *operations*. Operations are mental activities that serve as the basis of thinking. This contrasts with the physical and perceptual activities that are primary features of thinking in infancy and the pre-school years. During the period from approximately seven to eleven years of age, the child's reasoning is often called *logical* because of this newfound ability to use mental operations.

THE CONCRETE OPERATIONAL PERIOD: GENERAL CHARACTERISTICS

In the period of concrete operations, children use operations to solve problems and to reason. However, their thinking is tied to what is observable, or *concrete*. The child is able to think in terms of number, classes, and relationships. In order to do that, however, children need to be able to utilize two fundamental thinking procedures: *reversibility* and *conservation*. (We have already discussed reversibility. We will discuss the meaning of conservation later). •

Piaget has described logical operations as the ability to do three things:

1. *The ability to return to the original or starting point in a given thought process (reversibility)*. Piaget (1973) considered reversibility a basic mechanism for the development of logical thinking as well as for the integration of cognitive structures at the stage of concrete operations and beyond.
2. *The ability to organize objects into classes (classification)*. Children at the preoperational level classify objects on the basis of one perceptual quality, such as shape or color, and may overlook other characteristics (Sigel and Cocking, 1977). The concrete operational child can classify objects in terms of several dimensions simultaneously. Along with these sophisticated classification skills, the child learns to *decenter*, or to shift the focus from one attribute to another (you will recall that the preoperational child tends to *center* on only one attribute at a time). As the child's ability evolves and matures, she/he is able to organize objects into *hierarchies* that include superordinate classes (e.g., animal) and subclasses (e.g., dog, bird) (Sigel and Cocking, 1977).
3. *The ability to arrange objects along a continuum of increasing value (seriation)*. Ordinarily the child develops a relationship between objects in a descending or an ascending order (e.g., on such dimensions as length,

width, or size). Initially children cannot do this, particularly preoperational children. For example, if the preoperational child is given a group of sticks varying in size, he/she will probably have no difficulty finding the longest and shortest sticks but may have some difficulty ordering the sticks in between (Sigel and Cocking, 1977). The concrete operational child can make a total serial arrangement.

Once the seriation operation has been refined and perfected, the child can solve problems involving one-to-one correspondence. For example, given a group of dolls of varying size and a group of doll beds also of varied size, the concrete operational child can match both beds and dolls in a serial order, with bed sizes corresponding to doll sizes. This ability to make serial one-to-one correspondences is a prerequisite skill for understanding the formal school arithmetic functions as addition, subtraction, division, and multiplication (Sigel and Cocking, 1977).

DEALING WITH CONCEPTS

As a result of the acquisition of logical operations, the child is now able to deal with *concepts*. An example of the use of these three operations is the child's ability to reason and think in terms of *numbers*. In order to reason with numbers, the child must master the following prerequisite activities (Hunt, 1961):

1. *To perform reversible operations.*

$$\boxed{\begin{array}{l} \text{e.g., if } 2 + 2 = 4 \\ \text{then } 4 - 2 = 2 \end{array}}$$

   In this case, the child knows that for a given manipulation of a number, there is another manipulation that "cancels" that one or returns the entire process to its original state.
2. *To develop the logic of classes.* For example, 10, 20, 30, 40, and 50 are all units of 10.
3. *To arrange items or quantities of items in order (seriation).* For example, if the child knows that object A weighes more than object B and that object B weighs more than object C, then the child can order the objects in a serial relationship.

$$\boxed{\begin{array}{c} \text{A B C} \\ \text{Heavy} \quad - \quad \text{Light} \end{array}}$$

The mental operations described are used by the child to deal symbolically with many aspects of experience, including objects, numbers, and words. The child's mental operations are integrated into a total cognitive pattern that provides a way of generating concepts for representational thought (Piaget, 1950). The major differences between concrete operational thinking and adult (formal operational) thinking are twofold (Sigel and Cocking, 1977):

374

1. The child has limited experience and therefore limited knowledge.
2. The child uses mental operations in the context of concrete things.

CONSERVATION

As we pointed out in Chapter Seven, Piaget emphasized that one of the most important milestones of the child's thinking is *conservation* (the ability to recognize that two equal quantities remain equal as long as nothing is added or taken away). Depending on the particular situation, conservation can refer to substance, weight, volume, length, number, or space. Children develop the various types of conservation at different ages. For example, conservation of substance occurs at age six or seven. Conservation of weight occurs at age nine or ten, and conservation of volume at age eleven or twelve.

Before mastering any type of conservation, children generally go through three stages (Sigel and Cocking, 1977).

Stage I: No Conservation Present. In Stage I, children fail to conserve. They may focus on only one aspect or dimension of a problem without recognizing relationships between such dimensions as height, weight, length, and width. Furthermore, they are probably fooled by general appearances and cannot recognize the reversible nature of a problem.

Stage II: Transitional Period. During Stage II, the child vacillates between being able to conserve and failing to conserve. Children seem to be able to focus on more than one dimension of a problem at a time but are very inconsistent in their understanding of the relationship between those dimensions.

Stage III: Conservation with Logical Explanations. In Stage III, conservation occurs consistently whenever such problems arise. This consistency in all types of conservation problems usually does not occur until the child is ten or twelve. The logical explanations or justifications that accompany the solution of problems may take three forms (Sigel and Cocking, 1977):

1. *Justification based on reversibility.* When confronted with a clay cylinder that has been shaped from a clay ball, the child might say, "Wait a minute—you could make the clay worm into a ball again if you wanted to."
2. *Justification or explanation of conservation based on the concept of identity.* When confronted with equal amounts of water poured into different-shaped containers, the child might say, "It's the same water; you haven't done anything to it."
3. *Justification based on the concept of compensation.* When presented with the clay cylinder formed from a clay ball, the child might say, "The cylinder is skinnier than the ball, but the ball was fatter and shorter than the cylinder—so they both have the same amount of clay."

Thus, conservation is a competency that develops over time and that reaches its completion as a result of maturation and experience.

One of the features of being around young children is hearing them ask "why" when they confront things that puzzle them. The question "why" is often posed to parents and may deal with many matters, such as "Why do people die?" "Why are you my daddy?" "Why do people go to school?" (to infinity, or so it may seem to excited but weary parents). Many of the questions that children ask have to do with their developing conception of reality as well as their emerging notions of causality. In previous chapters, we discussed the development of causality as an outgrowth of sensorimotor activity. In this section, we examine causality as an instance of cognitive development in the six- to twelve-year-old child.

At the concrete level, the child begins to apply rational judgments to causality although the process is not complete until the period of formal operations. An example of causal thinking is Piaget's experiment involving children's understanding of atomism. In the experiment, the child is shown a glass of water into which ice cubes are poured. Children are then asked what happens after the ice melts in the glass of water. Preoperational children tend to respond by saying that the ice simply disappears. Concrete operational children have varied responses depending on their level of conservation skill:

1. The seven- to eight-year-old child thinks that the ice is still in the water; however, its weight and volumes have *not* been added or combined with the original water in the glass. Children at this age have not achieved conservation of weight or volume and, therefore, do not think that the ice has contributed to the weight or volume of the original water.

2. By the time children attain conservation of weight and volume, they recognize that several things have happened:
   a. The ice has not disappeared but has been *transformed* in the melting process.
   b. The weight and volume of the melted ice have been retained in a different form.
   c. The transformed ice does not increase the water level of the container.

The understanding of causation is very much related to the operations used in conservation. Furthermore, causation in the six- to twelve-year-old is also firmly rooted in the child's understanding of *object permanence* (see Chapter Six). In other words, because the ice disappears (in a simple perceptual sense) does not mean that the ice no longer exists. In the case of the melting ice, Piaget suggested that the concrete operational child comes to understand the *principle of atomism*. That is, objects are composed of particles (e.g., ice is composed of molecules and atoms) that, in the process of a physical change such as melting, change form and become smaller and thus invisible to the naked eye (Sigel and Cocking, 1977). The understanding of causality by the child requires, among other things, that the child lessen his/her egocentric perspective of the world.

Piaget suggested that this happens through a gradual *socialization* of thinking in which the child comes to recognize that peers and others may have different viewpoints. This process of *sociocentrism* (Sigel and Cocking, 1977) leads the child to reorganize his/her own thinking in general and his/her notions of causality in particular. Piaget (1954) described how this happens as a process of mutual interaction with other people:

[The child] makes the effort to adapt . . . he bows to the exigencies of . . . verification which are implied by discussion and argument, and this comes to replace egocentric logic with true logic created by social life. (p. 302)

Social and Personality Development

A discussion of the development of children's thinking leads us quite naturally to a discussion of the social and personality development of the school-aged child. Changes in the school-aged child's ability to think lead to important developments in social and personality development. We discuss two of these developments in this section: (1) social cognition, or the ways in which school-aged children think about their social worlds; and (2) moral development, or the ways in which children think about "right" and "wrong." Before we discuss these two features of personality development, it is important to note that we have already discussed a central aspect of school-aged personality: the development of self-concept and self-esteem (in the contexts of family, peer group, school, and neighborhood).

SOCIAL COGNITION

Social cognition is the way we form concepts about the social world (Forman and Sigel, 1979). Specifically, social cognition has to do with how we view ourselves *(self-knowledge)* and how we view the emotions, thoughts, and viewpoints of others (role taking). Historically, studies of children's thinking focused largely on the child's understanding of the nonsocial world. This situation has changed as a considerable amount of interest and research has focused on children's understanding of their social world. The study of the development of social cognition is important because it helps us to understand how children view other people. These social conceptualizations, in turn, are an important influence on how children relate to others. In summary, social cognition is a kind of conceptual "system" that may organize and determine social relationships.

Self-Knowledge. The question—"Who am I?"—is one that human beings come to grips with throughout the life span. As we pointed out in our discussion of infancy and the preschool years (see Chapters Six and Seven), this important question of selfhood is addressed even in those early periods of development. The infant's recognition of the distinction between "self" and "other" and the young child's understanding of the permanence of self are examples of how the question "Who am I?" is resolved. For the most part, children have already developed an emerging "personality" with individual styles of coping with the world by about age two (Murphy, 1962). The existence of such a personality pattern does not imply that the child is consciously aware of such a pattern (Forman and Sigel, 1979).

The development of conscious awareness of self seems to follow a pattern that is related to the child's level of cognitive development (Alschuler and Weinstein, 1976). Alschuler and Weinstein examined the conscious aware-

Children's Understanding of Death, or How Come the Gerbil Doesn't Move?

The title question has been known to strike terror into the heart of even the most experienced first grade teacher when the death of a classroom pet is discovered by a curious 6-year-old. The issues raised are more distressing when a classmate or a classmate's parent dies and questions are asked. The simplest path is that of silence, or of trying to dispose of the questions as swiftly and painlessly as possible. . . .

The conspiracy of silence that seems to exist among adults when it comes to discussing death with children has at least three basic roots. First, there is the adult's own emotional concern which may prevent him or her from confronting death-related issues. This may stem from actual experience or from fear of emotional losses. The second root is a general uncertainty about what to say or where to begin. It is hard to know what issues will be of immediate concern and which will be unimportant. Finally, there is the situation which combines the two mentioned above, when an emotional crisis such as the death of a parent or relative, for instance forces an anxious adult into the awkward position of having to explain what has happened to a frightened child. . . .

DEVELOPMENTAL TRENDS

Children's ideas about death develop along clear developmental lines and can be grouped by levels of mental functioning. A good example of this are the ideas children have about what causes living things to die. In the youngest group (under 6 or 7) the answers children tend to give to such questions are often magical and quite eccentric. Typically, they might include such causes of death as "Eating a dirty bug" or "Going swimming alone when your mother says no." In middle childhood (approximately ages 7 to 11) children tend to become more concrete in their reasoning, and they will typically cite as causes of death "cancer," "guns," "dope" or "poison." When children reach early adolescence (approximately age 12 and over), they become capable of more abstract formal reasoning and their explanations also take on a more abstract quality. Often they fall into such broad groups or general categories as "illness," "old age," "accidents," or "part of the body doesn't work right any more."

Large numbers of children under the age of seven may also fail to recognize the irreversibility of death. In answer to questions about how dead things can be brought back to life, such children might offer such answers as: "Take them to the emergency room," "Keep them warm and give them hot food" or "Take them to Grandma's house." In such cases the child has not yet developed the ability to break away from his own history of first-hand experiences. . . . he cannot realize the permanence of death. When he reaches the more concrete level of mental operations he will be able to incorporate the experiences of others. He will then know that the gerbil in the title is not "asleep". . . .

From G. P. Keecher, "Why Isn't the Gerbil Moving Anymore? Discussing Death in the Classroom—and at Home." *Children Today.* Washington, D.C.; January–February 1975, pp. 18–21, 36.

"It was my turtle. It died." Doug, age 12.

"It's a bird that died of old age." Robert, age 12.

ness of individuals ranging from preschoolers through adolescents. They asked their subjects to describe a memorable experience, including all relevant actions, thoughts, and feelings. Their analysis yields four levels of self-knowledge (see Table 8.1). Stage 1 (elemental) includes the preschool years with its emphasis on images of physical events, sometimes out of order. Stage 2 (situational) includes the beginning of the concrete operational stage of thinking as story images and symbols become more organized and more in-

Alschuler and Weinstein's Levels of Self-Knowledge

Stage 1: Elemental Stage

Subjects in this stage recount the memorable experience in a fragmented, list-like fashion. Events are incomplete and show little continuity. They are overt, external, and observable rather than subjective. There are no metasituational statements—that is, no statements that summarize several situations. The self in the story has to be inferred by the listener instead of being disclosed by the speaker. For example, "I was bit by a dog. The dog was big. It was raining. I slipped down."

Stage 2: Situational Stage

Subjects begin to describe subjective states, but the discussion seldom goes beyond the particular situation. The various parts of the recollected experience are connected in a causal chain. There are some attempts to define the general tone of the situation, but there is still no attempt to relate the situation to other situations. The subjects stay within one time frame rather than see consistency of self across past situations. The descriptions of internal states are rather global and lacking in nuances. For example, "I was bit by a dog. I screamed when he bit me. I think I was mad and afraid. It was a rather bad day. It upset me for a long time afterward."

Stage 3: Patterned Stage

Subjects begin to see themselves as consistent across situations. True hypotheses about self form and are tested against past experiences (for example, "I guess I must have problems with authority"). The person begins to see a pattern to his or her social behavior. The subject makes predictive statements about how he or she would probably react in a given situation, knowing what he or she knows about himself or herself. Situations are defined abstractly ("things that threaten me") rather than physically ("things that are hot"). Behavior is described dispositionally ("I have a tendency to get overly involved with members of the opposite sex" rather than overtly ("I try to kiss all the girls").

Stage 4: Process Stage

Subjects do more than describe their personality patterns. They also have an awareness of how they deal with their internal states. Subjects can describe the process by which they control and modify their feelings and moods ("I try to make my guilt work positively by setting realistic deadlines and then feeling anxious if it looks like I'm not meeting those deadlines"). The awareness of how "self directs self" is explicit, conscious. In the previous stage generalized patterns are merely described, but there is no evidence that the self is seen as a possible agent in the change itself. In this stage the self is seen as proactive in influencing internal states ("I began to give myself permission to express my true feelings").[1]

[1]This view of self-awareness in terms of stage is supported by the research of Peevers and Secord (1973) and Livesley and Bromley (1973), who identified similar stages in the verbal descriptions subjects gave of friends, someone they disliked, and themselves.

From "Self-Knowledge Development," by A. Alschuler and G. Weinstein. An unpublished manuscript written at the School of Education, University of Massachusetts, Amherst, 1976. Reprinted by permission of the authors.

terpretive (less bound by the actual appearance of events). Stage 3 (patterned) involves more developed concrete operational thinking in which subjects see themselves as consistent across many situations. Stage 4 (process) requires the use of formal operations (we will discuss this stage in Chapter Nine).

Role Taking. *Role taking* means the "growth of the cognitive skills that are required for a child to understand other people, their emotional states, their perspectives, and the differences between these perspectives and those held by the child himself or herself" (Forman and Sigel, 1979, p. 169). Research suggests that important changes occur in role-taking ability during the middle-childhood years. The four- to six-year-old child does not fully realize that each person has his/her own thoughts and feelings, which serve as a basis for action (Flavell, 1977). Between six and eight years, the child's egocentric perspective lessens. By age six, the child usually can infer that another person may have different perceptions of the same event. In addition, the six-year-old realizes that other people may act on the basis of personal thoughts or feelings. Furthermore, by this age, the child can understand whether another person's actions are accidental or intended (Shantz, 1975).

Selman (1973; Selman and Byrne, 1974) suggested that children go through several stages in understanding the thinking of others. In order for us to understand these stages of role-taking better, we will tell a story about Scott, Baby Elizabeth's nine-year-old brother.

SCENARIO: SCOTT AND THE BABY KITTEN

In the back of Scott's house was a rather sizable locust tree with many branches. Some of the branches were low enough so that Scott could reach them and lift himself into the tree. On noticing Scott's tree-climbing activities, Scott's father asked him to promise not to climb trees because of the potential danger.

One day Scott was faced with a choice between keeping his promise to his father and saving a baby kitten that was trapped in the locust tree.

The children in the Selman and Byrne research were told a story similar to the one about Scott and the kitten. They were asked to think about how Scott would feel as he decided what to do. Selman and Byrne found the following *stages of role taking* among children:

Level 0 (four to six years.) At Level 0, children can understand that another person may have thoughts or feelings that differ from their own. However, *they do not yet have the skills to assess what those feelings might be.* Children at this stage may assume that everyone in the story about Scott automatically understands what each person thinks and feels. Although children in this stage recognize that other people may have different thoughts and feelings, they *cannot* quite grasp the idea that other people are beings who live life in terms of these feelings and thoughts.

Level 1: subjective role-taking (six to eight years). At Level 1, children understand that *other people have personal reasons for their behavior.* Children even realize that others may be unaware of these personal reasons for actions. For example, in the story about Scott, children at this level would understand why Scott's friends might be puzzled by his reluctance to climb the tree to save the kitten (i.e., Scott's friends might not know about his promise to his father not to climb trees).

Level 2: self-reflective role-taking (eight to ten years). At Level 2, *children realize that they themselves can be the "objects" of the thoughts of other children.* They now realize not only that others have their own perspective but also that these others can make inferences about the perspectives of still others. In the story of Scott, for example, his friends can think about Scott's father's thoughts on Scott's dilemma as well as the father's probable reaction. Will he be furious? Will he "understand"? (Forman and Sigel, 1979).

Level 3: mutual role-taking (ten years and older). "At Level 3 . . . , the child begins to think about *two people's points of view simultaneously*" (Forman and Sigel, 1979, p. 172). With reference to the story about Scott, Level 3 children might pose the following question: "If Scott and his father discussed Scott's dilemma, what do you think they would decide *together*? Why?" Children at this level are able to take the *position of a third person* (even if they are participants in the event):

The child can look at the two-person interaction as an interaction, not just as a succession of one-way relations as in Level 2. Neither self nor other is given first-person priority—for example, "They both understand how the other might have been upset." . . . At level 2 the child understands that both parties have first-person views of the other's thinking about self, but these views are not coordinated into a third-person view of the interaction. The Level 3 child, instead, has constructed the concept of a mutuality of perspectives. (Forman and Sigel 1979, p. 172)

Moral Development

Moral development is one part of the total social development of the child. During the early years of childhood, it occurs, at first, in the family, and then the influences of the culture and the society are brought to bear as the child increasingly moves into peer and school circles. Throughout this transition, however, the family continues to be a primary influence. In this section, we examine the significant changes in moral development during the middle-childhood years.

What is meant by *moral development?* In simple terms, *morality* has been defined as "conscience," or a set of cultural—social rules for governing the appropriateness of social behavior that has been internalized by the individual (Kohlberg, 1964). Moral development, then, is the internalization and organization of these guiding principles over time. Moral development is directed toward the organization of priorities and values in social situations.

Piaget's Theory of Moral Development. Piaget believed that the child's progression in cognitive development (sensorimotor stage, preoperational stage, concrete operational stage, and formal operational stage) is *paralleled* by the child's moral development. In terms of the process of centration—decentration, the child moves in the following pattern (Lee, 1976):

Premoral Period (birth to seven years of age). The premoral period has two phases which have their counterparts in the sensorimotor and the preoperational stages of cognitive development. The focus of the early phase of the premoral period is on the self—a highly egocentric self. For about the first one and a half to two years, the infant begins life fairly incapable of moral judgments or moral behavior. The child is bound by an egocentrism of sensations, impulses, and generalized feelings. To a large extent, the sensorimotor infant is only beginning the process of differentiation between self and other. Therefore, all feeling (including moral emotion) is *centered* largely on the infant's body and actions (Lee, 1976).

The second or later phase of the premoral period is marked by a focus on the ''permanent object'' that the caretaker or the parent has come to be. The major characteristic of this phase is the shift from a focus on the *self* to a focus on the *authority* of that most prominent ''permanent object,'' the parent or the caretaker. This emphasis on adult authority continues through the preoperational stage until about age seven. Much like the thinking during the preoperational period, this later phase of premoral thought is marked by moral feelings that are not ''conserved'' or generalized to all situations. For example, just as preoperational children cannot ''conserve'' in different situations, (e.g., when a quantity of water is poured into a different-shaped beaker), they cannot extend parental rules to new situations. For example, children may find it perfectly appropriate to tell the truth to their parents and lie to their peers (Lee, 1976).

Moral Relationships Based on Mutual Respect (Ages eight to eleven). The obedience to authority of the previous period declines in favor of *autonomy* based on *mutual respect*. These moral feelings have their counterpart in the ability to conserve in the cognitive domain. In this period, the child moves from a focus on *authority* to a focus on *interactions* in *concrete* situations. For example, in the previous period, the child might share toys in the presence of his or her mother (in deference to the authority of his or her mother). In this new period, the child may note that other children do not play with or like a child who does not share toys (Lee, 1976).

The child ultimately becomes able to ''conserve'' or generalize sharing behaviors to many situations. What has happened is that the child is now capable of *reversible operations*. In the toy-sharing example, the child who stops sharing and incurs the wrath of his or her playmate(s) can return (mentally) to the beginning of the play sequence, where sharing resulted in positive interaction. The ability to reverse thinking and return to a starting point helps the child to develop and extend the principle of reciprocity and sharing. Piaget suggested that such ''reciprocal morality'' is *autonomous,* primarily because it is no longer ''dependent'' on the relationship of the child to an authority figure (as in the previous stage). The morality of middle childhood depends on the *mental relationships* between peers on an equal, give-and-take basis in a *concrete situation* (Lee, 1976).

The focus on the *concrete* distinguishes the moral behavior of middle childhood from that of the adolescent and the adult. Because the child focuses on the real, the immediate, and the concrete, there is the possibility that the child may become *inflexible* in his/her moral judgments. Even though the individual in middle childhood is less egocentric than the premoral child, he/she is still dependent for both cognitive functioning and moral judgments on what he/she perceives. The ''eye-for-an-eye'' level of morality may still be popular at this stage. It is not until the later stages of moral development in adolescence and adulthood that the individual is able to take unique motivational and

Huckleberry Finn's Conscience

Some of the most poignant descriptions of the development of conscience and moral judgement occur in literature. In the following passage, Mark Twain describes the thoughts of Huckleberry Finn as he argues with himself about the virtues of helping Jim—a runaway slave—to escape. Huck has learned that there is a reward for returning Jim. Both he and Jim are now escaping down the Mississippi River on a raft.

Jim said it made him all over trembly and feverish to be so close to freedom. Well, I can tell you it made me all over trembly and feverish, too, to hear him, because I begun to get it through my head that he was most free—and who was to blame for it? Why, me. I couldn't get that out of my conscience, no how nor no way. It got to troubling me so I couldn't rest; I couldn't stay still in one place. It hadn't even come home to me before what this thing was that I was doing. But now it did; and it stayed with me, and scorched me more and more. I tried to make out to myself that I warn't to blame, because I didn't run Jim off from his rightful owner; but it warn't no use, conscience up and says, every time, "But you knowed he was running for his freedom, and you could 'a' paddled ashore and told somebody."

From Clemens, S., *Huckleberry Finn* (1962).

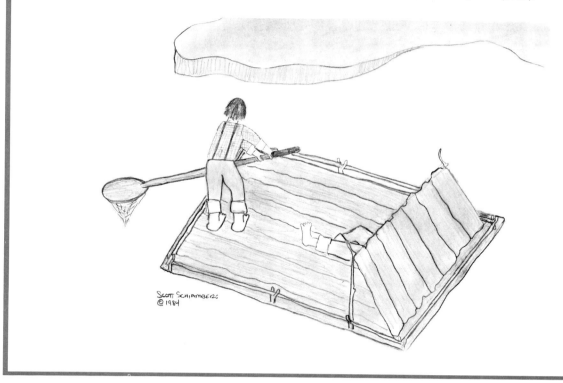

situational factors fully into account (e.g., "to temper justice with mercy") (Lee, 1976).

Moral Relativity (Age eleven to twelve). The relativity stage of moral development presumably begins sometime during the adolescent years, although, as we will see later, it is not certain that every human being attains this stage. With the attainment of *formal operational thinking,* the individual shifts from a focus on the *concrete* (centration) to a focus on the realistic application (taking all factors into account) of moral values and ideals to specific situations (Lee, 1976). We discuss this development in Chapter Nine.

Kohlberg's Theory of Moral Development. Using Piaget's theories as a starting point, Lawrence Kohlberg (1968) described moral development in terms of three levels of moral thinking: *preconventional, conventional,* and *postconventional* (see Tables 8.2 and 8.3).

Preconventional Level. The following are characteristic features of the preconventional level of moral thinking:

- The child defines wrong as "those things that I get punished for." Right is obeying the commands of authorities, such as teachers and parents.
- When moral judgment is fully developed at this level, the child defines right as whatever works out to his or her advantage.
- The criteria that a child uses to judge right and wrong are determined by his or her self-interest. Reasoning is concrete.
- Right, love, or kindness is something that one does.
- Rules are unchangeable commands from some higher authority. The understanding of rules is so limited that the application of them is very inconsistent.
- The child applies specific rules to specific situations.
- Right is what good people do.
- There are rules that govern the actions of the child's models.

During the first stage of this level (see Table 8.2), the child views adults as all-powerful and all-knowing authority figures and submits unquestioningly to them. During the second stage, "goodness" and "badness" refer to what does or does not satisfy one's needs. Although there may be some *apparent* instances of a morality based on mutual understanding, such events are almost always defined in a *self-satisfying* or egocentric way (e.g., "You do something for me, and I'll do it for you").

Conventional Level. As the child moves into the conventional level, the rules of the society tend to be viewed as literal and rigid. In the third stage (see Table 8.2), the child sees "good" behavior as imperative. The *intent* of the child's actions becomes important because good behavior is what elicits the approval of significant others. In Stage 4, the child becomes oriented toward authority and rules. Maintenance of rules and respect for authority become one's *duty.* Other characteristics of this level are that the child:

Becomes aware of intentions and the personal differences that should be considered when judging actions.

Becomes concerned about the way in which wrong actions and responses damage relationships between persons and in groups.

Sees all laws as having equal importance.

Postconventional Level. According to Kohlberg, the individual in the postconventional level of moral development is no longer tied to the rules of authority or society but is able to organize and reanalyze moral principles in particular situations. In the fifth stage (see Table 8.2), moral behavior is no longer governed by one's *duty* or by obedience of the *letter of the law* but by the

384

TABLE 8.2 **Kohlberg's Basis of Moral Judgment**

	Preconventional
LEVEL-I moral value resides in external, quasi-physical happenings, in bad acts, or in quasi-physical needs rather than in persons and standards.	Stage 1: Obedience and punishment orientation. Egocentric deference to superior power or prestige or a trouble-avoiding set. Objective responsibility. Stage 2: Naively egoistic orientation. Right action is that instrumentally satisfying the self's needs and occasionally others. Awareness of relativism and value to each actor's needs and perspective. Naive egalitarianism and orientation to exchange and reciprocity.
	Conventional
LEVEL-II moral value resides in performing good or right roles, in maintaining the conventional order and the expectancies of others.	Stage 4: Authority-and-social-order-maintaining orientation. Orientation to "doing duty" and to showing respect for authority and maintaining the given social order for its own sake. Regard for earned expectations of others. Stage 3: Good-boy orientation. Orientation to approval and to pleasing and helping others. Conformity to stereotypical images of majority or natural role behavior, and judgment by intentions.
	Postconventional
LEVEL-III moral value resides in conformity by the self to shared or sharable standards, rights, or duties.	Stage 6: Conscience or principle orientation. Orientation not only to actually ordained social rules, but to principles of choice involving appeal to logical universality and consistency. Orientation to conscience as a directing agent and to mutual respect and trust. Stage 5: Contractual legalistic orientation. Recognition of an arbitrary element or starting point in rules or expectations for the sake of agreement. Duty defined in terms of contract, general avoidance of violation of the will or rights of others, and majority will and welfare.

Reprinted from Lawrence Kohlberg, "Moral and Religious Education and the Public Schools: A Developmental View," In T. R. Sizer (Ed.), *Religion and Public Education.* Copyright © 1967 by Houghton Mifflin Company. Reprinted by permission.

TABLE 8.3
A Comparison of Piaget and Kohlberg on Moral Development.

Piaget	Kohlberg
Premoral period (birth–7 years)	Level I—Preconventional Stage 1: Obedience and punishment orientation Stage 2: Naively egoistic orientation
Concrete–transitional period (8–11 years)	Level II—Conventional Stage 3: Good–boy orientation Stage 4: Authority-and-social-order maintaining orientation
Moral relativity period (12 years and after)	Level III—Postconventional Stage 5: Contractual–legalistic orientation Stage 6: Conscience or principle orientation

principles that underlies the law. For example, the individual may support equal admission to professional schools not simply because "it's the law" but because of the underlying principle that all human beings are entitled to equality of opportunity. The individual operates in accordance with a "social contract." In the sixth stage, the individual is oriented toward moral decisions based on a "personal" ethical system. Kohlberg (1968) suggested that this system is based on "universal principles of justice, reciprocity and equality of human rights and respect for the dignity of human beings as individual persons" (p. 26). Whereas the Stage 5 individual was oriented toward a legalistic or social-contract approach, the Stage 6 individual attempts to develop a system that satisfies his or her own conscience. We will discuss the postconventional level of morality in greater detail in Chapter Nine.

Concepts of Justice. Children entering middle childhood tend to judge actions and behavior (both their own behavior and the behavior of others) in terms of physical results, satisfaction of needs, or obedience to authority. For example, a child who breaks five cups while helping his father set the table may regard himself as having committed a greater offense than the child who breaks only one cup in the act of reaching for some forbidden candy. In other words, the greater the physical damage, the greater the crime. The child does not incorporate motivational or situational factors into moral decision making.

SCENARIO: THE TALE OF THE BABY-SITTER
An example of the child's tendency to judge transgressions in terms of the unquestioned authority of the parent is the story of the babysitter. The following story also is an example of the research technique used by Piaget to assess levels of moral development in children. The story is told to two groups of children—a *premoral group* (birth to seven years of age) and a *transitional group* (eight to eleven years of age):

The all-powerful, all-knowing authority figure known as the parent.

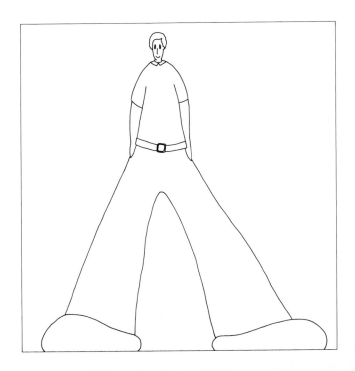

Middle Childhood: A Cultural Beginning

The Role of Parent and Teacher in the Child's Moral Development

The following are some suggestions and clues for parents or teachers who deal with the child as a "moral" individual.

Although each situation and each child are different, many parents and teachers want to provide an experience of justice in the home and in the school, and a variety of experiences to help the child see different viewpoints. In every home, an atmosphere of mutual respect of all persons is the most important starting point.

CLUES FOR PARENTS AND TEACHERS

Telling is the least effective technique for teaching morality.

Children can best "understand" moral reasoning at their own "level" or just one level above the level at which they are functioning.

One way to help children advance in their moral thinking is to involve them in trying to solve moral dilemmas (see the example of Scott and the kitten).

Kohlberg's research has shown that the children who reach the higher levels of moral development in their age group are those who have many associations and interactions with other children.

Another factor that relates to higher levels of moral development is the amount of exposure that a child has to ways of life different from her/his own.

Moral judgment matures most rapidly in an atmosphere of mutual respect.

Adults should admit mistakes when wrong.

Adults should consider the opinions and feelings of children.

Adults should encourage the children to consider the feelings of other family members when making decisions.

Parents should be "growing" people themselves and serve as models for the child.

A baby-sitter arrives at the home of Mr. and Mrs. Walker. Mr. and Mrs. Walker say good-bye to their child, Jeffrey, and leave for a dinner engagement. Two hours later, the Walkers return home. Mr. Walker walks immediately through the front door and over to Jeffrey. He begins to spank his son.

So ends the story. These statements are the *only* facts given to the children. Piaget then asks the children in each experimental group to describe what happened. Specifically, why was the child spanked?

The responses of the children presumably indicate their level of moral development:

1. *The premoral children are rather sure that Jeffrey must have done something wrong.* Otherwise, why would he have been punished by his father? The implication, of course, is that parents are unerring authority figures who never make mistakes.
2. The *transitional children* are much less certain about the appropriateness of the parental action. Although some agree with the view of the premoral group, a substantial number say that there just wasn't enough information given in the story for them to explain why Jeffrey was spanked. In other words, the transitional group is not as dependent on parental authority for defining moral behavior.

Summary

1. The period of middle childhood begins at age five or six with entrance into the formal school and concludes with the onset of puberty heralding the arrival of adolescence. As children enter the formal school, the stage is set for changes in the way they think, learn, interact with others, and organize their behavior. The child now begins more extensive interactions outside the family than in the preschool years.

2. During middle childhood, there is an increasing degree of "seriousness" about life as children begin to concentrate on what can be done and how well they can do it. This attitude contrasts with that of the preschool years when learning to do things was more incidental to the total life activities of the child. We refer to this increasing seriousness of middle childhood as an emerging *sense of competence*. Two important elements relate to this sense of seriousness or competence: the refinement of self-concept and skill learning.

3. Children learn and discover much about themselves in the family context. The school-aged child lives in two worlds: the adult or family world and the world of peers. The parent not only provides support for the child as a family member but also helps the child to manage the sometimes harsh judgments of the peer world. Coopersmith (1967) identified several major factors contributing to the development of child self-esteem.

The impact of siblings on the development of the child is not a simple one and depends on the interaction of a number of factors including the sex and age of the siblings, the spacing of siblings (proximity in age), the size of the family (the total number of children), and the mode of parent/child interaction.

4. The school-aged children's familiarity and participation in the community and neighborhood contexts depends, in part, on their *cognitive mapping skills*. There is considerable evidence that school-aged children are capable of rather sophisticated mapping skills. Children learn about the environment in two ways. First, children learn to orient themselves in an environment by relating to certain objects or reference points. Second, children learn the social features of the environment (i.e., what spaces are accessible to them, what "rules" govern the use of those spaces, and how well they perform activities in those spaces).

5. The learning of school skills and the social changes in the child that the school fosters, produce changes in the child's self-concept. Several specific issues are of interest in assessing the child's adaptation to the elementary school. What are the characteristics of teacher-child relationships? How do teachers help the child develop a positive self-concept? What impact do family peers have on the child's performance in school? What challenges confront the child on entering the school?

6. The peer group in middle childhood is composed of same-sex-individuals who all interact with one another to some extent. Children learn valuable things about themselves as a result of peer interaction. Between the age of six and eleven, there is a general shift in the overall structure and meaning of the peer group to the child.

7. During early childhood, play is characterized by make-believe games and the use of symbols or imagery. In middle childhood, games are often competitive or team activities which are structured by rules.

8. A discussion of the contexts of development in middle childhood would be incomplete without a look at the role of television. The reason is that television occupies a great deal of time in the typical child's life. It provides

children with many ideas and impressions about facets of life such as sex roles, violence, occupational roles, and family life.

9. By the end of early childhood, children have almost completed the development of the fundamental motor skills. These fundamental motor skills are extended to simple games in play situations (e.g., street hockey or tag).

10. During the years from five to seven, a number of qualitative changes occur in thinking processes. These changes accompany the child's first years in the formal school. As the *intuitive* period comes to an end, the child's thinking becomes more flexible, less dependent on perceptions and more dependent on logical operations. Between five and seven years, the child begins to use *operations*. During the period from approximately seven to eleven years, reasoning is often called ''logical'' because of this new-found ability to use mental operations. In this period of *concrete operations*, children use operations to solve problems and to reason. However, their thinking is tied to what is observable or ''concrete.''

11. Changes in the school-aged child's ability to think lead to important changes in social and personality development. Two of these developments include *social cognition* (i.e., the ways in which school-aged children think about their social worlds) and *moral development*.

Questions

1. What are the two primary sources of feedback for self-evaluation in middle childhood?
2. Identify and briefly describe several specific family experiences which have been found to be associated with the development of child self–esteem.
3. Identify and briefly describe several ways that teachers transmit expectations to students.
4. Briefly describe the general shift in the overall structure and meaning of the peer group between 6 and 11 years of age.
5. What is the general relationship between television viewing and aggressive behavior across all age groups?
6. Define and briefly discuss *reversibility* and *conservation* in relation to the thinking of school-aged children.
7. What is *social cognition?* Why is it important?

Bibliography

ALSCHULER, A., and WEINSTEIN, G. Self-knowledge development. Amherst, Massachusetts: School of Education. University of Massachusetts, 1976 (unpublished manuscript.

ALTUS, W. D. Birth order and its sequelae. *International Journal of Psychiatry,* 1967, *3,* 23–39.

BANDURA, A. *Principles of Behavior Modification.* New York: Holt, 1969.

BARCUS, E. Saturday children's television: A report of T. V. programming and advertising on Boston commercial television. ERIC Document Files No. ED 055 461. Action for Children's Television, Boston, 1971.

BELL, R. Q. A reinterpretation of the direction of effects in studios of socialization. *Psychological Review,* 1968, *75,* 81–95.

BERNSTEIN, B. Aspects of language and learning in the genesis of the social process. In D. Hynes (Ed.), *Language in Culture and Society.* New York: Harper & Row, 1965.

BERNSTEIN, B. Elaborate and restricted codes: Their social origins and some consequences. In A. G. Smith (Ed.), *Communication and Culture.* New York: Holt, 1966.

BIGNER, J. J. *Parent–Child Relations.* New York: Macmillan, 1979.

BRIGGS, D. C. *Your Child's Self-esteem.* New York: Doubleday, 1975.

BRONFENBRENNER, U. Who cares for America's children? Address presented at the National Association for the Education of Young Children, 1970.

BROPHY, J. E., and GOOD, T. L. Teacher's communication of differential expectations for children's classroom performance: Some behavioral data. *Journal of Educational Psychology,* 1970, *61,* 365–374.

BRUNER, J., and SHERWOOD, V. Peekaboo and the learning of rule structures. In J. Bruner, A. Jolly, and K. Sylva (Eds.), *Play: Its Role in Development and Evolution.* Hammondsworth, England: Penguin, 1976.

BUBER, M. *The Knowledge of Man.* New York: Harper & Row Publishers, 1965.

CBS BROADCAST GROUP. A study of messages received by children who viewed an episode of "Fat Albert and the Cosby Kids." New York: Office of Social Research, Department of Economics and Research, CBS Broadcast Group, 1974.

CLEMENS, S. *Huckleberry Finn.* New York: Macmillan, 1962.

CLINE, V. B., CROFT, R. G., and COURRIER, S. Desenitization of children to television violence. *Journal of Personality and Social Psychology,* 1973, *27,* 360–365.

COCHRAN, M., and BASSARD, J. A. Child development and personal social networks. *Child Development,* 1979, *50,* 601–603.

COLEMAN, J. S., CAMPBELL, E. Q., HOBSON, C. J., McPARTLAND, J., MOOD, A. M., WEINFIELD, F. D., and YORK, R. L. *Equality of educational opportunity.* Washington, D.C.: U.S. Government Printing Office, 1966.

COLLINS, H. L. The influence of prosocial television programs emphasizing the positive value of differences on children's attitudes toward differences and children's behavior in choice situations. Unpublished doctoral dissertation, Pennsylvania State University, 1974.

COOPER, H. M., BARON, R. M., and LOWE, C. A. The importance of race and social class information in the formation of expectancies about academic performance. *Journal of Educational Psychology,* 1975, *67,* 312–319.

COOPERSMITH, S. *The Antecedents of Self esteem.* San Francisco: Freeman, 1967.

CORBIN, C. B. *Becoming Physically Educated in Elementary School* (2nd Ed.), Philadelphia: Lea and Febiger Publishing Co., 1976.

CORBIN, C. B. *A Textbook of Motor Development.* Dubuque, Iowa: Brown, 1973 (second edition, 1980).

COSTELLO, J. The first grader's rites of passage. *Parents Magazine,* Nov. 1978.

DEWEY, J. *The School and Society.* Chicago: U. of Chicago P., 1943.

ECKERT, H. M. Age changes in motor skills. In G. L. Rarick (Ed.), *Physical Activity—Human Growth and Development.* New York: Academic Press, 1973.

ELLIS, G. T., and SEKYRA, F. The effect of aggressive cartoons on the behavior of first grade children. *Journal of Psychology,* 1972, *81,* 37–43.

ERIKSON, E. *Childhood and Society* (2nd ed.), New York: Norton, 1963.

ESPENSCHADE, A. S. *Monographs of the Society for Research in Child Development,* 1960, 5, (No. 1) (whole issue).

EPENSCHADE, A. S., and ECKERT, H. M. Motor development. In *Science and Medicine of Exercise and Sport.* (2nd ed.), W. R. Johnson and E. R. Buskirk (Eds.), New York: Harper, 1974 pp. 419–439.

EPENSCHADE, A. S., and ECKERT, H. M. *Motor Development.* 2nd ed. Columbus, Ohio: Merril, 1980.

FEATHERSTONE, J. Schools Where Children Learn. New York: Liveright Publishing Corporation, 1971.

FEIN, G. C., and CLARKE-STEWART, A. *Day Care in Context.* New York: Wiley, 1973.

FENTON, N. The only child. *Journal of Genetic Psychology,* 1928, *35,* 546–556.

FERRIS, P. *Dylan Thomas.* London: Hadley and Stoughton, 1977.

FESHBACK, S., and SINGER, R. *Television and Aggression.* San Francisco: Jossey-Bass, 1971.

FESHBACK, S., and SINGER, R. Television and aggression: A reply to Liebert, Sobol and Davidson. In G. A. Comstock et al. (Eds.), *Television and social behavior, Vol. 5: Television's effects: Further explorations.* Washington, D.C.: U.S. Government Printing Office, 1972.

FLAVELL, J. H. *Cognitive development.* Englewood Cliffs, N.J.: Prentice-Hall, 1977.

FORMAN, G. E., and SIGEL, I. E. *Cognitive Development: A Life-span View*. Monterey, Calif.: Brooks/Cole, 1979.

FRIEDRICH, L. K., and STEIN, A. H. Aggressive and prosocial television programs and the natural behavior of preschool children. *Monographs of the Society for Research in Child Development*, 1973, *38*(4, Serial No. 151) (whole issue).

FRIEDRICH, L. K., and STEIN, A. H. Prosocial television and young children: The effects of verbal labeling and role playing on learning and behavior. *Child Development*, 1975, *46*, 27–38.

GARBER, J., and SELIGMAN, M. E. P. *Human Helplessness: Theory and Applications*. New York: Academic Press, 1980.

GARMEZY, N. Vulnerable and invulnerable children: Theory, research, and intervention. American Psychological Association, MS 1337, 1976.

GARMEZY, N., and RUTTER, M. (Eds.) *Stress, Coping, and Development in Children*. New York: McGraw-Hill, 1983.

GARVEY, C. *Play*. Cambridge, Mass.: Harvard U. P., 1977.

GERBNER, G. Violence in television drama: trends and symbolic functions. In G. A. Comstock and E. A. Rubinstein (Eds.), *Television and social behavior*, Vol. 1. Media content and control. Washington, D.C.: U.S. Government Printing Office, 1972.

GILLIAM, T. B., KATCH, V. L., THORLAND, W., and WELTMAN, A., Prevalence of coronary heart disease risk factors in active children, 7 to 12 years of age, *Medicine and Science in Sports*, 1977, *9*, 21–25.

GLIDEWELL, J. C., KANTOR, M. B., SMITH, L. M., and STRINGER, L. A. Socialization and social structure in the classroom. In L. W. Hoffman and M. L. Hoffman (Eds.), *Review of Child Development Research*, Vol. 2, New York: Russell Sage Foundation, 1966.

GOERTZEL, V., and GOERTZEL, M. G. *Cradles of Eminence*. Boston, Massachusetts: Little Brown, 1978.

GORANSON, R. E. Media violence and aggressive behavior: A review of experimental research. In L. Berkowitz (Ed.), *Advances in Experimental Social Psychology*, Vol. 5. New York: Academic Press, 1970.

GUTIN, B., FOGLE, R. K., and STEWART, K., Relationship among submaximal heart rate, aerobic power, and running performance in children, *Research Quarterly*, 1975, *47*, 536.

HARTMANN, D. P. Influence on symbolically modeled instrumental aggression and pain cues on aggressive behavior. *Journal of Personality and Social Psychology*, 1969, *11*, 280–388.

HARTUP, W. W. Peer interaction and social organization. In P. H. Mussen (Ed.), *Carmichael's Manual of Child Psychology* (3rd ed.), Vol. 2. New York: Wiley, 1970.

HELLEBRANDT, F. A., RARICK, G. L., GLASSOW, R., and CARNS, M. L. Physiological analysis of basic motor skills: 1. growth and development of jumping. *American Journal of Physical Medicine*, 1961, *40*, 14.

HERZOG, E., and SUDIA, C. E. Children in fatherless families. In B. Caldwell and H. Riccuiti (Eds.), *Review of Child Development Research*, Vol. 3. Chicago: U. of Chicago P., 1973, 141–232.

HESS, R. D., and SHIPMAN, V. C. Early experience and socialization of cognitive modes in children. *Child Development*, 1965, *36*, 869–886.

HESS, R. D., and SHIPMAN, V. C. Maternal attitude toward the school and the role of the pupil: Some social class comparisons. Paper prepared for the Fifth World Conference on Curriculum and Teaching in Depressed Urban Areas, Columbia University, Teachers College, New York, June 1966.

HESS, R. D., and SHIPMAN, V. C. Maternal influences upon early learning: The Cognitive environments of urban preschool children. In R. D. Hess and R. M. Bear (Eds.), *Early Education: Current Theory, Research and Action*. Chicago: Aldine, 1968.

HILLIARD, T., and ROTH, R. M. Maternal attitudes and the nonachievement syndrome. *Personnel and Guidance Journal*, 1969, *47*, 424–428.

HOWE, M. J. *Understanding School Learning: A New Look at Educational Psychology*. New York: Harper & Row, 1972.

HUNT, J. McV. *Intelligence and Experience.* New York: Ronald, 1961.

ITTELSON, W. H., PROSHANSKY, H. M., RIVLIN, L. G., and WINKEL, G. *An Introduction to Environmental Psychology.* New York: Holt, 1974.

JACKSON, A. S., and COLEMAN, E., Validation of distance run tests for elementary school children, *Research Quarterly,* 1975, 47, 86.

JENCKS, C., BARTLETT, S., CORCORAN, M., CROUSE, J., EAGLESFIELD, D., JACKSON, G., McCLELLAND, K., MUESER, P., OLNECK, M., SCHWARTZ, J., WARD, S., and WILLIAMS, J. *Who Gets Ahead? The Determinants of Economic Success in America.* New York: Basic Books, 1979.

KAGAN, J. The child's sex-role classification of school objects. *Child Development,* 1964, 35, 1051.

KAGAN, J., and MOSS, H. A. *Birth to Maturity: The Fels Study of Psychological Development.* New York: Wiley, 1962.

KEECHER, G. P. "Why isn't the gerbil moving anymore?" Discussing death in the classroom—and at home. *Children Today.* Jan–Feb. 1975, 18–21, 36.

KELLOGG, R. L. A direct approach to sex-role identification of school-related objects. *Psychological Reports,* 1969, 24, 839–841.

KEOGH, J. F., Motor performance test data for elementary school children, *Research Quarterly,* 1970, 40, 600–602.

KITTRELL, E. Children and television: the electronic fix. *Children Today,* May–June 1978, 20, 24–25, 36–37.

KOCH, H. L., *Attitudes of children toward their peers as related to certain characteristics of their siblings. Psychological Monographs,* 1956(a), 70(426), 1–41.

KOCH, H. L. Sissiness and tomboyishness in relation to sibling characteristics. *Journal of Genetic Psychology,* 1956(b), 88, 231–244.

KOCH, H. L. Some emotional attitudes of the young child in relation to characteristics of his siblings. *Child Development,* 1956(c), 27, 393–426.

KOHLBERG, L. Development of moral character and moral ideology. In M. L. Hoffman and L. W. Hoffman (Eds.), *Review of Child Development Research,* Vol. 1. New York: Russell Sage, 1964.

KOHLBERG, L. Moral and religious education in public schools: a developmental view. In T. R. Sizer (Ed.), *Religion and Public Education.* Boston: Houghton Mifflin Co., 1967.

KOHLBERG, L. The child as a moral philospher. *Psychology Today,* September 1968, 25–30.

LABOV, W. The logical nonstandard english. In F. Williams (Ed.), *Language and Poverty.* Chicago: Markham, 1970.

LADD, F. Black youths view their environment: Neighborhood maps. *Environment and Behavior,* June 1970, 2(1), 86.

LEE, L. C. *Personality Development in Childhood.* Monterey, Calif.: Brooks Cole, 1976.

LEIFER, A. D., and ROBERTS, D. F. Children's responses to television violence. In J. P. Murray et al. (Eds.), *Television and social behavior, Vol. 2: Television and social learning.* Washington, D.C.: U.S. Government Printing Office, 1972.

LERNER, R. M., and BUSCH-ROSSNAGEL, N. A. (Eds.) *Individuals as Producers of Their Development: A Life-Span Perspective.* New York: Academic Press, 1981.

LERNER, R. M., and SPANIER, G. B. (Eds.) *Child Influences on Marital and Family Interaction: A Life-Span Perspective.* New York: Academic Press, 1978.

LIVESLEY, W. J. and BROMLEY, D. B. *Person Perception in Childhood and Adolescence.* London: Wiley, 1973.

LOVAAS, O. Effect of exposure to symbolic aggression on aggressive behavior. *Child Development,* 1961, 32, 37–44.

MACFARLANE, J., Perspectives on personality consistency and change from the guidance study. *Vita Humana,* 7, 1964.

MADGE, C. Public and private spaces. *Human Relations,* 1950, 3, 187–199.

MANGAROV, I. Bulletin Information. Bulgarian Olympic Committee, Year IX, 1964, 5, 22.

MENDELSON, G., and YOUNG, M. Network children's programming: A content analysis of black and minority treatment on children's television. ERIC Document Files No. ED 067 889. Action for Children's Television, Boston, 1972.

MILNE, C., SEEFELDT, V. and REUSCHLEIN, P., Relationship between grade, sex, race, and motor performance in young children. *Research Quarterly,* 1975, *47,* 726.

MINUCHIN, P. *The Middle Years of Childhood.* Monterey, Calif.: Brooks/Cole, 1977.

MINUCHIN, P. Differential use of the open classroom: A study of exploratory and cautious children. Final report to the national institute of education, 1976.

MINUCHIN, P., BIBER, B., SHAPIRO, E., and ZIMILES, H. *The Psychological Impact of School Experience.* New York: Basic Books, 1969.

MORENO, J. L. Who shall survive? Washington, D.C.: Nervous and Mental Diseases Publishing Co., 1934.

MUNROE, R. L., and MUNROE, R. H. Effect of environmental experience on spatial ability in an East African society, *Journal of Social Psychology,* 1971, *83,* 15–22.

MURPHY, L. B. *The Widening World of Childhood.* New York: Basic Books, 1962.

MUSSEN, P., and RUTHERFORD, E. Effects of aggressive cartoons on children's aggressive play. *Journal of Abnormal and Social Psychology,* 1961, *62,* 461–464.

NERLOVE, S. B., MUNROE, R. H., and MUNROE, R. L. Effect of environmental experience on spatial ability: a replication. Journal of Social Psychology, 1971, *84,* 3–10.

ORMISTON, K. H., and WILLIAMS, S. Saturday children's programming in San Francisco, California: An analysis of the presentation of racial and cultural groups on three network affiliated San Francisco television stations. ERIC Document Files No. ED 071 440. Committee on Children's Television, San Francisco, 1973.

PEEVERS, B. H. and SECORD, P. F. Developmental changes in attribution of descriptive concepts to person. *Journal of Personality and Social Psychology,* 1973, *27,* 120–128.

PIAGET, J. *The Psychology of Intelligence.* London: Routledge & Kegan Paul, 1950.

PIAGET, J. *The Construction of Reality in the Child.* New York: Basic Books, 1954.

PIAGET, J. *Child and Reality.* New York: Grossman, 1973.

PIAGET, J., INHELDER, B., and SZEMINSKA, A. *The Child's Conception of Geometry.* New York: Basic Books, 1960.

PIPPERT, R. A. A study of creativity and faith. Manitoba Department of Youth and Education Monograph, No. 4, 1969.

ROBERTS, F. The little backseat driver. *Parents Magazine,* Nov. 1978.

ROFF, M., and SELLS, S. B. Relations between intelligence and sociometric status in groups differing in sex and socio-economic background. *Psychological Reports,* 1965, *16,* 511–516.

ROSENBERG, B. G., GOLDMAN, R., and SUTTON-SMITH, B. Sibling age spacing effects on cognitive activity in children. *Proceedings, 77th Annual Convention of the American Psychological Association,* 1969, *4,* 261–262.

ROSENTHAL, R. The Pygmalion effect lives. *Psychology Today,* September 1973, 56–58ff.

ROSENTHAL, R., and JACOBSON, L. *Pygmalion in the Classroom: Teacher Expectation and Pupils Intellectual Development.* New York: Holt, 1968.

SEARS, P. S. Doll play aggressions in normal children: Influence of sex, age, sibling status, father's absence. *Psychological Monographs,* 1951, 65(6), (whole issue).

SEARS, R. R., MACCOBY, E. E., and LEVIN, H. *Patterns of Child Rearing.* New York: Harper & Row, 1957.

SEAVER, W. B. Effects of naturally induced teacher expectancies. *Journal of Personality and Social Psychology,* 1973, *28,* 333–342.

SELIGMAN, M. E. P. *Helplessness: On Depression, Development and Death.* San Francisco, California: W. H. Freeman, 1975.

SELMAN, R. L. A structural analysis of the ability to take another's social perspective. Paper presented at the Society for Research in Child Development meeting, 1973.

SELMAN, R. L., and BYRNE, D. F. A structural-developmental analysis of levels of roletaking in middle childhood. *Child Development,* 1974, *45,* 803–806.

SHANTZ, C. U. The development of social cognition. In E. M. Hetherington (Ed.), Review of child development research, Vol. 5, Chicago: U. of Chicago P., 1975.

SHIRLEY, K. W. The prosocial effects of publicly broadcast children's television. Unpublished doctoral dissertation, University of Kansas, 1974.

SIEGEL, A. E. Film-mediated fantasy aggression and strength of aggressive drive. *Child Development*, 1956, *27*, 365–378.

SIGEL, I., and COCKING, R. *Cognitive Development from Childhood to Adolescence: A Constructivist Perspective.* New York: Holt, 1977.

SINGER, J. L., and SINGER, D. G. Fostering imaginative play in preschool children: Television and life model effects. Draft for presentation at the Annual Meeting of the American Psychological Association, New Orleans, August 1974.

SPODEK, B. Alternatives to traditional education. Peabody Journal of Education, 1971, 48, 140–146.

STEIN, A. H., and Friedrich, L. K. Impact of television on children and youth. In E. M. Hetherington (Ed.) *Review of Child Development Research,* Vol 5. Chicago: U. of Chicago P., 1975.

STENDLER, C. B., and YOUNG, N. Impact of first grade entrance upon the socialization of the child: Changes after eight months of school. *Child Development,* 1951, *22,* 113–122.

SUTTON-SMITH, B., and SUTTON-SMITH, S. *How to play with your children (and when not to).* New York: Hawthorne Books, 1974.

TEDESCO, N. S. Patterns in prime time. *Journal of Communication,* 1974, *24,* 118–124.

TUCKMAN, B. W., and BIERMAN, M. L. Beyond pygmalion: Galatea in the classroom. Paper presented at the meeting of the American Educational Research Association, 1971.

WATSON, J. B. *Psychological Care of Infant and Child.* New York: Norton, 1928.

WHITING, B. B., and WHITING, J. W. M. *Children of Six Cultures: A Psychocultural Analysis.* Cambridge, Massachusetts: Harvard University Press, 1975.

WICKSTROM, R. L. *Fundamental Motor Patterns* (2nd ed.). Philadelphia: Lea and Febiger, 1977.

Suggested Readings

COOPERSMITH, S. *Antecedents of Self-Esteem.* San Francisco, California: Freeman, 1967. A thorough and well written analysis of the relationships of children's self esteem to parental attitudes and behaviors.

ELKIND, D. *The Hurried Child-Growing Up Too Fast Too Soon.* Reading, Massachusetts: Addison–Wesley, 1981. The book raises the provocative point that childhood as a phase of life may be disappearing.

JOHNSON, M. (ed.). *Toward Adolescence: The Middle School Years.* Chicago, Illinois: The University of Chicago Press, 1980. An excellent, up-to-date collection of essays on important facets of middle childhood including significant contexts areas of intervention and approaches to research.

MINUCHIN, P. P. *The Middle Years of Childhood.* Monterey, California: Brooks/Cole, 1977. An excellent integration and discussion of all aspects of middle childhood.

WILLIAMS, J. and STITH, M. *Middle Childhood* (2nd edition) New York: Macmillan, 1980. A readable discussion of all aspects of middle childhood with many practical suggestions.

WORELL, J. *Psychological Development in the Elementary Years.* New York: Academic Press, 1982. An excellent collection of reviews of research on important dimensions of middle childhood.

9
Adolescence

What Is the Period of Adolescence?

Adolescence is a critical period in human development because it is during this period that the individual begins to develop a stance toward the world, or an "identity" (Erikson, 1963, 1965). The period of middle childhood has introduced the child to elementary cultural skills (e.g., reading, writing, and social interaction skills). The period of adolescence requires the continued refinement and application of these skills to self-definition in relation to the culture. This process of self-definition in terms of a culture begins in early adolescence and culminates in later adolescence with the development of an identity that serves as the major mode of organizing individual behavior.

DEFINITION
Puberty. The period of time during which secondary sexual characteristics (e.g., the enlargement of the female breasts and the appearance of male facial hair) appear and accompany the attainment of biological sexual maturity.

FIGURE 9.1 The world of the adolescent has sometimes been called a "no man's land" between childhood and adulthood.

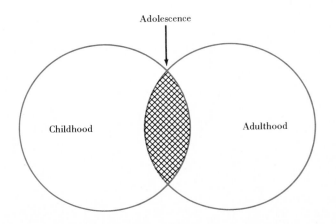

"Who am I?" is an important question for the adolescent.

Photographs by Darryl Jacobson

The period of adolescence begins with the onset of puberty. Puberty is a series of *biological* events that signals the coming of other changes. The end of adolescence comes with entrance into the world of the adult—a *social and psychological* event. Although there is little dispute that adolescence begins with the biological events of puberty, the end of adolescence is much less clear. When, for example, does a person become an adult? The answer to that question depends, of course, on the culture in which one lives. In many cultures, although not in ours, ceremonies called *rites of passage* are used to designate the arrival of adulthood (see Application Box: Rites of Passage and Figure 9.1).

There are many possible criteria for adulthood in our society. Some of these benchmarks are:

- Emotional independence from parents.
- Economic independence from parents (i.e., "making a living" at some job).
- Living away from one's childhood home.
- Graduation from high school or college.
- Commitment to a personal set of values or goals (i.e., a stance toward the world, an "identity").
- The minimum age for voting in public elections.
- Marriage and/or child rearing.

It is possible for the later adolescent to have some of the above characteristics and still not to be considered an adult.

What is the Period of Adolescence?

Who Are Adolescents?

Because of the increasing length of the adolescent period, it has become increasingly difficult to define it: there are few characteristics that fit both a twelve-year-old and a twenty-six-year-old. Therefore we adopt here a two-stage theory of adolescence: (1) *early adolescence* (twelve to sixteen years), or the high-school years, in which the major concern is with the development of the skills necessary for group interaction and group membership (Kagan and Coles, 1972); and (2) *later adolescence or youth* (seventeen to the middle or, in some instances, the late twenties), or the post-high-school years, in which the major concern is with the development of skills that build on prior experiences of group interaction. These skills are necessary if the individual is to stand by herself/himself in relation to the social system and culture.

During the high-school years the adolescent develops an identity in terms of the peer group. The process of identity formation continues into later adolescence with the development of the skills necessary to stand by oneself in the culture and the community. Having begun the process of identity crystallization through adaptation to physical changes in appearance, development of formal operations, and coping with peer pressures and values, the later adolescent is ready for a new phase of development. The lifelong process of identity development continues in later adolescence or youth with the establishment of several foundational components, including the organization of a career and a lifestyle, the evolution of a relatively mature value system, the acceptance of one's sexuality, and the development of autonomy from parents.

Youth, or later adolescence, is the stage that bridges the transition between adolescence and adulthood. Kenneth Keniston (1975) summarized the evolution of this "new" stage as follows:

> More than a decade's work with college and graduate students has convinced me that we have no psychology, apart from the work of Erik Erikson, adequate to understand the feelings and behavior of today's American youth. Millions of young people today are neither psychological adolescents nor sociological adults; they fall into a psychological no man's land. . . . I argue that the unprecedented prolongation of education has opened up opportunities for an extension of psychological development which in turn is creating a "new" stage of life. . . . I suggest that its central characteristic—the tension between selfhood and the existing social order—underlies many of the attitudes and behaviors of contemporary youth. (p. 5)

For our purposes, the definition of the age span for this period is approximately seventeen to twenty-five years of age. It should be noted, however, that this range of years could be expanded to as low as fifteen years of age or to as high as twenty-seven or twenty-eight years of age. In other words, some of the themes of the period we are calling *youth* are probably appropriate to some individuals whose chronological age would place them in early adolescence or young adulthood.

The primary factor that has created the stage of youth as a bona fide phase of development has been the extension of education (as a result of the increasing demands of a technological and industrialized society). It was this very same factor that produced the emergence of what we are calling *early adolescence* during the latter part of the nineteenth century. As a matter of fact, before the twentieth century, adolescence was rarely included as a stage of the

Rites of Passage

In many cultures, ceremonial rites of passage exist as a way of recognizing a change in relationships, status, or roles. We may look with some envy at societies in which rites of passage clearly proclaim that the boy is now a man, the girl an adult woman. In primitive societies, once the ceremony is over, the adolescent is "honored by new status and responsibilities," the parents or guardians relinquish authority, and all the responsibilities and privileges of adulthood are his (Hilgard and Atkinson, 1967). Possibly at an earlier time the marriage ceremony served as a rite of passage in Western society, but it no longer serves that function; many youths (particularly college students) marry while they are still financially dependent upon their parents. Similarly, the move away from home is not a genuine rite of passage, since for a major portion of youth it occurs upon entering college, when the parents still maintain financial responsibility. Some anthropologists argue that our society would function more smoothly if we had a clear, recognized rite which proclaimed at some point in development "you are an adult."

It is wishful thinking to believe that a simple ceremony would rid us of the confusion of becoming an adult. . . . Ceremonial assumption of roles is possible when the roles are unchanging, but it is no answer for a diversified and fast-changing society (Muuss, 1970).

Photograph by Burns Copeland

The search for identity is the price we pay for opening up many possibilities to each child.

From D. R. Matteson, *Adolescence Today.* Homewood, Ill. Dorsey Press, 1975, pp. 115–116.

life cycle. It was not until G. Stanley Hall's classic book *(Adolescence: Its Psychology and Its Relations to Physiology, Anthropology, Sociology, Sex, Crime, Religion and Education)* in 1904 that the period of adolescence was recognized as a prelude to adulthood. As Keniston (1975) pointed out, Hall's concept of adolescence was a reflection on what was really happening in America (and in other industrialized countries) at the turn of the century:

Nonetheless, Hall was clearly reflecting a gradual change in the nature of human development, brought about by the massive transformations of American society in the decades after the Civil War. . . . America changed from a rural agrarian society to an urban industrial society, and this new industrial society demanded on a mass scale not only the rudimentary literacy taught in elementary schools, but higher skills that could be guaranteed only through secondary education. (Keniston, 1975, p. 5)

As a function of the demands of society for even better-educated young people, the stage of youth has evolved in much the same manner that its predecessor, adolescence, emerged. For example, in 1900 only about 6.4 percent of young people completed high school, whereas nearly 80 percent do so today, and half of them begin college. In 1900, there were only 238,000 college students, whereas over 12 million students attended college in 1982 (U.S. Department of Health and Human Services, National Center for Educational Statistics, *Condition of Education 1983*). What seems to characterize these young people are two major features (Keniston, 1975):

1. They either have just formed or are working on a sense of identity. This emerging identity distinguishes youth or later adolescents from their younger high-school counterparts.
2. They have not decided major questions whose answers have historically defined adulthood: questions of lifestyle; questions of social role; matters of vocation; and questions of a general posture or stance toward the world.

The System of Adolescence: An Overview

In this section, we provide a total picture of what happens during the adolescent years. In keeping with our perspective, we will look at adolescence as a stage of life with two phases: early adolescence and later adolescence, or youth.

EARLY ADOLESCENCE: THE SELF IN CONTEXT

The central feature of the early-adolescent world is the organization and evaluation of the adolescent's self-concept in terms of the high school and peer group (see Figure 9.2). In a sense, it can be said that the individual is

FIGURE 9.2 The system of the early adolescent.

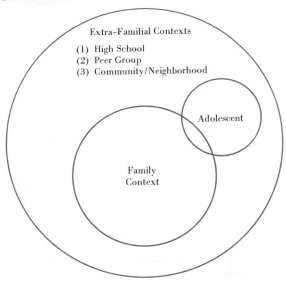

Extra-Familial Contexts

(1) High School
(2) Peer Group
(3) Community/Neighborhood

Adolescent

Family
Context

Adolescence

developing an identity in relation to the world of the high school and to the peer group (both in and out of school). This is a "group identity" as opposed to the identity formation of later adolescence, or a stance toward the world or the culture. The early adolescent is still very much influenced by his/her family. However, at this time, the discontinuities (as well as the continuities) between family values and the values of the peer group become apparent to the adolescent.

Group Identity Versus Alienation. During early adolescence, the individual is usually pressured to affiliate with a group of peers. This pressure comes from many sources, including the family, the school, and age-mates. The world of the early adolescent is characterized by the *preeminence of the peer group* as a source of influence. The adolescent's circle of friends defines her/him in terms of a specific subgroup with a meaning in the neighborhood and the community. Parents sometimes become concerned about the groups that the adolescent is spending time with. Sometimes there is even pressure from parents for the adolescent to affiliate with the "right" group. Indirectly, high-school teachers also exert pressure on adolescents to affiliate with groups by recognizing the *normality* of belonging to identifiable peer groups. Perhaps the most direct and intense pressure to identify with a peer group comes from the adolescent's age-mates, who support the affiliation as a standard norm of adolescence.

Like the individual in middle childhood, the early adolescent is involved in a process of *self-evaluation* based on experiences in the school and with the peer group. There is, however, a major difference in the self-evaluation of these two periods. The pressure of the peer group during middle childhood is not nearly as strong as during early adolescence. During middle childhood, there is relatively little emphasis on "belonging" and "affiliating" as primary features of self-identity. Being good at game skills, or "smart" in school, or good-looking, or a good "sport" or having some other positively evaluated characteristic is probably more important than being a member of a particular group. This attitude changes during early adolescence.

Early adolescence—"group" identity in the context of high school peers.

Photograph by Darryl Jacobson

General Characteristics of the Early Adolescent

General physical maturation. During this stage, males and females have parallel periods of physical growth. There is usually a somewhat dramatic rate of growth in the bones and muscles of the body. These changes have implications for participation in athletics or for sport skills.

Changes in sexual factors and reproductive capability. Closely related to changes in the skeletal and muscular dimensions of the body are changes in the reproductive systems. The psychological implications of these changes for the individual may include several reactions:

- A greater concern about and attention to the self as a result of the rapidity of the physical changes.
- Ambivalent feelings toward the self as a result of the recognition that changes have occurred. (The physical and sexual changes of early adolescence signal not only the beginning of a new phase of development but the end of a relatively comfortable and safe period—childhood. Early adolescents often resort to peers for support and approval at this time.)

Cognitive development. The changes in thinking skills that occur during early adolescence result in a more flexible and abstract view of the world and allow the early adolescent to understand logical sequences of action and to anticipate consequences of behavior. These skills lead to an ability to project action from the past and the present into a future dimension. The school-aged child in concrete operations was somewhat limited to the real objects of the present or the past. Adolescents, however, are able to exert greater control over their behavior and their world because of their skill in anticipating a future.

Social skills. The early adolescent develops relationships with peers of both sexes that are more mature than those of the school-aged child. Part of the reason is that adolescents' cognitive skills enable them to understand the perspectives of other people better.

The Contexts of Early Adolescence. *The Family.* The early adolescent is still very much involved in the family. The nature of family relationships, however, is changing as both parent and adolescent become aware of the needs of a maturing person. Increasingly the evaluation of the self occurs more and more outside the family.

The Neighborhood and the Community. In middle childhood, the individual began to develop "cognitive maps" of the major features of the neighborhood and a limited understanding of the general community, including the workings of government. In early adolescence, individuals begin to understand the community as a working organism. They may understand how resources are exchanged and how political organizations control them.

The Peer Group. Toward the end of middle childhood, the peer group becomes more formally organized. In early adolescence, the peer group becomes a prominent source of feedback for self-evaluation and the individual is concerned with the opinions of others. It is not uncommon to find adolescents in a state of mild euphoria about being supported by the peer group. On the other hand, they may be in a state of mild depression when subjected to pressures for compliance or conformity. Usually individuals adjust fairly well to the differences of various peer-group members and provide mutual support for trying out the roles and the various lifestyles of adulthood. Although most adults have perfected these skills of mutual interaction to a high level of efficiency, the early adolescent is exposed for the first time to the challenges of developing self-confidence in the face of pressures for conformity. Some individuals may be unable to affiliate with any existing group. In some instances, this inability results in a sense of alienation from the group, particularly if the individual *wants* to belong but does not possess the social or personality skills to do so. On the other hand, an individual who possesses these skills but who does not feel that the peer group can offer anything valuable may feel rather comfortable with a decision not to affiliate. Whether the early adolescent decides to affiliate with a particular group or not, the point is that the individual is confronted with an affiliation choice. It is safe to say that most adolescents become involved with some group. The peer group provides most adolescents with a needed *consensus* and *interpretation* of what is *real* and with *feedback* concerning the adolescent's self-image.

The High School. The world of the high school, including the peer group, introduces the adolescent to the formal cognitive and social skills needed for independent living or for continued education in later adolescence and youth.

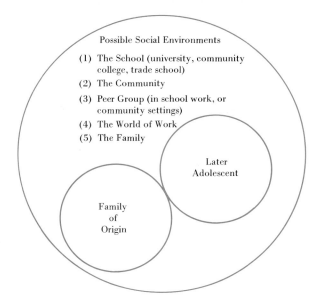

FIGURE 9.3 The system of later adolescence (youth). Youth may, in some cases, still be living at home. Or, they may have started a "new" family relationship of their own.

LATER ADOLESCENCE OR YOUTH: THE SELF IN CONTEXT

Figure 9.3 illustrates the "world" or the "system" of later adolescence. The essential difference between early and later adolescence is the increased autonomy and independence of the later adolescent years (see Figure 9.4). Several factors contribute to this emerging sense of independence:

- In some cases, living away from home.
- Thinking skills that allow independent problem-solving and contribute to an emerging lifestyle.
- Relatively stable and self-determined peer relations and friendships.

As the adolescent develops a more mature relationship with his or her parents, he or she also leaves the relatively stable world of the high-school

FIGURE 9.4 The evolution of identity from early to later adolescence.

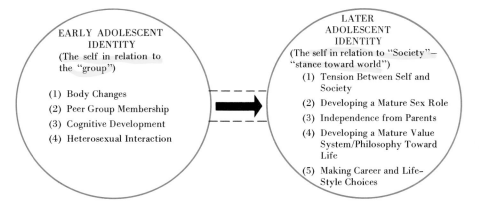

Later adolescence involves increased autonomy and independence.

Photograph by Darryl Jacobson

peer world for the uncharted seas of college or the world of work. These new experiences require the development of new self-regulatory skills. In the case of noncollege adolescents, career choice and vocational development may occur rather soon after high school. Although such individuals may, to some extent, experiment with various job roles or lifestyles, they are in many ways similar to young adults, whom we discuss in Chapter Ten. That is, they are confronted with the responsibility of supporting themselves, making a living, and, in some cases, supporting a family. for college-bound adolescents, continued experimentation and thinking about alternative careers and lifestyles is possible for a somewhat longer period of time.

As a result of either an initial job experience or continued role preparation and role experimentation in college, later adolescents usually become aware of the values and constraints of their society and culture. They may begin the "sorting" process of examining the options available to them. The idealism of the "desirable" may be transformed into the reality of the "possible."

As the individual progresses through the period of later adolescence and into early adulthood, one might wonder what has happened to the peer-group influence that has been so prominent since middle childhood. In early adolescence, the peer relationship usually occurs through group membership in the context of the high-school world. Peer relationships and friendships are ordinarily with individuals of similar age because of the organization of the high-school experience in terms of age. Peer relationships in later adolescence usually not as rigidly organized around age as in early adolescence.

The skills of peer interaction and group membership acquired during the high school years may prepare the individual for later participation in a given career or lifestyle. Several *major themes* or *issues* organize development and behavior in later adolescence or youth (see Figure 9.4).

The Tension Between the Self and Society. Whereas the early adolescent develops an identity in terms of the high-school peer group, later adolescents or youth must begin the process of determining who they are in relation to their culture and their society. This sense of identity may lead to the recognition of possible conflict between the self and the social order (Keniston, 1975).

Ambivalence toward both self and society and the attempt to make the two more congruent are central problems of youth. As Keniston (1975) suggested, "In youth, then, the potential and ambivalent conflicts between autonomous selfhood and social involvement—between the maintenance of personal integrity and the achievement of effectiveness in society—are fully experienced for the first time" (p. 10).

The attempt to deal with the tension between the self and society leads to what Keniston (1975) called the "wary probe." Whereas the early adolescent experiments with various roles or lifestyles with the aim of defining the self, later adolescents or youth attempt more serious and lasting ventures into the adult world. They can test aspects of the existing order more extensively and in a more precise fashion than early adolescents.

As later adolescents gain greater autonomy from the family, "probing" both the self and the society may become a central dimension of their lives. Through such "wary probing," each gradually comes to a "resolution" of the tension between herself of himself and society. This "resolution" is at the core

404

of what is meant by *identity* (Erikson, 1965). A positive resolution of the tension between the self and society does *not eliminate* the tension but recognizes and accepts it as a real and perhaps necessary ingredient of continued development.

One way to understand the meaning of this resolution is to examine Erikson's definition of *identity* as a "stance toward the world." (The polarities "identity versus self-diffusion" describe this process.) Identity involves a *balance* between the self and its relationship to or "stance" toward society. The meaning of this balance can be clarified further by a look at two extreme and inappropriate "resolutions" of the tension between the self and society:

- *Alienation from the self.* This "resolution" involves the affirmation of society but the denial of self. In other words, the individual resolves the tension between society and the self by ignoring the self and "selling out" or joining the "rat race."
- *Alienation from society.* This "resolution" reduces tension by simply eliminating or blocking out the reality of society, which is not the same thing as a rejection of society; rather, it is a denial that society exists. "Here the integrity of the self is purchased at the price of a determined denial of social reality and the loss of social effectiveness" (Keniston, 1975, p. 16).

An appropriate "identity" involves a balanced recognition of *both* the self and society.

Sex-Role Identity. The continued development of sex-role identity during later adolescence involves the mature acceptance of one's sexuality and the choice of an occupation and a life pattern that reflect this acceptance. Several important experiences that occur before later adolescence contribute to sex-role identity. For example, same-sex peer relationships during middle childhood and early adolescence help the child learn about intimacy between equals and norms for behaving as a male or a female. As children enter later adolescence, they encounter further expectations from adults, as well as peers, regarding mature sex-role behavior. These expectations include such things as holding a job and providing for a family for males and maternal–supportive behavior for females (later in this chapter we will see that many of these traditional expectations have changed or are in the process of changing). At the end of later adolescence, the young person has a sex-role identity that will serve as a basis for further growth in adulthood.

Autonomy and Understanding from Parents. As the individual approaches the end of childhood, the period of early adolescence sets a foundation for separation from the parents and a reliance on peer-group values. Although these values may not be totally different from parental values and beliefs, the fact that the individual is coming to rely more on extrafamilial sources for self-definition is the critical factor. Once this foundation is established, the individual is prepared for the next major step of self-definition in terms of culture, society, and community. The break with the family may be a gradual process in which both the adolescent and the family grow positively toward separation and independence, or the break may be more difficult (see Application Box: Leaving Home as the Capstone to Identity—a Family/Systems Perspective).

Leaving Home as a Capstone to Adolescent Identity—A Family/Systems Perspective

Every year virtually thousands of adolescents leave home for the first time to attend college or to work. Leaving home represents the beginning of adult status. Success in achieving full adult status as a psychologically autonomous individual may depend, to a large extent, on the impact of their departure on the *family system* (e.g., the attitudes of the parents toward their children and their own lives.)

Regardless of the timing or the manner of leaving home, many parents and young people are sometimes puzzled by the separation process. Is there a right or correct time for the adolescent to leave home? Our society offers few guidelines for assuring a smooth transition from adolescence to adulthood. How do parents know if they are pushing their children out of the nest too early or whether they are clinging too long to their offspring?

Several case studies will illustrate the variety of the timing of leaving home:

1. *Karen—Leaving Home Too Soon.* Some adolescents leave home before their parents think they are ready to do so. Karen was a 17-year-old who was living at home with her parents until two months before graduation from high school. At that time she had a violent argument with her mother about her right to stay out late at night and left home. Although she realized that her parents were upset about her departure, she felt that she could no longer live at home where she felt confined and unable to be anything more than a child.

2. *Brian—Leaving Home With ''No Hassle''.* Brian grew up in Fresno, California, and graduated from high school in 1979. In a scene that seemed to be right out of the movie *American Graffiti,* Brian boarded a plane and flew East to college. He returned home during summers and most vacations. After graduation Brian took a job with an advertising firm in Boston. Due to the re-

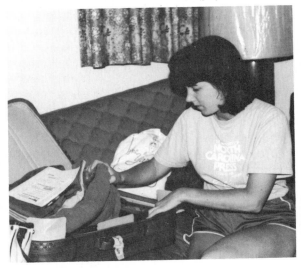

Photograph by Gale Schiamberg

quirements of his working activities, he was able to return home less and less regularly, usually only a few times a year. Brian's leaving home was a gradual process that seemed perfectly normal to both Brian and his parents.

3. *John—No Pressure to Leave Home.* John was 28 years old, the son of a retired construction worker in Sioux City, Iowa. He was the second of five children. John's older brother was married and lived nearby. His three younger sisters, aged 12, 17 and 19, also lived at home. John worked for a local radio station. He used part of his salary to help his family pay the bills. The family was always close and John never felt any pressure to leave home or, for that matter, to stay at home. Although he lived at home, John was treated as an adult and could come and go as he pleased.

Despite the variation in patterns of leaving home, there is evidence that, in both a psychological and a physical sense, leaving home is becoming more difficult. Since the late 1960s the percentage of young Americans living at home has increased by 25 percent. One reason for this increase is economic. That is, young people are finding it harder to find jobs and to financially establish themselves. In addition, the average age of marriage for both males and females has risen. This means, of course, that young people are living at home for longer periods of time before marriage then previous generations of youth.

An emerging body of research has demonstrated the important relationship of the adolescent's success in leaving home to the *family system* (Haley, 1980; Stierlin, 1974, 1975; Sullivan and Sullivan, 1980). In a series of studies at the National Institutes of Mental Health, Stierlin (1974) reported on the clinical profiles of 30 families who were referred to his group for family counseling because of a troubled adolescent child. Stierlin and his colleagues found that the adolescents' problems appeared to be linked to problems in the lives of their middle-aged parents.

The fathers of these adolescents appeared to be undergoing serious doubts about the direction of their own lives at the very moment their adolescent offspring seemed to have an array of options in love and work. These fathers were threatened by their child's movement toward adulthood. They responded to this situation with either total disengagement and lack of involvement or bickering criticism.

Stierlin and his colleagues found that the mothers of the adolescents were, like the fathers, involved in a crisis of their own at the time of adolescent separation. These mothers were confronted with the prospect of an "empty nest" or the loss of their child-rearing role. Many of these women responded by becoming overly involved in the lives of their children—to the point of meddling and intrusion of privacy—at the very time when these adolescents needed to be autonomous and independent.

A common result of this family profile of "resigned" fathers and "intrusive" mothers was an unhappy and frequently abrupt departure of the adolescent. In other instances, Stierlin found that when such adolescents remained at home, the relationship with their parents was characterized as a "running battle." Regardless of whether they left home or not, Stierlin found that these adolescents failed at the central tasks of adolescent identity formation—a beginning career orientation and meaningful interpersonal relationships outside the family.

The research of Stierlin and his colleagues has been supported by the findings of Jay Haley (1980). According to Haley, a family therapist, the time of greatest challenge or threat to a family system occurs when someone is entering the family (e.g., birth of a child) or leaving the family (e.g., the adolescent leaving the home or the death of a family member). Haley suggested that frequently when adolescents become involved in troublesome behaviors such as drug addiction, criminality, or school failure, the process of leaving home is *malfunctioning* for the *entire family system.* Haley frequently traced these adolescent problems to the need of some family members to preserve the stability of an unhealthy family system even at the price of damage to the psychological development of another family member. For example, the adolescent's problems often served to prevent the parents from addressing issues in their own relationship that might—when faced honestly and directly—result in divorce. Thus, if the adolescent's failures to successfully adapt in school, work, or intimate relationships regularly occupied parents' attention, then the family system could be saved. Unfortunately, the cost was high—the emotional growth of the adolescent.

Although most adolescents manage to leave home successfully, the question still remains—what is the significance of leaving home? The overall importance of leaving home lies in the challenge which such a separation from parents poses to childhood identity (e.g., dependency on parents). However, it is important to distinguish between *physically* leaving home (simply living at a physical distance, apart from one's family of origin) and *symbolically* leaving home. Symbolically leaving home is the process of identity formation necessary for the attainment of independent adult status. It can be attained whether or not the adolescent physically leaves home. In other words, the real significance of leaving home is as an inner process not an outer movement. Leaving home, then, is the capstone to adolescent identity which marks the beginning of adulthood.

School-Aged Parent   Early-Adolescent Parent   Youth-and-Early-Adulthood Parent

Although early adolescents may discover that their parents are not perfect and have weaknesses, in later adolescence the parents begin to be recognized as "persons" (human beings with strengths, weaknesses, concerns, problems, and products of their own historical situations). During early adolescence, the "hero worship" of parents begins to give way to a somewhat negative view. The early adolescent may become increasingly aware of parental weaknesses and shortcomings, and parents' "clay feet" may overshadow everything else. However, it is during youth that the parents may be rediscovered as "real" people (neither the "heroes" of childhood nor the "incompetents" of early adolescence). It is probably no accident that this understanding of parents as people begins during later adolescence, when youth are themselves probing the tensions between self and society.

An Internal Moral Code and an Emerging Philosophy of Life. For the young child, many moral issues were resolved in terms of the parents' point of view; that is, morality for the very young child was determined by the satisfaction of the child's needs or by rewards or punishments given by the parents ("preconventional morality"). Morality for individuals in middle childhood is determined by the fulfillment of parental expectations of the "right" role behavior ("conventional morality"). Both the preconventional and the conventional levels of morality are based on the child's subordinate role to adult authority. As adolescents gain autonomy from their parents and are able to think about such abstract concepts as justice and freedom (we will discuss the development of adolescent thinking later in this chapter), they become capable of developing their own reasons for moral decisions. Not every person or adult reaches this level of moral reasoning ("postconventional") (Kohlberg and Gilligan, 1972).

Career Choice and a Concept of the Future. The young person often has to make the choice of her/his life's work in the absence of actual experience in the world of work. There are some educational activities that can aid the individual in making an effective choice. Organized high school work experiences can give a person insight into the climate, expectations, and rewards that exist in a particular occupational area. Such experiences may also

408

provide information about how to gain access to a particular career (e.g., the necessary skills and training).

The Contexts of the Adolescent System

To understand adolescents fully, one needs to look at the culture in which they live as well as the social institutions with which they interact: educational institutions, economic institutions (e.g., work), and the family. In this section, we first examine the general cultural and social system as a context for adolescent development. Next we examine the principal institutions in which adolescents are socialized.

THE CULTURE AND THE SOCIETY AS A CONTEXT

In the world in which adolescents live, cultural and social values, norms, and expectations pervade their experience. The high-school years are, in some sense, a preparation for living in a given culture and society. The specific skills learned in the high school as well as the social skills developed through peer interactions are a basis for social adaptation to the world of work, to interpersonal relationships, and, for many individuals, to family life.

Preparation for adult responsibilities has become more difficult as the rate of social change has increased. Adjusting to changes in society or personal circumstances is not easy for some people. Because of rapid social change, the future has become less predictable, complicating the role of adolescents attempting to make vocational choices and of schools attempting to prepare individuals with the skills necessary for the future (Schiamberg, 1973).

THE COMMUNITY

In middle childhood, the individual experiences the excitement of "discovering" people and things in the community. The firehouse, the police station, the city hall, and the supermarket are part of the "concrete" world of middle childhood. They are there, it seems, to be innocently experienced, to be visited, or to be talked about. But certainly they are not to be seriously criticized or thought about in too much detail. In adolescence, this changes.

By adolescence, the neighborhood–community boundaries are expanded, and the adolescent has increasing freedom to explore the neighborhood and community. By adolescence, most individuals have experienced numerous independent trips in and around the community with their friends. During early adolescence, the child consolidates a notion of herself or himself as a resident of a city and perhaps of a state. The concept of national affiliation, however, does not appear to develop until around twelve years of age or after (Piaget and Inhelder, 1969).

Although the early and later adolescents' ability to think about their social worlds may be enhanced, their ability to interact meaningfully with the broad social community may still be limited because there has been, and increasingly continues to be, a traditional pattern of segregating adolescents from adults (Coleman, 1974). There are both advantages and disadvantages to such enforced separation (see Application Box: Adolescents and Rapid Social Change).

Adolescents and Rapid Social Change

We indicated that adolescence is a period of change for young people. All sorts of things are happening to the bodies of adolescents, to their thinking skills, and to their social relations with peers and parents. The adolescent is, in turn, trying to manage and organize these changes in some sort of reasonable way. As we pointed out, the identity of the later adolescent involves the organization of these changes in the self into a "stance toward the world" (Erikson, 1968). Now how do adolescents come to understand the nature of this "world" to which they must address themselves? Is this "world" relatively clear and understandable to both adolescents and adults? Are certain aspects of this world fairly clear and relatively constant over time? Or, does the rate of social change make it difficult for adolescents (or anyone, for that matter) to plan for a "future"?

Social change has always occurred; however, the difference today is the degree of change to which individuals are exposed. Using the metaphor of a clock, with each minute representing 50 years (60 minutes = 3000 years), the following somewhat startling conclusions follow: (1) the printing press was invented nine minutes ago; (2) the phonograph and the locomotive arrived three minutes ago; (3) the automobile and the airplane were invented two minutes ago; and (4) television appeared in the last ten seconds (Toffler, 1972). It is apparent that enormous numbers of social changes have occurred in a relatively short space of time, and there is little reason to expect that this increasing pace of social change will not continue. There is some reason to think it will get worse. The effects of technological change are usually not arithmetic (building one upon the other in additive fashion). Instead they are geometric in their impact on the social fabric, producing changes each of which produce other changes and so on (building one upon the other in multiplicative fashion). The invention of the printing press by Gutenberg was a technological innovation which made a dramatic impact upon the social system—a new media provided information,

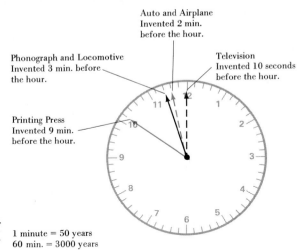

Auto and Airplane Invented 2 min. before the hour.

Phonograph and Locomotive Invented 3 min. before the hour.

Television Invented 10 seconds before the hour.

Printing Press Invented 9 min. before the hour.

1 minute = 50 years
60 min. = 3000 years

The increasing rate of social change (the clock as a metaphor).

helped to promote many on-going social changes such as the Protestant Reformation, and helped to pave the way for newer political forms. The social impact of the printing press was geometric (multiplicative), affecting many elements of society which, in turn, affected other elements (Toffler, 1972).

In recent years, what has changed is the *number of changes*. These are occurring simultaneously, with results as significant and perhaps more dramatic than those of the printing press. If the printing press had a profound influence on society, then imagine the simultaneous impact of the computer, the automobile, the television, and the laser beam. The degree to which human beings can tolerate continued social change and the resulting level of frustration and uncertainty is at best unclear.

Adapted from L. Schiamberg, *Adolescent Alienation*, Columbus, Ohio: Charles E. Merrill Publishing Co., 1973.

Arguments for and Against Segregation of Adolescents from Adults—What Do You Think?

Our society has changed in the past century from one in which the young . . . (14–24) were in frequent and continued contact with persons older than they to one in which adult contacts are confined to parents and teachers. The age segregation is extensive enough to deprive youth and adults from effective contact with one another. . . .

a. *Benefits of segregating youth from adults:* In the past the segregation of the young into schools was in part carried out as a protection for the young and in part as a custodial agency to free adults. It was protective for the young to shield them from the harsh work activities of adults and from the predatory behavior of adults. . . . The family and school were seen as proper places for youth and efforts were devoted to insulating them from other institutions less beneficial to them. This protection remains codified in child labor laws and school attendance laws of today. For adults, the school kept the young in custody, freeing adults for more efficient production in their work organizations.

Both these benefits still exist to some degree. . . . But the harsh labor from which children were protected has vanished in many work places and legal machinery has been developed to shield youth from exploitation. . . .

b. *Benefits of age integration . . .* When adults go off to work institutions from which the young are excluded . . . , work organizations increase their own efficiency, but at the expense of the incidental learning and experience that youth would otherwise have. So long as other institutions (such as the community and the extended family) made up some of these deficits, the fact was not apparent. But it is evident now that a major means by which skills, culture, ideas, and information is [*sic*] transmitted is vanishing as direct contacts between youth and adults in structured situations decline.

. . . age integration . . . brings benefits to adults. Some work situations have become routine and dull to persons in them. If a larger portion of adults' everyday environment, on the job or off it, were in association with youth, the interaction would be a livening one. . . .

An additional benefit . . . of social integration is that it facilitates social order and lessens the social conflict between ages.

YOUR VIEW

What do you think? Do the benefits of integrating youth with the adult community outweigh the benefits of segregation?

Reprinted from J. S. Coleman, *Youth: Transition to Adulthood,* by permission of The University of Chicago Press, 1974, pp. 130–132. Copyright © 1974.

THE FAMILY

Social Changes and the Family. Urbanization and mobility of families have had a dramatic impact on the role of the family in the lives of adolescents. Over the last fifty years, the dramatic movement to cities coupled with the geographic mobility between cities (about 17 percent of the population moved within the United States between 1980 and 1981. U.S. Bureau of the Census, 1983) has resulted in several changes influencing families. In the first place, these changes have tended to weaken the very neighborhoods and communities that we have been talking about throughout this book in the following ways:

1. The stability of communities, or organized entities of families with historical roots, has been seriously weakened.
2. The relationship between the family, the community, and its institutions has become less effective.
3. Finally, the accumulated result of these changes has made the family responsibilities of child rearing more difficult.

The magnitude of the social changes that have occurred are often seen in the reminiscences of the parents of adolescents when they themselves were growing up. Bronfenbrenner (1970) has made the following observations:

Everybody in the neighborhood minded your business. . . . If you walked on the railroad trestle, the phone would ring at your house, and your parents would know what you had done before you got back home. People on the street would tell you to button your jacket, and ask why you were not in church last Sunday. Sometimes you liked it and sometimes you didn't—but at least people "cared." (p. 96)

Children coming into adolescence in the last twenty years or so have probably been exposed to a much different concept of community and neighborhood.

Effects of Social Changes on Adolescent–Parent Relationships. Conger (1971) identified several important changes in the general nature of parent–adolescent relationships that have resulted from the social changes discussed:

The decline in adult authority. In an earlier generation in this country, adolescents were more likely to view the parents' contributions to the family in a positive light. "Father Knows Best" was not only the name of a television series but was a generally accepted standard of family life.

Margaret Mead (1970) examined this decline in authority in relation to the relevance of parental models. Mead argued that in earlier and more stable eras (she called these eras "postfigurative"), children as well as adolescents could realistically rely on their parents (as well as other adult figures) as guides for the appropriate social and vocational skills of adulthood. More recent times have seen the development of a "cofigurative" era, in which the young look less to parents and more to their peers for guidance.

Age segregation. Another feature of social change—and in particular, the growth of an urban and technology-oriented society—has been the reduction in interactions between age groups. As pointed out in the report of the 1970 White House Conference on Children, adolescents are

deprived not only of parents but of people in general. A host of factors conspire to isolate the young from the rest of society. The fragmentation of the extended family, the separation of residential and business areas, the disappearance of neighborhoods, zoning ordinances, occupational mobility, child labor laws, the abolishment of the apprentice system, consolidated schools, television, separate patterns of social life for different age groups, the working mother, the delegation of child care specialists—all of these manifestations of progress operate to decrease opportunity and incentive for meaningful contact between children and persons older, or younger, than themselves. (Children and Parents, 1970, p. 10)

Adolescent–Parent Relationships. Despite the current concern about the relevance of parental models, it still appears that parents constitute a vital

Despite current concerns about the relevance of parental influence, parents are still vital in helping the adolescent.

Photograph by Darryl Jacobson

force in helping the adolescent (Conger, 1971). The events of childhood and, specifically, the history of parent–child relationships that adolescents bring with them from childhood affect the way that adolescents react to the new demands of the period. For example, the overprotected child may find the adolescent peer society unwilling to provide such indulgence. Perhaps the most important feature of adolescent–parent interaction is how this mutual relationship helps the adolescent to develop a sense of independence (Erikson, 1968; Douvan and Adelson, 1966). In the words of Conger (1971):

> Without the achievement of separation and autonomy, the adolescent can hardly be expected to achieve mature heterosexual or peer relationships, confident pursuit of a vocation, or a sense of identity, which requires a positive image of the self as separate, unified, and consistent over time. (p. 1125)

It appears that parents who use democratic practices and frequent explanations to the adolescent of the reasons for their rules foster responsible, independent behavior in their children. Democratic parents accomplish this end in several ways.

Providing Opportunities for Autonomy. Autonomy is encouraged when parents *communicate* with their adolescents and provide appropriate levels of control in the context of ongoing activities. Adolescents who experienced "democratic" child-rearing practices (i.e., the adolescent is given the chance to participate in discussions of relevant family issues—including the adolescent's own activities and behavior—and participates in decision making, although the parents still retain ultimate authority) were more likely to think that their parents were fair and reasonable than children of autocratic parents (Elder, 1962; Bowerman and Bahr, 1973). Furthermore the development of a positive self-image and a sense of independence was related to parents who attempted to "legitimize" the exercise of their authority by frequently explaining the basis for their rules (Elder, 1963). Lack of confidence and adolescent dependence were commonly found among children of autocratic parents, who provided neither guidelines for behavior nor explanations of rules. In summary, it appears that a positive self-image (which is the basis of inde-

Photograph by Wayne Mason

pendence) is the result of democratic adolescent–parent relationships in which parents actively support adolescent opinions and participation in family affairs and actively encourage autonomous behavior (Rosenberg, 1965; Baumrind, 1968).

Promoting Positive Identification with the Parent. Parents who demonstrate both respect and love for their child (Conger, 1971) promote the adolescent's positive identification with the parent.

Providing Models of Reasonable Independence in a Democratic Framework. The parent demonstrates independent behavior to the adolescent in the normal course of his or her own behavior in family and community settings (Conger, 1971).

Adolescent–Parent Conflicts. A not uncommon experience is the intensification of adolescent–parent conflict during the period of adolescence. It is important to note, however, that although there seems to be an increase in such conflict (at least for boys), parent–child relationships are generally more positive than negative during adolescence (Matteson, 1975; Kandel and Lesser, 1972). However, several reasons have been suggested for the apparent "conflict of generations" during the adolescent years (Schiamberg, 1969).

The Different Content of Experience. The adolescents of any given time are likely to be living under a different set of historical circumstances than their parents when they were adolescents. For example, the content of experience for an adolescent during the American Depression of the 1930s was quite different from that of an adolescent during the more affluent 1960s. Differing adolescent experiences may lead to different expectations about appropriate adolescent values or behavior.

The Lack of Clearly Defined Steps Marking the Recession of Parental Authority over Children and Adolescents. As we pointed out, it is quite clear

"Could you redefine those commandments so as to make them more meaningful to the youth of today?"

Drawing by W. Miller; © 1971 The New Yorker Magazine, Inc.

when adolescence begins (the onset of puberty). However, it is not nearly so clear when the period of adolescence is over. This lack of clarity or absence of formal ceremonies (rites of passage) to mark the beginning of adulthood makes it less certain when parental authority over the adolescent ends.

Psychological and Social Differences Between Adolescents and Their Parents. On the psychological level, adolescents have often been described as "idealistic" (Schiamberg, 1969, 1973). On the other hand, adults are sometimes described as "realistic." This difference between the generations is often attributed to the "experience" of adults. Furthermore, this difference between the generations is not something new or recent. The ancient Greek philosopher Aristotle felt that the youth of his day were not only idealistic but also naive and overconfident of their knowledge and abilities. He said, "They think they know everything and are always quite sure about it. This, in fact, is why they overdo everything."

On the social level, there are differences in the "roles" of parent and adolescent. For example, the parent's role during childhood and, to some degree adolescence, is to supervise or oversee the development of the young person. Adolescents, on the other hand, need independent experiences to establish themselves as persons in their own right.

Adolescent–parent conflict or disagreement may be considered a normal activity in the process of adolescent self-determination (Elkind, 1968). The nature of the disagreements varies with the age of the adolescent and the maturity of the parent. Elkind pointed out that the issues that arise in these conflicts are real or imagined violations of three types of "contractual arrangements" between the parent and the adolescent:

- *The Bargain.* In this arrangement, the parent offers to reward (or to withhold punishment) in return for compliance by the child or the adolescent. Rather early in life, many children learn to negotiate such bargains successfully. Grounds for conflict may occur, for example, if the adolescent hears (or "thinks" he or she hears) his or her father agree to give him or her the car for Saturday night, providing the grass is mowed.

- *The Agreement.* This arrangement is more complex and lasts longer than the bargain. The parent(s) and the adolescent agree to abide by certain rules over time. For example, such rules might include the following:
  "If you (adolescent) agree to drive safely, then I (parent) feel comfortable giving you the car more frequently."
  "If you (parent) respect my right to privacy, then I (adolescent) would feel better about sharing some of my feelings with you."

- *The Contract.* This arrangement is the most complex and the least explicit of adolescent–parent relationships. In a contract, the parent and the adolescent interact with one another on the basis of *mutual expectations* that are unspoken (assumed). These expectations, in turn, derive from the history of parent–child bargains and agreements.

  Because contracts are seldom verbalized, their existence comes to light only in the breach. For example, an adolescent may say, "Despite how hard I work around the house and try to please my parents, it's never enough." Such a statement indicates a real or perceived breach of a contract.

Some Things Parents and Adolescents Disagree About

Although adolescents and their parents may disagree about numerous things, there are five major areas of conflict (Matteson, 1975). In the order of frequency, these areas are

- *Social life and customs.* Disagreements may center on such things as adolescent's dating partners, "quality" of the adolescent's friends, and peer activities.
- *Responsibility.* Parents tend to be critical of adolescents who display irresponsible behavior. For example, the adolescent who is often late to an after-school job or who always seems to "forget" that he/she promised to complete a household chore may incur the displeasure of the parent.
- *School.* School performance, behavior at school, and the adolescent's attitude toward school receive a good deal of attention from parents.
- *Family Relationships.* The nature of adolescent interactions with parents, siblings, or relatives attracts the attention of parents. Are the relationships characterized by tenseness, by superficiality, or, perhaps, by mutual understanding? Do some parents and adolescents have an uncanny habit of "goading" one another?
- *Values or Morals.* The numerous possibilities for disagreement include sexual values (e.g., premarital sexual relationships), the "value" of material things, appropriate career goals, and the "value" of education. The particular area of value conflict between parent and adolescent depends on the age and, to some extent, the sex of the adolescent.

Parents and adolescents are sometimes indifferent to each other's needs as developing human beings. Several reasons are given for such apparent insensitivity (Elkind, 1968; Schiamberg, 1969).

Parental Cultural Impoverishment. This is the parents' inability to anticipate future events or their tendencies to enter into restrictive contracts with the adolescent. Sometimes parents lack the experience to enable them to comprehend contemporary reality.

Parental Personality Constrictions. Because of their own personality needs, parents may be unable to cope with the adolescent's growing need for freedom. American parents tend to want to hold onto the adolescent. While the adolescent is struggling with the various changes in her or his life, her or his parents are often dealing with changes in their own lives. Conflicts over their own responsibilities make parents less able to respond to the adolescent's needs for independence (Scherz, 1967).

Mutual Insensitivity. Often parents may feel that youth are crazy and reckless, and too inexperienced to recognize that they are foolish and take chances. This assessment is presumably based on the parents' many years of experience. Parents may worry that their children will have accidents, get hurt, or get into trouble with the law. Adolescents feel that their parents are overly cautious and worry too much. Parents who are middle-aged tend to compare today's youth and their lifestyle with the way it was when the parents were growing up. Adolescents are sometimes idealistic and want instant reform. They may be annoyed when their parents do not agree with their thoughts. Finally, aging adults may become sensitive about growing old and may focus more and more attention on staying young. The adolescent wants to grow up but may never really "understand" or empathize with parents who are themselves growing old.

THE PEER GROUP AS A CONTEXT FOR DEVELOPMENT

Peer groups and friends provide the adolescent with an arena for much of the learning that occurs in early adolescence. In this section, we examine the following topics: (1) the functions of the peer group; (2) the structure of the peer group and how that structure changes over time; and finally, (3) the stages of peer-group development and friendships.

The Functions of the Peer Group. Peers play a vital role in the life of the adolescent as the adolescent's ties with parents become looser. Increasingly, relationships with peers of both the same and the opposite sex serve as an introduction and a prelude to later adult relationships in work and social relations. The functions of the peer group include the following.

The Provision of Primary Status. Primary status is the status that the individual earns through her or his own efforts and through the demonstration of her or his abilities and skills. It differs from attributed status, which comes from being a member of a given family. Peer groups help the adolescent to form a self-image by conferring a primary status.

Providing Norms for Governing Behavior. By moving into and forming peer groups that establish their own norms and standards of behavior, the adolescent is able to deviate from parental norms while having the support of significant others. This support is particularly important to the adolescent because of the initial confusion the early adolescent must experience when confronted with the mass of possible values, life styles, and vocations that comprise our society. Peer-group norms are designed to provide both guidelines for behavior and a source of common evaluation for appraising activities (Dunphy, 1963; Sherif and Sherif, 1964).

Facilitating Emancipation from the Family. We might begin by asking why it is necessary to be "emancipated" from the family. There are at least two good reasons. In the first place, as we pointed out earlier in our discussion of adolescent–parent relationships, healthy family relationships move naturally and normally in the direction of adolescent independence. The peer group builds on this trend. Second, because of the intensity of relationships in the modern nuclear family, the peer group serves a "distancing" function between parents and adolescents. That is, the peer group helps the parent to "see" the adolescent as an independent individual. Furthermore the adolescent begins to understand both the satisfaction and the pain of relating to others in an independent, adult fashion. These experiences help adolescents begin to appreciate their parents as people. (Youniss, 1980)

The Peer Group as a Testing Ground. The peer group allows adolescents to test themselves in a variety of roles. They can test abilities, emotions, feelings, values, and lifestyles within an empathic group. By observing and talking about how peers react to her or his way of thinking or behaving, the adolescent is further able to extend and refine her or his self-concept and range of behaviors. (Youniss, 1980)

What Do Adolescents Expect from Their Parents?

The following is a composite (and by no means all-inclusive) list of some parental characteristics that seem beneficial to the adolescent (Elder, 1964; Matteson, 1975; Elkind, 1968).

Parental interest and help. One of the ways that adolescents know their parents care about them is by their interest and their willingness to back the adolescents up and help them when necessary. Adolescents want attention from their parents.

Listening, understanding, and talking. A frequent complaint of adolescents is that their parents do not listen to their ideas or accept their opinions as relevant or try to understand their feelings or point of view. Adolescents seem to value sympathetic, "understanding" parents who feel that their child has something important to say and are willing, therefore, to communicate with her or him.

Love and acceptance. One of the components of love is acceptance. One way that love is shown is by knowing, and then accepting, the adolescent as he or she is, faults and all.

Trust. Some parents have difficulty trusting their adolescents. These parents tend to project their own fears, anxieties, and guilt onto the adolescent.

Photograph by Darryl Jacobson

Autonomy. One goal of every adolescent is to be accepted as an independent individual. As we have pointed out, such autonomy increases during adolescence. The shift in "emotional autonomy" during adolescence is not as dramatic as in "behavioral autonomy." The adolescent wants and needs parents who will grant independence, but in slowly increasing amounts, rather than all at once.

Peer-Group Structure. How are peer groups organized? What types of peer groups are there? In one of the earlier studies on the structure of adolescent peer groups and the organization of the "adolescent society," Coleman (1961) found that the "leading crowds" in high schools throughout the United States were similarly composed. There was a relatively large emphasis on athletics and popular girls and far less emphasis on academics or the brilliant student.

A replication of this early research (Eitzen, 1975) indicated that the adolescent hasn't changed much in the last fifteen to twenty years (at least, in terms of the support and prominence accorded various groups). Athletics were still of primary importance to the adolescent and to status in high school. To the question, "What does it take to be important?" the answer "good grades, honor roll" ranked fourth out of six items for boys and fifth out of six items for girls.

Crowds and Cliques in Peer Groups. The social structure of peer groups is composed of two basic subgroups: cliques and crowds (Dunphy, 1963). The *clique,* or the small grouping of two, three, or four friends, gives the adolescent the chance to establish some degree of companionship, security, and acceptance before moving out into the larger social scene or crowd. The *crowd* is the larger unit.

Cliques and crowds have differential functions. Most of the crowd, or large-group activities (dances, hayrides, parties, and so on) occur on weekends, whereas the cliques usually meet on weekdays. Crowd activities are more formally organized, whereas cliques meet informally during as well as before and after school. The predominant activity of cliques is conversation. They perform the function of organizing, publicizing, and evaluating crowd activities.

APPLICATION BOX

The Suicidal Adolescent

The thought of a teenager destroying his young life is so appalling that one tends to minimize the extent of this problem. However, the adolescent suicide rate has generally risen; the rate per 100,000 population for 15 to 24 year olds was 13.9 for white males in 1970 and 21.0 in 1979; 10.5 for black males in 1970 and 14.4 in 1979. The rate for females per 100,000 population was 4.2 for white females in 1970 and 5.1 in 1979 and 3.8 for black females in 1970 and 3.4 in 1979 [U.S. Bureau of the Census, *Statistical Abstract of the United States: 1982–83* (103rd ed.). Washington, D.C.: U.S. Government Printing Office, 1982)].

These figures become even more alarming when we realize that many suicides are not recorded as suicides but may be recorded as accidents.

For example, a physician may be reluctant to report a death as a suicide in order to "protect" a family he has served for a number of years. A death by suicide may be interpreted by the parents as a personal failure, whereas accidental death does not carry as heavy a burden of guilt. . . .

POSSIBLE DANGER SIGNS

Truancy from school and running away from home could be signs of a troubled teenager. Other signs to watch for are:

Exaggerated or extended apathy, inactivity, or boredom

Subtle signs of self-destructive behavior, such as carelessness and accident proneness

Loss of appetite or excessive eating

Decrease in verbal communication

Withdrawal from peer activities and from previously enjoyed activities

Substance abuse (drugs, alcohol)

Sleep disturbance (nightmares, difficulty falling asleep, early morning awakening)

Academic decline

Unusually long grief reaction following a loss (death, divorce, girlfriend/boyfriend relationship)

Tearfulness

Depressive feelings such as sadness or discouragement, when they are more than transient, and especially if found in association with the breakdown of relationships with significant others

Recent hostile behavior (e.g., arguments with parents, unruly behavior in school)

Recent increase in interpersonal conflict with significant others

A decrease in or inability to tolerate frustration

Almost any sustained deviation from the normal pattern of behavior should be taken seriously and evaluated further.

Taken from Hart, N. A. and Keidel, G. C., "The Suicidal Adolescent," *American Journal of Nursing,* 1979, pp. 80–84.

Peer relationships involve both crowds and cliques.

Photographs by Darryl Jacobson

Stage 3, the crowd in transition, marks the beginning of the *heterosexual clique.*

Photograph by Darryl Jacobson

Stages of Peer-Group Development. The development of the peer group in adolescence is marked by several distinct stages. Each of these stages serves to regulate and organize the adolescent's social development and particularly his/her heterosexual relationships (Dunphy, 1963) (see Figure 9.5).

Stage 1: The PreCrowd Stage. Stage 1 includes the isolated unisexual peer groups of late childhood and beginning adolescence. There is little interaction *between* groups and almost no organized dating. What is learned occurs primarily *within* the group.

Stage 2: The Beginning of the Crowd. Stage 2 includes unisexual peer groups and the *beginnings* of group-to-group heterosexual interaction. Such interaction is considered "daring" and is undertaken only in the presence of other group members. For example, arranging a date requires the support of fellow group members to bolster the courage of the "asker."

Stage 3: The Crowd in Transition. Stage 3 marks the beginning of the *heterosexual clique.* The upper-status members of the unisexual cliques begin to form an emergent heterosexual grouping. Those adolescents who belong to these emergent groupings still maintain membership in their unisexual groups.

Stage 4: The Fully Developed Crowd. Stage 4 is marked by heterosexual cliques in close association.

Stage 5: Beginning of Crowd Disintegration. With graduation from high school, the "glue" that held the heterosexual cliques together is no longer present. High-school heterosexual cliques are replaced by loose associations of couples.

Friendships. Whereas cliques and crowds operate as facilitators of social development in adolescence, intimate friendships (usually within peer groups) are important to self-development. The most important feature of adolescent friendship is the sharing of one's feelings and thoughts about important and everyday concerns.

As in the case of peer groups, there is a *developmental pattern of friendships* in adolescence (Douvan and Adelson, 1966).

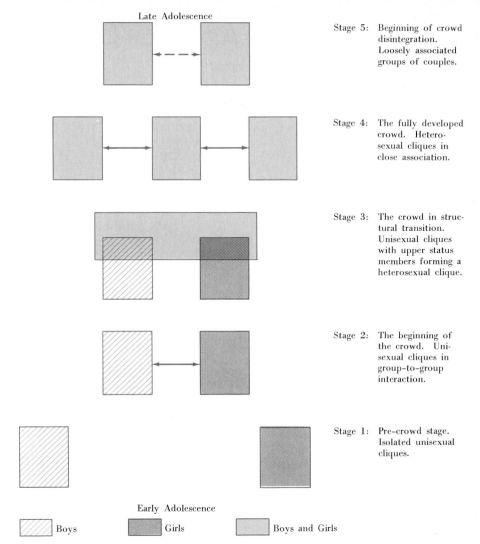

Late Adolescence

Stage 5: Beginning of crowd disintegration. Loosely associated groups of couples.

Stage 4: The fully developed crowd. Hetero-sexual cliques in close association.

Stage 3: The crowd in structural transition. Unisexual cliques with upper status members forming a heterosexual clique.

Stage 2: The beginning of the crowd. Unisexual cliques in group-to-group interaction.

Stage 1: Pre-crowd stage. Isolated unisexual cliques.

Early Adolescence

Boys   Girls   Boys and Girls

FIGURE 9.5 Stages of peer group development in adolescence.

Reprinted by permission from D. C. Dunphy, "The Social Structure of Urban Adolescent Peer Groups," *Sociometry,* 1963, 26(2), 230–246.

Superficial Sharing. Superficial sharing usually characterizes early adolescence. Friendship is based on the sharing of time, things, or mutual activity rather than on the sharing of thoughts or feelings. Douvan and Adelson (1966) described this stage of friendship as follows:

It is a busy age then [ages eleven to thirteen]; and the nature of friendship . . . reflects this business. . . . The friends focus more on activity—on what they are doing together—than they do on themselves. . . . We see this in the fact that girls at this period can tell us so little about friendship. When we ask what a friend ought to be like . . . the early adolescent mentions fewer qualities than older girls do. More important, the qualities she does mention are fairly superficial ones. For example, she wants a friend to do favors for her. She wants the friend to be . . . easy to get along with, cooperative and fair. (p. 186)

A Catalogue of "American Graffitti"— Types of Peer Groups

Analyses of the informal peer-group structure in the American high school have indicated several clearly identifiable groups (Reister and Zucker, 1968; Manaster, 1977). As you read the descriptions of the peer groups below, see if they resemble some of the groups during your high-school years. Are there some significant ones we have omitted? Do some now go by different names?

The "collegiates." These individuals are socially active in the high school and tend to be oriented toward the values and attitudes of the high-school establishment (including teachers, principals, and other students with "status").

The "hoods" or "greasers." These individuals act rougher and tougher than others. They are often noticeable by their dress, which might include leather jackets, boots, or a particular hairstyle. The "Fonz" of the television program "Happy Days" is a likely candidate.

"True individuals." These individuals may be identified by their clothes, hairstyle, or attitudes. Over the last twenty years, this peer group has been given various titles, including "beatniks," "hippies," "yippies," and "freaks."

The "quiet" kids. These individuals seem to be quite independent and to "go their own way." To most of their age-mates, they appear to be somewhat of a mystery. "Who are they?" and "Where have I seen you before?" are common responses to them. Although they may belong to a group, it is probably outside the school.

"Intellectuals." These are students who are serious about their studies. They are usually particularly interested in several school subjects. These individuals are known to others through their academic performance and sometimes through such symbols as briefcases loaded with books.

"Kids going steady." These individuals usually spend a great deal of time together, as well as with other couples.

The "jocks." These are individuals who participate in organized high-school team sports. In addition to association during game and practice sessions, they may associate closely with one another at other times.

Based on your own high school experiences, you may recall some additional groups. If so, describe them below:

Name _____
Characteristics _____

Name _____
Characteristics _____

Photographs by Darryl Jacobson

Heterosexual peer relations become more common in the high school years.

Photograph by Richard Levin

Superficial sharing usually characterizes early adolescence.

Photograph by Darryl Jacobson

Intense Sharing. Intense sharing occurs in early to middle adolescence. During this time of trying on roles, sampling lifestyles, testing the limits of personal abilities, and acknowledging sexual changes, the adolescent requires the *continuous* and intense support of a friend. Friendship during this period may be marked by a *feverish* or desperate quality because of relative insecurity about self-concept, dating, or sexual changes.

Douvan and Adelson (1966) described this stage of friendship in girls (fourteen, fifteen, and sixteen years old) as follows:

What stands out . . . is the stress placed on security in friendships. They want the friend to be loyal, trustworthy and a reliable source of support. . . . Why so much emphasis on loyalty? We imagine that part of the reason is that friendship is less a mutuality than it appears to be at first. The girl is less interested in the other than she thinks; what she seeks in the other is some response to, and mirroring of, the self. She needs the presence of someone who is undergoing the same trials, discoveries and despairs. . . . Through the sharing of knowledge and affects, she is relieved, to some extent, of the anxiety and guilt which accompanies [sic] the emergence of sexuality. (pp. 188–189)

Realistic Sharing. Realistic sharing is characteristic of late adolescence, youth, and adulthood. Friendship is based on what each partner brings to the relationship. Now there is a much greater stress on the *personality* of the friend.

Although these stages of friendship apply generally to boys and girls, there are some notable differences (Douvan and Adelson, 1966):

1. Girls may be socialized to place more emphasis on interpersonal relationships. Boys, on the other hand, may be socialized toward achievement, assertiveness, and activity. Therefore, girls may be disposed, more than boys, to use interpersonal, intimate methods of problem solving.
2. Boys are more concerned than girls with asserting and maintaining their independence from authority figures such as parents or teachers. Therefore, the boy develops a ganglike alliance:

Intense sharing as a stage of friendship occurs in early to middle adolescence.

Photograph by Darryl Jacobson

To this end he needs the gang . . . with whom he can confirm himself as autonomous and maintain a wall of resistance to authority. Even when the boys' close friendship group is small in number, they are apt to give it a ganglike definition, for example, calling themselves "The Three Musketeers" or "The Four Horsemen." Girls, . . . even when they are part of a large group of friends, tend to form centers of intimate two- and three-somes. (p. 194)

EDUCATION AS A CONTEXT FOR DEVELOPMENT

Adolescents spend a considerable amount of their time in schools. The school is the social mechanism for helping the adolescent to become a contributing member of society. There continues to be an important relationship between individual economic success and attending school. In addition, the school serves as a major socializing institution for the acquisition of interpersonal skills and socially responsible behavior.

The High School. High-school education in the United States has been dominated by one major type of organization: the comprehensive public school. This type of high school includes a wide variety of curricula and, to some extent, a variety of students from different social levels. Increasingly, American high school education has come to be characterized by large urban school districts with students assigned to schools on the basis of the neighborhood where they live. This trend toward largeness has been stimulated by several factors, such as the urbanization of American society and the growth of the population (particularly through the 1950s) (Coleman, 1974).

There have been growing problems with the comprehensive public school in relation to the needs of adolescents. These problems include the multiplicity of bureaucratic devices needed to manage such institutions; the absence of consumer choice; the large size of single age-grade levels; the segregation of races, social classes, and ethnic groups; and institutional similarity or blandness (see Application Box—Does the Large Comprehensive High School Inadvertently Encourage Adolescent—Adult Conflict?).

Several major studies have revealed some of the critical problems in the modern American high school (DeCecco and Richards, 1975; National Panel on High School and Adolescent Education, 1976). DeCecco and Richards examined 757 school districts and found the atmosphere of these schools to be one of tension and anger. Students expressed their unhappiness through defiance of authority, vandalism, absence, and disruption of classroom activities. Teachers showed their anger by using repressive disciplinary techniques and expelling students for relatively minor violations. School administrators often blamed both teachers and students for school problems. In addition, they aggravated tense situations by siding with one ethnic group against another and by making themselves unavailable to teachers or students.

The National Panel on High School and Adolescent Education (1976) found that many of the problems of the high school were due to "deficiencies" in the system. The panel found some of the following problems:

- High-school education does not provide many students with experiences designed to develop adult responsibilities and values.
- High schools too often treat teenagers as immature children.

Adolescents spend a considerable amount of their time in school.

Photograph by Darryl Jacobson

The comprehensive high school includes many educational experiences.

Photograph by Darryl Jacobson

- The typical high school is too big to be managed effectively.
- The schools have been asked to take responsibility for the "total" education of children. In the past, the responsibility for such a vast undertaking was more broadly shared with the family, the community, and religious organizations.

The panel concluded that many teachers, administrators, and students were making sincere efforts to make the system work. However, the panel suggested that their efforts were not likely to meet with success unless the entire approach to secondary education is revamped. Some of the panel's suggestions were the following:

Comprehensive Education (Rather than the Comprehensive High School). Adolescents should have the opportunity to learn through a variety of institutional arrangements. A good deal of the teenager's education should occur in the community (outside of the school).

Participatory Education. In order for adolescents to learn about adult roles and responsibilities, they need to be involved in the real world of the community. Adolescents should become involved in several types of community centers: a community career-education center, a community arts-and-crafts center, and a community center for government.

Reduction of Compulsory Attendance and All-Day Sessions. The panel recommended that formal instruction be curtailed to about two to four hours a day. The rest of the day would be spent in "participatory" programs such as those discussed above.

Education of the "Intellect." The panel recommended that the primary focus of formal high-school instruction be the cognitive or intellectual dimensions. Presumably this focus would be advisable—and possible—if the noncognitive goals were handled through the "participatory" programs outside the school.

YOUR VIEWS

The panel's recommendations are, of course, subject to evaluation and criticism. Do you think they are reasonable? Are they workable in our society? Why? Why not? Can you think of examples from your own experiences where these recommendations have been adopted?

Education and the Transition to Adulthood and Work. As we indicated, the aims of education include some emphasis on preparation for an occupation as well as on the socialization of the young. Another way of putting this is that schools have traditionally fostered the development of two types of goals and skills:

1. *Cognitive or academic skills* (e.g., mathematics, writing, biology, chemistry), which have been the traditional responsibility of the school.
2. *Nonacademic content or skills,* which attempt to incorporate "real-life" situations into educational experiences (e.g., driver education) or which incorporate elements that are viewed as important to the development of the "whole" person.

Both of these types of skills are viewed as important for the transition to adulthood. However, over the course of the existence of the public school, there has always been some level of debate as to what should be taught in the school (see Application Box—What Should Be Taught in the High School?).

Experiential Learning, Values, and Identity. Over the last several years, there has been a tendency to question the socialization role of formal schooling. Although the role of schools—including college and university education—is important in contributing to the development of values and identity structure, some researchers suggest that many of the important features of the individual's personality are developed prior to adolescence and independent of schooling (Jencks, Smith, Acland, Bane, Cohen, Gintis, Heyns, and Michelson, 1972; Kagan and Moss, 1972; Emmerich, 1964; Kohlberg, LaCrosse, and Ricks, 1972). For example, general intelligence and basic personality factors, such as activity–passivity, are established in childhood (Kagan and Moss, 1972). Jencks et al. (1972) suggested that although level of educational attainment is important, one's family and life experiences are more important than anything else in determining occupational and life success.

The importance of experience has led to consideration of "experiential" or "action" learning. Graham (1975) summarized this position as follows:

Does the Large Comprehensive High School Inadvertently Encourage Adolescent–Adult Conflict?

A school that is large, amorphous and bland is likely to have the unintended consequence of promoting socialization by the youth culture. The assembling of large numbers of youth along age-and-grade lines encourages them to create worlds of their own. At the same time, the increasing specialization and segregation of teaching encourages teachers, the only adults in the setting, to withdraw from those worlds. And there is little linkage provided by a sense of common purpose and a community of experience. The school has always been a setting, it is fair to say, in which there is some natural struggle between adults and youth. But the large comprehensive school changes the nature of the struggle from largely informal conflict and accommodation between teachers and students to a more formal one in which one major bloc feels impelled to elaborate rules and add more agents of control—even the police—while the other side, or a good share of it,

moves collectively to avoid the rules and to weaken the will to participate and learn.

Reprinted from J. S. Coleman, Youth: Transition to Adulthood, by permission of the University of Chicago Press, 1974, p. 152. Copyright © University of Chicago Press, 1974.

Experience in a job, in voluntary service, or by means of some other opportunity to handle novel responsibility is important and perhaps essential to the transition to adulthood and this transition is marked by progress through successive stages of cognitive development, social role perspectives, and moral judgment. For most young people the experiences needed for development cannot all be found in school; greater opportunities for experience with responsibility in school are needed. (p. 191)

What Should Be Taught in the High School?

One of the implications . . . of social changes . . . is that the nonschool portions of a youth's environment have dwindled in scope and force while the school portions have increased. One consequence has been to introduce into schools some things that were once outside in the form of extra-curricular programs, work-related programs, community projects and other activities. This is one kind of solution: to bring into the school certain of those non-cognitive activities that are deemed valuable to the development of youth or at least those activities for which there is some demand on the part of youth or the community.

Another solution, however, is to take the opposite approach: to confine formal schooling to those cognitive skills that are traditional to it and to devise new organizational arrangements outside the formal structure of the school for those non-academic activities important to the movement into adulthood. Such an approach very likely implies a reduction in the time spent in formal educational settings, rather than the increase inherent in the first solution. An example of this solution is cooperative education programs in high school in which a young person typically spends half his day in school and half on the job working for an employer. . . .

The central defect of the school for activities other than transmission of academic knowledge and skills is that schools are not well organized for other activities. Schools are apart from society while the non-academic portions of becoming an adult, such as gaining the capacity to take responsibility and authority, learning to care for others who are dependent, acquiring the ability to take decisive action, learning how to work, achieving a sense of self respect, are directly part of society. . . .

Photograph by Richard Levin

The essential difficulty of schools in handling activity other than academic learning is the position of the child or youth within the school. He is a dependent, and the school is responsible for shepherding his development. Yet if youth is to develop in certain ways involving responsibility and decision-making, the responsibility and dependency are in the wrong place. To reorganize a school in such a way that young persons have responsibility and authority appears extremely difficult, because such reorganization is incompatible with the basic custodial function of the school.

Reprinted from J. S. Coleman, Youth: Transition to Adulthood, *by permission of the University of Chicago Press, 1974, pp. 141–143. Copyright © University of Chicago Press, 1974.*

YOUR VIEW

What do you think? Do you agree with Coleman's argument? Why? Why not?

Research on the relationship between experiential learning and cognitive–moral development in youth suggests that the transition from adolescence and youth to adulthood is optimally completed when young people have the benefit of both academic and experiential education (Coleman, 1974; Kohlberg and Turiel, 1974; Graham, 1975).

The College Experience. If adolescents go on to postsecondary education, there is usually a longer delay before they become "full-fledged" adults. There is, of course, a considerable variety of postsecondary institutions: comprehensive public universities, private universities, private liberal arts colleges, and church-related schools, to name a few. For the most part, college and university students have been accorded a greater freedom and more adult privileges than have their younger counterparts in the high school (there are, of course, exceptions, such as variable drinking ages, which may exclude

---

APPLICATION BOX

Identity-Seeking and College Youth

It is our opinion that college students typically do not have a firm sense of identity and typically have not undergone an identity crisis. College students seem to experience identity crisis toward the end of senior year or during their early post-college experience. A male or female's disillusionment with first-job experience or graduate study, or a female's disappointment with being at home with small children is often the jolt that makes them ask what their education was for and why they are not as delighted with their lives as they had been led to believe they would be by parents and friends. Or instead of disillusionment, the feeling may be the constant tinge of doubt about whether the initial career choice (often made in high school and followed single-mindedly through college) was wisely made. . . .

What students often interpret as an identity crisis in college may be more of a crisis of "instrumental competence" or a crisis of "interpersonal competence." A person who is unable to choose his course and then work or who is unable to get along with significant peers may be experiencing a problem of autonomy or of intimacy, in its adolescent sense.

Reprinted from G. W. Goethals, and D. Klos, *Experiencing Youth: First-Person Accounts.* Boston: Little, Brown and Company, 1970, p. 129.

Photograph by Darryl Jacobson

some college students). In addition, there is considerable variety in educational experiences within institutions. For example, some programs have a clear career orientation (e.g., engineering, business, and teaching), and others are of a more general nature. On the whole (and, again, there are some exceptions), the greater freedom accorded to college students coupled with the variety of programs has created an atmosphere of relative satisfaction.

Impact of College on Values. Value changes and the consolidation of identity in the college setting are largely the result of the social environment. This environment includes a number of factors, such as the values that the student brings to the college experience, the student's interaction with peers, and the value orientation of the student's major field of specialization. Identity formation is also influenced by educational experiences that involve thinking, raising questions, and learning occupational skills.

The impact on values and the consolidation of identity of the college experience are, in some cases, quite clear (Pace, 1963; Thistlethwaite, 1960). Newcomb (1961, 1963) found that over the course of four years at Bennington College, student political attitudes changed from initially conservative values, reflecting family and community of origin, to relatively liberal values. Newcomb pointed to a number of factors supporting this change, including the orientation of the college, the attitudes of the faculty members, and relationships with psychologically close age-mates (e.g., friends and roommates) or admired individuals. However, the maintenance of these value changes requires a social support network (Newcomb, 1961, 1963). Such a network includes both friends and peers during the college years and one's marital partner or close associates after college.

Other research has reported changes in values in the college years because of commitment to a particular subject matter or curriculum (Huntley, 1965). For example, the humanities majors scored high in aesthetic values, and science majors scored high in theoretical and religious values. Huntley suggested that incoming freshmen bring with them a value orientation that guides their choice of major. In turn, their choice of major and curriculum tends to crystallize their value structure even further.

THE WORLD OF WORK

The choice of an occupational direction is a part of the overall process of identity formation in youth. Work and vocation set the tone for adult life and constitute integrating forces in determining what one's daily activities are, whom one associates with, where one lives, and how much physical and intellectual energy one expends.

Earlier in this century, most twenty-year-old adolescents were already involved in full-time employment or homemaking, that is, earning a living, organizing a marriage, and raising children. (As we shall see in Chapter Ten, these now are common responsibilities of early adulthood.) After World War II, this pattern of immediate involvement in work and adult activity changed substantially. These changes have included the following.

Education. The trend toward more years of formal education has tended to isolate youth from firsthand job experience.

Unemployed Teenagers—A Time Bomb?

The jobless statistics among youth are among the more somber and gloomy statistics of national unemployment. The 1983 report of the U.S. Department of Labor, Bureau of Labor Statistics shows that youth (sixteen to nineteen years of age) had a jobless rate that was almost two and a half times as high as the national average for all workers (see Figure 9.6). The jobless rate among blacks and other minorities (16–19 years old) was even more grim—more than double the rate for white youths. The implication of those high levels of youth unemployment are monumental in terms of the destruction of human beings and the frustration of human potential. The spillover of frustration could take the form of riots or increased crime.

The Alienation of Youth from Work. With the historical changes in the working world, the young person has been less involved in the work environment. The work of parents becomes less visible to children, and there are fewer opportunities for children to watch their parents at work, to talk with them about their work, or to work with them in the work setting. An emotional detachment from work characterizes some young people. Many children shift from positive attitudes and images of work toward negative ones. As they move through childhood and early adolescence, they appear to reject entire categories of work prematurely and irrationally. This phenomenon narrows the range of potential vocational choices (Borow, 1976).

Work Dysfunctions in Youth. For many youngsters from lower-socioeconomic or minority backgrounds, negative experiences with neighborhood, school, and work have often created obstacles to vocational development and adjustment to work. Many of these youth hold negative self-images as potential workers and lack realistic pictures of the world of work. A serious problem in the United States is the widespread unemployment of such youth (see the application box on teenage unemployment; also see Figure 9.6).

An Oversupply of Young Workers. During the 1960s and the early 1970s, schools, colleges, and universities in the United States had to cope with mushrooming enrollments that were the result of the so-called baby boom after World War II. As this large population "bubble" has moved out of the schools and entered the prime age bracket for work (twenty-five to forty-four years of age), there is some concern that meaningful jobs may be more difficult to find (see Table 9.1).

Physical and Sexual Changes in Adolescence

Up to this point, our discussion of the significant contexts of adolescence has presupposed certain changes in the adolescent. In the remainder of this chapter, we will focus on the individual adolescent. We will discuss changes in the way the adolescent thinks, developments in the adolescent personality, and, in this section, the physical and sexual development of the adolescent.

TABLE 9.1

Size of Population Aged 14–24, 1890–2050, and Percentage Change per Decade

Year	Size (in million)	Percentage Change
1890	14.2	
1900	16.5	+ 16
1910	20.0	+ 21
1920	20.8	+ 4
1930	24.8	+ 20
1940	26.3	+ 6
1950	24.5	− 7
1960	27.3	+ 11
1970	40.3	+ 48
1980	46.5	+ 15
1990	38.7	− 17
2000	40.0	+ 3
2025	40.3	+ 1
2050	40.2	0

Sources: 1890–1940. U.S. Bureau of the Census. *U.S. Census of Population: 1960. General Population Characteristics, United States Summary.* Final Report PC(1)–1B. U.S. Government Printing Office, Washington, D.C., 1961. Table 47.

1950–1980. U.S. Bureau of the Census, Department of Commerce, *Statistical Abstract of the United States 1981.* 102nd Edition.

1990–2050. U.S. Bureau of the Census, Department of Commerce, *Current Population Reports,* Series P–25, No. 922, Projections of the population of the United States 1982–2050 (Advance Report). Washington, D.C.: U.S. Government Printing Office, October 1982, Table 2, pp. 9, 11–13.

FIGURE 9.6 Youth unemployment.

Source: U.S. Department of Labor, Bureau of Labor Statistics, 1983; Labor Force Statistics Derived from the Current Population Survey: *A Data Book,* Vol. 1, Bulletin 2096, September, 1982.

GENERAL PHYSICAL MATURATION

The general growth rate of body tissue slows down from birth through childhood. However, the onset of puberty is marked by a considerable increase in this growth rate. There are increases in body size, changes in body shape and composition, and a rapid development of reproductive organs and secondary sexual characteristics. Many of these changes are similar for both sexes, although most are sex-specific. Three facts about this adolescent growth activity have remained constant as accurate descriptors of the process (Tanner, 1971):

1. *Girls* usually develop *earlier* than *boys.*
2. For both girls and boys, the *rate* of development is different for individuals.
3. The *sequence* of biological changes has remained the same as in the past (see Table 9.2).

Although these three characteristics have remained an accurate general description of adolescent physical growth, some of the specific events of growth are now occurring *earlier* than in the past. For example, the onset of puberty in females (i.e., the menarche, or first menstruation) appears to be occurring at earlier ages (see Figure 9.7). In addition, both children and adolescents appear to be taller now than at similar ages in the past (see Figure 9.8). Tanner (1978) has pointed out that most of this trend toward greater size in adolescents and children is the result of *more rapid maturation rather than greater ultimate size.* In earlier historical periods, final adult height was not

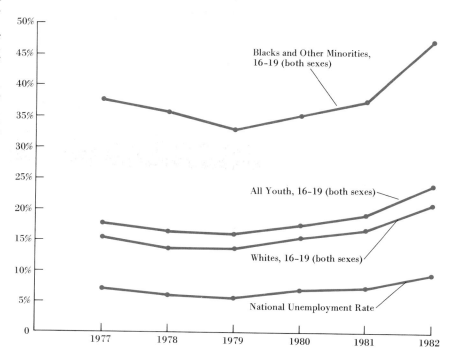

Blacks and Other Minorities, 16–19 (both sexes)

All Youth, 16–19 (both sexes)

Whites, 16–19 (both sexes)

National Unemployment Rate

Physical and Sexual Changes in Adolescence

431

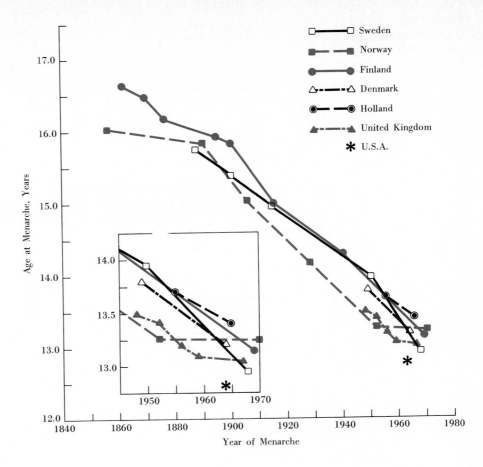

FIGURE 9.8   Secular trend in
growth of height—Swedish boys
and girls measured in 1883,
1938–1939, and 1965–1971.

From Ljung, Bergsten-Brucefors,
and Lindgren, 1974.

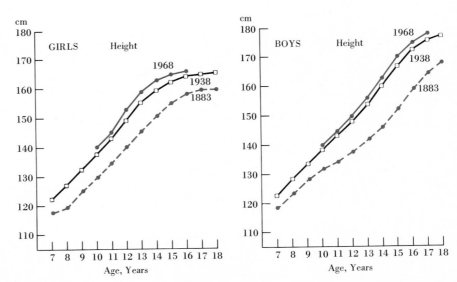

TABLE 9.2
The Sequence of Physical Changes in Males and Females

Females	Males
Skeletal growth.	Skeletal growth.
Breast development.	Enlargement of testes.
Straight pigmented pubic hair.	Straight pigmented pubic hair.
Maximum adolescent growth spurt (speed or "tempo" of growth is the fastest).	Early voice changes (e.g., voice "cracks"). Ejaculations (e.g., nocturnal emissions or "wet dreams").
Kinky pigmented pubic hair.	Kinky pigmented pubic hair.
Menstruation (the first menstruation is called the *menarche*).	Maximum adolescent growth spurt. Appearance of downy facial hair.
Appearance of hair in underarms and on forearms.	Appearance of hair in underarms and on forearms.
	Late voice change.
	Appearance of coarse pigmented facial hair and chest hair.

Based on information in J. M. Tanner, *Growth at Adolescence* (second edition). Oxford: Blackwell, 1962 and J. M. Tanner, *Education and Physical Growth* (second edition). New York: International Universities Press, 1978.

reached until about twenty-five years of age. Later adolescents now reach it at eighteen to nineteen years of age (Tanner, 1971). Therefore, we might conclude that the *sequence* of physiological changes (see Table 9.2) has remained the same; however, the *timing* is different for certain changes (Tanner, 1978).

Body Growth and Energy Levels. The extent of the adolescent growth spurt during this period is quite remarkable. For a period of about a year, the *velocity* or *rate* of growth almost doubles. A boy grows at the same rate during this year as he did during the first two years of life. Tanner (1971) described the situation as follows:

Admittedly during fetal life and the first year or two after birth developments occurred still faster, and a sympathetic environment was probably even more crucial, but the subject himself was not the fascinated, charmed, or horrified spectator that watches the developments, or lack of developments of adolescence. (p. 907)

During this year period, boys usually grow between 3–5 inches (7–12 cm) and girls grow between 2½–4½ inches (6–11 cm). The age at which the "peak" or maximal growth period occurs is approximately 14.0 years for boys and 12.0 years for girls (see Figure 9.9). The two-year difference in peak growth appears to remain constant (i.e., if for a particular group of boys the average "peak" age is 13.5 years, then the average "peak" age for a comparable group of girls tends to be 11.5 years) (Tanner, 1971).

The changes that occur in early adolescence are brought about by hormones that are either secreted for the first time or secreted in higher amounts (Tanner, 1971). Hormones then act on specific *targets* or *receptors,* which are often not concentrated in a specific organ or tissue. For example, the hormone

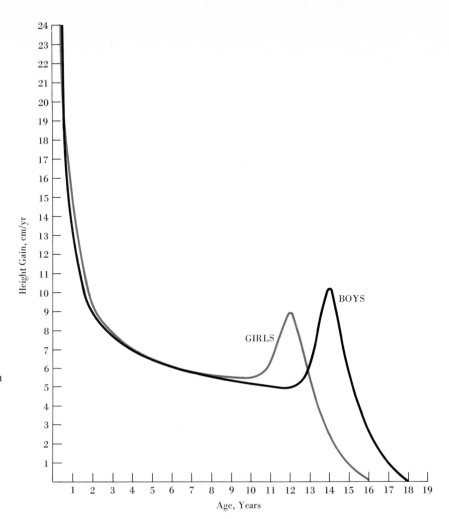

FIGURE 9.9 Typical individual velocity curves for height in boys and girls. The age at which the "peak" or maximal growth occurs is 14.0 years for boys and 12.0 years for girls.

From J. M. Tanner, R. H. White-house, and M. Takaishi, "Standards from Birth to Maturity for Height, Weight, Height Velocity and Weight Velocity; British Children, 1965, *"Archives of the Diseases of Childhood, 41* (1966), 455–471.

testosterone acts on several receptors located in the male penis, in facial skin, in the cartilage of the shoulder joints, and in parts of the brain (Tanner, 1971). These hormonal activities result in the release of specific sexual "energy," which can be channeled in numerous directions (Tanner, 1971). A good part of early adolescence is spent in learning both the meaning and the constructive channeling of this adolescent "energy." It is probably no accident that only when the hormonal and physical changes in early adolescence have completed their course, individuals are able to direct their attention to other matters of self-development (Tanner, 1971).

As hormones act on the various receptors in the body, changes begin to occur in practically all the skeletal and motor dimensions of the body. Tanner (1971) described the overall process as follows:

Most of the spurt in height is due to acceleration of trunk length rather than length of legs. There is a fairly regular order in which the dimensions accelerate; leg

Adolescence

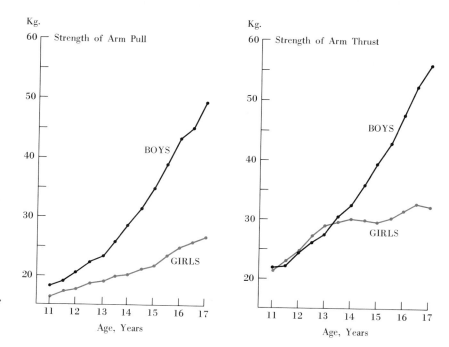

FIGURE 9.10   Strength of arm pull and arm thrust from ages eleven to seventeen years. Mixed longitudinal data for sixty-five to ninety-five boys and sixty-six to ninety-three girls in each age group.

From J. M. Tanner, *Growth at Adolescence*, 2nd ed. Oxford: Blackwell Scientific Publications, 1962; data from H. E. Jones, *Motor Performance and Growth*. Berkely: University of California Press, 1949.

length as a rule reaches its peak first, followed by the body breadths, with shoulder width last. Thus a boy stops growing out of his trousers (at least in length) a year before he stops growing out of his jackets. The earliest structures to reach their adult status are the head, hands and feet. At adolescence, children, particularly girls, sometimes complain of having large hands and feet. They can be reassured that by the time they are fully grown their hands and feet will be a little smaller in proportion to their arms and legs and considerably smaller in proportion to their trunk. (p. 911)

Boys have a marked increase in muscle size at adolescence. Boys' muscle widths reach a "peak" velocity of growth that is considerably greater than that of females. This increase in muscle size leads to an increase in strength for boys (see Figure 9.10). It should also be pointed out that boys are not only much stronger than girls at adolescence (probably, in part, because of larger muscles) but also have larger hearts, larger lungs, and a greater capacity for carrying oxygen in their blood (Tanner, 1971). Furthermore, girls have a considerably smaller increase in red blood cells and hemoglobin (see Figure 9.11). It is possible that these biological and physical differences, as well as social stereotypes of femininity, produce the apparent athletic superiority of males over females during adolescence and beyond. Furthermore, these factors may also contribute to the traditional lack of interest in sports and athletic skills by females. This situation is beginning to change.

Motor Performance. Sex differences in relation to motor activities begin to become apparent during the early adolescent years and are quite pronounced during middle and later adolescence and beyond. It should be em-

Physical and Sexual Changes in Adolescence

435

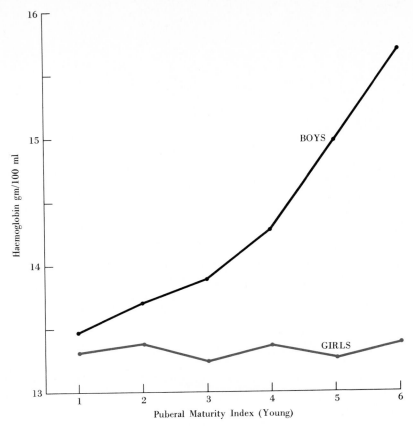

FIGURE 9.11 Blood hemoglobin level in girls and boys according to stage of puberty; cross-sectional data. Puberal maturity or "puberal age" describes the degree of maturity of an individual at puberty. Puberal age is measured as a scheme of six categories, which represent successive stages in transition from the degree of physical immaturity that exists before puberty through to maturity.

From J. M. Tanner, "Growth and Endocrinology of the Adolescent," in L. I. Gardner ed., *Endocrine and Genetic Diseases of Childhood and Adolescence.* Philadelphia: Saunders, 1969. Data from H. B. Young," Aging and Adolescence," *Developmental Medicine and Child Neurology,* 5 (1963), 451–460.

phasized that motor *learning* capabilities do *not* differ between the sexes; rather, physiological–anatomical differences, differential socialization, and related interest and motivation, taken together, probably account for sex-differentiated performance. Although it is not likely that the strongest females will ever equal the strongest males in activities involving sheer strength and power, two points are important here:

- Females are probably capable of both learning and performing motor skills at much higher levels than has generally been demonstrated in research to date.
- *Not all* athletic, sport, and general movement skills require excessive strength and power to perform effectively. For example, the most productive home-run hitter in major league baseball history, Hank Aaron, was *not* the strongest man on his team. If anything, his sheer strength was probably average to slightly above average. However, the total *power* required to hit a baseball a considerable distance is a function of both the *strength* of the hitter and the *speed* or velocity at which the bat travels in meeting the ball. Aaron's superior bat-swinging speed (probably the result of superb coordination of wrists and arms) resulted in home-run production unequaled by "stronger" men.

436

Adolescent Obesity—Are Females More Likely than Males to Be Overweight?

One of the major reasons for the problems that some teenage girls encounter with their nutritional status is the difference between the nutritional needs of males and females during adolescence. Female adolescents have an earlier maturational pattern as well as a social–cultural deemphasis on physically vigorous activity. The general nutritional needs of girls reach a peak between the ages of eleven and fourteen and continue thereafter to decline gradually until they are physically mature. In contrast, the nutritional needs of boys continue to rise throughout the period from the ages of eleven to eighteen and remain at that level until about age twenty-two. Therefore it is apparent that a boy consumes a much larger number of calories during the adolescent years than a girl. Because the female adolescent requires many fewer calories than the boy, she must get all the nutrients that she needs from a more restricted quantity of food:

In order to provide the necessary calcium, iron and vitamins in her diet, it is necessary for her to concentrate

Photograph by Darryl Jacobson

on eating a well balanced diet with only a few additional frills permitted. The teenage boy, on the other hand, is confronted with the delightful responsibility of consuming a large number of calories, and it is likely that many boys will unconsciously meet their needs for the various nutrients simply by attempting to satisfy their ravenous appetites. (McWilliams, 1975, p. 298)

SEXUAL CHANGES

The adolescent spurt in skeletal and muscular features is closely related, in time, to the rapid development of the sexual and reproductive organs. In girls, the general course of sexual maturity takes from one and one-half to six years, and in males, the duration of the changes is from two to five years. The general sequence of events is summarized in Figure 9.12.

Sexual Maturation in Boys. The onset of puberty in boys usually occurs at about age twelve. Puberty includes more than one event. The first indicator of puberty in boys is the increased growth of the testes and the scrotum (the pouch of skin that contains the testes). Slightly later, there is a small growth of pubic hair, which proceeds gradually until the general growth spurt (see Figure 9.12). About a year after testicle growth begins, accelerations occur in height and in the size of the penis. Shortly after the height spurt, the adolescent's larynx enlarges. The voice begins to deepen when the growth of the penis is near completion. About two years after the beginning growth of pubic hair, axillary hair (under the arms) and facial hair appear (Tanner, 1978).

Physical and Sexual Changes in Adolescence

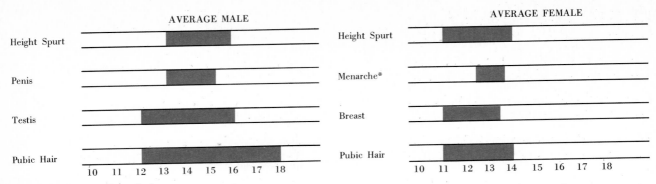

| AVERAGE MALE | | | | | | | | | | AVERAGE FEMALE | | | | | | | | |

Height Spurt

Penis

Testis

Pubic Hair

Height Spurt

Menarche*

Breast

Pubic Hair

10 11 12 13 14 15 16 17 18

10 11 12 13 14 15 16 17 18

FIGURE 9.12 Sexual changes in the average adolescent male and female. The shaded bars indicate the range of years during which the changes occur.

Based on statistics from Tanner, J. M., *Growth At Adolescence,* 2nd ed. Oxford: Blackwell, 1962 and Tanner, J. M., *Education and Physical Growth,* 2nd ed. New York: International Universities Press, 1978.

The growth of facial hair seems to follow a pattern. At first, there is an increase in length and pigmentation (coloring) at the corners of the upper lip. This increase in length and coloring spreads above the lips to complete the mustache. Hair then appears on the upper part of the cheeks, below the lower lip, and finally along the sides of the chin (Tanner, 1978).

Sexual Maturation in Girls. In girls, the beginning of puberty is marked by an increase in size of the breasts or, in some cases, by the initial appearance of pubic hair. Breast enlargement usually begins in the tenth year and continues for about three years until the full size is attained. In addition to an increase in general size, the breasts undergo other changes. The area around the nipples becomes darker in color and enlarges. Ordinarily pubic hair appears when a girl is approximately eleven years old (Tanner, 1978).

The first menstruation (menarche) is often regarded by adolescents and parents as a landmark event in female sexual maturity. Interestingly enough,

"Dear, this book says some rather profound things about adolescents."
"Well, between you and me, an adolescent is simply a person who can't pass a mirror without looking twice."

it occurs relatively late in the pubertal sequence. Most American girls have their menarche at about age thirteen (see Figure 9.12). The occurrence of the menarche marks a relatively mature stage of female uterine growth. However, the menarche does *not* usually signify the attainment of complete reproductive functioning. For example, a female is less likely to become pregnant near her menarche than she is five or six years later. Full reproductive maturity is not attained until the early twenties (Tanner, 1978).

Adolescent Reactions to Physical Changes. The changes that we have discussed do not, of course, go unnoticed by the adolescents themselves or their peers. Adolescents may become somewhat self-conscious about their physical appearance. They may spend significant time and energy in assessing how their peers view these changes. It has been suggested that adolescents and their peers may be comparing themselves with a mythical *body ideal* (Schonfeld, 1963). Through exposure to television, movies, and magazines, adolescents come to learn that there may be an ideal body type for males and females. Males, for example, may be expected to look relatively slim and to be slightly muscular. Female adolescents may perceive that boys prefer girls with a slender figure, well-developed breasts, and long legs (Wiggins, Wiggins, and Conger, 1968). Deviations from such idealized norms of physical appearance may affect the way some adolescents are treated by others and how they view themselves (Dwyer and Mayer, 1967).

Early and Late Maturation. Studies of early- and late-maturing boys (Jones and Bayley, 1950) showed that the early maturers tended to be stronger, taller, and better coordinated than the later maturers. In addition, early maturers were found to be less well poised, more immoderate in their behavior, and more tense and anxious than late maturers. These findings were confirmed in later studies (Faust, 1960; Elkind, 1967; Blos, 1970). Some of these differences seemed to persist over time even when the physical differences between early and late maturers was no longer present. For example, when early maturers reached their thirties, they tended to have higher occupational status and to be more socially active than late maturers (Jones, 1957). On the other hand, there is some reason to think that there are some favorable results of relatively late maturation. Early maturers appear to achieve in a more conforming manner and to be more conventional in their thoughts and attitudes than late maturers. Late maturers seem to be more flexible and adaptive and are better able to tolerate ambiguity (Jones, 1965).

In the case of females, early maturation may make a girl somewhat conspicuous at first. She may appear older than the boys in her class. However, this disadvantage may be offset as she reaps some benefits of early maturation, including increased attention and expectations of more mature and socially responsible behavior (Faust, 1960).

Cognitive Development

The maturational events that we have described accompany the development of a new cognitive competence. Just as there is a spurt in physical and sexual development, there is also an intellectual and cognitive "spurt." The changes that take place in adolescent intellectual growth are both quantitative and qualitative.

DEFINITIONS

Quantitative changes in thinking. Alterations in the total "amount" of a particular skill or ability. For example, an increase in verbal skills during adolescence would represent a *quantitative* change in a skill that was present during middle childhood (e.g., an increasing precision in the use of words to label objects, people, or actions).

Qualitative changes in thinking. Changes in the manner or process of cognitive functioning. For example, learning to use abstract labels (e.g., *justice, freedom*) without having to refer to concrete instances or examples of these abstractions is a *qualitative* change in thinking.

QUANTITATIVE CHANGES IN INTELLIGENCE

During middle childhood, mental growth tends to be fairly even. During adolescence, however, some abilities and skills appear to develop more than others. It appears that intellectual skills tend to become more specialized during adolescence, and individuals may demonstrate what appears to be emerging special interests, such as an aptitude for science or verbal skills.

This differentiation and specialization of abilities is sometimes heavily weighted by social–cultural factors. For example, it has been noted that adolescent girls may continue to develop verbal skills while their scientific and mathematical abilities appear to languish. On the other hand, adolescence often marks the surge of boys in science and mathematics. Some of this specialization might well be attributed to individual personality differences. However, it is also likely, in our culture, that males are expected to do well in science and mathematics, whereas females are expected to do well in verbal skills. These differences in ability may be the result of sex-role stereotypes that may be ingrained in our culture.

Another quantitative change in intelligence has to do with the continuity of mental skills from childhood to adolescence. Will the child who is first in her or his third-grade class in arithmetic continue to perform at a comparable level in high-school algebra and geometry classes? On the whole, a child's intellectual standing tends to remain about the same throughout childhood and adolescence. However, changes in the child's or the adolescent's life circumstances sometimes result in dramatic changes in relative intellectual standing. For example, the adolescent who associates with a peer group that does not value or support school skills may show a decline in school performance.

QUALITATIVE CHANGES IN INTELLIGENCE

In order to understand the qualitative changes in adolescent cognitive development, one must first understand the last of Piaget's stages of cognitive development: *formal operations*. You will recall that the individual in middle childhood was at the state of *concrete operations* (see Chapter 8). What are the major differences between the thinking of the child in the concrete operational stage and the adolescent in the formal operational stage? The following are three qualitative changes in the thinking of adolescents.

The Separation of Possibility and Reality. In the first place, concrete operational children focus their thinking on *relations between objects that they can classify, categorize, and order* (see Chapter 8). In formal operational thinking, the adolescent or adult can think about the *possible* as well as the *real*. Instead of being limited to dealing with things as they *are*, the adolescent can now deal with things as they might be (and related hypotheses).

The Use of Symbols to Represent Other Symbols. The adolescent who has reached the level of formal operations has developed the ability to use a *second-order symbolic system;* that is, the adolescent has the ability to work with relationships between *symbols that represent other symbols*. For example, the early adolescent can now learn algebra because she/he can now work with second-order symbols (e.g., *X* and *Y*) to represent first-order symbols (e.g., 5 and 10).

In the case of algebraic equations, the child in the concrete operational stage is able to solve the equation *only* if all elements are presented in terms of concrete, first-order symbols.

$$5 + X = 10$$
$$X = 5$$

The concrete operational child needs visual clues and props to be able to deal with complex symbolic relationships such as mathematical equations. On the other hand, adolescents can work exclusively with second-order symbols. Therefore, they can solve the boxed equation as well as many others without needing to refer to concrete examples or reference points.

The Ability to Coordinate Multiple Factors in Problem Solving. Adolescents are able, in a *systematic fashion*, both to raise and to test hypotheses about the solution to a given problem. On the other hand, when a younger child is presented with a problem, he or she may not proceed systematically, by abandoning solutions (hypotheses) that do not work and trying alternatives. Rather, the child may persist with a hypothesis that does not fit the facts, perhaps even trying to make the facts fit the hypothesis. The adolescent is able to test one hypothesis after another systematically, until the correct solution is discovered.

Furthermore, adolescent problem-solving is marked by the ability to deal with *many facts simultaneously*. For example, the adolescent recognizes that getting to the picnic on time depends on several factors, including the total distance, the speed of the automobile, and the total time needed to travel the distance. The child may be able to handle two factors but probably cannot understand how multiple determinants (e.g., distance, speed, and time) interrelate and contribute to a given solution. In addition to these three qualitative changes in adolescent thinking, there are several other notable ones.

Reasoning About Verbal Propositions. A child in the period of concrete operations can reason about things or concrete objects but cannot reason about verbal propositions. For example, if a child is shown three objects of varying size, he or she will be able to see that if A is bigger than B, which, in

Early adolescence marks the beginning of introspection.

Photograph by Darryl Jacobson

turn, is bigger than C, then A must be bigger than C. However, if he/she is presented with a verbal description of a situation, such as ''Jeff is taller than Scott and Scott is taller than Bruce,'' the child will probably be unable to arrive at the logical conclusion that Jeff is taller than Bruce. The reason for this limitation with regard to verbal propositions is that the child is dependent on *concrete* objects for successful problem-solving. Adolescents can solve word problems because they are able to think about and with symbols and words that transform concrete experiences (Elkind, 1971).

Introspection and Examination of One's Own Thinking. In early adolescence a thinking process begins that will characterize both adolescence and adulthood: the ability to think introspectively about one's own thoughts. Adolescents can talk about their beliefs and thoughts on a wide range of subjects. They can articulate many experiences that were mainly at the level of feeling and emotion in middle childhood. However, they appear to be somewhat more tactful than the child, who might simply state what is on her or his mind—no matter how potentially embarrassing. The adolescent seems to be more aware than the child that her or his thoughts are private even though she or he is capable of discussing them (Elkind, 1971).

The Ability to Understand Metaphor. Whereas the child almost always takes things literally, the adolescent is able to understand the symbolic meaning of metaphors, such as ''stubborn as a mule.'' The child has difficulty understanding such metaphors and other symbolic expressions because he or she cannot ''operate'' on words without concrete examples. He or she cannot sense the multiple meanings and levels of meaning in a metaphor, probably because his or her thinking is limited to the concrete, literal meaning (Elkind, 1971).

Thinking in Terms of Ideals and Contrary-to-Fact Conditions. The ability to think about the meaning of words—independent of concrete instances—leads the adolescent to the creation of *ideals* and ideal states. This new-found ability to think in terms of ideals and absolutes sometimes brings the criticism from adults that the adolescent is living in a ''dream world,'' is ''unrealistic,'' or is simply not ''down-to-earth.''

Thinking about ideals has another important facet for adolescents. It permits them to plan for the future by allowing them to project possible situations into a meaningful future. The concept of *future orientation* becomes an important organizational feature of the adolescent's life process. The *future orientation* of the adolescent is a way of developing goals and organizing immediate activities in a meaningful way. Furthermore, the ability to organize activities meaningfully in terms of a future is an important skill in adulthood.

Another result of thinking about ideals is the inevitable—and sometimes painful—comparisons of ''what is'' with ''what could be.'' These comparisons are often the basis for new perspectives on the family, the school, and the community. As we will see, sometimes the adolescent's recognition of the gap between the ideal and the real is the basis for minor or major conflicts between the adolescent and the parent.

Distinctions between the ideal and the real may come painfully close to home. The adolescent may come to realize the difference between what he or she is and what he or she would like to be. Such recognition can lead to many

Adolescence

commonly observed adolescent behaviors, such as day-dreaming, temporary stupors, or moodiness, on the one hand, and to attempts to narrow the gap between reality and the ideal world (e.g., trying out roles or dressing like a "cool dude"), on the other.

The Progression of Adolescent Thinking

In the above discussion, we have presented the general dimensions of early adolescent (ages twelve to sixteen) thinking. There are, however, important differences within the early adolescent period. Elkind (1971) described these differences as follows:

By and large the young adolescent [12 to 16 years] tends to be rather flighty as a consequence of the rapid changes that have been occurring in him. Because the changes are new he is more preoccupied with them than he will be later when he is more accustomed to his enlarged body, deeper voice, and awakened sexual interest and curiosity. The young person has to adjust not only to the new changes in his body, but also to new changes in his thinking abilities. Certain phenomena of early adolescence reflect this adjustment period. . . . the twelve- and thirteen-year-old can now deal with possibilities and consider many new alternatives in any given problem-solving situation. Initially this is a somewhat terrifying experience because while the young person can see the many possible alternatives, he does not have the background or experience upon which to make a choice. It often appears, as a consequence, that young adolescents are hopelessly dependent and indecisive. . . . By the age of fifteen and sixteen, however, young people have more experience in decision-making and have a better idea of the relative importance of things. (p. 127)

The new-found cognitive skills of idealization are usually exercised first in the home. Parents are the first to feel the strength of these skills, as they may be compared with other parents or against an ideal and found wanting. As Elkind suggested, "In early adolescence not only is the grass greener in the other person's yard, but the house is bigger and more comfortable and the parents are nicer" (p. 128). After the family and the parents, the child's critical judgment may be turned toward the school and the teacher. Whereas young children are more concerned with the teacher's personality or how "nice" or "mean" the teacher is, the adolescent may become concerned about the teacher's competence in addition to his/her personality. By the time the individual reaches the middle to the latter part of adolescence, criticism shifts to more general social issues, social values, or social institutions, such as government and religion.

Does Every Adolescent Attain Formal Operations?

Piaget (1969) originally hypothesized that the onset of formal operations occurred at about the ages of eleven or twelve and stabilized at around fourteen to fifteen years of age. Subsequent research, however, has indicated a more complex situation (Neimark, 1975; Martorano, 1977). The onset of formal operations does not appear to be related to such factors as intelligence, cultural background, or the amount and quality of education (Neimark,

1975). Higgins-Trenk and Gaite (1971) found that many adolescents do not attain formal operations until the late teen years or early twenties, if at all. About 50 percent of these authors' subjects (mean age 17.7 years) were not performing at the level of formal operations. Similarly, Martorano (1977) found, using a sample of females in the sixth through twelfth grades, that not even the twelfth graders consistently performed at the level of concrete operations across all ten tasks in the experiment. These findings seem to suggest that all adolescents may not be grappling with the results of changing cognitive patterns; however, the vast majority *are* dealing with physical, sexual, hormonal, and emotional changes.

Although not all adolescents attain formal operations during early adolescence, there is evidence that some older adolescents may go beyond formal operations, or to a second phase of formal operations. This phase has been called *problem finding,* in contrast to the *problem solving* that characterizes formal operations (Arlin, 1975). Thus, the thinking of some older adolescents fifteen to twenty years old might be characterized as "divergent" (moving toward new or creative solutions or the identification of problems) rather than "convergent" (moving toward known or accepted solutions to problems). This type of thinking characterizes the older adolescent who raises questions about the social system and its institutions. Intelligence is identified by the quality of the *questions asked* rather than the arrival at known conclusions. Parents or teachers may often respond to such thinking with comments like "That's a good question!"

Social and Personality Development

Throughout the years of childhood, the self is defined largely by the child's experiences in the family, in the elementary school, and, to some extent, in peer activities. The changes that we have described to this point may force the adolescent to reexamine this self so that it will be consistent with these changes. The adolescent integrates new skills in logical thinking, moral development, and sexual identity with the possibilities for a more independent social life. In this section, we discuss this process of integration of the self-concept as it relates to three major dimensions of adolescent personality: vocational identity, sexual identity, and moral identity.

A VIEW OF ADOLESCENCE: ERIK ERIKSON—ON ADOLESCENT EGO IDENTITY

According to Erikson (1950, 1968), the primary task that confronts the adolescent is the establishment of ego identity. He views the establishment of ego identity as the development of a "stance toward the world." However, *identity formation neither begins nor ends with adolescence.* Rather, Erikson considers it a lifelong process. It is during adolescence that the major features of this identity are sketched out.

Erikson suggests that adolescence might be viewed as a "psychosocial moratorium" between childhood and adulthood. In other words, adolescence is a socially recognized time for experimentation and testing of lifestyles and roles. A major aspect of this moratorium is a search for what to *believe in,* what to *live for,* and what to be *loyal to.*

444

OCCUPATIONAL IDENTITY

An important element of the adolescent's self-concept is his or her occupational identity. Adolescents are expected to define themselves, in part, in terms of some vocation. In the future, it is quite likely that vocational development will continue to increase in importance as a significant element in female identity.

A Developmental Perspective. How does the adolescent decide on an appropriate career direction or on a specific job? Here, we review the developmental theory, of Ginzberg (1972). By examining this theory, we may see the various features of development of vocation at each age level, from childhood through later adolescence and early adulthood. Ginzberg has suggested that the individual continually makes adjustments in aspirations and motivation that limit and refine vocational choices.

GINZBERG'S STAGE THEORY
(GINZBERG, 1972)

Ginzberg suggested that individuals move through four major psychological periods as a part of the process of making vocational choices. Each stage represents a compromise between what is wished for and what is possible.

The fantasy period. The fantasy stage begins in early childhood and lasts until about age eleven or twelve. As early as age four or five, children

Identity Concerns—Who Are You?

Most people answer "Who are you?" by referring to roles and extrinsics, not to themselves. "I am Charley Jones, a sophomore at Dartmouth, 19 years old, Sigma Chi, a history major" and so on. If you probe a little deeper, you may get a little closer to the person; he may tell you something more about his thoughts, hopes, and dreams— but the answers will still be superficial. "I plan to go to graduate school in physics. I am hoping to study in France next year. I'm pinned to a girl, but I'm not sure we'll get engaged."

People don't give real answers to the question because they don't know the answer and because they are afraid to expose themselves. They are so used to wearing masks that they do not know what is underneath them, and they may even be afraid to find out—afraid that their real self is much less attractive than their ideal or pseudo-self. . . .

The approach suggested here is essential because identity problems are different from most other problems. They can *never* be completely solved. Some day you may think that you have discovered who you really are, but then a new demand or opportunity will reveal unsuspected aspects of your personality. Solving identity problems is therefore a life-long task which requires developing both a realistic conception of who you are now and a way of responding to life and yourself which enables this self-conception to grow. . . .

The first and most important step is to take the problem seriously. Finding out who you are is the *most* important thing you will ever do—you cannot do it casually or quickly. It takes time and effort, and it creates serious discomfort. You cannot find your real self without giving up some of your defenses, and giving them up invariably creates anxiety. Defenses are self-deceiving and self-defeating, but they do protect you. When you weaken or destroy them, you will feel the anxiety they existed to prevent.

This anxiety is so painful that most people are afraid to weaken their defenses. From time to

Top photograph by Darryl Jacobson; bottom photograph by Shan Rucinski

time they lift their masks and try to look beneath them, but they immediately feel frightened and pull their masks down again.

Since your natural desire to avoid the pain of anxiety will make you want to avoid weakening your defenses, you must decide that finding yourself is important enough to justify the pain, time, and effort.

If you will not make that decision, if you refuse to pay the price, you will not solve the problem.

And 30 years from now you will look back on your life and say: "I blew it." You may have satisfied all of your conscious needs and climbed to the top of the pyramid, but you will know that you are a failure.

Abridged from pp. 30, 33, and 45 in *A Student's Survival Manual,* by Alan N. Schoonmaker. Copyright © 1971 by Alan N. Schoonmaker. Reprinted by permission of Harper & Row, Publishers, Inc.

are able to state vocational preferences. These are simply wishes that are usually based on a limited relationship with the working world. For example, when asked what they would like to be when they grow up, children may offer such responses as "I want to be a policeman" or "I want to be a fireman."

The tentative period (ages eleven to about eighteen). This stage begins in later childhood and early adolescence, when the individual begins to take into account his/her own interests and capabilities when considering a vocation.

There are four substages during this period. In the *interest stage* (ages eleven to twelve), the child begins to recognize the need to consider a vocation as well as identifying activities that are liked and disliked. These activities are generally similar to vocational activities.

The *capacity stage* (ages twelve to fourteen) coincides with the onset of formal operations as the individual begins to assess and understand the prerequisite aptitudes, training, and education necessary for given professions.

The *value stage* (ages fifteen to sixteen) involves the recognition of personal values, orientations, and goals as important dimensions of a vocational choice. The individual begins to recognize that given vocations have a particular relationship to her or his values, so that some vocations may be more suited to her or his value structure than others.

The *transition stage* (ages seventeen to nineteen) is a period of consolidation during which aptitudes, interests, and values are focused on the necessity of making a realistic vocational decision.

The realistic period (eighteen to the early twenties). The realistic period is composed of two substages. In the *exploration stage,* the individual tests his or her tentative vocational choices against the demands of a vocation and personal values, aptitudes, and interests. During the *crystallization stage,* the individual develops a clear picture of a vocational goal, including specific occupations.

The specification period. The specification period is usually reached during the early twenties and occurs when the individual makes a commitment to a particular vocation. This happens when the individual begins to train for a particular vocation or actually enters that vocation.

In summary, Ginzberg's theory suggests that career decisions are made through a continual process of compromise between individual values, interests, and capabilities and vocational task demands.

Evidence for a Developmental Perspective. The developmental approach to vocational choice has been supported in other research. Research on the relationship between thinking or cognitive functioning and vocational preferences has demonstrated results comparable to those of Ginzberg. For example, the vocational preferences of children under eleven indicates that their choices are largely subjective (Jordaan and Heyde, 1978). At this age, children have not assessed their own aptitudes or interests in relation to a proposed occupation. By the time they are sixteen years old, adolescents are much more realistic about what they are likely to achieve and more specific about what they want to do (Douvan and Adelson, 1966). For example, the high-school senior is more likely to say that she or he would like to be a pediatrician rather than simply a physician.

Sex Role, Identity, and Marriage

As a social institution, marriage has been, in the past, a traditional rite of passage from childhood or adolescence to adult independence and responsibility. Traditionally males have developed active vocational commitments that allowed them to "provide for" a family. In the past, women presumably were socialized for marriage as the primary dimension of their identity. Appropriate sex-role behaviors learned in childhood and adolescence *were* designed to facilitate this ultimate goal: marriage and child rearing (see Table 9.3).

Marriage for many young people today is no longer a social institution necessary for the attainment of adult status and personal security. Rather, it is viewed more and more as an optional relationship, perhaps as a commitment to shared growth with a significant other person during the adult years. Furthermore, sexual behavior is viewed as a natural and acceptable part of life, and many earlier restrictions are no longer appropriate (Dreyer, 1975). As changes have occurred in youth attitudes toward sexual relationships, in youth sexual behavior, and in traditional concepts of family functioning, the views of youth toward marriage have also changed. Youth are placing far less emphasis on the traditional notion of marriage as a social institution that provides social stability and continuity. Instead many see marriage as *one* source of personal growth and development (Dreyer, 1975). In such a marital relationship, each partner is free to play whatever roles are most comfortable or practical. Family roles are determined by mutual agreement rather than by the stereotypes of traditional masculine–feminine roles.

During the 1970s, the institution of marriage appeared to undergo some rather profound changes. Despite the continued and historical popularity of marriage, marriage rates have declined or at least leveled off during the last twenty years. For example, in 1965, 73.2 percent of the total population was married (persons 18 and over) while there were 64.9 percent married in 1981. Meanwhile, divorce rates have dramatically increased from 2.9 percent in 1965 to 6.7 percent in 1981 (U.S. Bureau of the Census, 1982–83).

TABLE 9.3
Stereotypes of the Differences Between Females and Males

Females differ from males in that females are . . .		
Well-founded	**Unfounded**	**Debatable**
Higher in verbal ability	More social	More fearful, timid, and anxious
Lower in visual–spatial ability	More suggestible	Lower in activity level
Weaker in mathematical ability	Higher in self-esteem	Less competitive and more cooperative
Less aggressive	Better at rote learning	Less dominant
More afraid to be successful, especially in mixed-sex competition, but less so for black females than for white females	Better at simple repetitive tasks	More compliant
	Poorer at higher-level cognitive processing	More nurturant
	Less analytical	More maternal
Poorer at problem solving	More affected by environment	
More easily able to maintain their sex-role identity	Less affected by environment	
	Lower in achievement motivation	
	More auditory, but less visual	

From *Adolescents Today* (2nd ed.) by J. S. Dacey, p. 63. Copyright © 1982, 1979 by Scott, Foresman & Co. Reprinted by permission.

Sex Roles. *Sex-Typing of Social Roles.* Historically, the result of industrialization was to create a more rigid patterning of sex roles. Men were given exclusive rights to the instrumental and task roles, both inside and outside the family. Women were given exclusive rights to the expressive and interpersonal roles, primarily within the family. A number of historical changes have contributed to the breakdown in traditional sex roles. These include (1) the education of women; (2) the perfection of birth control technology; and (3) the advent of feminist thinking in the contemporary women's movement (Douvan, 1975).

The education of women. The change in women's educational attainment has resulted in some changes in ideas about the marriage relationship and expectations about adult roles. The increased education of women has also had a profound impact on women's expectations for intellectual stimulation in their lives. Until relatively recently, educated women had usually not found employment opportunities equivalent to their education. As a result of educational preparation, increased social acceptance of career women, and improved opportunities, many women now *expect* and *find* acceptable combinations of work and marriage roles.

Birth control technology. A strong basis for the reduction in family size has been modern birth-control techniques. According to Douvan (1975), birth control technology has led to a separation of sex and its natural consequences, which has led to a separation of maternity from the core of feminine identity. Such a separation allows a woman to develop an identity as a fully integrated human being. *Historically,* many girls were socialized to anticipate motherhood as the fulfillment of their identity. The woman's self-definition was a reflection of others: who her husband was, what he did, and what her children did.

The women's movement. The increased education of women as well as the absolute control over conception has dramatically influenced the development of ideological feminism. The conflicts and discrepancies experienced by women—particularly the more educated women—gave rise to the so-called women's liberation movement. A significant result of the feminist movement has been the general acceptance by most of the population of proposals to eliminate discrimination in the hiring of women as well as to guarantee "equal pay for equal work." Such notions as the equalization of the role of male and female in child care and family maintenance have been given some support (Douvan, 1975).

Sex-Role Preferences Among Young Women. Dreyer (1975) suggested that among modern young women there are four major orientations or types of sex-role preferences. According to Dreyer (1975), these women could be described as follows:

- *Role synthesizers*

they attempt to combine what they feel are the best elements of both the traditional feminine and the traditional masculine roles into a life-style which emphasizes high levels of personal achievement. These young women are self-critical perfectionists who tend to be outstanding both in and out of school. They look forward to careers in such fields as medicine, law, business, architecture, and professional sports, and they expect to combine these careers with a happy marriage and children. (p. 215)

- *Role innovators*

they seek new activities, responsibilities and status for themselves as women. In general, these young women have practical goals, such as "getting a good job," "making something of myself," and "having enough money to be happy," and they see their "feminine" role attributes as ways to accomplish these personal ends. . . . These women look forward to marriage and children but expect to work in order to help the family finances. They do not seek equality with men in work situations because they feel that they can accomplish more of their personal goals by appearing "feminine" than by acting like men. (p. 215)

- *Role traditionals*

they conform to most of the stereotyped attitudes and behaviors of the "ultra domesticated" woman. These women have widely varying abilities both in school and out, but they share the same basic aspiration and hope of finding a loving husband who will be a good provider and father to their children. They have limited educational and occupational goals and see both school and work as a waiting period before marriage when they will devote all their attention to husband and family. (pp. 215–216)

- *Role-diffused*

they seem totally uncertain about almost everything in their lives. Very often the women in this group have past histories of great ability and accomplishment; they seem to be lost, however, in a flood of alternatives and decisions which threaten to overwhelm them. When asked about goals these young women give vague and unclear answers about going to college or getting a job but they do not know where or in what field. These women appear subdued, worried and embarrassed by their own

tentativeness. Their role behavior is similarly confused but tends to be more traditionally feminine than any other, most likely because it is an easy pattern of behavior to
fall back upon in times of doubt. (p. 216)

Female youth appear to be involved in a process of reorganizing and rede-
fining sex roles. What has changed is that, most women, not just college-educated women, are beginning to sense the contradictions between a fully
human identity and the limitations of the traditional "feminine" role. Young
women have apparently gone beyond the choice of either a "feminine" role
or a "modern" role and are developing combinations of roles in which they
get married, go to school, have children, and take up a career. Whereas the
mothers of today's youth might have had the choice—if there was a choice—
between either a family *or* a career, the dilemma of many young women of
today is the organization and management of both a family *and* a career.

Implications of Changes in Female Sex-Roles. As a result of the changes in
sex-roles and the preferences of female youth, many interesting and important consequences have occurred.

Androgyny and changes in male sex-role choices. One result of changing female
sex-roles has been an increasing flexibility in general sex-role behavior, so
that traditional "male" and "female" roles are being incorporated into
"human" sex-roles (*androgyny*). This trend, in turn, has resulted, in a long
overdue recognition that the personality characteristics associated with the
traditional roles of male and female represent an unrealistic division of
human traits.

The unsettling of traditional norms and role expectations. The changes described have created opportunities and choices that were not widely available
in earlier times. In addition, these changes have placed men and women in
positions of ambiguity, anxiety, and uncertainty. The role expectations that
have historically organized the relationships between male and female in an
industrial society have changed. When behavior becomes subject to choice, it
also becomes subject to potential conflict, anxiety, uncertainty, and problems.

Sexual Behavior and Attitudes. *Sexual Behavior.* Research indicates
that there has been an increase in the number of young people who engage in
premarital sexual intercourse (Sorensen, 1973; Zelnik and Kantner, 1977,
1978a; Spanier, 1979) (see Figure 9.13). It is, however, difficult to generalize
about sexual behavior for the whole American population because there are
definite regional differences.

The results of all the studies of sexual behavior among youth support the
idea that there have been dramatic changes including a general leveling off of
differences among various groupings of young people (social classes, males,
and females), as well as a disappearance of racial differences in sexual behavior patterns (Kinsey, Pomeroy, Martin, and Gebhard, 1953; Cannon and
Long, 1971; Zelnik and Kantner, 1977; Sorenson, 1973). For example, the
traditional "double standard" that made it more acceptable for males than for
females to engage in premarital sexual intercourse has apparently disappeared. Research indicates that both males and females have premarital sexual relations in approximately equal numbers (Zelnik and Kantner, 1977). In
addition, social-class differences as initially reported in the 1950s seem to
have disappeared. Recent data indicate that there appears to be little differ-

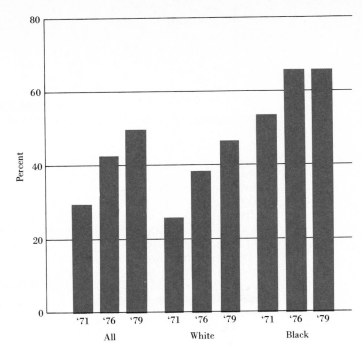

FIGURE 9.13 Percentage of females 15–19 years who had intercourse before marriage by race, 1971, 1976, and 1979.

From M. Zelnick and J. F. Kanter. Sexual activity, contraceptive use and pregnancy among metropolitan-area teenagers: 1971–1979. *Family Planning Perspectives*, 1980, *12*, 5, pp. 230–238.

ence among social classes in the ages at which sexual relations begin as well as in the type of sexual acts practiced (Zelnik and Kantner, 1977). A third trend is that racial differences are also beginning to disappear. This trend is somewhat more complex, as there are differences between black female youth and white female youth aged fifteen to nineteen years for initial sexual intercourse. Black women tend to begin having sexual intercourse at an earlier age. However, these initial differences level out and decrease after age twenty (Zelnik and Kantner, 1977, 1978a).

One interesting finding is that both knowledge about sexual reproduction and the use of contraceptive techniques have not kept pace with the changes in sexual mores (Zelnik and Kantner, 1977, 1978a). Zelnik and Kantner (1978b) found that about 75 percent of their sample of sexually active teenagers had used contraceptive methods at some time, but almost two out of three had failed to use any method in their last sexual intercourse. Furthermore, only 40 percent of the females in the sample had a correct understanding of the period of greatest risk of pregnancy during their monthly cycles. Surprisingly most of these female youth thought that the time of greatest risk was *during* the menstrual period. In addition, a large number of them seemed to *feel* that even without the protection of a contraceptive device, one could not easily become pregnant.

Teenage Pregnancy. Zelnik and Kantner (1978b) estimated that there are almost 800,000 premarital pregnancies each year among the fifteen–nineteen year age group. Jaffe and Dryfoos (1976) have estimated that 30,000 girls under age fifteen become pregnant each year in the United States. In recent years fewer girls have been marrying before the age of eighteen or boys before the age of twenty; however, *more* females under the age of eighteen are having babies *and* trying to raise them (see Application Box—Teenage Pregnancy—A Systems Perspective).

As contraceptive information is so relatively widespread, why are so many teenage girls becoming pregnant? Several factors may be relevant (Wuerger, 1976; Polsby, 1974; Sklar and Berkov, 1974):

- Emotional problems and lack of adjustment.
- A poor self-concept, including low self-esteem.
- Extreme inability to communicate with parents or peers about sexual matters resulting in a gross misunderstanding of sexual facts and an absence of valid information.
- A desire to punish a parent toward whom the adolescent is angry.
- The absence of the self-control necessary to take proper precautions against pregnancy.

Changing Attitudes Toward Sex. There is evidence that the attitudes of youth toward sex have changed. Jarl E. Dyrud (1974) summarized this position as follows:

We are all aware that in the past decade there has been something special about the way the popular culture has taken up sex as a preoccupation, or rather an obsession. I don't mean pornography either. I mean the new sexual mythology that views orgasm as a panacea for all of life's dreariness. . . .

Even if sexual behavior has not changed dramatically, the meanings have. Words are powerful determinants of how we think of ourselves—how we feel about ourselves. They define success and failure. As Ogden Nash, the poet Laureate of Baltimore, put it: "Sticks and stones may break my bones, but words can break my heart." (p. 21)

There appears to be a greater liberalization of attitudes toward sexual behavior, particularly among unmarried persons. Studies have demonstrated that over the last twenty years an increasing number of both male and female youth approve of premarital sexual intercourse (Christensen and Gregg, 1970; King, Balswick, and Robinson, 1977; Yankelovich, 1972). Furthermore, the greater acceptability of sexual relationships is related to the perceived *context* in which sex occurs, which appears to be the serious or potentially long-term relationship (Dreyer, 1975). Male and female youth tend to feel that sexual relationships are acceptable within such a framework.

Sexual behavior among youth appears to be part of the attempt of youth to achieve a sense of identity through affectionate, emotionally involving forms of physical intimacy. The increasing acceptability of premarital sexual behavior carries with it anxieties and tensions that were not present in past generations (Hunt, 1973; Stratton and Spitzer, 1967; Offer, 1972).

The picture is not a totally positive one. The meanings that youth attach to premarital sexual relations are not entirely positive, as many youth experience anxiety and uncertainty accompanying sexual behavior:

The data demonstrate a tremendous variability among adolescents in their attitudes toward sex. About 50 percent are comfortable about it and 50 percent are not.

Another study shows that when college students were asked about their current love affairs, 25 percent of the females and 35 percent of the males responded that they were more active sexually than they want to be.

Teenage Pregnancy—A Systems Perspective

Perhaps one of the most serious problems of adolescence is teenage pregnancy (girls who become pregnant during the high school years at approximately 13–17 years of age). Indeed, there appear to be few areas in the life of the adolescent that do not hold the potential to be negatively affected by a pregnancy.

1. *The adolescent mother as system: Blockage of the developmental tasks of adolescence.* Many of the developmental tasks of adolescence are omitted in order for the teenage mother to fulfill adult or parental responsibilities (Klein, 1978; Osofsky and Osofsky, 1978). For example, there is often a failure to remain in school, a failure to develop what might be considered a stable family, and a failure to enter a vocation and become relatively self-supporting. There is little doubt that these failures are heavy psychological burdens for both the adolescent and her family (Klein, 1978).

   These failures at the tasks of adolescence represent the closing of doors that typically serve as the transition from childhood to adulthood autonomy. Frequently, if these transitional tasks are not successfully managed during the adolescent years, the requirements and frustrations of being a teenage parent may prevent their completion at a later time.

2. *The crisis in the family system.* Sometimes the pregnant teenager may be viewed, particularly by other family members, as the individual who has caused a permanent crisis or strain in the family system.

   In spite of the fact that the adolescent's parents may move toward a posture of acceptance during the course of the pregnancy, Osofsky and Osofsky (1978) have determined that the most frequently occurring initial parental response is the traditionally anticipated one of anger. This anger is one mechanism of crisis generation and is often accompanied by a strong sense of shame and guilt. Through their work with parents, these two researchers have observed family members to view the pregnancy event as the symbol of

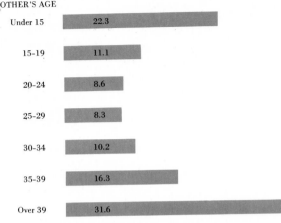

MOTHER'S AGE

Under 15	22.3
15–19	11.1
20–24	8.6
25–29	8.3
30–34	10.2
35–39	16.3
Over 39	31.6

Fetal-death ratios by age of mother (total of 37 reporting states and the District of Columbia, 1978).

Source: U.S. Department of Health and Human Services. Public Health Service, National Center for Heath Statistics, Vital Statistics of the United States 1978, Vol. 11—Mortality Part A.

failed aspirations for the whole family. This view of the pregnancy as a pervasive failure may provoke guilt surrounding "what went wrong," as well as questioning within the parents themselves regarding any role they may have played that might have inadvertently contributed to the occurrence of this problem. The total picture of familial response to the pregnancy event spans the full range of positive and negative attitudes, but the situation is open throughout the entire process to the potential for crisis (Bolton, 1980, p. 115).

3. *Prenatal care and the infant system.* For a number of reasons, the teenage mother is in a high-risk situation both for herself and her infant. These risks include the biological immaturity of the expectant mother and the frequent reluctance of the teenage mother to seek proper prenatal care. Infants born to teenage mothers have a greater risk of having a lower birth-weight than infants born to mature women. This increased risk is due to the association of teenage pregnancy with the absence of adequate prenatal care, poor maternal nutrition, and the poor socioeco-

nomic status of the mother. Likewise, there is a greater risk for infant death among very young teenage mothers (Monkus and Bancalari, 1981). (See diagram—Infant Death Rate per 1,000 Live Births by Mother's Age). Furthermore, the relationship between teenage pregnancy and child abuse has raised serious concerns.

Does the age of parents have anything to do with child abuse? Professionals who work closely with school-aged parents believe it is a serious problem. They feel that the dangerous age is when children are from one to three years old. During these years babies are able to move actively about and require constant attention but are still too young to understand why they should or shouldn't do things. DeLissovoy (1973) found that school-aged parents are apt to expect too much too soon of their babies. For example, mothers expected babies to sit up alone by 12 weeks, while records show that the average baby is not able to do so until 28 weeks. Young fathers expected even faster development. Very young parents showed a low tolerance for crying. DeLissovoy says, ''This low tolerance (of crying), combined with unrealistic expectations of development, contributed to their impatience with their children—and to their sometimes cruel treatment of them.'' He reports babies as young as six or seven months being hit or spanked in his presence (Nye, 1975).

This bit of information can be interpreted in many ways. Possibly they feel guilty about their behavior, or they do more things, because they think the adult world expects it from them. It is possible, too, that his or her partner demands more sex than either really wants to give. But no matter how the data are interpreted, we end up with the young adult in conflict over his or her sexual behavior. (Offer, 1972, pp. 81–90)

MORAL DEVELOPMENT AND AN EMERGING PHILOSOPHY OF LIFE

One of the consequences of the adolescent search for identity is the clarification of values. Adolescents begin the process of organizing the set of values that will help them deal with life experiences. They are formulating a ''philosophy of life.'' The changes in adolescent thinking that we have described lay the foundation for the development of this philosophy of life.

Moral Stages in Adolescence. The school-aged child is characterized by a level of moral reasoning in which concern for maintaining the rules or expectations of the family, school, or group is the primary focus. You may remember that Kohlberg (1964; Kohlberg and Turiel, 1974) referred to this as the ''conventional'' level of moral reasoning. ''Right'' behavior for the school-aged child is based on at least two central factors:

- The authority of parents, teachers, or other adults who hold these values.
- The child's identification with these adults (i.e., the child considers these adults important enough to try to please them).

According to Kohlberg (1981), the adolescent may enter a stage of moral reasoning known as the *postconventional* level, at which ''right'' or ''moral'' behavior is determined by the *individuals themselves.* In contrast to the school-aged child, the adolescent determines what is right independent of the expectations of other people (e.g., parents, teachers, and other adults). The adolescent may still arrive at a moral principle that is similar or even identical to that of significant adults or society at large. However, the critical factor is that these moral principles are self-developed. Right action is defined in terms of ethical principles that are based on what the individual thinks is right. These are usually universal principles of justice, equality, and respect for the dignity of human beings.

The new cognitive tools of adolescents (i.e., abstract reasoning) encourage them in their quest for a consistent set of principles or a philosophy of life (Kohlberg, 1964; Kohlberg and Gilligan, 1972; Kaczkowski, 1962). Adolescents come to appreciate the fact that there may not be a single "correct"

TABLE 9.4
Action-Learning Assignments Related to Moral Development and Role-Taking

---

Action-Learning Assignment

Stage 1
Carrying out orders in prescribed ways as in well defined, military assignments; some fixed rate production or assembly work. One's concern is for oneself, to receive reward or avoid punishment. Rules are to be obeyed.

Stage 2
Piece rate jobs, e.g., fruit picking at so much a basket, some sales clerk assignments, some assignments helping others. Pay or approbation is based on the quantity and quality of work performed. One's responsibility is for self and, in part, for others. One's concern is to be fairly treated.

Stage 3
Group work as at some hamburger stands, secretaries in a pool, some kinds of sales work, some shared production work or group bench work, some responsibilities for helping others, e.g., child care. One's desire is to do one's share and be liked by peers, employers, or the persons served. Loyalty is to the "group" whether it is viewed as peers or employers. One's concern is for self and others.

Stage 4
Carrying out responsibilities in the absence of group support. Some supervisory or instructional assignments. Some kinds of legal or correctional work. Some sales work involving the influencing of others. Some assignments helping others. Work is according to rules or precedents which are to be maintained. Loyalty is to the company or the labor organization. Judgment is exercised but within prescribed limits. One's concern is for Self and Others, to do one's duty according to rules and convention.

Stage 5
Positions of decision-making in the presence of conflict. Some personnel work or counseling; some work involving responsibilities for others; negotiated policy formation and decision-making, some legislative work, negotiating goals and standards, cooperatively establishing or revising rules and procedures in light of underlying principles. One's concern is for Self and for Others according to fundamental principles of fairness and utility.

From R. Graham, "Youth and Experiential Learning." In, R. J. Havighurst and P. H. Dreyer (Eds.), *Youth*. Chicago: University of Chicago Press, 1975.

position on moral behavior. For example, are premarital sexual relations simply immoral and wrong in all cases? Or are they defensible for some adolescents who are presumably mature enough to avoid problems? The messages that the adolescent receives from family, peers, religious groups, and the school may indeed be conflicting. The adolescent's attempt to resolve or at least understand these inconsistencies is an important motivation for developing a philosophy of life. This process of developing such a moral stance toward the world has its *beginning* during adolescence. However, the process is not completed until at least the early twenties, if it is completed at all (Kohlberg, 1981). The "conventional" morality of the school-aged child may be the highest level of moral reasoning reached by some people (Kohlberg, 1981).

Moral Development and Experience. Kohlberg (1981) suggested that during the teens and early twenties, educational programs can be developed that will stimulate higher stages of moral development. The relationship between experiential learning and moral development has been demonstrated for high-school students (Sprinthall and Mosher, 1970), for college students (Gilligan, 1977), and for young adults in prison (Hickey, 1974). Graham (1975) has suggested that there is a relationship between "action-learning" experiences and moral development (see Table 9.4). Various tasks and experiences (e.g., household chores, being a street-crossing guard, secretarial activities) encourage the development of moral processes as well as an understanding of social roles.

A Special Issue— Drug Use

In negotiating the challenges of adolescence, young people undoubtedly will encounter peers who use drugs or may, themselves, experiment with drugs. For our purposes, a drug will be defined as any substance (with the exception of food) which, when taken by an individual, alters one or more of the functions (e.g. excitation level, sensory perceptions, heart rate, blood pressure) of the individual (Katchadourian, 1977). The health hazards resulting from the abuse of drugs by adolescents constitutes a serious problem for adolescents and society. Table 9.5 shows several types of drugs which can be abused by adolescents as well as how the drug is taken into the body, the primary physical and behavioral signs associated with abuse, and the medical implications resulting from abuse.

Johnston, Bachman, and O'Malley (1982), using national data on adolescent drug use (based on relatively large, representative surveys of eight graduating classes of high school seniors, 1975–1982, in public and private schools across the United States), established several key findings:

- *Alcohol* use has remained relatively stable since 1975, though at relatively high levels (see Table 9.6). Nearly all young people have tried alcohol by the end of their senior year (93%) and the great majority (70%) have used it in the prior month (see Figure 9.14, p. 461).
- *Cigarette smoking* has declined since 1975 (see Table 9.6). Nonetheless, 70% of all young people have smoked cigarettes by the end of their senior year.

TABLE 9.5
**Drug Classification
Summary**

Name	Slang Name	Classification	How Taken
Heroin	H, Horse, junk, stuff, harry	Narcotic	Injected or sniffed
Morphine	White stuff, M	Narcotic	Injected or swallowe
Barbituates	Barbs, blue devils, candy, peanuts, phennies	Hypnotic sedative	Injected or swallowe
Alcohol	Booze	Hypnotic sedative	Swallowed
Amphetamines	Bennies, dexies, speed, lid proppers, pep pills	Stimulant	Swallowed or inject
Cocaine	Gold dust, coke, flake, star dust	Stimulant	Sniffed or injected
Tobacco	Fag, coffin nail	Stimulant-sedative	Smoked, sniffed or chewed
LSD	Acid, sugar, big D	Hallucinogen	Swallowed
Glue	—	Hydrocarbon	Inhaled
Marijuana	Pot, grass, hashish, tea, reefers	Cannibis	Smoked

Based on information in U.S. Public Health Service, *Resource Book for Drug Abuse Education*, Washington, D.C.: Govt. Printing Office, 1969, pp. 34–35 and Vaughan, V.C. and McKay, R. J. (Eds.) *Textbook of Pediatrics* (10th ed.). Philadelphia: Saunders, 1975.

Of this number, approximately 30% have smoked in the prior month, a substantial proportion of whom are, or soon will be, daily smokers (see Figure 9.14). Cigarettes are used *daily* by more young people than any other category of drugs (21%). However, *daily* cigarette smoking decreased from 1977 (28.8%) to 1981 (20.3%) and appears to have stabilized in 1982 (21.1%). It appears that the rather large drop in daily smoking rates was in response to both personal concerns about the health consequences of use and perceived peer disapproval of use.

Behavioral Effects	Physical Effects	Medical Complications	Physical Dependence Potential	Mental Dependence Potential
uphoria, lethargy, possible coma	Constricted pupils loss of appetite, respiratory depression	Addiction, injection-site infection, tetanus	Yes	Yes
uphoria, lethargy, possible coma	Constricted pupils, loss of appetite, respiratory depression	Addiction, injection-site infection, tetanus	Yes	Yes
lurred speech, short attention span, violence, drowsiness	Constricted pupils, needle marks	Addiction with severe withdrawal symptoms, possible convulsions, toxic psychosis	Yes	Yes
s above	Constricted pupils	Addiction, gastritis, central nervous system depression	Yes	Yes
yperactivity, insomnia, loss of appetite, irritability, paranoia	Dilated pupils, high blood pressure, weight loss	Hepatitis, injection-site infection, psychosis	No?	Yes
estlessness, hyperactivity, occasional depression or paranoia	High blood pressure	Nausea, vomiting, inflammation or perforation of nasal septum	Yes	Yes
ariable	Shortness of breath, cough, nervousness	Long term effects may include emphysema, lung cancer, loss of appetite, cardiovascular problems	Yes?	Yes
uphoria, hallucinations, confusion	Dilated pupils, occasional high blood pressure	Primarily psychiatric, particularly dangerous for individuals with previous or unrecognized mental problems	No	No?
uphoria, confusion	Nonspecific	Asphyxiation may result from plastic bag used to inhale fumes	No	No?
1ild intoxication, euphoria	Poor coordination, delayed response time	Occasional psychiatric problems	No	Yes

- Approximately ⅔ of all American young people (64%) try an illicit drug (e.g., marijuana, cocaine, or other drug that is illegal unless used under a physician's supervision) before they finish high school. (Alcohol and cigarettes are, of course, legal drugs).
- Marijuana use increased substantially from 1975 (47.3%) to 1979 (60.4%) and has remained relatively stable to 1982 (58.7%) (see Table 9.6). Marijuana is by far the most widely used illicit drug with 59% reporting some use by high school graduation, 44% reporting some use in the previous year, and 29% reporting some use in the past month (see Figure 9.14). The *daily* use of marijuana increased dramatically from 1975 (6.0%) to 1978

TABLE 9.6 Trends in Lifetime Prevalence of Sixteen Types of Drugs

	Percent Ever-used								
	Class of 1975	Class of 1976	Class of 1977	Class of 1978	Class of 1979	Class of 1980	Class of 1981	Class of 1982	'81–'82 Change
Approx. N =	(9400)	(15400)	(17100)	(17800)	(15500)	(15900)	(17500)	(17700)	
Marijuana/Hashish	47.3	52.8	56.4	59.2	60.4	60.3	59.5	58.7	−0.8
Inhalants[a]	NA	10.3	11.1	12.0	12.7	11.9	12.3	12.8	+0.5
Inhalants Adjusted[b]	NA	NA	NA	NA	18.7	17.6	17.4	18.0	+0.6
Amyl & Butyl Nitrites[c]	NA	NA	NA	NA	11.1	11.1	10.1	9.8	−0.3
Hallucinogens	16.3	15.1	13.9	14.3	14.1	13.3	13.3	12.5	−0.8
Hallucinogens Adjusted[d]	NA	NA	NA	NA	18.6	15.7	15.7	15.0	−0.7
LSD	11.3	11.0	9.8	9.7	9.5	9.3	9.8	9.6	−0.2
PCP[c]	NA	NA	NA	NA	12.8	9.6	7.8	6.0	−1.8s
Cocaine	9.0	9.7	10.8	12.9	15.4	15.7	16.5	16.0	−0.5
Heroin	2.2	1.8	1.8	1.6	1.1	1.1	1.1	1.2	+0.1
Other opiates[e]	9.0	9.6	10.3	9.9	10.1	9.8	10.1	9.6	−0.5
Stimulants[e]	22.3	22.6	23.0	22.9	24.2	26.4	32.2	35.6	+3.4ss
Stimulants Adjusted[e,f]	NA	NA	NA	NA	NA	NA	NA	27.9	—
Sedatives[e]	18.2	17.7	17.4	16.0	14.6	14.9	16.0	15.2	−0.8
Barbiturates[e]	16.9	16.2	15.6	13.7	11.8	11.0	11.3	10.3	−1.0
Methaqualone[e]	8.1	7.8	8.5	7.9	8.3	9.5	10.6	10.7	+0.1
Tranquilizers[e]	17.0	16.8	18.0	17.0	16.3	15.2	14.7	14.0	−0.7
Alcohol	90.4	91.9	92.5	93.1	93.0	93.2	92.6	92.8	+0.2
Cigarettes	73.6	75.4	75.7	75.3	74.0	71.0	71.0	70.1	−0.9

NOTES: Level of significance of difference between the two most recent classes:
  s = .05, ss = .01, sss = .001.
    NA indicates data not available.

[a] Data based on four questionnaire forms. N is four-fifths of N indicated.

[b] Adjusted for underreporting of amyl and butyl nitrites (see text).

[c] Data based on a single questionnaire form. N is one-fifth of N indicated.

[d] Adjusted for underreporting of PCP (see text).

[e] Only drug use which was not under a doctor's orders is included here.

[f] Adjusted for overreporting of the non-prescription stimulants. Data based on three questionnaire forms. N is three-fifths of N indicated.

From L. D. Johnston, J. G. Bachman, and P. M. O'Malley. *Student drug use, attitudes, and beliefs: National Trends 1975–1982.* National Institute of Drug Abuse, Department of Health and Human Services. Washington, D.C.: U.S. Government Printing Office, 1982, p. 32.

(10.7%) and dropped substantially by 1982 (6.3%). As in the case of cigarette smoking, the drop was also in response to personal concern about health consequences and perceived peer disapproval.

- The most widely used class of illicit drugs (other than marijuana) was stimulants (28%) (see Figure 9.14). Stimulants were followed, in use, by inhalants (18%), cocaine (16%), sedatives (15%), hallucinogens (15%), tranquilizers (14%), other opiates (10%), and heroin (1.2%).

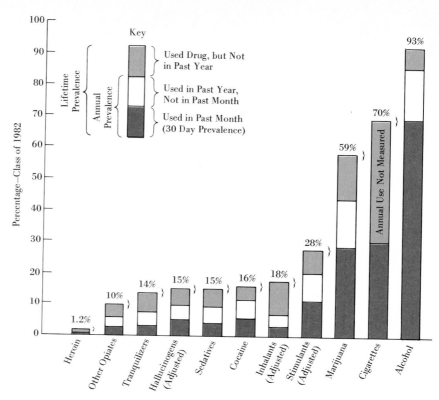

FIGURE 9.14 Prevalence and recency of use of 11 types of drugs, class of 1982.

From L. D. Johnson, J. G. Bachman, and P. M. O'Malley. *Student drug use, attitudes, and beliefs: National trends 1975–1982.* National Institute of Drug Abuse, Department of Health and Human Services. Washington, D.C.: U.S. Government Printing Office, 1982, p. 17.

Note: The bracket near the top of a bar indicates the lower and upper limits of the 95% confidence interval.

- According to Johnston, Bachman, and O'Malley (1982), these are truly alarming levels of substance use and abuse, whether by historical standards or in comparison with other countries. In fact, they still probably reflect the highest levels of *illicit* drug use to be found in any nation in the industrialized world.

Summary

1. Adolescence is a critical period in human development because it is during this period that the individual begins to develop a stance toward the world or an "*identity*." Adolescence begins with the onset of puberty and ends with the entrance into the world of the adult—a social and psychological event. Although there is little dispute that adolescence begins with the biological event of puberty, the end of adolescence is much less clear. When, for example, does a person become an adult?

2. Since there are few characteristics that apply to both a twelve year old and a twenty year old, we will adopt a two-stage theory of adolescence: *early adolescence* and *later adolescence* or *youth*. The central feature of early adolescence is the development of a "group identity" in relation to the world of the high school and peer group. The primary characteristic of later adolescence is the clarification of the self in relation to society as a whole (i.e., an identity that reflects a stance toward the world).

3. In adolescence, the neighborhood/community boundaries are expanded. The adolescent has increasing freedom to explore the neighborhood and community. However, their ability to interact with the broad social community may still be limited by traditional patterns of age segregation.

4. The most important feature of parent-adolescent interaction is how this *mutual relationship* helps the adolescent to develop a sense of independence. Parents who use democratic practices and frequent explanations to the adolescent of the reasons for their rules foster responsible, independent behavior in their children. Sometimes adolescent-parent conflict is intensified.

5. Peer groups and friends provide the adolescent with an arena for much of the learning that occurs in early adolescence. Significant features of the peer context include the *functions of the peer group*, the *structure of the peer group* and how that structure changes over time, and the *stages of peer group development and friendship*.

6. Adolescents spend a considerable amount of their time in schools. High school education in the United States has been dominated by one major type of organization—the comprehensive public school. Several major studies have revealed some of the critical problems in the modern American high school.

7. The choice of an occupational direction is a part of the overall process of identity formation in youth.

8. Although the general growth rate of body tissue slows down from birth through childhood, the onset of puberty is marked by a considerable increase in this growth rate. There are increases in body size, changes in body shape and composition, and a rapid development of reproductive organs and secondary sexual characteristics. Three facts remain constant as accurate descriptions of the process. (a) Girls usually develop earlier than boys. (b) For both boys and girls the rate of development is different for individuals. (c) The sequence of biological changes has remained the same as in the past although, for some changes, the onset may be earlier than in the past.

9. The changes which take place in adolescent intellectual growth are both *quantitative* and *qualitative*. Not all adolescents attain formal operations during early adolescence. There is evidence that some older adolescents may go beyond formal operations.

10. The adolescent integrates new skills in logical thinking, moral development, and sexual identity with the possibilities for a more independent social life in formulating a self–concept. Three major dimensions of this newly integrated self–concept include a vocational identity, a sexual identity, and a moral identity.

Questions

1. What event marks the beginning of adolescence? What events mark the end of adolescence?

2. What is the central theme of early adolescence? How is this theme different from the concerns of later adolescents?

3. Give several reasons why parents of adolescents who use democratic practices with frequent explanations of the reasons for rules foster responsible and independent behavior in their children.

4. Briefly describe four functions of the peer group during adolescence.

5. Identify and briefly describe two qualitative changes in adolescent thinking.

6. After examining the stages of Ginzberg's theory of vocational development, consider whether you think the theory is realistic and accurate.

Adolescence

Bibliography

ARLIN, P. K. Cognitive development in adulthood: A fifth stage? *Developmental Psychology,* 1975, *11*(5), 602–606.

BAUMRIND, D. Authoritarian vs. authoritative parental control. *Adolescence,* 1968, *3,* 255–272.

BLOS, P. *The Young Adolescent: Clinical Studies.* New York: Free Press, 1970.

BOLTON, F. G. *The Pregnant Adolescent: Problems of Premature Parenthood.* Beverly Hills, California: Sage, 1980.

BOROW, H. Career development. In J. F. Adams (Ed.), *Understanding Adolescence* (3rd ed.), Boston: Allyn and Bacon, 1976, 489–523.

BOWERMAN, C. E., and BAHR, S. J. Conjugal power and adolescent identification with parents. *Sociometry.* 1973, *36,* 366–377.

BRONFENBRENNER, U. *Two Worlds of Childhood: U.S. and U.S.S.R.* New York: Russell Sage Foundation, 1970.

CANNON, K. L., and LONG, R. Premarital sexual behavior in the sixties. *Journal of Marriage and the Family,* February 1971, *33,* 36–49.

Children and parents: Together in the world, Report of Forum 15, 1970. White House Conference on Children. (Washington, D.C.: Superintendent of Documents, 1971).

CHRISTENSEN, H. T., and GREGG, C. F. Changing sex norms in America and Scandinavia. *Journal of Marriage and the Family,* November 1970, *32,* 616–627.

COLEMAN, J. S. *The Adolescent Society.* New York: Free Press, 1961.

COLEMAN, J. S. *Youth: Transition to Adulthood.* Chicago: U. of Chicago P., 1974.

CONGER, J. J. A world they never knew: The family and social change. *Daedalus* Fall 1971, *100,* 1105–1138.

DACEY, J. S. *Adolescents Today* (2nd ed.), Santa Monica, Calif.: Goodyear Publishing Co., 1982.

DeCECCO, J. P., and RICHARDS, I. K. Civil war in the high schools. *Psychology Today,* 1975, *9*(6), 51–52, 120.

DeLISSOVOY, V. Child care by adolescent parents. *Children Today,* July–August 1973, 22–25.

DOUVAN, E. Sex differences in the opportunities, demands and developments of youth. In R. L. Havighurst and P. H. Dreyer (Eds.), *Youth.* Chicago: U. of Chicago P., 1975, 27–45.

DOUVAN, E., and ADELSON, J. *The Adolescent Experience.* New York: Wiley, 1966.

DREYER, P. Sex, sex roles and marriage among youth in the 1970's. In R. J. Havighurst and P. H. Dreyer (Eds.), *Youth.* Chicago: U. of Chicago, 1975, pp. 194–223.

DUNPHY, D. The social structure of urban adolescent peer groups. *Sociometry,* 1963, *26*(2), 230–246.

DWYER, J., and MAYER, J. Variations in physical appearance during adolescence. Part I: Boys. *Postgraduate Medicine,* 1967, *41,* 99–107.

DYRUD, J. E. The sexual revolution: Fact or fantasy? *University of Chicago Magazine,* January–February 1974, *66,* 21.

EITZEN, D. S. Athletics in the status system of male adolescents: A replication of Coleman's *The Adolescent Society. Adolescence,* 1975, *38*(10), 265–276.

ELDER, G. H. Structural variations in the child rearing relationship. *Sociometry,* 1962, *25,* 241–262.

ELDER, G. H. Parental power legitimation and its effect on the adolescent. *Sociometry,* 1963, *26,* 50–65.

ELDER, G. H. Variations in adolescent perceptions of family power structure. *American Sociological Review,* 1964, *29,* 551–567.

ELKIND, D. Egocentrism in adolescence. *Child Development,* 1967, *38,* 1025–1034.

ELKIND, D. Exploitation and the generational conflict. Paper presented at the meeting of the American Psychological Association, San Francisco, 1968.

ELKIND, D. *A Sympathetic Understanding of the Child Six to Sixteen.* Boston: Allyn and Bacon, 1971.

EMMERICH, W. Continuity and stability in early social development. *Child Development,* June 1964, *35,* 311–333.

ERIKSON, E. *Childhood and Society*. New York: Norton, 1950.

ERIKSON, E. *Childhood and Society* (2nd ed.), New York: Norton, 1963.

ERIKSON, E. (ED.). *The Challenge of Youth*. New York: Doubleday, 1965.

ERIKSON, E. *Identity: Youth and Crisis*. New York: Norton, 1968.

FAUST, M. S. Developmental maturity as a determinant in prestige of adolescent girls. *Child Development*, 1960, *31*, 173–184.

GILLIGAN, C. In a different voice: women's conceptions of self and of morality. *Harvard Educational Review*, 1977, *47*, 481–517.

GINZBERG, E. Toward a theory of occupational choice: A restatement. *Vocational Guidance Quarterly*, 1972, *20*, 169–176.

GOETHALS, G. W., and KLOS, D. *Experiencing Youth: First-Person Accounts*. Boston: Little, Brown and Company, 1970.

GRAHAM, R. Youth and experimental learning. In R. J. Havighurst and P. H. Dreyer (Eds.), *Youth*. Chicago: U. of Chicago P., 1975.

HALEY, J. *Leaving Home*. New York: McGraw-Hill, 1980.

HALL, G. S. *Adolescence: Its Psychology and its Relation to Physiology, Anthropology, Sociology, Sex, Crime, Religion and Education*, 2 volumes. New York: Appleton, 1904.

HART, N. A., and KEIDEL, G. C. The suicidal adolescent. *American Journal of Nursing*, 1979, 80–84.

HICKEY, J. Stimulation of moral reasoning in delinquents. In L. Kohlberg and E. Turiel (Eds.), *Recent Research in Moral Development*. New York: Holt, 1974.

HIGGINS-TRENK, A., and GAITE, A. Elusiveness of formal operational thought in adolescence. *Proceedings of the 79th Annual Convention of the American Psychological Association*, 1971.

HILGARD, E. R., and ATKINSON, R. C. *Introduction to psychology*. New York: Harcourt, Brace, 1967.

HUNT, M. Sexual behavior in the 1970's. *Playboy Magazine*, October 1973, *20*, 200–201.

HUNTLEY, C. W. Changes in the study of values during the four years of college. *Genetic Psychology Monograph*, 1965. *71*, 349–383.

JAFFE, F. S., and DRYFOOS, J. G. Fertility control services for adolescents: access and utilizations. *Family Planning Perspectives*, 1976, *8*, 167–175.

JENCKS, C., SMITH, M., ACLAND, H., BANE, M. J., COHEN, D., GINTIS, H., HEYNS, B., and MICHELSON, S. *Inequality: A reassessment of the effect of family and schooling in America*. New York: Basic Books, 1972.

JOHNSTON, L. D., BACHMAN, J. G., and O'MALLEY, P. M. *Student drug use, attitudes, and beliefs: National Trends 1975–1982*. Washington, D.C.: National Institute of Drug Abuse, U.S. Government Printing Office, 1982.

JONES, M. C. The later careers of boys who were early—or late—maturing. *Child Development*, 1957, *28*, 113–128.

JONES, M. C. Psychological correlates of somatic development. *Child Development*, 1965, *36*, 899–911.

JONES, M. C., and BAYLEY, N. Physical maturing among boys as related to behavior. *Journal of Educational Psychology*, 1950, *41*, 129–248.

JORDAAN, J. P., and HEYDE, M. B. *Vocational development during the high school years*. New York: Teachers College Press, 1978.

KACZKOWSKI, H. Sex and age differences in the life problems of adolescents. *Journal of Psychological Studies*, 1962, *13*, 165–169.

KAGAN, J., and COLES, R. *Twelve to sixteen: Early adolescence*. New York: Norton, 1972.

KAGAN, J., and MOSS, H. A. *Birth to maturity*. New York: Wiley, 1972.

KANDEL, D. B., and LESSER, G. *Youth in two worlds: United States and Denmark*. San Francisco: Jossey-Bass, 1972.

KATCHADOURIAN, H. *The biology of adolescence*. San Francisco: Freeman, 1977.

KENISTON, K. Prologue: Youth as a stage of life. In P. Dreyer and R. J. Havighurst (Eds.), *Youth*. Chicago: U. of Chicago P., 1975.

KING, K., BALSWICK, J. O., and ROBINSON, I. E. The continuing premarital sexual revolution among college females. *Journal of Marriage and the Family*, 1977, *39*, 455–459.

KINSEY, A., POMEROY, W. B., MARTIN, C. E., and GEBHARD, P. H. *Sexual behavior in the human female*. Philadelphia: Saunders, 1953.

KLEIN, L. Antecedents to teenage pregnancy, *Clinical Obstetrics and Gynecology*, 1978, *32*, 1151–1159.

KOHLBERG, L. Development of moral character and moral ideology. In M. L. Hoffman and L. W. Hoffman (Eds.), *Review of child development research*, Vol. 1. New York: Russell Sage Foundation, 1964.

KOHLBERG, L. *The Philosophy of Moral Development*. New York: Harper & Row, 1981.

KOHLBERG, L., and GILLIGAN, C. The adolescent as a philosopher: The discovery of the self in a post-conventional world. In J. Kagan and R. Coles (Eds.), *12 to 16: Early adolescence*. New York: Norton, 1972, 144–179.

KOHLBERG, L., and TURIEL, E. (Eds.). *Recent research in moral development*. New York: Holt, 1974.

LJUNG, B. O., BERGSTEN-BRUCEFORS, A., and LINDGREN, G. The secular trend in physical growth in Sweden. *Annals of Human Biology*, 1974, *1*, 245–256.

MANASTER, G. *Adolescent development and the life tasks*. New York: Allyn and Bacon, 1977.

MARTORANO, S. C. A developmental analysis of performance on Piaget's formal operations tasks. *Developmental Psychology*, 1977, *13*, 666–672.

MATTESON, D. R. *Adolescence Today*. Homewood, Ill.: Dorsey, 1975.

McWILLIAMS, M. *Nutrition for the Growing Years* (2nd ed.). New York: Wiley, 1975.

MEAD, M. *Culture and Commitment: A Study of the Generation Gap*. New York: Doubleday, 1970.

MONKUS, E., and BANCALARI, E. Neonatal outcome. In K. G. Scott, T. Field, and E. Robertson (Eds.), *Teenage parents and their offspring*. New York: Grune and Stratton, 1981, 131–144.

MUUSS, R. Puberty rites in primitive and modern societies. *Adolescence*, 1970, *5*, 109–128.

National Panel on High School and Adolescent Education. *The education of adolescents*. Washington, D.C.: U.S. Department of Health, Education, and Welfare, 1976.

NEIMARK, E. D. Intellectual development during adolescence. In F. D. Horowitz (Ed.), *Review of child development research* (Vol. 4). Chicago: University of Chicago Press, 1975.

NEWCOMB, T. *The Acquaintance Process*. New York: Holt, 1961.

NEWCOMB, T. Persistence and regression of changed attitudes: Long-range studies. *Journal of Social Issues*, 1963, *19*, 3–14.

NYE, F. I. *School-Age Parenthood*. Pullman, Wash.: Cooperative Extension Service, Extension Bulletin 667, 1975.

OFFER, D. Attitudes toward sexuality in a group of 1500 middle class teenagers. *Journal of Youth and Adolescence*, 1972, *1*, 81–90.

OSOFSKY, J. D., and OSOFSKY, H. S. Teenage pregnancy: Psychosocial considerations, *Clinical Obstetrics and Gynecology*, 1978, *21*, 1161–1173.

PACE, C. R. Differences in campus atmospheres. In W. W. Charters, Jr., and N. L. Gage (Eds.), *Readings in the social psychology of education*. Boston: Allyn and Bacon, 1963.

PIAGET, J., and INHELDER, B. *The Psychology of the Child*. New York: Basic Books, 1969.

POLSBY, G. K. Unmarried parenthood: Potential for growth. *Adolescence*, Summer 1974, *9*(34), 272–284.

REISTER, A. E., and ZUCKER, R. A. Adolescent social structure and drinking behavior. *Personnel and Guidance Journal*, 1968, *46*, 304–312.

ROSENBERG, M. *Society and the Adolescent Self-image*. Princeton, N.J.: Princeton U. P., 1965.

SCHERZ, F. The crisis of adolescence in family life. *Social Casework*, 1967, *48*, 209–215.

SCHIAMBERG, L. Some sociocultural factors in adolescent–parent conflict: A cross-cultural comparison of selected cultures. *Adolescence,* 1969, *4,* 333–360.

SCHIAMBERG, L. *Adolescent Alienation.* Columbus, Ohio: Merrill, 1973.

SCHONFELD, W. A. Body-image in adolescents: A psychiatric concept for the pediatrician. *Pediatrics,* 1963, *31,* 845–855.

SCHOONMAKER, A. N. *A Student's Survival Manual,* New York: Harper & Row, Publishers, Inc., 1971.

SHERIF, M., and SHERIF, C. W. *Reference Groups.* New York: Harper & Row, 1964.

SKLAR, J., and BERKOV, B. The American birth rate: Evidence of a coming rise. *Science,* 1974, *189,* 693–700.

SORENSON, R. C. *Adolescent Sexuality in Contemporary America: The Sorenson Report.* Cleveland: World, 1973.

SPANIER, G. B. *Human Sexuality in a Changing Society.* Minneapolis: Burgess, 1979.

SPRINTHALL, N. A., and MOSHER, R. Psychological education in secondary schools. *American Psychologist,* October 1970, *25,* 911–924.

STIERLIN, H. The adolescent as delegate of his parents, *Adolescent Psychiatry,* 1975, *4.*

STIERLIN, H. *Separating Parents and Adolescents: A Perspective on Running Away, Schizophrenia, and Waywardness.* New York: New York Times Book Company, 1974.

STRATTON, J., and SPITZER, S. Sexual permissiveness and self evaluation: A question of substance and a question of method. *Journal of Marriage and the Family,* August 1967, *29,* 434–441.

SULLIVAN, K., and SULLIVAN, A. Adolescent-parent separation. *Developmental Psychology,* 1980, *16*(2), 93–99.

TANNER, J. M. *Growth at Adolescence* (2nd ed.). Oxford: Blackwell, 1962.

TANNER, J. M., WHITEHOUSE, R. H., and TAKAISHI, M. Standards from birth to maturity for height, weight, height velocity and weight velocity; British Children, 1965, *Archives of the Diseases of Childhood,* 1966, *41,* 455–471.

TANNER, J. M. Sequence, tempo and individual variation of the growth and development of boys and girls aged twelve to sixteen. *Journal of the American Academy of Arts and Sciences,* Fall 1971, *100,* 907–930.

TANNER, J. M. Trends towards earlier menarche in London, Oslo, Copenhagen, the Netherlands and Hungary. *Nature,* 1973, *243,* 95–96.

TANNER, J. M. Growth and endocrinology of the adolescent. In L. I. Gardner (ed.), *Endocrine and Genetic Diseases of Childhood and Adolescence.* Philadelphia: Saunders, 1969.

TANNER, J. M. *Education and Physical Growth* (2nd ed.). New York: International Universities Press, 1978.

THISTLETHWAITE, D. L. College press and changes in study plans of talented students. *Journal of Educational Psychology,* 1960, *51.*

TOFFLER, A. *Future Shock.* New York: Random House, 1972.

U.S. BUREAU OF THE CENSUS, DEPARTMENT OF COMMERCE. *Statistical Abstract of the United States,* 1981. 102nd Edition.

U.S. BUREAU OF THE CENSUS, DEPARTMENT OF COMMERCE. *Current Population Reports,* Series P-25, No. 922, Projections of the population of the United States 1982–2050. (Advance Report). Washington, D.C.: U.S. Government Printing Office, October 1982, Table 2, pp. 9, 11–13.

U.S. BUREAU OF THE CENSUS. *U.S. Census of Population: 1960. General Population Characteristics. United States Summary.* Final Report PC(1)-1B. U.S. Government Printing Office, Washington, D.C., 1961. Table 47.

U.S. BUREAU OF THE CENSUS. Geographical mobility: March 1980 to March 1981. *Current Population Reports, Population Characteristics,* Series P.20, No. 377, Jan. 1983.

U.S. BUREAU OF THE CENSUS. *Statistical Abstract of the United States: 1982–83* (103rd Edition). Washington, D.C.: U.S. Government Printing Office, 1982.

U.S. DEPARTMENT OF HEALTH AND HUMAN SERVICES. NATIONAL CENTER FOR EDUCATIONAL STATISTICS. *Condition of Education, 1983.* Washington, D.C.: Government Printing Office, 1983.

U.S. Department of Health and Human Services, Public Health Service, National Center for Health Statistics. *Vital Statistics of the United States,* 1978. Vol. II-Mortality Part A.

U.S. Department of Labor, Bureau of Labor Statistics, 1983.

U.S. Department of Labor, Bureau of Labor Statistics. *Labor Force Statistics Derived from the Current Population Survey: A Data Book,* Vol. I, Bulletin 2096, September 1982.

U.S. Public Health Service. *Resource Book for Drug Abuse Education.* Washington, D.C.: U.S. Government Printing Office, 1969.

Vaughan, V. C., and McKay, R. J. (Eds.). *Textbook of Pediatrics* (10th ed.). Philadelphia: Saunders, 1975.

Wiggins, J. S., Wiggins, N., and Conger, J. C. Correlates of heterosexual somatic preference. *Journal of Personality and Social Psychology,* 1968, *10,* 82–90.

Wuerger, M. K. The young adult, stepping into parenthood. *American Journal of Nursing,* August 1976, 76(8).

Yankelovich, D. *The Changing Values on Campus.* New York: Pocket Books, 1972.

Young, H. B. Aging and adolescence. *Developmental Medicine and Child Neurology,* 1963, *5,* 451–460.

Youniss, J. *Parents and Peers in Social Development.* Chicago: University of Chicago P., 1980.

Zelnik, M., and Kantner, J. F. Sexual and contraceptive experience of young unmarried women in the United States, 1976 and 1971. *Family Planning Perspectives,* 1977, *9,* 55–71.

Zelnik, M., and Kantner, J. F. First pregnancies to women aged 15–19: 1976 and 1971. *Family Planning Perspectives,* 1978(a), *10,* 11–20.

Zelnik, M., and Kantner, J. F. Contraceptive patterns and premarital pregnancy among women aged 15–19 in 1976. *Family Planning Perspectives,* 1978(b), *10,* 135–142.

Zelnik, M., and Kantner, J. F. Sexual Activity, Contraceptive Use and Pregnancy Among Metropolitan-Area Teenagers: 1971–1979. *Family Planning Perspectives,* September/October, 1980, Vol. 12, No. 5, pp. 230–238.

Suggested Readings

Coleman, J. S. (ed.) *Transition to Adulthood.* Chicago, Illinois: The University of Chicago Press, 1974. An important book with many insights and policy recommendations.

Douvan, E., and Adelson, J. *The Adolescent Experience.* New York: Wiley, 1966. A comprehensive and thorough analysis of a variety of issues related to adolescent development, based on data from 3000 males and females.

Elkind, D. *A Sympathetic Understanding of the Child Six to Sixteen.* Boston, Massachusetts: Allyn and Bacon, 1971. An excellent description of all facets of child and adolescent development.

Joyce, J. *Portrait of the Artist as a Young Man.* New York: B. W. Huebsch, 1916. A very interesting autobiographical novel by the famous writer James Joyce, illustrating many of the classical features of adolescence.

Schiamberg, L. *Adolescent Alienation.* Columbus, Ohio: Charles E. Merrill Publishing Company, 1973. A discussion of the meaning of alienation for adolescents, including cross cultural analysis and practical suggestions for applying a systems perspective to youth problems.

TANNER, J. M. *Education and Physical Growth* (2nd edition). New York: International Universities Press, 1978. A thorough discussion of the dynamics of the growth spurt preceding adolescence and the accompanying physiological changes.

WRIGHT, R. *Black Boy*. New York: Harper & Row, 1965. An interesting autobiography of growing up as a black child and adolescent in the pre-civil-rights South.

10

Early Adulthood: The Entry Years

The period of early adulthood is the beginning of the period of maturity.

Photograph by Rich Schwartz

Who Are Young Adults?

Studies of child development have plotted every nuance of growth and given us comforting labels such as Terrible Twos and the Noisy Nines. Adolescence has been so carefully deciphered, most of the fun of being impossible has been taken out of it. But after meticulously documenting our periods of personality development up to the age of 18 or 20—nothing. Beyond the age of 21, apart from medical people who are interested only in our gradual physical decay, we are left to fend for ourselves on the way downstream to senescence, at which point we are picked up again by gerontologists. . . .

The years between 18 and 50 are the center of life. The unfolding of maximum opportunity and capacity. But without any guide to the inner changes on the way to full adulthood, we are swimming blind. When we don't "fit in" we are likely to think of our behavior as evidence of our inadequacies, rather than as a valid stage unfolding in a sequence of growth, something we all accept when applied to childhood.

From Gail Sheehy, *Passages: Predictable Crises of Adulthood.* New York: Bantam Books, 1976, pp. 14–15.

The entry of the individual into adulthood represents a major transition in the human life cycle. Up to this point, in our discussion of the developing person we have focused on physical *growth* as well as the *development* of thinking, social relationships, and personality. Such growth and development are, as we have seen, important and exciting in themselves. In addition, the growth and development through adolescence can be viewed as a *preparation* for the period of maturity or adulthood. In the remainder of this book, we focus on the *application* of these developments to the independent living of adulthood.

The period of early adulthood usually brings the beginning of a commitment to a career, the beginning of marriage (or, in some instances, an alternate family form), and, sometimes, the beginning of parenthood. Figure 10.1 illustrates the place of these typical events of early adulthood in the total life span. Adolescence provides the foundation for early adulthood in the form of a relatively stable identity. The years of early adulthood are based on this beginning definition of selfhood.

The timing of such social milestones of early adulthood as marriage, parenthood, and career development varies from one individual to another. This variation is based on a number of factors, including the differing cultural demands of different socioeconomic classes, nationalities, and ethnic groups, as well as individual personality differences and historical events (e.g., wars, economic depressions, or recessions) (see Table 10.1). For example, marriage may occur anywhere from the age of fifteen throughout the life span. Or it may not occur at all. Again, clarification of commitment to an occupation may vary from the individual who, at twelve, wants to (and eventually does) become a lawyer, to the adult at forty who wants to "change gears" by embarking on a new career. Because of such *normal* variability in the development of adult activities, it is difficult, if not impossible, to pinpoint precisely the stages of adulthood on the basis of age alone. When we suggest chronological age ranges (e.g., an early adulthood that extends from the early twenties to the middle or late thirties), we are really suggesting an arbitrary time period during which many individuals appear to have made certain life choices.

470

Child I—"Do you really think there's life after death—like the minister said?"
Child II—"I dunno—I just wonder sometimes if there's life after adolescence?"

FIGURE 10.1 The human life line. The ages of important events are approximate because there are considerable individual and sex differences in the order of these milestones.

Reprinted from Kimmel, D. C., *Adulthood and Aging.* New York: Copyright © 1974, 1980, by John Wiley & Sons, Inc.

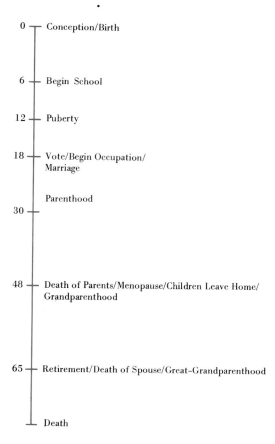

0 — Conception/Birth

6 — Begin School

12 — Puberty

18 — Vote/Begin Occupation/ Marriage

Parenthood

30 —

48 — Death of Parents/Menopause/Children Leave Home/ Grandparenthood

65 — Retirement/Death of Spouse/Great–Grandparenthood

— Death

Who Are Young Adults?

TABLE 10.1
Consensus in a Middle-Class, Middle-Aged Sample Regarding Various Age-Related Characteristics

	Age Range Designated as Appropriate or Expected	Percentage Who Concur	
		Men (N = 50)	Women (N = 43)
Best age for a man to marry	20–25	80	90
Best age for a woman to marry	19–24	85	90
When most people should become grandparents	45–50	84	79
Best age for most people to finish school and go to work	20–22	86	82
When most men should be settled on a career	24–26	74	64
When most men hold their top jobs	45–50	71	58
When most people should be ready to retire	60–65	83	86
A young man	18–22	84	83
A middle-aged man	40–50	86	75
An old man	65–75	75	57
A young woman	18–24	89	88
A middle-aged woman	40–50	87	77
An old woman	60–75	83	87
When a man has the most responsibilities	35–50	79	75
When a man accomplishes most	40–50	82	71
The prime of life for a man	35–50	86	80
When a woman has the most responsibilities	25–40	93	91
When a woman accomplishes most	30–45	94	92
A good-looking woman	20–35	92	82

Source: B. L. Neugarten, J. W. Moore, and J. C. Lowe, "Age Norms, Age Constraints, and Adult Socialization," *American Journal of Sociology,* 1965, 70(6), 710–717, Table 1. Reprinted by permission from the *American Journal of Sociology,* copyright © 1965 by the University of Chicago.

Neugarten and Moore (1968) have identified three periods or stages of adulthood:

1. *Early adulthood:* the twenties and thirties.
2. *Middle age or middle adulthood:* the forties, fifties, and early sixties.
3. *Old age:* sixty-five and over.

The Concept of Maturity

Whereas the periods of childhood, adolescence, and youth are seen as preparatory stages, the period of adulthood is viewed as the fulfillment of these earlier periods. It is the period of *maturity.* What is meant by maturity? This is not an easy question to answer. There are, of course, legal definitions of *maturity.* For example, a person is considered mature enough to vote at the age of eighteen, and an individual is mature enough to drive a car, in some states, at sixteen. Furthermore, there are more diffuse social definitions of maturity: someone who is financially independent, someone who has a job, someone who is married and/or is a parent.

I know of no greater fallacy, nor one more widely believed, than the statement that youth is the happiest time of life.

As we advance in years, we grow happier if we live intelligently. The universe is spectacular, and it is a free show. Difficulties and responsibilities strengthen and enrich the mind. To live abundantly is like climbing a mountain or a tower.

To say that youth is happier than maturity is like saying the view from the bottom of the tower is better than the view from the top. As we ascend, the range of our views widens. The horizon is pushed farther away. Finally, as we reach the summit, it is as if we had the world at our feet.

William Lyon Phelps, *Autobiography with Letters.* New York: Scribner, 1939.

Most theories of personality describe maturity as something that develops or crystallizes during early adulthood. Among these various theories, there appears to be agreement on several psychological characteristics of maturity: the ability to be affectionate and sexually responsive, the ability to love and be loved, the ability to be sociable (to have friends), and the ability to be nurturant to other selected human beings. Furthermore, mature persons are clearly aware of who they are, what are their personal strengths and weaknesses, and what is best for them. Most theories of the mature person also include the characteristic of an interest in and an ability to perform productive work. The mature person is not static but constantly adapts and organizes the self in relation to the demands of adult life. Maturity is not a final *product* but a continual *process* of *becoming*—becoming better able to cope with the decisions, tasks, and problems of adult life.

Another way of thinking about maturity—or happiness, for that matter—is as a congruence between one's perception of oneself and how one is actually doing (i.e., how others perceive that self). Birren and Reedy (1978) suggested that in a mature person, there is such a congruence. In other words, the mature person sets realistic goals that are neither beyond his or her skills and abilities nor beneath his or her potential (see Figure 10.2). *Whereas the period of youth* (see Chapter Nine) *involves the crystallization of identity, early adulthood involves the exploration of the still-uncharted depths of that identity.*

FIGURE 10.2 One definition of maturity involves the agreement, or congruence, between one's subjective perception of the self and how others perceive that self.

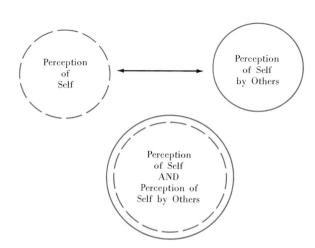

However maturity is defined or whatever combination of characteristics is included in such a definition, maturity appears to be both a gradual and a cumulative process. There is no precise chronological age at which maturity occurs, although it is fairly clear that the early adult years appear to be a time during which a sense of maturity emerges.

Frames of Reference for Looking at Adult Development

Before we describe the specific features of early adulthood in greater detail, we will examine several frames of reference for looking at adult development. Every human being has unique life circumstances and enters adulthood with a unique set of abilities, skills, and personal strengths and weaknesses. Frames of references as well as organized theories can provide us with some understanding of the general characteristics of adult life. What general features of adult experience, if any, are shared by most adults? What features of adulthood are specific to each individual? A frame of reference, or theory, can at least start us thinking about such questions. Theories of adult development heighten our awareness of the milestones of adulthood. In this section, we examine several perspectives on adulthood that are notable for at least one of the following reasons:

- They represent commonly held viewpoints about adulthood.
- They have influenced study and research on adults.

AN INTERLUDE:
WILLIAM SHAKESPEARE ON THE HUMAN LIFE CYCLE
Shakespeare's perception of adulthood and the life cycle as seven stages (from Shakespeare's *As You Like It,* Act II, Scene vii):

All the world's a stage,
And all the men and women merely players.
They have their exits and their entrances,
And one man in his time plays many parts,
His acts being seven ages. At first the infant,
Mewling and puking in the nurse's arms.
Then the whining schoolboy with his satchel
And shining morning face, creeping like snail
Unwillingly to school. And then the lover,
Sighing like furnace, with a woeful ballad
Made to his mistress' eyebrow. Then a soldier,
Full of strange oaths and bearded like the pard,
Jealous in honor, sudden and quick in quarrel,
Seeking the bubble Reputation
E'en in the cannon's mouth. And then the justice,
In fair round belly with good capon lin'd,
With eyes severe and beard of formal cut,
Full of wise saws and modern instances;
And so he plays his part. The sixth age shifts
Into the lean and slipper'd pantaloon,
With spectacles on nose and pouch on side;
His youthful hose well sav'd, a world too wide
For his shrunk shank, and his big manly voice,
Turning again toward childish treble, pipes

And whistles in his sound. Last scene of all,
That ends this strange eventful history,
Is second childishness and mere oblivion—
Sans teeth, sans eyes, sans taste, sans everything.

A Chronological Viewpoint

The chronological viewpoint is quite simple and also quite common. Adult development and behavior are explained in terms of a person's "calendar-year" age, or chronological age. If this perspective is used, a thirty-year-old is expected to be physically and psychologically "younger" than a fifty-year-old. Although the chronological viewpoint has a certain ring of "common sense," it is an inadequate explanation for adult behavior. Chronological age becomes less important as people grow older because they show considerable variability as they age (Dibner, 1975). It is not uncommon to find some older adults who act or look "younger" than some chronologically younger adults (see Application Box: A Fifty-Two-Year-Old Hockey Star or the Inadequacies of a Chronological Perspective on Adulthood).

Chronological age is a poor way of measuring aging for the following reasons:

- Individuals *vary* in their *overall rate* of aging; a person might age much more or much less during one particular time period than during any other (Dibner, 1975). Therefore, chronological age is a poor indicator of individual skill or physical well-being.
- Aging is not a uniform process; a person can be at different "ages" in terms of mental ability, physical status, creativity, and other functions (Butler, 1975).

A Biological Perspective

A biological view of adulthood and aging emphasizes physical changes in the human body as the primary indicators of aging. These changes in functioning can occur in several ways (Dibner, 1975) (we will discuss many of these changes in more detail later in this chapter and in the next two chapters):

- *Structural changes in human cells.* The human body is made up of many billions of cells. Every minute of life may witness the death of about 3 billion of these cells. Fortunately, at the same time, about the same number of cells are created through cell division. As human beings age, however, their cells may lose this capacity to proliferate (increase in number). On the other hand, some old cells can become cancer cells that proliferate uncontrollably.
- *Changes in the overall performance of body organs* (e.g., heart, lungs, eyes). With increasing age, the functioning of many body organs is reduced in effectiveness or efficiency. For example, with age, there is a gradual decline in "nighttime" vision and in hearing certain tones.
- *Age-related diseases.* As body cells and organs age, the overall biological functioning of adults may be reduced by such age-related diseases as heart disease, stroke, arthritis, and cancer.

A Fifty-Two-Year-Old Hockey Star, or the Inadequacies of a Chronological Perspective on Adulthood

Physically demanding sports such as hockey are for young people in the prime of their physical and mental lives. After all, these sports require a physical endurance and stamina that simply cannot be found in older men and women. Right? Not so!

On a December evening in 1979 in the Detroit Olympia Stadium, a hockey player named Gordie Howe skated quickly down the ice and took a hard shot at the opposing team's goal net. The shot was blocked by a player who was born in 1955. In 1955, Gordie Howe was already a ten-year veteran in the National Hockey League. The blocked shot was not a serious loss for Mr. Howe. He had already amassed more goals over his career than any other player in the history of professional hockey. All this—and still playing at the age of fifty-two.

Photograph courtesy of UPI

A biological perspective is accurate in the sense that physical changes do, in fact, occur throughout the life span. Furthermore, most of these changes occur during a particular time in the life cycle. For example, the onset of puberty occurs at adolescence, the female menopause occurs during the period of middle adulthood, and the gradual decline in visual capabilities begins during young adulthood.

The limitation of the biological perspective is that it does not take into account other important factors in the development of adults. Although biological changes do occur, individuals differ in their response to such events. Some adults appear to retain great vitality in the face of a decline in their physical skills. Other adults drift into a state of disinterest or depression. In any case, although biological changes occur, they may not completely account for adult behavior.

A CULTURAL PERSPECTIVE

To some extent, adulthood is a social and cultural concept. You will recall that the definition of maturity may include social permission to do certain things (e.g., drive a car, vote, and drink alcoholic beverages.) Whether one is recognized as an adult depends, in part, on the cultural definition of adulthood (Stegner, 1976). What it means to be an adult differs from one culture to another (Kessler, 1976). For example, an older adult in India may be revered and respected for his or her wisdom. In some industrialized countries, older people represent a "burden" to be carried by society without any apparent return.

A DEVELOPMENTAL PERSPECTIVE

The life-span approach to human development is viewed as a process of stages that build on one another (Elder, 1975). Such a perspective has several important characteristics:

- It is concerned with both biological and psychological changes.
- It emphasizes that life, at any stage of development, is a changing and growing process.
- It involves the study of the individuals in the contexts of their lives (e.g., family, work, community, school).

In this section, we examine several developmental-stage theories. We are particularly interested in how these theories treat adulthood. A review of these theories will alert us to some of the critical features of adulthood to be discussed in this and the following two chapters.

Buhler's Theory of Human Development. One of the pioneers in the study of adult development was Dr. Charlotte Buhler (1933, 1961). In the early part of the twentieth century, Buhler, a clinical psychologist, undertook a study of development throughout the life span and developed a five-phase theory of human development that was based on an intensive analysis of more than two hundred biographical studies. Buhler suggested that *self-fulfill-*

ment was the most important feature of healthy, happy development. Self-fulfillment involves the continual actualization of a lifelong orientation toward a goal or a set of goals.

Buhler's developmental conceptualization of goal attainment includes the following five phases (Buhler, 1968a, 1968b) (see Table 10.2).

Phase I: Childhood (Birth to about Age Fifteen). The self-determination of life goals does not occur in Phase I of development, although children obviously engage in many activities that will prepare them for the future. The child's concept of time as well as of the future is still rather general and vague.

Phase II: Adolescence and Young Adulthood (Approximately Ages Fifteen to Twenty-Five). In Phase II, individuals first begin to understand the idea that their lives are, to some extent, under their own control. During this phase, there is a tendency to be idealistic and to expect to find simple or perfect answers to life's problems. According to Buhler, individuals resolve this phase by becoming flexible and adaptable in dealing with normal concerns, conflicts, and problems.

Phase III: Young and Middle Adulthood (Approximately Ages Twenty-Five to Forty-Five or Fifty). Whereas the previous phase was characterized by tentative life goals, Phase III is characterized by the movement toward more specific and definite life goals. This is a period during which the individual has a rich personal life in which career development has stabilized, marriage and/or children provide nurturant interpersonal relationships, and one has a circle of friends in the community. Although individuals are presumably clearer about their goals during this period of life, they are not always able to attain them. According to Buhler, many adults encounter hindrances to self-fulfillment, including disappointment over their chosen careers or marriage partners. In other instances, they may have emotional problems and conflicts that direct considerable energy away from the attainment of life goals. In still other cases, Buhler suggested, individuals may simply be too immature to integrate the elements of their lives into a meaningful pattern.

Phase IV: Mature Adulthood (About Ages Forty-Five to Sixty-Five). According to Buhler, Phase IV is primarily a period of self-assessment. Individuals assess their past and the goals that have guided them up to this point. In so doing, healthy individuals revise their goals and plans in terms of their present family activities and status, their present physical condition, and their current career status. Buhler suggested that healthy and happy individuals feel fulfilled if their decisions (based on self-assessment) result in improved

TABLE 10.2
Buhler's Theory of the Course of Human Life

Age	Phase of Development
0–15	The child at home; prior to the self-determination of goals.
15–25	Preparatory expansion, experimental self-determination of goals.
25–45	Culmination: clear and specific self-determination of goals.
45–64	Self-assessment of the results of striving for those goals.
65 up	"Experience of fulfillment or failure, with the remaining years spent in either continuance of previous activities or a return to the need-satisfying orientation of childhood" (Horner, 1968, p. 65).

Adapted from D. C. Kimmel, *Adulthood and Aging* (2nd ed.), New York: Wiley, 1980, p. 8.

Early Adulthood: The Entry Years

interpersonal relations with significant others as well as improved career performance. As in the previous phase of adult development, not all individuals are able or willing to take stock in their previous activities and current developmental status. According to Buhler, some people are not aware of the aspects of their personalities that lead to interpersonal difficulties in the family or at work or to limited success in their careers.

Phase V: Old Age (Age Sixty-Five or Seventy and Beyond). The major characteristic of Phase V is a gradually developing sense of the totality and completeness of one's life. The appreciation of the totality of life can lead to a sense of fulfillment with the perception of goals achieved or to a sense of disappointment with the recognition of goals never achieved. Buhler suggested that most older people attain a sense of partial fulfillment in which many life goals were achieved tempered by many disappointments. This partial fulfillment culminates in a sense of resignation.

Erikson's Stages of Adulthood. In Chapter Two, we discussed Erik Erikson's eight stages of human development. Here, we will briefly review the stages relevant to adulthood.

APPLICATION BOX

Adulthood in Muslim Societies

Islam has a conception of adulthood. Though Muslim tradition is not self-consciously occupied with it, especially as opposed to childhood or youth, it does provide a notion of what the fully matured person should be. A Muslim legal concept that is close to our own sense of adulthood defines the "mukallaf"—the legally and morally responsible person—as one who has reached physical maturity, is of sound mind, may enter into contracts, dispose of property, and be subject to criminal law. Above all, he is responsible for the religious commands and obligations of Islam . . .

. . . Muslim religious writings discuss the spiritual and psychological issues involved in the development of an integrated adult personality. . . . One crucial theme is the balance between confidence and humility. . . . In this view, a man must balance the tides of helplessness, worthlessness and inadequacy with his experience of confidence . . . so that he may without false enthusiasms or false despair proceed with the life that scripture, society and his own convictions require of a Muslim adult.

Taken from Ira M. Lapidus, "Adulthood in Islam: Religious Maturity in the Islamic Tradition," *Daedalus,* Spring 1976, pp. 93–108.

YOUR OPINION

Although the ideas of maturity in Islamic tradition describe adulthood for Muslims, are there any similarities to your own ideas of adulthood? Are there any differences?

- *Identity Versus Identity (Role) Diffusion.* Although we discussed the meaning of identity in Chapter Nine, we would like to emphasize here that there is no simple separation between this stage and the other—more clearly adult—stages of development. That is, identity is modified by the experiences of adult life.
- *Intimacy Versus Isolation.* Erikson (1968) summarized this stage as follows:

Sexual intimacy is only part of what I have in mind, for it is obvious that sexual intimacies often precede the capacity to develop a true and mutual psychosocial intimacy with another person, be it in friendship, in erotic encounters, or in joint inspiration. The youth who is not sure of his identity shies away from interpersonal intimacy or throws himself into acts of intimacy which are "promiscuous" without true fusion or real self-abandon.

Where a youth does not accomplish such intimate relationships with others—and, I would add, with his own inner resources—in late adolescence or early adulthood, he may settle for highly stereotyped interpersonal relations and come to retain a deep "sense" of isolation." (pp. 135–136)

- *Generativity Versus Stagnation.* This is the seventh stage of life, involving the development of something that will outlive the individual, and is usually accomplished through parenthood and/or occupational achievements.
- *Integrity Versus Despair.* This is the final stage of development and involves the evaluation of one's life and accomplishments. Have they been meaningful? Did they have a purpose? Were my goals accomplished?

Individuals define themselves as adults during the early twenties.

Photograph by Sylvia Byers

Levinson's Theory. Levinson's theory of adult development was derived from interviews and personality tests of forty men aged eighteen to forty-seven (Levinson, 1978). Levinson maintained that adulthood, like childhood, is made up of stages or periods, each of which has unique "tasks." As individuals move through each phase of adulthood, they develop what Levinson calls "life structures." Life structures are the personal meanings that individuals attach to their experiences in family, work, community, and friendship. Levinson divided adult life into the following stages.

Leaving the Family. The phase of leaving the family begins sometime in late adolescence, when the individual graduates from high school, and extends to about age twenty or twenty-four. The major event in this phase is the development of emotional and financial independence as individuals move out of their parents' home.

The tasks of this passage are to locate ourselves in a peer group role, a sex role, an anticipated occupation, an ideology or world view. As a result, we gather the impetus to leave home physically and the identity to "begin" leaving home emotionally. (Sheehy, 1976, p. 39) (Levinson's research on adult development was the basis for Sheehy's book, *Passages.*)

Getting into the Adult World. According to Levinson, individuals define themselves as adults during the twenties.

The Trying Twenties confront us with the question of how to take hold in the adult world. Our focus shifts from the interior turmoils of late adolescence—"Who am I?" "What is truth?"—and we become almost totally preoccupied with working out the externals. "How do I put my aspirations into effect?" "What is the best way to start?" "Where do I go?" "Who can help me?" (Sheehy, 1976, pp. 39–40)

Early Adulthood: The Entry Years

Like Buhler, Levinson and his associates suggested that many adult problems derive from goals that are not realistic. Levinson suggested that the ability to reorient goals is a determining factor in how well adults cope with life.

The Age-Thirty Transition. At about age thirty, people begin to take stock of their lives. According to Levinson, this stock taking may involve a rethinking about one's career, marriage partner, or life goals. Although Levinson's research focused primarily on male subjects, it also appears that females go through the same reexamination process (Sheehy, 1976). For example, a housewife at about this age might decide to return to school to pursue a career.

"What do I want out of this life, now that I'm doing what I ought to do?"
A restless vitality wells up as we approach 30. Almost everyone wants to make some alteration. If he has been dutifully performing in his corporate slot, he may suddenly feel too narrowed and restricted. . . . If she has been at home with children, she itches to expand her horizons.
The restrictions we feel on nearing 30 are the outgrowth of the choices of the twenties, choices that may have been perfectly appropriate to that stage. Now the fit feels different. . . . (Sheehy, 1976, p. 198)

Settling Down. Levinson suggested that the early thirties are marked by the setting of goals (e.g., corporate vice-president, supervisor, a specific income level) to be attained within a certain period of time. This phase of life is characterized by the orderly pursuit of these goals and/or interests.

Life becomes less provisional, more rational and orderly in the early thirties. We begin to settle down in the full sense. Most of us begin putting down roots and sending out new shoots. People buy houses and become very earnest about climbing career ladders. . . . (Sheehy, 1976, p. 43)

Becoming One's Own Person: The Deadline Decade. In the late thirties, individuals begin the process of reexamining the identities that they have forged for themselves in the first half of life. Levinson pointed out that one symptom of this process is that some people become increasingly uncomfortable or feel constrained by those who have authority over them. Particularly in the case of men, there is a tendency to discard one's mentor (an older individual who has taken an interest in the young adult's career).

We have reached the halfway mark. Yet even as we are reaching our prime, we begin to see there is a place where it finishes. Time starts to squeeze.
. . . Such thoughts usher in a decade between 35 and 45 that can be called the Deadline Decade. All of us have the chance to remake the narrow identity by which we defined ourselves in the first half of life. And those of us who make the most of the opportunity will have a full-out authenticity crisis. . . .
"Why am I doing all this?" "What do I really believe in?" (Sheehy, 1976, pp. 43–44)

An Evaluation of Developmental Theories. One of the major criticisms of any stage theories of adult development is that they do not take into account the timing of biological, social, and personal events in relation to historical time (see Figure 10.3). The theories we have discussed emphasized biological and social age-related events. Another approach that may help us to understand adult development is to examine the events of history (the

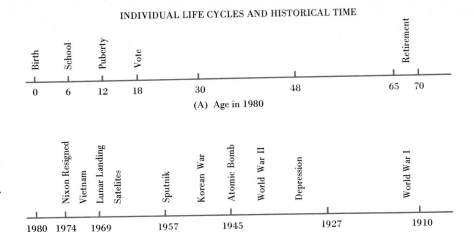

FIGURE 10.3 Intersection of individual lifeline (A) with the historical time line in 1980 (B).

Reprinted from Kimmel, D. C., *Adulthood and Aging.* New York: Copyright © 1974, 1980, by John Wiley & Sons, Inc.

historical time line) that coincide with the social and biological events of individual development (the individual lifeline). For example, in Figure 10.3, a person who was fifty to fifty-five years of age in 1980 (top line drawing) was a young child during the Great Depression and probably negotiated the events of adolescence and young adulthood during the waning years of that economic crisis and the beginning of World War II.

What were the "lessons" of the Depression? Those who experienced the Depression as adults or children probably learned to value a good job and economic security. Furthermore, they may have participated in a community and family life in which material goods were at a premium. An overriding lesson learned by those who came to maturity during this period was that material resources can never be taken for granted. Money as a motivator of human behavior became important for this generation. As these children of the Depression continued through their life cycle, the world began to change. During World War II, the nation emerged from the economic depression of the 1930s into a period of economic growth, development, and relative abundance. Many of the young adults who are now in college or who were in college during the last ten to fifteen years were probably born into this postwar world of economic abundance. Those individuals have been exposed to a different set of historical factors than their parents. Historical factors play a role that supplements the general features of adult development.

The Young Adulthood System: An Overview

The theories that we have just discussed point to some significant features of young adulthood. Figure 10.4 is a representation of the world of the young adult. The diagram indicates that the young adult has moved out of the family or origin and is an independent individual. This movement toward autonomy and independence is a normal process. It is the culmination of the individual's physical, social, cognitive, and personality development up to this time. In the remainder of this chapter, we discuss the features of the young adult's world. For simplicity, we have divided that world into two parts: an "internal" world and an "external" world.

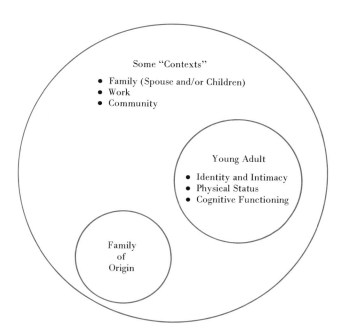

Some "Contexts"
- Family (Spouse and/or Children)
- Work
- Community

Young Adult
- Identity and Intimacy
- Physical Status
- Cognitive Functioning

Family
of
Origin

FIGURE 10.4 The system of young adulthood.

ORGANIZING AN EXTERNAL WORLD

During young adulthood, the major efforts of activity are *external*. That is, they are directed at the social world: beginning a family, finding a job, or achieving an intimate relationship with a marital partner, children, or other persons.

Social Interaction. Social relationships provide the basis for continuing development in adulthood. The young adult enters into a set of relationships among family, among friends, and at work. From these experiences, the young adult develops a *social network*, which includes friends, family members, and co-workers, who provide a *social resource* for continued development. When we discuss the contexts of early adulthood (later in this chapter), we will describe how these social networks serve as frameworks for psychological growth (see Figure 10.5).

Autonomy and Independent Living. We indicated in Chapter Nine that later adolescents or youth had some measure of autonomy and independence from their parents and that some later adolescents are more autonomous than others. For example, the nineteen-year-old high-school graduate who has a full-time job and a family and is economically self-supporting is more "autonomous" than the nineteen-year-old college student, who is still being supported by hs or her parents. Young adulthood is probably the first time when most individuals are, without question, *really on their own*. Young adults are in a position where they must make their own decisions and own up to the consequences.

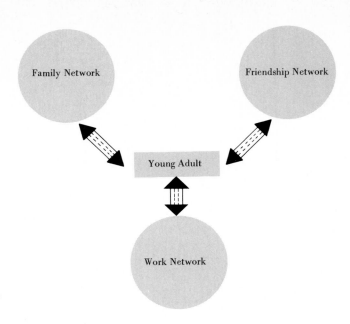

Family Network

Friendship Network

Young Adult

Work Network

FIGURE 10.5 The social networks of the young adult provide a support system for development.

ORGANIZING AN INTERNAL WORLD

As the young adult engages in work, family, and community activities, there are accompanying changes in the individual's internal world. These changes occur in several areas:

Identity and Intimacy. The identity fashioned in adolescence is shared and tested in close relationships with significant others (including marriage and other intimate relationships).

Physical Status. The young adult is generally at the peak of physical prowess and health. Between young adulthood and middle adulthood, there is, of course, some decline in physical–biological features. However, this decline is gradual and, in some instances, almost unnoticeable.

Intellectual and Cognitive Functioning. Intellectual and cognitive skills are relatively stable from later adolescence through middle age (approximately age twenty to age fifty) (Knox, 1977; Cunningham and Birren, 1976). If intelligence is defined as the ability to derive knowledge from education or experience ("crystallized" intelligence), then intelligence increases during the adult years.

The Contexts of the Young Adulthood System

The development of the adult involves both activity in the significant contexts of adult life and the interpretation of this activity by the individual. In this section, we examine several important contexts: the family, the community, and the world of work. In the next section, we discuss the developments of a personal "meaning" for these activities.

THE FAMILY

Of all the features of the world of young adulthood, the family is of prime importance because shifts in family-role performance affect all other aspects of adult development. Family-role changes, such as marriage, parenthood, divorce, and widowhood, affect adult self-concepts, work performance, and general happiness.

The Family Life-Cycle in Adulthood. The family life-cycle is marked by a series of transitions or stages characterized by *changes in adult roles*. Table 10.3 describes some of the major family life-cycle events associated with each stage of adulthood (see also Figure 10.6). As you read the table, you may wonder what happened to singles, childless couples, late marriages, and other less common patterns. The answer is that they are not included on the table mainly because marriage and the associated role changes still constitute the pattern for the vast majority of adults (Knox, 1977). We will discuss the less common—although *increasingly significant*—family patterns later in this section. Before doing that, however, we will discuss the role changes in the family life-cycle for young adults: mate selection, marriage, and parenthood.

Mate Selection. Marriages occur as a result of a process that involves some of the following features: dating, courtship, and a formal marriage ceremony. Mate selection appears to occur in accordance with one of the following principles:

DEFINITIONS

Principle of homogamy. Mates are chosen on the basis of similarity of age, race, religion, ethnic origin, educational level, social class, and personality. The principle of homogamy suggests that "Like attracts like."

TABLE 10.3
The Family Life-Cycle in Adulthood

Stage of Adulthood	Family Life-Cycle Events
Young Adulthood Approx. 18–25 years Approx. 25-late 30s	• Marriage • Beginning of parenthood • First child starts school
Middle Adulthood Approx. late 30s–65 years	• Children leave home for work, marriage, or college • Relationship to married children, their spouses, and their offspring ("grandparenting") • Adjustments in relationship with aging parents • Adjustments in relationship between husband and wife after children have left home

Later Adulthood
Approx. 65 years and beyond
	• Retirement
	  -Change of living arrangements
	  -Transition from work
	• Death of spouse

Photograph (center) by Darryl Jacobson; photograph (right) by Irving Rader

FIGURE 10.6 The family life cycle.

Adapted from Duvall, E. M., *Marriage and Family Development* (5th ed.). Philadelphia: J. B. Lippincott, 1977, Figure 19.3, p. 474. Reprinted by permission. This information and diagram are a modification of Table 3.2 in this book. Permission for Table 3.2 covers this figure.

1. Married Couples (without children).
2. Childbearing Families (oldest child, birth–30 months).
3. Families with Preschool Children (oldest child, 30 months–6 years).
4. Families with Schoolchildren (oldest child, 6–13 years).
5. Families with Teenagers (oldest child, 13–20 years).
6. Families as Launching Centers. (first child gone to last child leaving home).
7. Middle-aged Parents (empty nest to retirement).
8. Aging Family Members (retirement to death of both spouses).

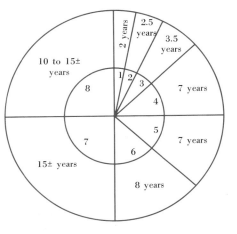

Principle of complementarity. Mates are chosen on the basis of different characteristics (particularly, with reference to personality). In effect, the principle of complementarity suggests that "Opposites attract one another."

Does research evidence support the notion that "Opposites attract" (complementarity) or that "Like attracts like" (homogamy)? As might be expected in such a complex and totally "human" process as mate selection, the evidence is not all on one side (Levinger, Senn, and Jorgensen, 1970; Murstein, 1972). However, most evidence seems to suggest that homogamy is the most frequent or common basis of mate selection (Kerckhoff and Davis, 1962; Murstein, 1970). Presumably a homogamous choice promotes a relationship in which there will be less conflict over such factors as religion, socioeconomic class, and educational level. Homogamy is probably also the result of other forces, such as parental interest and general social pressures.

Finding a Partner. Some people may think that finding a marriage partner is simply a matter of choosing from an unlimited variety of people. The process, of course, is not completely arbitrary. Rather, research evidence suggests that finding a partner is a "filtering-out" process (Murstein, 1970; Edwards, 1969; Kerckhoff and Davis, 1962).

486

THE "FILTERS" OF MATE SELECTION

In finding a mate, there are *three primary filters* at work. In the first place, *external factors* such as physical attractiveness and propinquity (physical nearness) operate to bring people together. For example, if a female college student sees a male student in her medieval history course who appears handsome or otherwise attractive, she may arrange to meet him. When this meeting occurs, a second filter begins to operate: sorting out *similarities of background*. Are the individuals from similar or different religious, social, or ethnic backgrounds? After these factors are sorted, several possible decisions may be made:

- "No chance we could be more than casual friends."
- "I like what I see, so far. Let's go farther."
- "A 'holding pattern' is in order. I really can't tell what's going on here. Maybe I'll be back—maybe I won't."

If it is necessary, the third filter involves *accepting and "loving" one another as individuals*. This means going beyond mutual acceptance simply as members of the same social group to "Do I like the individual as a 'person'?"

Marriage. Marriage may be viewed as a rite of passage that signals the transition from the roles of singlehood to the new roles of the married couple (see Figure 10.7). These new roles involve the couple's relationship, their relationship to their parents, their relationship to other couples, and their relationship to society as a whole.

An important task of the early phase of marriage is the establishment of mutually satisfying patterns of living together, including patterns of sexual interaction. Included in this task are the development of modes of conflict resolution, the development of decision-making styles, and the development of role patterns in the family, including the division of family responsibilities. For most couples, the first few years of marriage constitute a major transition in their lives—perhaps one of the most dramatic transitions in the family life-cycle. During the early years of marriage, the couple attempts to establish its own family structure. Despite the "romantic" notions that prevail about marriage, the first few years may sometimes prove to be rocky. The major sources of marital problems in the early years are sex, living conditions and finances, general incompatibility, and parental interference (Rollins and Feldman, 1970). Disenchantment may play a large role in the relatively high rate of divorce during the early years of marriage.

INTERLUDE:
YOUNG ADULT EXPECTATIONS FOR MARRIAGE.
ARE THEY UNREALISTIC?

One of the notable features about modern marriage is the increasing rate of failure (see the figure). Koller (1974) suggested that much of the blame for this situation resides with the married couple (see the table) and that many newly married couples are quite immature and unrealistic about life and marriage.

Birdwhitsell (1970) suggested that the problem is not with the married couple but with society as a whole, which portrays the institution of marriage idealistically. For example, the tendency in the media is to picture marriage as some sort of "perfect" experience without flaws or problems:

FIGURE 10.7 Marriage is a rite of passage that signals the transition to new roles.

Photograph by Irving Rader

It requires but little reflection to see that the American family, as idealized, is an overloaded institution. It is easy to see, too, that the goals set by the concept are unattainable and leave people failing both as spouses and as parents. (p. 195)

The Expectations and Realities of Marriage

Before Marriage	After Marriage
Dreaming	Reality
Could walk away from problems	Must face problems
Making promises	Fulfilling promises
Choice of partner	Partner chose
One kinship network	Two kinship networks
Need consult only oneself	Must consult with another
Contemplate different roles	Play a definite role

Based on *Families: A Multigenerational Approach*, by M. R. Koller. Copyright © 1974 by McGraw-Hill Book Company. Used with the permission of McGraw-Hill Book Company.

Marital Adjustment. Although differences of opinion commonly arise between marriage partners, it is the importance of these issues to the partners that determines the degree of conflict. That is, some issues are of *direct* importance to the marriage (e.g., money, child-rearing, extramarital relationships), and others are *peripheral* to the relationship (e.g., "Why does the encyclope-

Divorce rate—selected years, 1950–1982.

Fowler, 1983

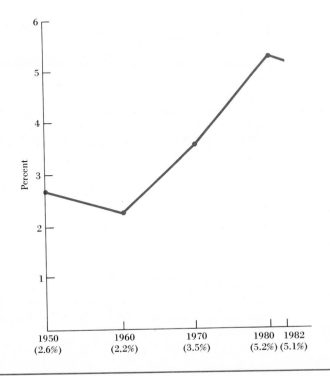

| 1950 | 1960 | 1970 | 1980 | 1982 |
| (2.6%) | (2.2%) | (3.5%) | (5.2%) | (5.1%) |

Conflict in the early years of marriage: *"Honey, you know I prefer to have the end of our toothpaste tube rolled rather than squeezed!"*

dia salesman always come when I'm at home and you're at work?"). Basic conflicts arise over fundamental "rules" of the marital relationship. For example, if a particular marital arrangement requires that the husband work to support the family, then a husband refusing to work would be breaking a fundamental "rule." The breaking of such a basic rule could also be the basis for a serious marital conflict.

COMMUNICATION IN MARITAL RELATIONSHIPS

Two types of communication are important in a marital relationship:

- *Tacit communication.* This is a way of conveying a message without using spoken language. One example of tacit communication is "body language" (e.g., two conversationalists sitting in adjacent chairs and leaning toward each other may be communicating their mutual interest through their "body language").
- *Explicit communication.* This is the direct transmission, usually through verbal language, of ideas or feelings from one person to another.

Both explicit and tacit communication are used to transmit information between husband and wife. If correctly used, explicit communication conveys, in precise terms, the message of the spouse. If incorrectly used, explicit communication can be vague or unclear at one extreme or blunt and insensitive at the other extreme. An example of an intentionally vague explicit communication is the *double message:*

Wife (to husband): "I really don't care if you finish painting the door, but I won't have time to iron the shirt you need tomorrow."

Marital difficulties are caused not only by poor communication skills but also by an overall atmosphere of hostility in a relationship. Even when a couple are perfectly capable of communicating their feelings and receiving "signals" from their spouse, negative emotions may prevent them from doing so.

Parenthood. The next stage in the traditional family life cycle is parenthood. This stage begins with pregnancy and the birth of the first child. Many young couples have come to question the need for having children or may postpone beginning a family. In spite of these trends, approximately 94% of all ever-married women aged 40 to 44 will have borne at least one child (U.S. Bureau of the Census, 1983).

Why do parents decide to have children? In traditional societies (e.g., the United States prior to industrialization), parents need children as productive and economic contributors to the family. For example, if the parents own a farm, many "helping hands" are clearly an advantage. This is not to suggest, of course, that the only reason parents in a traditional society have children is economic.

In some industrialized societies, children (and the aged) are sometimes viewed as economic responsibilities or "burdens" because they cannot be, or are not allowed to be, economically productive. Therefore, parents in an industrialized society have children largely for psychological reasons: love, emotional gratification, or companionship (Yorburg, 1974).

INTERLUDE:
THE VALUE OF CHILDREN TO A MARRIAGE?—SOME VIEWS

It's true in a technical sense, of course, that with all the contraceptive devices available today, people can decide not to have children. But in a deeper sense, one can only really make a free choice in an unprejudiced social context. And we don't have that today.

Everything in our society—from tax laws to television shows to women's magazines to the most casual conversation—is oriented toward parenthood. It's very difficult to even consider whether you shouldn't have children when everyone is pressuring you to "have kids and find out what you're missing."—A woman who decided not to have children. (Katz, 1975, p. 162)

What people think they're missing, says NON (National Organization of Nonparents), is something that many of them are totally unsuited for—a child-centered life that fails to live up to the glorified picture usually painted of [parenthood]. NON believes that "the motherhood myth," as they call it, is a leftover from the early days of this country, when mortality rates were high, the vast wilderness needed settling, and large numbers of children were considered an important adjunct to a pioneering homestead. When that day passed, NON says, the idea that it was the duty and glory of every woman to procreate was kept alive by "babysell"—the efforts of business and advertising to depict motherhood as chic, fun and glamorous, so that more and more consumer goods could be sold to an unsuspecting, continually expanding population. (Katz, 1975, p. 163)

Personal Experience. Among all the activities of life, parenthood is a unique experience. It is a part of life, of personal growth, that simply cannot be experienced in any other way, and hence is literally an indispensable element of the full life. (Berelson, 1975, p. 173)

Personal Pleasure . . . pleasure of having them, caring for them, watching them grow, shaping them, being with them, enjoying them. This reason . . . is typically the first one mentioned to the casual inquiry: "because I like children." Even this reason has its dark side, as with parents who live through their children, often to the latter's distaste and disadvantage. But that should not obscure a fundamental reason for wanting children: love. (Berelson, 1975, p. 173)

From B. Katz, "Cooling Motherhood," and B. Berelson, "The Value of Children," in J. G. Wells (Ed.), *Current Issues in Marriage and the Family.* New York: Macmillan, 1975.

Photographs by Darryl Jacobson

The major transition in this stage is a shift in roles from wife and husband to mother and father. This shift really represents the addition of new roles rather than the complete elimination of preparental roles. Furthermore, the couple needs to adjust to the presence of a third member. The birth of a first child is a significant transition in family life and brings with it some potential problems of adjustment (Rossi, 1968; Anthony and Benedek, 1970). As we indicated in our discussion of infancy (see Chapter Six), the infant is a demanding creature that does not wait patiently for its needs to be satisfied.

There may be many reasons for unsatisfactory adjustment to parenthood. The following are three primary factors (Knox, 1977):

1. Negative attitudes toward pregnancy.
2. Feelings of parental inadequacy. Many parents are not prepared for the role transition to parenthood, which requires attention and seemingly complete time involvement with the newcomer to the family. The lack of preparation and lack of experience with infants—particularly when the first child is born—can lead to feelings of inadequacy and being overwhelmed with things to do.
3. Unwillingness to accept role changes.

Alternative Life Patterns. The foregoing descriptions have focused primarily on the young-adult family life cycle, with emphasis on adults who marry, have children and organize their family lives around these events.

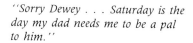

"Sorry Dewey . . . Saturday is the day my dad needs me to be a pal to him."

DENNIS THE MENACE ® used by permission of Hank Ketcham and © by Field Enterprises Inc.

Although the majority of adults follow this pattern, there are alternative (and equally *valid*) life patterns. Included in these patterns are adults who never marry (singles), new family arrangements that result from remarriage, marriages that end in separation or divorce, childless couples, adults who may marry late in life, and alternative family forms (e.g., communal living). During the past decade, there has been increasing attention to the future directions of the family (Glenn and Weaver, 1977; Heckman, Bryson and Bryson, 1977; Kempler, 1976).

Living Alone. Single adults in the United States include the divorced, the widowed, and the never-married. They constitute approximately 40 percent of all individuals 15 years of age and above. Among these singles 18 percent are widowed, 16 percent are divorced, and 65 percent have never married (U.S. Bureau of the Census, *Marital Status and Living Arrangements:* March, 1982, 1983). Furthermore, population data suggest that throughout most of early adulthood (up to approximately 34 years of age) the numbers of those who have never married has substantially increased from 1970 through 1982 (U.S. Bureau of the Census, *Marital Status and Living Arrangements:* March 1982, 1983). The 20-to-24-year age group currently has the largest proportion of never married persons among those individuals beyond the teen years. From 1970 to 1982, the population of never married for this age group rose from 35.8 to 53.4 percent for women and from 54.7 to 72.0 percent for men. It is, of course, possible that these young adults are simply postponing their first marriages in comparison to earlier cohorts (e.g., the 1970 group) who married earlier. However, considerable increases in the proportion of never marrieds for the age groups of 25 to 29 and 30 to 34 suggest that many persons may be electing to never marry at all (U.S. Bureau of the Census, *Marital Status and Living Arrangements:* March 1982, 1983).

There is considerable mythology about the lives of singles. For example, there are unfounded myths that unmarried women are somehow inadequate, emotionally disturbed, or latent lesbians (Baker, 1968; Adams, 1971). The attitude of society toward single women is summarized by a twenty-year-old woman, as follows:

> I was brought up with the idea that not getting married was the worst thing that could happen to you. If you didn't get married, your life was doomed to loneliness. (Boston Women's Health Book Collective, 1971)

Research evidence suggests that single women have a higher level of mental health than married women (Bernard, 1972). Bernard found that among women over thirty years old, married women were more likely than single women to suffer from psychological distress (e.g., nervousness and insomnia), severe neurotic symptoms, and depression.

Another myth about the single female is that she lives a fast-paced, sex-filled life. In fact, most single women tend to lead rather conventional lives (Starr and Carns, 1972). Rather than participating in continual sex orgies, they appear to be largely concerned about such conventional matters as finding a good place to live and finding a meaningful job. Singlehood may also allow women to explore life and to be involved in various social movements. The following statement by a group of women in Boston expresses this position:

Early Adulthood: The Entry Years

Together we are trying to explore our independence and find positive identities for ourselves—not in isolation from other people, but outside of relationships that feel limiting or confining. We have different fantasies for the future. Some of us want more intimate relationships. But in our lives outside of couples we've got a lot of strength and joy—alone and as part of a group. What we've learned from being single is much more than the skills of survival in a "transitional" state. And we look forward to new options for women in the future. (Boston Women's Health Book Collective, 1971)

In the case of the single man, the myths have also proved to be unfounded. Unlike the myth of the female as "loser," the myth of the single male proclaims him to be a "winner." A mystique about the single man seems to pervade our culture. It is an image of power, toughness, and freedom.

The life of the single man contradicts this stereotype of masculine freedom and happiness. Generally the research evidence suggests that the single man suffers more from psychological and physical problems than the married man (Bernard, 1972; Gilder, 1974). We are not suggesting, of course, that the absence of marriage "causes" these problems. One could speculate that there may be basic personality or health factors that limit interest in or opportunities for marriage (i.e., the absence of marriage is a *symptom* rather than a *cause*). On the other hand, one could argue that the marital relationship tends to ease anxiety about acceptance as a person.

Childless Couples. This group includes those couples who have never had children, either because they chose not to do so or have been unable to do so. Some couples may become particularly frustrated if they wish to have children and cannot. This frustration may lead to marital conflict.

Couples who choose not to have children may do so for various reasons. Both husband and wife may have careers that they do not wish to have disrupted by having children. Other couples may be unwilling to assume the responsibility of rearing children. Others may be aware of a genetic defect that they do not wish to risk transmitting to children. Still others may realize that they are not interested in or suited for the parent role.

Childless marriages may be satisfying and fulfilling, providing both partners have either chosen not to have children or have accepted the reason(s) that they cannot have children.

Usually the couple in a childless marriage are better adjusted to their status if they have some major interests or life activities that provide meaning and direction for their lives (Knox, 1977). Where there are problems in a childless marriage, these are likely to focus on a loss of richness from family experience or a lack of connection with the future (Veevers, 1973).

Divorce. An increasing number of marriages end in divorce (Carter and Glick, 1970) (see Figure 10.8). Over the last two decades, there has been a relatively high level of dissatisfaction and disenchantment with marriage during the parenting phases of marriage, with a relative increase in satisfaction during the post parenting years (Rollins and Feldman, 1970). Even though some couples experience more satisfaction in the years after children have left the home, about one in five married couples still indicate that they are unhappy with married life during the postparental phase (Campbell and Converse, 1975). This dissatisfaction may account for an increase in conflict and divorce at this time.

According to data on couples getting a divorce in 1980 (U.S. Department of

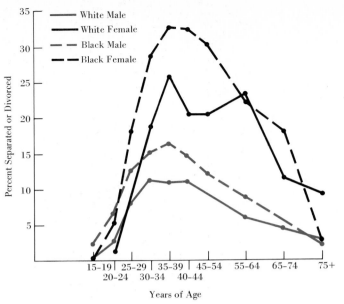

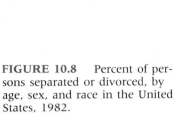

FIGURE 10.8 Percent of persons separated or divorced, by age, sex, and race in the United States, 1982.

Source: U.S. Bureau of the Census, "Marital Status and Living Arrangements: March 1982." *Current Population Reports,* Population Characteristics, Series P-20, No. 380. Washington, D.C.: U.S. Government Printing Office, 1982.

Health and Human Services, 1983), 38 percent had been married for less than five years; 28 percent had been married for 5–9 years; 15 percent, 10–14 years; and 19 percent had been married 15 years or more. It is clear from these statistics that the first four years of marriage account for a disproportionately large number of divorces (38%). There is a continued decline in divorces after 5 years of marriage with a modest increase (19%) at 15 years of marriage and after. This increase has often been attributed to the decline in marital satisfaction associated with adolescent-aged children (Rollins and Feldman, 1970).

People who become divorced vary to a large extent in the reasons associated with divorce:

Compared with marriages that do not end in divorce, a higher proportion of divorced couples entered marriage under the following circumstances:

1. a very brief period of courtship or engagement that provided too little opportunity to get to know each other and prospective in-laws;
2. major differences in religious or ethnic backgrounds of the two families;
3. marriage at a very young age (teenage marriages have twice the divorce rate that marriages during the twenties have);
4. forced marriage as a result of pregnancy;
5. overly romantic and unrealistic expectations about marriage; and
6. unsatisfactory marital role models usually because either or both of the . . . couple's parents had unhappy marriages. (Levinger, 1966; Burchinal, 1965 . . .)

(From Knox, 1977, pp. 123–124)

A primary cause of divorce is dissatisfied or unhappy people. Sometimes people who are unhappy or emotionally distraught enter marriage with the unrealistic expectation that it will solve their problems. Unfortunately that is

Early Adulthood: The Entry Years

The Children of Divorce

Three current trends highlight the need to direct attention to children of divorce. The first is the continuing high divorce rate in the United States. The second is the high remarriage rate and the third, the rising percentage of divorces which involve young children. . . .

The impact of divorce on children has produced substantial literature concerned with the psychological and emotional effects of parental separation. Much of the research suffers from two sources of distortion. The adjustment of children of divorced parents tends to be measured against the norm of children from intact, presumably well-functioning families, rather than against children in homes where there is substantial parental dissension, the pre-divorce norm. In addition, case studies are often done on samples of children seen in treatment, and these may not be representative of all children of divorce. Furthermore, there has been little follow-up study of children after the crisis period is past. . . .

Children of divorce experience many problems shared by other children, and some unique trauma of their own. In common with most children in single-parent families, and with many children of minority groups, they are likely to be at risk of poverty. But they are also subject to special legal problems, custody issues and parental dissension. Depending on their age and develop-

mental phase, they may need special help to integrate the emotional impact of separation, and their parents may utilize peer supports as well as professional counseling. Finally, the high remarriage rate and growing numbers of children in step-relationships have created a new national phenomenon—a new demographic entity, not of children of divorce but of children of remarriage.

Reprinted from S. Jenkins, "Children of Divorce," *Children Today.* Washington, D.C., March–April 1978, pp. 16–20, 48.

usually not the case, as marriage brings with it major role transitions that, as we have seen, require emotionally stable people who are firmly rooted in their own identities. A much higher proportion of divorced people (compared with happily married people) are tense, depressed, hypercritical, or generally poorly adjusted adults (Pinard, 1966).

Other influences on divorce include factors associated with family functioning, particularly during the parenthood phase of the family life cycle. Individuals who have not successfully negotiated the role transitions of living with a spouse may be particularly vulnerable because of the additional role tasks of parenthood. Societal factors such as the religious and social acceptance of divorce or the availability of employment for women may encourage or discourage divorce among families in an unhappy situation.

Divorce is usually an upsetting and even a traumatic event for the couple and for their children. General life satisfaction appears to be lower for di-

Strengths and Weaknesses of Six Family Forms

My appraisal of the strengths and weaknesses of each of six different family forms, based on a review of empirical studies, clinical reports and my own research activity, follows.

THE SINGLE CAREER FAMILY

Intact nuclear family consisting of husband, wife and offspring living in a common household where one partner, usually the husband, is the provider. (Represents 13 percent of all households.)

Strengths

Maintains its position as the primary structure for potential socialization of members over the life cycle.

Is the primary unit for taking care of disabled, deviant and dependent members.

Is among the best adapted in terms of fitting the demands of the corporate economic structure.

Weaknesses

Is easily broken, with increasing intervention of organizations and expenditure of monies to maintain individuals of broken marriages and new family forms.

The single breadwinner of the working class is unable to provide adequately for its maintenance. Among the middle classes, there is difficulty in providing an expected quality of life.

THE DUAL CAREER FAMILY

Intact nuclear family consisting of husband, wife and offspring living in a common household where both partners work. (Represents 16 percent of all households.)

Strengths

Competent structure to provide maximal income for maintenance and to achieve quality of life aspirations.

Highly adequate form for effecting goals of gender equality. It provides work options for both marital partners and opportunity to share household tasks and marital responsibilities.

Weaknesses

Dependence on kin and institutional support systems for effective maintenance and functioning.

Developing but still non-institutionalized values and means to harmonize the career activities and ambitions of both partners and the roles concerned with marital relationships and parenting.

THE SINGLE-PARENT HOUSEHOLD

With children under age 18. (Represents 16 percent of all households.)

Distribution of Adult Americans by Type of Household

Household Type	Percentage of All Households
Heading single-parent families	16
Other single, separated, divorced or widowed	21
Living in child-free or post-child-rearing marriages	23
Living in extended families	6
Living in experimental families or cohabiting	4
Living in dual-breadwinner nuclear families	16
Living in no wage-earner nuclear families	1
Living in single-breadwinner nuclear families	13

Strengths

Many adults who can function as socialization models for children are potentially available. Adults other than parents may be more effective in teaching and socializing children.

If supported appropriately, the single parent can achieve greater self-expression than a married counterpart; accountability is limited to children.

For a significant number of single-parent families, which result as a consequence of separation and divorce, the removal or absence of a violent parent results in a nurturant and liveable family form.

Weaknesses

Need for support systems for parenting, economic and health maintenance and social relationships—often scarce or unavailable in particular communities.

The insufficiency of finances endemic to this family form often results in higher morbidity and

expenditure of third party monies for maintenance and survival. Another consequence of economic deficiency is the pressure for some to remarry in order to obtain such support, with
increased probability that the previous marriage
experience will be repeated.

For some families, when the single parent is
gainfully employed and substitute parents are
unavailable or ineffective, the socialization is
done by peers, and the behavior of children may
be viewed as deviate and delinquent.

THE REMARRIED NUCLEAR FAMILY

Husband, wife and offspring living in a common household. (Represents 11 percent of all
households.)

Strengths

Previous marital experiences may result in an
increased number (actual incidence unknown) of
stable marriages.

Parenting, which may formerly have been the
function of a single adult, may be shared with the
new partner and his or her older children.

For some, there is improved economic status as
a consequence of shared income.

Weaknesses

The difficulties in blending two formerly independent households into one functioning unit
may result in extreme psychic stress for some
members.

Formations consisting of two large-size families
may require substantial economic help, counseling and other supports in order to survive.

Economic and social commitments to individuals of previous marriages may restrict the development of adequate, stable relationships in the
new marriage.

THE KIN FAMILY

Consisting of bilateral or intergenerational-
linked members living in the same household.
(Represents six percent of all households.)

Strengths

Maintenance of familial values and transmission
of accumulated knowledge and skill are likely
occurrences.

Multiple adults are available for socialization
and shared household and work responsibilities.

Weaknesses

Demands for geographical mobility are not easily
met.

From one perspective, the resistance to changes
which threaten the maintenance of this family
form can reduce the motivation of individuals to
achieve in the society.

EXPERIMENTAL FAMILIES

Individuals in multi-adult households (communes) or cohabitating. (Represents four percent
of all households.)

Strengths

In communal forms, a large number of individuals are available to form a support system to meet
individual needs, a situation especially important
to individuals in transition from one family form
to another, such as recently divorced women with
small children.

Individuals not ready or unwilling to make a
commitment to a long-term partnership can experience economic and social sharing, psychic
growth and open communication and interpersonal relationships.

Weaknesses

Few of these forms have developed strategies,
techniques or economic bases to sustain their activities or achieve their goals.

In a large number of experimental family
forms, role responsibilities are not clearly deline-
ated or articulated, with consequential difficulties
in implementing parenting, economic, household
and other functions.

Reprinted from M. B. Sussman, "The Family Today—Is It an
Endangered Species?" *Children Today.* Washington, D.C.,
March–April 1978, pp. 32–37, 45.

vorced individuals than for any other group (Campbell and Converse, 1975).
For the young adult, a divorce following a relatively short marriage may be
viewed as correcting a mistake—and may be less traumatic, therefore, than
the end of a relatively long marriage. However, for young adults, the end of a
longer marriage may be more upsetting because of the major readjustments

required, particularly if young children are involved. Knox (1977) identified the following adjustments that affect most couples involved in a divorce:

1. Concern about the forthcoming divorce.
2. The divorce itself.
3. The use of children as a "weapon" in disputes between the divorcing couple.
4. Changed feelings.
5. The results of perceived personal and interpersonal failure.
6. Children who live with one parent.
7. Attitudes of friends, relatives, and peers.
8. Possible remarriage.

The welfare of children is also a major concern in divorcing families. Marital conflict is upsetting to children, particularly when it involves uncertainties and loyalty divided between parents.

THE COMMUNITY

Throughout our discussion of life-span development, we have indicated the vital role of the neighborhood and the community as a context for human development. An important dimension that emerges during early adulthood is a network of social relationships in addition to those at work and in the family. The importance of this community–social network is that it serves both to support and to diversify the resources of adults and their families.

Such social networks differ depending on the circumstances of individuals and their families. American adults engage in a broad range of activities depending on marital state, sex, socioeconomic level, and age. Social participation (besides work and family) may involve activities such as participation in organizations, political activities, religious organizations, recreational events, public–community events, and informal activities.

During the years of courtship and the early years of marriage, patterns of social participation by men and women become more similar and shift toward activities preferred by women (Knox, 1977). During early and middle adulthood, the extent of parental responsibilities tends to concentrate social participation in child-related activities. In middle age, a great deal of the woman's social participation is in family and community activities, whereas men's social participation tends to involve work-related activities. In spite of the variety of specific social-participation patterns, a developmental shift begins in early adulthood and continues more strongly and consistently to middle age; Knox (1977) pointed out a shift from the physically vigorous activities of late adolescence and young adulthood to the more interpersonal emphasis of middle adulthood (see Figure 10.9).

THE WORLD OF WORK

"I'm a 'machine,'" says the spot welder. "I'm caged," says the bank teller. "I'm a mule," says the steelworker. "A monkey can do what I do," says the recep-

498

FIGURE 10.9 The Developmental Shift in Social Participation Patterns. Beginning in young adulthood there is a shift from more physically vigorous social activities to more interpersonal (and less physically active) activities.

Photograph by Bruce Hecht

tionist. . . . To earn one's bread by the sweat of one's brow has always been the lot of mankind. At least, ever since Eden's slothful couple was served with an eviction notice. The Scriptual precept was never doubted, not out loud. No matter how demeaning the task, no matter how it dulls the senses and breaks the spirit, one must work.

From Louis Terkel, *Working.* New York: Pantheon Books, 1974, p. 11.

Occupational life-cycle. The occupational life-cycle includes the following phases:

1. Exploration and establishment during late adolescence and early adulthood.
2. Mid-career adjustments.
3. Termination of occupational activity (as a result of retirement or death).

Launching a Career. The process by which adults enter jobs varies greatly. Many factors contribute to job choice, including the value of work to the individual, personality factors such as decisiveness and particular preferences, and available opportunities. Work provides adults with a number of important opportunities, including earning a living, demonstrating competence, supporting and validating self-esteem, engaging in social interaction, and meeting challenges (see Figure 10.10). Decisions that later adolescents and young adults make regarding mate selection, peer groups, and education also influence occupational choice.

Traditional views of occupational development as a "one-shot" process that occurs primarily during late adolescence and young adulthood have gradually given way to the notion that occupational development occurs throughout adulthood. In previous generations, individuals entered careers

FIGURE 10.10 Young adults are engaged in a wide variety of activities.

Left photograph by Darryl Jacobson; Right photograph by Gale Schiamberg

with a sense of the finality of a lifetime commitment (Marcia, 1966). It is becoming increasingly common for adults to change careers in midlife. Some of these shifts may be due to changes in the job market for some skills. In other cases, such career shifts may reflect changes in personal goals.

The success of occupational development in young adulthood is reflected by both satisfaction and productivity. Job satisfaction is generally the result of factors associated with both job characteristics and individual characteristics, such as interests and abilities (Healy, 1973; Quinn, Staines, and McCullough, 1974).

Young Women in the Work Force. The occupational pattern of women differs in significant ways from that of men. Large numbers of women are found in certain occupations that require "nurturing" behavior (e.g., nursing) or routine–precision activities (e.g., typists, clerical workers, receptionists). From the available research evidence, it is not clear how much of this occupational "focusing" is due to limited alternatives (access to jobs), or to particular talents, or to both factors (Veroff and Feld, 1970; Kreps, 1976). Sex-role stereotyping undoubtedly plays a role.

In comparison with previous generations of women, today more young women are employed out of the home and more of them are working when their children are young (see Figure 10.11).

Some young women prefer to devote most of their adult lives to being mothers, wives, and homemakers. Others have long-term career interests to which they wish to devote their primary attention without marrying or having children. Still others attempt to combine homemaking and career goals. Although some young adult women continue in the work force out of choice, others may do so out of necessity, that is, to help support the family.

Early Adulthood: The Entry Years

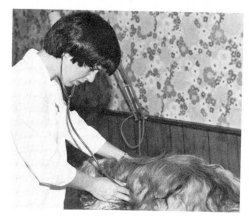

FIGURE 10.11 Young women are engaged in a wide range of vocational roles.

Top left photograph by Darryl Jacobson; bottom left photograph by Gale Schiamberg; right photograph by Irving Rader

An Oversupply of Young Workers?

The baby boom that came after World War II, producing a huge population bulge, has shifted from the campus to the office and the factory, and there may not be enough promotions or good jobs to go around in the next decade.

In 1975 there were 39 million workers in the "prime" 25-to-44 age bracket, so called because those ages are perceived as the years of ambition as well as skill. In 1990 there are expected to be 60.5 million workers in this bracket.

"This remarkable bunching of the work force will have far-reaching consequences for the job market," said Richard B. Freeman, professor of economics at Harvard University and director of labor economics research for the National Bureau of Economic Research.

'INCREASINGLY DENSE MARKET'

"They will have to jostle and elbow to find room in an increasingly dense labor market environment," said Arnold Weber, professor of economics and public policy and provost at Carnegie-Mellon University. "Competition will be intense and disappointment more widespread. This disappointment will be deepened by the fact that, on average, these workers will be better educated than many of their superiors."

From J. Flint, "Oversupply of Young Workers Expected to Tighten Jobs Race," *The New York Times,* June 25, 1978.

Some Problems of the Working Woman

Equal pay for equal work? Even when the earnings of men and women employed in the same occupation groups throughout the year are compared, sharp differences may be noted. The following trends are of interest (U.S. Department of Labor, 1983):

- Working women are in the same relative earnings position compared to men as they were in the past, averaging about $6 for every $10 earned by men (see diagram and table below).
- In some occupations, women's wages are closer to parity with men's wages. For example, in elementary school teaching, women earn roughly [82] percent as much as men. But in other areas, such as sales, women average only a little more than half of men's earnings.
- Occupations ranking high in terms of women's earnings typically do not rank among those with the highest concentrations of female workers. The very highly paid professional and managerial occupations are still predominantly male.

Sexual harassment. The man I was working for thought he could pinch me. . . . When I told him to stop, he just continued but when I gave notice, he stopped. Then he propositioned me and I gave notice again. He finally understood, but it was six months of pure hell. I was a wreck but I needed the money. He said I was taking it too seriously, and it was all a joke. What made him think that he had the right to do it?—employed woman (Nemy, 1975)

Comparison of the Weekly Earnings of Men and Women, 1981

Occupation	Men	Women	Women's Earnings as a Percentage of Men's
Professional technical (accountants, computer specialists etc.)	$439.00	$316.00	71.8%
Engineers	547.00	371.00	67.8%
Physicians, dentists, and related practitioners	495.00	401.00	80.9%
Nurses, dietitians, and therapists	344.00	326.00	94.7%
Elementary-school teachers	379.00	311.00	82.2%

Source: Rytina, N. F., Earnings of men and women: A look at specific occupations, *Monthly Labor Review*, U.S. Department of Labor, April 1982, 105, pp. 25–31.

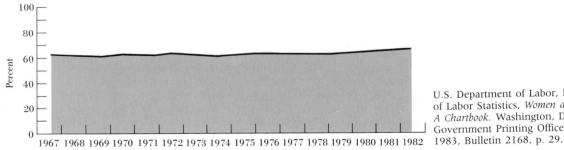

Women's Earnings as a Proportion of Men's Earnings

U.S. Department of Labor, Bureau of Labor Statistics, *Women at Work: A Chartbook.* Washington, D.C.: U.S. Government Printing Office, April 1983, Bulletin 2168, p. 29.

Usual weekly earnings by sex, 1967–1982. Women's earnings continue to average about 60 percent of men's earnings.

"First-Job" Experiences

The new graduate comes from college to his first job in industry prepared to be a company president. He is ambitious, enthusiastic and ready. Then come the realities of the business world. Within a year, he is very likely to suffer a serious loss of motivation, to find himself facing the thought of quitting the job that once seemed so promising as a career opportunity, or to stop trying so hard, to ease off and lapse into a kind of apathy. What is wrong? . . .

In my interviews with graduates after they had been on the job for six months to one year, almost every one stated in one way or another that he was shocked by the degree to which his "good ideas" were rejected, the way they were undermined, sidetracked, or even sabotaged.

What else does the graduate discover during his first year on the job? . . .

- "Things are more disorganized than I expected."
- "I ran into conflict with procedures . . . shaped by people far higher up . . . the informal methods of handling things, you can't buck that."
- "The company has a program of planned frustration of keeping you one step behind all the time; as soon as you master one thing, you discover so many other barriers. . . ."

- "The number of unproductive people in the corporation is simply astounding. . . ."
- "All the problems boil down to communication and human relations. . . ."

Not only does the graduate find his rational ideals upset, he also becomes emotionally involved in a way that he did not anticipate. . . .one of their most difficult problems was learning to accept emotionally the reality of the organization's human side.

With many graduates, their basic approach was not how to work in and around the human organization, but rather how to make the human organization go away. The legitimacy and reality of the human aspects of the company were being resisted at an emotional level, and the graduates were expressing a strong wish to exist in a world that by their own definition was totally rational.

The degree to which the graduate is able to accept the human organization at the emotional level may be directly related to his potential as a manager or executive.

From E. Schein, "The First-Job Dilemma," *Readings in Educational Psychology Today.* New York: Random House-CRM, 1970, pp. 51–55.

The Development of the Self in Young Adulthood

PHYSICAL CHANGES

Most young adults are at the peak of physical development. From about twenty-five through fifty years of age, the decline in physical–biological features is gradual. Most male adults reach the full adult height at approximately 21.2 years (Roche and Davila, 1972). At twenty-five to thirty years of age, the adult reaches a peak of maximum muscular strength with a subsequent 10 percent loss of strength between ages thirty and sixty (Bromley, 1974; Espenschade and Meleney, 1961; Timiras, 1972). This development is particularly reflected by the number of young adults who win contests and set athletic records that require strength and short bursts of energy. Maximum strength during the period sixty to seventy years of age is about 80 percent of what it was in the twenties (de Vries, 1974).

Physical endurance, or the ability to engage in work or exercise over an extended period of time, also declines with age. The decline in physical endurance is not as rapid as the decline in muscle strength, particularly at moderate levels of performance. Many older adults are able to compensate for this decline by pacing themselves in work and recreation activities so that they can consistently maintain a high level of performance. The decline in physical endurance does not appear to be as great for physically active adults as for sedentary people who do little exercise (Milne and Milne, 1968; Astrand, 1968; Timiras, 1972; deVries, 1974).

The Senses. In human interaction, the ability to communicate effectively is determined in a large part by the use of the senses (vision, hearing, speech, touch, taste, and smell). In our discussion of infancy and childhood (see Chapters Six, Seven and Eight), we pointed to the vital role of the senses in organizing the world of the developing human being. As adulthood progresses, individuals must adjust to and organize their world in relation to a decline in sensory functioning. This decline may make it difficult for older adults to make discriminations at lower levels of intensity; that is, older adults may have difficulty hearing the softest sounds, smelling the faintest aromas, and seeing the dimmest lights.

Vision and visual adaptation are the sharpest at age twenty. Visual adaptation at age twenty also reflects the cumulative conditions such as farsightedness (hyperopia) and nearsightedness (myopia). Some life-cycle trends for certain aspects of eye functioning are described in Figure 10.12:

FIGURE 10.12   Vision and age for seven indices of visual acuity: (1) central nervous system; (2) pupil size; (3) adaptation rate; (4) light threshold; (5) visual acuity; (6) lens accommodation; (7) contrast.

From Knox, A. B., *Adult Development and Learning.* San Francisco: Jossey-Bass, 1977, p. 278. Reprinted by permission.

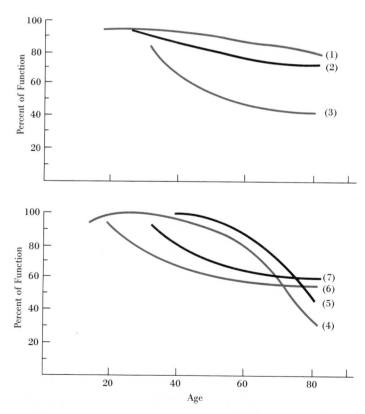

1. *Central nervous system.* There is a gradual decline in central nervous system functioning, which usually does not become apparent until old age. These changes affect all behavior, including vision. The general effect of these changes is a slowing down of almost all functions and processes.

2. *Pupil size.* Less light enters the eye in older adults than in younger adults because of a decline in the diameter of the pupil with age. This situation may be particularly difficult for older individuals in poorly lit settings (Birren, Casperson, and Botwinick, 1950).

3. *Adaptation rate.* It takes an older adult a substantially longer time to become adapted to the light than a younger adult.

4. *Light threshold.* When the eye becomes adapted to the dark (a process that takes longer for older adults), there is a decline with age in the minimum intensity of light that can be seen. It has been suggested that this minimum intensity must be doubled every thirteen years beyond age twenty to be seen by the adult's dark-adapted eye (McFarland and Fisher, 1955; Knox, 1977).

5. *Visual acuity.* Visual acuity, usually measured with a conventional eye chart, increases during childhood and adolescence, remains stable from about twenty through fifty years of age. At age fifty a slow but accelerated decline begins (Knox, 1977).

6. *Lens accommodation.* The muscle action and elasticity of the lens allow it to change its roundness or flatness so that the viewed image falls directly on the retina. There is little change in lens accommodation during adolescence; however, between ages twenty and fifty, there is a distinct loss of lens elasticity. After age fifty, the decline in lens accommodation is more gradual. (Knox, 1977).

   A related age trend is the interaction between age and nearsightedness and farsightedness. Both nearsightedness and farsightedness tend to increase between adolescence and the start of middle age (Morgan, 1958). This trend is sometimes reversed in old age.

7. *Contrast.* With increasing age, adults require more contrast between a viewed object and its background.

The overall impact of these age-related trends in human vision is that in early adulthood, most adults are aware of few changes. At about the age of forty, most adults notice some changes.

Reaction Time. Between young adulthood and old age, there is a gradual increase in time of responding. *Reaction time* (the time lag between when a person sees, hears, smells, or touches an object and when she or he starts to respond) decreases rapidly during childhood. A plateau is reached during early adulthood. The peak period of reaction time is reached just before the age of twenty, and there is a subsequent increase in time of responding through middle adulthood and old age (Birren, Woods, and Williams, 1980; Welford, 1977).

Physical Health. During early adulthood, most instances of disability, restricted activity, or death are due primarily to *acute conditions.*

DEFINITIONS

Acute conditions. These include infectious diseases (e.g., influenza or pneumonia, temporary digestive disorders) and accidents (e.g., sprains, broken bones, and lacerations).

Chronic conditions. These include age-related diseases such as arthritis, coronary heart disease, and arteriosclerosis.

There is a life-cycle shift from the acute or functional conditions of young adulthood to the chronic or degenerative (irreversible) conditions of middle adulthood and old age. Before age forty, the vast majority of deaths are caused by infectious diseases and accidents. After age forty, the number of deaths due to chronic conditions begins to increase markedly (Knox, 1977).

The three major causes of death in the human life cycle are:

1. Accidents.
2. Cardiovascular diseases.
3. Cancers (neoplasms).

Figure 10.13 describes the relationships among these three factors. During childhood, adolescence, and young adulthood, accidents are the primary cause of deaths. By middle age, cardiovascular diseases become the major cause of death for men. Cancer is the major cause of death for middle-aged

FIGURE 10.13 Deaths due to cancers, major cardiovascular diseases, and accidents.

Based on information from U.S. Department of Health and Human Services, Public Health Service, National Center for Health Statistics, *Vital Statistics of the United States,* 1978, Vol. 11, Part A. DHSS Pub. No. (PHS) 83-1101. Washington, D.C.: U.S. Government Printing Office, 1982, pp. 1-10, 1-11, 1-14, 1-15, 1-24, and 1-25. Graphs designed by Gale Schiamberg.

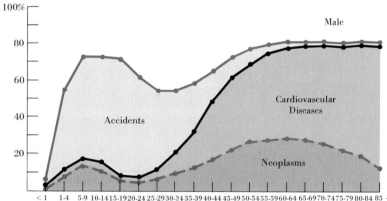

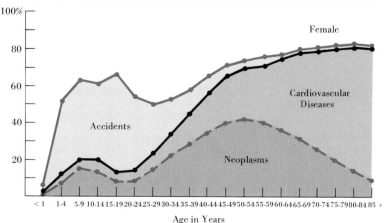

Age in Years

Young adults often engage in regular exercise and running to increase endurance and strengths.

Photographs by David Kostelnik

women. In old age, cardiovascular diseases are the major cause of death for men and women.

Because of their high death rate from accidents, *accident prevention* is an important consideration for young adults. One factor that contributes to the high number of accidents during young adulthood is the adventuresome nature of people at this age. However, most accidents during this period are not the result of direct attempts to create a risky situation; rather, they result from carelessness. Furthermore, such accidents seem to occur at times and in places where hazards and the likelihood of injuries are high (e.g., on the highway). Whereas fires, drownings, and similar accidents are the primary cause of *accidental* death during childhood and adolescence, motor vehicle accidents, shootings, drownings, and poisonings are more prevalent during early adulthood. It is interesting that there are no types of fatal accidents that are prevalent in the age range from twenty-five to sixty-four (Rodstein, 1964; National Safety Council, 1975).

In every setting in which young adults find themselves, there are times when the risk of accidents is high. An awareness of risk coupled with accident-prevention practices could reduce accidents. For example, in the work setting, safety practices such as the use of protective guards around moving machinery, safety shoes and hats, and warning lights can greatly reduce the occurrence of accidents. In the home, *areas* such as the kitchen, *objects* such as toys or electrical appliances, and *times* such as late afternoon are often associated with accidents. In the case of driving, accidents are associated with holidays, speed, alcohol, and the onset of precipitation (Knox, 1977).

INTERLUDE:
EXERCISE AND HEALTH IN EARLY ADULTHOOD

Another way for young adults to reduce accidents is to maintain a level of physical conditioning that exceeds the daily requirements for peak performance. Regular physical exercise may help to increase endurance as well as the ability to recover from muscle fatigue. The trend toward increased participation of both male and female young adults in physical fitness programs may be important in preventing cardiovascular problems as well as making them "feel good." During early and middle adulthood regular physical exercise tends to improve cardiovascular functioning, particularly for sedentary people. There appear to be significant benefits from exercise in young adulthood (Mitchell and Blomquist, 1972).

Many aspects of physical health are associated with regular exercise that is appropriate for the individual. In general, regular and moderate exercise related to work or recreation contributes to good posture, vitality, endurance, strength, circulation. . . .In addition to emotional satisfaction and relaxation for sleep, exercise may develop collateral circulation that increases the capacity to respond to increased demand and helps prevent coronary heart disease (Knox, 1977, p. 294).

INTELLECTUAL AND COGNITIVE FUNCTIONING OF YOUNG ADULTS

With regard to intelligence and cognitive functioning, there is reason to think that young adults reach an individual peak of performance (Baltes and Schaie, 1974). It is important to note that age is not the only factor that may influence intelligence in young adulthood. Both educational and health backgrounds are just as important as age in determining intelligence in adulthood (Botwinick, 1973). Nonetheless, young adulthood is likely to be a time in which the individual has maximum flexibility in forming new concepts and in shifting from one perspective to another. Memory and creativity may also be at a peak (see Figure 10.14)

FIGURE 10.14   Intellectual functioning is at a high level in young adulthood.

Photograph by Darryl Jacobson

Early Adulthood: The Entry Years

Limitations in Measurement of Adult Mental Ability. Tests of general intelligence, or "omnibus" tests, derive a single score (e.g., IQ) for an individual by combining scores on several subtests. Omnibus tests include the Stanford–Binet and the Wechsler Adult Intelligence Scale (WAIS) (Wechsler, 1958). At present, there are no really effective instruments or tests for estimating adult learning ability. There are at least three reasons for this situation (Knox, 1977):

1. Many of the most popular and widely used adult intelligence tests (e.g., the WAIS) were derived, in both format and theory, from comparable tests for children and adolescents (e.g., the Wechsler Intelligence Scale for Children or WISC), rather than being based on a realistic understanding of adult experience.
2. These tests of child and adult intelligence are based on several questionable assumptions (Knox, 1977):
   - Children, adolescents and adults have equal access to a fund of knowledge and experience. (This is probably not true in light of the marked differences between middle-class and poor individuals.)
   - More intelligent people learn more effectively and efficiently and therefore perform at higher levels on ability tests. (If individuals are not motivated, they may not do anything very well.)
3. Rather few intelligence-test items correspond to the types of skills and competencies that adults have actually acquired or actually use in real-life situations.

Tests and other estimates of learning ability are really indications (or at least, they are assumed to be indications) of an individual's *ceiling* capacity (potentially maximal level of functioning). It has been a rather consistent observation that in everyday life, individuals perform well below this ceiling capacity (Knox, 1977). What this underperformance means for adult cognitive functioning is that *even if* ability (or ceiling) scores on intelligence tests decline, the result has no practical effect on performance (see Figure 10.15).

Longitudinal, Cross-sectional, and Cross-sequential Studies of Adult Intelligence. Three ways of estimating trends in adult intelligence are longitudinal studies, cross-sectional studies, and cross-sequential studies.

Longitudinal studies of learning ability involve the administration of intelligence tests to the same individuals over time. Although longitudinal findings are a reasonable indication of age trends, their results can be misleading. Such

FIGURE 10.15   Capacity, performance, and age.

From Knox, A. B., *Adult Development and Learning.* San Francisco: Jossey-Bass Publishers, 1977, p. 414.

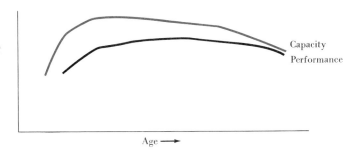

findings may not account for social changes or life-cycle changes that alter the types of learning activities relevant during the stages of adulthood. Furthermore, longitudinal studies may provide an inflated estimate of the long-term development of intelligence simply because fewer of the less able adults survive (Knox, 1977; Riegel, Riegel, and Meyer, 1967; Baltes, Schaie, and Nardi, 1971).

Longitudinal studies indicate a high level of stability of intellectual skill between twenty and fifty years of age and beyond (see Figure 10.16) (Tuddenham, Blumenkrantz, and Wilkin, 1968; Piaget, 1972; Furry and Baltes, 1973; Cunningham, Clayton, and Overton, 1975; Cunningham and Birren, 1976).

Cross-sectional studies of adult learning ability usually involve the administration of intelligence tests to a representative sample of adults at various ages (the same individuals are not followed in time, as is the case in longitudinal research). Cross-sectional studies of learning ability indicate a gradual decline of ability during adulthood (Horn and Cattell, 1966; Fozard, Nuttall and Waugh, 1972) (see Figure 10.16). However, these cross-sectional findings are an inadequate indicator of age trends because of the differences between young adults and older adults in degree of formal education, health, and interest in learning and in the values internalized during adolescence and youth.

Cross-sectional studies provide evidence that there is a broad range of learning abilities in adulthood. Research indicates that the most cognitively able individuals increase their learning quite rapidly during childhood and adolescence and then reach a plateau during young adulthood (Knox, 1977). On the other hand, less intellectually able individuals increase in learning ability much more slowly, reach a plateau earlier, and then decline more rapidly.

Cross-sequential Studies. In order to resolve the problems of both the longitudinal and cross-sectional methods in describing the progression of adult intelligence, the cross-sequential method was developed (see discussion in Chapter Three). Schaie (1965, 1973) and Baltes (1968), suggested methodological strategies which involved the combination of cross-sectional and longitudinal approaches. In general, the results of studies using this method (Schaie and Labouvie-Vief, 1974; Schaie and Parham, 1977), question the notion of an inevitable, age-related, and universal decline in intelligence. Instead, they demonstrate that cohort-related factors (e.g., the impact of historical events such as economic recessions and depressions, wars, or the his-

FIGURE 10.16 Mental abilities and age based on longitudinal and cross-sectional studies.

From Owens, W. A., "Age and Mental Ability: A Second Adult Follow-up," *Journal of Educational Psychology,* 1966, *57,* 311–325. Copyright 1966 by the American Psychological Association. Reprinted by permission of the author, W. A. Owens.

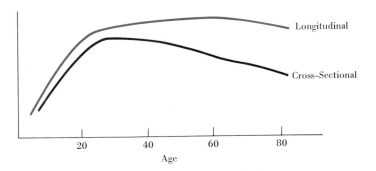

torical improvement in education) are much greater in impact on adult cognitive functioning than simple age changes. Stability or even increases in cognitive functioning are indicated as characteristic of most of early adulthood, middle age, and the early phases of old age. However, decline in some, but not all, abilities appears late in life during the late sixties or early seventies.

The clarification of the reasons for this late-life decline or, in some cases, stability requires a more detailed assessment of the factors or antecedents of cognitive functioning that operate *within* cohort effects or age effects. These antecedents include the following factors:

Biological/Physiological Factors. Since old age is accompanied by some degenerative biological/physiological changes (e.g., decline in nerve conduction velocity, decline in maximum breathing capacity, decline in kidney functioning, decline in heart pumping capacity, and so on), there is good reason to consider the possibility that cognitive functioning declines with physiological decline (particularly of the central nervous system) (Horn, 1978; LaRue and Jarvik, 1982). Research on the interaction of overall health and cognitive functioning in adulthood suggests the following relationships:

1. When biological/physiological factors are intact, cognitive functioning is largely independent of biological functioning.
2. When the biological/physiological base is damaged by injury or illness, a direct relationship between cognitive functioning and biological/physiological factors develops. (Birren, Butler, Greenhouse, Sokoloff, and Yarrow, 1963; Eisdorfer and Wilkie, 1977).

Learning-related Factors. These include the characteristics of learning situations to which older adults are exposed, such as practice, feedback, or general educational design. Research suggests that for some types of learning activities, appropriately designed educational programs result in performance of middle-aged and older adults which is both stable (rather than declining) as well as similar to the performance of young adults (Denney, 1982). Such findings suggest that age-related performance declines may be based on educational experience rather than on age, per se.

Social-Environmental Factors. These refer primarily to the attitudes, values, and behaviors which originate in the *contexts* of adulthood and which may encourage or even force older adults into roles or behaviors that stimulate a decline in cognitive functioning. The postretirement years may result in environmental circumstances that discourage social and intellectual development (Labouvie-Vief, 1977; Kuypers and Bengston, 1973).

Fluid and Crystallized Intelligence. The theory of fluid and crystallized intelligence (Cattell, 1963; Horn, 1967; Cattell, 1976) has provided a useful way of looking at the shifts in adult learning skills.

Fluid Intelligence. Fluid intelligence is an underlying or basic capacity that results from the interaction of human physiology and early human experience. This form of intelligence consists of the ability to form concepts, to use abstract reasoning, and to perceive complex relationships. Presumably fluid intelligence is independent of education and experience. That is why it is "fluid" or can "flow into" or be applied to a wide range of intellectual activities. Examples of the kind of activities or tests that are used to measure fluid intelligence include grouping letters and numbers, pairing related words (analogies), or remembering a series of digits (short-term memory).

Crystallized Intelligence. Crystallized intelligence involves the application of formal reasoning and abstraction and perception of complex relations to tasks that have been learned. Crystallized intelligence is dependent on education and experience. It is measured by tests of general information, vocabulary, arithmetical reasoning, or social situations that presumably assess how much knowledge the individual has derived from her or his experiences.

Fluid and crystallized intelligence, taken together, account for the majority of the abilities that adults use in their thinking and problem solving. Many life problems or issues can be resolved by the use of either of the two. Over the life span, an individual probably develops a "cognitive style," so that he or she may solve problems through "brilliance" (or fluid intelligence) or by applying accumulated "wisdom" (or crystallized intelligence).

Both fluid and crystallized intelligence increase during childhood and adolescence. Fluid intelligence, however, tends to decline gradually during adulthood (Tuddenham, Blumenkrantz, and Wilkin, 1968; Fozard and Nuttall, 1971). On the other hand, crystallized intelligence continues to increase gradually throughout adulthood (Schaie and Strother, 1968; Blum, Jarvik, and Clark, 1970; Cunningham, Clayton, and Overton, 1975). It is interesting that in an ongoing national educational assessment (U.S. National Assessment of Educational Progress, DHEW, 1976), achievement test score results were higher for adults than for seventeen-year-olds. The continued growth of crystallized intelligence, however, depends on a continuing process of meaningful cultural involvement including information seeking, reflection, and educational activity (Campbell, 1965).

Adult performance on omnibus intelligence tests represents a mixture of both fluid and crystallized intelligence. Therefore, omnibus measures tend to remain somewhat stable throughout the adult years. The reason for this apparent stability is that the decline in fluid intelligence is balanced out by the increase in crystallized intelligence (see Figure 10.17).

PERSONALITY DEVELOPMENT

General Trends. The development of personality during young adulthood may be described in terms of several general trends.

Gradual Stabilization of the Self-concept. The sense of self that began to emerge in adolescence becomes even sharper and clearer in the young adult years (White, 1966). Young adults continue to refine their self-concepts through experiences gained in the family, at work, and in the community.

Interpersonal Flexibility. Interpersonal flexibility is a continuation of a trend that was developed in adolescent friendships (see Chapter Nine). During adolescence and young adulthood, the individual learns to interact with others as "people" in their own right. Prior to young adulthood or later adolescence, the individual may have been concerned more with interpersonal relationships as a way of handling growing up. For example, adolescent girls sometimes develop close friendships with other girls as a way of handling the physical and sexual changes of adolescence. Adolescent boys may develop ganglike social interactions as a way of managing their feelings about "authority" figures. Young adults are, in a sense, freed of some of these concerns and can relate in a more open and honest fashion.

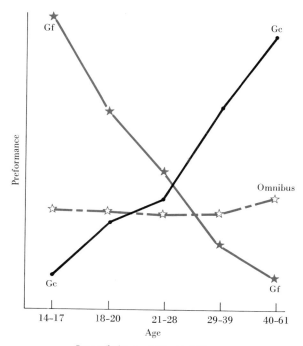

FIGURE 10.17 Fluid and crystallized intelligence patterns with age.

From Horn, J. L., "Organization of Data on Life-span Development of Human Abilities," in L. R. Goulet and P. B. Baltes, Eds., *Life-span Developmental Psychology.* New York: Academic Press, 1970.

Gc stands for crystallized intelligence.
Gf stands for fluid intelligence.

Deepening Interests. Interests develop throughout life. However, it is often not until young adulthood that the individual has the time and the confidence to pursue them at a deeper level. For example, the young adult who has been generally interested in photography may purchase a precision camera, read books on photography, or learn to develop her or his own pictures.

Humanization of Values. During young adulthood, the individual develops a "mellow" or "humanized" view of values. Experience in the family, the world of work, and the community help young adults to realize that the world is not perfect. This recognition of life's imperfections leads to the development of a value system suited to the realities of experience.

Expansion of Caring. The general trend of human development from birth on is toward less *egocentrism.* That is, the child moves away from a conception of himself or herself as the center of world to an appreciation and understanding of the perspectives of others.

Due to physical and sexual changes the adolescent may become self-conscious and concerned primarily about the self. However, this adolescent egocentrism is very likely only a temporary setback. The young adult is able to become seriously concerned about and involved in the welfare of others.

The Self-concept. The individual does not experience any dramatic changes in the self-concept from adolescence to young adulthood. Rather, there is a combination of stability with some change (Block, 1971). The young adult remains basically the same person as he or she was in adolescence. Young adults, however, do tend to show a greater ability to cope with problems and a greater sense of competence in relation to the world (Block, 1971; Neugarten, Berkowitz, Crotty, Gruen, Gutmann, Lubin, Miller, Peck, Rosen, Shukin, and Tobin, 1964; Gutmann, 1970).

Sex-role learning has a bearing on how males and females demonstrate competence. As we indicated in our prior discussions of sex-role learning, cultural expectations may have a profound influence on the behavior of males and females. If, for example, women "learn" that "appropriate" female behavior is to be passive and irrational, then they may be less likely than men to develop a sense of control over their lives. It is not uncommon to find women attributing their success to "luck" rather than to their skill or rationality, particularly if they are in competition with men (Deaux, 1976).

Young adults now appear to be going beyond traditional sex-role stereotypes. For example, many young adults no longer think of the ideal male as being a rugged dominant figure (a likeness of the late movie actor John Wayne). Rather, both sexes see the ideal male as one who is caring, self-confident, warm, and intelligent (Tavris, 1977). These traits represent a mixture of "traditional" role expectations for males and females.

Summary

1. The period of early adulthood usually brings the beginning of a commitment to a career, the beginning of marriage (or, in some instances, an alternate family form), and, sometimes, the beginning of parenthood. Adolescence provides the foundation for early adulthood in the form of a relatively stable identity.

2. Whereas the periods of childhood, adolescence, and youth are seen as preparatory stages, the period of adulthood is viewed as the fulfillment of these earlier periods. It is the period of *maturity*.

3. There are several frames of reference for looking at adult development: the chronological viewpoint, the biological perspective, the cultural perspective, and the developmental perspective.

4. During young adulthood, the major efforts of activity are external. That is, they are directed at the social world: beginning a family and finding a job or achieving an intimate relationship with a marital partner, children, or other persons. However, as the young adult engages in work, family, and community activities, there are accompanying changes in the *internal* world of the young adult.

5. Of all the features of the world of young adulthood, the family is of prime importance because shifts in family role performance affect all other aspects of adult development. Major *role changes* in the family life-cycle for young adults may include mate selection, marriage, and parenthood. Although the majority of adults follow the pattern of marriage and childrearing, there are *alternate life patterns*. Included in these alternate patterns are singlehood, new family arrangements resulting from remarriage, marriages ending in separation or divorce, childless married couples, adults who marry late in life, and experimental family forms (e.g., communes).

6. An important dimension of the community-neighborhood context (and, to some extent, the work experience) is a network of social relationships. The importance of this network is that it serves both to support and diversify the resources of adults and their families.

7. The occupational life cycle includes the following phases: (a) exploration and establishment, (b) mid-career adjustments and (c) retirement.

8. Most young adults are at the peak of physical development. From about 25 through 50 years, the decline in physical/biological features is gradual. During early adulthood, most instances of disability, restricted activity, or death are due primarily to *acute* (rather than *chronic*) conditions.

9. With regard to intelligence and cognitive functioning, young adults reach an individual peak of performance. There are serious limitations in the measurement of adult mental ability using standardized tests. Three ways of estimating trends in adult intelligence are cross-sectional, longitudinal, and cross-sequential studies. The theory of fluid and crystallized intelligence has provided a useful way of looking at the shifts in adult learning skills.

10. General trends in personality development during young adulthood include: the gradual stabilization of the self-concept, interpersonal flexibility, deepening interest, humanization of values, and the expansion of caring.

Questions

1. What is the concept of maturity and why does it crystallize during early adulthood?
2. Mate selection appears to occur in accordance with one of two principles. What are they? Give a brief description of each.
3. Discuss the advantages and disadvantages of the following "alternate" life patterns: singlehood, the childless couple, and the divorced family.
4. Are women treated equally in the world of work?
5. Distinguish between *acute* conditions and *chronic* conditions as these relate to the physical health of young adults.

Bibliography

ADAMS, M. The single woman in today's society: A reappraisal. *American Journal of Orthopsychiatry,* 1971, *41*(5), 776–786.

ANTHONY, E., AND BENEDEK, T. (EDS.). *Parenthood: Its Psychology and Psychopathology.* Boston: Little, Brown, 1970.

ASTRAND, P. O. Physical performance as a function of age. *Journal of the American Medical Association,* 1968, *205,* 105–109.

BAKER, L. G., JR. The personal and social adjustment of the never-married woman. *Journal of Marriage and the Family,* August 1968, *30,* 473–479.

BALTES, P. B. Longitudinal and cross-sectional sequences in the study of age and generation effects. *Human Development,* 1968, *11,* 145–171.

BALTES, P. B., AND SCHAIE, K. W. Aging and I.Q.: The myth of the twilight years. *Psychology Today,* March 1974, *7,* 35–40.

BALTES, P. B., SCHAIE, K. W., AND NARDI, A. H. Age and experimental mortality in a seven-year longitudinal study of cognitive behavior. *Developmental Psychology,* 1971, *5,* 18–26.

BERELSON, B. The value of children: A taxonomical essay. In J. G. Wells (Ed.), *Current Issues in Marriage and Family.* New York: Macmillan, 1975, pp. 168–176.

BERNARD, J. *The Future of Marriage.* New York: World, 1972.

BIRDWHITSELL, R. L. The idealized model of the American family. *Social Casework,* April 1970, *51*(4), 195–198.

BIRREN, J. E., BUTLER, R. N., GREENHOUSE, S. W., SOKOLOFF, L. AND YARROW, M. R. (EDS.). *Human Aging: A Biological and Behavioral Study.* Washington, D.C., U.S. Government Printing Office, 1963.

BIRREN, J. E., CASPERSON, R. C., AND BOTWINICK, J. Age changes in pupil size. *Journal of Gerontology,* 1950, *5,* 216–221.

BIRREN, J. E., AND REEDY, M. E. *Psychology of the adult years.* Belmont, Calif.: Brooks-Cole, 1978.

BIRREN, J. E., WOODS, A. M., AND WILLIAMS, M. V. Behavioral slowing with age: causes, organization and consequences. In L. W. Poon (Ed.), *Aging in the 1980's.* Washington, D.C.: *American Psychological Association.* 1980.

BLOCK, J. *Lives Through Time.* Berkeley, Calif.: Bancroft, 1971.

BLUM, J. E., JARVIK, L. F., AND CLARK, E. T. Rate of change on selective tests of intelligence: A twenty-year longitudinal study of aging. *Journal of Gerontology,* 1970, *25,* 171–176.

BOSTON WOMEN'S HEALTH BOOK COLLECTIVE. *Our Bodies, Ourselves.* New York: Simon & Schuster, 1971.

BOTWINICK, J. *Aging and Behavior.* New York: Springer, 1973.

BROMLEY, D. B. *The Psychology of Human Aging* (2nd ed.). Middlesex, England: Penguin, 1974.

BUHLER, C. *Der Menschliche, Lebenslauf als Psychologicshes Problem.* Leipzig: Verlag Von S. Herzel, 1933.

BUHLER, C. Old age and fulfillment of life with considerations of the use of time in old age. *Acta Psychologica,* 1961, *19,* 126–148.

BUHLER, C. The course of human life as a psychological problem. *Human Development,* 1968a, *11,* 184–200.

BUHLER, C. The developmental structure of goal setting in group and individual studies. In C. Buhler and F. Massarik (Eds.), *The Course of Human Life.* New York: Springer, 1968b.

BURCHINAL, L. G. Trends and prospects for young marriages in the United States. *Journal of Marriage and the Family,* 1965, *27,* 243–254.

BUTLER, R. N. *Why Survive? Being Old in America.* New York: Harper & Row, 1975.

CAMPBELL, A., AND CONVERSE, P. *Monitoring the Perceived Quality of Life.* New York: Russell Sage Foundation, 1975.

CAMPBELL, D. P. A cross-sectional and longitudinal study of scholastic abilities over twenty-five years. *Journal of Counseling Psychology,* 1965, *12,* 55–61.

CARTER, H., AND GLICK, P. C. *Marriage and Divorce: A Social and Economic Study.* Cambridge, Mass.: Harvard U.P., 1970.

CATTELL, R. B. Theory of fluid and crystallized intelligence: A critical experiment. *Journal of Educational Psychology,* 1963, *54,* 1–22.

CATTELL, R. B. Fluid and crystallized intelligence. *Psychology Today,* 1976, *3,* 56–62.

CUNNINGHAM, W. R., AND BIRREN, J. E. Age changes in human abilities: A 28-year longitudinal study. *Developmental Psychology,* 1976, *12*(1), 81–82.

CUNNINGHAM, W. R., CLAYTON, V., AND OVERTON, W. Fluid and crystallized intelligence in young adulthood and old age. *Journal of Gerontology,* 1975, *30*(1), 53–55.

DEAUX, K. *The Behavior of Men.* Belmont, Calif: Brooks-Cole, 1976.

DENNEY, N. W. Aging and cognitive changes. In B. Wolman (Ed.), *Handbook of Development Psychology.* Englewood Cliffs, New Jersey: Prentice Hall, 1982, 807–827.

deVRIES, H. A. *Physiology of Exercise* (2nd ed.). Dubuque, Iowa: Brown, 1974.

DIBNER, A. S. The psychology of normal aging. In M. G. Spencer and C. J. Dorr (Eds.), *Understanding Aging: A Multidisciplinary Approach.* New York: Appleton, 1975.

DUVALL, E. M. *Marriage and Family Development.* (5th ed.). Philadelphia: Lippincott, 1977.

EDWARDS, J. N. Family behavior as social exchange. *Journal of Marriage and the Family,* 1969, *31,* 522–526.

EISDORFER, C. AND WILKIE, F. Stress, disease, aging and behavior. In J. E. Birren and K. W. Schaie (Eds.). *Handbook of the Psychology of Aging.* New York: Van Nostrand Reinhold, 1977.

ELDER, G. H. Adolescence in the life-cycle. In S. E. Dragastin and G. H. Elder (Eds.), *Adolescence in the life-cycle.* Washington, D.C.: Hemisphere, 1975, pp. 1–22.

ERIKSON, E. H. *Identity: Youth and Crisis.* New York: W. W. Norton, 1968.

ESPENSCHADE, A., AND MELENEY, H. E. Motor performances of adolescent boys and girls of today in comparison with those of 24 years ago. *Research Quarterly of the American Association for Health, Physical Education, and Recreation,* 1961, *32,* 186–189.

FLINT, J. Oversupply of young workers expected to tighten jobs race. *The New York Times,* June 25, 1978.

FOWLER, J. The American Family: Social statistics. *Congressional Research Service,* Report No. 83-102 EPW. Washington, D.C.: The Library of Congress, 1983, p. 5.

FOZARD, J. L., AND NUTTALL, R. L. GATB scores for men differing in age and socioeconomic status. *Journal of Applied Psychology,* 1971, *55*(4), 372–379.

FOZARD, J. L., NUTTALL, R. L., AND WAUGH, N. C. Age-related differences in mental performance. *Aging and Human Development,*1972, *3,* 19–43.

FURRY, C. A., AND BALTES, P. B. The effect of age differences in ability: Extraneous performance variables in the assessment of intelligence in children, adults, and the elderly. *Journal of Gerontology,* 1973, *28,* 73–80.

GILDER, G. *Naked nomads.* New York: Quadrangle, 1974.

GLENN, N. D., AND WEAVER, C. N. The marital happiness of remarried divorced persons. *Journal of Marriage and the Family,* May 1977, *39*(2), 331–337.

GUTMANN, D. Female ego styles and generational conflict. In J. Bardwick et al., *Feminine personality and Conflict.* Belmont, Calif: Brooks-Cole, 1970.

HEALY, C. C. The relation of esteem and social class to self-occupational congruence. *Journal of Vocational Behavior,* 1973, *3,* 43–51.

HECKMAN, N. A., BRYSON, R., AND BRYSON, J. B. Problems of professional couples: A content analysis. *Journal of Marriage and the Family,* May 1977, *39*(2), 323–330.

HORN, J. L. Intelligence—Why it grows, why it declines. *Transaction,* 1967, *4,* 23–31.

HORN, J. L. Organization of data on a life-span development of human abilities. In L. R. Goulet and P. B. Baltes (Eds.), *Life-span Developmental Psychology: Research and Theory.* New York: Academic Press, 1970.

HORN, J. L. Human ability systems. In P. B. Baltes (Ed.), *Life-Span Development and Behavior* (Vol.1), New York: Academic Press, 1978.

HORN, J. L., AND CATTELL, R. B. Age differences in primary mental ability factors. *Journal of Gerontology,* 1966, *21,* 210–220.

HORNER, A. J. The evolution of goals in the life of Clarence Darrow. In C. Buhler and F. Massarik (Eds.), *The Course of Human Life.* New York: Springer, 1968.

JENKINS, S. Children of divorce, *Children Today.* Washington, D.C.: March–April 1978, *48,* 16–20.

KATZ, B. J. Cooling motherhood. In J. G. Wells (Ed.), *Current Issues in Marriage and The Family.* New York: Macmillan, 1975, pp. 161–164.

KEMPLER, H. L. Extended kinship ties and some modern alternatives. *Family Coordinator,* April 1976, *25*(2), 143–149.

KERCKHOFF, A., AND DAVIS, K. Value consensus and need complementarity in mate selection. *American Sociological Review,* 1962, *27,* 295–303.

KESSLER, J. B. Aging in different ways. *Human Behavior.,* 1976, *5,* 56–60.

KIMMEL, D. C. *Adulthood and aging.* New York: Wiley, 1974 (2nd ed. 1980).

KNOX, A. B. *Adult Development and Learning.* San Francisco: Jossey-Bass, 1977.

KOLLER, M. R. *Families: A Multigenerational Approach.* New York: McGraw-Hill, 1974.

KREPS, J. M. (ED.). *Women and the American Economy.* New York: Prentice-Hall, 1976.

KUYPERS, J. A. AND BENGSTON, V. L. Social breakdown and competence: A model of normal aging. *Human Development,* 1973, *16,* 181–201.

LABOUVIE-VIEF, G. Adult cognitive development: In search of alternative interpretations. *Merrill-Palmer Quarterly,* 1977, *23,* 227–263.

LAPIDUS, I. M. Adulthood in Islam: Religious maturity in the Islamic tradition. *Daedalus,* Spring 1976, Vol. 102, 93–108.

LARUE, A. AND JARVIK, L. F. Old Age and biobehavioral changes. In B. Wolman (Ed.), *Handbook of Developmental Psychology.* Englewood Cliffs, N.J.: Prentice Hall, 1982, 791–806.

LEVINGER, G. Sources of marital dissatisfaction among applications for divorce. *American Journal of Orthopsychiatry,* 1966, *36,* 803–807.

LEVINGER, G., SENN. D. J., AND JORGENSEN, B. Progress toward permanence in courtship: a test of the Kerchoff-Davis hypothesis. *Sociometry,* 1970, *33,* 427–433.

LEVINSON, D. *The Seasons of a Man's Life.* New York: Alfred A. Knopt, 1978.

MARCIA, J. E. Development and validations of ego-identity status. *Journal of Personality and Social Psychology,* 1966, *3*(5), 551–558.

McFARLAND, R. A., AND FISHER, M. P. Alterations in dark adaption as a function of age. *Journal of Gerontology,* 1955, *10,* 424–428.

MILNE, L. J., AND MILNE, M. *The Ages of Life: A New Look at the Effects of Time on Mankind and Other Living Things.* New York: Harcourt, Brace, 1968.

MITCHELL, J. H., AND BLOMQUIST, G. The effects of physical training on sedentary American men. *Cardiac Rehabilitation,* 1972, *2*(4), 33–36.

MORGAN, M. W. Changes in refraction over a period of twenty years in a nonvisually selected sample. *American Journal of Optometry,* 1958, *35,* 281–299.

MURSTEIN, B. I. Stimulus-value role: A theory of marital choice. *Journal of Marriage and the Family,* 1970, *32,* 465–482.

MURSTEIN, B. I. Interview behavior, projective techniques, and questionnaires in the clinical assessment of marital choice. *Journal of Marriage and the Family,* 1972, *36,* 462–467.

NATIONAL SAFETY COUNCIL. *Accident facts.* Chicago: National Safety Council, 1975.

NEMY, E. Women speak out against sexual harassment at work. *The New York Times,* August 19, 1975, p. 38.

NEUGARTEN, B. L., MOORE, J. W., AND LOWE, J. C. Age norms, age constraints, and adult socialization. *American Journal of Sociology,* 1965, *70*(6), 710–717, Table 1.

NEUGARTEN, B. L., BERKOWITZ, H., CROTTY, W. J., GRUEN, W., GUTMANN, D. L., LUBIN, M. I., MILLER, D. L., PECK, R. F., ROSEN, J. L., SHUKIN, A., AND TOBIN, S. S. *Personality in Middle and Late Life.* New York: Atherton, 1964.

NEUGARTEN, B. L., AND MOORE, J. W. The changing age-status system. In B. L. Neugarten (Ed.), *Middle Age and Aging.* Chicago: U. of Chicago P., 1968.

PARIS, B. L., AND LUCKEY, E. F. A longitudinal study in marital satisfaction. *Sociological and Social Research,* 1966, *50,* 212–222.

PHELPS, W. L. *Autobiography with Letters.* New York: Scribner, 1939.

PIAGET, J. Intellectual evolution from adolescence to adulthood. *Human Development,* 1972, *15,* 1–12.

PINARD, M. Marriage and divorce decisions and the larger social system: A case study in social change. *Social Forces,* 1966, *44,* 341–355.

QUINN, R., STAINES, G. AND McCULLOUGH, M. Job satisfaction: Is there a trend? U.S. Department of Labor, Manpower Research Monograph No. 30. Washington, D.C.: U.S. Government Printing Office, 1974.

RIEGEL, K. F., RIEGEL, R. M., AND MEYER, G. A study of the dropout rates in longitudinal research on aging and the prediction of death. *Journal of Personality and Social Psychology,* 1967, *5,* 342–348.

ROCHE, A. F., AND DAVILA, G. H. Late adolescent growth in stature. *Pediatrics,* 1972, *50*(6), 874–880.

RODSTEIN, M. Accidents among the aged: Incidence, causes and prevention. *Journal of Chronic Diseases,* 1964, *17,* 515–526.

ROLLINS, B. C., AND FELDMAN, H. Marital satisfaction over the family life cycle. *Journal of Marriage and the Family,* 1970, *32,* 20–28.

ROSSI, A. The transition to parenthood. *Journal of Marriage and the Family,* 1968, *30,* 26–39.

RYTINA, N. F. Earnings of men and women: A look at specific occupations, *Monthly Labor Review,* U.S. Department of Labor. April 1982, *105,* pp. 25–31.

SCHAIE, K. W. A general model for the study of developmental problems. *Psychological Bulletin,* 1965, *64,* 92–107.

SCHAIE, K. W. Methodological problems in descriptive development research on adulthood and aging. In J. R. Nesselroade and H. W. Reese (Eds.), *Life-Span Developmental Psychology: Methodological Issues.* New York: Academic Press, 1973.

SCHAIE, K. W. AND LABOUVIE-VIEF, G. Generational and cohort-specific differences in adult cognitive functioning: A fourteen year study of independent samples. *Developmental Psychology,* 1974, *10,* 305–320.

SCHAIE, K. W. AND PARHAM, I. A. Cohort-sequential analyses of adult intellectual development. *Developmental Psychology,* 1977, *13,* 649–653.

SCHAIE, K. W., AND STROTHER, C. R. Cognitive and personality variables in college graduates of advanced age. In G. A. Talland (Ed.), *Human Aging and Behavior.* New York: Academic Press, 1968.

SCHEIN, E. The first-job dilemma. *Readings in Educational Psychology Today.* New York: Random House-CRM, 1970, 51–55.

SHAKESPEARE, W. *As You Like It.* Boston: Heath Publishing Co., 1896.

SHEEHY, G. *Passages: Predictable Crises of Adulthood.* New York: Dutton, 1976.

STARR, J. R., AND CARNS, D. E. Singles in the city. *Society,* February 1972, *9*(4), 43–49.

STEGNER, W. The writer and the concept of adulthood. *Daedalus,* 1976 *105*(4), 39–48.

SUSSMAN, M. B. The family today—is it an endangered species? *Children Today.* Washington, D.C.: March–April 1978, *45,* 32–37.

TAVRIS, C. Men and women report their views on masculinity. *Psychology Today,* January 1977, *10,* 34–43, 82.

TERKEL, LOUIS. *Working.* New York: Pantheon, 1974.

TIMIRAS, P. S. *Developmental Physiology and Aging.* New York: Macmillan, 1972.

TUDDENHAM, R. D., BLUMENKRANTZ, J., AND WILKIN, W. R. Age changes in AGCT: A longitudinal study of average adults. *Journal of Counseling and Clinical Psychology,* 1968, *32*(6), 659–663.

U.S. BUREAU OF THE CENSUS, DEPARTMENT OF COMMERCE. *Statistical Abstract of the United States: 1975.* Washington, D.C.: U.S. Government Printing Office, 1975.

U.S. BUREAU OF THE CENSUS. Marital status and living arrangements: March 1982. *Current Population Reports,* Population Characteristics, Series P-20, No. 380. Washington, D.C.: U.S. Government Printing Office, 1983.

U.S. BUREAU OF THE CENSUS. Fertility of American women. *Current Population Reports,* October 1979.

U.S. NATIONAL ASSESSMENT OF EDUCATIONAL PROGRESS. Department of Health, Education, and Welfare, 1976.

U.S. BUREAU OF THE CENSUS, SPECIAL DEMOGRAPHIC ANALYSES, CDS–80–8, *American Women: Three Decades of Change.* Washington, D.C.: U.S. Government Printing Office, 1983, p. 5.

U.S. DEPARTMENT OF HEALTH AND HUMAN SERVICES, PUBLIC HEALTH SERVICE, National Center for Health Statistics: Monthly Vital Statistics Report, Vol. 32, No 3, Supplement, Washington, D.C.: U.S. Government Printing Office, June 27, 1983.

U.S. DEPARTMENT OF HEALTH AND HUMAN SERVICES, PUBLIC HEALTH SERVICE. National Center for Health Statistics: *Vital Statistics of the United States,*1978, Vol 11, Part A. DHHS Pub. No. (PHS) 83–1101. Washington, D.C.: U.S. Government Printing Office, 1982.

U.S. NATIONAL CENTER FOR HEALTH STATISTICS, PUBLIC HEALTH SERVICE, DEPARTMENT OF HEALTH, EDUCATION AND WELFARE, *Reports of the National Center for Health Statistics, Vital and Health Statistics.* Data from the National Health Survey, United States, July 1962–June 1963. No. 1000, Series 10, No. 1, 5, 9, 1963.

VEEVERS, J. E. Voluntary childlessness: A neglected area of family study. *The Family Coordinator,* 1973, *22,* 199–205.

VEROFF, J., AND FELD, S. C. *Marriage and Work in America: A Study of Motives and Roles.* New York: Van Nostrand, 1970.

WECHSLER, D. *The measurement of Appraisal of Adult Intelligence* (3rd ed.). Baltimore: Williams & Wilkins, 1958.

WHITE, S. *Lives in Progress: A Study of the Natural Growth of Personality* (2nd ed.). New York: Holt, 1966.

YORBURG, B. *Sexual Identity: Sex Roles and Social Change.* New York: Wiley, 1974.

WELFORD, A. T. Motor performance. In J. E. Birren and K. W. Schaie (Eds.), *Handbook of the Psychology of Aging.* New York: Van Nostrand Reinhold, 1977.

Suggested Readings

BIGNER, J. *Parent–Child Relations.* New York: Macmillan, 1979. A readable book on the course and nature of parent-child interaction through the child-rearing years of the family life cycle.

KIMMEL, D. *Adulthood and Aging* (2nd edition). New York: Wiley, 1980. An excellent book with a good discussion of all phases of adulthood.

KENISTON, K. *All Our Children.* New York: Harcourt, Brace Jovanovich, 1977. An excellent discussion of contemporary family life and the strains on the family.

LEVINSON, D. *Seasons in a Man's Life.* New York: Random House, 1978. A well written and very readable discussion of maturity.

SHEEHY, G. *Passages: Predictable Crises of Adult Life.* New York: E. P. Dutton, 1976. Part 3 of this book presents a readable and enjoyable account of young adulthood.

TROLL, L. E. *Early and Middle Adulthood.* Monterey, California: Brooks/Cole, 1975. A comprehensive introduction to early and middle adult development.

11

Middle Adulthood: The Prime of Life or the Beginning of the End?

Perhaps, the wisest thing of all said on the subject [of middle adulthood] was not a definition, jocular or grave, but a reminder and admonition [that] man comes as a novice to each age of life! This was what Dante meant centuries earlier when he began his **Divine Comedy** *with his famous lines: "In the middle of life's journey, I found myself lost in a deep forest." Middle age . . . no less than infancy, childhood, young adulthood, and old age, is a separate and special bracket of the total life experience and one which each of us comes to as a novice despite our education or sophistication; a novice in coping with changing conditions, changing feelings about ourselves with changing expectations, and changing abilities and responsibilities.*

From Sydney J. Harris, 1983

In this chapter, we focus on the individual who has reached the peak of development: the middle-aged adult. Physically the middle-aged adult is in fairly good health. However, the beginning signs of physical aging begin to emerge. For example, the individual may gain weight, particularly in the stomach and hips, hair may become gray or thinner, and the eyes may look less bright than in early adulthood. The individual may ask, "Is this the beginning of the end?" On the other hand, the individual has accumulated a broad range of social, personal, and work skills. For this reason, middle age has sometimes been viewed as the "prime of life." The primary concern of the middle-aged person could be viewed as that of the proverbial man who wondered aloud if his glass was half empty or half full.

Who Are Middle-Aged Adults?

When does middle age begin? This is a difficult question to answer, primarily because middle adulthood is not marked by any specific biological changes or any rites of passage. For our purposes, middle age is that period of life from approximately thirty-five years of age (when many individuals begin to reach peak levels of social, personal, and economic performance) to approximately sixty-five years of age (when many individuals retire from their occupations). Admittedly these are somewhat arbitrary boundaries for middle age. In the first place, chronological age is not a good indicator of a life period that is characterized more accurately by a "social clock" that begins with a peak period and ends not with decline and disintegration but with the onset of a new social period usually marked by retirement. Another obvious reason for the arbitrariness of the age range thirty-five to sixty-five is the variability of individuals as well as of their social clocks. Some twenty-seven-year-olds have most of the signs of middle age, including gray hair, as well as indications of social and career success marked by questioning of future directions. Some forty-seven-year-olds have the physical conditioning and apparent vigor of a twenty-five-year-old coupled with the enthusiasm of a teenager. Whereas one forty-five-year-old may fit the standard depiction of a middle-aged adult who is secure and settled—a mature and experienced individual—another forty-five-year-old may be insecure and undergoing an identity crisis reminiscent of adolescence.

INTERLUDE: SOME VIEWS ON BEING MIDDLE-AGED

In our youth-oriented society, childhood gets a lot of loving attention, old age is viewed with terror—and middle age is simply ignored. There isn't even an ac-

Who are middle-aged adults?

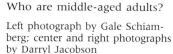

Left photograph by Gale Schiamberg; center and right photographs by Darryl Jacobson

cepted specific noun for a person in this last age group: "middle-ager," the only one listed in the unabridged Webster's, is a word you seldom hear used in ordinary conversation. . . . The truth is, once we've achieved that ill-defined state of being "grown up" we are not forever after through with growing and changing. Life is not the same at forty-five as at twenty-five; nor are we the same kind of people. (Fried, 1976, pp. 1–2)

Forty is a noticeably restless, introspective . . . moody . . . and melancholy person. Thirty is sunny, cheerful, hard working and obedient to the demands of daily routines. . . . When asked to describe his life, Forty will reply vaguely that it is "awful," "boring," "dull," or "depressing," without being able to say exactly why. Thirty is satisfied with familiar surroundings and content to play with his own toys. . . . It is not too much to say that Forty manages to make life miserable for those who must live with him, possibly because he seems unable to live with himself. (Fried, 1976, pp. 11–12)

My God, I realized that my life was half over. Death was always something that happened to the other guy—the old guy. But now I was becoming that older person. It bothered me. So I started taking stock of what I had done, and what was left for me to do. (A middle-aged man)

I always wanted to play the violin. When I went to college, girls who took music seriously were peculiar. Suddenly, it was as if some voice inside me said, now is the time, you'll never get another chance. I felt embarrassed, practicing at forty. It exhausts me and hurts my shoulder, but it makes me feel at one with something larger than myself. The universe suddenly becomes real and you're part of it. You feel as if you really exist. (A middle-aged woman, as quoted in Friedan, 1963)

Is it not possible that middle age can be looked upon as a second flowering? . . . The signs that presage growth, so similar, it seems to me, to those in early adolescence: discontent, restlessness, doubt, despair, longing, are interpreted falsely . . . as signs of approaching death. Instead of facing them, one runs away. . . . Anything, rather than stand still and learn from them. One tries to cure the signs of growth, to exorcise them, as if they were devils, when really they might be angels of annunciation. (Lindbergh, 1955)

The Middle Adulthood System: An Overview

As in early adulthood, the middle-aged adult has two primary responsibilities: to organize the external world, or the contexts of development, and to organize the internal world of the self (see Figure 11.1).

ORGANIZING THE EXTERNAL WORLD

The Family. In the family, middle-aged adults may feel pressures involving the psychological and financial support of children who are now adolescents and young adults. In addition, the middle-aged adult's own parents may be aging adults who also require support. In some instances, middle-aged adults may feel guilty about not being able to provide sufficiently (or what they perceive to be sufficiently) for their own parents. Middle age may be marked by the reevaluation of marriage as the children leave the home to establish their own lives and families. The "empty nest" may be the basis for redeveloping the marital interests of the preparental years, or in some cases, it may leave the husband and wife with nothing to occupy their joint energies and time.

The Community. Typical forms of community participation include involvement in religious activities, outdoor and indoor recreation, informal activities with family and friends, and voluntary clubs or organizations. There is a large variation in the types of community activities in which middle-aged adults may become involved. A vital dimension of such community participation is the quality of the *support network* of friends and other relationships which the middle-aged adult has developed.

FIGURE 11.1   The system of middle adulthood.

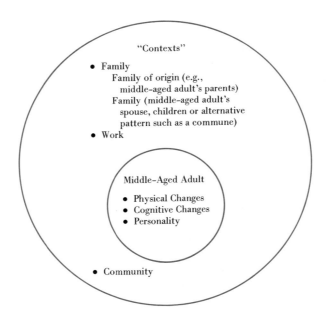

Work. Career development reaches its height during middle age. The individual has usually attained a high level of skill. In many occupations, it is the middle-aged adults who move into positions of leadership or prominence in their work. Middle-aged persons may be coming to grips with their actual career or life activities in relation to their adolescent or young adult aspirations. Career goals that were fashioned at an earlier time of life may now seem unrealistic or even impossible. Winning the Nobel prize, becoming corporation president by the age of forty, or becoming a fabulously wealthy entrepreneur may now seem to be aspirations that need to be reevaluated.

It is important to note that not all careers in middle adulthood follow a linear pattern from occupational entry in young adulthood, to possible attainment of occupational heights in middle adulthood, to retirement in later adulthood. Due to changes in the structure of western economies (e.g., movement from labor-intensive industries to technology-intensive industries utilizing computers), occupational careers for both men and women may involve holding several different types of jobs during a lifetime. Such transitions would likely involve temporary unemployment followed by retraining and re-entry into the labor market. In addition, the increasing participation of women in the work force has also created unique career patterns for women, which combine multiple roles of worker, mother, and housewife.

ORGANIZING THE INTERNAL WORLD

Physical Changes. While development and experience point toward a high point in the life cycle, there is nonetheless the uneasy recognition that the "beginning of the end" may be at hand. Wrinkled skin, extra body weight, graying hair, and a perceived decline in sexual vigor (particularly among men) are some of the physical changes that signal the onset of physical decline. There are also changes in sensory perception, such as gradual declines in vision and hearing. Changes in the appearance of the body are often accompanied by changes in the functioning of internal organs. For example, arteriosclerosis (a clogging of the walls of the arteries) may cause circulatory difficulties. High blood pressure may lead to heart problems.

A common adjustment that many middle-aged men and women make is to changes in sexual capacity. Women experience the *menopause,* or "change of life." At that time, menstrual periods cease and women are no longer able to bear children. Men may experience a *climacteric,* which comes later than the female menopause. The male climacteric is a somewhat vague concept because the reproductive functioning of men does not diminish as markedly as it does for females. Usually there is a slight decline in testicular functioning; however, males can remain sexually fertile into old age. For both sexes, achieving orgasm may take longer and it may be less intense than in earlier years. For men and women sexual activity changes but it does not stop.

Intellectual and Cognitive Activity. As we indicated in the previous chapter, mental skills remain fairly stable through young adulthood and middle age. Evidence for this sustained cognitive functioning includes the numerous cultural, community, and educational activities that middle-aged adults perform at a high level.

Personality Development. Personality development in middle age is marked by several themes:

Middle age as a transition Adolescence represents a transition from childhood to adulthood. So, too, can middle age be thought of as a transition from young adulthood to the stability and retrenchment of the older years. As in adolescence, the social and behavioral changes to come may be marked by biological events. Just as the onset of puberty heralded the coming of changes in adolescence, so, too, the female menopause or the male climacteric may signal the gradual decline of physical skills and the approach of other changes (e.g., retirement, children leaving the home, a sense of lost youth).

Middle age as a time of achievement Middle age is a time when individuals reach the peak of success and achievement (Erikson, 1967). People usually reach the pinnacle of their careers at this time. They have attained a high level of work skill and may be of great value to their companies or organizations. If they are self-employed (e.g., as a physician or a small business owner), they may have achieved their highest level of success by middle age. Middle-aged women who return to the work force or continue their education may also be demonstrating a need to achieve.

Middle age as a time for reevaluation Although the reevaluation of one's life might, to some extent, be a characteristic of many life stages, reevaluation during middle age has a special quality because middle-aged people may be more aware of how the decisions and events of the past have fashioned the direction of the future. Whereas the adolescent may be faced with a large number of *potential* careers or lifestyles, the middle-aged adult may be faced with more limited choices. They may ask such questions as "Shall I continue in the same direction?" "What is the meaning of my life?" "Where am I going?" Some writers have labeled this period of questioning a "mid-life crisis" (Sheehy, 1976). We prefer not to view this period as a "crisis," with all the connotations of an emergency and the attendant emotions of fear and anxiety. Rather, the questioning of the life process associated with middle age might be better seen as a normal, natural, and even inevitable result of growth and development. (see Application Box: Is There A Midlife Crisis?, p. 527)

INTERLUDE: AUTHOR JAMES BALDWIN ON MIDDLE AGE

Though we would like to live without regrets and sometimes proudly insist that we have none, this is not really possible, if only because we are mortal. When more time stretches behind than stretches before one, some assessments, however reluctantly and incompletely, begin to be made. Between what one wishes to become and what one has become there is a momentous gap. . . . Some of us are compelled, around the middle of our lives, to make a study of this baffling geography.

James Baldwin.

Middle Adulthood: The Prime of Life or the Beginning of the End?

Is There a Midlife Crisis?

Dr. Robert N. Butler, noted gerontologist, psychiatrist, and author, was the first director of the National Institute on Aging—a component of the federal government's National Institutes of Health at Bethesda, Maryland. His book *Why Survive? Being Old in America* won a Pulitzer Prize. . . .

In this interview, Dr. Butler (who is in his 50s) discusses coping with the problems of late middle life with Washington (D.C.) independent writer Natalie Davis Spingarn. . . .

Spingarn: Dr. Butler, we're talking here about problems that occur during the years 50 to 65. Are there signs that point to what some have called "the midlife crisis"?

Butler: The "crisis," in Schopenhauer's terms, is that moment in time when you begin to count backward from death rather than forward from birth. That's the first sign. The second is a tendency to take inventory of where you are; the third, having taken stock, to make certain decisions. These decisions can range all the way from . . . [to] breaking up a marriage, or to renewing a relationship which already exists—even to midlife career changes, which are intriguing.

Spingarn: Are there other signs?

Butler: Middle age is also a time when people's oral dependencies seem to get greater. They get carried away by eating, smoking, drinking. It becomes very difficult for them to control their waistlines. . . . At the same time, there's an increasing amount of "body monitoring"—you are more attentive to your body. . . .

Spingarn: So, for most people, just *being* middle-aged is a problem?

Butler: No, I'm glad you asked that question. Middle age has some joyful aspects; it can be a marvelous period. You reach the prime of your fulfillment, in the sense that you finally really know where you are. You hold positions of influence and power. (If you don't hold such positions then, it's likely you never will—unless, like Colonel Sanders, you can parlay a social security check into a chicken empire.) Problems emerge as you see your opportunities being eaten up by time—as you question whether you have achieved what you hoped to achieve.

Spingarn: Is there any one quality you can identify that makes some people more able to deal with the problems of middle age than others?

Butler: Generally, I would say that people who are reasonably open and flexible are maybe the most fortunate. . . .

Spingarn: What suggestions do you have for us then?

Butler: It helps to maintain three broad types of fitness—social, personal, and physical fitness, not necessarily in that order.

By *social fitness,* I mean keeping, developing, and working on your relationships—and not just assuming they will happen. This is very much a part of successful, effective middle years. It may not necessarily result in a Perle Mesta, parties-every-night kind of sociability, but in a quiet life. The cues between friends of long standing are often so simple and clear that they hardly need to say certain things to communicate effectively. This kind of simplification—including the capacity to stay silent and say nothing at all for a period of time without feeling embarrassed or troubled—is very delicious, very pleasant.

By *personal fitness,* I mean using your head—reading, thinking. Or, if you are not "intellectual," developing yourself in terms of making things, doing things. This can go all the way from taking courses to being a very good observer—a bird watcher, for example.

And I think we have certainly underestimated *physical fitness* in our culture. We're so "busy" watching football, or driving a car, that we think we are exercising. Yet it's quite clear that a significant amount of what we call "aging" is physical deterioration.

If you keep physically active, your muscles remain firmer, stronger, and more solid. And eating decently—good nutrition—is another important part of physical fitness. . . .

The Contexts of the Middle Adulthood System

In this section, we examine the significant contexts of middle adulthood: the family, the community, and the work setting. Each of these contexts provides an opportunity for the middle-aged adult to organize her/his experiences.

THE FAMILY

In Chapter Ten, on young adulthood, we traced the development of the family life-cycle through its early phases, including the premarital period, the marriage, the birth of the first child, and the family with preschool children (see Figure 10.6). We examined the role changes and transitions inherent in each of those phases. In this section, we discuss the phases of the family life-cycle that typically coincide with the years of middle adulthood: the family with school-aged children, the family with adolescents, the family as launching center, and the postparental family (see Figure 10.6).

The time during which a married couple raises children is one of the busiest phases of the family life-cycle. In addition, the financial cost of raising children is a sizable sum. The earning capability of the head of an average household does not reach a peak until he or she is between forty-five and fifty-five years of age (see Figure 11.2). This is helpful, of course, if there are still children in college. However, it does not provide much consolation for the married couple who are raising children during the expensive years of elementary and high school.

The arrival of children in a family usually puts pressure on the family finances. In addition, young children create a busied family situation that tends to reduce the intimacy and communication of the average couple; when children compete for the attention of their parents, the parents are likely to have less time for each other. Couples with children have been found to talk to one another about half as often as couples without children (Duvall, 1971). When conversation does occur, it frequently revolves around the children. Frequency of sexual intercourse is reduced after the birth of children (Pineo, 1961). All of these factors taken together represent normal "stresses" that are

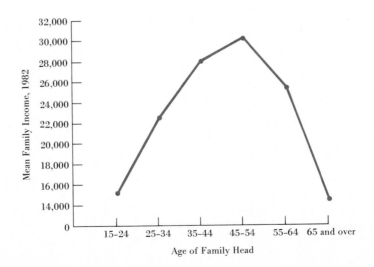

FIGURE 11.2 Earnings normally reach their peak in middle age.

The $147,000 Child—and Counting: The Financial Cost of Raising a Child

Parenthood requires not only a high level of emotional maturity and ability to manage a household but a high level of financial awareness and unselfishness. According to one analysis, a two-parent family with an income of approximately $29,500 can expect to expend about $147,000 (in 1982 dollars) to raise and educate (including four years at a private residential college) a child born in 1980 (Olson, 1983). Although this figure is not the same for all families, it is nonetheless useful in assessing the average costs of raising a child. It is important for parents and anyone who is considering marriage and child rearing to be aware of the realistic costs of child rearing, as well as of the progression of such expenses by child age.

The figure of $147,000 is somewhat more meaningful with the following qualifications:

- Girls are approximately 10 percent more expensive to raise than boys.
- About one third of total cost for both boys and girls comes during the last four years. This primarily reflects the high costs during later adolescence of college expenses.
- The total cost of large families are, as expected, more than those of smaller families (one or two children).

- Each additional child costs less than the first child.

The costs of child rearing tend to increase generally with the age of the child. The costs of preschool children (including infants) are less than those for elementary school children, which are, in turn, less than those for a high school student. There is one major exception to younger children being less expensive than older ones. Because of initial one-time expenses of pregnancy, birth, and early medical bills, early infancy is more expensive than the toddler or preschool years. However, once the child reaches first grade, he or she will probably continue to make friends and join outside activities, which continue to increase child-rearing expenses throughout childhood and adolescence.

The costs of child rearing are typically broken down into the following categories: housing, food, clothing, transportation, health care, and "other" or miscellaneous items (largely costs of recreation) (Olson, 1983; Family Economics Research Group, 1983). For Olson (1983), food and housing constitute the bulk of child rearing expenses at approximately 59%, transportation at approximately 12%, medical care at 8%, clothing at 4%, and other (including education at a private, four-year residential college) at 17%.

placed on a marital relationship with the arrival of children. A married couple who are aware of these strains and are "understanding" of one another and tolerant about the needs of children are likely to fare reasonably well.

The Family with School-Aged Children. The phase of the family lifecycle between the child's first day at school and the onset of adolescence creates a whole new set of experiences for the parents and the child. During this phase, children move out into new areas of life in the school, in peer relationships, and in the neighborhood (see Chapter Eight). Children may seek out new things to do, such as joining clubs and participating in other recreational activities. Parents tend to be cautious about the safety of their

"Could I leave this here 'til my folks figure out where they're gonna get the money to buy a new car?"

DENNIS THE MENACE ® used by permission courtesy of Hank Ketcham and © by Field Enterprises Inc.

children in playing outdoor games, crossing streets, or fighting with peers. The parents of school-aged children may become involved in planning activities that take place in the school, such as Thanksgiving programs or school carnivals, and they tend to take on larger, more time-consuming projects than the parents of preschool children. As a result of their experiences with the schools, these parents may begin to develop a philosophy and an attitude toward education.

TABLE 11.1

Marital Satisfaction by Present Stage of the Family Cycle

Stage of Family	Husband's Degree Satisfied (Percentage)			Wife's Degree Satisfied (Percentage)			Each Sample
	Very	*Quite*	*Less*	*Very*	*Quite*	*Less*	*(N)*
Establishment	55	39	6	74	22	4	51
New parents	69	23	8	76	18	6	51
Preschool children	61	31	8	50	33	17	82
School-aged children	39	45	16	35	44	21	244
Adolescent children	44	41	15	17	68	15	227
Launching center	9	25	65	8	16	76	64
Postparental	24	13	63	17	13	70	30
Aging family	66	30	4	82	14	4	50
Total of all stages	44	37	19	45	33	22	799

Source: Adapted from B. C. Rollins and H. Feldman, "Marital Satisfaction over the Family Life Cycle," *Journal of Marriage and the Family,* February 1970, *32*(1). Copyrighted 1970 by the National Council on Family Relations, 1219 University Avenue Southeast, Minneapolis, Minnesota 55414. Reprinted by permission.

The Family with Adolescent Offspring. The adolescent period may be a particularly difficult one for both adolescents and their parents (see Table 11.1). During this period, adolescents have a good deal of freedom and may spend most of the day away from home and away from the supervision of adults. It is during this period that many of the principles of moral behavior that parents have emphasized as important throughout childhood may be tested by the adolescent. During this phase of the family cycle, parents may be called on to balance their attempts to give the adolescent the freedom to make his or her own decisions with their attempts to provide appropriate limits and emotional support for the adolescent. Some of the issues that often occur in this period include career choices for the adolescent, the selection of a college, sexuality and dating, and the use of alcohol or drugs. Parents may sometimes feel that their adolescents resent their help.

The adjustment of each adolescent to her/his own emerging sense of adulthood is unique. The adolescent on the verge of this transition often presents a special challenge to parents. The attempts of adolescents to attain a sense of identity may lead them to be assertive with their parents. This assertiveness, in turn, may contribute to increased intergenerational strife.

The general pattern of adolescent—parent relationships involves an increase in intergenerational conflict from the early to the later teens, with reduced conflict during young adulthood. During the period of adolescence, parents begin to accept—or rather, learn to accept—the growing independence of their adolescent offspring.

For many couples in this phase of the family life-cycle, marriage no longer occupies the central position that it did earlier. Husbands may be heavily involved in occupational and community activities. Wives may be dissatisfied because they are "taken for granted" by both their husbands and their adolescent offspring. Communication between the parents of adolescents appears to occur even less frequently than between parents of younger children. A considerable amount of intellectual and emotional energy is apparently required to manage family affairs. Sometimes little energy is left for the husband—wife relationship. One study showed that almost 98 percent of wives reported having very little interaction with their husbands after a "trying" day (Duvall, 1971). Some of these difficulties are evidenced by the increasing divorce rate

Families with school-aged children.

Photograph by Sara Chandler

Families with adolescent offspring.

Photograph by Sylvia Byers

between the ages of forty-one and forty-five (Carter and Glick, 1970). There appear to be two peak periods for divorce during the family life-cycle, one in the early years of marriage (see Chapter Ten) and the second during middle adulthood (at forty-one to forty-five years of age).

The Family As Launching Center. The launching-center phase of the family life cycle involves the departure of the children from the family into separate living arrangements or into families of their own. When the children are no longer at home, the parents can no longer interact on the basis of the parental role. This stage, therefore, involves the redefinition of the parents' roles in relation to their children. The parents are involved in "letting go of" their children and adjusting to the independence of their children. The period of launching appears to involve some conflict and upset for parents, particularly for the mother if her center of interest and time involvement has been primarily the family. This conflict may be the case not simply because of the shift in the mother's role but also because the menopause may be occurring at this time. Furthermore, the husband may be in the midst of his career, highly involved in his work, and somewhat removed from the scene. On the other hand, the husband may be coming to grips with the "realities" of his occupational and life situation and therefore, might be somewhat preoccupied with his own concerns. The interaction of these factors may well make this a particularly difficult time for parents (see Table 11.1). In fact, the role shifts and life concerns of the parents coupled with the typical life choices in adolescence may result in a co-occurence of "identity" crises. Such a situation may not facilitate honest and open communication between generations.

The Postparental Family or the "Empty Nest." The postparental phase or the "empty nest" spans the time from the launching of the children to retirement. On the average, this is approximately a fifteen-year period of

In marriage, communication skills may not come naturally.

time until the male retires at about age sixty-five. For some couples, the empty-nest phase is a welcome period in which marital satisfaction begins to increase, particularly in comparison with the launching phase. The departure of the children may allow the couple to regain some of the intimacy that they had in the early years of marriage.

> We seem to get along better than when the kids were with us. I mean we always got along pretty well but now it's better. We're by ourselves now and that sure makes a difference. I seem to really appreciate being with him now. I think that we can be more ourselves now without worrying so much about the kids. (A postparental wife)

> You know, this is going to be the first year when all the kids are gone. To tell you the truth, I don't know if the two of us can stand being together in the same house for all that time. (A concerned postparental husband)

Relieved of some financial responsibility for their children, many couples can enjoy some of the luxuries that were not possible during the financially tighter years of marriage. As we have pointed out, income may now be at a peak, enabling the married couple to do such things as travel or buy things that they have always wanted.

Although many couples adapt quite well to the changes of the postparental phases, others may find it a more difficult period. Although raising children may have been a demanding responsibility, some parents find it difficult to adjust to a childless state. This adjustment may be particularly hard for women who have defined themselves primarily as mothers (Bart, 1970). For such women, the empty nest may produce depression or a loss of meaning in life. It is likely that this adverse reaction to the empty nest may lessen somewhat as women move away from the strictly traditional definitions of identity (Troll, 1971).

The empty-nest phase may be hard on some husbands—however, for different reasons than for some wives. Coinciding with the peak of the male adult's career, this phase causes some individuals depression over the realization that they have gone as far as they can in their work. If his income and job status have reached a peak, the man may become depressed because the ultimate direction is downhill.

By the time middle-aged adults have reached the postparental phase of the family life-cycle, two new major events are likely to have occurred:

1. *Providing care for aging parents.* At some point during middle adulthood, the couple are faced with providing some type of care for their aging parents. The middle-aged couple also begin to assume a role as a "middle" generation, trying to meet the needs of both aging parents and their own young-adult offspring. (see Application Box: Middle-Aged Adults and Their Parents: Guilt or a New Mutuality, p. 534)

2. *Becoming grandparents.* This change involves a shift in roles as the middle-aged couple become more aware of their own increasing age. The majority of new grandparents are satisfied with this role change (see Table 11.2). Neugarten and Weinstein (1964) found that the meaning of the grandparenting role varied considerably:

Middle-Aged Adults and Their Parents: Guilt or a New Mutuality?

The following discussion provides two opposing perspectives on the relationship of middle-aged adults and their aging parents:

For the adult child [the middle-aged adult], the most dominant and pervasive issue regarding intergenerational relationships is the subject of guilt. The expression of guilt feelings was pervasive not only during interviews with adult children, but also with aging parents, practitioners, and researchers who were professionally involved in family relationships. The middle generation in particular expressed difficulty in coping with and resolving feelings of guilt in conjunction with feelings of responsibility. Often, the adult daughter or son felt responsible for the general well-being of parents and frequently could not improve their parents' general satisfaction with life. These feelings were frequently expressed in relation to nursing home admissions. The middle generation frequently responded to the loneliness, lack of income and mobility, depression, and dissatisfactions of an aging parent with feelings of guilt, helplessness, and resentment. (Hirschfield and Dennis, 1979, p. 3)

ON THE OTHER HAND . . .

It is easy for the middle generation to be trapped into believing that their relationships with aging parents run in one direction, particularly as the older person becomes more dependent. The stereotype "role reversal" typifies this belief. This model of parent–child relationships in the later years suggests that the adult child becomes parent to his own parents and that the burden of care falls only on the middle generation. . . . [This model reflects] the dynamics of the neurotic or immature chronologically aging parent–child pair, but as a model of normal behavior it is inappropriate and perhaps destructive.

It is, first of all, demeaning to old persons to suggest that they inevitably return to a state of childishness; rather it is the adult child who takes on the filial role, which involves being depended on and dependable insofar as his parent is concerned, but does not involve becoming a parent to his parent. . . . A mutuality develops between the older generation . . . [and the adult-child] . . . which did not occur earlier when the

Photograph by Darryl Jacobson

adult child was really a child and the aged parent was really fulfilling the role of parent. The concept of role reversal can also be very frightening to the middle generation, who may see themselves as being psychologically and practically overburdened and guilty if they accept this burden. . . . We [suggest] that we should turn our backs on outmoded and negative concepts such as guilt and role reversal as characterizing the fate of the middle-aged and aged. We should look toward different roles for both generations which rest firmly on the concepts of mutuality and shared responsibility. (Silverstone, 1979, pp. 114–115)

TABLE 11.2
Ease of Role Performance, Significance of Role, and Style of Grandparenting

	Grandmothers (N = 70) N	Grandfathers (N = 70) N
A. Ease of role performance:		
(1) comfortable—pleasant	41	43
(2) difficulty—discomfort	25	20
(insufficient data)	4	7
Total	70	70
B. Significance of the grandparent role:		
(1) biological renewal and/or continuity	29	16
(2) emotional self-fulfillment	13	19
(3) resource person to child	3	8
(4) vicarious achievement through child	3	3
(5) remote: little effect on the self	19	20
(insufficient data)	3	4
Total	70	70
C. Style of grandparenting:		
(1) the formal	22	23
(2) the fun-seeking	20	17
(3) the parent surrogate	10	0
(4) the reservoir of family wisdom	1	4
(5) the distant figure	13	20
(insufficient data)	4	6
Total	70	70

Top photograph by Bruce Hecht; bottom photograph by Brenda Golbus

Source: Reprinted from B. L. Neugarten and K. K. Weinstein, "The Changing American Grandparent," *Journal of Marriage and the Family,* May 1964, 26(2). Copyrighted 1964 by the National Council on Family Relations, 1219 University Avenue Southeast, Minneapolis, Minnesota 55414. Reprinted by permission.

Some felt it produced a sense of *biological renewal*—"Its through my grandchildren that I feel young again." Some felt a sense of *biological continuity*—"It's carrying on the family line." And some felt *emotional fulfillment*—"I can do for my grandchildren things I could never do for my own kids. I was too busy with my business to enjoy my kids, but my grandchildren are different. Now I have the time to be with them." (p. 200)

Grandparents usually relate to their grandchildren in one of five ways:

(1) *Fun-seeking.* [Many] grandparents prefer a "pleasure without responsibility" relationship with their grandchildren. It allows them to have fun with their grandchildren and avoid resistance to their advice as old-fashioned and unwanted interference. Instead, they emphasize playful informality and restrain their impulses to give advice. This fun-seeking relationship is especially widespread for grandparents under the age of sixty-five.

(2) *Formal.* Grandparents who have little significant interaction with grandchildren except special treats for special occasions have a similar but more restrained relationship than the fun-seeking grandparents.

(3) *Parent substitute.* Grandmothers and sometimes grandfathers may assume responsibility for the care of grandchildren because of the absence of a parent due to death, divorce or the necessity of working.

(4) *Family wisdom.* Grandfathers and sometimes grandmothers may develop a relationship that emphasizes the provision of special knowledge, skills, or resources to grandchildren.

Photograph top left courtesy of Louis and Miriam Schiamberg; photograph top right by Robert Spirtas; photographs at bottom by Darryl Jacobson

(5) *Distant figure.* Especially when there is substantial geographic or social distance some grandparents appear infrequently from afar for brief contact on special occasions with their grandchildren. (Knox, 1977, p. 112, based on Neugarten and Weinstein, 1964).

INTERLUDE: A DEFINITION OF A "GRANDMA"

The following perspective on grandparents was written by an elementary school child in response to a school assignment.

What is a grandma?

A grandma is a lady who has no children of her own, so she likes other people's little boys and girls.

A grandfather is a man grandmother. He goes for walks with the boys and they talk about fishing and things like that.

Grandmas don't have to do anything except be there. They're so old they shouldn't play hard. It is enough if they drive us to the supermarket where the pretend horse is and have lots of dimes ready.

Or if they take us for walks, they should slow down past things like pretty leaves or caterpillars. And they should never say, "Hurry up!"

Usually they are fat, but not too fat. They wear glasses and funny underwear. They can take their teeth and gums off.

They don't have to be smart, only answer questions like why dogs hate cats, and how come God isn't married.

536

They don't talk baby talk like visitors do because it is hard to understand. When they read to us they don't skip words and they don't mind if it is the same story.

Grandmas are the only grownups who have got time—so everybody should have a grandmother especially if you don't have television.

THE COMMUNITY

An important arena for the demonstration of adult competence is community activities. As in the case of career development, the middle-aged adult is usually at the peak of participation and influence in community activities. There is, of course, considerable variation in the kinds of activities that adults become involved in as well as the degree of involvement. Community activities may include organizations and clubs (e.g., Lions, Rotary, Elks), religious activities, indoor and outdoor recreation, political organizations, volunteer groups, and informal activities with family and friends.

Patterns of Activity. There is a relationship between socioeconomic status (in particular, level of education) and community participation. For example, white-collar adults tend to be more active in the community and to be engaged in more complex activities than blue-collar adults (Scott, 1957; Wright and Hymen, 1958). Throughout the adult years, white-collar workers tend to engage in more family-centered entertaining and occupationally related social participation than blue-collar adults (Knox, 1977).

Friendship. Friends are made in all the contexts of adulthood, including work, the family, and the community. In earlier times, one's friends were found in the extended family and among the neighbors in relatively stable communities. With the increasing mobility and "rootlessness" of modern life, it has been suggested that America is a "nation of strangers." Friendships have traditionally served the vital function of helping people to adapt to life situations through the sharing of mutual needs, concerns, and problems. In a mobile society, where neighborhoods and communities continue to exist physically but the people change, the art of making friends is an important skill (Knox, 1977).

It has been suggested that one of the developmental tasks of middle age is making an "art" of friendship (Havighurst and Orr, 1956). There is some evidence that this art of making friendships matures during middle adulthood. From late adolescence to the end of middle adulthood, the perception of the qualities of friendships becomes more precise and accurate (Lowenthal, Thurnher, Chiriboga, Beeson, Glay, Pierce, Spencer, and Weiss, 1975). The characteristics of an adult's *actual* friends coincide with the adult's *ideal* of a friend. Prior to middle adulthood, there may be a discrepancy between the *ideal* and the *actual* characteristics of friends (Knox, 1977). It is likely that by middle adulthood, the individual is more selective in choosing friends who will fulfill his/her expectations.

According to Lowenthal et al. (1975), individuals from late adolescence through the end of middle adulthood considered reciprocity (helping and sharing) to be the most important characteristic of ideal friends. Similarity of experiences and ease of communication with friends were also considered important dimensions of friendship. Lowenthal and her colleagues also found sex differences in friendship patterns. Women seemed to be more deeply involved in interpersonal relationships than men. Women considered reciprocity in the form of sharing and helping to be the most important characteristic of friendship. Men considered similarity of experiences as the primary basis of choosing and keeping friends.

Furthermore, Lowenthal et al. (1975) found the most complex friendships among the late middle-aged group. People in early adulthood and early middle age were more involved with their families and with establishing occupational security than with friends. Presumably, after job security and family relationships are dealt with, the middle-aged adult can develop complex friendships involving the appreciation of the unique, individual characteristics of others.

INTERLUDE: DIMENSIONS OF ADULT FRIENDSHIP

[Friendships] appear to be very important for most adults, especially during stressful periods. This type of sharing relationship entails trust and support. . . . Various dimensions . . . have been identified that describe aspects of close friendship that are important to adults.

- The most widespread dimension is *similarity of experience,* which includes shared experiences, activities, interests and ease of communication.
- The second dimension is *reciprocity,* in which the relationship is characterized as supportive, dependable, accepting, trustworthy and confidential.
- A third dimension is *compatibility,* which includes likeability and enjoyment.
- A fourth dimension is *structural* and includes geographic closeness, duration and convenience.
- A fifth is the contributions that some friends make as role models because of the respect and admiration that they engender, . . . the mentor relationship that they perform, or the help that they provide. (Knox, 1977, p. 229)

An Ecological Support Network. As indicated throughout this book, in virtually every stage or phase of the human life cycle the community/neighborhood is a vital context of human development. Middle adulthood is, of course, no exception. In addition to the provision of material resources (e.g., community centers and direct opportunities for involvement), the community/neighborhood may provide social supports through interpersonal interaction with friends, neighbors, or others. This social support can exert a dramatic impact on both the psychological and physical well-being of the middle-aged adult. The social support derived from these informal social networks can occur in several ways:

- *Protecting individuals from the negative effects of life stress* (French, Rodgers, and Cobb, 1974; see Application Box: Stress and Health, p. 556). For example, the potentially harmful effects of stressful life events such as the death of a spouse or child, divorce, or work problems may be lessened through social support networks.
- *Positively contributing to general psychological health.* (Moos, 1976). Informal social networks may help individuals maintain a positive sense of self-esteem by reaffirming their positive personality characteristics and their ability to help others.

Middle Adulthood: The Prime of Life or the Beginning of the End?

- *Exerting a beneficial influence on the maintenance of physical health.* (Dohrenwend and Dohrenwend, 1974). Studies of social support and physical illness suggest that social support networks are *associated with* recovery and positively coping with serious illness or injury (Moos and Tsu, 1977).

CAREER DEVELOPMENT AND WORK

Freud was once asked what he thought a normal person should be able to do well. The questioner expected a complicated, "deep" answer. But Freud simply said, "Lieben und arbeiten" ("to love and to work") (Erikson, 1968a, p. 136). As Freud indicated—and as we have pointed out throughout this book—work is one of the most important aspects of human development (see Figure 11.3). "Loving," or family life, and "working" are not unrelated in middle age.

Occupation and the Family. The relationship between the family and the occupational world of adulthood can be viewed as a *system* of interacting factors. The characteristics of one sphere may enhance or detract from the other sphere (see Figure 11.4). A sense of satisfaction and accomplishment in the work setting can influence the quality of family life. Frustrating work

FIGURE 11.3 Middle-aged individuals at work.

Photographs by Gale Schiamberg. Left photograph courtesy of Oldsmobile, Lansing, Michigan

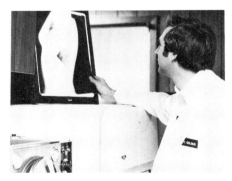

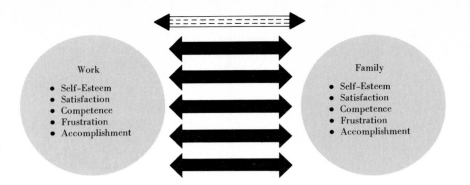

FIGURE 11.4 Work and family as a *system* of interacting factors.

environments can result in a greater need for a stable and nurturing family, an increased importance for family life and leisure-time activity, or additional tension felt by all family members as the individual transfers work frustrations to the family. As we indicated in Chapter Three, the family can be viewed as a system in its own right that is composed of interactions between family members, and between family members and other social institutions (including the school and work). When such institutional relationships become unbalanced and the family is required to compensate for a lack of satisfaction in other areas, the family is likely to be overburdened.

On the other hand, an unsatisfying family situation may put pressure on the work setting as the major source of satisfaction. Occupational activities can provide an escape from the frustrations of family life. In other cases, a rising professional or executive may be called on to put in long hours, weekends, or evenings for advancement. One result, unfortunately, may be additional family tension.

Patterns of Career Development. In the previous chapter, we discussed the process of occupational choice and entry in young adulthood. Career development during the middle years usually involves one of two general directions (Knox, 1977):

- *The career "peak."* The individual is at the peak of an occupation that was chosen during later adolescence or young adulthood. The individual has attained a high level of skill, influence, and financial standing relative to the general social status of the job.
- *The "transitional" career.* The individual is on the verge of a new occupation. For some adults, this change in vocation may be the result of a mid-life questioning and reexamination of life goals. For other adults, changing careers may reflect changes in the demands for certain skills over the years. As a result of such social or technological changes, it is becoming increasingly common for individuals to have multiple careers over their life span.

When we examine occupational patterns, we become aware that there is an occupational cycle just as there is a family life-cycle; that is, there are "turning points" in the progression of a typical occupation. Kimmel (1974) identified the three major turning points:

Middle Adulthood: The Prime of Life or the Beginning of the End?

1. *Entry into the occupation.* This point marks the conclusion of a process of occupational choice and is also one of the milestones marking the beginning of adulthood. The individual, having learned and practiced many of the roles involved in his new job during the period of anticipatory socialization, now actually enters the job for the first time. He is confronted by the "real" demands of the job, the "real" expectations, and the "real" rewards. Probably, these factors will differ from what he expected; and he will experience some conflict between the idealism of his earlier expectations and the actuality of the job.
2. *The middle years of the occupation.* This turning point contains elements similar to the crisis at the entry point in that it involves readjusting one's goals and idealistic hopes to what, at this stage, is perceived as one's realistic future possibilities in light of how much time is left in the occupation. . . . This crisis differs from the earlier occupational crisis, however, because it involves what may be called the "career clock." This "clock" . . . is the individual's subjective sense of being "on time" or "behind time" in his career development. During the middle years (approximately 40 to 55), a person typically becomes aware of the number of years left before retirement and of the speed with which he is attaining his own goals. If he is markedly "behind time," or if his goals are unrealistic, he begins to adjust his goals to be more consistent with what is likely to actually be feasible; he may also decide to change jobs before it is too late. . . .
3. *Retirement.* . . . It is a crisis point, in this sense, whether it results from an inability to find a job or is the next and final step in the career progression. (pp. 251–253)

Occupational Changes. Until recently, the typical pattern of occupational development was thought to involve entrance into a particular career in early adulthood and retirement from that career in later adulthood. Planning for this career trajectory was presumably made during adolescence, with appropriate education and training in high school, college, or professional schools.

This pattern has changed with the realization that adult development may result, in some cases, in changed career goals. Furthermore, the increasing application of technological innovations may result in greater unemployment and the need to retrain for new occupational directions. Initial occupational choice in adolescence and young adulthood is now being viewed as the first step in the *lifelong process* of career development (Sarason, 1977). For example, Sarason (1977) found that approximately 40 percent of 2300 biographical entries in *Who's Who* had experienced some type of career shift.

The significant personality factors which appear to influence career shifts are (1) the need to feel in control of one's destiny, (2) the willingness to take risks, and (3) the desire to try out new roles (Heath, 1976). In addition, other research suggests two primary sources of pressure to shift careers—internal and external pressures (Murray, Powers, and Havighurst, 1971). Four possible occupational patterns are identified as a function of these internal (personality) factors and external (situational) factors:

- The *routine career* pattern involves advancement based primarily on seniority. This type of career is characterized by the following combination of internal and external factors: low self-direction and little outside pressure to change.
- The *flexible career* pattern involves initiative for change and development coming primarily from the person. This type of career involves the following combination of internal and external factors: high self-direction and little outside pressure to change.

The Lives of Working People

Mike the Steelworker: Mike is 37 years old and works in a steel mill. He is married and has two children.

"I'm a dying breed. A laborer. Strictly muscle work . . . pick it up, put it down, pick it up, put it down. We handle between forty and fifty thousand pounds of steel a day (*laughs*) . . . . It's dying.

"You can't take pride any more. You remember when a guy could point to a house he built, how many logs he stacked. He built it and he was proud of it. . . .

"It's hard to take pride in a bridge you're never gonna cross, in a door you're never gonna open. You're mass-producing things and you never see the end result of it. . . .

"If you can't improve yourself, you improve your posterity. Otherwise life is worth nothing. . . . I'm sure the first caveman who went over the hill to see what was on the other side—I don't think he went there wholly out of curiosity. He went there because he wanted to get his son out of the cave. Just the same way I want to send my kid to college."

John the Copy Chief: John is 36 years old and works as a copy chief at an advertising agency.

"I am what is called a creative supervisor. Creative is a pretentious word. I have a group of about six people who work for me. They create radio commercials, print ads, billboards that go up on highways, television commercials too. . . . It's an odd business. It's serious but it isn't (*laughs*). Life in an advertising agency is like being at a dull party, interrupted by more serious moments. . . .

"They're aware that they're talking about little bears capering around a cereal box and they're arguing which way the bears should go. It's a silly thing for adults to be doing. At the same time, they're aware the client is going to spend a million dollars on television time to run this commercial."

John the Mail Carrier: John is 48 years old and has been a mail carrier for 10 years.

"I'm doing a job that's my life ambition. When I was in school, you said in the yearbook what you're most likely to be. I did say mailman. . . . This is a profession that everyone has looked up to and respected. They always say, 'Here comes the mailman'—pony express or something. . . . Everyone likes to receive mail. . . .

"You find that most people in the post office have two jobs. I have had two most of the time. My wife, she's working. If she wasn't, I don't know how we'd make it. . . .

"My day starts at four o'clock. I hit the floor. At five thirty I'm at work. . . .

"Constantly you walk. . . . I wear out on the average about three or five pairs of shoes a year."

Kitty the Occupational Therapist: Kitty is an occupational therapist at a major medical center in the Midwest.

"I'm an occupational therapist. It's an emerging profession—like medicine was, maybe a hundred years ago. . . .

"For several months I worked with hemiplegics, elderly people who've had a stroke. Half their body is paralyzed. First thing in the morning I'd get to the old men's ward and I'd teach them dressing. They didn't think they could do anything, but they could dress themselves. If people can take care of themselves, they have more self-esteem. . . .

"Patients I've worked with helped each other much more than I helped them. If I get five old men together—hemiplegics—and do some crazy things like tie a red ribbon on their affected arm, it gets to be a game or joke. They look at what the other guy is doing. . . . They learn about survival from each other."

From Studs Terkel, *Working.* New York: Pantheon, 1974, pp. xxxi–xxxii, 73, 271, 494–495.

- The *disjointed career* pattern may involve technological reasons for unemployment (e.g., the blue collar worker displaced because of automation) or unemployment due to lack of skill or experience (e.g., the widow having a hard time entering the job market after the death of her spouse). This career pattern involves the following combination of internal and external pressures: low self-direction and much pressure to change.
- The *sequential, orderly career* pattern involves a well-planned effort in making occupational progress and change. This career pattern involves the following combination of internal and external pressures: high self-direction and much pressure to change.

This typology of internal and external pressures for career organization and change was further supported by a study comparing the occupational shifts of two groups of men thirty and forty years of age (Clopton, 1973). One group made a midlife career shift whereas the other group did not. The two groups were matched on background factors such as birth order and college degrees, and on other characteristics such as degree of success in their original occupation and present family responsibilities. Results indicated that both personality factors and adult life experiences differed between those who shifted careers and those who did not. Those who changed careers had higher levels of self-esteem and self-acceptance than those who stayed in the same occupation. Also, the "changers" had experienced more momentous life events, such as death of a family member, divorce, or a sudden job loss, than those who did not change occupations. The changers gave three major reasons for their move (Clopton, 1973):

- The gradual disenchantment with their past job.
- The discovery of a new career that seemed more desirable and potentially more satisfying (in some cases, this involved the pursuit of a previous avocation or hobby as a career).
- The reorganization of life goals as a result of significant life events and changes.

The Contexts of the Middle Adulthood System

Who Is Happier—The Full-time Homemaker or the Employed Woman?

Changing social and sex roles have led to questions about the relative contributions of work and family roles to the quality of women's lives. The traditional view that women find primary personal fulfillment as spouses and mothers has been seriously questioned in recent years.

THE DYSFUNCTIONAL HOUSEWIFE ROLE?

Some studies have suggested or implied that the traditional role of housewife may be dysfunctional for at least the following reasons:

- Some researchers view the traditional housewife role as inadequate or insufficiently challenging. This is seen as particularly true for the development of self-esteem (Rossi, 1980; Maas and Kuypers, 1974). Therefore, the frequently documented finding that women have lower mental health levels than men is often attributed to the assumed frustrations and inadequacies of the housewife role (Gove and Tudor, 1973).
- An emphasis on the role of spouse and mother may set up women for personal disorganization and stress when this traditional role is lost during the postparental phase of family life (Stroud, 1981).

In contrast to this rather dismal picture, women involved in the labor force are *assumed* to have higher levels of self-esteem and to be generally happier than full-time homemakers (Feree, 1976). In this regard, the situation of the college-educated woman is assumed to be the primary argument for the destructive role of housewife in the emotional health of women. It is frequently argued that highly educated women experience a dramatic discontinuity between their potential for skilled work and the role of housewife which is *assumed* to involve minimal skills (Stroud, 1981).

MULTIPLE ROLES AND STRESS

There is some evidence that the role of employment in women's self-development may result in role conflict (Stroud, 1981). Because many working women are also wives and mothers, there is the increased possibility of personal stress and strain due to the demands of both the housewife role and the occupational role. This stress and strain can take many forms, including guilt on the part of the woman, who feels that her job prevents her from being a better companion to her husband or a better mother to her children. On the other hand, a working woman might also feel particularly frustrated that she cannot devote herself more completely to occupational achievement because of the demands of her family roles. While such role conflicts are more probable for working women, they are *not* inevitable. For example, a number of studies suggest that working mothers make a special effort to compensate for their absence by planning activities for their children and by setting aside time to be with them (Jones, Lundsteen, and Michael, 1967; Rapoport and Rapoport, 1971; Bronfenbrenner and Crouter, 1982).

RESEARCH ON LIFE SATISFACTION

The majority of studies on the contributions of work and family roles to women's life satisfaction seem to suggest that involvement in such multiple roles neither increases nor reduces overall life satisfaction (Wright, 1978; Baruch and Barnett, 1980). In other words, there is little difference in life satisfaction between women who work and those who are full-time housewives. While this generalization may be true for most working women, it is less accurate for highly-educated women. Among this latter group, working women appear to be consistently more positive about their self-esteem and their lives in general than full-time housewives (Campbell, Converse and Rogers, 1976; Stroud, 1981).

The general finding of no difference in overall life satisfaction between working and nonworking women may be an artifact (artificial result) of the design of the studies themselves rather than an accurate description of the actual situation. For example, many studies use broadly based samples of working women and housewives. The *employed* woman could include the following: those with diverse motivation for, and commitment to, work; those from low-status jobs and those from high-status jobs; those who are highly educated and those with minimal education; those who have been employed continuously and those who have only recently reentered the work force (Stroud, 1981). Such distinctions have important ramifications for satisfaction with work and with family roles. For example, there is evidence that the marriages of women who worked by choice tend to be happier than the marriages of those who must work because of economic necessity (Orden and Bradburn, 1969).

SOME CONCLUDING THOUGHTS

Although no simple answer is available for the question raised in the title of this application box (Who Is Happier?), some guidelines may be appropriate:

- The *sources* of satisfaction and self-esteem for women vary considerably depending not only on whether they work but on their personal characteristics (e.g., education, commitment to achievement in a career, or commitment to achievement as a parent).

- The *assumption* that the role of housewife (spouse and mother) is of such low order needs to be further examined in light of both the importance of the child-rearing function and the *family as a system.*

- In light of the high divorce rate as well as the importance of human self-actualization (from both a personal and social perspective), continued support needs to be given to women's occupational competence at all phases of the life-span.

Women's Career Cycles. In the case of women there have been significant shifts in labor-force participation. Between 1947 and 1980, the number of women in the labor force increased by 173 percent (from 16.7 to 45.6 million) in comparison to a 43 percent increase for men (from 44.2 to 63.4 million) (U.S. Department of Labor, 1982). This increase has been most dramatic for white and hispanic women. It has been less marked for black women who have historically worked in greater numbers because of economic necessity.

Although labor-force participation has increased so significantly, women tend to be concentrated largely in certain types of jobs. In 1980, women were overrepresented (in comparison to their overall numbers in the labor force) in clerical and service occupations. For example, 98 percent of secretaries and 96 percent of nurses were women while only 1.8 percent of engineers were women (Henle and Ryscavage, 1980). In addition, there is a significant gap in earnings between men and women (see Application Box: Some Problems of Working Women, Chapter 10, p. 502).

In the 1920s the typical working woman was usually unmarried, under 30 years of age, and generally from the lower socioeconomic class. Today, however, working women represent all socioeconomic classes, are drawn from a wider age range, and are frequently married, with children at home. There are many factors which contribute to the desire of women to work including the following (Kamerman and Hayes, 1982):

- The desire and need for supplemental family income.
- The need for self-development, independence, or social contact.
- A high level of achievement motivation or a desire for status.
- The increasing social acceptance of the need for some women to work.
- The recognition of, and reduction in, sexual discrimination.

In discussing the occupational careers of women, it is important to recognize several different groups of working women:

- Unmarried women, with no children, in an occupational role.
- Married women, without children, in an occupational role.
- Married or divorced women, with children at home, in an occupational role.
- Married or divorced women in an occupation role, whose children have left home.

Given these four alternative groups, it is possible to imagine a wide variety of career patterns. For example, unmarried women (with no children) in an occupational role could include those who are in a professional job and intend to remain in that role with no intention of getting married. It could also include those who may be using a job to establish an economic base for later marriage and childbearing, with a possible return to the labor market at a later time. Working married women whose children have left home might be involved in continuous and uninterrupted occupational roles. On the other hand, they could be middle-aged women entering the job market for the first time. From these few examples, it should be clear that women follow a much greater variety of occupational career patterns than men.

Within this wide variety of occupational cycles, women may experience situations which strain their adaptation skills. The relative contributions of the housewife role and the occupational role to women's sense of psychological well being has been the subject of considerable debate. Some researchers have suggested that the female work role is liberating, whereas the housewife role is inadequate and insufficient for self-development (Maas and Kuypers, 1974; Rossi, 1980). On the other hand, it has been suggested that involvement in both the housewife role and work role neither improves nor reduces general satisfaction with life (Baruch and Barnett, 1980; Wright, 1978). (See Application Box: ''Who Is Happier—The Full-Time Homemaker or the Employed Woman?'' p. 544).

The Development of the Self in Middle Adulthood

The development of the self in middle adulthood is a potentially exciting and challenging process. Not all adults, of course, respond as if it were. The physical changes of middle age sometimes produce a disquieting feeling that although the end of life may not be imminent, it is in sight. Other adults simply ''work through'' the period of middle age, giving no evidence whatsoever of any crisis. In this section, we discuss the physical, cognitive, and personality changes that occur in the middle adult years.

INTERLUDE: BETWEEN ADOLESCENCE AND SOCIAL SECURITY

Somewhere between adolescence and Social Security, the roller coaster of life pauses at the top of the rise before plunging into what looks depressingly like All Down Hill. This is middle age.

Not all people get there at the same time. Psychologists place the beginning of feeling and/or appearing middle-aged anywhere between 35 and 55. And like riders on the conventional roller coaster, not all people react the same way.

Some scream. Some close their eyes tightly and wait for this unpleasant experience to go away and for things to be as secure as they were before. Some hang on with grim determination and gritted teeth, utterly miserably. Some laugh and enjoy it. (Naunton, 1976) (Reprinted with permission from *The Miami Herald*).

Middle Adulthood: The Prime of Life or the Beginning of the End?

PHYSICAL CHANGES IN MIDDLE AGE

For many adults, the first signal of coming changes in social relationships and personality which are associated with aging are the changes in their general appearance, sensory perception, sexual functioning, or health.

Appearance. There is rather little change in an individual's physical appearance during early adulthood. Middle adulthood is marked by dramatic changes in appearance.

- *There is a tendency to gain weight.* Body fat is about 10 percent of total body weight in adolescence. By middle adulthood, fat is about 20 percent of body weight (Bischof, 1976).
- *There is a redistribution of body fat.* The abdomen and hips become larger and the bust and chest become smaller (compared with the stomach and hips).
- *Changes in hair* (particularly in men) are also obvious in middle age. The hairline recedes and baldness increases, as does graying of the hair.
- The *skin* becomes *less elastic.*
- General *posture* and *movements become less smooth.*

Sensory Functioning

Vision. There are several age-related trends in visual functioning, most of which were discussed in the previous chapter. The overall effect of these changes (including such factors as pupil size, adaptation to light, and lens accommodation) is that by about age forty, adults become aware of some changes in vision, many of which seem to occur rather abruptly in middle

"Grampa—are you going to have a baby?"

The Development of the Self in Middle Adulthood 547

adulthood. Before age sixty-five, less than half of all adults require corrective lenses. However, after age sixty-five, almost nine out of ten adults require corrective lenses (Knox, 1977).

Hearing. The occurrence of hearing loss is less than 1 percent for persons under twenty-five years of age. At about forty-five years, that rate begins to increase. Most of the loss is in the high frequencies of sound. Most men seem to hear better at the lower frequencies than women, and in turn, women hear better at the higher frequencies than men. Men seem to experience greater hearing loss beyond fifty years of age than women, probably because of greater exposure to occupational noise.

Other Senses. There are other gradual changes in sensory functioning during middle adulthood. Changes in taste occur after age fifty. The taste buds begin to atrophy inside the cheeks, at first, and then progressively toward the back of the tongue. The sensitivity to sweetness is almost three times less in old age than in young adulthood.

After age forty, sensitivity to smell also declines significantly. A sixty-year-old person is able to identify faint aromas less than 50 percent as often as a 20-year-old (Knox, 1977). Sensitivity to pain increases at about forty-five years of age and continues to increase beyond sixty years (Woodruff, Friedman, Siegelaub, and Collon, 1972).

Movement Skills. There is a widely recognized decline in movement skills during the adult years. Research on performance and work in maturity and old age has traditionally emphasized manifestations of aging in all behavioral functions, with the implication that aging changes are all deteriorative and negative. The studies summarized by Welford (1959) noted these main changes: (a) an increase in reaction time (the time lag between what a person sees, hears, feels, or otherwise senses, and when the person begins to respond) and an increase in work performance time with age; (b) increasing variability of performance with age; and (c) greater performance losses in more complex tasks with age. Welford concluded that aging is manifested in an altered capability of the brain to channel and store information. As a result, older persons do not respond as fast as younger persons.

Toward the end of middle age, it becomes increasingly difficult to sustain a fast pace in work-related movements. For example, some adults find it difficult to maintain a long series of complex movements such as those involved in playing a violin or a guitar (Fozard, Nuttall, and Waugh, 1972). Although there is evidence of a decline in movement skills, there is no evidence that this decline causes a decline in job performance (Birren, 1964). In other words, the accumulated wisdom and expertise of older individuals more than compensate for any decrease in dexterity or speed (see Figure 11.5).

Sexuality and the "Change of Life." During middle adulthood, sexual changes occur in both males and females.

SOME DEFINITIONS
"Change of life." A general term applying to both males and females and referring to the sexual alterations of middle age. It means the conclusion of one phase of life and the beginning of another.

FIGURE 11.5 Although there is a decline in manual skills at the end of middle age, the accumulated experience and knowledge of adults more than compensate for this loss.

Photograph by Darryl Jacobson

Climacteric. Webster's New Collegiate Dictionary defines this term as "a major turning point or critical stage." It is most frequently applied to the gradual loss of reproductive capability in middle age by both men and women. The end of the climacteric is more dramatic in women because it is marked by an unmistakable signal: menstruation stops (i.e., the menopause).

Menopause. The end point of the female climacteric. The word *menopause* derives from two Greek words that mean "month" and "cessation." It refers to the time in a woman's life when the monthly reproductive function (i.e., the process of ovulation, the discharge of the unfertilized egg, and the monthly menstrual flow) ceases. Menopause results from the cessation of the hormone estrogen. The absence of estrogen leads to the end of the process of ovulation, which, in turn, leads to the end of the monthly menstrual flow.

The male climacteric. The gradual lessening of fertility in males. As the body ages, the production of both sperm and the male hormone, testosterone, drops off (Fried, 1976). These declines are usually so gradual that there is relatively little impact on the fertility of the male. Unlike the female menopause, the male reproductive function does not end. It usually continues into old age despite lowered levels of testosterone and sperm (Kimmel, 1980).

Symptoms of the Menopause. The decline of estrogen in females may affect the entire body system, producing symptoms that may be disturbing to some women. Most menopausal women have either no serious problems or only minor ones. In only about 25 percent of women is medical help required (Kirby, 1973). Some of the most talked-about symptoms of the menopause are sweating and hot flashes. During a hot flash, the woman's body becomes very hot; perspiration and chilliness follow. Hot flashes are probably the most annoying of all symptoms. In most cases, they stop at the conclusion of the menopause.

The range of menopausal symptoms has been treated with tablets or injections of artificial estrogen (Wilson, 1966; Kantor, Michael, Boulas, Shore, and Ludvigson, 1966). The apparent benefits of estrogen-replacement therapy in reducing or avoiding menopausal symptoms have come into question. Some research indicates an increasing risk of cancer of the uterine lining with estrogen treatment (Smith, Prentice, Thompson, and Herman, 1975; Finkle and Ziel, 1975). However, more research will be necessary to fully clarify the risks of estrogen-replacement therapy.

INTERLUDE:
THE PSYCHOLOGICAL REACTION OF WOMEN TO MENOPAUSE

Women comment on menopause. Some women (particularly those with higher educational levels) felt that menopause was of no real social–psychological consequence:

"Why make any fuss about it?"

"I just made up my mind I'd walk right through it, and I did. . . . "

"I saw women complaining, and I thought I would never be so ridiculous. I would just sit there and perspire if I had to. At times you do feel terribly warm. I would sit and feel the water on my head, and wonder how red I looked. But I wouldn't worry about it, because it is a natural thing, and why get worried about it? I remember one time, in the kitchen, I had a terrific hot flash. . . . I went to look at myself in the mirror. I didn't even look red, so I thought, 'All right. . . . the next time I'll just sit there, and who will notice? And if someone notices, I won't even care. . . . ' "

Other women confessed to considerable fear:

"I would think of my mother and the trouble she went through; and I wondered if I would come through it whole or in pieces. . . . "

"I knew two women who had nervous breakdowns, and I worried about losing my mind. . . . "

"I thought menopause would be the beginning of the end . . . gradual senility closing over, like the darkness. . . . "

"I was afraid we couldn't have sexual relations after the menopause—and my husband thought so, too. . . . "

"When I think of how I used to worry! You wish someone would tell you—but you're too embarrassed to ask anyone. . . . "

From Neugarten, B. L., Wood, V., Kraines, R., Loomis, B., "Women's Attitudes Toward the Menopause," *Vita Humana*, 1963, 6(3), 140–151.

Psychologically the menopause may produce varying reactions in women. Some women become depressed and unhappy at the thought that they are losing their youth, their attractiveness, or "themselves." Such reactions are usually in the minority. Most women seem to go through the menopausal period without any psychological problems.

To some extent, the reaction of a woman to menopause depends on her age (Neugarten, Wood, Kraines, and Loomis, 1963). In the comments of women quoted in the box, there appears to be more fear of menopause among younger women who have not experienced it than among those who have. Women over the age of forty-five seem to see more positive changes after menopause has passed than younger women (see Table 11.3). Furthermore

Middle Adulthood: The Prime of Life or the Beginning of the End?

TABLE 11.3   Attitudes Toward Menopause: By Age

Illustrative Items	A 21–30 (N = 50)	B 31–44 (N = 52)	C 45–55 (N = 100)	D 56–65 (N = 65)
	Percentage Who Agree, in Age Groups			
Negative Affect				
Menopause is an unpleasant experience for a woman	56	44	58	55
Women should expect some trouble during the menopause	60	46	59	58
In truth, just about every woman is depressed about the change of life	48	29	40	28
Post-Menopausal Recovery				
Women generally feel better after the menopause than they have for years	32*	20*	68	67
A woman gets more confidence in herself after the change of life	12*	21*	52	42
After the change of life, a woman feels freer to do things for herself	16*	24*	74	65
Many women think menopause is the best thing that ever happened to them	14*	31	46	40
Extent of Continuity				
Going through the menopause really does not change a woman in any important way	58*	55*	74	83
Control of Symptoms				
Women who have trouble with the menopause are usually those who have nothing to do with their time	58	50*	71	70
Women who have trouble in the menopause are those who are expecting it	48*	56*	76	63
Psychological Losses				
Women worry about losing their minds during the menopause	28*	35	51	24*
A woman is concerned about how her husband will feel toward her after the menopause	58*	44	41	21*
Unpredictability				
A woman in menopause is apt to do crazy things she herself does not understand	40	56	53	40
Menopause is a mysterious thing which most women don't understand	46	46	59	46
Sexuality				
If the truth were really known, most women would like to have themselves a fling at this time in their lives	8*	33	32	24
After the menopause, a woman is more interested in sex than she was before	14*	27	35	21

Source: Neugarten et al., ''Women's Attitudes Toward the Menopause,'' 1963, 6(3), 140–151. Reprinted with permission from *Vita Humana* (now *Human Development*), published by S. Karger AG, Basel.

*Subjects who checked ''agree strongly'' or ''agree to some extent'' are grouped together. The difference between this percentage and the percentage of Group C is significant at the 0.05 level or above.

middle-aged women are more likely than younger women to find that menopause is not associated with any major changes in life.

Sexuality and Sexual Performance. Sexuality in the last half of life has been the subject of continued research and discussion. To date, most of these investigations have served to dispel two primary myths (Weiler, 1981):

- *The myth of the asexual older person.* Numerous studies have demonstrated that both sexual interest and activity persist well into later life (Kinsey, Pomeroy, and Martin, 1948; Masters and Johnson, 1966).
- *The myth that impotence, sexual disinterest, and a lack of sexual activity are expected and irreversible eventualities.* Clinical studies of sexuality in the last half of life have demonstrated both the life-span potential for sexual response and the reversibility of some sexual disorders in later life (Masters and Johnson, 1966, 1970).

The research on aging and sexuality has come largely from three primary studies which have served as the basis for much of our current knowledge on the topic.

1. *The Kinsey Studies* (1948, 1953). This cross-sectional research was the earliest to examine adulthood and sexuality. Kinsey and his colleagues concluded that while sexual activity was likely to continue into the later years, there was, nonetheless, a general decline in all measures of sexual response across adulthood. For example, levels of sexual activity gradually decreased for both men and women.

2. *The Masters and Johnson Clinical Studies* (1966, 1970). These studies involved 150 women and 212 men, aged 50 and above. The focus was on the *physiology* of sexual response. For example, in the female the decline in the sex hormones—estrogens and progestogens—may result in changes in the vagina (e.g., decreased lubrication or decreased vaginal size) which may produce pain during intercourse. For men, sexual orgasm may occur more slowly.

The Masters and Johnson research dispels a frequent misconception that any decline in the frequency or quality of sexual activity in middle age and beyond is due exclusively to these physiological changes. They pointed out that the maintenance or reduction in sexual activity during the adult years could result from many social-psychological factors. For women, a warm and secure relationship with an appropriate man was the primary factor in continuity of sexual activity. For men, significant factors included boredom or monotony in the sexual relationship, concern about money matters, mental fatigue, concern about family or work matters, and a fear of sexual failure (Masters and Johnson, 1966, 1970).

3. *The Duke University Aging Studies* (Pfeiffer, Verwoerdt, and Davis, 1972; Pfeiffer and Davis, 1972). The data from these cross-sectional reports were based on a sample of 502 white men and women from 46–71 years of age. The results of the studies were as follows:

- Sexual activity declined gradually over time for both men and women.
- Sexual interest declined over time (although the decline was slower than for sexual activity).
- Men were more sexually active than women during middle adulthood, although the gap narrowed with age.

552

- Although declines in sexual activity and interest were evident, nonetheless the majority of men and women in the studies were still sexually active and sexually interested (for example, only 6 percent of the men and 33 percent of the women indicated they were no longer interested in sex).
- For men the major determinants of sexual interest and activity in later life were past sexual experience, age, health status, and social class.
- For women, the major determinants of sexual interest and activity in later life were the availability of a socially appropriate and capable male partner, age, and enjoyment from sexual experiences at a younger age.

The three primary sources of data on sexuality in later life—the Kinsey studies, the Masters and Johnson clinical reports, and the Duke studies—help to dispel the myths of asexuality and sexual dysfunction in later adulthood. *However, all three sources appear to support the idea that sexual activity and sexual interest do, in fact, decline.* More recent longitudinal analysis of the Duke University data (Pfeiffer and Davis, 1972; Pfeiffer et al., 1972) suggest that even this finding of gradual decline may be inaccurate (George and Weiler, 1981). George and Weiler (1981) suggest that instead of a pattern of gradually declining sexual activity and interest, a more likely and accurate pattern is one of maintenance and stability with a relatively abrupt cessation in sexual activity. This abrupt cessation would presumably occur at whatever point the older individual experiences a life event (e.g., a serious deterioration of one's own health, the deterioration of a spouse's health, or the death of a spouse) which might force the cessation of sexual activity.

Physical Health. In the adult years, people tend to get more chronic illnesses and fewer acute illnesses (McCammon, 1970). As we indicated in Chapter Ten, acute illnesses are of short-term duration and curable, whereas chronic illnesses are long term and incurable (e.g., arthritis or diabetes).

Chronic Illnesses. Certain chronic diseases begin to appear in middle adulthood. Between the ages of fifty and sixty, (particularly in men), diabetes reaches its peak. Shortly after forty, arthritis becomes more frequent.

Cardiovascular problems (i.e., problems relating to the heart and the circulatory system) also increase during middle age. These problems include the following:

Arteriosclerosis. Sometimes called *hardening of the arteries,* this condition results from the accumulation of substances such as cholesterol on the walls of arteries (see Figure 11.6).

FIGURE 11.6   The diameter of arteries is reduced by arteriosclerosis.

Photograph from Timiras, P. S., *Developmental Physiology and Aging.* New York: Macmillan, 1972, p. 481. Courtesy of Dr. E. S. Evans.

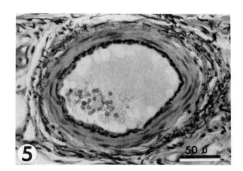
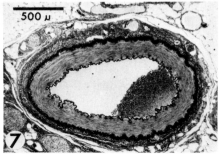

Type A Behavior and Your Heart

Can an individual's personality cause heart problems? There appears to be a relationship between how people respond to life situations and whether they are candidates for a heart attack (Friedman and Rosenman, 1974; Glass, 1976).

- *Type A Personalities.* These individuals are likely to have heart problems. They are "engaged in a relatively *chronic struggle* to obtain an *unlimited* number of *poorly defined* things from their environment in *the shortest period of time*" (Friedman and Rosenman, 1974, p. 7). These people are hard-driving, aggressive, competitive, ambitious, and successful. They try to do more and more in less and less time; they find it hard to relax; and they never have enough time to do all that they want to do (Friedman and Rosenman, 1974).
- *Type B Personalities.* These individuals are less likely to have heart attacks than Type As. In many ways, they are the opposite of the Type A personality. They tend to be relaxed and easygoing and rarely feel pressured.

ARE YOU TYPE A OR TYPE B?

Friedman and Rosenman (1974) determined the personality type (A or B) of an individual with a questionnaire. The following questions are a brief adaptation of that questionnaire. Try it and see how you do.

1. Do you always move, walk, and eat rapidly?
   yes   no
2. Do you become unduly irritated when the car ahead of you moves too slowly?
   yes   no
3. Do you indulge in *polyphasic* thinking or behavior (try to think or do two things at once)?
   yes   no
4. Do you always feel vaguely guilty when you relax and do absolutely nothing for several hours or several days?
   yes   no
5. Do you rarely observe the more important and interesting objects in your surroundings?
   yes   no
6. Do you rarely have time to become the things worth *being* because you are too preoccupied with getting the things worth *having?*
   yes   no
7. Do you always try to bring the theme of any conversation around to those subjects that especially interest you?
   yes   no
8. Do you believe that whatever success you have achieved has been due in *good* part to your ability to do things faster than others?
   yes   no
9. Do you translate and evaluate your own life and things around you in terms of numbers?
   yes   no
10. When you meet a Type A person, do you find yourself compelled to challenge him or her rather than feeling compassion for his or her affliction?
   yes   no

WHAT TO DO IF YOU ARE TYPE A

Friedman and Rosenman have produced a set of "drills" to reduce Type A behavior.

These drills involve establishing new habits through exercise and an examination of one's philosophy of life. Some examples of daily drills:

1. Quit trying to think of more than one thing at a time.
2. Quit trying to do more than one thing at a time.
3. Practice listening quietly to others.
4. Deliberately do some things more slowly than usual—and enjoy it.
5. Do not make unnecessary deadlines.
6. Learn to leave some projects unfinished.
7. Find some time each day for doing *nothing*— seek total body relaxation and peace of mind.

Based on M. Friedman and R. H. Rosenman, *Type A Behavior and Your Heart.* New York: Knopf, 1974.

Arteriosclerosis is a process that probably begins as early as childhood, continues through adulthood, and progressively limits the elasticity of artery walls.

Fatty streaks appear during the first decade, fibrous plaques appear from the second decade onward, and by the forties there is sufficient thickening and blocking of arteries so that clinical problems increasingly occur, such as bulges in artery walls (aneurysms), death of some heart tissue caused by insufficient blood supply (infarcts), moving blood clots (thromboses), death of peripheral tissues (gangrene), and hemorrhages of cerebral arteries (strokes). (Knox, 1977, p. 263)

Coronary heart disease. This condition has to do with changes in the coronary arteries of the heart. Between young adulthood and middle age, there is approximately a 25 percent reduction in the cross section of the coronary arteries (Knox, 1977). Coronary heart disease is sometimes associated with cigarette smoking, cholesterol levels, and high blood pressure (Smith and Bierman, 1973; Timiras, 1972) There is some evidence that personality patterns may be associated with heart disease (Friedman and Rosenman, 1974). (see Application Box: "Type A Behavior and Your Heart).

Hypertension (high blood pressure). High blood pressure plays a direct role in the deaths of nearly sixty thousand men and women each year in the United States. Most of these people are in their fifties. Hypertension is an illness that involves the interaction of physical and emotional factors. For example, it is associated with the accumulation of substances on the walls of the arteries—a physical factor. In addition, it is associated with the way an individual reacts to stress—an emotional factor. Continuous arousal and stress can sometimes result in sustained levels of high blood pressure (Henry and Cassel, 1969; Timiras, 1972). Even though there is a tendency for blood pressure to increase with age, some people appear to develop healthy techniques, early in life, for managing stress that help them throughout adulthood. Others appear less able to handle potentially stressful situations (see Application Box: "Stress and Health." p. 556).

COGNITIVE FUNCTIONING AND LEARNING

As in the case of sexuality and sexual performance in middle adulthood, there are myths about the cognitive functioning and learning skills of middle-aged adults.

Myth 1: Intelligence declines in adulthood. By the time you reach middle age, you just can't think the way you used to. After all, who could think straight anyway with all the aggravation that you have? Right? (Well, we certainly hope not. See discussion below.)

Myth 2: Adults can't effectively learn new things. (or "You can't teach an old dog new tricks"). Middle-aged adults are supposed to be "set in their ways"—so set, in fact, that they cannot or will not learn new ways of thinking or doing things.

As for Myth 1, we indicated in Chapter Ten that intelligence and cognitive skills tend to remain rather stable in adulthood. In fact, reasoning and verbal

Stress and Health

WHAT IS STRESS?

When we experience an event that is unexpected or undesirable (i.e., a crisis-provoking event), we physiologically respond by producing excess energy. The feelings generated within us because of this excess energy have commonly been labeled *stress*. Long-term stress can result in very real health problems, such as depression, personality changes, anxiety ulcers, heart attacks, nervousness, headaches, alcoholism, and nervous breakdown.

STRESS AND ILLNESS ON THE HIGH SEAS

Two research scientists at the University of Washington—Thomas Holmes and Richard Rahe (1967)—were interested in examining the relationship between stress and physical disease.

Could stress cause illness? In 1967, they developed a rating form (see the table) that ranked stressful events (e.g., divorce, death of a spouse, pregnancy) on a point scale. Each stressful event was assigned a value in terms of its severity. (For example, divorce had a "scale impact" of 73 points, and a "change in schools" had a value of 20 points.) Holmes and Rahe administered the rating form to a group of U.S. Navy men who were about to sail on a year-long cruise. The investigators were interested in the relationship between the stressful events that each sailor had experienced in the year prior to the cruise and the illnesses that they might experience during the cruise year.

One year later, the ship returned to home port. Holmes and Rahe examined the medical records

The Holmes–Rahe Readjustment Rating Scale

Event	Scale of Impact	Event	Scale of Impact
Death of a spouse	100	Son or daughter leaving home	29
Divorce	73	Trouble with in-laws	29
Marital separation	65	Outstanding personal achievement	28
Jail term	63	Wife begins or stops work	26
Death of close family member	63	Child begins or ends school	26
Personal injury or illness	53	Change in living conditions	25
Marriage	50	Revision of personal habits	24
Fired from a job	47	Trouble with boss	23
Marital reconciliation	45	Change in work hours or	
Retirement	45	conditions	20
Change in health of family member	44	Change in residence	20
Pregnancy	40	Change in schools	20
Sex difficulties	39	Change in recreation	19
Gain of new family member	39	Change in church activities	19
Business readjustment	39	Change in social activities	18
Change in financial status	38	Mortgage or loan for lesser purchase	
Death of a close friend	37	(car, TV, etc.)	17
Change to different line of work	36	Change in sleeping habits	15
Change in number of arguments with		Change in number of family	
spouse	35	get-togethers	15
Mortgage or loan for major purchase		Change in eating habits	15
(home, etc.)	31	Vacation	13
Foreclosure of mortgage or loan	30	Christmas	12
Change in responsibilities at work	29	Minor violations of the law	11

Adapted with permission from T. H. Holmes, and R. H. Rahe, The social readjustment rating scale. *Journal of Psychosomatic Research*, 1967, *11*, 213–218. Copyright © 1967, Pergamon Press, Ltd.

of the crew. Whey they compared these medical records with the precruise stress-rating forms, they found an interesting pattern. The amount of stress to which an individual had been subjected in the year prior to the cruise was directly related to the severity of the physical illnesses suffered during the cruise.

PREVENTIVE MEASURES
The following suggestions are for using the Social Readjustment Rating Scale for the maintenance of your health and prevention of illness:

1. Become familiar with the life events and the amount of change they require.
2. Put the Scale where you and the family can see it easily several times a day.
3. With practice you can recognize when a life event happens.
4. Think about the meaning of the event for you and try to identify some of the feelings you experience.
5. Think about the different ways you might best adjust to the event.
6. Take your time in arriving at decisions.
7. If possible, anticipate life changes and plan for them well in advance.
8. Pace yourself. It can be done even if you are in a hurry.
9. Look at the accomplishment of a task as a part of daily living and avoid looking at such an achievement as a "stopping point" or a "time for letting down."
10. *Remember*, the more change you have, the more likely you are to get sick. Of those people with 300 or more Life Change Units for the past year, almost 80% get sick in the near future; with 150 to 299 Life Change Units, about 50% get sick in the near future; and with less than 150 Life Change Units, only about 30% get sick in the near future.

So, the higher your Life Change Score, the harder you should work to stay well.

Thomas H. Holmes, M.D., Professor of Psychiatry and Behavioral Sciences RP-10, University of Washington, Seattle, Washington 98195.

skills may actually improve (Birren, 1976). The middle-aged individual's ability to think is, on the whole, likely to be as good as in early adulthood.

In addition, *creativity* shows no apparent decline during middle adulthood (Dennis, 1966). Studies of the total productivity of creative people suggest that the peak of performance may be reached in middle age or, in some cases, in later adulthood (see Figure 11.7). For scientists, the period from forty through about sixty years of age was marked by a fairly constant stream of production, with a relative decline from sixty through seventy. It is interesting to note that for scientists, the period from twenty to twenty-nine years was

FIGURE 11.7 Percentage of total output as a function of age. The humanities, sciences, and arts are represented by the means of several specific disciplines.

Data are from Dennis, W., "Creative Productivity Between the Ages of 20 and 80 Years," *Journal of Gerontology,* 1966, *21,* 1–8. Reprinted from Jack Botwinick, *Cognitive Processes in Maturity and Old Age,* Figure 21. Copyright © 1967 by Springer Publishing Company, Inc., New York. Used by permission.

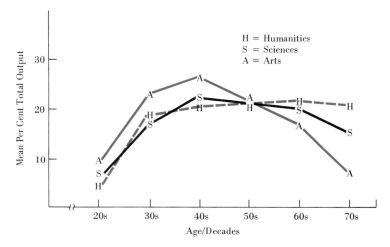

FIGURE 11.8 Creative work in the humanities may continue through middle age and beyond. The philosophers Bertrand Russell and Alfred North Whitehead are good examples.

the least productive—less productive, in fact, than the decade from sixty to seventy years. Artists were the only group for whom the period from sixty to seventy was less productive than the period from twenty to twenty-nine. Creativity in the humanities appeared to be sustained from about thirty through seventy years of age (see Figures 11.7 and 11.8). Even when "peaks" are reached in middle age, people can continue some creative activities well into later adulthood. Simply because a peak is reached does not mean that all work ceases after that time. Furthermore, "declines" do not necessarily represent changes in skill:

declines are, perhaps, more the result of noncognitive factors than intellectual changes. That is, following some major creative work, the scientist would be likely to be given greater responsibilities (department chairman or director of research, for instance), to become more involved in more scientific and governmental committees, and to find that there is less time and energy left over for creative productivity. (Kimmel, 1980, p. 363)

As for Myth 2, almost any adult is able to learn almost any formal and informal subject and skill, provided she or he is given sufficient time and attention. Although there is admittedly a trend toward an increasing range of individual differences in adulthood (see the discussion of fluid and crystallized intelligence in Chapter Ten), adults can still learn new things if their self-confidence has not been eroded. Self-confidence is particularly important because some adults tend to underestimate their learning ability by overemphasizing their limited formal school experiences. They also tend to underestimate the large gains made in practical and specific knowledge and experience (crystallized intelligence) (Knox, 1977).

Adults continue to learn informally throughout their lifetime in the worlds of work, family, and community or neighborhood. Many adults engage in self-directed learning activities as well as in formal part-time educational programs (see Figure 11.9). In most cases, when adults engage in sustained and

systematic learning activities, the intent is to improve their performance. In other words, adults typically want to use what they learn. Knox (1977) has identified the following *factors that have a primary influence on learning in adult-hood:*

Condition. Physiological condition and physical health can affect learning and cognition in various ways. Sensory impairment, such as poor vision or hearing loss, can restrict sensory input. . . . Ill health can restrict attention given to external events. . . .

Adjustment. The effective assessment or facilitation of learning is less likely when there is substantial personal or social maladjustment in the learning situation. Social maladjustment is usually associated with learner defensiveness and anxiety and should not be confused with moderate levels of arousal and motivation. If a person believes that he or she can deal with a situation, it may be a challenge, if not, it may be perceived as a threat. People deal best with failure when they have experienced many successes. Support and assistance is [sic] especially important for adults with few recent educational experiences.

Relevance. The adult's motivation and cooperation in the learning activity is [sic] more likely when the tasks are meaningful and of interest to the learner. Active interest and participation are more likely when the learner helps identify objectives, selects learning tasks, and understands procedures.

Speed. Especially for older adults, time limits and pressures tend to reduce learning performance. Optimal learning performance is more likely when learners can proceed at their own pace.

Status. Socioeconomic circumstances are associated with values, demands, constraints, and resources that can affect learning ability. Level of formal education tends to be the status index most highly associated with adult learning. The influence of status on learning depends on the type of learning activity. For example, for learning the metric system, oral communications might be more effective for blue collar adults, and white collar adults might learn abstract concepts through written communication more effectively. . . .

Outlook. Personal outlook and personality characteristics, such as open mindedness or defensiveness, can affect the way in which an adult deals with specific types of learning situations. (Knox, 1977, pp. 410–411)

The Development of the Self in Middle Adulthood

PERSONALITY DEVELOPMENT

DEFINITIONS

Differentiation of personality. The increasing complexity and specialization of the self-concept. As individuals mature, they develop specific interests, values, and roles that contribute to a unique self.

Integration of personality. An "organization" of the many dimensions of the self into a unit that is coherent, so that the dimensions of the self "hold together" as part of the "same" person. In other words, there is a consistency of self across different roles (e.g., parent, worker, friend) and over time.

Throughout life, there is some degree of tension between personality *differentiation* and personality *integration*. During late adolescence and early adulthood, this tension is reflected in the search for identity (Erikson, 1968b). Too much differentiation may result in role diffusion or inadequate identity definition. Premature integration too soon may result in faulty identity decisions. One of the primary themes of personality development in adulthood is the adult's attempt to achieve an integrated sense of self in the face of the many differentiated roles that the adult is expected to play (e.g., worker, spouse, parent, and community member).

In many cases, being middle-aged implies being in a position of relative power and authority, particularly in relation to what comes before—early adulthood—and what comes after—later adulthood. One way to think about this phase of life is in terms of *developmental tasks*. Some of the developmental tasks which are characteristic of middle adulthood include the following (Havighurst, 1972; Cytrynbaum, Blum, Patrick, Stein, Wades, and Wilk, 1980):

- Accepting physical limitations and the prospect of mortality.
- Helping school-aged children and adolescent offspring negotiate their own developmental tasks.
- Relating to aging parents.
- Maintaining or developing leisure activities.
- Maintaining or reorienting work skills.
- Maintaining or developing social ties and friendships.

These developmental tasks represent activities of personal development which are common to many middle-aged adults and which characterize some of the arenas in which personality development occurs.

The Self-Concept. Although adolescence tends to be the period that is commonly associated with the stabilization of the self-concept in the form of an identity, the self actually evolves throughout life. During adulthood, the individual's experiences in work, in the family, and with friends interact to influence the adult's notion of self. For many adults, work provides a strong contribution to the individual sense of worth.

Middle-aged adults appear to show continuity in their sense of self (Giele, 1980). For the most part, there are not radical shifts in personality dimensions from adolescence through middle adulthood. However, one personality dimension for which there is good evidence of a change is introversion (Neugarten, 1977). The findings on this dimension suggest that introversion increases with age over the second half of life. Aside from this single finding, other research attempting to demonstrate change over the second half of life for other personality dimensions (e.g., rigidity, creativity, morale, and cautiousness) has been inconclusive for the following reasons:

- The samples used in these studies have varied considerably in terms of health, socioeconomic level, and education making them difficult to compare.
- Questionnaires and other instruments have been used which have unknown meaning for older adults.
- "Still another problem is that in most studies of personality and aging, the investigator has asked if change is age-related without considering also whether or not marriage has intervened, or parenthood, or job failure, or illness, or widowhood" (Neugarten, 1977, p. 636).

In recent years, there has been a surge of interest in the evolving self in adulthood. Early research (Erikson, 1950; Havighurst, 1957) has been expanded on by other efforts that have concentrated on young adulthood and middle age (Levinson, Darrow, Klein, Levinson and McKee, 1974; Lowenthal, Thurnher, Chiriboga, Beeson, Glay, Pierce, Spencer, and Weiss, 1975; Gould, 1975; *Daedalus,* 1976).

Adults tend to become increasingly varied in their outlooks and self-concepts. Some adults become more tolerant of themselves, more self-directed, and more aware of situational complexities (Gould, 1975). The sequence of the development of the self in middle adulthood seems to follow a general pattern (Knox, 1977).

The late twenties and early thirties. Most of this period is characterized by a settling down, an order, and a striving.

The late thirties and early forties. This period is characterized by a general reorientation of both outlook and activity. Knox (1977) described this period as follows:

Some of the abstract commitments and aspirations that were formed in adolescence and young adulthood begin to wane. During this period most adults become more eager to share the joys and sorrows of human experience, and the quality of friendships becomes more important. The earlier sense of adult self that largely reflected role relationships as worker, spouse and parent seems inadequate. The reexamination of the fit between the current sense of self and the structure of participation that evolved leads to the mid-life transition that is becoming increasingly widespread. (Knox, 1977, pp. 345–346)

The mid-forties and early sixties. This period involves an increasing variability in the sense of self. Many individuals develop stability, competence, responsibility, and maturity during this period (Neugarten, 1968). Knox (1977) described this period as follows:

The quest for the adolescent dream has been replaced by protection of gains. Under favorable personal and societal conditions, the older adult is able to extract wisdom from the mental struggle between a sense of integrity and a sense of despair about the meaning and worth of one's life. Such wisdom reflects a detached yet active concern with life in the face of physical decline and death (. . . Levinson et al., 1974; Gould, 1975; Erikson, 1976). (Knox, 1977, p. 347)

Sex-Role Changes. An emerging body of empirical evidence suggests that sex roles become less rigid in the second half of life (Livson, 1983; Sedney, 1977; Guttmann, 1977). According to Livson (1983) there are three life-span stages of gender development, the last of which corresponds to the last half of life:

- A global, undifferentiated stage during the first few years of life in which concepts of gender are largely *unorganized*.
- A highly differentiated or conforming stage (which begins in middle childhood) in which sex roles are *rigidly polarized*.
- An integrated stage which involves the *combination* of previously polarized sex roles.

According to Livson (1983), the sex-role integration of the final stage is not fully established until mature adulthood. While it is possible that some adolescents may reach this integrated stage, it is likely that they may do so only tentatively. In response to the demands of early adulthood roles, these adolescents will probably regress to the polarized second stage of gender development. Livson suggests that the roles of early adulthood—marriage, parenthood, and career building—tend to maintain polarized male-female sex roles. The reason is that in order to efficiently and effectively perform the roles of achieving occupational success, nurturing children, and becoming a *traditional* husband or wife, individuals presumably need the clear guidelines of polarized sex roles. It is not until middle age when children leave home, work goals change, and retirement looms as a possibility, that the traditional roles of *nurturing* female and *achieving* male become less prominent and demanding. According to Livson (1983, p. 109), "Individuals may now [in middle age] allow themselves to reclaim unused parts of their personalities."

Livson (1976) also found that the ability to integrate sex roles—to become *androgynous*—was related to overall mental health. Both males and females who were psychologically healthiest at age 50 also shared the highest androgyny. In her study, the only individuals who failed to improve in psychological health at age 50 were highly feminine, submissive, and dependent women (i.e., women who were oversocialized to the traditional female sex role and were, therefore, not androgynous). However, men who were oversocialized to the traditional masculine sex role (i.e., men who were not androgynous) were not inhibited in later development and continued to improve in psychological health. Livson suggests that even traditional (non-androgynous) male sex roles allow for more growth options than traditional female roles.

The evidence is fairly clear that men and women become more like each other somewhere in the middle years of life. However, men and women follow *different paths* over the life cycle in arriving at this integration of sex roles. Men are socialized to attain their identity at much younger ages than women.

Their (men) childhood experiences and their adult roles stress separateness, independence, and competence in the outside world. As a result, men form their identity earlier in life. Men, in this sense, are early maturers. (In my opinion, Erikson's [1950] model proposing identity formation as the central task of adolescence fits men more than women.)

There are advantages as well as disadvantages to both of these developmental paths. Women suffer more than men from depression and mental illness, particularly during the first half of life, and they devalue themselves more. On the other hand, women may acquire more role flexibility. Women follow a clearcut, linear path through life. They experience more discontinuities in role (marital, parental, and occupational) and life-styles than do men over the life span (Maas and Kuypers, 1974). They adapt to more complex or conflicting role demands (for example, work and family) and experiment with more role options (jobs, volunteer work, continuing education, and organizational activity). Women, in brief, are more likely than men to learn to cope with change, as a result, they may be better equipped to cope with change in later life. There is some evidence to suggest that women do adapt better than men to aging (Kuhlen, 1964). (From Livson, 1983, p. 123)

Summary

1. When does middle age begin? This is a difficult question to answer primarily because middle adulthood is not marked by any specific biological changes or any rites of passage. For our purposes, middle age is that period of life from approximately thirty-five years of age (when many individuals reach peak levels of social, personal, and economic performance) to approximately sixty-five years of age (when many individuals retire). Admittedly, these are somewhat arbitrary boundaries.

2. As in early adulthood, the middle-aged adult has two primary tasks: to organize the external world or the contexts of development and to organize the inner world of the self.

3. The phases of the family life-cycle that typically coincide with the years of middle adulthood are: the family with school-aged children, the family with adolescents, the family as launching center, and the postparental family.

4. An important arena for the demonstration of adult competence is community activities. As in the case of career development, the middle-aged adult is usually at a peak of participation and influence in community activities. There is, of course, considerable variation in the type and degree of activities in middle adulthood.

5. Career development reaches its height during middle age. In many occupations, it is the middle-aged adult who moves into positions of leadership or prominence. Middle aged persons may assess their actual career or life activities in relation to their prior aspirations.

6. For many middle-aged adults, the first signal of the coming changes in social relationships and personality which are associated with aging are changes in general appearance, sensory perception, sexual functioning, or health. Wrinkled skin, extra body weight, and graying hair are some of the physical changes. There are also changes in sensory perception such as gradual declines in visual acuity and hearing. Changes in the appearance of the body are often accompanied by changes in the functioning of internal organs or organ systems (e.g., arteriosclerosis and high blood pressure).

7. Intellectual and cognitive functioning remain fairly stable throughout middle age. Evidence for this sustained cognitive functioning includes the numerous cultural, community, and educational activities that middle-aged adults perform.

8. One of the primary themes of personality development in adulthood is the attempt to achieve an integrated sense of self in the face of the many differentiated roles that the adult is expected to play. Adults tend to become increasingly varied in their outlooks and self-concepts. Some adults become more tolerant of themselves, more self-directed and more aware of situational complexities.

Questions

1. Is there a clear, distinct, and agreed upon age at which middle adulthood begins? Why or why not?
2. In what sense is middle age frequently a time for re-evaluation?
3. Is there a mid-life crisis? Why? Why not?
4. What does the "empty nest" mean with reference to middle age? Do you think that all middle-aged adults have the same reaction to the "empty nest?" Why? Why not?
5. Define the following terms and briefly discuss their importance: menopause, male climacteric, Type A personality, Type B personality, and arteriosclerosis.

Bibliography

BART, P. B. Mother Portnoy's complaints. *Trans-action*, November–December 1970, *8*, 69–74.

BARUCH, G. K., and BARNETT, R. C. On the well-being of adult women. In L. A. Bond and J. C. Rosen (Eds.), *Competence and Coping During Adulthood*. Hanover, N.H.: University Press of New England, 1980.

BIRREN, J. E. *The Psychology of Aging*. Englewood Cliffs, N.J.: Prentice-Hall, 1964.

BIRREN, J. E. Aging: the psychologist's perspective. In R. H. Davis (Ed.), *Aging: Prospects and Issues*. Los Angeles: University of Southern California Press, 1976, 16–28.

BISCHOF, L. J. *Adult Psychology*. New York: Harper and Row, 1976.

BOTWINICK, J. *Cognitive Processes in Maturity and Old Age*. New York: Springer, 1967, Figure 1.

BRONFENBRENNER, U., and CROUTER, A. C. Work through time and space. In S. Kamerman and C. D. Hayes (Eds.), *Families That Work: Children in a Changing World*. Washington, D.C.: National Academy Press, 1982, 39–83.

CAMPBELL, A., CONVERSE, P., and RODGERS, W. *The Quality of American Life: Perceptions, Evaluations and Satisfactions*. New York: Russell Sage Foundation, 1976.

CARTER, H., and GLICK, P. C. *Marriage and Divorce: A Social and Economic Study*. Cambridge, Mass.: Harvard U. P., 1970.

CLOPTON, W. Personality and career change. *Industrial Gerontology*, 1973, *17*, 9–17.

CYTRYNBAUM, S., BLUM, L., PATRICK, R., STEIN, J., WADES, D., and WILK, C. Midlife development: A Personality and Social Systems Perspective. In L. W. Poon (Ed.), *Aging in the 1980's: Psychological Issues*. Washington, D.C.: American Psychological Association, 1980, 463–474.

Daedalus, Spring 1976, *105*, (2) Special Issue on Adulthood.

DENNIS, W. Creative productivity between the ages of 20 and 80 years. *Journal of Gerontology*, 1966, *21*, 1–8.

DOHRENWEND, B. P., and DOHRENWEND, B. S. *Stressful Life Events*. New York: Wiley, 1974.

DUVALL, E. M. *Family Development* (4th ed.). Philadelphia: Lippincott, 1971.

ERIKSON, E. H. *Childhood and Society*. New York: Norton, 1950.

ERIKSON, E. H. Identity and the life cycle: Selected papers. *Psychological Issues Monographs*, Vol. 1, No. 1. New York: International Universities Press, 1967.

ERIKSON, E. H. Inner and outer space: Reflections in womanhood. In N. W. Bell and E. F. Vogel (Eds.), *A Modern Introduction to the Family*. New York: Free Press, 1968a.

ERIKSON, E. H. *Identity: Youth and Crisis*. New York: Norton, 1968b.

ERIKSON, E. H. Reflections on Dr. Borg's life cycle. *Daedalus*, Spring 1976, *105*(2), 1–28.

Family Economics Research Group, Updated estimates of the cost of raising a child. *Family Economics Review*, 1983, *4*, 30–31.

FEREE, M. Working-class jobs: Housework and paid work as sources of satisfaction. *Social Problems*, 1976, *23*, 431–441.

FINKLE, W. D., and ZIEL, H. K. Increased risk of endometrial carcinoma among users of conjugated estrogens. *New England Journal of Medicine*, 1975, *293*(23), 1167–1170.

FOZARD, J. L., NUTTALL, R. L., and WAUGH, N. C. Age-related differences in mental performance. *Aging and Human Development,* 1972, *3,* 19–42.

FRENCH, J. R. P., RODGERS, W. L., and COBB, S. Adjustment as person-environment fit. In G. Coelho, D. Hamburg, and J. E. Adams (Eds.), *Coping and Adaptation.* New York: Basic Books, 1974.

FRIED, B. *The Middle Age Crisis.* New York: Harper & Row, 1976.

FRIEDAN, B. *The Feminine Mystique.* New York: Norton, 1963.

FRIEDMAN, M., and ROSENMAN, R. H. *Type A Behavior and Your Heart.* New York: Knopf, 1974.

GEORGE, L. K., and WEILER, S. J. Sexuality in middle and late life: The effects of age cohort and gender. *Archives of General Psychiatry,* 1981.

GIELE, J. Z. Adulthood as transcendence of age and sex. In N. J. Smelser and E. H. Erikson (Eds.), *Themes of Work and Love in Adulthood.* Cambridge, Massachusetts: Harvard University Press, 1980, pp. 151–173.

GLASS, D. C. Stress, competition and heart attacks. *Psychology Today,* 1976, *10*(7), 54–57, 134.

GOULD, R. Adult life stages: Growth toward self-tolerance. *Psychology Today,* 1975, *8*(9), 74–78.

GOVE, W., and TUDOR, J. Adult sex roles and mental illness. *American Journal of Sociology,* 1973, *78,* 812–835.

GUTMANN, D. L. The cross-cultural perspective: Notes toward a comparative psychology of aging. In J. E. Birren and K. W. Schaie (Eds.), *Handbook of the Psychology of Aging.* New York: Van Nostrand Reinhold, 1977, 302–321.

HARRIS, SYDNEY J. What is Middle Age? In L. B. Schiamberg (Ed.), Proceedings of the National Conference on Middle Adulthood. Sponsored by the National Endowment for the Humanities. E. Lansing, Mich.: Michigan State University, 1983.

HAVIGHURST, R. J. The social competence of middle-aged people. *Genetic Psychology Monographs,* 1957, *56,* 297–375.

HAVIGHURST, R. J. *Developmental Tasks and Education.* (3rd ed.). New York: McKay, 1972.

HAVIGHURST, R. J., and ORR, B. *Adult Education and Adult Needs.* Chicago: Center for the study of liberal education for adults, 1956 (Available from Syracuse University, Publications in Continuing Education).

HEATH, D. H. Adolescent and adult predictors of vocational adaptation. *Journal of Vocational Behavior,* 1976, *9,* 1–19.

HENLE, P., and RYSCAVAGE, P. The distribution of earned income among men and women, 1958–1977. *Monthly Labor Review.* April 1980, 3–10.

HENRY, J. P., and CASSEL, J. C. Psychosocial factors in essential hypertension: Recent epidemiological and animal experimental evidence. *American Journal of Epidemiology.* 1969, *90,* 171–200.

HIRSCHFIELD, I. S., and DENNIS, H. Perspectives. In P. K. Ragan (Ed.), *Aging Parents.* Los Angeles: Ethel Percy Andrus Gerontology Center, University of Southern California P., 1979, pp. 1–10.

HOLMES, T. H., and RAHE, R. H. The social readjustment rating scale. *Journal of Psychosomatic Research,* 1967, *11,* 213–218.

HUNT, M. *Sexual Behavior in the 1970's.* New York: Dell, 1974.

JONES, H. E. Consistency and change in early maturity. *Vita Humana,* 1960, *3,* 17–31.

JONES, J. B., LUNDSTEEN, S. W., and MICHAEL, W. B. The relationship of the professional employment status of mothers to reading achievement of sixth grade children. *California Journal of Educational Research,* 1967, *43,* 102–108.

KAMERMAN, S., and HAYES, C. D. (Eds.), *Families that Work: Children in a Changing World.* Washington, D.C.: National Academy Press, 1982.

KANTOR, H. L., MICHAEL, C. M., BOULAS, S. H., SHORE, H., and LUDVIGSON, H. W. The administration of estrogens to older women: A psychometric evaluation. *Proceedings of the 7th International Congress of Gerontology,* 1966.

KIMMEL, D. C. *Adulthood and Aging.* New York: Wiley, 1974.

KIMMEL, D. C. *Adulthood and Aging*. (2nd ed.). New York: Wiley, 1980.

KINSEY, A. C., POMEROY, W. B., and MARTIN, C. R. *Sexual Behavior in the Human Male*. Philadelphia, Pennsylvania: Saunders, 1948.

KINSEY, A. C., POMEROY, W. B., and MARTIN, C. R. *Sexual Behavior in the Human Female*. Philadelphia, Pennsylvania: Saunders, 1953.

KIRBY, I. J. Hormone replacement therapy for postmenopausal symptoms. *Lancet,* 1973, *2,* 103.

KNOX, A. B. *Adult Development and Learning*. San Francisco: Jossey Bass, 1977.

KUHLEN, R. G. Aging. In J. E. Birren (Ed.), *Relations of Development and Aging*. Springfield, Illinois: Thomas, 1964, 209–246.

LEVINSON, D. J., DARROW, C. M., KLEIN, E. B., LEVINSON, M. H., and McKEE, B. The psychosocial development of men in early adulthood and the mid-life transition. In D. E. Ricks, A. Thomas, and M. Roff (Eds.), *Life History Research in Psychopathology,* Vol. 3. Minneapolis: University of Minnesota P., 1974.

LINDBERGH, A. M. *Gift from the Sea*. New York: Pantheon, 1955.

LIVSON, F. B. Sex-Roles. Paper presented at the meeting of the Gerontological Society, 1976.

LIVSON, F. B. Gender identity: A life-span view of sex-role development. In R. B. Weg (Ed.), *Sexuality in the Later Years: Roles and Behavior*. New York: Academic Press, 1983, 105–127.

LOWENTHAL, M. F., THURNHER, M., CHIRIBOGA, D., BEESON, D., GLAY, L. E., PIERCE, R., SPENCER, D., and WEISS, L. *Four Stages of Life: A Comparative Study of Women and Men Facing Transitions*. San Francisco: Jossey-Bass, 1975.

MAAS, H., and KUYPERS, J. A. *From thirty to seventy*. San Francisco, California: Jossey-Bass, 1974.

MASTERS, W. H., and JOHNSON, V. E. *Human Sexual Response*. Boston: Little, Brown, 1966.

MASTERS, W. H., and JOHNSON, V. E. *Human Sexual Inadequacy*. Boston: Little, Brown, 1970.

McCAMMON, R. W. *Human Growth and Development*. Springfield, Ill.: Thomas, 1970.

MOOS, R. H. *The Human Context: Environmental Determinants of Behavior*. New York: Wiley, 1976.

MOOS, R. H., and TSU, V. D. The crisis of physical illness: an overview. In R. H. Moss (Ed.), *Coping With Physical Illness*. New York: Plenum, 1977.

MURRAY, J. R., POWERS, E. A., and HAVIGHURST, R. J. Personal and situational factors producing flexible careers. *The Gerontologist,* 1971, *11,* 4–12.

NAUNTON, E. Middle aging: Downhill all the way, *The Miami Herald,* May 23, 1976.

NEUGARTEN, B. L. (Ed.). *Middle Age and Aging*. Chicago: U. of Chicago P., 1968.

NEUGARTEN, B. L. Personality and the aging process. *The Gerontologist,* 1972, *12,* 9–15.

NEUGARTEN, B. L. Personality and Aging. In J. E. Birren and K. W. Schaie (Eds.), *Handbook of the Psychology of Aging*. New York: Van Nostrand Reinhold, 1977, 626–649.

NEUGARTEN, B. L., and WEINSTEIN, K. The changing American grandparent. *Journal of Marriage and the Family,* 1964, *26*(2), 199–204.

NEUGARTEN, B. L., WOOD, V., KRAINES, R., and LOOMIS, B. Women's attitudes toward the menopause. *Vita Humana,* 1963, *6*(3), 140–151.

OLSON, L. *Costs of Children*. Lexington, Massachusetts: Lexington Books, 1983.

ORDEN, S., and BRADBURN, N. Working wives and marriage happiness. *American Journal of Sociology,* 1969, *74,* 392–407.

PFEIFFER, E., and DAVIS, G. C. Determinants of sexual behavior in middle and old age, *Journal of the American Geriatric Society,* 1972, *20,* 151–158.

PFEIFFER, E., VERWOERDT, A., and DAVIS, G. C. Sexual behavior in middle life. *American Journal of Psychiatry,* 1972, *128,* 82–87.

PINEO, P. Disenchantment in the later years of marriage. *Marriage and Family Living,* February 1961, *23,* 3–11.

RAPOPORT, R., and RAPOPORT, R. *Dual-Career Families*. Baltimore, M.D.: Penguin, 1971.

ROLLINS, B. C., and FELDMAN, H. Marital satisfaction over the family life cycle. *Journal of Marriage and the Family,* February 1970, *32*(1), 20–28.

ROSSI, A. S. Aging and parenthood in the middle years. In P. B. Baltes, and O. G. Brim, (Eds.), *Life-Span Development and Behavior* (Vol. 3) New York: Academic Press, 1980, 138–207.

SARASON, S. B. *Work, Aging and Social Change: Professionals and the One Life–One Career Imperative.* New York: The Free Press, 1977.

SCOTT, J. C. Membership and participation in voluntary organizations. *American Sociological Review,* 1957, *22,* 315–326.

SEDNEY, M. A. Sex-role development in adulthood: Growing beyond polarities. Paper presented at the 85th annual meeting of the American Psychological Association, San Francisco, 1977.

SHEEHY, G. *Passages: Predictable Crises of Adult Life.* New York: E. P. Dutton, 1976.

SILVERSTONE, B. Issues for the middle generation: Responsibility, adjustment, and growth. In P. K. Ragan (Ed.), *Aging Parents.* Los Angeles: Ethel Percy Andrus Gerontology Center, University of Southern California P., 1979, pp. 107–115.

SMITH, D. C., PRENTICE, R., THOMPSON, D., and HERMAN, W. Association of extrogenous estrogen and endometrial carcinoma. *New England Journal of Medicine,* 1975, *293*(23), 1164–1167.

SMITH, D. W., and BIERMAN, E. L. *The Biologic Ages of Man.* Philadelphia: Saunders, 1973.

SPRINGARN, N. D. Coping with the mid-life crisis. *Dynamic Maturity,* March 1977, 11–14.

STROUD, J. G. Women's careers: Work, family, and personality. In D. Eichorn, J. Clansen, N. Haan, M. Honzik, and P. Mussen (Eds.), *Present and Past in Middle Life.* New York: Academic Press, 1981, 353–390.

TERKEL, S. *Working.* New York: Pantheon, 1974.

TIMIRAS, P. S. *Developmental Physiology and Aging.* New York: Macmillan, 1972.

TROLL, L. The family in later life: A decade review. *Journal of Marriage and the Family,* 1971, *33,* 263–290.

U.S. BUREAU OF THE CENSUS. Money income of households, families, and persons in the United States: 1981, *Current Population Reports: Consumer Income,* Series P-60, No. 137, March 1983, Table 10, p. 27.

U.S. DEPARTMENT OF LABOR. Bureau of Labor Statistics. Employment and Earnings (January). Washington, D.C.: U.S. Government Printing Office, 1982.

WEILER, S. J. Aging and sexuality and the myth of decline. In R. W. Fogel, E. Hatfield, S. B. Kiesler, and E. Shanas (Eds.), *Aging: Stability and Change in the Family.* New York: Academic Press, 1981, 317–327.

WELFORD, A. T. Psychomotor performance. In J. E. Birren (Ed.), *Handbook of Aging and the Individual.* Chicago: U. of Chicago P., 1959.

WILSON, R. A. *Feminine Forever.* New York: Evans, 1966.

WOODRUFF, R. M., FRIEDMAN, C. D., SIEGELAUB, A. B., and COLLON, M. F. Pain tolerance: Differences according to age, sex, and race. *Psychosomatic Medicine,* 1972, *34,* 548–556.

WRIGHT, C., and HYMEN, H. Voluntary association memberships of American adults— Evidence from national sample surveys. *American Sociological Review,* 1958, *23,* 284–294.

WRIGHT, J. D. Are working women really more satisfied? Evidence from several national surveys. *Journal of Marriage and the Family,* 1978, *40,* 301–313.

Suggested Readings

ASLANIAN, C. B., and BRICKELL, H. M. *Americans in Transition: Life Changes As Reasons For Adult Learning.* New York: College Entrance Examination Board, 1980. A well-written examination of the relationship between life transitions, such as loss of a job or divorce, and the need for adult education.

EICHORN, D. H., CLAUSEN, J. A., HAAN, N., HONZIK, M. P., and MUSSEN, P. H. (Eds.). *Present and Past in Middle Life*. New York: Academic Press, 1981. A longitudinal study of numerous aspects of middle adulthood, including interpersonal dimensions, health, sex role changes, women's careers, and social maturity.

GOULD, R. *Transformations*. New York: Simon and Schuster, 1978. An excellent discussion of the changes in middle age as well as practical suggestions for coping with these changes.

LERNER, R., and SPANIER, G. *Child Influences on Marital and Family Interaction: A Life-Span Perspective*. New York: Academic Press, 1978. A readable and scholarly collection of articles on the impact of the child on the quality of marital and family relationships.

LEVINSON, D. *The Seasons of a Man's Life*. New York: Knopf, 1978. The author provides an interesting and stimulating discussion of mid-life career adjustments, and marriage and emotional crises.

TROLL, L. E. *Early and Middle Adulthood*. Monterey, California: Brooks/Cole, 1975. A comprehensive description of middle adulthood.

VAILLANT, G. *Adaptation to Life*. Boston, Massachusetts: Little, Brown, 1977. Focuses on the results of a study of adult adaptation and mental health.

WEG, RUTH B. (Ed.). *Sexuality in the Later Years: Roles and Behavior*. New York: Academic Press, 1983. A comprehensive collection of research reviews on significant physical and personality dimensions of adult sexuality.

WHITBOURNE, S. K., and WEINSTOCK, C. S. *Adult Development: The Differentiation of Experience*. New York: Holt, Rinehart and Winston, 1979. A thorough examination of middle and later adulthood with careful consideration of identity, intimacy, and cognitive development.

12

Later Adulthood and Aging

NOTHING IS FOREVER

From the time you are conceived until after your death, you are in a state of dynamic change. Some changes result primarily from processes going on within the organism; some evolve largely as the result of relationships with other organisms. . . . As you become older, you change in size, appearance, awareness of the world, intellectual capacity, sexual drives and innumerable other ways. As you undergo change, the perceptions others have of you undergo similar (although not necessarily congruous) change.

Moreover, the others who are perceiving you are themselves undergoing change. Your parents change from people who control you to people with whom you can interact on some basis of equality to people you may have to care for. Your children change from weak, helpless infants to independent adults. Brothers and sisters, teachers and clergymen, neighbors and friends, and employers, coworkers and employees are all changing. A permanent relationship with someone of the opposite sex (and occasionally of the same sex) is established. It grows, changes its course many times and is eventually broken by death, by separation, or by psychological withdrawal.

NOTHING IS FOREVER

From R. A. Kalish, *Late Adulthood: Perspectives on Human Development.* Monterey, Calif.: Brooks/Cole, 1975.

Photograph by Darryl Jacobson

Who Are Older Adults?

A common age often given for the beginning of later adulthood is sixty-five. The selection of sixty-five as the boundary between middle age and later adulthood is an arbitrary choice. Why sixty-five? The use of this age was borrowed from the social legislation of Otto von Bismarck, who was the chancellor of Germany in the 1880s. This definition of old age (sixty-five years old and over) has been used in other countries (including the United States) primarily as a social way of determining the age of retirement from some jobs or the age at which some social benefits become available (e.g., Social Security payments or health-care benefits).

Beyond providing us with an arbitrary age for retirement, sixty-five is nearly irrelevant in describing other aspects of adult functioning. For example, simply knowing that an adult is sixty-five years old tells us little about his or her general health, creativity, physical or psychological endurance, or mental capacities. Older adults vary considerably in their physical status and behavior. In fact, older adults vary more in biological and behavioral functioning than young and middle-aged adults (Botwinick and Thompson, 1968). If we know that someone is thirty-five years old, we can probably make some rather accurate predictions about what that person can do: a thirty-five-year-old can probably walk a mile, read a magazine or newspaper, and use eating utensils to feed herself or himself (to name a few behaviors). However, if we try to predict even such minimal behaviors for a seventy-five-year-old, our predictive accuracy diminishes considerably.

NUMBERS OF ELDERLY ADULTS

Total Number. One of the most significant demographic trends of the twentieth century has been the aging of the population in most industrialized nations. In the United States in 1900 only 3.1 million people, or four percent of the total population, were 65 years of age or older. By 1980 that number had increased eight times, reaching 25 million individuals, or 11 percent of the population. By the year 2000, it is projected that almost 32 million persons will be 65 years of age or older (12 percent of the total population) (see Figure 12.1). Furthermore, it is expected that the ranks of the population of adults 65 years old and older will increase rapidly during the second and third decades of the twenty-first century when the children of the post World War II "baby boom" reach later adulthood (individuals who were born between 1946 and 1964 are commonly considered to be the "baby boom" generation). (White House Conference on Aging, 1981).

Important changes are occurring within the aging population itself. That is, the older population is itself, growing older. The 75-plus segment of the older adult population (65 years and over) is presently the fastest growing age group in the United States (see Figure 12.2). In the year 1900, there were fewer than one million persons over 75 years of age and only 100,000 persons over 85 years of age. However, by 1980, the number had grown to 9.5 million persons aged 75 and older and 2.3 million persons 85 and over. While the total population of adults 65 years and above has increased eightfold since 1900, the population of adults 85 and over has grown 22 times since 1900 (White House Conference on Aging, 1981). The enormous increases in the 75–84 population and the 85-plus population have vast implications for future economic, social, and health care policies for older adults.

What is old age?

Photograph by Darryl Jacobson

"To be seventy years young is sometimes more cheerful and hopeful than to be forty years old."
Oliver Wendell Holmes

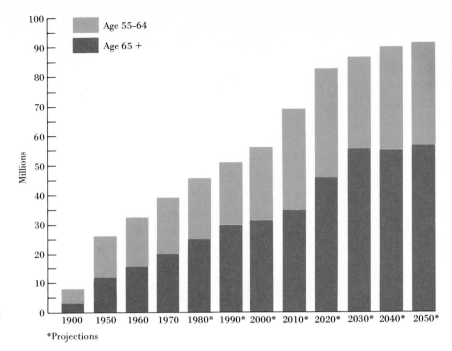

FIGURE 12.1 Number of persons aged 55–64 and 65 and over, 1900 and 1950 to 2050.

Source: White House Conference on Aging, *Chartbook on Aging in America*, 1981, p. 3.

Another perspective for thinking about these demographic changes in the older adult population is the increased life expectancy of older adults. In 1900, the average adult life expectancy was only 47 years and, as mentioned, only 4 percent of the population was over 65 years of age. The probability of a marriage lasting into a couple's forties or fifties was rather small. Retirement was hardly a concern. The most recent estimates of average life expectancy indicate that it reached a record 72.3 years in 1978 (U.S. Dept. of Health and

FIGURE 12.2 Distribution of the older population by age group, 1950 and 1980 to 2030.

Source: White House Conference on Aging, *Chartbook on Aging in America*, 1981, p. 3.

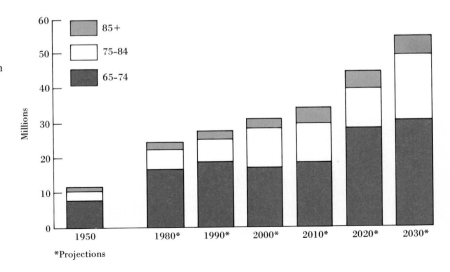

Later Adulthood and Aging

Human Services, National Center for Health Statistics, 1981). This increase has been the result of two major factors.

1. *A substantial reduction in infant mortality.* During the first half of this century, most of the increase in average life expectancy was primarily due to declines in deaths at younger ages. That is, more people lived to older ages; however, once there, they were not living any longer than their ancestors who reached such ages (U.S. Dept. of Health and Human Services, National Center for Health Statistics, 1981).

2. *A dramatic improvement in health care.* From 1950 to 1978, average life expectancy *at age 65* increased more than it did during the first half of the century. The largest gains have occurred since 1970 due to significant declines in deaths due to heart disease and stroke.

In 1978, white females had the highest life expectancy at age 65 with an average of 18.4 years remaining. They were followed by females of other races (18.0 years) males of races other than white (14.1) and white males (14.0) (see Figure 12.3).

If declining mortality rates continue, particularly at 65 years and above, the number of people in the older age group may increase even more than current projections.

Men and Women. Is the population of older people composed equally of men and women? Or, put another way, do men and women have the same life expectancy? In 1980, approximately 15 million women were over sixty-five years old compared with 10.5 million men (U.S. Bureau of the Census, 1982). Until about age twenty-four boys tend to outnumber girls in the population of the United States (see Table 12.1). After that age, a shift occurs. Females outnumber males from that point on. In the age group sixty-five and over, there are over 4½ million more women than men (U.S. Bureau of the Census, 1983).

FIGURE 12.3 Life expectancy at age 65, 1970 to 1978.

Source: U.S. Department of Health and Human Services, National Center for Health Statistics, 1981.

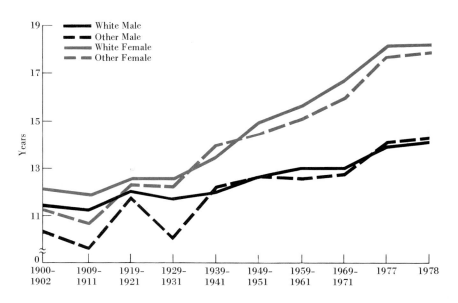

TABLE 12.1
**Number of Males per 100
Females by Age**

Age in Years	Males per 100 Females
Under 15	104.6
15 to 24	101.7
25 to 34	98.3
35 to 44	96.2
45 to 54	93.4
55 to 64	87.9
65 to 74	76.6
75 to 84	59.0
85 and over	43.7

Source: U.S. Bureau of the Census, Department of Commerce, "1980 Census of Population." *General Population Characteristics,* PC 80-1-B1. Washington, D.C.: U.S. Government Printing Office, 1983, Table 41, p. 23.

OTHER POPULATION CHARACTERISTICS

Marital Status. The fact that women live longer than men has an impact, of course, on the marital status of older adults (see Table 12.2). Most elderly women are widows; they have simply outlived their husbands. Likewise, most elderly men are married. There are almost six times as many widows as widowers among the elderly (U.S. Bureau of the Census, 1983a). This imbalance of men and women represents a concern of the aged. It is considerably easier for an elderly man to remarry than for an older woman.

Living Arrangements. Where do the elderly live? One of the most common myths about older adults is that large numbers of them live in such institutions as hospitals for chronic diseases, nursing homes, or mental institutions. In reality, only about 5 percent of the elderly are in such institutions (U.S. Bureau of the Census, 1983a) (see Figure 12.4). Almost 95 percent of the elderly are on their own in the community. They may be living alone or with nonrelatives, or living with a spouse, or living with other relatives.

Significant differences in living arrangements exist by age and sex for the elderly (see Figure 12.4). Living arrangements for older women have shown marked changes in recent years as the proportion of older women living in family settings (living with a spouse or living with other relatives) has sharply

TABLE 12.2
**Marital Status
of Older Persons
by Sex and Age: 1980**

| Sex and age | Percentage Distribution | | | |
	Single	Married	Widowed	Divorced
Male				
65–74 years	4.9	83.0	8.2	3.9
75 years and over	3.5	72.0	22.1	2.5
Female				
65–74 years	5.4	50.1	40.1	4.4
75 years and over	6.2	23.3	68.2	2.3

Source: United States Bureau of the Census, *Statistical Abstracts of the United States* (103rd Edition). Washington, D.C.: United States Government Printing Office, 1982–83.

FIGURE 12.4 Living arrangements of the 65+ population by sex and age group, 1979.

Source: White House Conference on Aging, 1981, *Chartbook on Aging in America,* p. 17, I-8, 1981.

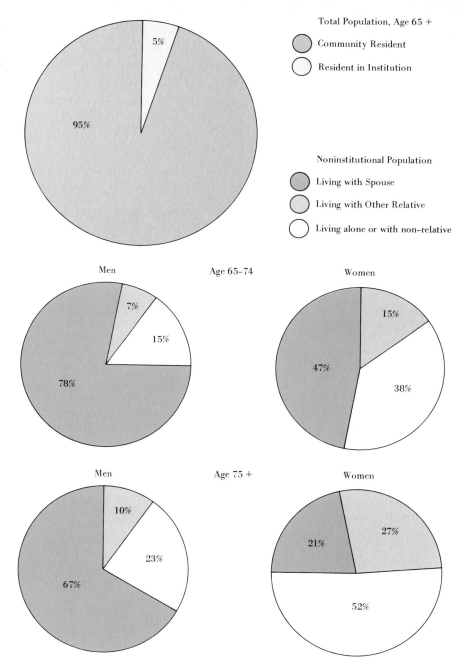

Total Population, Age 65 +

⬤ Community Resident

◯ Resident in Institution

Noninstitutional Population

⬤ Living with Spouse

◯ Living with Other Relative

◯ Living alone or with non–relative

Men   Age 65–74   Women

Men   Age 75 +   Women

declined while the proportion maintaining their own households has increased dramatically. Most men live in a family setting with their spouse throughout later adulthood (78 percent of all males, ages 65–74 and 67 percent of all males 75 and older). In contrast, only 47 percent of all women age

65–74 lived in a husband–wife household. This figure drops even more to only 21 percent of all women age 75 and above who live with their husbands. By age 75 slightly more than one-half of all women (52 percent) head up their own households (live alone or with a nonrelative) as contrasted to only 23 percent of all men who do so.

Racial and Ethnic Makeup. Whites constitute by far the largest segment of the older adult population (see Figure 12.5). In 1980 approximately 23 million persons aged 65 and over were white (about 90 percent of all older adults, 65 years and above). This was followed by 2.1 million or 8.2 percent who were black, 539,000 or 2.3 percent who were of Hispanic origin, and 514,000 or 2.0 percent who were of "other" races (i.e., American Indians, Eskimos, Aleuts, Asians, and Pacific Islanders).

Income. Unfortunately, poverty is often associated with being old. In 1979, the poverty rate was 15.1 percent for the elderly and 11.6 percent for the total U.S. population. Furthermore, an additional 2.3 million persons or 10 percent of the older adult population were classified as "near poor," with incomes barely above the poverty level. Therefore, in aggregate numbers, 25 percent of the older adult population were either poor, or near poor, in 1979. (White House Conference on Aging, 1981).

Certain groups are disproportionately represented in the ranks of the elderly poor. Older women, particularly those who live alone, are far more likely to be poor than older men. Minority groups are also overrepresented among the elderly poor (White House Conference on Aging, 1981). A large percentage of the income of the elderly poor must go toward necessities.

Most of [their] money must go for food, shelter and medical expenses—the essentials of existence. . . . [This spending pattern] has given rise to the old myth that the aged can live on less because they do not need as much for clothing, transportation, entertainment, recreation or education as the young. The truth is simply that the elderly are not able to afford these items, which for younger people are considered necessary for mental health, social status, avoidance of isolation, and growth of the individual. (Butler and Lewis, 1982, p. 15).

FIGURE 12.5 Percent of population aged 65 and over in each color and race group, 1980.

Source: White House Conference on Aging, 1981, *Chartbook on Aging in America*, p. 23, I-11, 1981.

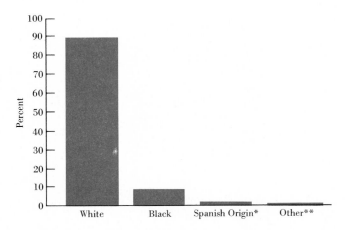

*Spanish Origin may be of any race.
**Other includes American Indians, Eskimos, Aleuts, Asians, and Pacific Islanders.

Later Adulthood and Aging

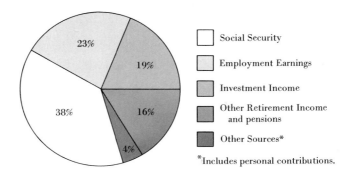

FIGURE 12.6 Percent of aggregate money income of older persons by source.

Sources: White House Conference on Aging, 1981, *Chartbook on Aging in America*, p. 61, III-6, 1981; Upp, 1983, pp. 9–10.

Social Security

Employment Earnings

Investment Income

Other Retirement Income and pensions

Other Sources*

*Includes personal contributions.

There are four major sources of income for the 65 and older population (see Figure 12.6):

- Social Security benefits (38 percent);
- Employment earnings (23 percent);
- Investments (19 percent);
- And other retirement income and pensions (16 percent).

Taken together these four sources provide 96 percent of the total money income of older adult population. The remaining 4 percent comes from other sources including personal contributions (White House Conference on Aging, 1981).

Although most Social Security recipients have more than one source of income, Social Security is the major source of income for a large number of older adults. Originally only intended to be an income base, Social Security nonetheless provided half of the total income for nearly 60 percent of couples and was the sole source of income for 20 percent of single beneficiaries 85 years and above in 1978 (White House Conference on Aging, 1981). Several trends have created a serious strain on the Social Security system. These trends include the rapid increase in the size of the older population, the trend toward early retirement of workers, the reduction in the number of workers whose earnings provide the funds for the Social Security system, and the large growth in the number of Social Security recipients. By the end of 1979 there were 18.6 million retired persons compared to 12.6 million a decade earlier—a 50 percent increase. During that same period the work force increased by only 27 percent (White House Conference on Aging, 1981).

Employment. One of the most dramatic changes in the U.S. labor force in the twentieth century has been the significant reduction in the proportion of older men in the labor force. In 1900, almost 67 percent of men aged 65 and over were in the work force. By 1980, the figure was only 20 percent. Projections indicate that this trend will continue throughout the 1980s despite the increased number of the population of men over 65 years of age. This trend could be reversed if social policies were altered to favor older workers and delay retirement.

The current trend toward "early retirement" is indicated by the increasing number of persons who claim Social Security benefits prior to age 65. One-third of all Social Security recipients presently retire at 62 years of age. Cur-

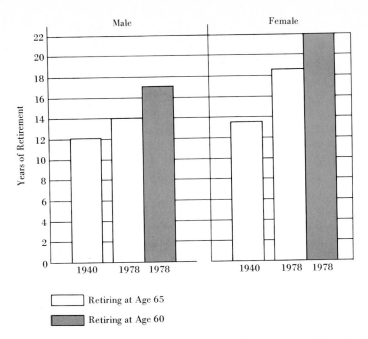

FIGURE 12.7 Years of retirement (average life expectancy), by sex, 1940 and 1978.

Source: White House Conference on Aging, 1981, *Chartbook on Aging in America*, p. 43, II-5, 1981.

rently almost 60 percent of all retired workers receiving Social Security payments are getting "reduced benefits" because they started drawing their benefits prior to age 65. The trend toward early retirement and the increased life expectancy of older adults has resulted in a lengthening of the years the average person spends in retirement (see Figure 12.7). After age sixty-five or seventy, the opportunities for older adults to work is restricted by two primary factors (In 1978, the U.S. Congress amended the Age Discrimination in Employment Act to abolish mandatory retirement in federal civil-service jobs and generally to raise the mandatory retirement age from sixty-five to seventy years of age):

- *The Social Security ceiling on earnings.* A limit is placed on the maximum amount that an older person can earn if he or she wishes to collect a full Social-Security payment. If more than this specified limit is earned, the Social Security check is reduced. (As of 1983, retirees under 65 years of age could earn up to $4,920.00 without penalty of reduction in Social Security income. Individuals between 65–69 years could earn $6,600.00 without penalty. Retirees who were 70 years and older were not subject to an earnings penalty.)
- *Age discrimination in employment.* There is often a bias against hiring and retaining older workers because it is assumed, erroneously, that older workers can no longer perform satisfactorily (see Application Box: Job-Related Stereotypes of Older Adults).

INTERLUDE: ELDERLY BLACK WORKERS

Black aged men participate in the labor force in the same proportions as whites; but they earn less, do harder physical work, and are in poorer health (. . . they die an average of seven and a half years sooner than white males). Elderly black

Later Adulthood and Aging

15.1 percent of the elderly adults in the United States are poor.

Photograph by Darryl Jacobson

women are more likely to work than white women, indicating their greater need to support themselves or supplement their husband's earnings. They, like black men, earn less, usually doing domestic and service work. Retirement by choice is less an option because blacks' retirement benefits are often meager, in line with their previous low earnings. Indeed there may be no benefits at all. When they can no longer work, the black elderly are simply mustered out of the labor market. They frequently must turn to Supplemental Security Income (SSI) as the only income source available. Thus SSI programs have a disproportionate number of aged blacks on their rolls compared to whites and it is important to understand why.

From R. N. Butler and M. I. Lewis, *Aging and Mental Health.* 3rd ed. St. Louis: Mosby, 1982, p. 17.

The Later Adulthood System: An Overview

As in early and middle adulthood, old age can be viewed from two primary perspectives: the organization of an external world and the organization of an internal world (see Figure 12.8).

THE ORGANIZATION OF AN EXTERNAL WORLD

There are several important "contexts" of development in which older adults usually operate. These contexts include the following.

Job-Related Stereotypes of Older Adults

The question of age stereotypes in the working world was examined by Rosen and Jerdee (1976b). Specifically they were interested in the relationship of the age of the worker to managerial decisions. In their study, they presented forty-two business students (all in their twenties) with six situations requiring a managerial decision. There were two versions of each situation, and each business student was given six "memos" that described the focal person or worker as either "younger" or "older." Each management student received only one version (younger or older) of the six memos to minimize awareness of the intent of the study. A photograph of the worker accompanied four of the memos.

The six memos involved the following situations:

1. A newly employed shipping-room employee who seemed to be unresponsive to customer service calls.
2. Managerial consideration of a candidate for promotion to a marketing position that would require "a high degree of creative innovative behavior" and "fresh solutions to challenging problems."
3. Managerial consideration of hiring a person for a position requiring knowledge of the field as well as the ability to make "quick judgments under high risk."
4. An employee's request to transfer to a higher-paying and more physically demanding job.
5. A production staff worker's request to attend a conference on "new theories and research relevant to production systems."
6. A managerial decision whether to retrain or terminate a computer programmer whose skills had become outdated with the introduction of changes in computer operations.

The results of the study were as follows:

The younger shipping-room employee was seen as being capable of change, and a managerial reprimand was suggested to solve the problem. On the other hand, the older shipping-room worker was not expected to alter his behavior.

The management students suggested that he should be replaced.

Of the management students who reviewed the younger candidate, 54 percent recommended promotion to the marketing job. Only 24 percent recommended that the older candidate be promoted. It should be noted that the candidates had identical qualifications.

Of the management students who reviewed the younger candidate for the "risk-taking" job, 25 percent recommended selection. Only 13 percent of those who reviewed the older candidate recommended hiring that person.

The older worker who wished to transfer to a more physically demanding job was much less likely to have the request approved than a younger worker.

The older production worker was significantly more likely to be refused permission to attend the conference than the younger worker.

The older computer programmer was much more likely to be fired than to be retrained.

Rosen and Jerdee concluded that managerial assumptions about the physical, mental, and emotional makeup of older workers resulted in management decisions that were neither fair nor in the best interests of older workers. This study was seen as supporting a previous one (Rosen and Jerdee, 1976a) that showed that managers stereotyped older workers as overly cautious or slow to make decisions, lower in physical capacity, resistant to change, uncreative, untrainable, and generally uninterested in technological change. The current study confirmed that management decisions dealing with such important matters as the hiring, retention, retraining, and in-service education of older workers suffered simply because of the age of the worker.

YOUR OPINION
- Do you think that the results of the Rosen and Jerdee study accurately portray the situation in the American work setting?
- Can you think of examples of family, friends, or others who have suffered from age-based job biases?

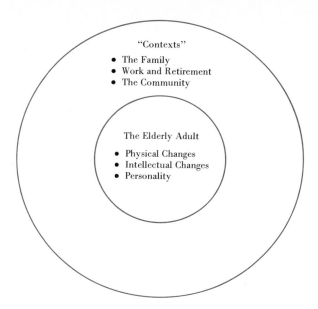

"Contexts"
- The Family
- Work and Retirement
- The Community

The Elderly Adult
- Physical Changes
- Intellectual Changes
- Personality

FIGURE 12.8 The system of later adulthood.

The Family. Several significant adaptations in family relationships occur in later adulthood. Aged individuals and their adult children ideally develop a mature relationship based on a realistic blending of dependency and reciprocity (see Chapter Eleven). In addition the married older couple may continue to adapt to the "empty nest."

The *role of grandparent* is an important aspect in the lives of some elderly adults. About 70 percent of people over age sixty-five have grandchildren. There are several reasons that grandparenting is important in the lives of older adults:

1. "Being a grandparent may take on special meaning to the elderly as other areas of role-performance become closed to them" (Kalish, 1975, p. 80).
2. Furthermore, grandparents can have meaningful relationships with their grandchildren while experiencing minimal obligation and responsibility.
3. The role of grandparent provides many older adults with a sense of human continuity and biological renewal (a sense of immortality through the grandchild) (Neugarten and Weinstein, 1964).

The end of marriage in later adulthood—usually through the death of one partner (usually the husband) creates a new role—widowhood—for the surviving partner. This new role requires adaptive skills.

The Community. There are several significant dimensions of the older adult's relationship to the community, including the changing nature of friendships and participation in community activities and the quality of housing for the elderly. Successful adaptation to changes in community organization, housing, and friendship patterns is an important basis for the morale and life satisfaction of older adults (Kalish, 1975).

Work and Retirement. One of the major role changes in the lives of older adults is retirement. Throughout childhood, adolescence, and adulthood, work has loomed as a major factor in the identity of the individual. For many adults, the important—if not the central—role of work in the determination of the life process must now be reexamined.

THE ORGANIZATION OF AN INTERNAL WORLD

The changes in the self that characterize later adulthood are the result of several factors, including physical and biological changes, intellectual changes, and changes in personality.

Physical Changes. The elderly experience many changes in their outward appearance and their biological functioning, such as the loss of hair and teeth, skin wrinkles, fading eyesight and hearing, and changes in posture. Relatively little is known about the origins of these changes, and many have been thought to be the consequences of aging. However, there is reason to think that some changes in body appearance and function may be due to diseases

---

APPLICATION BOX

Good-Bye to Ageism

Modern research indicates that a high proportion of the mental and attitudinal changes seen in "old" people are not biological effects of aging. They are the results of role playing. When women were expected to faint at the sight of blood, or black people to be amiable Uncle Toms, some of them did and were; now that those roles are seen to be demeaning or ridiculous, they don't and aren't. . . .

The trouble with the part we assign to "the old" is that it is a destructive part. They are supposed to be physically and intellectually infirm, slow on the uptake and rigid in their ways.

The salient fact is obvious enough. "Old" people are people who have lived a certain number of years, and *that is all.* If they have physical problems, so do younger people. . . .

The real curse of being old is the ejection from a citizenship traditionally based on work. In other words, it is a demeaning idleness, nonuse, not being called on any longer to contribute, and hence being put down as a spent person of no public account, instructed to run away and play until death comes out to call us to bed. . . .

When you are "old" you will feel no different and be no different from what you are now or were when you were young, except that more experiences will have happened. In age your appearance will change, however, and you may encounter more physical problems. When you do, these will affect you only as physical problems affect a person of any age. An "aged" person is simply a person who has been there longer than a young person. . . .

Getting these attitudes over to people, "old" and not old, is probably the main outstanding task of social gerontology. Aging as a physical change is relatively unimportant compared with aging as a social nonevent. The only necessary losses of age (necessary because some of them occur to everyone) are physical. All the other losses we see as the natural consequences of being over 60, over 70, or over 80 are unnecessary, organizational, conventional.

Reprinted from *A Good Age* by Alex Comfort. Copyright © 1976 by Mitchell Beazley Publishers, Ltd. Used by permission of Crown Publishers, Inc. pp. 10–13, 16, 28–29, 31–33.

(e.g., heart or bone diseases) or to exposure to some environmental elements (e.g., cigarette smoke or polluted air) (Butler and Lewis, 1982).

Changes in body function and physical health play an important role in determining the available energy and adaptive skills of older adults.

Older people experience a good deal more acute and chronic disease than the younger population. Specific physical disabilities and diseases such as cardiovascular (heart-related) and locomotor afflictions (e.g., arthritis) are particularly debilitating. . . . Perceptual losses of eyesight and hearing can deplete energy and cause social isolation. However, although 86 percent of the elderly have one or more chronic health problems, 95 percent are able to live in the community. Their conditions are mild enough to enable 81 percent of the elderly to get around with no outside assistance. (Butler and Lewis, 1982, p. 28).

Intellectual Changes. On the whole, there does not appear to be a decline in intellectual abilities with age. Usually, good physical health, sufficient educational experiences, and a reasonably stimulating environment are enough to sustain intellectual and cognitive capacities.

Personality Changes. Sometimes older people are described as being irritable, mean-tempered, forgetful, depressed, rigid, or dependent, to name only a few personality descriptors. In many—perhaps most—cases, there are inaccurate descriptions of an older adult's personality. Such general assessments often do not distinguish among continuous personality traits (relatively constant throughout an individual's life), emotional responses to physical illnesses, and responses to the loss of loved ones or friends.

The Contexts of the Later Adulthood System

In this section, we discuss the significant contexts of later adulthood: the family, the community, and work, including retirement.

THE FAMILY

The Myth of the "Alienated" Elderly. One of the myths of family life in later adulthood is that American families abandon their elderly. Supposedly the modern nuclear family is a streamlined unit that requires mobility and emotional self-sufficiency and has no room for older parents or grandparents. Although this description may sound like a classical picture of the nuclear family, it is not true that older adults are left to shift for themselves.

Statistics indicate that approximately 20 percent of elderly adults in the United States live alone. The vast majority of these people are divorced, widowed, or unmarried. Many are women. Although they may have children, they apparently prefer to live apart from them. The majority of elderly adults (approximately 80 percent) do, however, live with family members. *Most older people prefer to live with their spouse or alone for as long as such independent living is possible.* Only when this is not possible do they wish to move in with family members (Butler and Lewis, 1982).

Many policymakers seem to have accepted as facts three common myths about old people and their families: first, that older people are alienated from their children;

second, that older people, particularly those living alone, are isolated; and third, that families are unwilling or unable to care for their frail elderly members.

Contrary to these myths, the family . . . is the major resource of its older members for emotional and social support, crisis intervention, and bureaucratic linkages. Using data from three successive nationwide probability surveys of noninstitutionalized persons aged 65 and over made in 1957, 1962, and 1975, Shanas [1978, 1979] [found that] older people are not alienated from children and other relatives, that most old people living alone either had daily visitors or visited other people, and that about twice as many people were bedfast and housebound at home as were in institutions of all kinds. (From Shanas and Sussman, 1981, pp. 218–219).

Relationships between adults and their aging parents can take many forms. If they live close together, then they may visit each other often or do many things together, including shopping, recreation, and religious activities. If they do not live close together, then they may still telephone one another, write letters, and get together at special family events, such as anniversaries, reunions, funerals, or birthday parties.

Family support patterns can include giving gifts, financial assistance, and emotional support. It is interesting to note that the proportion of older parents who help their adult children is larger than the proportion of adult children who help their aging parents (Kivett, 1976). Older parents appear not to have high expectations of support, especially financial assistance, from their children (Watson and Kivett, 1976). Only 7 percent of aging parents receive financial help from relatives, whereas 12 percent of adult children receive financial assistance from their aging parents. Aging parents offer such help to their adult children in spite of their own limited resources (Watson and Kivett, 1976).

Grandparents. Grandparenthood is a common experience for older adults. Some 70 percent of all older people have grandchildren. Almost 32 percent of adults over sixty-five have great-grandchildren (Butler and Lewis, 1982). There are many different *styles* of grandparenting (see Chapter Eleven). Interactions between grandparents and grandchildren may include several kinds of experiences (Smith, 1965):

- Short and long visits.
- Exchange of letters, telephone calls, and other forms of communication.
- Exchange of gifts.
- Sharing of experiences.

AN INTERLUDE ON GRANDPARENTHOOD

Grandparenthood is a new lease on life because grandparents—grandmothers more intensely than grandfathers—relive the memories of the early phase of their own parenthood in observing the growth and development of their grandchildren. Grandparenthood is, however, parenthood one step removed. Relieved from the immediate stresses of motherhood and the responsibilities of fatherhood, grandparents appear to enjoy their grandchildren more than they enjoyed their own children. . . . Since they do not have the responsibility for raising the child. . . . their love is not as burdened by doubts and anxieties as it was when their own children were young. (Benedek, 1970, p. 201)

Family Support Systems for the Aged Individual— An Ominous Future?

Despite the continuing importance of family support systems for the aged, historical changes have created new constraints on families in caring for aging kin. Demographic change has reduced the number of descendents to whom an older person may turn for assistance. Change in women's social roles, particularly the rise in work outside the home, has fostered obligations which compete with duties toward aging parents. Transformations of the economy have decreased parents' power to insure their support by grown offspring. . . .

DEMOGRAPHIC CHANGES IN INTERGENERATIONAL RELATIONSHIPS

. . . Today's middle-aged adult is more likely to have a living parent than his counterpart in the past. Despite the improved survival chances of offspring, the aging parent, having raised fewer children, will have fewer descendents to call upon for assistance than did his own parent. The increasing mobility of American society has been indicted for restricting the older generation's day-to-day access to younger kin, but declining fertility is the demographic process more profoundly affecting the availability of younger family members. . . .

WOMEN'S CHANGING SOCIAL ROLES

Children routinely provide to aging parents services, companionship, financial aid, gifts, advice, and counsel. These family exchanges often reveal a sexual division of labor in the care of older kin. Lopata (1973) . . . found . . . sons helpful in managing funeral arrangements and financial matters while their daughters fostered closer emotional ties by giving services and visiting. As the mainstay of family support systems, it is daughters who have taken widowed mothers into their homes. . . .

The care of aging parents is but one of a number of competing responsibilities confronting mature women. Children and spouses also pose demands. . . .

Postwar years have witnessed dramatic changes in the social roles of women in the United States. Increasingly, women work for pay outside the home. . . . Although their jobs may offer personal satisfactions in terms of career accomplishment, social contacts, or just keeping busy, most women admit that they work because they need the money. . . .

It is uncertain how many working women might quit their jobs in order to furnish daily care to older kin who are sick or senile. We do know that [by March 1981, a record 8.2 million children below age 6—45 percent of all preschoolers—had working mothers (Grossman, 1982).] . . . If so many mothers are willing to trust the care of small children to others in order to work, women are probably willing to delegate responsibility for . . . aging parents as well. These trends in women's roles outside the home portend a future in which the family can no longer offer day-to-day care to aged who can no longer care for themselves.

DECREASING PARENTAL POWER

Historical changes in the economic organization of society have operated to reduce the economic clout which aged parents can exercise over grown children, because material legacies are of lessened importance to the financial success and security of offspring. Today, one's livelihood commonly derives from a job rather than from the family farm or business enterprise. . . .

Reprinted by permission of *The Gerontologist*/the *Journal of Gerontology*, 1977, *17*(6), 486–491.

Photograph by Darryl Jacobson

Although the grandparent role may be a meaningful and satisfying one for *some* older people, it may *not* be a significant role for others. Wood and Robertson (1976) found that life satisfaction of older adults was significantly related to their friendships and organizational activities rather than to their grandparent role activities. Wood and Robertson stated: "This supports Blau's contention (1973) that an older person who has a single good friend is more able to cope with old age than one who has a dozen grandchildren but no peer-group friends" (1976, p. 299).

How do grandchildren respond to grandparents? When we look at the relationship from the perspective of the child, we find that the feelings of grandchildren are important to the overall quality of the relationship. Children's feelings toward their grandparents depend on such things as the child's perception of the grandparent (e.g., kind, helpful, nasty), the parent's relationship to the grandparents, the child's perception of older people in general, and the grandparent's actual behavior toward the grandchildren (Kahana and Kahana, 1970, 1971). Children's responses to their grandparents also vary in terms of the child's age. Younger children react positively to gifts, small favors, and open expressions of affection. Older children seem to respond more favorably to shared activities or having fun with the grandparent (Butler and Lewis, 1982).

The Elderly Married Couple. During the period of later adulthood, the couple is usually retired from work, so both partners spend more time together at home than in middle adulthood. Marital relationships that may have been held together in previous years because both husband and wife were busy with jobs or with their children and could therefore avoid encoun-

Later Adulthood and Aging

tering one another may now become difficult and stressful. There appears to be no consensus among researchers on whether the later years of marriage are more or less satisfying than the earlier years of marriage. There is some evidence that the later years of marriage are marked by increasing unhappiness (Pineo, 1968; Blake, 1974). On the other hand, other researchers seem to find an increase in marital satisfaction in the later years (Rollins and Cannon, 1974; Stinnett, Carter, and Montgomery, 1972).

INTERLUDE: THE DIVERSITY OF MARRIED LIFE IN LATER ADULTHOOD

[The] lengthening [well into later adulthood] of the "couple alone again" period [the empty nest] has been accompanied by a number of new patterns of relationships between husbands and wives, most of them still unstudied. Many contradictory statements have appeared in the family literature. For example, there are . . . reports that marriages are more likely to break up when the children leave home, with a secondary peaking in divorce rates comparable to that [at the] beginning [of] marriage. . . . These reports are counterbalanced by other reports of the phenomenon of *second honeymoons* when husband and wife are alone again. . . . Furthermore, others have said that couples now have greater opportunity for sharing activities, both household chores and leisure activities, and that this leads to greater enjoyment of their marriage. There are reports that sexuality terminates for most couples at this time, counterbalanced by reports of revitalized sexuality. There are reports of heightened marital satisfaction—but these are often tied to reports of cooling down of interpersonal interactions. Unfortunately, most of our research information is still so tenuous for these later years that we must proceed cautiously in drawing anything but tentative conclusions. It would not be too-farfetched to presume that *diversity* [italics ours] of marital style in later years is even greater than in earlier years. After all, variation increases in almost every other measure with each succeeding decade of life.

From L., Troll, S., Miller, and R. C., Atchley, *Families in Later Life.* Belmont, California: Wadsworth Publishing Company, Inc., 1979, p. 40.

Widowhood. The increasing percentage of widowhood in the United States is illustrated in Figure 12.9. The plight of older widows in American society, as well as empirical research on their life situation, has received shockingly minimal attention. This is particularly sad in light of the fact that almost 75% of all women are widows by 80 years of age (see Figure 12.9). In fact, the older widow in American society has remained a somewhat invisible person (Schiamberg, Spell, and Chin, 1984). This lack of recognition is not surprising in light of the historical pattern (now being partially reversed) of minimizing the status of women at the various levels of human development (e.g., working women, divorced women, and displaced homemakers).

Although there is some anticipatory socialization for the death of a spouse (particularly because of the death of friends), the death of a spouse is a difficult and upsetting experience. Woodruff and Birren (1975) described the changes in a widow's life as follows:

Clearly, widowhood means the loss, reorganization and acquisition of social roles. In ceasing to be a wife, a woman can no longer function as her husband's nurse, confidant, sex partner, or housekeeper, but she may have to assume unfamiliar roles like financial manager, handyman, or worker. (Woodruff and Birren, 1975, p. 103)

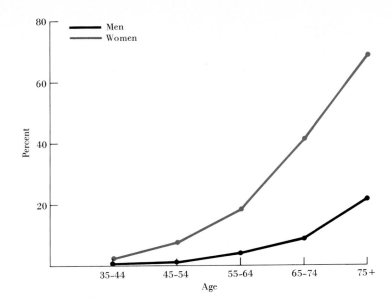

FIGURE 12.9 Widowhood as a percentage of the population by age and sex, 1978.

Source: U.S. Bureau of the Census, 1982–83.

Remarriage after the death of a spouse does occur among older adults. However, they encounter greater difficulty in finding new mates. Limitations of physical mobility, finances, and energy make courtship activities more difficult in later adulthood. It is not surprising, therefore, to find that older people marry long-time acquaintances (McKain, 1972). Men are much more likely than women to remarry after the age of sixty-five. There are two major reasons for this situation:

- After age sixty-five, there are four times as many single, never married, widowed, or divorced women as men (U.S. Bureau of the Census, 1983b).
- Older women may be restricted by social custom from marrying younger men (this factor may considerably reduce the number of available "candidates").

The higher death rates among men and the higher remarriage rate among widowers (men) has resulted in five times as many widows as widowers among the elderly (Miller, 1978). The death of a spouse is a different experience for women and men (Troll, et al., 1979). For a woman, being a widow may challenge the basis of *identity*. Women for whom the *role of wife* is the primary dimension of identity may have more difficulty adapting to widowhood than women who can turn to other roles (e.g., worker, organization volunteer, etc.).

For women, family roles are affected by widowhood. Lopata (1973, 1979) has indicated that contacts with children increase somewhat although few widows move in with their children. Instead, they prefer "intimacy at a distance" rather than possible involvement in the dilemmas of home management or child rearing. Patterns of mutual aid (between widows and their children) are usually changed such that widows grow closer to their daughters while their sons take on a more "distant" helping role (e.g., financial planning).

Widowhood—A Systems Perspective

The status of widowhood illustrates one of the central ideas of this book—the *systems* perspective. Widowhood can be viewed as a *system* in which the widow or widower reorganizes *a self-identity* in relation to the significant *contexts* of life (e.g., family, community, friends and neighbors, and work-retirement).

Helena Znaniecka Lopata has written widely on widowhood and is recognized as a leading authority in this area of inquiry. Her books include *Widowhood in an American City* (1973) and *Women As Widows: Support Systems* (1979). Both books deal with her research on an urban sample of widows in Chicago. For the latter book, Lopata extensively interviewed a sample of 301 widows, fifty years of age or older, from sixty Chicago-area neighborhoods. Lopata identified the social support systems that aid in the reintegration of widowed women into the community and the broader society.

Photograph by Darryl Jacobson

WIDOWHOOD AS A SYSTEM: SOME DEFINITIONS

1. A *support.* An "action or object which the society generally defines as necessary or helpful in maintaining a style of life of a category of its members" (Lopata, 1979, p. 4). Lopata identified four primary supports:

Economic. These include such things as social security payments, pension benefits, financial investments, or financial help from children.
Emotional. These include feelings of closeness, enjoyment, confidant relationships, help in a crisis, or comfort when feeling depressed. These can be provided by children, friends, the self, or no one.
Service. These include receiving help with transportation and shopping, or being cared for by a friend when ill.
Social. These include such activities as visiting friends, entertaining friends, or participation with friends, siblings, or children in recreational activities or attending sports events.

2. *Resources.* People, institutions, or roles which provide economic, social, service, or emo-

tional supports. These resources include the following:

Personal resources. These include such things as abilities, a sense of independence or competence, educational level, or money.
Children and kin as resources.
Friends and neighbors as resources.
Community resources. This category includes the helping professions, doctors, and church leaders.
Societal resources. This category includes the social roles widows are encouraged or discouraged from performing, and economic-providing groups such as the Social Security Administration.

3. *A support system.* A "set of similar supportive actions or objects involved in social action" (Lopata, 1979, p. 4). For example, an emotional support system might involve children, friends and neighbors, memories of the deceased husband, and support from a new husband.

4. *A support network.* The "people with whom a person is involved in supportive interaction" (Lopata, 1979, p. 4). The Table (below) indicates the *frequency of occurrence* of various *people* in the provision of the four primary supports (economic, emotional, service, and social) of aging widows. The three most frequent categories of people are children (8.4), the late husband (8.0), and friends (6.0). Since the widow will have spent many years in marriage, it is not surprising to find that the late husband is a valuable resource for support (e.g., economic—Social Security payments, pensions, etc.; *emotional*—a positive memory of the late husband often helps in negotiating the difficulties of widowhood). What is surprising—and somewhat alarming—is the relatively large number of times (3.2) that *no one* meets the needs of aging widows.

Frequencies of Categories of People Appearing in Support Systems of Chicago Area Widows

Persons	Mean
Self	4.1
No one	3.2
Late husband	8.0
Present husband	0.9
Boyfriends	0.5
Children	8.4
Parents	1.0
Siblings	2.9
Other relatives	3.5
Friends	6.1
Other persons, groups	3.2

Reprinted by permission of H. Z. Lopata, *Women As Widows: Support Systems.* New York: 74. Copyright © 1979 by Elsevier-Science Publishing Co., Inc.

In addition, the impact of widowhood on a woman's friendship patterns is determined by the number of the widow's friends who are *already* widows (Troll, et al., 1979). If a woman is one of the first in her group of friends to become a widow, she may find herself being avoided by her friends who are themselves uncomfortable with prospects of grief and death. Furthermore, if social interaction is on a couple basis, the widow may feel awkward. On the other hand, if the woman is one of the last of her social group to become a widow, then she may find extensive support and understanding for her situation among her friends.

The impact of widowhood on men appears to be no less devastating than for women. Widowers are not as likely to experience an identity crisis as widows since *traditional* male roles usually emphasize work and/or community activities, in addition to the role of husband (Troll, et al., 1979). On the other hand, men are more likely than women to respond to bereavement by feeling that they have "lost a part of themselves" (Glick, Weiss, and Parkes, 1974).

Women usually respond to bereavement for a spouse by feeling deserted or abandoned. Furthermore, women are much more likely than men to have a *close confidant* with whom they can share their intimate and personal problems of widowhood and reduce the pains of loneliness (Petrowsky, 1976; Atchley, 1957b; Powers, Keith, and Goudy, 1975).

INTERLUDE: THE FAMILY IN LATER ADULTHOOD—A CONCLUDING THOUGHT

The family is the focus of many of the life changes associated with aging, such as the dispersal of offspring and a loss of a spouse. While the family is a source of life change, it is also a resource for change. The [family] aid network, the intergenerational investments of emotion, and the [mutual] support of marital relationships all may [relieve] the stressful personal disorganization which can accompany life's transitions. The family may fall short of meeting the needs of some older people,

Young and Old Together—The Reintegration of the Generations

"Oh no, not me, I'm not going to get that old!"

"That's awful—being old is being sick, helpless and ugly. I just don't want to get old."

Children, even those as young as three, simply do not want to grow old, as the above comments indicate. To children, old people are those who are wrinkled and sad; they chew funny, walk with canes and sit in wheelchairs all day. When asked what they knew about old people, or how they feel about growing old, children interviewed in a study conducted by the University of Maryland typically responded with mixed feelings. Although they frequently rejected the elderly on the basis of physical and behavioral stereotypes, the children had had limited contact with older people and did not really know any older persons outside of their family unit.[1]

Children's stereotypic thinking about older persons and the aging process is potentially harmful. In order for children to develop the positive self-concepts necessary for a fulfilling life, they must be able to adapt to their own changing, growing and aging selves. Only when they can see the elderly positively, as individuals, will they be able to develop positive interpersonal relationships with those older than they and thus realize their full potential.

It may be that children stereotype the elderly because they simply do not know, or have contact with, persons so much older than themselves. It's difficult to dispel conventional notions about a group of people when there is no contact with the individuals who make up that group. Children need to have contact with older persons in many different roles and settings. As they come to know the elderly in a variety of satisfying roles and lifestyles, they will learn to question their existing ideas of older people as unhappy, inactive or sick members of society.

BENEFITS OF YOUNG AND OLD TOGETHER

Involving the elderly as volunteers and regular participants in classrooms is beneficial for children, teachers, parents and older persons. In

Great Britain the Old People's Council actively encourages contacts between old and young people, believing that as the young learn to adjust to their own aging, they will be able to treat the elderly with dignity and respect. The social and personal problems of the aged in 40 years, according to the Council, will be diminished in proportion to the amount of involvement between the elderly and today's youth. The Council believes that some problems of caring for the elderly—for dependent parents for example—may be based on children's attitudes toward their own aging and the older people they know.[2]

. . . For many older people, working with children is useful, fulfilling and enriching in and of itself. Children, while expressing negative attitudes toward the physical aspects of aging, also expressed love and affection for the elderly. "They're good, wonderful; they love you, you can sit on their lap and they'll talk to you" were some comments children made when asked what they knew about older people. Children will receive a large measure of this love and affection. In return, to feel loved, wanted and valued, to receive the attention of children, is often more reward than the elderly person ever thought of receiving.

RESOURCES

(The following organizations can be contacted for help in locating older people willing to visit the classroom or to volunteer their time to work with children.)

ACTION Regional Office (Foster Grandparents)
320 Walnut Street
Philadelphia, Pennsylvania 19106

SERVE (Community Service Society of
  New York)
Committee on Aging
105 East 22nd Street
New York, New York 10010

RSVP (Retired Senior Volunteer Program)
14 S. Perry Street
Rockville, Maryland 20850

National School Volunteer Program
300 N. Washington St.
Alexandria, Va. 22314

ORGANIZATIONS

(These organizations are concerned with all aspects of aging and might be contacted for additional resources specifically concerned with aging and the elderly.)

Administration on Aging
Department of Health [and Human Services]
Washington, D.C. 20402

American Association of Retired Persons
National Retired Teachers Association
1901 K Street, N.W.
Washington, D.C. 20006

National Council on Aging
1828 L Street, N.W.
Washington, D.C. 20036

Gerontological Society
1 Dupont Circle
Washington, D.C. 20036

[1] Jantz, R., Seefeldt, C., Galper, A. and Serock, K. *Children's Attitudes Toward the Elderly.* Final Report to American Assoc. of Retired Persons, Washington, D.C., July 1976.
[2] National Old People's Welfare Council, *Annual Report of the Year Ending March 31, 1966,* British Information Services, London, 1966.

From C. Seefeldt, Young and old together. *Children Today.* Washington, D.C.: U.S. Department of Health, Education, and Welfare, January–February 1977, pp. 23–25.

and its inadequacies may be even more apparent if . . . society fails to provide adequately for older citizens. Nevertheless, the American family shows remarkable solidarity in the face of a mobile and changing world. Mutual affection and concern seem here to stay.

From D. S. Woodruff and J. E. Birren, *Aging: Scientific Perspectives and Social Issues.* New York: Nostrand, 1975, p. 105.

THE COMMUNITY

The readjustment required of older married persons at the death of a spouse may also be mirrored when close friends and neighbors pass away. Such changes are indeed common in later adulthood and represent a significant modification in the *social support* network of older adults. The level of community interactions that we have traced from the early childhood years reaches a peak in middle adulthood when the individual has developed a relatively high level of community interactions with friends and neighbors. These friends and neighbors, as well as the involvement with community organizations constitute a part of the adult's total *social network*—a network that, along with the family, provides support for the adult. Increasing research is being devoted to these social networks in old age as well as the general issue of older adult-environment interaction (Rowles and Ohta, 1983).

An issue that has frequently been raised with reference to the relationship of the elderly adult to the community is the matter of the *age segregation* of older adults from other age groups (e.g., children, youth, or young adults). It has been suggested that in relation to the potential contribution of older adults (e.g., their experience in, and knowledge about, child rearing and occupational skills), the segregation of many older adults into a limbo status of retirement and non-involvement is a national tragedy (see Application Box: Young and Old Together—The Reintegration of the Generations, p. 591).

Friends and Neighbors. What is the meaning of friendship in later adulthood? Relationships may range all the way from *casual contacts* with people over the years to *intense and continuous* relationships (Clark and Anderson, 1967). For our purposes, the former could be called *associates* and the latter could be called *friends.* Older women appear to have more *friends* than older men; older men have more *associates* than older women (Clark and Anderson, 1967). Furthermore, older women seem to rely—more than men—on friendships as a way of dealing with life problems or concerns (Powers, et al., 1975; Petrowsky, 1976).

When neighbors and friends die and when buildings and houses are torn down to make room for new shopping centers, office buildings, or so-called urban-renewal projects, both the people who may directly provide social and emotional support and the symbols (buildings, organizations, houses) of these relationships are no more. Now the individual must replace these relationships and symbols with new ones.

Kalish (1975) described some of the difficulties of the relocation of older adults:

When older people are relocated to new neighborhoods because of urban renewal or other factors, their social integration is diminished or destroyed—sometimes only temporarily, but often permanently. Although they may find new friends and confidants, this takes time. Also, they frequently find that housing in the new neighborhoods is some distance away from friends, distance that affects their network of social relationships. Of course, when an elderly person leaves his community to live with his adult children or to enter a long-term care facility, the same disruptions occur. His interrelationships with his family or his new relationships formed within the institution occasionally replace his old ties but in many instances he never finds substitutes. (p. 88)

Housing. Almost 30 percent of elderly adults in the United States live in substandard housing (Butler and Lewis, 1982). There are two reasons for this situation:

- Older adults have limited incomes, and many live in outright poverty.
- Although as many as two thirds of all elderly own their own homes, these homes were purchased perhaps thirty to forty years earlier and have become substandard (Butler and Lewis, 1982). As the cost of maintenance,

property taxes, and utilities has gone up considerably, needed home repairs and upkeep have become increasingly difficult for older adults on limited incomes.

Where do older people live? Although approximately two thirds of older adults own their own homes, the remaining one third live alone in rented housing, with relatives, or in a variety of living arrangements. Such arrangements may include low-income housing, retirement villages, or nursing homes (see Application Box: Types of Living Arrangements for Older Adults). The choice of where to live (if there is a choice) is a highly individual matter. It reflects several factors, including the personality and lifestyle of older adults as well as their physical and mental health, and their financial resources.

Relocation. An issue that many elderly adults and their families have to face with increasing frequency is relocation of the older adult. Whether or not the move has positive or negative consequences depends on several factors (Pastalon, 1983):

- The *degree of choice*. Did the elderly adult make the move voluntarily or unvoluntarily?
- The *degree of environmental change*. Was the move made from one residential home to another or from a home to an institution?
- The *health and the personality* of the elderly adult prior to the move.
- The *degree of preparation* for the move (e.g., prior visits to the new location or personal counseling).

Many studies have examined the impact of a *voluntary* move for an older adult from one residential home to another. Carp (1967) examined a group of 352 older adults who had applied for public housing. Of this group, 204 were admitted and relocated whereas 148 were not. The vast majority of those who became residents of the housing project were much more satisfied with their living arrangement than those who did not become residents. In addition, the residents had increased social relationships and activities, better health and morale (based on self reports), and required fewer services than the non–resident group. One factor that contributed substantially to the high level of satisfaction was the fact that the relocated subjects moved to an environment that was significantly better than the one they left. A follow-up study eight years later (Carp, 1977) found that a higher percentage of the nonresidents had died compared to the residents. Carp (1977) suggested that the new living environments may have produced greater satisfaction and reduced stress, which led to improved health. Other studies generally support the conclusion that voluntary relocation from one home to another is usually positive in outcome (Lawton and Yaffe, 1970; Wittels and Botwinick, 1974; Storandt and Wittel, 1975).

Research on *involuntary* relocation from one home to another generally suggest negative consequences related to the move (Brand and Smith, 1974; Shahinian, Goldfarb and Turner, 1968). Specifically, older adults with physical or mental health problems were found to be consistently vulnerable to such a move.

In some cases, it becomes necessary for older adults to move from their homes to an institution. Sometimes health factors make it extremely difficult for some older adults to care for themselves at home. In other instances, the

Types of Living Arrangements for Older Adults

RETIREMENT COMMUNITIES

During the past twenty-five years, many elderly adults have moved to retirement communities, particularly in Florida, California, and Arizona. These are communities inhabited exclusively by the elderly. Community activities are usually designed exclusively for and by the elderly. Some of these communities have rules that restrict residence to people who are over fifty years of age. Such rules vary from community to community. Retirement communities offer the elderly an opportunity to purchase homes, usually on a long-term payment plan. The choice of living in a retirement community reflects individual factors. Some older adults prefer not to live in such a community for fear of being isolated from other age groups. Still other elderly adults find the presence and activities of children and youth to be tension-producing and feel great satisfaction in living in communities that directly address the needs of the elderly.

MOBILE HOMES

Some adults find mobile homes particularly attractive. Many trailer courts have a high percentage of elderly residents. Some older adults appreciate the low cost and the informality of such a living arrangement. Others do not like the lack of privacy or the small living space (Kalish, 1975).

RETIREMENT HOTELS

Retirement hotels are often older hotels or apartment houses that have been converted to housing for older adults. Retirement hotels or apartments are usually in or near a city and provide the elderly access to many activities and services. Some retirement hotels provide limited maid or meal service. Although they are closer to the "action," retirement hotels may have the disadvantage of exposing residents to the higher crime rates of cities (Kalish, 1975).

NURSING HOMES

When older people can no longer take care of themselves and have no one to take care of them, they often go into nursing homes. Most of the residents of nursing homes are women simply because women live longer than men. About 50 percent of all nursing-home residents have no living relatives. The average age of nursing-home residents is seventy-eight years. Between 60 and 80 percent of them are poor. Approximately 85 percent of nursing home residents die during an average stay of about one year (Rogers, 1979).

decision to move to an institution is much more difficult because the older adults may be able to do some living tasks (e.g., feeding self, dressing, or bathing) and not others (e.g., cooking and shopping) (see Application Box: Home Is Where the Heart Is—And Where Care for the Elderly Can Occur, p. 596).

What is the impact of institutionalization on an older adult? Most of the studies on institutional relocation have focused on moves from the home to an institution and from one institution to another institution. While the focus of much of this research has been on the impact of moving on death rates, the results have been mixed. Some studies report a relationship between institutionalization and mortality rates (Lieberman, 1975; Marlowe, 1973). Other studies indicate no such relationship (Gutman and Herbert, 1976; Borup, Gallego, and Heffernan, 1979).

Another focus of the research on institutionalization has been on the factors related to adaptation to an institutional setting. Lieberman (1975) found that the most important predictor of successful relocation was the *degree of environ-*

Home Is Where the Heart Is—And Where Care for the Elderly Can Occur

Home is extraordinarily significant to many older persons. It is part of their identity, a place where things are familiar and relatively unchanging, and a place to maintain a sense of autonomy and control. Some insist on remaining at home "at all costs" to their emotional and physical health and personal security. Such tenaciousness can be laid to a desire for freedom and independence; a fear of loss of contact with familiar and loved people, places and things; a fear of dying because of the reputation of hospitals and nursing homes as "houses of death" from which there is no return; and a trepidation about change and the unknown, which frightens people of all ages. In this nation of homeowners where 67 percent of older people own their homes, the idea of a personal house is deeply ingrained; and communal living is viewed as a loss of personal liberty and dignity.

WHAT IS A "HOME?"

The notion of home can refer primarily to the four walls surrounding one, to the neighborhood in which one is located, or to the possessions that make one feel at home. Home may mean certain other individuals living with one or it may mean neighbors, pets and plants. It can either be a place where one has lived a good part of one's life or be a new place, as when older people move into a retirement community or leave the farm for a home in town. This home is whatever the "concept of home" means to each person.

ADVANTAGES OF HOME CARE

. . . In general we believe that home care offers the best treatment location except when people . . . require inpatient medical treatment. But it is beneficial only when the home is an adequate place to begin with or can be made adequate by selected interventions.

- One of the most obvious advantages of home care is that most older people prefer it.
- Care at home offers better morale and security as long as proper services are given to provide comfort, support and direct treatment of physical and emotional ills.
- Relatives and service personnel such as homemakers and home health aides can often give more individualized care than nursing staffs in institutions. . . .
- Familiar surrounds are reassuring. . . .
- Older people and their families can receive not only medical and psychiatric care but also social and economic help.

Photograph by Darryl Jacobson

. . . The older person and the people in his life receive a different view of illness and treatment. Instead of being whisked off to the hospital or an institution, people remain where their care can be observed and participated in.

From R. N. Butler and M. I. Lewis, *Aging and Mental Health.* 3rd ed. St. Louis: Mosby, 1982, pp. 255–257.

YOUR VIEW

- Do you think that home care is an alternative that should be more fully explored or supported by families and government agencies? Why? Why not?
- Can you think of some older adults whom you know who could benefit from such a program?
- If you were designing a home care program for the elderly, which of the following skills do you think would be necessary for independent living? Why? Why not?

Orientation to time, places, and people.
Ability to dress self.
Ability to bathe self.
Ability to do shopping.
Ability to climb stairs.

Ability to manage money.
Toileting and continence.
Ability to follow instructions (particularly for medication).
• Any others?

mental change (i.e., the dissimilarity between the new and old environments) involved in the move. Specifically, the frequency of emotional breakdown due to relocation increased as the degree of environmental change increased. In this regard, there is evidence that relocation preparation programs, including visits to the institution prior to the move and advance counseling, can significantly reduce the stress of moving (Pastalan, 1976).

In addition, the physical health and personality of the older adult were significant adaptational factors. Lieberman (1975) found that a minimal level of physical health and cognitive ability were required for successful adjustment to a move. However, beyond these underlying or basic factors, certain personality characteristics were important. Those relocated adults who were best able to cope with the institution were demanding, aggressive, and self-involved (Lieberman, 1975).

INTERLUDE: NURSING-HOME CARE—SOME PROBLEMS

There is considerable variety in nursing homes. Some may be more like hospitals, offering intensive medical services while others may offer minimal nursing service to older adults who are relatively physically well. Some institutions limit care to those of a particular religious or ethnic group. Some institutions may be part of chain-owned and run for a profit, while others may be non-profit organizations.

In addition, there is continual debate over the *quality* of nursing home care. Some institutions provide excellent programs, others do not (Butler, 1975). The latter programs are a concern for all who are interested in the welfare of older adults.

They often have few or no nurses, and hardly qualify as homes. Robert Butler (1975) often visited them, frequently disguising himself as a family member. Sometimes he saw "patients lying in their own urine and feces. Food is frequently left untouched on plates" (p. 263). On the basis of such observations Butler also lists "a grim catalog of medical deficiencies" (p. 264). In many cases drug prescriptions are wrongly administered, fundamental hygiene standards are neglected; and in order to keep down food costs, meals are often inadequate to the point of malnourishment. Few of the homes have social or therapeutic programs . . . (Gottesman, Quarterman, and Kohn, 1973). The employees are often grossly overworked, and just as grossly inefficient and untrained. The patients themselves are often treated in a highly authoritarian manner. Such care is no bargain at any price (Rogers, 1979, p. 325)

WORK AND RETIREMENT

Throughout this book, we have pointed to the significance of work in the lives of human beings. It is important for families and children. It is important for adolescents as a critical consideration in the shaping of an identity. And it is a dynamic aspect of early and middle adulthood.

Retirement represents a major transition in the lives of adults. Men have traditionally had to grapple with the changes associated with retirement. And now that women have increasingly entered the job market, retirement will be a common concern of males and females.

What Is Retirement? There are three common ways of thinking about retirement.

Retirement as an Event. Retirement is an occasion that marks the transition from middle age to the later years of adulthood. For some individuals, retirement may also mark the end of a period of work and the beginning of a period of relative leisure. In some cases, this event is marked by a special ceremony. For example, a company may hold a dinner reception for retiring workers during which fellow workers may speak or present gifts. Whether or not there are such ceremonies, the meaning of retirement is probably best understood from the perspective of the individual (Maddox, 1966).

Retirement as a Status. After the event of retirement, the individual moves into a relatively new social position with accompanying expectations and roles. The major characteristics of this new status are often a general decline in the standard of living and a reduction in the number of roles played.

Retirement as a Process. The process of retirement involves working through the conflicts and concerns inherent in a major life transition. These concerns have to do with such factors as the individual's health, whether retirement is mandatory or voluntary, and the meaning that the individual personally attributes to retirement.

Health Factors and Retirement. Many persons retire because of poor health (Foner and Schwab, 1981). In a study of men who began receiving Social Security benefits in 1969, Rubin (1976) found that 43 percent had

"I'm coming out of retirement, Martha. I've been offered two cents each for every lizard I can catch!"

DENNIS THE MENACE ® used by permission of Hank Ketcham and © by Field Enterprises, Inc.

"When I was young, I was amazed at Plutarch's statement that the elder Cato began at the age of eighty to learn Greek. I am amazed no longer. Old age is ready to undertake tasks that youth shirked because they would take too long."

W. Somerset Maugham

Photograph by Darryl Jacobson

health related work limitations when they retired at age sixty-five. Rubin also found that for those men who retired at age sixty-two, 61 percent had health-related problems. Health factors were also important for women who retired. Approximately one third of women who retired indicated that health was the primary reason (Reno, 1976). It is clear that biological decline—specifically disease and poor health—is a major factor in a person's decision to retire (Birren, Butler, Greenhouse, Sokoloff, and Yarrow, 1963). Disease and poor physical health prior to retirement may be related to consequent emotional and mental problems (Lowenthal, 1964).

Does retirement lead to major emotional or physical health problems? The folklore of aging seems to include many stories of adults who retire in perfect health only to succumb to serious emotional or physical problems. Existing evidence, however, is not clear on this question. Many persons report an improvement in health rather than a decline in health following retirement (Eisdorfer, 1972). Reports of improved health may, of course, relate to the individual's general feeling of satisfaction about retirement. Some individuals do not make such a successful adaption to retirement:

Work has long been recognized as a useful defense that occupies minds and bodies and keeps feelings in control. This brings to mind the individuals who get sick, anxious or upset on Sundays, holidays or vacations and feel fine once they are back at work. In retirement, these symptoms can become everyday occurrences unless work-substitutes and a satisfactory new lifestyle are found; otherwise perfectly healthy men and women may develop headaches, depression, gastrointestinal symptoms and oversleeping. . . . Irritability, loss of interest, lack of energy, increased alcoholic intake, and reduced efficiency are all familiar and common reactions. (Butler and Lewis, 1982, p. 128 and 130)

The Meaning of Retirement. Whether retirement is *voluntary* (selected as an option) or *compulsory* (a mandatory requirement) has an impact on the meaning of retirement to the individual. Kimmel (1974) summarized this effect as follows:

The meaning of this shift in roles (retirement) is also affected by the characteristics of the retired status and the range of social roles that are associated with it. That is, does the retired person choose the retired status because it is desired, or is he forced into a status of a "non person" who is socially defined as worthless and useless? What roles is he expected to play according to the age norms of the society? How meaningful are those roles for him? How much status do they provide? Is he able to maintain a decent income, or is he forced to live a standard below the federally-defined poverty level? (p. 258)

To understand the meaning of retirement, we have first to understand the meaning of work. For some individuals, work constitutes the primary source of meaning in their lives. For such people, retirement is never a voluntary choice. Rather, such individuals retire, when they do, because they are required to do so. They thoroughly enjoy their work and would choose to continue doing it. For such individuals, satisfaction in retirement will depend, in part, on their ability to continue working. For other elderly adults, work appears to be much less important. Shanas and her associates (Shanas, Towsend, Wedderburn, Friis, Milhoj, and Stehouwer, 1968) found that fewer than 20 percent of their sample of retired persons indicated that they actually missed the work itself. About 17 percent indicated that their greatest loss in retirement was the absence of contact with fellow workers and friends.

In addition to the meaning of work in an individual's life, there is considerable evidence that the following factors are related to positive adjustment in retirement (Eisdorfer, 1972; Keahy and Seaman, 1974; Atchley, 1975a; Beverly, 1975; Foner and Schwab, 1981; Glamser, 1981):

- A relatively high level of income prior to retirement.
- A relatively high standard of living during retirement.
- Good health.
- A relatively high level of education.
- Preretirement planning.

Preretirement Planning. One of the important factors in promoting positive adaptation to retirement is preretirement planning, or preparation for the new set of roles that may occupy one's time when formal work roles come to an end. Some aspects of preretirement planning include:

1. Developing or ensuring that an adequate income will be available at retirement.
2. Anticipating new roles that are available in the family or the community.
3. Developing or continuing an interest that may be extended into leisure-time pursuits.

Leisure Activities and Retirement. What kinds of activities and involvement characterize retirement? The kinds of activities available are in-

Work is an important source of life satisfaction for many older adults.

Photograph by Darryl Jacobson

deed numerous. Some of the most popular activities include reading, visiting friends and relatives, gardening, taking walks, watching television, and engaging in educational or creative interests (Kalish, 1975). Some older adults may continue with formal work activities, at least on a part-time basis.

One of the issues that confronts retired persons is "structuring" their time. Prior to retirement, an adult's time is structured or organized around activities in the family (e.g., child care or housework), in the community, or in the work setting. After retirement, the individual may be confronted with large blocks of unstructured time. Depending on their individual preferences, some older adults derive pleasure in filling this time with unplanned experiences, and others prefer to organize their time around numerous leisure or work activities.

INTERLUDE: THE DAY SAM SELIGMAN RETIRED

Last Thursday, when the last of the giant black linotype machines was hauled from the composing room of the *Post-Dispatch*, Sam Seligman's job went with it. In a few days, Sam will be going too, walking through the revolving glass doors on Twelfth Street and running—as he always does—to the corner of Eleventh and Locust.

There, Sam will catch the bus he has been catching for more than 20 years in St. Louis and ride out to his wife and home in University City. Only this time, Sam will not be riding alone. With him will go not only a grand tradition and sense of nostalgia, but a slice of newspaper history itself.

Now 74 years old, Sam Seligman does not know what he will do with the rest of his life. All he knows is that he will not be glad or sad.

"When I was 19 years old," he said, "I was walking up Franklin Avenue one day and I made up my mind I would *never* be glad or sad. All I would be is satisfied. I'd looked at my relatives, my friends and neighbors, and they seemed to have so many troubles. I didn't want to be troubled; all I wanted to be was satisfied. And my friend, I'm very satisfied."

Sam Seligman is a legend at the *Post-Dispatch*, but more than that he represents the resilience, guts and spirit of one of America's most cherished memories; a link with the roaring days of console radios and no TV sets, of extra editions and *Stop The Presses* and *Read All About It!* and a stack of tightly bound newspapers tumbling onto a street corner from the back of a speeding truck. . . .

Now Sam is standing amid the hum, staccato and whirr of a modern *Post-Dispatch* composing room. Around him are the winking lights of computers and the loud silence of cutting, splicing and pasting news into cold type. A new era has come, and Sam is leaving, but he is resolute in his commitment to satisfaction.

"I've never worked a day in my life," he said. "My hobby was setting type. It kept me young. I'll never forget what an old-timer told me when I was just a kid starting out. 'Can you believe it?' he said. 'They're paying you to enjoy yourself.'"

"He was a pro," said one of Sam's bosses. "One of the best. He came from those days when, if you made a mistake, you had to correct it on your own time. Linotype operators like Sam, they just didn't make mistakes."

Sam Seligman says he cannot remember many of the stories he set in type through the years, the datelines from around the world and the names of famous correspondents who brought the news of the day into the hands of the reading public.

"I found out that if I knew what I was setting, my work just wasn't that good," he said. "I learned that concentration was the important thing, not reading what you were setting.

"But you know, it seemed like whenever they needed something in a hurry they always gave it to me. They knew I'd really go to town on it. I guess they all knew I really loved what I was doing; that when I said I never worked a day in my life, I meant it."

From Gary Ronberg, St. Louis Post-Dispatch, Tuesday, November 19, 1974, p. 3D. Reprinted by permission.

Retirement and Social Policy. Although it is possible to plan for and successfully adapt to retirement, nonetheless, the *limits of individual adaptation to retirement* are spelled out in current social policies toward retirement. Although it is surely important to consider the ways in which older adults adjust to and *cope* with retirement, such a focus is not sufficient if it leads us to ignore the larger or *macrolevel* processes of current social policies toward older adults. In the area of retirement, these broad social policies take the form of the general removal of older men and women from the work force in a fashion that may be limiting for them and for society as a whole (McCluskey, 1981). Such a policy of forced retirement may have been appropriate in an earlier era when there were large numbers of young workers who both needed jobs and could help to support (through their Social Security payroll taxes) retired older adults. As a result of population changes, this situation no longer exists. Declining birth rates are resulting in fewer young adult workers, and improved health care practices are resulting in more healthy older adults. (It is estimated that beginning in 1985, the 20–24 age population will peak as a result of the high birthrates in the 1950's and 1960's "baby boom". This peaking or population "bulge" will then continue to move through higher age brackets leaving, in its wake, a reduced number of young workers) (U.S. Bureau of the Census, 1983a). This scenario requires a re-examination of current practices of compulsory retirement (see Application Box: Careers for Older Adults).

The Development of the Self in Later Adulthood

In this section, we examine the changes in the self that occur in later adulthood. Specifically we will look at physical changes (health, sensory functioning, and motor skills), cognitive functioning, and changes in the personality.

PHYSICAL CHANGES

Physical Health. From middle age to later adulthood, there are some important changes in general health status. For example, heart disease and hypertension increase from middle adulthood to later adulthood; on the other hand, deaths due to cancer decrease (see Figure 12.10).

SOME HEALTH STATISTICS

- Contrary to the stereotype, the older population as a whole is healthier than is commonly assumed. In 1980, 92 percent of elderly persons (interviewed in a national survey) described their own health as fair, good, or excellent as compared with others of their own age; only 8 percent said their health was poor (U.S. Department of Health and Human Services, *1980 Health Interview Survey,* forthcoming).
- About 40 percent of the elderly population reported that, for health reasons, a major activity had been limited (compared with about 20 percent

602

Careers for Older Adults

For generations American society has striven successfully to eliminate health hazards, improve health care and diet, and broaden educational opportunity. The result has been the evolution of perhaps the largest, healthiest, best educated, and longest-lived population . . . in history. However, the supreme irony is that just at the point when we should be capitalizing on [this] valuable asset . . . , society continues to follow public and private policies designed to shunt it aside. A chronological guillotine is sprung to separate senior men and women from the work force just when many of them are in their prime. Little thought is given to continuing them in useful capacities either in their original jobs or in some related area of employment, as paid, self-employed, or volunteer workers. . . . Layoff or involuntary retirement, or simply the absence of invitations bring a halt to their productive lives with devastating effects upon their personal lives. (McCluskey, 1981, pp. 31–32).

DESIRE TO WORK

Do older adults really wish to continue working or would they prefer to retire? According to a Harris study (1979), the answer to this question is as follows:

- 48 percent of currently employed adults, 50–64 years, who were surveyed said they wished to continue working after age 65.

- 53 percent of retired adults who were surveyed said they wished they had never quit their job.

SOME PRACTICAL STEPS FOR DEVELOPING OLDER ADULT CAREERS

The National committee on Careers for Older Adults prepared a report entitled *Older Americans: An Untapped Resource* (1978). In addition to a careful discussion of why older adults are a valuable resource, there are numerous suggestions for utilizing this resource. The committee document lists several basic steps:

- Counseling, training, and placement services need to be provided for older adults.
- Employers need to re-examine personnel policies and practices relating to older adults (e.g., flexibility in working hours, skill requirements, and fringe benefits for part-time older workers—particularly health benefits and disability).
- Community, trade, and education organizations need to encourage persons interested in self-employment.
- Major attention should be given to the transportation needs of older adults.

of the population 45 to 64 years old). However, 54 percent reported no limitations of any kind in their activities (U.S. Department of Health and Human Services, *Current Estimates from the National Health Interview Survey, United States, 1981, 1982*).
- Not until ages 85 and over do about half of the population report being limited or unable to carry on a major activity because of a chronic illness [U.S. Department of Health and Human Services, *The Need for Long Term Care: Information and Issues,* No. (OHDS) 81-20704, 1981].
- More than 80 percent of the noninstitutionalized very old (85 years and over) were able to take care of their own daily needs (e.g., dressing, eating, bathing, and toileting). [U.S. Department of Health and Human Services, *The Need for Long Term Care: Information and Issues,* No. (OHDS) 81-20704, 1981].
- Whereas *acute* conditions (e.g., infectious diseases having a relatively sudden onset and short duration) were predominant at the turn of the century, *chronic* conditions (e.g., those conditions marked by a long duration of frequent recurrence such as arthritis, heart disease, diabetes,

Cause of Death	Middle Age		Later Adulthood		
	45–54	55–64	65–74	75–84	85+
1	Heart Disease 30.9	Heart Disease 36.8	Heart Disease 40.7	Heart Disease 44.4	Heart Disease 48.2
2	Cancer 30.2	Cancer 31.2	Cancer 26.4	Cancer 18.0	Stroke 15.5
3	Accidents 6.5	Stroke 5.2	Stroke 8.0	Stroke 12.7	Cancer 9.9
4	Cirrhosis of the Liver 5.2	Accidents 3.3	Influenza & Pneumonia 2.2	Influenza & Pneumonia 3.6	Influenza & Pneumonia 5.7
5	Stroke 4.5	Cirrhosis of the Liver 3.1	Diabetes 2.1	Diabetes 2.0	Arterio-sclerosis 4.3
All Other	All Other 22.7	All Other 20.4	All Other 20.6	All Other 19.3	All Other 16.4

FIGURE 12.10 Leading causes of death by age, 1978.

Source: White House Conference on Aging, 1981. *Chartbook on Aging in America*, p. 79, IV-3, 1981.

and hypertension) are now the most prevalent health problem for elderly persons.

• Heart disease, stroke, and cancer account for over 75 percent of all deaths in the 65 and over population (White House Conference on Aging, 1981).

• The use of hospitals increases dramatically with advancing age. While individuals who are 65 years and above constitute slightly more than 11 percent of the population, they account for more than 25 percent of total hospital stays (White House Conference on Aging, 1981).

Sensory Processes. There is a decrease in the efficient functioning in nearly all the senses with time. Decline in smell and taste may ultimately affect nutrition. Decline in proprioception (perception of one's position in space) may affect balance and coordination.

Vision. One of the most apparent changes in visual capacity with age is the increased difficulty of seeing objects close at hand. This visual problem is called *presbyopia* or *farsightedness*. It is due primarily to the loss of elasticity in the lens of the eye (McFarland, 1968) (see Figure 12.11). Eyeglasses are normally used to correct this problem. Unfortunately, there are no available devices to compensate for another problem, a loss in the ability with age to adjust to changes in light, which can be a particular problem for older adults who must do night driving. In night driving, a person must be able to adapt to the bright headlights of an approaching automobile and then, just as quickly, adjust to the relative darkness of the road ahead. In addition, the peripheral vision of older adults shows significant reductions, which may lead to difficulty in seeing objects (such as cars) approaching at an angle (McFarland, 1964, 1968; National Safety Council, 1983) (see Figure 12.12).

By about age sixty-five, almost 50 percent of all adults have a visual acuity of 20/70. (In a standard test of visual acuity using block letters at a distance of 20 feet, 20/70 vision means that the eye sees at 20 feet what can be seen by the normal eye at 70 feet.) This is almost five times as many as those who have 20/70 visual acuity at forty-five years of age (Kalish, 1975). Of approximately 500,000 individuals in the United States who are considered legally blind, 53 percent are sixty-five years old or older. However, only one percent of the elderly are legally blind. (National Society for the Prevention of Blindness, 1978. White House Conference on Aging, Mini White House Conference on Aging and Vision, American Foundation for the Blind, 1981.)

Hearing. As we indicated in the previous chapters, loss of hearing is rather slight in early and middle adulthood. From about age sixty-five on, decreases

"The spiritual eyesight improves as the physical eyesight declines."
Plato

Photograph by Darryl Jacobson

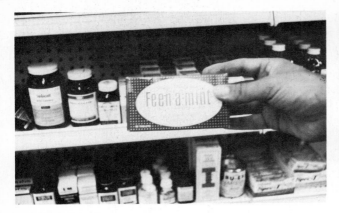

FIGURE 12.11 Normal vision versus simulation of vision with age-related deficiencies.

From L. Pastalon, "The Empathic Model," *Journal of Architectural Education,* 1977 *31* (1), 14–15. Reprinted by permission.

in auditory functioning occur, mostly at the higher sound frequencies (Corso, 1971).

One of the major results of hearing deficits is the difficulty of many older people in understanding the speech of others. It is therefore important for those who interact with older adults to recognize the following:

1. Hearing loss may often be accompanied by a sense of confusion and insecurity because the loss of "background noise" may create a sense of "deadness" in the environment (Ramsdell, 1965).

FIGURE 12.12 Number of drivers in all automobile accidents per 100 drivers in each age group.

National Safety Council, *Accident Facts.* Chicago, Illinois: National Safety Council, 1983, p. 54.

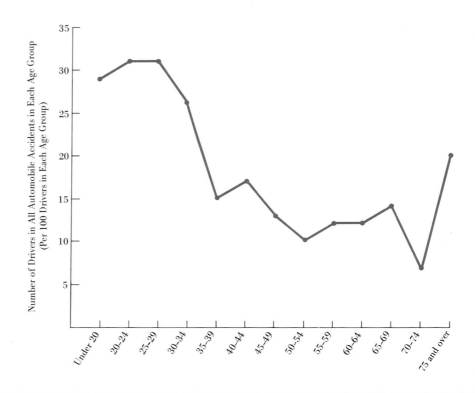

2. Hearing aids may be necessary and should be encouraged (approximately 1 in 20 individuals over age sixty-five use hearing aids, as contrasted with 1 in 200 under sixty-five) (Knox, 1977).
3. When one is talking to hard-of-hearing adults, it is important to enunciate words clearly.

Movement and Motor Skills. Older persons generally require a longer time to make movements, take longer to start their movements (i.e., have a longer reaction time), and have less muscular strength than younger persons (see Figure 12.13). A number of factors contribute to reduced motor performance.

Changes in Bone. There is a fairly widespread decrease in bone mass by later adulthood. This condition is called *osteoporosis.* It frequently results in increased stress on the weight-bearing areas of bone, which may lead to greater likelihood of fractures (Woodruff and Birren, 1975). In addition, processes of calcification in cartilage and ligaments occur in a larger number of adults (Smith and Bierman, 1973). Many older adults demonstrate a loss of elasticity in some joints as well as the beginnings of degeneration in joint cartilage.

Muscle. Both muscle size and strength decline with age (see Figure 12.13). The loss of muscle size may itself be a result of other factors, including decreasing activity and changes in connective and circulatory tissues next to the muscles (Woodruff and Birren, 1975; deVries, 1974, 1977).

Nervous System. A major reason for the slowness in motor performance of older adults is assumed to result from changes in the nervous system (including the changes in sensory functioning already discussed).

A consistent finding in research on aging adults is the increase in reaction time with age. This increase in reaction time is manifested in a decline in speed in tasks ranging from simple (the length of time required to press a

FIGURE 12.13 Age decrement in muscle strength in a coordinated movement (cranking).

Adapted from N. W. Schock and A. H. Norris, *Physical Activity and Aging,* Vol. 4 of *Medicine and Sport,* D. Brunner, and E. Jokl, Eds. Basel, Switzerland: S. Karger AG, 1970.

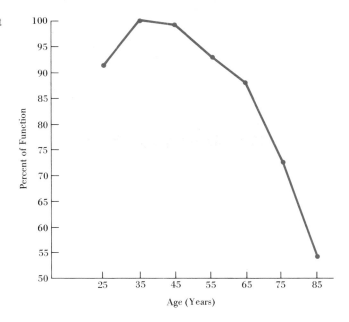

button after a light goes on) to more complex (writing or typing). This decrease in speed can range from 20 percent for simple tasks to as much as 50 percent for more complex tasks (Welford, 1977). One explanation of these changes is that the central nervous system becomes "sluggish" with age, slowing down reaction time (Birren, 1974; Birren, Woods and Williams, 1980). According to Birren (1974, p. 808), this increasing slowness "reflects a basic change in the speed with which the central nervous system processes information."

It has been hypothesized that this sluggishness may be due to one or more of the following factors: irreversible neural deterioration (loss of brain cells as well as changes in the properties of nerve cells and nerve fibers); decreased blood flow to the brain (a potentially reversible condition); or inadequate concentration on, or attention to, the tasks at hand (Birren, Woods, and Williams, 1980). It is important to recognize that physical exercise can significantly improve reaction time in older adults by improving blood flow to the brain and generally increasing the amount of oxygen in the blood (Botwinick, 1978; Spirduso and Clifford, 1978). Furthermore, poor concentration and attention may result from any situation (whether in the laboratory or real-life settings) which create extreme anxiety or indifference in the older adult. Adults who have begun to think of themselves as losing accuracy and agility may demonstrate anxiety over the possibility of making an error or being slow *or* may "give up" by indicating indifference.

What is the human significance of a relative decline in sensory and motor skills? As we have pointed out in previous chapters and earlier in this chapter, the changes that result from aging can to some extent be adapted to in a positive fashion. The ability of people to adapt successfully is a function of several factors, including the degree of sensorimotor changes, and the personality of the individual. Does the individual perceive his or her "cup" to be half empty or half full? Kalish (1975) described the implications of sensorimotor decrements as follows:

If a person suffers from a decrement in hearing or from an arthritic condition severe enough to make walking or even buttoning his clothing difficult, the impact can be . . . [great]. Even though decrements occur only very gradually and sometimes not at all, and even though substitute satisfactions are often readily available, we live in an era in which the notion of personal growth is extremely important. The realization that growth in certain tasks will no longer occur can be very depressing, especially since it often coincides with other losses, such as the death of friends or the recognition that another promotion will probably never be awarded. Coming to terms with these problems, while still being able to engage in substitute activities and retain a high sense of life satisfaction, is the major demand made on the aging. (p. 33)

A Systems Perspective to Health in Later Adulthood. Traditionally many of the biological and physiological changes which occur in adulthood have been simply assumed to "happen", independent of any significant control by the individual (Schiamberg, 1983). However, recent research suggests that many of the symptoms of physical decline (e.g., stiffness in joints, osteoporosis or thinning of bones, muscle weakness, and so on) are primarily the result of lifestyle factors such as *disuse* or simply being *out of shape* (Smith and Stoedefalke, 1980; deVries and Hales, 1982).

Lifestyle is the learned pattern of self-regulating and controlling personal behaviors such as diet, smoking, stress management, and exercise. It is the result of life-span socialization in the significant contexts of human development, including the family, the school, the work setting, and the community/ neighborhood. Therefore, the lifestyle patterns of older adults are the accumulated experience of a lifetime.

For many years, it has been recognized that lifestyle factors such as diet, stress control, and smoking may have a negative impact on health (U.S. Surgeon General, 1980). More recently, the role of exercise in lifespan health, particularly for older adults, has come to be appreciated. The research of deVries and his colleagues (deVries and Adams, 1972a; deVries and Adams, 1972b; deVries and Hales, 1982) has demonstrated that vigorous exercise (e.g., walking, jogging, swimming, calisthenics, and stretching) has dramatic effects on older adults in toning muscles, improving joint flexibility, and promoting cardiovascular fitness. In addition, deVries and his colleagues found the following significant changes in older adults as a result of a program of vigorous exercise:

- A marked *increase in oxygen capacity* (the best single indicator of individual vigor). Walking and jogging, in particular, resulted in deeper and easier breathing and improved cardiovascular endurance and efficiency.
- Drop in *blood pressure.*
- Loss of *fat.*
- Drop in *nervous tension.* Subjects reported more restful sleep, less anxiety, and reduced aches and pains.
- Increase in *muscle strength.*

While this research has demonstrated the positive results of exercise on the health and well-being of older adults, other research has begun to demonstrate the possibility of stabilizing—or partially reversing—some deleterious outcomes previously associated with aging. Smith, Reddan, and Smith (1981) have shown that osteoporosis (i.e., the decrease in bone mass with age, which causes bones to become brittle and, in some cases, crack under stress) can be slowed or partially reversed. The rate of osteoporosis appears to be the greatest between 45 and 70 years of age and to be particularly prominent for females (Smith, Khairi, Norton, and Johnston, 1976). The subjects for the Smith study were 80 females between the ages of 69–95 years of age. Smith et al., (1976) found that a control group who did not participate in the exercise program had continued osteoporosis (a loss of bone marrow content of over 3 percent) while the exercise group actually reversed their osteoporosis (a bone marrow gain of 1.5 percent).

In summary, current research is helping to reverse the longstanding myth that the deteriorating consequences of aging are inevitable and independent of any action by the older adult. This position is summarized by Bortz (1982, p. 1203), as follows:

A review of biologic changes commonly attributed to the process of aging demonstrates the close similarity of most of these to changes subsequent to a period of enforced physical inactivity prompting the suggestion that at least a portion of the changes is in reality caused by disuse and, as such, is subject to correction.

It has been suggested that many individuals can maintain—or even improve—some intellectual abilities.

Photograph by Shan Rucinski

COGNITIVE FUNCTIONING

As we have indicated in the previous two chapters, the evaluation and measurement of intelligence is, at best, an uncertain and inexact process. Part of the difficulty is in defining exactly what intelligence is. Is intelligence doing well on intelligence tests? Is intelligence doing well in school settings? Is intelligence relating effectively to people and having lots of friends? Is intelligence making lots of money? Clearly, depending on who develops the definition, *intelligence* could mean almost anything, an important idea to bear in mind when we are discussing changes in intelligence during later adulthood. The multiple and varied aspects of intelligence would make it unfair and unreasonable to suggest that elderly adults experience a decline in all phases of cognitive activity.

Age and Intelligence. Research on the patterns of cognitive functioning in later adulthood indicates several directions of change (Blum, Foshage, and Jarvik, 1972; Eisdorfer, 1963; Jarvik, Kallman, and Falek, 1962). Abilities that require speed, physical activity, or immediate memory seem to decline more than those that are untimed or are dependent on experience. This finding does not mean that older adults are less intelligent than young or middle-aged adults. Rather, it suggests that because of slower reaction times, measured intelligence scores may be lower than for younger adults (Bischof, 1976; Kimmel, 1980). It has been suggested that many individuals can maintain—or even improve—some intellectual abilities (e.g., verbal skills) well into old age (Baltes and Schaie, 1974; Botwinick, 1967). On the other hand, older adults may have particular difficulty with tasks requiring visual and motor coordination.

Memory. Learning and memory are very much related to one another; it is virtually impossible to separate one from the other, and changes in age that affect one will affect the other (Botwinick, 1970). Memory is usually divided into two categories:

1. *Short-term memory*. This process of remembering is characterized by the recall of material for a brief period of time, for example, when you remember a new telephone number just long enough to dial it and then you forget it.
2. *Long-term memory*. This process of remembering is characterized by the recall of material over a longer period of time, for example, when an older adult recalls childhood experiences.

Long-term memory appears to be resistant to the effects of aging. Vocabulary skills, information from previous experiences, and information from one's personal history are usually not lost with aging.

Why does short-term memory seem to decline in *some* people with age? Several explanations have been offered (Kimmel, 1980):

- Loss of memory through *disuse.*
- Loss of memory through *interference* with a larger store of information accumulated in life experiences.
- Loss of memory through *neurochemical change* (i.e., the reduction of brain cells).

At present, the last two theories—interference and neurochemical change—in combination appear to be the best explanation for short-term memory loss in older adults (Kimmel, 1980). It is important to keep in mind that it is *not* correct to conclude that with advancing age there is progressive loss of memory. Rather, the data indicate *only* that some older adults suffer memory decline (Botwinick, 1967). Many older adults have an excellent memory and continue to perform as well as young persons in learning tasks (Arenberg and Robertson-Tchabo, 1977).

''There is a wicked inclination in most people to suppose an old man decayed in his intellect. If a young or middle-aged man, when leaving a company, does not recollect where he laid his hat, it is nothing; but if the same inattention is discovered in an old man, people will shrug their shoulders and say 'His memory is going.'''
  Samuel Johnson

From Boswell, J. *Life of Samuel Johnson,* Vol. IV. Philadelphia, Pennsylvania: Claxton, 1980, p. 181.

Photograph by Darryl Jacobson

INTERLUDE: WHAT IS "SENILITY?"

To begin with, "senility" is not, properly speaking, a medical diagnosis at all but a wastebasket term for a range of symptoms that, minimally, includes some memory impairment or forgetfulness, difficulty in attention and concentration, decline in general intellectual grasp and ability and reduction in emotional responsiveness to others. This condition, as studies at the National Institutes of Health [N.I.H., *Human Aging: A Biological And Behavioral Study*, 1974] and elsewhere have made clear, is not an inevitable consequence of age, per se. Rather, it is a reflection of any of a variety of different problems including . . . destruction of central-nervous-system cells, or emotional states such as severe depression. For example, the depression of an older person may be inner preoccupation . . . manifesting itself as disturbed concentration, forgetfulness and withdrawal. The term "senility" should be discarded altogether in favor of "emotional and mental disorders" in old age. More than semantics is involved here. Viewing disorders in this way would encourage a . . . broader perspective on the everyday problems and disorders of old age.

From R. N. Butler, *Why Survive? Being Old in America.* New York: Harper & Row, 1975, p. 232.

PERSONALITY PATTERNS AND CHANGES

It is important to point out that the way people regard themselves is probably the most important factor in their overall happiness. This is particularly true of aging individuals (Schwartz, 1975). Like individuals in other phases of the life span, the elderly are able to organize their activities in a meaningful way when they perceive themselves as competent, self-regulating human beings—and are treated that way by others.

Being a competent person in later adulthood does, of course, involve more than one way of approaching life. In other words, there is undoubtedly more than one way to "age" successfully. Because of the unique personality as well as the differing life circumstances of each person, there are a variety of ways of adapting to old age.

Patterns of Aging. Several explanations have been proposed for successful aging, such as disengagement theory, activity theory, and continuity theory.

Disengagement Theory. Disengagement theory stresses mutual withdrawal by both society and the individual. The individual's withdrawal is often associated with decreased emotional involvement in the activities and social relationships that characterized middle age (Cumming and Henry, 1961). Social disengagement may take many forms, including the separation of individuals from their possessions (e.g., when individuals move from private residences to institutions), the loss of prestige and authority when individuals retire, or the loss of family members or close friends through death.

Disengagement theory was originally based on a cross-sectional study of 275 adults who lived in Kansas City and ranged in age from fifty to ninety years (Cumming and Henry, 1961). According to Cumming and Henry, society disengages or withdraws from the individual because of the social necessity of bringing younger people into roles held by older adults. Individuals presumably withdraw from society because of their awareness of reduced capabilities and the relatively short time left to them prior to death. Cumming and Henry (1961) described disengagement theory as follows:

Photograph by Darryl Jacobson

Youth, Large, lusty, loving—
  youth full of grace, force,
  fascination.
Do you know that Old Age
  may come after you with
  equal grace, force
  fascination?
    Walt Whitman

From Kreymborg, A. (Ed.), *Anthology of American Poetry* (2nd rev. ed.) New York: Tudor Publishing Company, 1941.

an inevitable mutual withdrawal or disengagement, resulting in decreased interaction between the aging person and others in the social system he belongs to. The process may be initiated by the individual or by others in the situation. . . . His withdrawal may be accompanied from the outset by a preoccupation with himself. (p. 14)

Almost as soon as disengagement theory appeared, criticisms also emerged. On the whole, these criticisms centered on the following issues.

The assumed inevitability of the process of disengagement. Is the mutual withdrawal of the individual and society an automatic process that occurs at about the same time for all individuals? What about older adults who choose to stay "engaged" and, in fact, do so?

The lack of attention to the role of personality factors. The process of disengagement would seem to be influenced by the personality of the older adult (Atchley, 1971). For example, an elderly person who might be described as aloof, detached, or uninvolved would be expected to have little difficulty "disengaging" from work or family roles.

Activity Theory. In contrast to disengagement theory, activity theory suggests that older adults must compensate for the loss of roles experienced in later adulthood. Rather than disengage, older adults need to maintain a moderately active lifestyle. Blau (1973) summarized the essential idea of activity theory as follows:

the greater the number of optional role resources with which the individual enters old age, the better he or she will withstand the demoralizing effects of exit from the . . . roles ordinarily given priority in adulthood.

The proponents of activity theory assert that active involvement has a positive impact on morale, self-concept, and a general sense of well-being (Havighurst and Albrecht, 1953; Maddox, 1970; Havighurst, Neugarten, and Tobin, 1968; Lipman and Smith, 1968).

Activity theory is not without its limitations. A major criticism has been that it represents an oversimplification of the complex and highly individual process of aging. For example, not all activities provide support for the older adult's self-concept by substituting for the lost roles of middle adulthood. Simply busying oneself with hobbies, pastimes, or "filler" activities that do not represent dominant cultural roles may not lead to better adjustment (Gubrium, 1973).

Continuity Theory. In light of the limitations of both disengagement theory and activity theory, continuity theory has been introduced as a broader view of the complex process of aging (Atchley, 1972). Continuity theory suggests that later adulthood may involve a combination of disengagement from some roles and a continued performance of other roles.

Atchley (1972) described continuity theory as follows:

Continuity theory holds that in the process of becoming an adult, the individual develops habits, commitments, preferences and a host of other dispositions that become a part of his personality. As the individual grows older, he is predisposed toward maintaining continuity in his habits, associations, preferences, and so on. . . . Continuity theory implies that there are many possible adaptations to aging rather than just a few. (p. 36)

Continuity theory emphasizes the complexity of aging. This is both an advantage and a disadvantage. It is an advantage in that complexity and individuality come close to explaining the reality of aging. On the other hand, this complexity is difficult to measure or describe.

Continuity theory suggests that later adulthood may involve a combination of disengagement from some roles and continuation of other roles.

Photograph by Gale Schiamberg

Later Adulthood and Aging

Personality Patterns in Older Adults. As we have seen in our consideration of general theories or patterns of aging, it is not always possible to apply a single theory to all older adults. Each human being is unique. Gerontologists (those who study older adults) have identified some interesting *personality types.*

Reichard, Livson, and Peterson (1962) analyzed the adaptive patterns of eighty-seven men ranging in age from fifty-five to eighty-four. These authors were able to identify five major personality types that described the majority of the men in their sample. In addition, they found that the personalities of the men had not changed much throughout most of adulthood. Well-adjusted men were categorized as in the "mature," "rocking-chair," or "armored" categories. Less-well-adjusted men were characterized as either "angry" or "self-haters."

The mature type. These men seemed to enjoy life, to accept themselves, and to find satisfaction in their activities and relationships with others. In short, these men made the best of their situation without regrets for what had occurred in the past.

The "rocking-chair" men. This group was also judged to be "successful" in their older years, although their approach to life was more passive than that of the "mature" group. These men looked forward to retirement and to the opportunity to be free of responsibility. To some extent, these individuals were content to be dependent on others.

The "armored" men. This group were afraid of the consequences of growing old. They avoided confronting these matters through compulsive activity. They usually kept tight control over their emotions. This mode of aging was also judged to be relatively successful because these men seemed to stay happy (even at the expense of avoiding reality).

The last two modes of aging were seen as unsuccessful.

"Angry" men. These individuals could not reconcile themselves to growing old and were, in many cases, afraid of death.

The "self-haters." These individuals were generally upset about the results of aging and their particular situation. They tended to blame themselves for their current problems and looked forward to death as a release from their misery.

In another study that identified older adult personality types (Neugarten, Berkowitz, Crotty, Gruen, Gutmann, Lubin, Miller, Peck, Rosen, Shukin, and Tobin, 1964, Neugarten, et al., 1968; Neugarten, 1972), Neugarten found four types of aging, which were similar to the Reichard et al. ones. The Neugarten studies examined personality in relation to life satisfaction and activity level (see Table 12.3). For fifty-nine men and women aged seventy to seventy-nine, Neugarten found the following four types of personality:

Integrated personalities. These individuals had competent egos, intact cognitive abilities, high levels of life satisfaction, and relatively complex inner lives. Neugarten identified three types of integrated personalities:

1. *The reorganizers.* These individuals were highly active and had restructured their lives by substituting new activities for old ones. They tended to be involved in a rather broad range of activities.

TABLE 12.3
Personality Type in Relation to Activity and Life Satisfaction (N = 59)

Personality Type	Role Activity	Life Satisfaction High	Medium	Low
Integrated	High	9	2	
	Medium	5		
	Low	3		
Armored–defended	High	5		
	Medium	6	1	
	Low	2	1	1
Passive–dependent	High		1	
	Medium	1	4	
	Low	2	3	2
Unintegrated	High		2	1
	Medium	1		
	Low		2	5
	Total	34	16	9

Source: Neugarten, B. L., Havighurst, R. J. and Tobin, S., "Personality and Patterns of Aging." In B. L. Neugarten (Ed.), *Middle Age and Aging.* Chicago: University of Chicago Press, 1968, pp. 173–177.

2. *Focused people.* In contrast to the "reorganizers," focused adults concentrated their energies on one or two roles (e.g., parent, husband, volunteer).
3. *The disengaged.* These people differed from the reorganizers and the focused people because they demonstrated a relatively low level of activity. By preference, they had withdrawn into a contented and self-contained life.

The "armored–defended" personalities. These individuals were characterized by their striving, achievement motivation and generally guarded emotions. Neugarten identified two types of armored–defended individuals:

1. *The "holding-on" pattern.* These individuals maintained or "held on" to the life pattern and activities of middle age as long as possible. These older adults had a high or medium level of activity and scored high on life satisfaction.
2. *"Constricted" individuals.* These older adults tried hard to defend themselves against the perceived threat of aging by limiting their social interactions. They achieved a fairly high level of life satisfaction accompanied by a medium to low level of activity.

Passive–dependent personalities.

1. *The succorance-seeking.* These individuals had high dependency needs. As long as they could find someone to depend on, they were rather satisfied with life.
2. *Apathetic people.* These people appeared to have been relatively passive and indifferent throughout adulthood. They achieved a medium to low level of life satisfaction.

The unintegrated personalities. These individuals had highly disorganized patterns of aging. They had psychological problems that included emotional disturbances and general decline in thought processes. According to Neugarten, these individuals had both a low level of activity and a low level of life satisfaction.

Self-concept and Self-esteem. As people move into later adulthood, the self-concept tends to become much more dependent on *inner* thoughts and feelings than on *external* factors (e.g., other people's opinions) (Neugarten, et al., 1964). (This was a *general* trend which Neugarten found primarily in men.) For example, Neugarten, et al. (1964) found the following:

> Forty-year-olds see the environment as one that rewards boldness and risk-taking and to see themselves possessing energy . . . [equal to] the opportunities presented in the outer world. Sixty-year-olds seem to see the environment as complex and dangerous, no longer to be reformed in line with one's own wishes and to see self as conforming . . . to outer world demands. (p. 189)

Neugarten referred to this change as a change from *active mastery* to *passive mastery* of the environment. As older adults come to adopt passive mastery as a way of viewing the world, they move from an outer-world to an inner-world orientation. According to Neugarten, their preoccupation with their inner world becomes greater and their ability to relate emotionally to other people declines. Furthermore, their ability to attribute activity and emotion to other people also declines.

Differences between the sexes also appear with age. While older men move from an active involvement with the world to a more passive, self-centered position, women seem to move in the opposite direction—from passive to active mastery. They may become more domineering and aggressive.

INTERLUDE: ON BLOODY-MINDEDNESS

Bloody-mindedness is a British Army term without an exact American equivalent. It subsumes feistiness, cussedness, and orneriness, with overtones of heroic obstinacy in not being put down, in defying popes, presidents, priests, professors, pundits, and people generally when defending your own patch and your own right to be yourself. Bloody-mindedness is the chief adaptive character of man . . . and it is the ultimate resource of the senior person. "Do not go gentle" said the Welsh poet Dylan Thomas, "into that good night." (Comfort, 1976, p. 45)

> Do not go gentle
> into that good
> night.
> Old age should
> burn and rave
> at close of day
> Rage, rage
> against the
> dying of the
> light.
>
> Dylan Thomas

Kermode, F. and Hollander, J. (Eds.), *Oxford Anthology of English Literature,* Vol. 1. New York: Oxford University Press, 1973.

There is stability in self-concept throughout the adult years.

Photograph by Darryl Jacobson

Although there are some general changes in personality as already indicated, older adults still continue to see themselves as they have always been. Rather than there being dramatic changes in self-concept during older adulthood, there is *stability* throughout the adult years (Neugarten, et al., 1964, 1972).

As we pointed out earlier in this chapter, later adulthood is marked by many *role changes*. For example, widowhood, retirement, and disability are all role changes often associated with aging. These role changes do not produce the alterations in self-concept that one might expect (Atchley, 1972). Atchley identified two reasons for this stability of self-concept:

• Older adults depend less on feedback from others and more on their own inner standards.
• Older adults continue to think of themselves in terms of former roles despite changes. For example, an older adult might continue to think of himself or herself as a plumber, a lawyer, or an engineer long after retirement.

The ability to maintain this consistency and stability of self-concept is associated with positive adjustment to the role changes in later adulthood (Lieberman, 1975). One might expect that the self-esteem of older adults would decline because of changes in social roles. However, this does not appear to be the case. Older adults who perceive themselves as having done well in the past continue to think of themselves as doing well in later adulthood. Likewise, those who have negative views of themselves are likely to maintain these negative feelings into later adulthood (Reichard, et al., 1962). Atchley (1972) suggested that "the key to positive self-esteem in old age may in some cases reside in the past."

In many cases, older adults "fight back" by refusing to accept the negative labels and beliefs associated with aging. For example, some older adults simply do not view themselves as "old." Bengston, Cuellar, and Ragan (1977) found that many individuals over age seventy identified themselves as middle-aged rather than elderly or old. Another study (Riley and Foner, 1968) showed that younger people were more critical than older adults of their own shortcomings.

An important dimension of individual self-esteem at all ages is the perception of *competence* and *being in control* (at least, as much as possible) of one's life. Research on older adults suggests that a positive sense of self-esteem is associated with making decisions for oneself (Langer and Rodin, 1977).

Death and Dying

The personal realization that life has a limit—an end—has a marked effect on how adults interpret their life experience. For example, a middle-aged adult who has attained family and occupational goals may now wonder about the "meaning" of life in relation to the years remaining. The older adult who is near death may begin a "life review" process (Butler, 1968). The life review involves the recall of previous life experiences and the attempt to organize these events into a meaningful pattern.

When we experience the death of another person whom we care about, we may begin to realize the finite aspects of life as well as to think about a sometimes difficult topic: our own deaths. The recognition of death as a reality of human experience may be greeted by a variety of cognitive and emotional responses. The meaning of death varies with the developmental level of the individual. For example, death may mean one thing to a five-year-old child and quite another to a forty-nine-year-old businessman who thinks his heart may have "skipped a beat" or an eighty-eight-year-old woman with terminal cancer.

Most Americans grow up in a culture in which the topic of death is virtually taboo, much as the topic of sex was taboo to our Victorian ancestors (Shneidman, 1973). Although young people may have had some experiences with death, it is usually not until the middle years of life that individuals begin to see it as a personal reality. Furthermore, middle-aged adults are more likely to fear death than the young or the old (Riley, 1970).

THE MEANING OF DEATH

When we think about someone else's death or our own death, we experience many thoughts and feelings. For example, we may *think* of death as a relief, a new beginning, a meaningless ending to a meaningless experience, or a total mystery, to name only a few possible viewpoints. Our *feelings* about death may also be variable: resentment, fear, loneliness, helplessness, peacefulness, awe, sadness, or anger, to name only a few emotions. To some extent, our reactions to death are both individual and personal *and* similar to those of people of the same age (see Interlude: Subjective Life Expectancy).

INTERLUDE: SUBJECTIVE LIFE EXPECTANCY

Death of a parent or of one special person often makes the difference. Simply knowing a person's age does not tell us whether he or she realizes death as an authentic personal fact. Similarly, knowing a person's age does not tell us how the future is imagined. Try for yourself the following exercise in *subjective life expectancy.* . . .

1. I expect to live to age (circle your answer).
   25 30 35 40 45 50 55 60 65 70 75 80 85 90 95 100.
2. I want to live to age (circle your answer).
   25 30 35 40 45 50 55 60 65 70 75 80 85 90 95 100.

The thoughts and feelings that flashed through your mind in answering these questions may be more important than the answers themselves. Perhaps you were able to catch some of your assumptions, fears and hopes. . . .

- Would you have answered this pair of questions the same way five years ago?
- Will you have the same thoughts and feelings about the length of your life when you are 5, 10 or 20 years older?
- Compare your choices to those of your peers.

There are probably some elements in your subjective life expectancy that other people your age tend to share. But there are probably other thoughts and feelings that are more personal.

From R. J. Kastenbaum. Death, Society and Human Experience (2nd ed.). St. Louis: The C. V. Mosby Co., 1981, pp. 132–133.

Young Children and Death. The concept of death changes as children grow older. Preschool children do have death-related experiences that engage their thoughts and feelings. For example, a fallen leaf or a dead bird may allow the preschool child to raise questions such as: "How come the leaf fell? What will it do now?" These first encounters with death can be opportunities for parents and children to focus together on concepts such as *permanence* and *impermanence*. Very young children may not yet understand the concept of object permanence (see Chapter Five). A clear understanding of the idea of permanence would seem to precede the understanding of when things "are no more." For example, simply because the child cannot see a tree on a dark night does not mean that the tree is "gone forever." However, when young George Washington chopped down the cherry tree (if he did), that cherry tree was indeed "all gone" and "no more."

There does appear to be a developmental pattern in young children's understanding of death. Nagy (1948) identified three stages of death interpretation in children.

- *Death as a temporary, "sleeplike" experience* (children three to five years old).
- *Death as a "personification"* (children five to nine years old). In this stage, children may think of death as an "angel" or a "monster." Although death may be viewed as final or permanent for some people or some things, it is not seen as necessarily universal. For example, some children think that others will die but that they can avoid death.
- *Death as universal, final, and personal* (begins at approximately age nine or ten). This is the adult perspective of death. It is universal, final, and touches "me."

Adults and Death. One might assume that the adult who has the advantage over young children of high-level thinking processes and additional life experience would demonstrate a mature approach to death. Although this expectation may hold for some adults, it does not hold for all of them.

Accepting death is an important aspect of mature adulthood.

Photograph by Darryl Jacobson

Later Adulthood and Aging

Youth and young adulthood are often times of busy involvement—of attaining things or preparing to attain them. Such a time may not lend itself to a mature attitude toward death despite the more capable thinking skills of young adults. Compared with middle-aged adults and the elderly, youth have had fewer personal experiences with death (Shneidman, 1973).

INTERLUDE: "YOUTH: TOO ALIVE TO DIE?"

"Somebody else who happens to have my name may grow old some day, and may even die. But that's not really 'me.' I am here right now, and I'm as full of life as can be. It's the only way I know to be. I have always been young, never old, always alive, never dead. Sure, I have a good imagination: but to see myself, really see myself as old or dead—say, that's asking too much!"

This is the implicit credo of youth that I have observed in our society over the past two decades. Perhaps it has been around much longer, and perhaps it has now started to change. . . . Most of us, however, have grown up in a society that celebrates youth. . . . Very little systematic preparation is provided, or expected, to meet the challenges of later life and of death. Both aging and death share a cloudy, dimly perceived existence on the far distant mental horizon. . . . the young adult may have a sense that both old age and death are conditions that do not really apply to him.

From R. J. Kastenbaum. *Death, Society and Human Experience.* (2nd ed.). St. Louis: The C. V. Mosby Co., 1981, pp. 126–127.

The middle-aged adult is likely to have had more personal experience with death. He or she is likely to have experienced the death of a parent or a friend. Therefore, the middle-aged adult often comes to grips with death as an authentic fact that applies to him or her. As we indicated above, middle-aged individuals are more fearful of death than either young adults or the elderly.

Although death may be less frightening for some older adults, they do talk and think about it more than younger adults. Several reasons have been suggested for a decline in the fear of death in old age (Kalish, 1976):

- *Older adults may put less value on life.* They may feel that they have completed their important life projects. They may also be in serious discomfort because of ill health.
- People who reach older ages may feel that they have lead a full life—at least from the perspective of time and length.
- Older people who experience the death of a spouse and close friends may come to accept their own deaths as inevitable.

At some point, the older adult may recognize that there is really rather little time left. Life's end is at hand. Some individuals may now prepare themselves for what may appear to be the "ultimate disengagement" (Kastenbaum, 1977). Why wait any longer to be with the people one loves or appreciates, to do the things that one has never "had the time to do?"

INTERLUDE: ON DEATH AND TRIVIALITY

Death is the end of living, not the end of "old age," but obviously the longer we live the more realistically we are obliged to view it. It is something which, because it represents the end of experience, no normal person welcomes. Some cultures celebrate and in a sense "affirm" death, thus taking it into the sweep of experience. Our culture tends to deny or sentimentalize it, and push the deceased person out by the back door. . . . All that the "proximity of death" does to age is to add value to living, to reduce our tolerance of triviality and to increase our anger with those who, or those attitudes which, cause us to waste a store of time and experience that we cannot afford to dissipate or have destroyed. (Comfort, 1976, pp. 60–61)

In the time remaining before death, individuals are likely to change their relationship to themselves and to society: "He will spend less time under the control of other people's demands and expectations, retain more time to use as he sees fit for himself" (Kastenbaum, 1977, p. 147). Part of this time may involve the process of "life review" (Butler, 1968). When older adults recognize their limited time, many begin to examine the kind of life they have lived: "What kind of person have I become?" "Am I satisfied with my life?" "Would I do anything differently?" According to Butler, older adults who conclude that they are reasonably satisfied with life may find it easier to die.

THE PROCESS OF DYING

What happens when people die? Are there fairly consistent patterns of adaptation to dying that young and old alike experience? Kubler-Ross (1969) has proposed a series of stages of grief that dying persons and their families must negotiate prior to death. Her stages of dying were developed while working with terminal cancer patients. Although these stages may *not* necessarily reflect the way in which *all* old people approach death, they are both relevant and accurate depictions of the experience of dying for many human beings. According to Kubler-Ross, individuals pass through five stages as death approaches:

Denial. Most people react with shock when informed that they are going to die. Even adults (who as we have seen have the cognitive skills to understand death) are unready to accept the fact that they are dying: "Wait a minute—it can't be me—there must be some mistake!" Denial is often viewed as a defense mechanism that helps the individual to cushion the initial shock of impending death.

One physician reported an incident in which he had the uncomfortable role of explaining to a middle-aged woman that she was dying of cancer. She was in the hospital undergoing tests for cancer and knew of the possibility. When the physician told her that she *had* cancer, she responded, "I'm glad I don't have cancer."

Anger. When individuals come to realize that denial no longer works, they typically experience feelings of rage, anger, or resentment. The individual may be saying to himself or herself, "Why me? How come it's not happening to someone else?" This stage is particularly difficult for the medical staff and for the family because the anger of the dying person may be aimed at them. It is particularly important for family, friends, and medical people to be understanding and forgiving during this stage.

The . . . family is received with little cheerfulness and anticipation, which makes the encounter a painful event. They can either respond with grief and tears, guilt or shame, or avoid future visits, which only increases the patient's discomfort and anger. (Kubler-Ross, 1969, p. 51)

Bargaining. The individual in this stage hopes that somehow death can be delayed or even postponed. In some cases, the dying person may believe that he or she can strike a bargain to "be good" or "be better" in return for an extension of time: "If God has decided to take us from this earth and he did not respond to my angry pleas, He may be more favorable if I ask nicely" (Kubler-Ross, 1969, p. 82).

Depression. When dying people realize that nothing more can be done to deny or postpone their deaths and that they can only look forward to more pain and medical treatment, they may become engulfed in depression. Kubler-Ross identified two types of depression: *reactive depression* resulting from a loss that has already occurred (e.g., one's health) and *preparatory depression* resulting from an expected future loss (e.g., family relationships).

One approach to helping people through this period is being a good listener. Allowing the person to express his or her depression and to "mourn" past and future losses paves the way for the final stage.

Acceptance. Acceptance is a stage during which the dying person shows little feeling or emotion. He or she is resigned to impending death. Kubler-Ross described this period as one of calm peacefulness—a final pause before the "long journey." Furthermore, Kubler-Ross suggested that the dying person's family may need more assistance during this stage than the dying person.

INTERLUDE: THE "RIGHT TO DIE"

Medical science has continued to make advances in sustaining life for both reversible and irreversible (terminal) conditions. For many terminally ill individuals, some life functions can be maintained even though there is virtually no hope for recovery. Many people therefore suggest that the terminally ill should have the "right to die" if they so choose (Aiken, 1978). The "living will" is an attempt to do this:

THE LIVING WILL

To my family, my physician, my lawyer, my clergyman
To any medical facility in whose care I happen to be
To any individual who may become responsible for my health, welfare, or affairs

Death is as much a reality as birth, growth, maturity and old age—it is the one certainty of life. If the time comes when I, _____, can no longer take part in decisions for my own future, let this statement stand as an expression of my wishes while I am still of sound mind.

If the situation should arise in which there is no reasonable expectation of my recovery from physical or mental disability, I request that I be allowed to die and not be kept alive by artificial means or "heroic measures." I do not fear death itself as much as the indignities of deterioration, dependence, and hopeless pain. I therefore ask that medication be mercifully administered to me to alleviate suffering even though this may hasten the moment of death.

This request is made after careful consideration. I hope you who care for me will feel morally bound to follow its mandate. I recognize that this appears to place a heavy responsibility upon you, but it is with the intention of relieving you of such responsibility and of placing it upon myself in accordance with my strong convictions that this statement is made.

Signed_____

Date_____

Witness_____   Witness_____

Copies of this request have been given to _____

_____

CARE FOR DYING PERSONS

In many instances, the traditional treatment of dying persons in institutional settings (e.g., hospitals, nursing homes) is not particularly suited to them or to their families (Kastenbaum, 1981). You may recall (in Chapter 4 on birth) that questions were raised about the suitability of hospitals, delivery techniques, and hospital practices for the newborn and the family. The same questioning can be applied to institutional arrangements for the dying person.

INTERLUDE:
THE HOSPICE—AN INNOVATION IN
CARE FOR THE DYING

The best known hospice today is St. Christopher's, a facility that has been serving London since 1968. . . . The best of contemporary health-care expertise is applied but with a concern for what in a former day would have been known as the spiritual well-being of the patient as well as for his physical well-being. . . .

The family of the terminally ill person is not merely tolerated at a hospice such as St. Christopher's. Instead, the family is both an agency and a recipient of care. The philosophy of care encompasses the entire family unit. Many family members not only visit their own kin but also befriend other patients. This permeability of the hospice much reduces the likelihood of social isolation for the patient and the sense of helplessness for the family. . . .

A person who has been with seriously and terminally ill patients in other environments is likely to observe a different attitude among most patients at St. Christopher's. There is less anxiety and obvious suffering, more serenity and a sense of security. . . . One gets the impression that it is neither the general atmosphere nor the specific treatment procedures that produce [sic] the favorable effects. Rather, it seems to be the integration of the humane impulse and clinical expertise. . . . Particular [care is given] to the control of pain. . . . Relief from seemingly endless and meaningless suffering makes it possible for many terminally ill people to call upon their own personal resources to adapt to their situation and to be more responsive to others. When the high priority given to pain management is successful it makes a dramatic difference in the patient's sense of well-being and, obviously, a difference to the family and staff as well. . . .

The philosophy and practice of St. Christopher's Hospice suggests [sic] that it is not a wild fantasy to integrate an encompassing concern for the dying person with all the relevant resources of contemporary medicine.

From R. J. Kastenbaum, *Death, Society and Human Experience* (2nd ed.). St. Louis: The C. V. Mosby Co., 1981, pp. 201–206.

Summary

1. A common age given for the beginning of later adulthood is sixty-five—the age of retirement. Beyond providing us with an arbitrary age for retirement, sixty-five is nearly irrelevant in describing other aspects of adult functioning. Older adults vary more in biological and behavioral functioning than young and middle aged adults.

One of the most common myths about older adults is that large numbers of them live in such institutions as hospitals for chronic diseases, nursing homes, or mental institutions.

2. One of the myths of family life in later adulthood is that American families abandon their elderly. It is not the case that older adults are left to shift for themselves. Considerable research has demonstrated the support of older adults through strong family ties.

Grandparenthood is a common experience for older adults. Being a grandparent may, in some cases, take on an important meaning to older adults as other activities (e.g., work) are closed to them. There are many different styles of grandparenthood.

The end of marriage—usually through the death of one partner (probably the husband)—creates a new role, widowhood. After age sixty-five, less than half of older women are living with their spouses.

3. The readjustment of older married persons at the death of a spouse may also be mirrored when close friends and neighbors pass away.

4. There are three common ways of thinking about retirement: (a) as an event, (b) as a status, and (c) as a process. Whether retirement is voluntary or compulsory has an impact on the meaning of retirement to the individual.

5. From middle age to later adulthood, there are some important changes in the general health status. In addition, there is a decline in the efficient functioning in nearly all the senses with time. Older persons generally require a longer time to make movements, take longer to start their movements (i.e., have a longer reaction time) and have less muscular strength than younger persons.

6. The multiple and potentially diverse definitions of intelligence make it both unfair and unreasonable to suggest that elderly adults experience a decline in all phases of cognitive ability. Research on the patterns of cognitive functioning in later adulthood indicates several directions of change. Abilities that require speed, physical activity, or immediate memory seem to decline more than those that are dependent on experience or are untimed.

7. Like individuals in other phases of the life-span, the elderly are able to organize their activities in a meaningful way when they perceive themselves as competent, self-regulating human beings—and are treated that way by others. Because of the unique personality and differing life circumstances of each person, there are a variety of ways of adapting to old age. Several explanations have been proposed for successful aging such as disengagement theory, activity theory, and continuity theory.

As people move into later adulthood, the self-concept tends to become much more dependent on *inner* thoughts and feelings than on *external* factors (e.g., other people's opinions). Differences between the sexes appear with age as older men move from active involvement to passive mastery whereas, older women move in the opposite direction—from passive to active mastery. Rather than there being dramatic changes in self-concept during older adulthood, there is *stability* throughout the adult years.

An important dimension of individual self-esteem at all ages including old age is the perception of "being in control" of one's life. Positive self-esteem in later adulthood is associated with making decisions for oneself.

8. The older adult who is near death may begin a "life review" process. Life review involves the recall of previous life experiences and the attempt to organize these events into a meaningful pattern.

9. Most Americans grow up in a culture in which the topic of death is virtually taboo much as the topic of sex was taboo to our Victorian ancestors. To some extent our reactions to death are both individual and personal and similar to those of people of the same age. Kubler-Ross has proposed a five-stage process of grief and dying. The stages are denial, anger, bargaining, depression, and acceptance.

10. In many instances, the traditional treatment of dying persons in institutional settings is not particularly suited to them or to their families. The *hospice* concept is a relevant and promising innovation in holistic and integrated care for dying persons and their families.

Questions

1. Who are the elderly? How many are there? What are some common living arrangements for older adults? Are there more widows than widowers? Why?

2. Briefly explain each of the following: disengagement theory, activity theory, and continuity theory. What are the strengths and weaknesses of each theory?

3. Describe the changes in sensory systems which occur in old age. Which problems of vision can be corrected and which ones cannot?

4. What is ageism? How prevalent do you think it is?

5. Discuss the problems inherent in measuring the intelligence of the elderly.

6. Discuss the stages in adaptation to dying as described by Kubler-Ross.

7. Define the following terms: a living will and hospice.

Bibliography

AIKEN, L. R. *The Psychology of Later Life.* Philadelphia: W. B. Saunders, 1978.

ARENBERG, D., and ROBERTSON-TCHABO, E. Learning and aging. In J. E. Birren and K. W. Schaie (Eds.), *Handbook of the Psychology of Aging.* New York: Van Nostrand, 1977.

ATCHLEY, R. C. Disengagement among professors. *Journal of Gerontology,* 1971, *26,* 476–480.

ATCHLEY, R. C. *The Social Forces in Later Life: An Introduction to Social Gerontology.* Belmont, Calif.: Wadsworth, 1972.

ATCHLEY, R. C. *The Sociology of Retirement.* Cambridge, Mass.: Schenkman, 1975a.

ATCHLEY, R. C. Dimensions of widowhood in later life, *The Gerontologist,* 1975b, *15*(2), 176–178.

BALTES, P. B., and SCHAIE, K. W. Aging and the I.Q.: The myth of the twilight years. *Psychology Today,* March 1974, *7,* 35–40.

BENEDEK, T. Parenthood during the life cycle. In E. D. Anthony (Ed.), *Parenthood.* Boston: Little, Brown, 1970.

BENGSTON, V. L., CUELLAR, J. B., and RAGAN, P. K. Stratum contrasts and similarities in attitudes toward death. *Journal of Gerontology,* 1977, *32*(1), 76–88.

BEVERLY, E. V. Turning the realities of retirement into fulfillment. *Geriatrics,* 1975, *30*(1), 126–139.

BIRREN, J. E. *The Psychology of Aging.* Englewood Cliffs, N.J.: Prentice-Hall, 1964.

BIRREN, J. E. Translations in gerontology—from lab to life: Psychophysiology and speed of response. *American Psychologist,* 1974, *29,* 808–815.

BIRREN, J. E., BUTLER, R. N., GREENHOUSE, S. W., SOKOLOFF, L., and YARROW, M. R. (Eds.). *Human aging: A biological and behavioral study.* Pub. No. (HSM) 71-9051. Washington, D.C.: U.S. Government Printing Office, 1963.

BIRREN, J. E., WOODS, A. M., and WILLIAMS, M. V. Behavioral slowing with age: Causes, organization and consequences. In L. W. Poon (Ed.), *Aging in the 1980s,* Washington, D.C.: American Psychological Association, 1980.

BISCHOF, L. J. *Adult Psychology.* New York: Harper & Row, 1976.

BLAKE, J. Can we believe recent data on birth expectations in the United States?'' *Demography,* February 1974, *11*(1), 25–44.

BLAU, Z. S. *Old Age in a Changing Society.* New York: New Viewpoints, a division of Franklin Watts, 1973.

BLUM, J. E., FOSSHAGE, J. L., and JARVIK, L. F. Intellectual changes and sex differences in octogenarians. *Developmental Psychology,* 1972, *7,* 178–187.

BORTZ, W. M. Disuse and aging. *Journal of the American Medical Association,* 1982, *246*(9), 1203–1208.

BORUP, J. H., GALLEGO, D. T., and HEFFERNAN, P. G. Relocation and its effect on mortality. *The Gerontologist.* 1979, *19,* 135–140.

BOSWELL, J. *Life of Samuel Johnson,* Vol. IV. Philadelphia, Pennsylvania: Claxton, 1870, 181.

BOTWINICK, J. *Cognitive Processes in Maturity and Old Age.* New York: Springer, 1967.

BOTWINICK, J. Geropsychology. In P. H. Mussen and M. R. Rosenzweig (Eds.), *Annual Review of Psychology.* Palo Alto, Calif.: Annual Reviews, 1970.

BOTWINICK, J. *Aging and behavior* (2nd ed.). New York: Springer, 1978.

BOTWINICK, J., and THOMPSON, L. W. Individual differences in reaction time in relation to age. *Journal of Genetic Psychology,* 1968, *112,* 73–75.

BRAND, F., and SMITH, R. Life adjustment and relocation of the elderly. *Journal of Gerontology,* 1974, *29,* 336–340.

BUTLER, R. N. Toward a psychiatry of the life cycle. In L. A. Epstein, and A. Simon, (Eds.), *Aging in Modern Society.* Washington, D.C.: American Psychiatric Association, 1968.

BUTLER, R. N. *Why survive? Being old in America.* New York: Harper & Row, 1975.

BUTLER, R. N., and LEWIS, M. I. *Aging and Mental Health.* (3rd ed.). St. Louis: Mosby, 1982.

CARP, F. The impact of environment on old people. *The Gerontologist.* 1967, *7,* 106–108.

CARP, F. Impact of improved living environment on health and life expectancy. *The Gerontologist,* 1977, *17,* 242–249.

CLARK, M., and ANDERSON, B. G. *Culture and Aging: An Anthropological Study of Older American Adults.* Springfield, Ill.: Thomas, 1967.

COMFORT, A. *A Good Age.* New York: Crown, 1976.

CONSUMER CLEARINGHOUSE. *Social Security Explained.* Chicago: Commerce Clearinghouse, 1980.

CORSO, J. F. Sensory processes and age effects in normal adults. *Journal of Gerontology,* 1971, *26,* 90–105.

CUMMING, E., and HENRY, W. E. *Growing Old: The Process of Disengagement.* New York: Basic Books, 1961.

DEVRIES, H. A. *Vigor Regained.* Englewood Cliffs, N.J.: Prentice-Hall, 1974.

DEVRIES, H. A. Physiology of physical conditioning for the elderly. In R. Harris and L. J. Frankel (Eds.), *Guide To Fitness After Fifty.* New York: Plenum Press, 1977, pp. 47–52.

DEVRIES, H. A., and ADAMS, G. M. Comparison of exercise responses on old and young men: II. The cardiac effort/total body effort relationship. *Journal of Gerontology,* 27(2), 244–248, 1972a.

deVries, H. A., and Adams, G. H. Comparison of exercise responses on old and young men: II. Ventilatory mechanics. *Journal of Gerontology, 27*(3), 349–352, 1972b.

deVries, H. A., and Hales, D. *Fitness After Fifty.* New York: Charles Scribner's and Sons, 1982.

Eisdorfer, C. The WATS performance of the aged. *Journal of Gerontology, 1963, 18,* 169–172.

Eisdorfer, C. Adaptation to loss of work. In F. Carp (Ed.), *Retirement.* New York: Behavioral Publications, 1972.

Foner, A., and Schwab, K. *Aging and Retirement.* Monterey, CA.: Brooks/Cole, 1981.

Glamser, F. D. The impact of pre-retirement programs on the retirement experience, *Journal of Gerontology, 1981, 36,* 244–250.

Glick, I. O., Weiss, R. S., and Parkes, C. M. *The First Year of Bereavement.* New York: Wiley, 1974.

Gottesman, L. E., Quarterman, C. E., and Kohn, G. M. Psychosocial treatment of the aged. In C. Eisendorfer and M. P. Lawton (Eds.), *The Psychology of Adult Development and Aging.* Washington, D.C.: American Psychological Association, 1973.

Grossman, A. S. More than half of all children have working mothers. *Monthly Labor Review,* U. S. Department of Labor, Bureau of Labor Statistics, 1982, 105, 41–43.

Gubrium, J. F. *The myth of the golden years: A socio-environmental theory of aging.* Springfield, Ill.: Thomas, 1973.

Gutman, G. M., and Herbert, C. P. Mortality rates among relocated extended care patients. *Journal of Gerontology, 1976, 31,* 352–357.

Harris, Louis, and Associates, Study of American Attitudes Toward Pensions and Retirement: A Nationwide Survey of Employees, Retirees, and Business Leaders. Commissioned by Johnson and Higgins, conducted by Louis Harris and Associates, Inc., Feb. 1979.

Havighurst, R. J., and Albrecht, R. *Older people.* New York: McKay, 1953.

Havighurst, R. J., Neugarten, B. L., and Tobin, S. S. Disengagement and patterns of aging. In B. L. Neugarten (Ed.), *Middle age and aging.* Chicago: U. of Chicago P., 1968.

Jantz, R., Seefeldt, C., Galper, A., and Serock, K. *Children's Attitudes Toward the Elderly.* Final Report to American Assoc. of Retired Persons, Washington, D.C., July 1976.

Jarvik, L. F., Kallman, F. J., and Falek, A. Intellectual changes in aged twins. *Journal of Gerontology, 1962, 17,* 289–294.

Kahana, B., and Kahana, E. Grandparenthood from the perspective of the developing grandchild. *Developmental Psychology,* April 1970, 3, 98–105.

Kahana, B., and Kahana, E. Theoretical and research perspectives on grandparenthood. *Aging and Human Development, 1971, 2,* 261–268.

Kalish, R. A. *Late Adulthood: Perspective on Human Development.* Monterey, Calif.: Brooks-Cole, 1975.

Kalish, R. A. Death and dying in a social context. In R. H. Binstock and M. E. Shanas (Eds.), *The Handbook of Aging and the Social Sciences.* New York: Nostrand, 1976, pp. 483–509.

Kastenbaum, R. *Death, Society and Human Experience.* St. Louis, Mo: The C. V. Mosby Co., 1981.

Keahy, S. P., and Seaman, D. F. Self-actualization and adjustment in retirement. *Adult Education, 1974, 24,* 220–226.

Kermode, F., and Hollander, J. (Eds.). *Oxford Anthology of English Literature,* Vol. 1. New York: Oxford University Press, 1973.

Kimmel, D. C. *Adulthood and Aging.* New York: Wiley, 1974. (2nd ed., 1980).

Kivett, V. R. The aged in North Carolina: Physical, social and environmental characteristics and sources of assistance, Technical Bulletin No. 237. Raleigh, N.C.: Agricultural Experiment Station, 1976.

Knox, A. B. *Adult Development and Learning.* San Francisco: Jossey-Bass, 1977.

KREYMBORG, A. (Ed.), *Anthology of American Poetry* (2nd rev. ed.). New York: Tudor Publishing Company, 1941.

KUBLER-ROSS, E. *On Death and Dying.* New York: Macmillan, 1969.

LANGER, E., and RODIN, J. The effects of choice and enhanced personal responsibility for the aged: A field experiment in an institutionalized setting. *Journal of Personality and Social Psychology,* 1977, *34,* 191–198.

LAWTON, M., and YAFFE, S. Mortality, morbidity, and voluntary change of residence by older people. *Journal of the American Geriatric Society.* 1970, *18,* 823–831.

LIEBERMAN, M. A. Adaptive processes in late life. In N. Datan and L. H. Ginsberg (Eds.), *Life Span Developmental Psychology: Normative Life Crises.* New York: Academic Press, 1975, 135–160.

LIPMAN, A., and SMITH, K. J. Functionality of disengagement in old age. *Journal of Gerontology,* 1968, *23,* 517–521.

LOPATA, H. Z. *Widowhood in an American City.* Cambridge, Mass.: Schenkman, 1973.

LOPATA, H. Z. *Women as Widows: Support Systems.* New York: Elsevier-North Holland, 1979.

LOWENTHAL, M. F. Social isolation and mental illness in old age. *American Sociological Review,* 1964, *29*(1), 54–70.

MADDOX, G. L. Retirement as a social event in the United States. In J. C. McKinney and F. T. DeVyver (Eds.), *Aging and Social Policy.* New York: Appleton, 1966.

MADDOX, G. L. Themes and issues in sociological theories of human aging. *Human Development,* 1970, *13,* 17–27.

MARLOWE, R. A. Effects of environment on elderly state hospital relocatees. Paper presented at the annual meeting of the Pacific Sociological Association, Scottsdale, Arizona, May 1973.

MCCLUSKEY, N. G. Careers for older Americans. In N. G. McCluskey, and E. F. Borgatta (Eds.), *Aging and Retirement: Prospects, Planning and Policy.* Beverly Hills, California: Sage, 1981, 31–46.

MCFARLAND, R. A. The sensory and perceptual processes in aging. In K. W. Schaie (Ed.), *Theory and Methods of Research on Aging.* Morgantown, West Virginia University Library, 1968.

MCFARLAND, R. A., TUNE, G. S., and WELFORD, A. T. On the driving of automobile by older people. *Journal of Gerontology,* 1964, *19,* 190–197.

MCKAIN, W. A new look at older marriages. *The Family Coordinator,* 1972, *21,* 61–69.

MILLER, S. J. Will the real 'older woman' please stand up? In M. M. Seltzer, S. L. Corbett and R. C. Atchley (Eds.), *Social Problems of the Aging: Readings,* Belmont, California: Wadsworth, 1978.

NAGY, M. The child's view of death. *Journal of Genetic Psychology,* 1948, *73,* 3–27.

NATIONAL COMMITTEE ON CAREERS FOR OLDER AMERICANS. *Older Americans: An Untapped Resource.* New York: Academy for Educational Development, 1978.

NATIONAL INSTITUTES OF HEALTH. *Human Aging: A Biological and Behavioral Study,* 1974.

NATIONAL OLD PEOPLE'S WELFARE COUNCIL. *Annual report of the year ending March 31, 1966,* British Information Services, London, 1966.

NATIONAL SAFETY COUNCIL. *Accident Facts.* Chicago, Illinois: National Safety Council, 1983, p. 54.

NATIONAL SOCIETY FOR THE PREVENTION OF BLINDNESS, 1978. White House Conference on Aging, Mini White House Conference on Aging and Vision, American Foundation for the Blind, 1981.

NEUGARTEN, B. L. Personality and the aging process. *The Gerontologist,* 1972, *12*(1), 9–15.

NEUGARTEN, B. L., BERKOWITZ, H., CROTTY, W. J., GRUEN, W., GUTMANN, D. L., LUBIN, M. I., MILLER, D. L., PECK, R. F., ROSEN, J. L., SHUKIN, A., and TOBIN, S. S. *Personality in Middle and Late Life.* New York: Atherton, 1964.

NEUGARTEN, B., HAVIGHURST, R., and TOBIN, S. Personality and patterns of aging. In B. Neugarten (Ed.), *Middle Age and Aging.* Chicago: U. of Chicago P., 1968.

NEUGARTEN, B. L., and WEINSTEIN, K. K. The changing American grandparent. *Journal of Marriage and the Family*, 1964, *26*, 199–204.

PASTALAN, L. Report on the Pennsylvania nursing home relocation program. Interim Research Findings, Institute of Gerontology, University of Michigan, Ann Arbor, 1976.

PASTALAN, L. The empathic model, *Journal of Architectural Education*, 1977, *31*, 1, 14–15.

PASTALAN, L. Environmental displacement: A literature reflecting old-person—environment transactions. In G. D. Rowles and R. Ohta (Eds.), *Aging and Milieu: Environmental Perspectives on Growing Old*. New York: Academie Press, 1983.

PETROWSKY, M. Marital status, sex, and the social networks of the elderly, *Journal of Marriage and the Family*, 1976, *38*(3), 749–756.

PINEO, P. Disengagement in the later years of marriage. In B. Neugarten (Ed.), *Middle Age and Aging*. Chicago: U. of Chicago P., 1968.

POWERS, E. A., KEITH, P., and GOUDY, W. H. Family relationships and friendships. In R. C. Atchley (Ed.), *Environments and the Rural Aged*. Washington, D.C.: Gerontological Society, 1975.

RAMSDELL, D. A. The psychology of the hard of hearing and deafened adult. In H. Davis and R. Silverman (Eds.), *Hearing and Deafness*. New York: Holt, 1965.

REICHARD, S., LIVSON, F., and PETERSON, P. G. *Aging and Personality: A Study of 87 Older Men*. New York: Wiley, 1962.

RENO, V. "Retired Women Workers." In Social Security Administration, *Reaching Retirement Age: Findings from a Survey of Newly Entitled Workers*, 1968–1970. Washington, D.C.: U.S. Govt. Printing Office, 1976.

RILEY, J. W. What people think about death. In O. B. Brim et al., (Eds.), *The Dying Patient*. New York: Russell Sage Foundation, 1970, pp. 30–41.

RILEY, M. W., and FONER, A. *Aging and Society. Vol. 1: An Inventory of Research Findings*. New York: Russell Sage Foundation, 1968.

ROGERS, D. *The Adult Years*. Englewood Cliffs, N.J.: Prentice-Hall, 1979.

ROLLINS, B., and CANNON, K. L. Marital satisfaction over the family life cycle: A reevaluation. *Journal of Marriage and the Family*, 1974, *36*(2), 271–282.

RONBERG, G. *St. Louis Post-Dispatch*, Tuesday, November 19, 1974, 3D.

ROSEN, B., and JERDEE, T. The nature of job-related stereotypes, *Journal of Applied Psychology*, 1976(a), *61*, 180–183.

ROSEN, B., and JERDEE, T. The influence of age stereotypes on managerial decisions, *Journal of Applied Psychology*, 1976(b), *61*, 428–432.

ROWLES, G. D., and OHTA, R. J. (Eds.), *Aging and Milieu: Environmental Perspectives and Growing Old*. New York: Academic Press, 1983.

RUBIN, L. Disabling Health Conditions Among Men. In Social Security Administration, *Reaching Retirement Age: Findings from a Survey of Newly Entitled Workers 1968–1970*. Washington, D.C.: U.S. Govt. Printing Office, 1976.

SCHIAMBERG, L. Is growing old inevitable? A systems perspective to biological changes and educational priorities in later adulthood. Paper presented at the annual meeting of the American Educational Research Association, Montreal, Canada, April, 1983.

SCHIAMBERG, L., SPELL, J., and CHIN, C. Aging Widows. A paper presented at the Annual Meeting of the American Educational Research Association, New Orleans, Louisiana, 1984.

SCHWARTZ, A. N. Self esteem: linchpin of quality of life for the aged. Paper presented at the annual meeting of the American Association for the Advancement of Science, New York, 1975.

SEEFELDT, C. Young and old together. *Children Today*, Washington, D.C.: U.S. Department of Health, Education, and Welfare, January–February 1977, 23–25.

SHAHINIAN, S., GOLDFARB, A., and TURNER, H. Death rate in relocated residents of nursing homes. New York State Department of Mental Hygiene, Office of the Consultant on Aging. Albany, New York, 1968.

SHANAS, E. The unmarried old person in the United States: Living arrangements and care in illness, myth and fact. Paper prepared for the International Social Science Research Seminar in Gerontology, Markaryd, Sweden, August 1963.

SHANAS, E. Final Report. National Survey of the Aged. A Report to the Administration on Aging, 1978.

SHANAS, E. Social myth as hypothesis: The case of the family relations of old people. *The Gerontologist,* 1979, *19*(1), 3–9.

SHANAS, E., and SUSSMAN, M. B. The family in later life. In R. W. Fogel, E. Hatfield, S. B. Kiesler, and E. Shanas (Eds.), *Aging: Stability and Change in the Family.* New York: Academic Press, 1981, 211–231.

SHANAS, E., TOWNSEND, P., WEDDERBURN, D., FRIIS, H., MILHOJ, P., and STEHOUWER, J. (Eds.), *Old People in Three Industrial Societies.* New York: Atherton, 1968.

SHNEIDMAN, E. S. *Deaths of Man.* New York: Quadrangle, 1973.

SHOCK, N. W., and NORRIS, A. H. *Physical Activity and Aging, with Special Reference to the Effect of Exercise and Training on the Natural History of Arteriosclerotic Heart Disease.* Vol. 4 of *Medicine and Sport,* D. Brunner and E. Jokl (Eds.), Basel, Switzerland: S. Karger AG, 1970.

SMITH, D. M., KHAIRI, M. R. A., NORTON, J., and JOHNSTON, C. C., JR. "Age and activity effects on rate of bone mineral loss," *Journal of Clinical Invest. 58,* 716–721, 1976.

SMITH, D. W., and BIERMAN, E. L. (Eds.), *The Biologic Ages of Man.* Philadelphia: Saunders, 1973.

SMITH, E. L., JR., REDDAN, W., and SMITH, P. Physical activity and calcium modalities for bone mineral increase in aged women. *Medicine and Science in Sports and Exercise,* 1981, *13,* 60–64.

SMITH, E. L., JR., and STOEDEFALKE, K. *Aging and Exercise,* Hillside, New Jersey: Enslow Publishers, 1980.

SMITH, H. E. Family interaction patterns of the aged: A review. In A. M. Rose and W. A. Peterson (Eds.), *Older People and Their Social World.* Philadelphia: Davis, 1965.

SPIRDUSO, W. W., and CLIFFORD, P. Replication of age and physical activity effects on reaction and movement time. *Journal of Gerontology,* 1978, *33,* 26–30.

STINNETT, N., CARTER, L. M., and MONTGOMERY, J. E. Older person's perceptions of their marriages. *Journal of Marriage and the Family,* 1972, *34*(4), 667–672.

STORANDT, M., and WITTELS, I. Maintenance of function in relocation of community dwelling older adults. *Journal of Gerontology,* 1975, *30,* 608–612.

TREAS, J. Family support systems for the aged, *The Gerontologist,* 1977, *17*(6), 486–491.

TROLL, L., MILLER, S., and ATCHLEY, R. C. *Families in later life.* Belmont, California: Wadsworth, 1979.

UNITED STATES BUREAU OF THE CENSUS. Projections of the population of the United States by age and sex: 1972 to 2020. *Current Population Reports,* Series P-25, No. 493. Washington, D.C.: U.S. Government Printing Office, 1972.

UNITED STATES BUREAU OF THE CENSUS. *Statistical Abstracts of the United States* (103rd ed.). Washington, D.C.: U.S. Government Printing Office, 1982–83.

U.S. BUREAU OF THE CENSUS, DEPARTMENT OF COMMERCE. 1980 census of population. General Population Characteristics, PC 80-1-B1. Washington, D.C.: U.S. Government Printing Office, 1983a, Table 41, 23.

U.S. BUREAU OF THE CENSUS, DEPARTMENT OF COMMERCE. Marital status and living arrangements: March 1982 Current Population Reports, Population Characteristics, P-20, No. 380, May 1983b.

U.S. DEPARTMENT OF HEALTH AND HUMAN SERVICES. Public Health Service. National Center for Health Statistics. *1980 Health Interview Survey,* forthcoming.

U.S. DEPARTMENT OF HEALTH AND HUMAN SERVICES. Public Health Service. National Center for Health Statistics. B. Bloom, *Current Estimates from the National Health Interview Survey, United States, 1981.* Vital and Health Statistics. Series 10, No. 141, DHHS Publication No. (PHS) 83-1569. Washington, D.C.: U.S. Government Printing Office, October 1982, Table 14, p. 24.

U.S. Department of Health and Human Services. *Federal Council on Aging. The Need for Long Term Care: Information and Issues*. DHHS Publication No. (OHDS) 81-20704. Washington, D.C.: U.S. Government Printing Office, 1981, pp. 27–29.

United States Department of Health, Education and Welfare. *Health in the later years of life*. Selected data from the National Center for Health Statistics. Washington, D.C.: U.S. Government Printing Office, 1971.

Upp, M., Relative importance of the aged, 1980, *Social Security Bulletin, 46*, No. 1, January 1983, pp. 9–10.

U.S. Surgeon General. *Healthy People*. Washington, D.C.: U.S. Government Printing Office, 1980.

Watson, J. A., and Kivett, V. R. Influences on the life satisfaction of older fathers. *The Family Coordinator*, 1976, *25*(4), 482–488.

Welford, A. T. Motor performance. In J. E. Birren, and K. W. Schaie (Eds.), *Handbook of the Psychology of Aging*. New York: Van Nostrand Reinhold, 1977.

White House Conference on Aging. Aging and blindness, special concerns session report. Washington, D.C.: U.S. Government Printing Office, 1972.

White House Conference on Aging. *Chartbook on aging in America, 1981*, Washington, D.C.: U.S. Government Printing Office, 1981.

Wittels, I., and Botwinick, J. Survival in relocation. *Journal of Gerontology*, 1974, *29*, 440–443.

Wood, V., and Robertson, J. The significance of grandparenthood. In Jaber F. Gubrium (Ed.), *Time, Roles, and Self in Old Age*. New York: Human Sciences Press, 1976.

Woodruff, D. S., and Birren, J. E. *Aging: Scientific Perspectives and Social Issues*. New York: Nostrand, 1975.

Suggested Readings

Atchley, R. *The Social Forces in Later Life* (3rd edition) Belmont, California: Wadsworth, 1980. An excellent comprehensive introduction to human aging with particular emphasis on social and sociopsychological aspects.

Birren, J. E. and Schaie, K. W. (Eds.). *Handbook of the Psychology of Aging*. New York: Van Nostrand Reinhold, 1977. A good collection of readings covering a multitude of topics relating to older adults.

Butler, R. N. *Why Survive? Being old in America*. New York: Harper and Row, 1975. A Pulitzer Prize-winning book on aging in America, readable and enjoyable.

Butler, R. N., and Lewis, M. *Aging and Mental Health* (3rd edition) St. Louis, Missouri: Mosby, 1982. A comprehensive and thorough discussion of the status changes and problems facing aging adults.

Comfort, A. *A Good Age*. New York: Crown Publishers, 1976. A provocative, interesting, and thoroughly enjoyable discussion of the situation of aging adults.

Fogel, R. W., Hatfield, E., Kiesler, S. B., and Shanas, E. (Eds.). *Aging: Stability and Change in the Family*. New York: Academic Press, 1981. This book is an excellent collection of reviews of research which focus on the vital role of family and later adulthood.

Kalish, R. A. *Late Adulthood: Perspective on Human Development*. Monterey, California: Brooks/Cole, 1975. An excellent introductory discussion to the general aspects of aging.

McCluskey, N. G., and Borgatta, E. F. *Aging and Retirement: Prospects, Planning and Policy*. Beverly Hills, California: Sage, 1981. This is a very thorough and readable discussion of such matters as aging and national retirement policies and individual planning for retirement.

Rowles, G. D., and Ohta, R. J. (Eds.). *Aging and Milieu: Environmental Perspectives on Growing Old.* New York: Academic Press, 1983. This is an excellent and well-written collection of reviews of research on selected environmental perspectives, such as environmental learning and relocation.

Timiras, P. S. *Developmental Physiology and Aging.* New York: Macmillan, 1972. A detailed and technical account of the biochemical changes occurring throughout the lifespan and an excellent discussion of the degenerative process in old age.

Glossary

Accommodation In Piaget's theory of intelligence, the process of modifying existing schema in order to account for the novel properties of objects or events. See also *Assimilation*.

Activity theory The theory of aging which suggests that productive, industrious, or active people adjust best in old age. See also *Disengagement* and *Continuity*.

Acuity (visual) The ability to see objects clearly and to resolve detail.

Adolescence The period of development which begins with the onset of puberty and ends with the legal, social, and psychological status of adulthood.

Adduction The action of drawing a body limb toward or past the median axis of the body.

Adrenal glands Two ductless glands located one above each kidney. See *Adrenal medulla* and *Epinephrine*.

Adrenal medulla The inner portion of the adrenal gland which secretes epinephrine. See *Epinephrine* and *Adrenal glands*.

Ageism Discrimination against or stereotyping of elderly adults.

Affect The emotion, feeling, or mood of a person.

Afterbirth This includes the placenta, its membranes, and the remainder of the umbilical cord, all of which are expelled in the final stage of labor.

Allelle Any of several possible genes found at a given position or locus on a chromosome.

Alimentary canal Those organs that compose the food tubes in man and animals.

Amino acids Substances from which organisms build proteins.

Amniocentesis A means of detecting fetal abnormalities by inserting a hollow needle through the abdomen of the pregnant woman and withdrawing a sample of amniotic fluid for analysis.

Amnion   The inner membrane of the sac which surrounds and protects the developing ovum and fetus.

Amniotic fluid   A liquid in the amnion in which the developing fetus is suspended and protected from external jarring as well as from any pressure exerted by the mother's internal organs.

Anal stage   In the psychoanalytical theory of Freud, the second stage of psychosexual development during which the central features of development focus on elimination or toilet training activities.

Apgar Test   A commonly used measure for assessing appearance, heart rate, activity, muscle tone, reflex irritability, and respiration in the newborn infant. The sum total of the score can vary from 0 to a high of 10 points.

Arteriosclerosis   The thickening or hardening of the artery walls which makes a person more susceptible to stroke, heart attack, or senility.

Arthritis   The inflammation or deformation of one or more joints accompanied by chronic stiffness, swelling, and pain.

Assimilation   In Piaget's theory of cognitive development, the incorporation of the novel aspects of objects or events into existing schemata or structures of intelligence. See also *Accommodation*.

Attachment   The primary social bond which develops between the infant and its caretaker.

Autonomic nervous system   A division of the nervous system which regulates vital internal organs. It operates involuntarily. See *Central nervous system* and *Sympathetic nervous system*.

Autonomy   The ability of the human being to self-regulate or determine its own behavior.

Autosome   All chromosomes with the exception of sex chromosomes.

Babbling   A stage of prelinguistic speech which begins around three to four months and is characterized by the simple repetition of consonant or vowel sounds.

Babinski reflex   A response of the newborn infant in which the toes extend or fan out when the sole of the foot is gently stroked. As the infant's nervous system matures, the infant's toes will curl downward when the sole of the foot is stroked.

Behavior   Any human action or reaction in relation to internal, external, or self-generated stimulation (includes complex social and biological activities).

Behavior modification   The use of concepts from learning theory, in particular, reinforcement, association, and repetition to change behavior.

Behaviorism   The school of psychology which emphasizes that an organism's behavior is largely the result of the learning produced by external factors such as reinforcement.

Blastocyst   The cluster of cells that begins to differentiate into distinct parts during the germinal period of prenatal development.

Blastula   The cluster of cells that composes the prenatal organism during the first few days following conception.

Canalization   A model for the development of genetic traits in which such traits can be thought of as a ball rolling down a canal. When the canals are fairly deep, the environment will have limited influence in changing the direction of the ball. At other times (sensitive periods) when the canals are shallow, the environment may play a significant role.

Centering   The tendency in thinking to concentrate on some outstanding or prominent characteristics of an object to the exclusion of other characteristics.

Central nervous system (CNS)   The brain, spinal cord and the nerves arising from each. See *Autonomic nervous system* and *Sympathetic nervous system*.

Cephalocaudal development   Physical growth and motor development that occurs from the head downward.

Cerebral dominance   The fact that one hemisphere (half of the brain) prevails over the other in terms of the control of body movements or regulation of other behaviors.

Cervix   The narrow canal connecting the vagina and the uterus.

Cesarean section   A surgical operation in which the walls of the abdomen and uterus are cut for the purpose of delivering a child.

Chorion   The outer membrane of the sac that surrounds and protects the developing fertilized egg.

Chromosomes   The thin, rod-like strings of genes present in the nucleus of each cell of the human body which contain the genetic material necessary for directing cell activities.

Cognitive development   The qualitative and quantitative changes throughout the lifespan in thinking, organizing perceptions, and problem solving.

Cognitive map   An internal mental representation of the environment.

Cohort   In the design of research, a group of individuals born at the same time or during the same historical period.

Competence   The feeling or sense that a person is capable of exercising mastery over the environment.

Conception   The union of sperm and egg signaling the beginning of life.

Concrete operations   In Piaget's theory of cognitive development, the stage which begins when the child can use thought processes involving reversible transformations of actual or concrete objects or events in the child's immediate experience.

Congenital   Refers to the characteristics or defects acquired *during* the period of gestation and persisting after birth as distinguished from those characteristics acquired by heredity.

Conservation   The realization that changes in perceptual characteristics of an object or objects do not change the real physical characteristics of that object or those objects. For example, rearranging one row of objects into two rows does not change the number of objects.

Continuity theory   The theory which holds that successful aging involves combinations of disengagement from some roles and continued performance or activity in others, in keeping with the tendency of human beings to maintain or continue habits, associations, and preferences. Continuity theory emphasizes the complexity of aging. See also *Activity theory* and *Disengagement theory*.

Contraception   The voluntary prevention of pregnancy.

Control   The intentional manipulation of any condition of a research investigation such as the selection of participants or subjects.

Conventional level or stage   The stage or level of moral reasoning in which correct or moral behavior means the maintenance of the standard social order and expectations of others. See also *Postconventional stage* and *Preconventional stage.*

Correlation coefficient   A statistical index for measuring the relationship or correspondence between changes in two variables. A perfect correspondence is +1.00; no correspondence is 0.00; a perfect correspondence in opposite directions is −1.00.

Crib death   This little understood syndrome results in the death of approximately 7,000 to 10,000 young babies each year. The babies (usually 6 months of age or younger) typically die in their sleep with no clear or apparent cause for death (also called *Sudden Infant Death Syndrome* or SIDS).

Critical period   A time of maximum sensitivity to or readiness for development of a particular biological/physiological process or behavior pattern/skill.

Crossing over   The tendency of chromosomes to exchange genes prior to cell division.

Cross-sectional study   Research that compares different age groups (e.g., eight, ten, and twelve year olds) at a specific point in time. See also *Longitudinal study.*

Cross-sequential designs   This research design combines both the longitudinal and cross-sectional approaches by initially doing a cross-sectional sample of subjects and then following these same subjects longitudinally over time. See also *Cross-sectional study* and *Longitudinal study.*

Crystallized intelligence   The skills, abilities, and information that are acquired by means of experience, socialization, and education. See also *Fluid intelligence.*

Cytoplasm   Everything within the cell with the exception of the nucleus.

Deprivation dwarfism   The reduction in the secretion of growth hormone and the accompanying decline in growth resulting from emotional stress in children. See also *Somatotrophin (growth hormone).*

Developmental task   Refers to a particular learning experience that tends to occur at a given stage of life and that individuals must successfully negotiate to meet cultural requirements.

DNA (deoxyribonucleic acid)   Complex chemical molecules which contain the genetic code or blueprint that determines the makeup of cells.

Dependence   The reliance on other people for assistance, nurturance, or comfort.

Dilation   Being stretched or open beyond normal limits.

Disengagement theory   The theory of aging which holds that successful adaptation and adjustment in later adulthood is characterized by the mutual withdrawal of the individual from society and society from the individual. See also *Activity theory* and *Continuity theory.*

Dizygotic (DZ) twins   Refers to twins that develop from two separate fertilized eggs (fraternal twins). See *Monozygotic twins.*

Dominant gene   A form of a gene that is always expressed in the phenotype when paired with the same or different gene.

Down's Syndrome   A condition resulting from an extra chromosome in the fertilized egg; results in various physical abnormalities and mental re-tardation in the affected child.

Ecology of human development As defined by Bronfenbrenner, the ecology of human development is the scientific study of the progressive and mutual accommodation between the human being and the significant contexts in which that person lives.

Ecosystem Living organisms interacting with their environments.

Ectoderm The outermost cell layer in the developing embryo from which structures such as the skin and nervous system develop.

Egocentrism A self-centered style of thinking in which the individual is unable to consider the perspective or point of view of others. According to Piaget, egocentrism is characteristic of the preoperational child.

Embryo The period of prenatal life from the second to the eighth week; comes after the germinal period and is followed by the fetal period.

Endocrine gland A ductless gland which secretes a hormone directly into the blood.

Endoderm The innermost of the three cell layers of the embryo from which many visceral organs and the digestive tract develop.

Enzyme A protein that promotes reactions in a living system.

Epinephrine A hormone secreted by the adrenal gland which can cause sudden bodily changes during anger or fright. Also called *Adrenalin*. See also *Adrenal medulla* and *Adrenal gland*.

Epistemology The branch of philosophy which deals with determining the nature of human knowledge.

Extended family The family which consists of three generations (parents, children, and grandparents) and, in some cases, other blood relatives all living under the same roof.

Eye-hand coordination The ability to integrate visual and motor activities for reaching and grasping.

Fallopian tube The tube that conveys eggs from the ovary to the uterus; fertilization occurs in the Fallopian tube.

Family of origin The family to which one is born.

Family of procreation The family which an individual starts as an adult.

Feedback The effects of activity that are sensed by a responding system and used to regulate subsequent activity.

Fertilization The union of an egg cell with a sperm.

Fetus The prenatal organism from the eighth week after conception until birth.

Field study A study in which the investigator examines naturally occurring behavior and may control only some features of the situation.

Fluid intelligence A type of intelligence involving the ability to solve novel problems. It is influenced primarily by neurological factors.

Formal operations In Piaget's theory of intelligence, this is the final stage of cognitive development characterized by the ability to think abstractly.

Fraternal twins See *Dizygotic twins*.

Gamete A mature reproductive cell (e.g., egg or sperm).

Gender The sex of a person.

Genes   The elements of heredity which are found in chromosomes and which contain the codes for transmitting inherited characteristics.

Genetic epistemology   The science or study of the origins of knowledge (most frequently associated with Piaget).

Geriatrics   The medical study and care of aging adults.

Germinal period   The first stage of prenatal development extending from conception through the first two weeks after conception during which time the fertilized egg is primarily engaged in cell division.

Gerontology   The study of the psychology and sociology of aging persons.

Gestation period   The span of time between fertilization and birth.

Gonads   The sex glands (testes in males and ovaries in females).

Grammar   The structural principles for organizing a language.

Grasping reflex   The tendency of the newborn during the first few weeks of life to clutch at objects placed in its hands.

Handedness   An individual's hand preference.

Hemoglobin   An iron-containing protein compound which gives red blood corpuscles their color.

Heredity   The total sum of all characteristics which are biologically transmitted from parents to offspring at conception.

Heritability   An estimate of the relative contribution of genetics to a given trait or behavior. The estimate is based on a sample of individuals.

Heterosexual   Attraction to and interaction with members of the opposite sex; seeking and finding gratification with a member of the opposite sex.

Holophrases   One word sentences that occur at about age one.

Hypertension   Abnormally high blood pressure.

Hypothalmus   A part of the brain located at the base of the brain, above the pituitary gland. The hypothalmus controls body functions such as temperature, water balance, and the release of pituitary hormones. See also *Pituitary gland*.

Hypothesis   A tentative interpretation of a given set of data based on supportive findings; a prediction of a solution to a given problem.

Icterus neonatorum   See *Jaundice*.

Identical twins   See *Monozygotic twins*.

Identification   The socialization process by which a person takes on the characteristics of a significant and/or admired other and incorporates these characteristics into one's own personality.

Identity   The sense of self or who one is.

Imitation   The process of repeating or copying another person's (model's) words, gestures, or behaviors.

Independence   Self-reliance.

Infancy   The stage of human development which extends from birth through the development of relative independence in feeding, movement, and language at approximately two years of age.

Intelligence   A broad term which refers to an individual's abilities in a wide variety of cognitive areas including mathematical/number skills, language skills, and problem solving.

Intuitive thinking   The third stage of Piaget's theory of cognitive development in which the four to seven year old child's thinking is characterized by reliance on immediate perceptions and experiences rather than on flexible operations.

Jaundice   A condition characterized by the yellowish pigmentation of the skin, tissues, and body fluids due to the deposit of bile pigments. See also *Icterus neonatorum.*

Juvenile   Relating to an older child or an adolescent.

Karotype   A chart in which photographs of chromosomes are arranged according to size and structure.

Kinesthetic   The perception or sense of one's body position or movement.

Lactation   The presence and secretion of milk which occurs automatically in the breasts of the mother of a newborn infant.

Life span   The length of an individual's existence.

Lifestyle   The relatively permanent organization of individual activity including the balance between work and leisure and the general pattern of family and social relationships.

Long-term memory   The storing of events over a lengthy period of time.

Longitudinal study   Research that examines the same subjects over a specified period of time.

Lymph   This is a clear liquid part of blood that enters tissue spaces and tiny lymph vessels which come together to form enlargements called lymph nodes or lymph glands. Lymph is purified in these nodes before being returned to the blood. The entire lymph system helps fight infections and supports the immunity of the body to illness.

Lymph glands   Lymph nodes.

Male menopause (climacteric)   An imprecise term for the gradual physical and psychological changes in middle-aged men.

Marijuana (or marihuana)   A drug derived from *Cannabis sativa* containing tetrahydrocannabinal (THC). It has sedative-hypnotic effects and can reduce tension and induce the experience of a "high."

Maternal deprivation   The lack of opportunities for interaction with a mother or primary caregiver.

Maturation rate   The general tempo at which various biological, behavioral, and personal characteristics emerge and develop in the individual as a result of growth and development.

Meiosis   The process of cellular division which results in daughter cells each receiving half the number of chromosomes and thereby becoming gametes.

Memory   The process of recalling or reproducing what has been learned in the past as a way of predicting and organizing present and future activities. See also *Long-term memory* and *Short-term memory.*

Menarche   The beginning of regular menstrual periods for the female; occurs during adolescence.

Menopause   The cessation of the menstrual cycle as well as the ability to bear children.

Menstrual cycle   The cyclical discharge of blood and discarded uterine tissue which occurs on a monthly basis in females from the menarch through the menopause (except during pregnancy).

Mesoderm The middle layer of the three basic layers of embryonic cells; it is the basis for the formation of the alimentary canal, digestive glands, muscle structure, and bones.

Metabolism The physical/chemical changes that occur in the human body for the purpose of building up, repairing, and supporting existing structures as well as for breaking down (as in digestion) and removing (as in elimination of) body wastes.

Mitosis The process of cell division that results in two cells identical to the parent cell.

Model In social learning theory, the person who is imitated.

Mongolism See Down's syndrome.

Monozygotic (MZ) twins Twins who develop from the same fertilized egg or ovum (identical twins). See also *Dizygotic twins.*

Moral conduct A complex form of behavior consisting of three primary components: thinking or cognition, feeling, and action.

Moral development The nature and the lifespan course of an individual's moral thoughts, feelings, and actions.

Morality The sense or judgment of what is right or wrong behavior.

Moro reflex The startle reaction of the newborn, characterized by the extension of both arms to the sides of the body with fingers outstretched, closely followed by the retraction of the arms to the midline of the body.

Morphemes The smallest and most basic meaningful units of a language; composed of phonemes which are combined to produce basic words, suffixes, or prefixes. See also *Phonemes.*

Motor skill Body movement actions which require coordination of muscles (e.g., walking, jumping).

Mutation Any change in a gene, usually from one allele to another, which results in the production of new forms.

Mutual following (adaptation) The changes in behavior which result from two or more people adjusting their movements or general behavior in response to the movement or behavior of others, and vice versa. See also *Social tracking.*

Myelin A white, fatty substance which coats some nerve fibers thereby channeling nerve signals along fibers and reducing random spread to other neurons.

Myelinization The process by which nerve fibers acquire a myelin sheath.

Naturalistic study The observation of behavior without any intervention or interference by the investigator.

Nature The genetic and biological factors which contribute to human development. See also *Nurture.*

Neonate The technical term for a newborn infant up to about two to four weeks of age.

Neuron A brain cell (approximately 10 billion such cells in the average adult brain).

Norephinephrine A crystalline compound occurring with epinephrine, which constricts the diameter of blood vessels and mediates the transmission of sympathetic nerve impulses. See also *Sympathetic nervous system.*

Norm A brief description of the essential features of a skill or personal/social attribute as well as the approximate age(s) it appears in the average child.

Normative   Relating to or based on averages, standards, values, or established norms.

Nuclear family   A household grouping that include a mother, a father, and their children. See also *Extended family*.

Nurture   The influence of environmental factors on human development. See also *Nature*.

Object permanence   The awareness that a person or an object continues to exist even when out of sight.

Observational learning   The changes in thinking and behavior which result from watching others.

Operant conditioning   Conditioning or learning that occurs when an organism is reinforced for emitting a response.

Oral stage   In Freud's psychosexual theory of development, the first stage of life during which the mouth is the primary focus of interaction with primary caregivers.

Osteoporosis   A thinning or loss of bone characterized by a decreased mineral mass and an enlarged bone cavity.

Ovary   The female reproductive gland in which egg cells or ova are produced.

Overextension   A generalization in the apparent meaning of a word such that it is used to include or refer to dissimilar events or objects.

Overt behavior   Responses that are easily seen and recorded.

Ovulation   The release of the ovum or egg into one of two Fallopian tubes.

Ovum   An egg or the female sex cell (gamete).

Parathyroid glands   The four small ductless glands embedded in the thyroid gland (see *Thyroid gland*).

Parturition   Delivery of the baby.

Peer   Any individual at a comparable level of development, age, and/or social status.

Peer group   The collection of persons who constitute one's associates.

Perception   The recognition and organization of sensory behavior.

Peripheral nervous system   The nerves communicating with the central nervous system and other parts of the body. See also *Central nervous system*.

Personality   The characteristics and relatively stable pattern of thought, feeling, and action of an individual.

Pharynx   The muscular throat cavity extending from the soft palate to the nasal cavity.

Phenotype   The observable characteristics that are the result of genetic and environmental contributions. See also *Genotype*.

Phonemes   The sounds of a given language that are the building blocks of morphemes. See also *Morpheme*.

Pituitary gland   A ductless gland located at the base of the brain and composed of two lobes. The anterior lobe secretes hormones such as growth hormones, *gonadotropic* hormones that influence the reproductive organs, and hormones which stimulate other endocrine glands. The posterior lobe secretes two hormones: *oxytocin* (regulates blood pressure and stimulates smooth muscles) and *vasopressin* (regulates water resorption in the kidneys). See also *Hypothalmus*.

Placenta   The organ that conveys food and oxygen to the developing prenatal organism and discharges waste.

Postconventional stage   In Kohlberg's theory of moral development, the final and most sophisticated level of moral development involving the organization of self-determined moral principles rather than simply conforming to the principles or expectations of others. See also *Conventional stage* and *Preconventional stage*.

Postpartum   The time immediately following birth, usually the first week of life.

Preconventional stage   In Kohlberg's theory, the first level of moral development in which moral decisions are based on whether an action has positive or negative consequences or whether it is rewarded or punished by parents or caretakers. See also *Conventional stage* and *Postconventional stage*.

Prenatal   The stage of human development from conception to birth.

Prepared childbirth (Lamaze)   The method of childbirth where the woman acquires knowledge about the physiological processes in childbirth as well as learning exercises that make delivery somewhat easier.

Prosocial behavior   Activity intended to help or assist others.

Protein   A molecule containing amino acids.

Proximodistal development   The progressive growth of the human body from a central to external direction. See also *Cephalocaudal development*.

Puberty   The period of time during which secondary sexual characteristics (e.g., the enlargement of the female breast and the appearance of male facial hair) appear and accompany the attainment of biological sexual maturity.

Quickening   The first movements of the fetus that the pregnant woman can readily perceive.

Range of reaction   The potential for development of a specific genetic endowment given variable environments.

Reaction time   The time interval between the signal to make a response and the actual response.

Recessive gene   The subordinate member of a pair of genes whose trait does not appear, unless paired with another recessive gene.

Reciprocal interaction   A relationship in which the behavior of each participant is influenced by the responses of the other person.

Reflex   An unlearned behavior which occurs naturally in a given situation.

Reversibility   In Piaget's theory, the awareness that an operation (mental thought process) can be restored or reversed to an original condition (e.g., a clay rod can be rolled into a ball and then back to a rod).

RNA (ribonucleic acid)   Molecules that convey the information in the DNA to the cytoplasm of the cell so that appropriate amino acids can be formed.

Ribosome   Small spherical bodies in the cytoplasm; the cite of protein synthesis; composed of protein and RNA.

Rooting reflex   An early reflex response of babies that includes head turning movements and attempts at sucking when the cheek is touched.

Schema (plural schemata)   In Piaget's terminology, the organization of actions or thoughts into a unified whole or mental construct.

644

Secondary sex characteristics Physical characteristics that appear at the time of puberty including breast development, enlargement of the penis, deepening of the voice in males, pubic hair in males and females. These characteristics are differentiated according to sex but they are not necessary for sexual reproduction.

Self-concept The characteristics and attributes one applies to oneself.

Senility Mental incapacities brought about by increasing age.

Sensorimotor stage The first stage in Piaget's theory of cognitive development (birth to two years) during which children experience their environment through action and develop schemata which reflect this experience.

Separation anxiety The negative reaction of some infants to the absence of the primary caregiver and the attempts made to regain contact with this object of attachment.

Seriation The ability to sort objects or other stimuli according to characteristics (e.g., size, color).

Sex chromosomes The single pair of chromosomes that determines the sex of the organism (XX = female; XY = male).

Sex-linked inheritance The pattern of inheritance in which characteristics are conveyed on the X chromosome, transmitted by the female and expressed in the male.

Sex roles The patterns of behavior which are considered appropriate for each sex.

Sex-role identification The integration of the awareness of social and cultural expectations associated with each sex, awareness of one's gender, preference for a sex-role, and the close emotional association with the same-sex parent.

Sex-role preference The positive value given to a set of expectations and standards held for a gender group.

Sex-typing The process of learning the behaviors appropriate for a gender.

Short-term memory The type of memory associated with the immediate perception of information (e.g., telephone numbers).

Sibling A brother or sister.

Skeletal muscles Voluntary muscles, such as the biceps in the arm.

Smooth muscles The muscles which act involuntarily and are found lining the walls of the stomach, arteries, and intestines.

Social class A social level which is differentiated from other social levels or strata by such characteristics as income, occupation, or education.

Social role The set of expectations or standards associated with a given position.

Social tracking Mutual following in which the actions of one participant serve as the basis of the response of another person, and vice versa. There are three primary modes of social tracking: tactual, visual, and auditory tracking. See *Mutual following.*

Socialization The process of transmitting and enforcing social and cultural norms and values to the new members of a group.

Sociogram A graphic representation of preferences and rejections in social interaction.

Somatotrophin Growth hormone secreted by the anterior lobe of the pituitary gland. See also *Pituitary gland.*

Sperm (spermatozoon; *plural* spermatazoa) The male sex cell (gamete).

State   The cyclic variation in an infant's wakefulness, sleep, and activity.

Stranger anxiety   The negative reactions which occur when infants are separated from primary caregivers and in the presence of unknown (strange) people. It usually occurs during the 6th or 7th months of infancy.

Sympathetic nervous system   This nervous system is made up of two rows of nerve cords which lie on either side of the spinal column. The functions of the sympathetic nervous system include the regulation of the heart, the secretion of endocrine glands, and the action of smooth muscles.

System   A set of interrelated objects or components which are tied together by feedback relationships.

Systems perspective   See *Ecology of human development.*

Tactual tracking   Mutual following between two people using touch (e.g., as in a parent holding a clinging infant or in sexual intercourse).

Temperament   An individual style of relating to people and situations including behavioral style or characteristic mood.

Teratogenic   Capable of causing an organic malformation.

Testis (*plural* testes)   The male reproductive gland; also known as a testicle.

Thymus   It is thought to be a ductless gland, located above the heart, whose function helps the body to fight diseases.

Thyroid gland   The ductless gland, located on either side of the larynx, which regulates metabolism.

Toddlerhood   The period of human development from about fifteen to thirty months.

Toxemia of pregnancy   A disorder whose symptoms include persistent nausea and vomiting or in some cases, hypertension and a rapid increase in weight due to retention of water in the tissues and albumin in the urine.

Trachea   The windpipe.

Umbilical cord   The cord connecting the prenatal organism to the placenta through which the developing fetus receives nourishment.

Uterus   The pear-shaped muscular organ in which the prenatal organism develops until birth.

Vagina   The female genital canal or passage from the uterus to external opening of the genital canal (vulva).

Validity   The extent to which a given measure actually assesses what it purports to measure.

Venereal disease   An infection transmitted by sexual intercourse.

Vernix   The white greasy substance that covers the newborn and lubricates it for the passage through the birth canal.

Vernix caseosa   The oily covering of the newborn secreted by its skin glands.

Visual acuity   The ability to see objects, particularly small details. See also *Acuity.*

Visual tracking   The ability to follow an object with one's eyes and, as appropriate, to adjust body movements in accordance with visual feedback.

Vital capacity   The air-holding capability of the lungs.

Wechsler Adult Intelligence Scale (WAIS)   A standardized individual intelligence test for adults which measures both verbal and performance abilities.

X Chromosome A sex-determining chromosome of which the female has two (XX) and the male has only one (XY).

Y Chromosome A sex-determining chromosome which when paired with the X chromosome produces a male (XY).

Zygote The cell formed by the union of male and female gametes.

Name Index

Ellis, R. W. B., 124
Emerson, P. E., 227
Emmerich, W., 426
Engel, W. R., 212
Engen, T., 159
Enright, R. D., 312
Erikson, E., 30, 31–39, 79, 236, 329, 396, 398, 405, 410, 413, 444, 479–480, 526, 539, 560, 561
Erlenmeyer-Kimling, L., 61
Erlich, S., 152
Ervin, S., 221
Ervin-Tripp, S., 221
Espenschade, A. S., 372, 503
Ewy, D., 149
Ewy, R., 149

Fagan, J. F., 157
Fagen, R. E., 249
Falek, A., 610
Fantz, R. L., 157, 169, 227
Farson, R., 254
Fasold, R., 303
Faust, M. S., 439
Fawl, C. L., 314
Featherstone, J., 351
Fein, G. C., 351
Feld, S. C., 500
Feldman, H., 71, 493, 494, 530
Fenton, N., 338
Feree, M., 544
Ferris, P., 346
Feshbach, L., 314
Feshback, S., 361
Field, J., 159
Finkle, W. D., 550
Fischer, L. K., 165
Fishbein, H. D., 66
Fisher, C. W., 41
Fisher, M. P., 505
Flavell, J. H., 205, 380
Flint, J., 501
Forman, G. E., 377, 380, 381
Foshage, J. L., 610
Fozard, J. L., 510, 512, 548
Fraiberg, S., 170, 305
Fraisse, P., 289
Frankenburg, W. K., 196
Franklin, C. C., 312
Freedman, A. M., 165–166
Freedman, D. G., 228
Freeman, R. B., 501
French, J. R. P., 538
Freud, S., 29–31, 32, 33, 34, 36, 38, 39, 307–308, 539
Frey, K. S., 309
Fried, B., 523, 549
Fried, M., 261
Friedan, B., 523
Friedman, C. D., 548
Friedman, M., 554, 555
Friedrich, L. K., 360, 361, 364, 365

Friis, H., 599–600
Frommer, E. A., 140
Frost, R., 180
Fryer, J. G., 103
Fuller, B., 58
Furry, C. A., 510
Furstenberg, F., 258

Gaite, A., 444
Gallatin, J. E., 15
Gallego, D. T., 595
Galper, A., 592
Gans, H., 261
Garbarino, J., 46–47, 64, 258, 259
Garber, J., 346
Gardner, L. I., 274, 276–277
Garmezy, N., 345
Garvey, C., 290, 291, 292, 293, 358
Gebhard, P. H., 451
Gelles, R., 258
Gelman, R., 301
George, L. K., 553
Gerbner, G., 365
Gesell, A., 15–18, 19, 82
Gewirtz, J. L., 228, 233
Giele, J. Z., 560
Gilder, G., 493
Gilliam, T. B., 363
Gilligan, C., 408, 456, 457
Ginsburg, H., 304
Gintis, H., 426
Ginzberg, E., 445, 447–448
Glass, D. C., 554
Glassow, R., 369
Glay, L. E., 537, 561
Gleicher, P., 261
Glenn, N. D., 492
Glick, P. C., 493, 532
Glidewell, J. C., 356
Glucksberg, S., 299
Gluecksohn-Waelsch, S., 103
Goertzel, M. G., 344
Goertzel, V., 344
Gold, S., 265
Goldfarb, A., 594
Goldman, R., 338
Good, T. L., 348
Goranson, R. E., 361
Gordon, T. E., 255
Gottesman, I. I., 66
Gottesman, L. E., 597
Gottlieb, B., 258
Gould, R., 561
Gove, W., 544
Graham, R., 428, 456, 457
Green, E. H., 314
Greenfield, P. M., 289
Greenhouse, S. W., 511, 599
Gregg, C. F., 453
Gruen, W., 514, 615
Grusec, J. E., 132, 310, 312, 313
Gump, P., 4, 41

Gutmann, D. L., 514, 562, 615
Guttmacher, A. F., 148

Haaf, R. A., 227
Haith, M. M., 169
Haley, J., 407
Hall, A. D., 249
Hall, 30
Hall, G. S., 18, 399
Haller, W., 185
Halton, A., 127
Halverson, H. M., 199
Hand, M., 312
Hanes, M. L., 305
Hanks, C., 223
Hanlon, C., 223
Harper, P. A., 165
Harpring, E. B., 61
Harris, S. J., 522
Hart, N. A., 419
Hart, R. A., 265
Hartmann, D. P., 361
Hartup, W. W., 266, 352
Havighurst, R. J., 9, 537, 541, 560, 561, 614
Hayes, C. D., 545
Hayward, D. G., 265
Healy, C. C., 500
Heath, D. H., 541
Heckman, N. A., 492
Heffernan, P. G., 595
Heimer, C. B., 165–166
Helfer, R., 140
Hellbrugge, T., 162
Hellebrandt, F. A., 369
Henle, P., 545
Henry, J. P., 555
Henry, W. E., 612–613
Hensen, S. A., 132
Herman, W., 550
Hersh, S. P., 173
Hertzig, M. E., 65
Herzog, E., 186, 339–340
Hess, R. D., 302, 349–350
Hetherington, E. M., 308
Heyde, M. B., 448
Heyns, B., 426
Hickey, J., 457
Higgins-Trenk, A., 444
Hildebrand, V., 316
Hilgard, E. R., 399
Hilliard, T., 349
Hirsch, J., 68–69
Hirschfield, I. S., 534
Hobson, C. J., 349
Hoffman, M. L., 312, 313
Holland, V. M., 298
Hollander, J., 617
Holmes, T. H., 556–557
Holt, J., 254
Honzik, M. P., 63
Horn, J. L., 510, 511

Horn, J. M., 64
Hornstein, H. A., 313
Horowitz, F. D., 64
Howe, M. J., 348
Howes, C., 238
Hubel, D. H., 66–67
Hunt, J. McV., 19
Hunt, M., 453
Hunter, W. S., 289
Huntington, T. S., 143
Hutt, C., 157–158
Hutt, S. J., 157–158, 161, 162
Hymen, H., 537

Iannotti, 312
Immelmann, K., 41
Ingram, D., 215
Inhelder, B., 341, 409
Ittelson, W. H., 262, 340

Jacklin, C., 309
Jackson, G., 350
Jacobson, L., 253, 347–348
Jaffe, F. S., 452
James, L. S., 154
Jantz, R., 592
Jarvik, L. F., 61, 511, 512, 610
Jencks, C., 350, 426
Jenkins, S., 495
Jensen, A. R., 59
Jerauld, R., 168
Johnson, D. L., 305
Johnson, V. E., 552
Johnston, L. D., 457, 461
Jones, J. B., 544
Jones, M. C., 439
Jones, R. S., 10
Jordaan, J. P., 448
Jorgensen, B., 486
Julia, J., 170

Kaczkowski, H., 456
Kagan, J., 227, 338, 346, 402, 426
Kalafat, J., 227
Kallman, F. J., 610
Kamerman, S., 545
Kandell, D. B., 414
Kanter, R. M., 74, 185
Kantner, J. F., 451–452
Kantor, D., 250
Kantor, H. L., 550
Kantor, M. B., 356
Kastenbaum, R. J., 619, 621, 622, 624
Katch, V. L., 363
Katchadourian, H., 457
Katz, B., 490
Kaye, H., 159
Keecher, G. P., 378
Keidel, G. C., 419
Kellogg, R. L., 295, 346
Kelly, D. H., 193
Kempe, C., 140

Kempler, H. L., 492
Keniston, K., 399, 400, 404, 405
Kennell, J. H., 139–140, 142, 150–151,
    168, 169, 170, 171
Kephart, W. M., 183
Kerckhoff, A., 486
Kermode, F., 617
Kessen, W., 169
Kessler, J. B., 477
Kimmel, D. C., 478, 540–541, 549, 558
King, K., 453
King, R. A., 313
Kinsey, A. C., 451, 552
Kirby, I. J., 549
Kittrell, E., 362
Klaus, M., 139–140, 142, 150–151, 168,
    169, 170, 171
Klein, E. B., 561
Klein, L., 454
Klima, E. S., 221
Klinger, E., 293
Kloostermann, G. J., 141
Knobloch, H., 165
Knox, A. B., 484, 485, 491, 493, 494,
    498, 505, 506, 507, 508, 509, 510, 536,
    537, 538, 540, 548, 555, 558, 559, 561
Koch, H. L., 338
Kohlberg, L., 309, 381, 384–386, 408,
    426, 428, 455, 456
Kohn, G. M., 597
Kolars, J. C., 168
Koller, M. R., 487
Korn, S., 65
Korner, A., 161
Kounin, J. S., 41
Kraines, R., 550
Krauss, R. M., 299
Krebs, D., 310
Kreger, N., 168
Kreps, J. M., 500
Kuhlen, R. G., 563
Kutz, S., 291
Kuypers, J. A., 511, 544, 546, 563

Labouvie-Vief, G., 510, 511
Labov, W., 304–305, 351
La Crosse, 426
Ladd, F., 341
Lamb, M., 144, 235
Lang, R., 169
Lantz, E., 169
Lapidus, I. M., 479
LaRue, A., 511
Latz, E., 227
Lazar, J., 40
Leboyer, F., 148–150, 151
Lee, L. C., 381, 382, 383, 384
Lehr, W., 250
Leifer, A. D., 361
Lenard, H. G., 157–158, 161, 162
Lenneberg, E. H., 212
Lennon, R., 312

Lerner, M. J., 311
Lerner, R. M., 33, 54, 344
Leslie, G. R., 183
Lesser, G., 304, 305, 414
Lett, F. E., 40
Levenson, S., 261
Levin, H., 84, 315, 338
Levin, K., 173
Levine, S., 161
Levinger, G., 486, 494
Levinson, D., 480–481, 561
Levinson, M. H., 561
Levitt, M. D., 112
Levy, J., 211
Levy, N., 160
Lewin, K., 40, 314
Lewis, M. I., 227, 235, 576
Lewis, T., 157
Liebman, J. C., 265
Liley, A. W., 126
Lilienfeld, A. M., 126
Limber, J., 222
Lind, J., 171
Lindbergh, A. M., 523
Lindzey, G., 60
Lipsitt, L. P., 159, 160, 192
Lipton, E. L., 165
Littman, R. A., 266
Livesley, W. J., 379
Livson, F. B., 562, 563, 615
Locke, J., 19
Loehlin, J. C., 60, 63, 64
London, P., 310
Long, G. T., 311
Long, R., 451
Loomis, B., 550
Lopata, H. Z., 588, 589–590
Loring, W. C., 261
Lovaas, O., 360
Lowe, C. A., 348
Lowe, J. C., 472
Lowe, M., 292
Lowenthal, M. F., 537, 538, 561
Lubin, M. I., 514, 615
Ludvigson, H. W., 550
Lundsteen, S. W., 544
Lynn, D., 235

Maas, H., 544, 546, 563
McAlpine, W., 168
McCarthy, D., 212
McCartney, K., 65
McClearn, E. G., 57
McCleary, E. H., 141
McClelland, K., 350
Maccoby, E. E., 84, 309, 315, 338
McCullough, M., 500
McCurdy, R. N. C., 124
McDougall, D., 308
McFarland, R. A., 505
MacFarlane, A., 141, 159, 160
MacFarlane, J. A., 159–160, 345

McGinty, D. J., 192
McGurk, H., 44
McKee, B., 561
McKenna, J., 225, 227
McKinney, J. P., 313
McNeill, D., 217
McPartland, J., 349
McWilliams, M., 437
Maddox, G. L., 8–9
Madge, C., 341
Mahler, S., 265
Maier, H. W., 31–32
Manaster, G., 422
Mangarov, I., 372
Manheim, L. A., 312
Mansfield, A. F., 308
Marantz, S. A., 308
Marcia, J. E., 500
Marcus, R. F., 312
Martin, C. E., 451
Martin, C. R., 552
Martorano, S. C., 443, 444
Marx, J. L., 57, 243
Masters, W. H., 552
Matteson, D. R., 399, 414, 416, 418
Mauer, D., 157
Mayer, J., 274, 439
Mead, M., 412
Meier, R. A., 260
Meleney, H. E., 503
Meltzov, A., 161
Mendelson, G., 365
Meyer, G., 510
Michael, W. B., 544
Michal, C. M., 550
Michaud, E., 289
Michelson, S., 426
Milgram, S., 260, 261
Milhoj, P., 599–600
Miller, D. L., 514, 615
Miller, D. T., 311
Miller, M. E., 314
Miller, S. M., 308, 587
Milne, C., 282
Milne, L. J., 504
Milne, M., 504
Minuchin, P., 352, 353
Miranda, S. B., 157
Mischel, W., 309
Mitchell, J. H., 508
Moerk, E. L., 301, 302
Monkus, E., 455
Montagu, M. F. A., 127
Mood, A. M., 349
Moore, J. W., 472
Moos, R. H., 538
Moreno, J. L., 355
Morgan, M. W., 505
Mosher, R., 457
Moss, H. A., 338, 426
Mowrer, O. H., 314
Mueller, E., 300

Mueser, P., 350
Muir, D., 159
Munroe, R. H., 341
Munroe, R. L., 341
Muntjewerff, W. J., 157–158
Murdoch, G. P., 183
Murphy, L. B., 377
Murphy, M. N., 272
Murray, J. R., 541
Murstein, B. I., 486
Musella, D., 41
Mussen, P., 312, 360
Muuss, R., 399

Nardi, A. H., 510
Nash, J., 275
Naunton, E., 546
Neill, A. S., 254
Neimark, E. D., 443–448
Nelson, A. K., 451
Nelson, K., 212, 213, 215, 301
Nelson, P. A., 40
Nelson, S. A., 312
Nerlove, S. B., 341
Ness, S., 312
Neugarten, B. L., 9, 472, 514, 550, 551, 560, 561, 614, 615, 617, 618
Nevis, S., 227
Newcomb, T., 429
Nichols, R. C., 63
Nicholson, S., 265
Nuttall, R. L., 510, 512, 548
Nye, F. I., 455

Offer, D., 453
Olejnik, A. B., 313
Oliver, R. R., 289
Olneck, M., 350
Olson, L., 529
O'Malley, P. M., 457, 461
Ormiston, K. H., 365
Orr, B., 537
O'Shea, G., 140
Oskarsson, M. K., 57
Osofsky, H. S., 454
Osofsky, J. D., 454
O'Toole, J., 74–75
Overton, W., 510, 512

Pace, C. R., 429
Paden, L. Y., 64
Palermo, D. S., 298
Papousek, H., 235
Parham, I. A., 510
Parisi, D., 215
Parke, R., 144, 235, 236
Pasamanick, B., 126, 165
Pastalon, L., 257
Patrick, R., 560
Patterson, G. R., 266
Pavlov, I., 20, 21
Peck, R. F., 514, 615

Peer, A., 127
Peisack, E., 298
Perry, D. G., 308, 311, 313
Perry, E., 183
Perry, J., 183
Peterson, L., 311
Peterson, P. G., 615
Pfeiffer, E., 552, 553
Phelps, W. L., 473
Piaget, J., 25–28, 82, 83, 199–206, 228, 230, 237, 284, 286, 289, 290, 293, 298, 344–345, 351, 372, 373, 374, 375, 376–377, 381–384, 385, 387, 409, 443, 510
Pierce, R., 537, 561
Pilon, R., 159
Pinard, M., 495
Pineo, P., 528
Pippert, R. A., 347
Plantz, M. C., 259
Pollowy, A. M., 40
Polsby, G. K., 453
Pomeroy, W. B., 451, 552
Powers, E. A., 541
Pratt, K. C., 160
Prechtl, H. F. R., 155, 161, 162, 225, 227
Prentice, R., 550
Proshansky, H. M., 340

Quarterman, C. E., 597
Quinn, R., 500

Rabin, A. I., 233
Racki, G., 185
Radke-Yarrow, M., 313
Ragan, P. K., 618
Rahe, R. H., 556–557
Rapoport, R., 544
Rarick, G. L., 369
Rau, L., 308
Read, K., 267–268, 271, 294
Rebelsky, F., 223
Redler, E., 312, 313
Reichard, S., 615–618
Reister, A. E., 422
Reuschlein, P., 282
Rheingold, H. L., 228
Richards, I. K., 424
Richards, M. P. M., 160
Richardson, S., 273
Richmond, J. B., 165
Ricks, 426
Rider, R. V., 165
Riegel, K. F., 510
Riegel, R. M., 510
Rivlin, L. G., 340
Roberts, D. F., 361
Roberts, F., 337
Robinson, I. E., 453
Robson, K. S., 170, 227
Roche, A. F., 503
Rodgers, W. L., 538
Rodstein, M., 507

Troll, L., 533, 587, 588, 590
Tsu, V. D., 539
Tuckman, B. W., 349
Tuddenham, R. D., 510, 512
Tudor, J., 544
Tulkin, S. R., 302
Turiel, E., 428, 455
Turleau, C., 126
Turner, H., 594

Valenstein, A. F., 143
Van den Daele, L. D., 165
Vandenberg, S. G., 66
VandeWorde, G. F., 57
Veevers, J. E., 493
Veroff, J., 500
Verwoerdt, A., 552
Vinacke, W. E., 289
Vincent, M. M., 132
Volpe, E. P., 112
Vore, D. A., 124
Vorster, J., 223
Vuorenkoski, V., 171

Waddington, C. H., 66
Wades, D., 560
Walbek, N. H., 310
Walters, R. H., 23, 316
Ward, S., 350
Warren, R. L., 257
Wasz-Hackert, O., 171
Waters, E., 237
Watson, J. B., 19–20, 344
Watson, J. S., 237
Waugh, N. C., 510, 548

Weaver, C. N., 492
Weber, A., 501
Wechsler, D., 509
Wedderburn, D., 599–600
Weiler, S. J., 552, 553
Weinberg, R. A., 64
Weinfeld, F. D., 349
Weinstein, G., 377, 379–380
Weinstein, K. K., 533
Weintraub, D., 166
Weisberg, P., 228
Weisberg, R., 299
Weiss, J., 4, 41
Weiss, L., 537, 561
Weissbrod, C. S., 313
Welford, A. T., 505, 548
Weltman, A., 363
Wertheimer, M., 157, 227
Whatley, J., 291
White, B. L., 198
White, G. M., 310
White, R. W., 28
White, S., 21–22, 512
Whiting, B. B., 345
Whiting, J. W. M., 345
Wicker, A. W., 41
Wickstrom, R. L., 369
Widdowson, E. M., 274, 276
Wiesel, T. N., 66–67
Wiggins, J. S., 439
Wiggins, N., 439
Wilk, C., 560
Wilkie, F., 511
Wilkin, W. R., 510, 512
Wilkins, L. P., 193

Willerman, L., 64
Williams, J., 350
Williams, M. V., 505
Williams, S., 365
Wilson, R. S., 61, 62, 63, 550
Winkel, G., 340
Winnicott, D. W., 233
Wittig, B. A., 227
Wolff, P., 161, 165, 227, 228, 237
Wolfram, W., 303
Wood, V., 550
Woodruff, R. M., 548
Woods, A. M., 505
Wortis, H., 165–166
Wright, C., 537
Wright, H., 40
Wright, J. D., 544, 546
Wuerger, M. K., 453

Yaffe, S., 166
Yankelovich, D., 453
Yarrow, M. R., 511, 599
Yorburg, B., 489
York, R. L., 349
Young, M., 365
Young, N., 347
Youniss, J., 417

Zahn-Waxler, C., 313
Zelnik, M., 451–452
Ziel, H. K., 550
Zigler, E., 309
Zimiles, H., 352
Zucker, R. A., 422

Subject Index

Adolescence (*cont.*)
maturation in. *See* growth in; sexual changes, *herein*
motor performance in, 435–436
nutrition and, 437
peer group and, 75–76
boys and, 423–424
cliques and, 419
crowds and, 419, 420, 421
development of, 420, 421
early adolescence and, 401, 402
friendships distinct from, 424–425, 427–428
functions, 417
group identity and, 401
later adolescence and, 404
structure, 417, 422–423
personality development, 444
ego identity and, 444
moral identity, 455–457
occupational identity, 445, 447–448
self-fulfillment, 478
sex-role identity, 448–455
philosophy of life developing in, 455–457
puberty, 396–397; *see also* sexual changes, *below*
rites of passage and, 397, 399
school and
college, 428–429
comprehensive education versus, 425
experiential learning and, 426–428
high school, 78, 402, 424–428
participatory education and, 420
transition to adulthood and work and, 425–426
work attitude and, 429
self-concept. *See* personality development, *above*
sexual behavior in
attitudes toward, 453, 455
contraception, 449–450, 452
pregnancy, 452–453, 454–455
premarital, 451–452, 453, 455
sexual changes
in boys, 433, 437–438
early and late, 439
in girls, 433, 438–439
menarche, 431, 432, 438–439
reaction to, 439
sequence of, 433
social change and, 409, 410
age segregation and, 412
family and, 411–412
society and, 404–405, 409
suicide and, 419
television and, 361
traditional emphasis on, 4
work and, 429–430
Adulthood
adolescence separated from, 411
biological view of, 475, 477

chronological viewpoint of, 475, 476
criteria for, 397
cultural perspective, 477
developmental-stage theories of, 377
Buhler on, 477–479
Erikson on, 479–480
evaluation of, 481–482
Levinson on, 480–481
generativity versus stagnation in, 480
Hall on, 16
historical factors shaping, 482
identity versus role diffusion in, 480
increase in population of adults and, 4
integrity versus despair in, 480
intimacy versus isolation in, 34, 38, 480
life structures, 480–489
in Muslim societies, 479
self-fulfillment in, 477–479
Shakespeare on, 474–475
see also Aging; Early adulthood; Later adulthood; Middle adulthood
Adventure playground, 265, 266
Age-mates. *See* Peer group
Age segregation, adolescence and, 412
Ageism, 582; *see also* Later adulthood
Aggression
modeling and, 266–267
in preschool years, 314–317
television and, 360–361, 362
Aging, 608
biological view of, 475, 477
continuity theory and, 9
disengagement theory and, 9
Hall on, 16
see also Adulthood; Later adulthood
Alcohol consumption
in adolescence, 457, 458–459, 460, 461
prenatal development and, 130, 131–132
Alert inactivity, in neonate, 162
Alienation from the self, in later adolescence, 405
Allele, 100, 101
Amniocentesis, 110–111
Amphetamines, 458–459
Anal expulsive fixations, 30
Anal retentive fixation, 30
Anal stage, of psychosexual development, 30
Analgesics (sedatives), prenatal development and, 129–130
Androgyny, 451
in middle adulthood, 562
Anemia, 124
Anesthetics (pain killers), prenatal development and, 129–130
Anger, as stage of dying, 622–623
Angry men, as personality type in later adulthood, 615
Antigens, 125
Apgar test, 154

Apnea, Sudden Infant Death Syndrome and, 192
"Armored-defended" personalities, in later adulthood, 616
Armored men, as personality type in later adulthood, 615
Art, in preschool years, 295–298
Arteriosclerosis, in middle adulthood, 553, 555
Arthritis, in middle adulthood, 553
Ascribed status, 189
Assimilation, cognitive development and, 27
Associationism, 20
Athletic skills, peer group popularity and, 356; *see also* Motor development
Atomism, causation and, 376
Attachment, 224–238
activity initiative in seeking proximity and contact stage, 229, 230
clinging and, 225, 228–229
crying and, 225, 228
cuddling and, 227
definition, 224–225
discriminating social responsiveness stage, 229–230
exploration and, 232
father and, 233
fear and, 232
following and, 225, 227
goal-corrected partnership stage, 230
grasping and, 228–229
listening and, 227
looking and, 227
as love between parent and child, 226
maternal deprivation and, 233
multiple caregiving and, 233
play and, 232
rooting reflex and, 225, 227
separation anxiety and, 232–233
smiling and, 225, 227–228
stages in the development of, 229
stranger anxiety and, 232
sucking and, 225, 227
as a system, 225
undiscriminating social responsiveness stage, 229
vocalizing and, 228; *see also* Language development *see also* Maternal–infant bonding
Authoritarian parent, 254, 256
Authoritarian teacher, 347
Authoritative parent, 256
Authoritative teacher, 347
Authority, adolescence and, 412
Autonomy
in adolescence, 403–404, 413–414, 417
in early adulthood, 483
in toddlerhood, 238
Autonomy versus shame and doubt, 33, 34

Babbling, language development and, 211

Babinski reflex, 155, 157, 158, 160
Baby biographies, development studied with, 82, 83
Barbiturates, 458–459, 460
Bargaining
    with parents in adolescence, 415
    as stage of dying, 623
Bayley Scales of Infant Development, 194
Behavioral stages, in development, 17–18
Behaviorism
    beginnings of, 19–20
    as deterministic, 23
    Dewey on, 22–23
    evaluation of, 22
    Watson on, 19–20
Biological clocks, 162
Biological determinants of development.
        See Heredity
Biological maturation, language development and, 211
Biorhythmicity, between mother and infant, 170
Biotin, Sudden Infant Death Syndrome and, 193
Birth. See Childbirth
Birth control, 449–450, 452
Birth defects, 103–112
    amniocentesis for, 110–111
    congenital, 106, 107
    environment and. See Prenatal development
    genetic counseling for, 109
    maternal age and, 126
    prematurity and, 167
    prenatal diagnosis of, 110
    transmission, 104–105, 106–108
Birth order, middle childhood and, 338–339
Black English, 303–304
Blacks, language development and, 303–305
Blastocyst (blastula), 113–114
Bloody-mindedness, in later adulthood, 617
Body (somatic) cells, 98
Bonding. See Maternal-infant bonding
Botulism, Sudden Infant Death Syndrome and, 193
Bouncing, in preschool years, 282
Brain, 270
    association areas of, 211
    cerebellum, 270
    cerebral cortex, 155, 270–271
    growth in preschool years, 269–271
    lateralization, 211
    myelinization, 270
    reticular formation, 271
Brain stem, 155
Brazelton Neonatal Assessment Scale, 194
Breast-feeding
    cry of newborn and, 171
    rooting and, 225, 227

Caesarean birth, 147–148
Canalization, heredity and environment and, 66–67
Cancer, death from, 506–507
Cardiovascular problems. See Heart disease
Career development, 540–541
    adolescence and, 408–409, 445, 447–448
    career peak, 540
    launching a career, 499–500
    middle childhood and, 330
    occupational life cycle, 449
    transitional career, 540
    see also Work
Castration anxiety, 31
Catching, in preschool years, 282
Cattell Measurement of Intelligence of Infants and Young Children, 194
Causality
    in middle childhood, 376–377
    sensorimotor period and, 200, 202, 203
Centering, in intuitive period of thinking, 373
Central nervous system. See Nervous system
Cephalocaudal development, 7–8
    of motor development, 194
    of muscle development, 192
Cerebellum, 270
Cerebral cortex, 155, 269–270
Change of life, 548; see also Middle adulthood
Child abuse, 46–47, 455
Child care centers, 40, 234, 268, 271
Childbirth
    Caesarean birth, 147–148
    episiotomy, 145
    at home or in hospital, 141, 147
    hospital programs for families, 173–174
    as interactional process, 138–139
    labor and delivery, 143–147
        contractions, 143
        dilation, 145
        expulsion, 145–147
        placenta delivery, 147
        real versus false, 143–144
    Lamaze method, 148, 149
    Leboyer method, 149–150, 151
    parental reaction after, 150–152
    rooming-in, 173–174
Children, 4
    death viewed by, 619–620
    decision to have, 489–490, 493
    divorce effects on, 495, 498
    family and, 529–530
    health of, 507
    grandparents viewed by, 586
    later adulthood viewed by, 591–592
    moral development of, 381–382, 387
    self-fulfillment and, 478
    see also Infancy: Middle childhood;
        Preschool years; Toddlerhood

Chromosomes, 56, 96
    autosomes and, 102
    sex chromosomes, 102–103
Chronic conditions, 506
Chronological age, adulthood and, 475, 476
Cigarette smoking
    in adolescence, 457–459, 460, 461
    prenatal development and, 131
Circadian rhythm, 162, 163
    of newborn, 170
Classical conditioning, 21
Classification
    in middle childhood, 373, 374
    in preschool years, 288
Classroom, organization of and academic performance, 351–352, 353; see also School
Cleft lip, 104
Cleft palate, 104
Climacteric (male), 525, 549; see also Menopause
Climbing, in preschool years, 279–280, 281
Clinging, attachment and, 225, 228–229
Clinical method, development studied with, 82–84
Clinical studies, development studied with, 82
Cliques, in peer groups, 419, 420–421
Clubfoot, 104
Cocaine, 458–459, 460, 461
Cognitive capacities, 583
Cognitive development, 56
    accommodation, 27
    adaptation to environment and, 25, 26
    assimilation, 27
    centering, 373
    conservation, 286–288, 375
    definition, 199
    equilibrium, 27
    moral development and, 381–384, 385, 387
    operations, 373
        concrete operational period and. See Middle childhood
        formal, 28, 440–442, 443–444
    organization, 27
    reversibility, 373
    schemata, 27
    stages of, 27–28
        concrete operations. See Middle childhood
        formal operations, 28, 440–442, 443–444
        intuitive period, 372–373
        preoperational period. See Preschool years
        sensorimotor period. See Infancy
    see also Adolescence; Cognitive theory;
        Intelligence
Cognitive mapping skills, in middle childhood, 340, 341

Cognitive theory, 25–29; *see also* Cognitive
    development
Cohabitating, 497
College, experience of, 428–429
Communes, 497
Communication
    in marriage, 489
    in preschool years, 298–301
    see also Language development
Community, 72, 256–257, 259
    in adolescence, 79, 402, 409, 411
    in early adulthood, 80, 498, 524
    in later adulthood, 81, 581, 592–593
    in middle adulthood, 80–81, 524, 537–
        539
    in middle childhood, 78, 333, 340–343,
        345, 524, 537–539
    prosocial behavior and, 313
    see also Neighborhood; Preschool years
Competence, middle childhood and, 328–
    330
Competitive play, in preschool years, 295
Complementarity, mate selection and, 486
Complex genetic transmission, 11
Complex sentences, development of
    formation of, 222
Comprehensive education, for adolescents,
    425
Conception, 94–95
Concepts
    in middle childhood, 374–375
    in preschool years, 288–289
    see also Cognitive development; Spatial
        concepts; Time concepts
Concrete operations. *See* Middle childhood
Conditioned reflex, 21
Conditioning theory, 20, 21
Congenital defects, 106, 107; *see also* Birth
    defects
Congenital heart malformations, 104
Congenital rubella syndrome, 105
Congenital syphilis, 105
Conjugal family. *See* Nuclear family
Conservation
    in middle childhood, 375
    in preschool years, 286–288
Continuity theory, aging and, 9
Contraception, 449–450, 452
Contract, with parents in adolescence, 415
Contractions, in birth process, 143
Conventional level, of moral development,
    384, 385
Cooing, language development and, 211
Cornelian Corner, 172
Coronary heart disease. *See* Heart disease
Correlation coefficient, 57
Creativity
    art in preschool years and, 295–298
    middle adulthood and, 557–558
Crib death. *See* Sudden Infant Death
    Syndrome
Critical periods. *See* Sensitive periods

Cross-sectional designs
    of adult intelligence, 509
    development studied with, 85–87
Cross-sequential design
    of adult intelligence, 509
    development studies with, 86
Crossing over, 98–100
Crowding, effects of, 260–261
Crowds, in peer groups, 419, 420–421
Crying
    attachment and, 225, 228
    language development and, 211
    in neonate, 162, 170–171
Crystallized intelligence, 484, 511, 512,
    513
Cuddling, attachment and, 227
Cultural stereotypes, television and, 364–
    365
Culture
    adolescence and, 409
    adulthood defined by, 477
    development and, 76–77
    language and, 302–305
Cystic fibrosis, 104
Cytoplasm, 97

Darwinian reflex. *See* Grasp reflex
Day care, working mother requiring, 40,
    234, 268, 271
Death and dying, 618–626
    adults and, 620–621, 622
    care for, 624
    dying process and, 622–623
        acceptance, 623
        anger, 622–623
        bargaining, 623
        denial, 622
        depression, 623
    hospice for, 624
    life expectancy and, 573–574
        subjective, 619
    living will, 623–624
    meaning of, 619–622
    right to die, 623–624
    on triviality and, 621–622
    widowhood, 587–590
    young children and, 619–620
Decentering, in middle childhood, 340,
    341
Deductive reasoning, 286
Deep structure, of language, 209
Deficit hypothesis, of language
    development, 303, 304–305
Denial, as stage of dying, 622
Density, effects of, 260–261
Deoxyribonucleic acid (DNA), 96, 97–98
Dependent variable, in experiment, 84
Depression, as stage of dying, 623
Deprivation dwarfism, 274, 276
Deserving norm, prosocial behavior and,
    311
Designed play setting, 265

Determinism, learning theorists and, 23
Development
    definitions, 7
    determinants of
        biological, *see* Heredity
        culture, 76–77
        environment, 56, 69–77
        family, 70–71, 73, 77
        neighborhood, 72
        peer groups and friends, 75–76
        school, 72–73
        systems theory and, 54–56
        watermelon theory and, 54–56
        work, 73–75
    differentiation, 8
    from life-span perspective, 2–4
    methods of studying, 81–89
        baby biographies, 82, 83
        clinical method, 82–83
        clinical studies, 82–84
        cross-sectional designs, 85–86
        cross-sequential design, 86–87
        ethics and, 87–88
        experimental research, 84–85, 87
        interview, 83–84
        longitudinal designs, 85, 86
        naturalistic observations, 82
        naturalistic studies, 81–82
        time sampling, 82
    as a normative science, 19
    as orderly and sequential, 8–9
    periods of. *See* Early adolescence; Early
        adulthood; Infancy; Later
        adolescence; Later adulthood;
        Middle adulthood; Middle
        childhood; Prenatal period;
        Preschool years; Toddlerhood
    qualitative change in, 4
    quantitative change in, 4
    sensitive periods of, 10, 66–67
    sequences of, 16–18; *see also* periods of,
        above
    theories of, 14; *see also* Behaviorism;
        Cognitive development; Learning
        theories; Maturation theories;
        Psychoanalytic tradition; Systems
        theories
    see also Growth
Developmental-stage theories, 477; *see also*
    Adulthood
Diabetes mellitus, 104, 553
    prenatal development and, 132
Difference hypothesis, of language
    development, 303
Differentiation
    growth and development, 8
    of personality, 560
Dilation, in labor, 145
Direct teaching, in preschool, 268
Discipline
    by parents, 251–253, 254, 256, 313,
        315–316

by teacher, 347
Discriminating social responsiveness, in attachment, 229–230
Diseases
   acute versus chronic, 505, 506
   age-related, 475
   in preschool years, 274
   see also Health; Heart disease; Prenatal development
Disengagement theory
   aging and, 9
   of personality in later adulthood, 612–613
Division of labor, family and, 187–188
Divorce, 493–495, 497–498
Dizygotic twins, 60
DNA (deoxyribonucleic acid), 96, 97–98
Dominant gene, 100–101
Down's syndrome, 104, 107–108, 126
Dramatic play, in preschool years, 293–294
Drawing, in preschool years, 295–298
Drugs, 457–461
   prenatal development and, 129, 131
Dual career family, 188, 497
Duke University Aging Studies, 552–553
Dwarfism, deprivation, 274, 276–277
Dying. *See* Death and dying

Early adolescence. *See* Adolescence
Early adulthood, 470, 482–483
   autonomy in, 483
   cognitive and intellectual skills during, 484, 508
   community and, 498
   death viewed by, 621
   family and, 79, 485–498; *see also* Marriage
      adjustment to, 491
      having versus not having children, 489–490, 493
   identification of, 6, 78–80, 470–472
   identity versus role diffusion in, 480
   interests developed in, 513
   interpersonal flexibility in, 512
   intimacy versus isolation in, 34, 38, 480, 484; *see also* Marriage
   maturity and, 472–474
   peer group and, 75, 76
   physical changes during, 484, 503–508
      central nervous system, 505
      exercise and, 507–508
      health, 506–508
      muscular strength, 503
      physical endurance, 503–504
      reaction time, 505
      vision, 504–505
   self-concept and, 512, 513–514
   sex-role learning during, 514
   social interaction during, 483
   social networks of, 483, 498
   values in, 513

see also Adulthood; Marriage; Work
Ecological environment, Bronfenbrenner on, 42–43
Ecology, 44
   of human development, 41–43
   see also Systems theories
Economic system, educational experiences influenced by, 43
Ecosystems, 49; *see also* System theories
Ectoderm, in prenatal development, 115
Education. *See* School
Ego identity, 444; *see also* Adolescence; Identity
Ego integrity versus despair, 34, 39
Ego psychology. *See* Psychoanalytic tradition
Egocentrism, in preschool years, 283, 285
Elderly. *See* Later adulthood
Electra Complex, 31, 308
Embryo, 95
Embryonic stage, of prenatal growth, 113, 114–116
Emotional stress, effect on unborn child, 127–128
Empathy, prosocial behavior and, 312
Empty-nest phase, of family, 532–533
Endoderm, in prenatal development, 115
Entrainment, maternal–infant bonding and, 169–170, 171
Environment
   adaptation to the
      Erikson on, 33
      Piaget on, 25, 26, 27
   Bronfenbrenner on, 42
   development and, 56, 69–77
   in system theory, 40–41, 42, 43, 45
   see also Heredity; Prenatal development
Enzyme, 97
Epigenetic principle, psychosocial development and, 33
Epilepsy, 111
Episiotomy, in labor, 145
Equality norm, prosocial behavior and, 311–312
Equilibrium, cognitive development and, 27
Equity norm, prosocial behavior and, 311–312
Erythroblastosis fetalis, 105, 124–126
Ethics, in research, 87–88
Ethological-biological theories, aggression in preschoolers explained by, 314–315
Ethologists, 41
Exercise
   in early adulthood, 507–508
   heart disease in childhood and, 363
   in later adulthood, 608–609
   see also Motor development
Exosystems
   Bronfenbrenner on, 43
   Community and, 259

Expectations
   of parents, 253
   of teacher, 347–349
Experience, moral development and, 456, 457
Experiential learning, adolescence and, 426–428
Experimental method, 84
Experimental research, development studied with, 84–85, 87
Exploration, attachment in infancy and, 232
Expressive component, of language, 208
Expulsion, in labor, 145
Extended family, 77, 184, 186
Extinguishing behavior, 21
Eye-to-eye contact, maternal–infant bonding and, 169, 170–171

False labor, 143
Family
   adaptiveness of, 251
   alternative patterns
      childless, 493
      cohabitation, 497
      communes, 497
      divorced, 82, 493–495, 497–498
      dual-career, 496
      extended, 77, 184, 186
      kin, 497
      nuclear, 77, 184, 496
      remarried nuclear, 497
      single-parent, 186, 339–340, 496–497
      single status, 492–493
   change and, 180–183
   community influence on, 262–263
   definition, 183, 184, 186
   development and, 70–71, 73, 77
   developmental stages of, 70–71
   functions, 186–188
      economic, 187–188
      emotional support and companionship, 189
      as intermediary between society and family member, 186–187
      legitimizing sexual relations, 188
      reproduction, 188–189
      socialization of children, 188
      status and role provision, 189
   infancy and. *See* Attachment; Maternal–infant bonding
   language development and, 215–216, 222–223
   leaving the, 480
   openness of, 251
   organizational complexity of, 250–251
   of orientation, 183
   preschool years and, 253–254, 255, 301–302, 317
   of procreation, 183
   school and, 73
   size of and birth control, 449–450

Icterus neonatorum, 153
Ideal versus real, in adolescence, 442–443
Identical twins, 60
Identification, psychoanalytic interpretation of, 308
Identity. *See* Adolescence; Sex-role identity
Identity versus role diffusion, in psychosocial development, 34, 37–38, 405, 480
Illness. *See* Diseases
Imitation
　language development and, 209
　neonate and, 161
　social learning theorists and, 23–25
　see also Modeling
Independence. *See* Autonomy
Independent variables, in experiment, 84
Indirect teaching, at the preschool level, 267
Individuality, of personality, 65
Inductive reasoning, 286
Industry versus inferiority, in psychosocial development, 34, 36–37, 329–330
Infancy
　approximate ages of, 6
　child abuse and, 46–47, 455
　intelligence in, 194; *see also* sensorimotor period in, *below*
　motor development, 194–199
　　language development and, 211, 212
　　locomotion, 196, 197, 198
　　order of, 194–196
　　prehension, 198–199
　oral stage, 29, 30
　personality and selfhood in. *See* Attachment; Maternal–infant bonding
　physical growth, 190–191
　　muscle development, 192
　　skeletal development, 191–192
　primary contexts of, 78
　sensorimotor period in, 27, 199–206
　　causality and, 200, 202, 203
　　memory and, 206
　　object permanence, 196, 198, 199–201, 226
　　representations and, 202–203
　　space and, 200, 204
　　time and, 205–206
　smile in, 237
　sociable self emerging in, 235–238
　Sudden Infant Death Syndrome, 192–193
　as system, 180–181
　trust in, 33, 34, 236–237
　see also Language development; Maternal–infant bonding; Neonate; Prematurity
Infant botulism, Sudden Infant Death Syndrome and, 193
Inflections, in language development, 220–221

Inhalants, 460, 461
Inheritance. *See* Heredity
Initiative versus guilt, in psychosocial development, 34, 36
Inner-city neighborhood, 260
Institutionalization, in later adulthood, 594–595, 597
Integrated personalities, 560
　in later adulthood, 615–616
Integrity versus despair, 480
Intelligence
　of adopted children, 63–64
　crystallized, 484, 511, 512, 513
　definition, 18
　in early adulthood, 484, 508–512, 513
　fluid, 511–512, 513
　genetic component of, 18
　gifted, 18–19
　heredity versus environment, 58–64
　individual differences in, 18
　in infancy, 194
　　sensorimotor period and. *See* Cognitive development
　intervention studies for, 64
　in later adulthood, 583, 610–612
　in middle adulthood, 525–526, 555–559
　peer group popularity and, 356
　prematurity and, 165
　tests of, 18, 509
　of twins, 60–63
　see also Adolescence; Cognitive development
Intentions, language development and, 218–219
Interactional perspective. *See* Systems theories
Interests, in early adulthood, 513
Interpersonal flexibility, in early adulthood, 512
Intervention studies, heredity and environment and, 64
Interview, development studied with, 83–84
Intimacy
　in early adulthood, 484. *See also* Marriage
　family providing, 189
Intimacy versus isolation, in psychosocial development, 34, 38, 480
Introspection, in adolescence, 442
Intuitive stage, in preoperational period, 283, 372–373
Irregular sleep, in neonate, 162
Islam, adulthood in, 479

Jaundice, in neonate, 153
Journal of Genetic Psychology, 16
Jumping
　in middle childhood, 368–369
　in preschool years, 279, 280
Junk playground, 265, 266
Justice, child's concepts of, 386–387

Juvenile delinquency, single-parent family and, 339–340

Kansas tradition, of system theory, 40–41
Kin family, 497
Kinsey Studies, 552, 553

Labor. *See* Childbirth
Labor force. *See* Work
Laboratory schools, for preschool children, 268
Lamaze method, of childbirth, 148, 149
Language, 207–209
　acquisition. *See* Language development
Language development
　babbling and, 211–212
　biological maturation, 211
　black children and, 303–305
　black English, 303–305
　brain development and, 211
　child's role in, 223
　complex sentences, 222
　cooing and, 211–212
　crying and, 211–212
　deficit hypothesis and, 303, 304–305
　difference hypothesis and, 303
　expansions in, 223
　family and, 215–216, 222–223
　father's role in, 223
　first words, 212–216
　imitation and, 209–210
　infant as language specialist, 210–211
　infant speaking own language, 210
　inflections, 220–221
　intentions, 218–219
　motor development and, 211, 212
　open words, 218
　overextension and, 213–215
　overregularization and, 220
　pivot words, 217–218
　questions, 221–222
　semantic relations in, 219
　sentences, 215
　telegraphic speech, 216, 217
　theories of, 208
　　learning theory, 208–209
　　psycholinguistic theory, 209
　　social learning theory, 209–210
　two-word combinations, 216–219
　vocalizing and, 228
　see also Preschool years
Latency stage, of psychosexual development, 30, 31
Later adolescence. *See* Adolescence
Later adulthood, 472, 485, 571
　activity theory and, 8–9
　ageism and, 582
　community and, 581, 592–593
　determination, 6, 571
　exercise and, 608–609
　family and, 81, 485, 581, 590, 592

Neonate, 124
Apgar test given to, 154
appearance, 152, 154
breast-feeding, 171, 225, 227
hearing in, 157–159
heartbeat, 153, 154
imitation and, 161
jaundice (icterus neonatorum) in, 153
nervous system of, 154–157, 158
pain sensitivity of, 160
parents and. *See also* Maternal–infant
bonding
reaction to, 150–152
states of neonate and, 165
reflexes in, 155–157, 158, 160
rhythms and, 161, 170
smell (olfaction) in, 159–160
states of, 161–163, 165
alert inactivity, 162
drowsiness, 162
irregular sleep, 162
operation of, 162–163, 165
regular sleep, 162
waking and crying, 162
taste (gustation) in, 160
teenage pregnancy and, 454–455
trends in caring for, 171–174
vision in, 157
see also Infancy; Maternal–infant
bonding; Prematurity; Prenatal
period
Nervous system
in early adulthood, 505
in later adulthood, 607–608
of neonate, 154–157, 158
Networks. *See* Social networks; Support
networks
New York Longitudinal Study, 65
Norm of reaction, heredity and
environment and, 66
Normality, definition, 10
Normative information, naturalistic studies
giving, 82
Normative science, development as, 19
Norms, 19
peer groups providing to adolescent, 417
prosocial behavior and, 311–312
sex role changes and, 451
Nuclear family, 77, 184, 496
Nursery schools. *See* Preschool programs
Nursing homes, for older adults, 595, 599
Nutrition
adolescence and, 437
preschool years and, 273–274

Object permanence, sensorimotor period
and, 200, 202, 203–205, 230, 376
Object play, in preschool years, 291–292
Observation, social learning theorists and,
23–25
Occupation. *See* Career development; Work
Oedipal Complex, 31, 307

Old age. *See* Later adulthood
Olfaction. *See* Smell
Omnibus tests, of intelligence, 509
Oncogenes, 57
One-parent family, 186, 339–340, 496–
497
Open classroom, 351–352
Open words, 218
Operant conditioning, 21
Operations. *See* Cognitive development
Opiates, 460, 461
Oral stage, of psychosexual development,
29, 30
Organization, cognitive development and,
27
Osteoporosis, 607, 609
Overextensions, in language development,
213–215
Overloaded environment, effects of, 261
Overregularization, in language
development, 220

Pain
middle adulthood and, 548
neonate's sensitivity to, 160
Palmar reflex. *See* Grasp reflex
Parent-cooperative nursery school, 268
Parent Effectiveness Training, 255
Parenting styles, 251–253
Parents
authoritarian, 254, 256
authoritative, 256
disciplinary techniques, 251–253, 254,
256, 313, 315–316
expectations of, effect on child's
behavior, 253
permissive, 254, 256
in preschool years, 253–254, 255, 301–
302, 317
prescriptive, 313
proscriptive, 313
prosocial behavior and, 312–313
styles of, 251–253
see also Attachment; Family; Fathers;
under Maternal; Neonate
Participatory education, for adolescents,
425
Passive-dependent personalities, in later
adulthood, 616
Pedagogical Seminary, 16
Peer group
definition, 352
development and, 75–76
in early adulthood, 80
in later adulthood and, 81
in middle adulthood, 80
in middle childhood, 78, 333–334, 352–
358
in preschool years, 75, 266–267, 317
in toddlerhood, 238
see also Friendships

Perceptual development, in preschool
years, 274–275, 285
Permissive parent, 254, 256
Permissive teacher, 347
Personal social networks. *See* Social
networks
Personality, 56, 612
activity level and, 65
child's role in, 65
developmental theories and. *See*
Development
differentiation of, 560
in early adulthood, 512, 513–514
heart problems and, 554
heredity versus environment and, 64–66
individuality and, 65
in infancy and toddlerhood, *see*
Attachment; Maternal–infant
bonding
integration of, 560
in middle adulthood, 526, 560–563
in preschool years, 305
sociability and, 65–66
see also Adolescence; Later adulthood;
Middle adulthood; Self-concept
Phallic stage, of psychosexual
development, 30–31
Phenotype, 67–68, 100, 101
Phenylketonuria (PKU), 100, 101, 105
Philosophy of life, in adolescence, 408,
455–457
Phonemes, of language, 207–208
Physical growth. *See* Growth
Physical health. *See* Health
Physiological jaundice, in neonate, 153
Piagetian theories. *See* Cognitive
development
Pivot words, 217–218
Placenta, 113, 147
Play
acceptance and rejection in, 361
attachment in infancy and, 232
importance of, 360
in toddlerhood, 238; *see also* Preschool
years
see also Friendships; Games; Middle
childhood; Preschool years
Polydactyly, 104
Possibility and reality, separation of in
adolescence, 441
Postconventional level, of moral
development, 384–386, 455–457
Preconceptual stage, in preoperational
period, 283
Pregnancy
acceptance of, 142
birth control and, 449–450, 452
decision to have children, 489–490
fathers reaction to, 143
at labor and delivery, 144
maternal–infant bonding during, 140,
143

mother's reaction to, 140, 143
quickening, 143
teenage, 452–453, 454–455
toxemia during, 125
trimesters of, 113, 121–122
see also Childbirth; Prenatal development
Prehension, in infancy, 198–199
Premarital sexual behavior, 453, 455
Prematurity, 104, 124, 165–168
Premoral period, of moral development, 381–382, 387
Prenatal development
   blastocyst (blastula), 113–114
   conception, 94–95
   ectoderm and, 115
   endoderm and, 115
   environmental influences on
      alcohol consumption, 130, 131–132
      cigarette smoking, 131
      drugs, 128–131
      maternal age, 126
      maternal diseases and disorders, 132
      maternal emotional state, 127–128
      maternal nutrition, 123–124
      maternal size, 126
      Rh-factor incompatibility, 124–126
   male versus female conception, 103
   mesoderm and, 115
   stages of, 112–113
      embryonic, 95, 113, 114–116
      fetal, 95, 113, 117–123
      germinal, 113–114
   zygote, 95
   see also Birth defects; Childbirth;
      Heredity; Neonate; Prematurity
Prenatal period, 6, 78; *see also* Prenatal
   development
Preoperational stage. *See* Preschool years
Prepared childbirth. *See* Lamaze method
Presbyopia, in later adulthood, 604–605
Preschool programs, 267–268
   child care centers, 40, 234, 268, 271
   prosocial behavior and, 313
Preschool years, 40, 249
   approximate ages of, 6
   brain growth in, 269–271
   cognitive development in. *See*
      preoperational period, *below*
   community and, 256–259
      community sense and, 260
      crowding of, 260–261
      density of, 260–261
      ecosystems and, 259
      housing and, 262, 263
      influence of, 260
      inner-city, 260
      macrosystems and, 259
      meaning of to child, 262–266
      microsystems and, 258–259
      overloaded, 261
      personal social networks in, 258

play and play settings in, 262, 264–266
   sociability and, 260
   stress and, 260
   urban renewal and, 263
drawing in, 295–298
growth in, 269–271, 272, 273
   illness and, 274
   nutrition and, 273–274
   socioeconomic status and, 274
   stress and, 274, 276–277
initiative versus guilt in, 34, 36
language development in, 283
   cognitive development and, 298
   communication and, 298–301
   culture and, 302–305
   parents and, 301–302
   play and, 292–293
   uses of language and, 300
motor development, 275, 277
   bouncing, 282
   catching, 282
   climbing, 279–280, 281
   fundamental motor skills, 277–282
   hopping, 280–281, 282
   jumping, 279, 280
   running, 280
   throwing, 281, 282
   walking, 280
parent–child interactions in, 253–254,
   255, 301–302, 317
peer group and, 75, 266–267, 317
perceptual development, 274–275, 285
personality development, 305
phallic stage, 30–31
physical appearance, 271–272
play in, 267, 289
   "adventure" or "junk" play setting,
      265, 266
   competitive play, 295
   definition, 290
   designed setting for, 265
   dramatic play, 293–294
   games with rules, 290–291, 293, 295
   with language, 292–293
   learning as, 275, 277
   modeling of behavior during, 252–253
   as motion and interaction, 291
   with objects, 291
   planned, 265
   preschool programs and, 267
   sensorimotor play, 290
   settings for, 262, 264–266
   symbolic, 283–284, 290
   toys and, 277
   traditional settings for, 265
preoperational period, 28, 282–283
   classification, 288
   conservation, 286–288, 298
   egocentrism in, 283, 285
   intuitive stage, 283
   language and, 298

limitations of, 284–286
   preconceptual stage, 283
   symbolic representation in, 283–284
   time concepts, 288–289
   transductive reasoning in, 285–286
primary contexts of, 78
see also Preschool programs
Prescriptive parents, 313
Pretend play. *See* Dramatic play
Primary status, peer groups providing to
   adolescent, 417
Primitive reflexes, 157
Problem finding, in adolescence, 444
Problem solving, in adolescence, 441–
   442
Project Head Start, 19
Proscriptive parents, 313
Prosocial behavior
   in preschool years, 310–314
   television and, 363–364
Protein, 97
Proximodistal development, 8
   of motor development, 194
Pruitt-Igoe housing complex, 263
Psychoanalytic tradition, 29
   Erikson and. *See* Psychosocial
      development
   evaluation, 39
   Freud and, 29–31
   sex-role identity in preschool years and,
      307–308
Psycholinguistic theory, language
   development and, 209
Psychosexual stages, of personality
   development, 29–31
Psychosocial development, 31–39
   adaptation and, 33
   epigenetic principle, 33
   Freudian theories versus, 31–32
   stages of
      autonomy versus shame and doubt,
         33, 34
      ego integrity versus despair, 34, 39
      generativity versus stagnation, 34, 38–
         39, 480
      identity versus role diffusion, 34, 37–
         38, 405, 480
      industry versus inferiority, 34, 36–37,
         329–330
      initiative versus guilt, 34, 36
      intimacy versus isolation, 34, 38, 480
      trust versus mistrust, 33, 34, 236–237
Puberty, 396–397; *see also* Adolescence
Public school. *See* School
Punishment, by parent, 315–316; *see also*
   Discipline
Pygmalion hypothesis, teacher–children
   interaction and, 347–348

Qualitative change
   in development, 5
   in intelligence in adolescence, 440